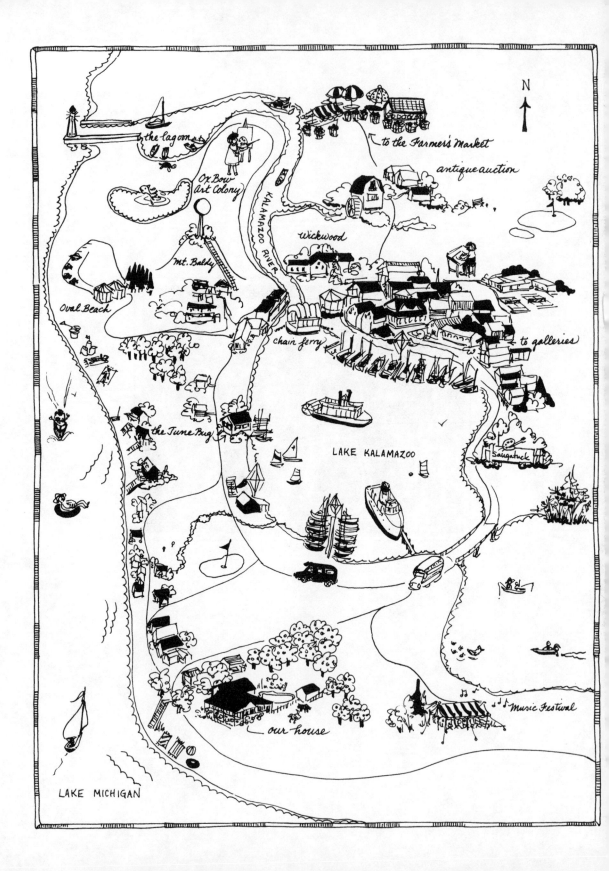

GREAT GOOD FOOD

LUSCIOUS LOWER-FAT COOKING

BY JULEE ROSSO

ILLUSTRATIONS BY CHRISTA WISE
DESIGN BY LESLEY EHLERS

CROWN/TURTLE BAY BOOKS

*A very special thanks to everyone at
Turtle Bay Books, for their spirit,
their style, and their energy
in helping to create* Great Good Food

Grateful acknowledgment is made to the following
for permission to reprint previously published material:
Little, Brown and Company and Curtis Brown Ltd.: "The Smelts" from
Verses from 1929 On by Ogden Nash. Copyright 1942 by Ogden Nash.
Excerpts from "The Chef has Imagination, Or, It's Too Hard to Do It Easy"
from *Private Dining Room* by Ogden Nash. First appeared in
Good Housekeeping. Copyright 1953 by Ogden Nash. Rights throughout
the world excluding the United States and Canada are controlled
by Curtis Brown, Ltd., New York. Reprinted by permission
of Little, Brown and Company and Curtis Brown Ltd.
Macmillan Publishing Company: Three lines from "The Song of
Wandering Aengus" from *The Poems of W. B. Yeats: A New Edition,*
edited by Richard J. Finneran (New York: Macmillan, 1983).
Reprinted by permission of Macmillan Publishing Company.

Published by Crown Publishers, Inc.
201 East 50th Street, New York, New York 10022.
Member of the Crown Publishing Group. Random House, Inc.
New York, Toronto, London, Sydney, Auckland

CROWN is a trademark of Crown Publishers, Inc.

Composition and Pre-press Production by Goodman/Orlick Design, Inc.

Manufactured in the United States of America on acid-free paper

Library of Congress Catalog Card Number: 92-56843

ISBN: 0-517-59645-8 (hardcover)
0-517-88122-5 (paperback)

10 9 8 7 6 5 4 3 2 1

First Edition

To
Mom, Wills, Kay,
Bert, and Bobbie

who are always there —
even when I plant impossible gardens

From the bottom of my heart my thanks to those who made this book grow with sunshine.

Toni Evans • Carole Lalli • Christa Wise • Lesley Ehlers • Deborah Hudgins • Pam Rugen • Tisha Winchester • Diane Robb • Nancy Newman • Kristin Crawford • Gerald McCauley • Alan Klavins • Nancy Baker • Deb Seymour/Rudecoff • Katy Keck • Sherry Bartholomew •

FARMERS MARKET

Susan Kamil •
Mitchell Ivers •
Rochelle Udell •
Beth Pearson • Judi
Orlick • Emily Pearl • Leon Friedman •
Richard Litner • Chip Gibson • Rob Singer •
Carie Freimuth • Tanis Donnaud • Della
Mancuso • Charles Rue Woods • Jose
Conde • Karen Steinig • Sandi Mendleson •
Leta Evanthes • Susan Wood • Amy
Edelman • The Women of Wickwood •

Fresh MELONS

CONTENTS

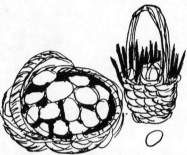

"The country habit has me by the heart." Vita Sackville West

I was well aware of the intensified interest in health and fitness in this country, but it really hit home one June evening several years ago. My husband and I had joined friends for an impromptu dinner. Typically, the men were outside at the grill, the women inside making salad. When I started out with the marinade to the grill crew, I could hardly believe my ears. Those three "manly men," all in their mid-forties, were discussing not golf but the benefits of skim milk over 2%!

Later, I held my breath as these food-loving but no-fancy-stuff guys dove into some desserts I'd been testing for this book—mousses made from nonfat dairy products, in six flavors. The mousses won raves all around, even after the "secret" ingredients were revealed.

We've come a long way in this country regarding our food habits. James Beard and Julia Child were our visionaries in the fifties and sixties. Julia's *The French Chef* was part of my own epiphany—I cooked my way through it, from start to finish. Then in 1974 I read Roy Andries de Groot's *Inn of the Flowering Hearth* and everything changed. Cooking had been a hobby, but suddenly I wanted to leave my career in advertising and fashion. I wanted to go off to the Valley of Chartreuse to chop carrots and share the passion of the two women who owned that inn. Sheila Lukins and I opened the Silver Palate gourmet takeout shop in New York City, and I learned what it's like to truly love what you do all day, every day. Our adventure was magnificent!

During the Silver Palate years, I was able to satisfy most of my curiosities. I love history and the study of cultures through food. I adore traveling and came to know this country well. I traveled time and again to Europe, the Caribbean, and Japan, to dig deeper into their culinary traditions. Having learned to cook using classic French ingredients, I became intrigued with Italian and Asian styles, the way they celebrate the seasons, and their respect for raw ingredients. In time, I developed my own approach, which is based on simplicity and integrity, along with a firm conviction that good food and good health are utterly compatible.

You Can Go Home Again

In the late eighties Sheila and I sold the Silver Palate. I wanted to be closer to my best pal—my mother—so I find myself today living happily in a cottage with a picket fence, on a cliff overlooking Lake Michigan, with my husband, Bill Miller (Wills to me), our dogs Black Jack (the Bouvier) and Kelly (a white Lab). Back home, I've rediscovered many of the basics I was brought up with. I grew up as a "gentleman" farmer's daughter—my father raised Black Angus beef, lambs, turkeys, and "walking-around" chickens, all naturally. Every year, we planted a huge garden of vegetables and herbs, and Mom and I canned the harvest.

Through my cooking workshops, I've become aware of the frustrations of today's home cooks who want to prepare meals every day that are more healthful, that have fewer fats and less cholesterol, and yet will please the palate. Their concerns are very real: We all are seeking a new way to eat for life. While it sometimes seems that no nutritional recommendation is valid for more than a few months, the need to significantly reduce total fat intake is a consistent message from the experts. Can this need coexist comfortably with the food revolution that began in the eighties, when the exotic became commonplace and flavors from around the world became part of the American food vernacular? Is plain, virtuous food the only way to deal with the food-health issue? I can't see why. The good news is that flavorful, lower-fat cooking is easier than I thought. The new recommendations, which are easily understood by becoming familiar with the food "pyramid," mean changing some habits, but there is nothing peculiar about the new regime. In a way, it can be as simple as adjusting the proportions—more vegetables, fruits, grains, and pasta; less meat and dairy. Just being aware makes the changes and choices easy. And best of all—the clean, clear, fresh tastes are memorable, satisfying and easy to trust every day.

Julee Rosso
Saugatuck, Michigan
Spring 1993

THE GREAT GOOD FOOD PHILOSOPHY

Great Good Food isn't a "diet" book—it's a celebration of magnificent flavors incorporated into a healthy, balanced lifestyle. This is a cookbook for people who love good food and enjoy cooking, and who want to develop sensible eating habits without sacrificing the pleasure of food. In writing *Great Good Food*, I had several priorities:

Taste Comes First

Taste determines what we eat. That's why most health regimens ultimately fail—they can't deliver the deep satisfaction of foods we truly enjoy. But there's no need to sacrifice pleasure for health, or to swap synthetic substitutes for "real" foods. You only need to be aware of what's in your favorite foods and to make smart choices.

Flavor Without Fat

Why is it so hard to give up fat? Because it's a vehicle for flavor. It's also a culinary medium, a moistener—and an unconscious habit. The problem is that fat makes people fat. It has more than twice the calories (9 per gram) of carbohydrates or proteins (both 4). A cup of flour has around 400 calories; a cup of oil, almost 2,000. Worst of all, high fat goes hand-in-hand with high cholesterol, a leading cause of heart attack and stroke.

In *Great Good Food*, I've focused on lowering fat levels in foods. I've replaced fat's rich taste with other intense, satisfying flavors. Today, I think of fat mostly as a flavor. I may add a tiny bit of butter at the very end of a dish if I really want the taste, olive oil if I want its fruity flavor. Otherwise, fat is no longer my cooking medium or taste of choice. The real surprise is that fat so often masks great, natural flavors. Without it, taste shines through. And eating lighter just feels better.

No Bad Foods, Just Good Food Choices

The idea is not to balance fat intake dish by dish or day by day, but over three or four days, eating fewer rich dishes and indulging less often. Remember, there are no bad foods!

My approach is like having a weekly "fat allowance." If you want to spend three days' worth of fat calories on chocolate cake, go ahead. But for the next few days, you'll have to "balance the expenditure" with equally appealing low-fat meals.

Follow the Seasons

I'm more determined than ever to use the freshest, most chemical-free ingredients I can find to make food taste terrific without fats. As much as possible, use whatever's available and in season, grow what you can if you enjoy gardening, shop the farmers' markets, follow the seasons, and see how seasonal foods naturally complement each other. The goal is not to overpower natural flavors but to enhance and emphasize them. And the best part is that this generally means less time in the kitchen.

HOW TO USE THIS BOOK

Each recipe in *Great Good Food* has been analyzed to help you plan meals intelligently. The nutritional values are evaluated per serving, or by the piece for such items as muffins or cookies. The nutritional breakdown is for calories, carbohydrates, protein, cholesterol, grams of fat, and the percentage of the total calories that comes from fat.

The Symbols

The symbols indicate the relationship of calories from fat to total calories. I've used the USDA's recommendation of 30% maximum fat in the diet as the standard for this book. That does not mean that each dish you cook and eat must not exceed 30% fat, but only that your diet overall should fall within that limit; some dishes may exceed it and some will fall below. The most sensible and sane way to manage your menus is to evaluate your fat intake over several days. So, if you enjoy my Midnight Torte at your friend's birthday party, don't feel guilty, just know that for 4 to 5 days you should choose dishes that come under the 30% fat limit. To keep you alert, I've assigned a few symbols to those dishes that exceed 30% (though most in this book are comfortably under.)

 Low-Cal/High Percentage Some dishes are so low in calories, the percentage of fat comes up disproportionately high. For instance, a whole pound of green beans—140 calories—has less than 1 gram of fat. Add 2 teaspoons of walnut oil and it jumps to 10 grams, or 40% of the calories in the dish. That seems high, but you don't need an advanced degree to know that 2 teaspoons of oil on a pound of beans serving 4 people is not very much.

 Fat Monitor Some dishes exceed the 30% limit, plain and simple. This is my "monitor" symbol; it lets you know that to keep your fat intake where you want it, you should balance this meal, on this day or during the next several days, with dishes that fall below 30%.

 Indulgence The devil made me do it! I've managed to recast some of my—and everyone's—favorite dishes to have far less fat than they traditionally do. Still, while they may be *lower*-fat, they are not all *low*-fat. And there are some recipes in here—just a few—that were too good not to share. (My best chocolate cake, for instance.) These are indulgences, and we all know that indulgences are once-in-a-while things.

Needless to say, some subjectivity came into play in allocating these symbols. It's hard to think of a full-course salad, for instance, as something to avoid in a healthful diet, even when it weighs in with 33% calories from fat. And in fact, it probably shouldn't be avoided. That's part of the point of this book—to be aware of what we are eating, monitor as we go along, and learn to maintain a balance. In time, it will become second nature.

NOTE: The recipes in this book were analyzed by the Nutrinfo Corporation.

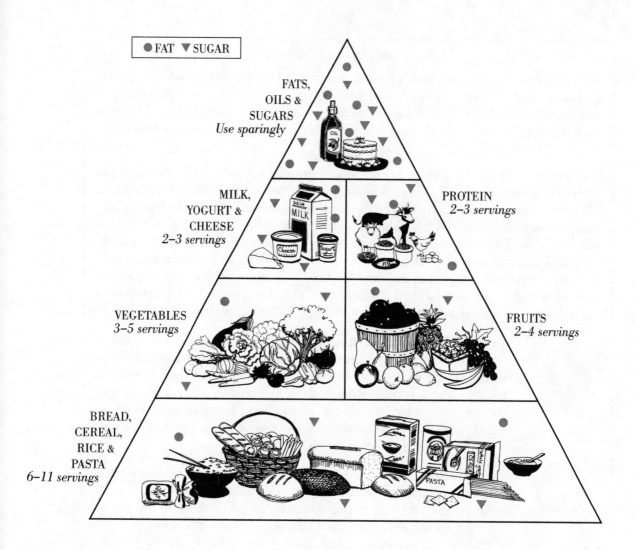

The USDA Food Pyramid

In 1992 the USDA (United States Department of Agriculture) Food Pyramid replaced the Four Basic Food Groups that for decades dictated a healthful diet. In the old scheme, the groups—vegetables and fruits; meat, fish, and poultry; dairy products; and beans and grains—were equal. Not anymore. The emphasis today is on carbohydrates, and fat, our biggest health concern, is in the narrowest segment. The pyramid is your daily guide for food intake—a menu for health.

Servings are meant to span a wide range of body sizes and activity levels. If you're a small, relatively sedentary woman, choose the lower amounts; if you're an athletic seventeen-year-old male, go for the maximum.

BREAD, CEREAL, RICE & PASTA

6–11 servings
Complex carbo-hydrates should make up more than half your daily diet. There are grains galore to choose from. The closer to "whole" they are, the greater the fiber, vitamins, and miner-als. Choose whole-grain cereals without added fat.

In bread, read the label and look for less than 2 grams of fat per 1-ounce serving and whole-grain clues like "100% whole-wheat flour," "stone-ground whole-wheat flour," "wheat berries," "sprouted wheat," "oat-meal," "rye," "millet," etc. Pasta comes in a wide variety of shapes and col-ors. Try the whole-wheat versions for more fiber and vitamins.

Rice has regained Amer-ican popularity as a great source of carbohydrates and offers a wide variety of tastes. Keep in mind that it's not rice, pasta, or bread that is fatty, but what you put on or serve with it.

Beans, peas, nuts, or seeds combined with whole grains provide the same high-quality protein as meat, fish, or poultry.

VEGETABLES

3–5 servings
Vegetables are far too important to be used as just side dishes or garnish-es. Virtually fat-free, they are full of fiber and rich in a variety of vitamins and minerals linked to disease prevention, particularly cancer. Beta-carotene, found in deep yellow and dark green vegetables such as carrots, spinach, winter squash, sweet potatoes, and pumpkins, is a major anti-carcinogen.

Cruciferous vegetables may be cancer-preventive, too: Brussels sprouts, cau-liflower, broccoli, broc-coflower, kale, mustard greens, cabbages, turnips, and rutabagas. Many con-tain vitamins B and C.

Try to eat vegetables both raw and cooked. Some, like carrots, yield 30% more beta-carotene after cook-ing, 50% after puréeing. Vitamin C–rich vegetables can lose up to half their nutrients when boiled, but only 15% when cooked in a microwave oven.

Choose a wider variety of darker greens—arugula, chicory, collards, dande-lions, kale, spinach, and watercress. And when dressing vegetables or sal-ads, have a light touch.

FRUITS

2–4 servings
Fruits aren't far behind vegetables as anti-carcinogens. The ellagic acid in grapes and straw-berries, for example, may be effective in preventing colon and esophageal can-cers. A natural flavoring agent in oranges and lemons may be anticar-cinogenic, too. Many fruits contain vitamins A, C, and E, which act as antioxi-dants, fighting molecules that can harm your body's natural healing ability.

Certain fruit pectins and gums lower cholesterol.

And fruit replaces high-sugar, high-fat treats, satis-fying your sweet tooth naturally. Furthermore, studies show that with at least two servings per day, fat consumption falls, which helps control weight.

PROTEIN

2–3 servings

It turns out that we need far less protein than anyone previously imagined. According to the American Heart Association, two 3-ounce portions of animal protein a day (an amount the size of a deck of cards) is quite sufficient. Limiting protein is a good idea because it is a natural carrier of fat and cholesterol.

The demands of health-minded consumers have encouraged breeders to raise leaner animals, and now leaner meat is actually becoming a reality.

Variety is important, but emphasize fish and poultry. Skinless, boneless chicken is tasty, lower in fat, and quick to prepare. White meat has less fat than dark. Try substituting ground chicken or turkey for ground beef, lamb, or veal. Fish is an excellent lean, protein-rich food. Some, like salmon and mackerel, have the added bonus of beneficial Omega-3 fatty acids. The American Heart Association recommends at least two fish meals per week. Game of all kinds is surprisingly lean, and now that it's farm-raised, it's milder in taste and more widely available.

Beans contain protein in amounts comparable to other protein-rich foods. They also provide fiber with virtually no fat. Include them in your diet.

In eggs, yolks are the culprits. Egg whites have no cholesterol and only 16 calories. Try substituting two egg whites for one egg in an omelette or make a frittata out of just whites. Nuts and seeds are good sources of protein, vitamins, and minerals, but are loaded with fat and calories (130 to 200 calories per ounce!). Walnuts, pecans, almonds, pistachios, peanuts, and hickory nuts are lowest in saturated fats.

Product	Protein (grams)	Calories	Fat (g)	Fat %	Carbohydrates (g)
One-cup serving					
Chick-peas	15	270	4	13%	45
Black beans	15	230	1	4%	41
Lentils	16	220	1	4%	38
White rice	4	230	trace	trace	50
Brown rice	5	230	1	4%	50
Pasta	6	190	1	5%	38
3½-ounce serving					
Sirloin	19	125	5	37%	0
Ground beef (lean)	17	192	13	61%	0
Lamb chops	16	122	6	45%	0
Pork loin	23	130	4	26%	0
Salmon	21	145	6	37%	0
Sole	19	91	1	12%	0
Shrimp (8 jumbo)	13	63	.7	10%	0
Scallops	17	87	1	8%	0

MILK, YOGURT & CHEESE

2–3 servings

The dairy group harbors two of the biggest diet dangers: fat and cholesterol.

But it also contains many wonderful low-fat and nonfat alternatives, rich in calcium, protein, and flavor. The secret's in the choosing.

Be on your guard for cheese labels that shout "lite" or "low-fat." This is one of the areas where there is the most confusion in labeling. Many such products still get half their calories from fat and are high in sodium.

"Light" may refer only to the sodium, not the fat. As the new labeling laws become effective, there are only a few cheeses that will qualify as lower in fat—part-skim mozzarella, fat-free cream cheese, low-fat goat cheese, nonfat cottage cheese—and they're not yet all available from coast to coast. On the other hand, it's almost impossible to buy whole milk yogurt anywhere.

Product *per one-cup serving*	Calories	Cholesterol (mg)	Fat (g)	% Fat
Heavy cream	821	326	80	97%
Whole milk	150	33	8	49%
2% milk	121	18	4.7	35%
Skim milk	86	4	.4	4%
Nonfat buttermilk	90	2	1	trace
Low-fat buttermilk	100	2	1	9%
Buttermilk	99	9	2	20%
Evaporated skim milk	198	10	.5	2%
Low-fat cottage cheese	164	10	2	11%
Nonfat cottage cheese	140	10	0	0%
Yogurt	150	30	8	40%
Low-fat yogurt	128	12	3	22%
Nonfat yogurt	120	0	1.4	10%
Sour cream	512	trace	48	84%
Low-Fat Blend (page xxvi)	142	5	2	12%
Nonfat Blend (page xxvi)	130	0	.7	5%
Light sour cream	400	0	32	72%
Ricotta	400	120	32	72%
Low-fat ricotta	160	60	8	45%
Cream cheese	792	176	80	91%
Low-fat cream cheese	640	40	56	79%
Fat-free cream cheese	200	40	0	0%
Mayonnaise	1600	80	176	99%
Light mayonnaise	800	80	80	91%
Part-skim mozzarella	576	128	40	63%
Parmesan	888	152	56	57%
Yogurt Cheese (page xxvi)	219	0	0	0%

FATS, OILS & SUGARS

You really do need some fat to absorb vitamins A, D, E, and K, and supply your body with essential fatty acids, but not getting enough fat is hardly the problem in America. The USDA recommends limiting fat intake to no more than 30% of total calories, and the national average is around 37%. Some experts think even 30% is too high. The choice is personal.

Some fats and oils actually aid in lowering cholesterol. Others, like Omega-3 fatty acids, have a preventive anticlotting action. Know what you're looking for, and choose and use wisely.

Saturated fats. Solid at room temperature, these artery-damaging fats are found in animal products like lard, meat fat, butter, and whole milk products, as well as tropical oils. Poultry and fish contain some, but less than red meat. These fats are the real villains; they have a greater impact on heart disease than dietary cholesterol. Experts recommend limiting them to no more than 7 grams a day.

Polyunsaturated fats are liquid at room temperature, and are found primarily in vegetable oils. They lower both LDL (bad cholesterol) and HDL (good cholesterol). Polyunsaturated Omega-3 fatty acids, found in fish such as salmon and mackerel (and leafy vegetables, and some seeds and oils) have an anticlotting action, effective in preventing heart attack and stroke.

Monounsaturated fats reduce only the damaging LDL, leaving HDL untouched. They are found in high amounts in olive, canola (rapeseed) and peanut oils. They remain liquid at room temperature, but become viscous or hard when refrigerated. There's a widespread agreement that olive and canola oils help lower cholesterol when they replace saturated fat, but you should still limit monounsaturated fats to 10–15% of total daily calories. And watch out for margarine. New studies indicate that in converting vegetable oils to solid margarine, "transfatty acids," which act like saturated fat, occur.

There are foods you wouldn't think contain fat—raspberries, for instance (it's in the seeds). And though it may be well known by now that avocados are very high in oil, few would suspect cloves, rice, beans, or grains of having any. So you can see that the pyramid's fat recommendation is as much a caution to beware of the total fat in your diet as a prescription for how many servings to consume.

Sugars. While the consensus is that sugars cause dental cavities but no other health problems, they contribute to obesity and squeeze out room for more nutritious foods by filling you up with empty calories. Experts recommend limiting consumption of refined sugars to 5% of total calories. Let fruit be your sweet treat.

Cholesterol is a waxy, fatlike substance that, with other blood fats, can clog the blood vessels, causing hardening of the arteries and sometimes triggering heart attack or stroke. If something you ate once had a liver, it had cholesterol. It's in meat, cheese—any animal product. Like other animals, you too manufacture the cholesterol in your own blood—60 to 80% of it.

TYPES OF OILS & FATS

All fats and oils have approximately 9 grams of fat or 100 calories per tablespoon.

	% Undefined Fatty Acids	% Polyunsaturated	% Monounsaturated	% Saturated	Chol. (mg)
Oils					
Almond	1	18	73	8	0
Avocado	12	13	71	4	0
Canola/rapeseed	4	30	59	7	0
Coconut	7	2	6	86	0
Corn	4	59	24	13	0
Cottonseed	4	52	18	26	0
Grapeseed	21	69	0	10	0
Hazelnut	5	10	78	7	0
Palm	5	9	37	49	0
Peanut	5	32	46	17	0
Olive	5	8	74	13	0
Safflower	78	13	9	0	0
Sesame	4	42	40	14	0
Soy	0	16	25	15	0
Sunflower	5	88	21	11	0
Vegetable	5	74	12	9	0
Walnut	5	67	24	9	0
Fats					
Chicken fat	4	21	45	30	24.1
Duck fat	0	14	51	35	13
Turkey fat	0	24	45	31	13
Lard	0	11	48	41	12
Butter	0	5	31	64	33

Chart based on analysis by Nutrinfo, Norwood, Massachusetts.

EVERY DAY, IT'S YOUR CHOICE

How to Figure Your Daily Fat Allowance in Calories and Grams

1. First, establish your health and weight goals. Take into consideration your sex, age, height, frame, current weight, activity level, and overall health. It's always a good idea to consult your doctor or nutritionist.

2. For instance, say you are a 130-pound woman who wants to maintain her weight. With the above considerations in mind, you may arrive at 1500 calories as ideal. If you also want to limit your calories from fat to 30% of your total calories (the USDA recommendation), 450 would be your limit.

3. If you also want to figure your daily allowance in grams, simply divide 450 calories by 9 (the number of calories per gram of fat) and you can easily see that your daily allowance is 50 grams from fat.

4. If, on the other hand, your goal is losing weight, you may arrive at 1200 calories a day. Then, you might also drop your maximum to 20% or 250 of your daily calories.

5. To keep track of fat grams, read labels and/or fat tables and add up your total every day. If you splurge on foods that contain more than your allowance, you will need to make up for it over the next 4 to 5 days.

The Fat/Calorie Equation

As you determine your daily calorie and fat intake, remember that a unit of fat has twice the calories of an equal unit of either protein or carbohydrates.

Calories per day	30% cal. from fat	25%	20%
3000	900 calories from fat (100 grams)	750 cal. (83 g)	600 cal. (67 g)
2500	750 calories from fat (83 grams)	625 cal. (69 g)	500 cal. (56 g)
2000	600 calories from fat (67 grams)	500 cal. (56 g)	400 cal. (45 g)
1500	450 calories from fat (50 grams)	375 cal. (42 g)	300 cal. (34 g)
1200	360 calories from fat (40 grams)	300 cal. (33 g)	240 cal. (27 g)

*Each calorie of fat = 9 grams

PERSONALIZING THE PYRAMID

The next step: thinking positively and making new health habits your own.

1. Eat three square meals and two snacks

Breakfast is a vital "jump-start" after perhaps 12 hours of fasting. It energizes and can help you keep from splurging later in the day, or eating "empty calorie" foods. You need complex carbohydrates for energy and fiber, a good source of protein, and an abundance of vitamins and minerals. Skip the high-fat, high-sugar doughnuts and bacon, but don't skip breakfast!

Lunch refuels and keeps you from overeating at dinner. Avoid the high-fat fast-food trap by choosing salads, soups, lean meat, and whole-grain sandwiches. Make soup the night before to heat up at work, pack a sandwich (tuck in a veggie or two), or take pasta and reheat it in the microwave oven. If you have lunch in a restaurant, order broiled fish or chicken.

Dinner should be a lot lighter than we're used to. Rather than a big piece of meat, make pasta, a vegetable stir-fry, soup, or salad the main event, with meat as an accent. Have a perfectly ripened fruit for dessert, perhaps dressed up with a yogurt sauce flavored with fruit purée.

"Legal snacks" (two a day) keep blood sugar steady and keep you from mindless munching. Choose sensibly from fresh foods: a baked potato, low-fat cheese and whole-grain crackers, low-fat popcorn, rice cakes, or fresh fruit and veggies. A smart snack helps curb impulsive eating.

Have a Great Good Day

Here's a day's menu based on the USDA's recommended 30% maximum fat allowance from total calories. In fact, the percentage for this hypothetical day is only 21%, in spite of three dishes that are significantly higher than 30%.

7:00 a.m.

Breakfast	Cal.	Fat(g)/%
Lime-Mint Slush	98	1/5
1 slice Edgecombs' Rye Bread	114	2/14
1 cup strawberries	55	.6/12
½ cup nonfat yogurt	61	.7/10
Coffee or tea	0	0/0

10:00 a.m.

Snack		
Granny Smith apple	77	.5/5

12:30 p.m.

Lunch		
Easy Caesar Salad	126	7/37
Herbed Croutons	74	4/49
Minted Pea Soup	71	2/19
1 slice Edgecombs' Rye Bread	114	2/14

4:00 p.m.

Snack		
Orange Tea	28	.1/4
Walnut-Raisin Toast	164	7/38

7:00 p.m.

Dinner		
Herbed Walleye	216	2/10
Five-Spice Rice	98	3/22
Oven-Roasted Veggies	35	1/11
Sautéed Spinach with Ginger	63	.5/6
1 cup honeydew melon	40	.2/0
2 tablespoons Mint Cream	16	.2/12
Total:	**1450**	**33.8/21%**

2. Eat more fiber

Nutrition experts recommend 30 grams of fiber a day (or about 2 grams per 100 calories). Our ancestors consumed about 100 grams, which is one reason we're fatter, and have higher cholesterol levels and greater rates of digestive cancers, in spite of eating less.

Fiber comes in two forms:
▲ Insoluble fiber forms bulk in the intestinal tract, decreasing the likelihood of intestinal polyps, colon cancer, hemorrhoids, appendicitis, diverticular disease, and irritable bowel syndrome. It's in wheat bran, whole grains and vegetables.
▲ Soluble fiber forms gels that delay the absorption of certain foods. Since it dissolves, it's ideal for cleaning out cholesterol and carrying away carcinogens. These pectins, gums, and other substances are found in oat bran, barley, citrus fruits, and most beans.

Choose the fiber found naturally in a wide variety of foods, rather than supplements. Cooked legumes are a particularly good source; a half cup provides an average of 5 grams of fiber and less than 1 gram of fat. Whole grains, fruits, and vegetables are also very good.

Eat a high-fiber diet, and you probably will consume a lot less fat while feeling satisfied by the same amount of food.

3. Exercise

Regular exercise enhances your overall health and sense of well-being. It makes you more energetic, while it increases your basal metabolism rate. You become a more efficient calorie-burner (better able to handle that occasional indulgence), a boost that can last for hours. The experts now say that without exercise, you can't lose weight and keep it off.
▲ Increase your physical activity—a minimum of 20 minutes of moderate exercise, three times a week.
▲ Step up your "lifestyle" activity—take the stairs, walk to the store, bicycle downtown, take up gardening . . . move!

"It's all right to drink like a fish—if you drink what a fish drinks."

Mary Pettibose Poole

4. Drink water

We're made primarily of water—warmed in winter, chilled in summer. It replenishes, cleanses, and makes us work more efficiently. Psychologists say we often snack when we're actually thirsty. So it only makes sense to drink an ample supply.

I start every day with a pick-me-up of ¼ cup lemon juice mixed with water. And I try to drink 8 to 10 glasses of water during the day. It's cleansing and doesn't make you feel jittery the way caffeine and sugar substitutes do. Keep a glass or bottle near you as you work.

VITAMINS
Good for You Nutrients

Vitamin A
- Keeps hair, skin, and mucous membranes healthy.
- Helps night vision.
- Promotes proper bone growth, teeth development, and reproduction.

The B Complex Vitamins, Including Niacin, Thiamine, Riboflavin, and Folic Acid
- Help your body absorb and metabolize carbohydrates and protein and use fats.
- Help in the formation of red blood cells.

Vitamin C
- Helps keep your capilaries, bones, and teeth healthy.
- Aids in the formation of collagen.
- Helps protect other vitamins from oxidation.
- May actually be a preventative for certain cancer-causing agents.
- Large doses may have an antihistamine effect, making your colds seem less severe (there's no evidence that it prevents colds or flu).
- With foods containing iron, can increase the iron you absorb.
- Aids calcium absorption.

Calcium
- Essential to building strong bones and teeth, blood clotting, and the functioning of muscles and nerves.
- Helps maintain cell membranes and aids in the absorption of B_{12} and the activation of enzymes. (Too much protein or fat interferes with calcium absorption and greatly increases calcium loss.)

Iron
- Helps muscles work.
- An essential part of hemoglobin, which carries oxygen from your lungs to your body tissues.
- Helps build healthy red blood cells (when iron becomes low or depleted, it may be a warning sign of anemia and many indicate the need for supplements).
- Coffee or tea after a meal can inhibit the absorption of iron from food.

Potassium
- Important for muscle contraction, maintaining fluid and electrolyte balance in the cells, and the transmission of nerve impulses.
- Helps release energy from carbohydrates, proteins, and fats.

"Tell me what you eat and I will tell you what you are."

Anthelme Brillat-Savarin

THE GREAT GOOD KITCHEN

LOWER-FAT COOKING TIPS

■ Learn to use liquids other than oil to moisten and baste:
- concentrated fruit juice
- fresh fruit and vegetable juices
- broths
- puréed fruits and vegetables
- wines, liqueurs, beer, fortified wine
- tea or coffee

■ Remember: Marinades don't have to include oil.

■ Defat whenever possible.

■ Build in time to let your stews, soups, and braised dishes cool so that the fats will rise to the top, congeal, and be easy to spoon off.

■ Use a defatting cup or ladle.

■ Tip the skillet or roasting pan so that most of the fat can be spooned off.

■ Cook rices, grains, and beans in defatted broth—add herbs, garlic, or shallots for even bigger taste.

■ Poach fish in tomato or vegetable broth.

■ Defat pan juices and use them as natural sauces.

■ Sprinkle fish before and during broiling or grilling with lemon juice and fresh herbs.

■ Make sauces from reduced stocks or juices thickened with arrowroot dissolved in water; add fresh herbs, and season with salt and pepper.

■ Thicken sauces with vegetable purées.

■ Make a "cream" sauce with low-fat buttermilk. Thicken 1 cup buttermilk with 1 tablespoon cornstarch; flavor with 3 to 4 tablespoons tomato sauce, mustard, pesto, puréed vegetables, or onion marmalade.

■ Cook with condiments—use mustards, preserves, or chutneys to give a tasty glaze to broiled or grilled foods.

- Add wines or other alcoholic ingredients early in the cooking so that their flavors will penetrate and concentrate. Use wine to deglaze a skillet. The alcohol and calories do not dissipate totally in cooking.
- Know your quantities. Many cooks don't measure, and you might not really know how much fat you're putting into a dish. Learn what a tablespoon of oil looks like, and 3 to 4 ounces of meat. Adjust your sights to know what a tablespoon of dressing on 2 cups of green salad looks like.
- Trim all extra fat from meat and poultry. You can leave the skin on poultry until after it's cooked—almost no fat will penetrate the flesh—but take it off before it goes to the table to avoid temptation.
- Use oil sprays for the lightest coating on pans. They come in a number of varieties—olive, canola, and butter-flavored.
- Find the perfect cookware: one that conducts and holds heat well, cleans easily, and is nonreactive. Most important, look for a surface that is nonstick or requires the smallest amount of oil for cooking.
- To really lightly dress a salad, use a spray bottle to barely coat the leaves.
- Don't throw your favorite old recipes away. Apply new methods, cut back on fat, substitute buttermilk for cream, sauté in broth—to enjoy familiar flavors with less fat.

THE GREAT GOOD PANTRY

For lower-fat cooking everyday, keep these tasty items in stock:

- ❏ Chicken broth
- ❏ Nonfat yogurt
- ❏ Low-fat or nonfat cottage cheese
- ❏ Low-fat or nonfat buttermilk
- ❏ Spices in small quantities to ensure freshness
- ❏ Fresh herbs
- ❏ All sorts of grains: rices, barley, wheat berries, millet
- ❏ All sizes and shapes of pasta
- ❏ All kinds of beans, lentils, and other legumes
- ❏ Mustards
- ❏ Oils for cooking (olive, canola)
- ❏ Oils for flavor (walnut, hazelnut, sesame, hot chile)
- ❏ Soy sauce
- ❏ Capers
- ❏ Anchovies
- ❏ Tomato paste
- ❏ Vinegars—red and white wine, balsamic, cider, herb- and spice-infused
- ❏ Onions, garlic, shallots, scallions
- ❏ Lemons and limes
- ❏ Potatoes—baking, new, Yukon Gold
- ❏ Whole-grain breads, pita bread, fat-free crackers
- ❏ Low-fat ricotta and mozzarella cheeses
- ❏ Kosher salt and sea salt
- ❏ Black, white, and dried green peppercorns
- ❏ Lettuces—Bibb, romaine, radicchio
- ❏ Mushrooms—fresh and dried
- ❏ Hot peppers
- ❏ Vanilla extract and beans
- ❏ Barbecue sauce
- ❏ Fortified wines

Low-Fat Blend

At the beginning of every week, I whip up a batch of this—2 cups of nonfat yogurt and 2 cups of low-fat cottage cheese mixed in the blender or by hand. I never use the food processor—it tends to break the mixture down and make it watery rather than creamy. I stash it in a plastic container in the fridge to use by the cup or spoonful in a myriad of ways. You'll see it used repeatedly throughout *Great Good Food* in mousses and sauces, and as a replacement for sour cream, mayonnaise, or heavy cream. If nonfat cottage cheese is available, so much the better, as the nutritional analysis shows.

YIELD: 2 CUPS

1 cup nonfat plain yogurt
1 cup low-fat or nonfat cottage cheese

Place the ingredients in a blender and blend until smooth. The mixture can be blended by hand. A food processor will not give the same consistency.

Cal. 142 Carb. 11g Protein 20g Chol. 5mg
Fat 1.8g/12% (with low-fat cottage cheese)
Cal. 130 Carb. 12g Protein 20g Chol. 0mg
Fat 0g/0% (with nonfat cottage cheese)
(analyzed per cup)

Yogurt Cheese

YIELD: 1 CUP

Place the yogurt in a cheesecloth-lined sieve or a fine-mesh strainer set over a bowl. Cover with plastic wrap. Set aside at room temperature overnight for at least 8 hours.

Cal. 14 Carb. 2g Protein 1g
Chol. 1mg Fat 0g/0%
(analyzed per tablespoon)

Buttermilk Biscuits

YIELD: 12 BISCUITS

2 cups all-purpose flour
1/4 cup sugar (for dessert biscuits only)
1 tablespoon baking powder
1/2 teaspoon baking soda
1/2 teaspoon salt
1 cup low-fat buttermilk
3 tablespoons canola oil
2 tablespoons vanilla extract

1. Preheat the oven to 425°. Lightly spray or wipe two 13 x 18-inch baking sheets with vegetable oil.
2. Place the flour, sugar, baking powder, baking soda, and salt in a medium-size mixing bowl and mix to combine. Add the buttermilk, oil, and vanilla, and mix with a fork until just blended. Do not overmix or the biscuits will be tough. Add an additional tablespoon of buttermilk if the dough seems too dry—this should be fairly sticky.
3. Drop the dough by heaping tablespoons, 1½ inches apart, onto the baking sheets. Bake for 10 to 12 minutes, until light golden brown. Remove from the oven and serve immediately.

Cal. 117 Carb. 18g Protein 3g Chol. 0mg
Fat 3.7g/29% (without sugar)
Cal. 133 Carb. 22g Protein 3g Chol. 0mg
Fat 3.7g/25% (with sugar)
(analyzed per biscuit)

Never-Fail Hollandaise

The taste's incredibly like classic hollandaise—but with the least amount of egg yolks and butter.

YIELD: 1 CUP

1 tablespoon cornstarch
2 tablespoons fresh lemon juice, strained
Salt
Cayenne
2 egg yolks
2 tablespoons unsalted butter

1. In the top a double boiler, slowly whisk ¾ cup water into the cornstarch. Stir in the lemon juice, salt, and cayenne to taste. Place the top over simmering water, and cook, stirring constantly, until slightly thickened, 2 to 3 minutes.

2. Remove the top from the heat. Whisk in the egg yolks, one at a time, and 1 tablespoon of butter. Replace over the water and cook until slightly thickened, about 3 minutes, stirring constantly.

3. When ready to serve, whisk in the remaining butter; taste and correct the seasonings.

Cal. **22** *Carb.* **1g** *Protein* **3g** *Chol.* **27mg**
Fat **2g/82%** *(analyzed per tablespoon)* %

Béarnaise Sauce

YIELD: 1 CUP

¼ cup white wine
2 tablespoons white wine vinegar
1 tablespoon finely minced shallot
Liberal grinding of white pepper
¼ teaspoon dried tarragon
⅛ teaspoon dried chervil
1 tablespoon minced fresh Italian parsley
1 tablespoon cornstarch
2 egg yolks, lightly beaten
2 tablespoons unsalted butter
Salt and freshly ground pepper

1. In a small nonreactive saucepan, combine the wine, vinegar, shallot, white pepper, tarragon, chervil, and parsley over medium-high heat. Bring to a low boil, reduce to 2 tablespoons, and strain. Discard the solids.

2. In the top of a double boiler over simmering water, whisk the cornstarch and ¾ cup of water. Stir until thickened, 3 to 4 minutes. Stir in the reduced vinegar mixture.

3. Remove the double boiler from the heat and whisk in the egg yolks and 1 tablespoon of butter. Place back over hot water and stir constantly until

thickened, about 4 more minutes. Do not overcook or let the mixture come close to a boil or it will curdle. Whisk in the butter and salt and pepper to taste. The sauce can be allowed to cool and gently reheated in a double boiler.

Cal. **23** *Carb.* **.8g** *Protein* **3g** *Chol.* **26.8mg**
Fat **2g/73%** *(analyzed per tablespoon)* %

Sugar Syrup

YIELD: 2 CUPS

2 cups sugar

In a small saucepan, combine 1 cup of water and the sugar. Bring to a boil and swirl the pan to dissolve the liquid. Cool, then pour into a container and keep covered in the refrigerator until needed.

Cal. **193** *Carb.* **50g** *Protein* **0g** *Chol.* **0mg** *Fat* **0g/0%** *(analyzed per ¼ cup)*

Chocolate Ganache

YIELD: 1½ CUPS

1 cup semisweet chocolate chips
1 cup Low-Fat Blend (opposite)
1 tablespoon espresso
1 tablespoon vanilla extract

1. In the top of a double boiler over simmering water, heat the chocolate until it is completely melted and smooth. Remove from the heat and cool until the chocolate is just warm to the touch, and stir in the espresso; do not allow it to set.

2. Place the Low-Fat Blend in a small mixing bowl. Gradually whisk the warm chocolate into the Low-Fat Blend until thoroughly incorporated. Blend in the vanilla until combined. Use immediately or refrigerate until needed.

Cal. **34** *Carb.* **4g** *Protein* **1g** %

Chol. **1mg** *Fat* **2g/48%** *(analyzed per tablespoon)*

It's About Broth

Whether homemade or store-bought, chicken broth seems indispensable, with uses that go far beyond the beloved chicken soup. In lower-fat cooking, chicken broth will be your best nonfat medium in various cooking methods, particularly sautéing.

Short of homemade broth, here are my usual fallbacks:

• Many gourmet shops and upscale supermarkets offer frozen chicken broth or stock, which is pretty acceptable.

• Chinese restaraunts often sell chicken broth or stock by the quart.

• As I roast a chicken and baste it with chicken broth, a more concentrated broth results. If I'm not serving it with the chicken, I freeze it and defat it later.

• There is one brand of canned chicken broth I rely on—College Inn. The various canned low-sodium or defatted broths on the market have little flavor, and unless you're on a very strict diet, they should be avoided altogether.

A hint: When opening the can, I only open it three-quarters of the way. Then, as I pour the broth through the small opening, the lid captures and removes most of the fat that has congealed on the surface.

Chicken Broth: A Comparison

Great Good Chicken Broth
Cal. **.1** *Carb.* **0g** *Protein* **0g** *Chol.* **0mg** *Fat* **0g/0%***

Canned, 99% fat free, low sodium %
Cal. **16** *Carb.* **1g** *Protein* **1g** *Chol.* **0mg** *Fat* **1g/50%***

Canned, regular
Cal. **22** *Carb.* **1.45g** *Protein* **1.34g** *Chol.* **0mg**
Fat **1.1g/45%*** %

(analyzed per cup)

Great Good Chicken Broth

I vary this recipe by adding lemon grass, sage, rosemary, dill, or ginger.

YIELD: 3½ QUARTS

1 chicken (4½ to 5 pounds), cut into pieces
4 chicken wings
2 garlic cloves
1 onion, peeled and quartered
4 scallions, cut into 2-inch pieces
4 carrots, peeled and cut into 2-inch pieces
4 celery ribs, cut into 2-inch pieces
2 cups fresh parsley leaves
2 bay leaves
Salt
½ teaspoon black peppercorns

In a large stockpot, place 5 quarts of cold water and all of the ingredients. Slowly bring to a boil; reduce the heat and simmer for 4½ hours, skimming and defatting whenever possible. Strain, reserving the chicken for another purpose if you like, and cool to room temperature. Use the broth immediately or store in the refrigerator for up to 1 week or in the freezer for 1 month.

Herbed Vegetable Broth

Use this as a basis for soup or stew, a broth for cooking grains or beans, for poaching fish, or any other way you might use chicken stock.

SERVES 6

1 cup coarsely chopped onion
1 cup scraped and coarsely chopped carrot
1 cup coarsely chopped celery, including some leaves
1 whole head garlic, papery outsides removed and tips cut off with a sharp knife to expose the flesh
2 strips lemon zest (2 x ½ inch)
2 bay leaves

2 sprigs fresh thyme
1 tablespoon dried oregano
4 sprigs fresh Italian parsley
1 small whole dried red chili
10 peppercorns
1 clove
One 2-inch cinnamon stick
¼ teaspoon salt

1. In a large Dutch oven or stockpot, combine all of the ingredients. Bring to a boil, cover and lower the heat to a simmer. Simmer gently for 1 hour. Remove from heat; cool to room temperature.
2. Strain the broth through a fine sieve, pushing down hard on the solids.

Cal. **0** *Carb.* **0g** *Protein* **0g** *Chol.* **0mg** *Fat* **0g/0%**
(analyzed per cup)

Beef Broth

YIELD: 2½ QUARTS

2 pounds beef soup bones
2 pounds lean beef, coarsely cubed
2 large onions, each cut into 8 pieces
1 rutabaga, peeled and coarsely chopped
2 celery stalks with leaves, coarsely chopped
2 carrots, coarsely chopped
4 tablespoons tomato paste
14 black peppercorns
5 sprigs fresh parsley
8 sprigs fresh thyme
8 garlic cloves, crushed
8 whole cloves
4 allspice berries
2 bay leaves
Salt

1. Preheat the oven to 450°.
2. Place the beef bones and cubes on a baking sheet. Brown them in the oven for 20 to 25 minutes, turning once or twice.

3. Place the beef in a large stockpot. Add all of the remaining ingredients and 4 quarts of cold water, or enough to cover by 2 inches; heat over medium heat to very slowly bring to a boil. Lower the heat, stir, cover, and simmer for 5 hours. From time to time, skim off any foam that accumulates.
4. Remove the pot from the heat and let cool to room temperature, uncovered. Defat the broth.
5. Strain the broth through a fine-mesh strainer. Discard the bones, meats, vegetables, and spices. Remove the grease from the surface.

Cal. **14** *Carb.* **0g** *Protein* **2g** *Chol.* **6mg** *Fat* **1g/46%** %
(analyzed per cup)

Onion Marmalade

Onions caramelized without any fat—simply through long simmering. This is great served as a condiment or an hors d'oeuvre, or atop pizza. It can add flavor to any number of dishes.

YIELD: 2 CUPS

2 tablespoons chicken broth (see opposite)
12 cups thinly sliced yellow onions
¼ cup balsamic vinegar

1. In a large saucepan over medium-high heat, warm the broth. Add the onion, cover, and cook until translucent and very soft, about 45 minutes.
2. Uncover, lower the heat, and simmer for 1 hour, stirring periodically. Add the vinegar and cook until the onion is caramelized, about 1 hour longer. Use immediately, or store in a glass or plastic container in the refrigerator for up to 10 days.

Cal. **23** *Carb.* **5g** *Protein* **1g** *Chol.* **0mg** *Fat* **1g/4%**
(analyzed per tablespoon)

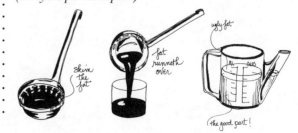

skim the fat

fat runneth over

ugly fat

the good part!

Flaky Pie Crust

To make pie crust delicate and flaky, it has to have fat—therefore, good pie is always an indulgence. But this one has no cholesterol.

YIELD: TWO 9-INCH SINGLE-CRUST PIES (16 SLICES)

2²/₃ cups all-purpose flour
¹/₄ teaspoon salt
4 tablespoons sugar
¹/₂ cup canola oil
6 tablespoons ice water
1 tablespoon skim milk

Place the flour, salt, and sugar in a large bowl, and blend well with a fork. Add the oil, and using a pastry blender or two table knives, cut the oil into the flour until the mixture resembles coarse crumbs. Sprinkle the water and milk over the mixture and blend it with a knife. Using your hands, gather the dough into two balls. Use immediately or wrap with plastic wrap and refrigerate until needed. When rolling the dough out, roll it between two sheets of waxed paper.

*Cal. **148** Carb. **19g** Protein **2g** Chol. **0mg***
*Fat **7g/43%** (analyzed per slice)*

Basic Bread

YIELD: 2 LOAVES (24 SLICES)

1 cup lukewarm water
2 tablespoons light brown sugar
1 package (¹/₄ ounce) active dry yeast
2 cups bread flour
1 cup rye flour
2¹/₂ teaspoons salt
2 tablespoons unsalted butter, softened
1 tablespoon cornmeal
1 egg
1 teaspoon sea salt

1. Place the water in a small bowl, sprinkle in the sugar and yeast, and stir to combine. Set aside for 10 minutes, until the mixture is foamy.

2. In the bowl of a food processor, combine the flours, salt, and butter. With the machine running, add the yeast mixture. Process until the dough cleans the sides of the bowl. If it seems too sticky, add a little flour. If it seems too dry, add a teaspoon of warm water. Process the dough for 10 minutes.

3. Spray or wipe a large bowl with vegetable oil. Add the dough and turn to coat evenly. Cover the bowl with plastic wrap and let the dough double in size, about 1¹/₂ hours.

4. Spray or wipe a large baking sheet with vegetable oil and dust it lightly with cornmeal.

5. Punch down the risen dough and divide in half. On a lightly floured surface, roll each piece into a 2 x 12-inch rectangle. Roll each rectangle up, jelly-roll fashion, along the long side. Pinch the ends and side seams to seal. Place the dough, seam side down, on the baking sheet. Cover with plastic wrap and let rise, until doubled in size, about 1¹/₂ hours. Preheat the oven to 425°.

6. In a small bowl, whisk the egg and ¹/₂ teaspoon salt. Brush the loaves with the mixture. With a very sharp knife, make three ¹/₄-inch-deep slashes on the top of each loaf. Sprinkle with the remaining salt. Place the loaves in the oven and bake for 20 minutes, until they are nicely browned and sound hollow when tapped on the bottom. Transfer the bread to a rack and allow to cool.

*Cal. **184** Carb. **37g** Protein **5g** Chol. **0mg***
*Fat **1.6g/8%** (analyzed per slice)*

Sourdough Starter

If you always have this on hand, you can bake great bread at the drop of a hat.

1 package (¹/₄ ounce) active dry yeast
2 cups lukewarm water
2 cups white flour

1. Place all of the ingredients in a glass bowl, crock, or jar. Stir with a wooden spoon—never use metal—until well blended; place in a warm place, uncovered, for 4 to 7 days.

2. Stir the mixture once a day, incorporating any crust that forms. After 4 to 7 days the starter will be light and foamy. Use at once or refrigerate until needed. To replenish, mix equal portions of water and flour with the original starter.

Plain Focaccia Dough

SERVES 12

1 pound potatoes, preferably Yukon Gold, peeled,
  boiled, and mashed
1 package ($^1/_4$ ounce) active dry yeast
$^1/_2$ teaspoon sugar
4 to 4$^1/_2$ cups all-purpose flour
1 teaspoon salt
1 tablespoon olive oil

1. Peel, boil, and mash the potatoes; you should have 2 cups. Reserve the water. Cool to lukewarm.
2. Meanwhile, in a small bowl combine the potato water, yeast, and $^1/_2$ teaspoon sugar, stirring to combine. Let the mixture proof (foam up) 8 to 10 minutes.
3. In the large bowl of an electric mixer fitted with a dough hook or beaters, combine 4 cups of the flour and the salt. Add the cooled mashed potatoes and yeast mixture. Beat the dough at medium speed 5 to 8 minutes. The dough will be wet and sticky. Add up to $^1/_2$ cup more flour. The dough will still be somewhat wet and sticky. Beat in the oil.
4. Lightly coat a large bowl with vegetable oil. Scrape the dough into the bowl, turning to coat. Cover the bowl with plastic wrap and refrigerate overnight.
5. The next day, punch the dough down and

proceed with the desired topping and specific baking instructions.
Cal. **184** *Carb.* **37g** *Protein* **5g** *Chol.* **0mg** *Fat* **1.6g/8%**

Sweet Focaccia

SERVES 12

1 pound potatoes, preferably Yukon Gold or
  Yellow Finn potatoes
1 package ($^1/_4$ ounce) active dry yeast
$^1/_2$ cup plus $^1/_2$ teaspoon sugar
4 to 4$^1/_2$ cups all-purpose flour
1 teaspoon salt
1 tablespoon unsalted butter, softened

1. Follow steps 1 and 2 for Plain Focaccia Dough.
2. In the large bowl of an electric mixer fitted with a dough hook or beaters, combine the remaining sugar, 4 cups flour, and the salt. Add the mashed potatoes and the yeast mixture. Beat until smooth, 5 to 8 minutes. The dough will be wet. Add up to $^1/_2$ cup more flour. The dough will still be quite wet and sticky. Beat in the butter.
3. Lightly spray or wipe a large bowl with vegetable oil. Scrape the dough into the bowl and turn to coat. Cover with plastic wrap and refrigerate overnight.
4. The next morning, punch down the dough and proceed according to your recipe.
Cal. **232** *Carb.* **46g** *Protein* **5g** *Chol.* **3mg** *Fat* **3g/11%**

Spring Fever

"Spring sprang suddenly onto the land."
Jean Giono

Spring Journal

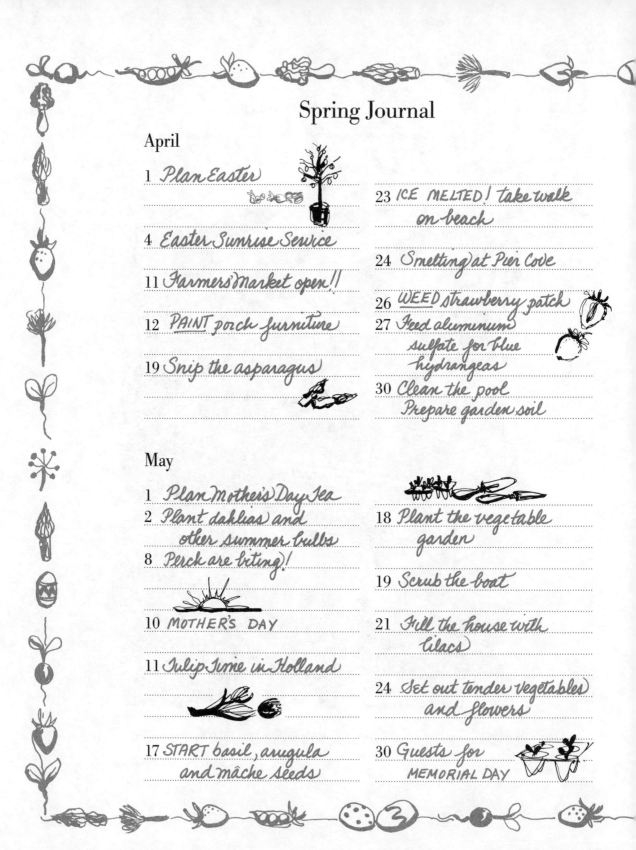

April

1 Plan Easter

4 Easter Sunrise Service

11 Farmers' Market open!!

12 PAINT porch furniture

19 Snip the asparagus

23 ICE MELTED! take walk on beach

24 Smelting at Pier Cove

26 WEED strawberry patch

27 Feed aluminum sulfate for blue hydrangeas

30 Clean the pool
   Prepare garden soil

May

1 Plan Mother's Day Tea

2 Plant dahlias and other summer bulbs

8 Perch are biting!

10 MOTHER'S DAY

11 Tulip Time in Holland

17 START basil, arugula and mâche seeds

18 Plant the vegetable garden

19 Scrub the boat

21 Fill the house with lilacs

24 Set out tender vegetables and flowers

30 Guests for MEMORIAL DAY

Opal Basil
Mache
Peas
Radishes
Basil
Aruqula
Red Leaf
Chard
Beets
Flowers all around

June

1 Yacht Club CLEAN-UP!
3 Plan Father's Day
4 Finish planting
5 Find espadrilles

8 START WEEDING!
10 FATHER'S DAY

11 It's too dry! WATER!!

14 Make strawberry pies
15 Press flowers

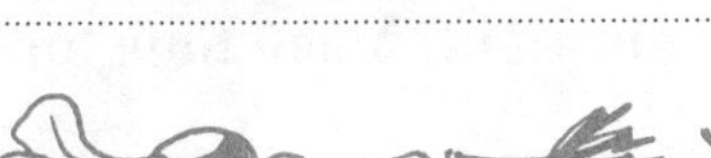
FLOWER PRESS

22 Plan Mid-Summer Nights Supper

24 Find straw hats

25 Pick peas, radishes, baby beets and sugar snaps

27 PAINT NEW FENCE!

28 Re-read Gift from the Sea

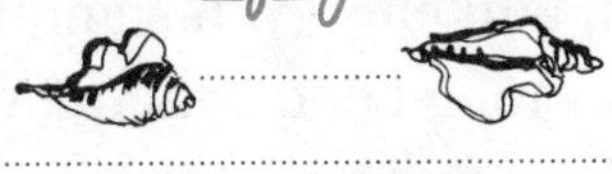

30 Take first midnight dip

Good Day Sunshine

Nothing beats breakfast on a spring morning. The air is cool and fresh. The first rays of sun steal over the horizon, building to a golden climax of light, warmth, and energy. It's another day. A new beginning.

Breakfast has long been championed as the most important meal of the day. It just happens to be my favorite. I'm a morning person, up early, ready to begin the day, and I've learned the way to start out right: Make time for breakfast.

FRESH FRUIT IN A GLASS

A fabulous way to begin your regimen of five fruits a day and start adding up fiber, vitamins A, B, C, and D, calcium, boron, thiamine, potassium, and very little fat. And fresh fruit starts off the day on a naturally sweet note, whether you're at home or on the go.

Red Berry Shake

Greet the day with a fresh rosy glassful, loaded with vitamin C and ready in seconds.

SERVES 2

1 cup fresh strawberries, hulled and halved
1 cup fresh pineapple chunks
½ cup fresh raspberries
2 tablespoons frozen limeade, defrosted

Process all of the ingredients in a blender until smooth. Serve immediately.

*Cal. **133** Carb. **34g** Protein **5g** Chol. **0mg** Fat **1g/7%***

Lime-Mint Slush

Bananas deliver a big energy punch. And they can replace the potassium depleted when you exercise.

SERVES 2

1 banana
6 mint leaves
Zest of 1 lime
1 cup skim milk
¼ cup ice cubes

Place the banana in a blender and purée. Add all of the other ingredients and blend until slushy. Serve immediately.

*Cal. **98** Carb. **20g** Protein **5g***
*Chol. **2mg** Fat **1g/5%***

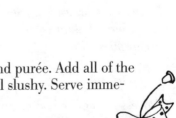

The Ideal Breakfast
Because your body can't store carbohydrates, you need a big boost every morning. You'll even think better. Start with complex carbohydrates, found in whole grains. They supply fiber and convert easily into glucose, vital for fueling the body's systems.

You need protein to get you going, too. Besides meat, good sources include cheese, yogurt, and other dairy products; nut butters; and legumes combined with whole grains, seeds, or nuts.

Avoid simple carbohydrates like those found in refined sugars. Fresh fruits supply all the natural sugar you want, plus fiber. But give up maple syrup on pancakes? Never! Just make it a sometime treat and use just a little.

Strawberry Slush

Sweetly strawberry, with an icy touch of tart.
SERVES 1
1 cup fresh strawberries, hulled and halved
1 tablespoon fresh mint leaves
Sugar
½ cup fresh orange juice
1 tablespoon fresh lemon or lime juice

In a blender, purée the strawberries and mint until very smooth. Add sugar to taste and strain if you like. Add the juices and serve immediately over ice.

*Cal. **107** Carb. **25g** Protein **2g** Chol. **0mg** Fat **.8g/6%***

Ginger-Melon Shake

SERVES 2
1 quarter cantaloupe, peeled, seeded, and cut into chunks
  (about 1 cup)
1 tablespoon crystallized ginger
1 cup skim milk
¼ cup ice cubes

Process the cantaloupe and ginger in a blender until very smooth. Add the milk and ice cubes and blend to desired consistency. Serve immediately.

*Cal. **87** Carb. **16g** Protein **5g** Chol. **2mg** Fat **.5g/5%***

Coffee Sip

Sip this cool coffee for your wake-up call.
SERVES 1
1 cup strong brewed coffee
¼ cup nonfat plain yogurt
½ cup skim milk
Sugar
¼ cup ice cubes

Process the coffee and yogurt in a blender until very smooth. Add the skim milk and sugar to taste. Add the ice cubes and blend to desired consistency; strain if you like. Serve immediately over ice.

*Cal. **81** Carb. **12g** Protein **7g** Chol. **2mg** Fat **.6g/6%***

Juicing It

You like to juice—for that concentrated energy in a glass. But you need fiber, too. So you don't juice every day. And when you do, you save as much of the fiber as you can to use in cookies, bread dough, cakes, salads, and pita sandwiches.

Carrot juice is by far the most popular vegetable juice. No wonder. It's sweet, bright, and serves as a fabulous base for adding highly concentrated vegetables and herbs.

Of course, fresh carrots are loaded with beta-carotene, which converts to vitamin A and helps in the prevention of some forms of cancer—not to mention their positive effect on vitality, appetite, and digestion. Add the darker green vegetables and you'll add chlorophyll, the vitamins A, C, E, K, and B_2 and iron and magnesium.

To get the maximum benefit from concentrated juices, drink them as quickly as possible after juicing. Every moment's delay means fewer benefits for you.

FRUIT SALADS

Luscious, perfectly ripened fruit—one of the best ways to welcome the day.

❀ For best flavor, choose what's in season, not forced. Ripen to perfection and serve at room temperature.

❧ Cut each fruit in a different way and a different size to appreciate its full flavor.

❧ Stir in freshly roasted, roughly chopped nuts; chopped crystallized or sliced preserved ginger; or crystallized angelica cut into small strips.

❧ Use a variety of fresh herbs to complement fruits—lemon balm, apple mint, orange thyme, or cinnamon basil.

▲ About 15 minutes before serving, add chopped dried apricots, pears, or pineapple; chopped dates; or whole raisins, sultanas (or golden raisins), or currants.

❧ Sprinkle with cooked wheat berries, cracked wheat, wild rice, or sesame seeds.

❀ Flaunt fruit salad convention: Make a glamorous mix of red currants, juicy pear, and a touch of kiwi fruit. The only rule: Use whatever's perfectly fresh and provides contrasts in color and texture.

❧ Sweeten with honey, brown sugar, or concentrated fruit juices such as carrot, orange, tangerine, or lime.

Rosy Berry Bowl

A rousing red, white, and blue way to begin the day.

SERVES 4

1 pint plus ⅔ cup raspberries
1 pint strawberries, hulled and halved
1 pint blueberries, washed
1 cup Low-Fat Blend (see Basics)
1 tablespoon honey
4 sprigs fresh mint

1. In a medium-size bowl, mix the 1 pint raspberries, the strawberries, and the blueberries, and set aside.

2. In a blender, process the Low-Fat Blend with the ⅔ cup of raspberries and the honey, and purée. Chill the sauce until serving time.

3. Place the berries in individual serving bowls and top with the sauce. Garnish with a sprig of fresh mint.

*Cal. **174** Carb. **37g** Protein **7g** Chol. **0mg** Fat **2g/8%***

Minty Fruit Bowl

SERVES 12

2 Granny Smith apples, cored and cut into bite-size pieces, peel left on

2 kiwi fruits, peeled, quartered, and sliced

2 cups seedless green grapes

1 medium-size ripe honeydew melon, cut into bite-size pieces

1 cup minced fresh mint

½ cup fresh lime juice

½ cup fresh lemon juice

3 tablespoons sugar

1 pint blackberries (or strawberries or raspberries), picked over and washed

2 sprigs fresh mint

1. Place the apple, kiwi, grapes, and melon in a large bowl and toss gently.

2. Add the mint, juices, and sugar; toss gently to combine thoroughly. Taste and adjust for sweetness.

3. Place in the refrigerator and chill for 2 to 3 hours. When ready to serve, let the mixture return to room temperature (½ hour). At the last minute, toss in the berries and garnish with fresh mint before serving.

*Cal. **109** Carb. **28g** Protein **1g** Chol. **0mg** Fat .5g/4%*

Great Start

Morning fruit supplies us with natural wonders:

- Valuable A, B, and C vitamins
- Minerals, including boron, magnesium, potassium, and iron
- Fiber
- Cleansing acids
- Natural fruit sugar
- Pure water

MINT CONDITION

"Plant a little mint, Madame, then step out of the way so you don't get hurt!" The British gardener wasn't kidding the lady of the house.

Mint demands a firm hand. A Mediterranean native spread by Roman legions throughout the Empire, it probably could have made the trip without assistance. Mint's vigorous underground runners defy all attempts to contain them—even with rocks, bricks, and cement barriers. Nothing short of a separate patch will thwart its cheerful mission to take over the yard.

I grew up with mint. I worked summers at Kalamazoo's Todd Mint Farm and have fond memories of sitting in the cool of the garden, enjoying a fresh-picked salad of early peas tossed with mint for lunch.

Start mint from cuttings. Then just let it grow. Despite its need for sun, water, and weeding, mint is tough stuff. Once you plant it, you'll never be without.

Mint comes in more than 400 varieties. Plant an assortment: spearmint, the classical cooking mint; peppermint for confections; apple, orange, grapefruit, pineapple, and ginger mint for their intriguing possibilities. Or try Corsican, the basis of crème de menthe, if you're truly mint-struck.

Berry Breakfast Pudding

Cut out even more fat by eliminating the nuts.

SERVES 8

1 cup wheat berries, rinsed and soaked in cold water
  overnight
  ½ cup chopped dried pears
  ½ cup chopped dried apples
4 cups skim milk
¼ cup sugar
1 cinnamon stick (4 inches)
½ teaspoon salt
1 egg
2 egg whites
1 teaspoon vanilla extract
2 cups fresh or frozen blueberries
Zest of 1 lemon
½ cup toasted almonds

1. Drain the wheat berries. In a large saucepan, combine the wheat berries with enough water to cover. Bring to a boil, lower the heat, and simmer gently for 30 minutes. Drain the wheatberries and return them to the saucepan.
2. Meanwhile, pour enough boiling water over the dried pears and apples to cover. Set aside.
3. Add the milk, sugar, cinnamon stick, and salt to the wheat berries. Cook over medium heat, stirring occasionally, until the mixture begins to thicken, about 35 minutes. Remove from the heat, and take out the cinnamon stick.
4. Preheat the oven to 325°.
5. In a small bowl, whisk the egg, egg whites, and vanilla. Beat ¼ cup hot wheat-berry mixture into the eggs; then slowly, while beating vigorously, add the egg mixture to the remaining hot wheat-berry mixture. Stir in the blueberries and zest.
6. Drain the pears and apples, and add to the mixture.
7. Spoon the mixture into a 2-quart soufflé or casserole dish. Sprinkle the top with almonds. Serve warm.

NOTE: The pudding can be made ahead and refrigerated, covered. Reheat at 300° for 30 minutes. Do not overcook.

Cal. 216 Carb. 33g Protein 9g Chol. 25mg Fat 6g/24%

Wheat Berries

They are whole, unprocessed wheat and a great-tasting grain to add to the assortment you keep in your pantry. They come from spring or winter wheat. The spring wheat berries ("farro" if imported from Italy) are soft and require only a half hour of soaking before cooking. Winterberries are hard and must soak overnight.

★ **GOOD FOR YOU** ★

Wheat berries are high in protein, carbohydrates, B vitamins, and the amino acids that give you lots of energy. One cup contains 110 calories and 770 units of protein.

Amish Friendship Bread

This is a traditional Amish bread that is lovingly passed from one friend to another. Usually, it has a nurturing time of eight days, during which you stir in various ingredients. Then, of course, there's additional kneading and rising. Here, that time is condensed into minutes.

YIELD: 4 LOAVES (64 SLICES)
2¾ cups skim milk
¼ cup low-fat buttermilk
4¾ cups all-purpose flour
¼ cup whole-wheat flour
3 cups plus 1 teaspoon sugar
1 package active dry yeast
⅔ cup canola oil
1¼ teaspoons baking powder
1 egg
1 teaspoon ground cinnamon
1 teaspoon vanilla extract
½ teaspoon salt
½ teaspoon baking soda
2 cups very coarsely chopped hazelnuts
2 cups dried cherries

1. Preheat the oven to 350°.
2. In a large nonreactive bowl, mix ¾ cup of the skim milk, the buttermilk, ¾ cup of the all-purpose flour, the whole-wheat flour, 1 teaspoon sugar, and the yeast. Set aside for 10 minutes or until the mixture starts to bubble.
3. In a large mixing bowl, place the remaining ingredients, except for the hazelnuts and cherries, and mix well. Add the milk mixture to the bowl and mix well. Fold in the hazelnuts and cherries.
4. Lightly wipe four 10 x 5 x 2-inch loaf pans with vegetable oil, divide the dough among the pans, and bake for 1 hour and 10 minutes, or until a toothpick inserted in the center comes out clean.

*Cal. **129** Carb. **22g** Protein **2g** Chol. **3mg** Fat **4g/27%** (analyzed per slice)*

Buttermilk

Real buttermilk—what's left after butter is churned—almost doesn't exist anymore. Today's commercial product is cultured. But it still brings goodness to baking and produces a fine uniform texture in cakes and breads. When there's none on hand, you can get similar results by adding something acidic—white or cider vinegar or lemon juice—to milk. Set it aside for a few minutes before adding to your batter.

★ GOOD FOR YOU ★

Whole buttermilk has 25 calories per ¼ cup, 2 grams protein, and .5 grams fat; low-fat has 25 calories, 2 grams protein, and .25 grams fat; nonfat has 23 calories, 2 grams protein, and only a trace of fat.

To make the best cup:
- Find the roast that best suits your taste. The middle range—not too light but not roasted to the burnt stage— is a good place to start. You can see the differences in the depth of color.
- Don't buy more coffee than you can use in a week or so.
- Store your beans (or ground coffee) in a glass, porcelain, or steel canister.
- Don't keep coffee in the freezer or refrigerator.
- Grind in pulses so you don't mash or burn the ground coffee.
- Use fresh cold water to make the best pot. If the water quality where you live isn't so great, use bottled water.
- Keep your coffeepot impeccably clean.
- The freshest pot makes the best cup.

GOOD MORNING MUFFINS

Nothing perks up the day like warm, fresh-from-the-oven muffins. Fill the tins before you hop in the shower. The muffins will be ready when you are.

Raspberry Muffins

Everybody's favorite. A light, lemony muffin filled with berries.

YIELD: 18 MUFFINS
2 cups sugar
1/4 cup canola oil
1 teaspoon minced lemon zest
1 egg
2 lightly beaten egg whites
1 cup Low-Fat Blend (see Basics)
2 1/2 teaspoons vanilla extract
2 teaspoons fresh lemon juice
2 cups all-purpose flour
1 tablespoon baking powder
1 pint raspberries
12 paper or foil muffin cups

1. Preheat the oven to 350°.
2. In a large bowl, cream the sugar, oil, and zest. Add the egg and egg whites and mix completely. Add the Low-Fat Blend and combine well. Add the vanilla and lemon juice and combine.
3. Slowly add the flour and the baking powder, stirring until completely blended.
4. When the batter is smooth, add the raspberries and gently mix until the berries are somewhat blended; do not overmix and break up the berries.
5. Place the paper cups in a muffin tin. Fill the cups three-quarters full with the batter. Place in the oven and bake for 25 minutes, or until a toothpick inserted in the center of a muffin comes out clean.
NOTE: Blueberries make an equally terrific muffin.

*Cal. **172** Carb. **33g** Protein **3g***
*Chol. **9mg** Fat **3g/17%***
(analyzed per muffin)

Morning Glory Carrot Muffins

Our favorite carrot cake—in mini muffin form. You can add ½ cup chopped walnuts, but remember that they will increase the fat values.

YIELD: 18 MUFFINS

2 cups all-purpose flour
2 cups light brown sugar
2 teaspoons baking powder
1 teaspoon salt
2 teaspoons ground cinnamon
1 teaspoon ground ginger
½ teaspoon ground cloves
¼ cup canola oil
½ cup applesauce
1 egg
1 egg white
2 teaspoons vanilla extract
2 jars (2½ ounces each) strained carrot baby food
½ cup fresh carrot or orange juice
4 ounces unsweetened crushed pineapple in its own juice
¾ cup loosely packed unsweetened shredded coconut

1. Preheat the oven to 350°. Lightly spray or wipe muffin tins with vegetable oil. Mix the flour, brown sugar, baking powder, salt, cinnamon, ginger, and cloves in a large mixing bowl.
2. Add the oil, applesauce, egg, egg white, vanilla, strained carrots, juice, and crushed pineapple and its juices. Mix well. Stir in the coconut.
3. Fill the muffin tins two-thirds full. Bake for 20 to 25 minutes, or until a toothpick comes out clean.
4. Turn the muffins out onto a wire rack. Once cooled, store them in an airtight container.

Cal. **168** *Carb.* **30g** *Protein* **2g** *Chol.* **10mg** *Fat* **5g/23%**

Warm Bran Muffins

This batter keeps well in the refrigerator for up to a month, so you can make fresh muffins every day.

YIELD: 72 MUFFINS

3 cups bran cereal
3 cups bran flakes
¾ cup unsweetened applesauce
2 cups hot water

Try It with Honey

Greeks considered it the nectar of the gods. Romans used it as currency. Large jars of honey were buried in tombs with Egyptian royalty to sustain them in the afterlife.

The flavors of honey are determined solely by the flower preference of the bees that made it. Some of my favorites: lavender, sage, raspberry, thyme, and wildflower.

I treat myself at breakfast with a dollop of special honey on crunchy toast, a scone, or an English muffin.

★ GOOD FOR YOU ★

Honey is high in carbohydrates, B$_2$, iron, and potassium, with only 64 calories per tablespoon and no fat.

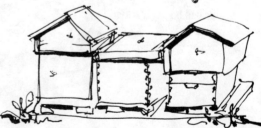

4 egg whites, lightly beaten
5 cups whole-wheat flour
2 cups sugar
¼ cup canola oil
1 egg
1 quart low-fat buttermilk
1 teaspoon salt
1 tablespoon plus 1 teaspoon baking soda
1 tablespoon ground ginger
4 tablespoons ground cinnamon
2 tablespoons ground nutmeg

1. Preheat the oven to 350°. Lightly spray or wipe the muffin tins with vegetable oil.
2. Place all of the ingredients in a large mixing bowl. Stir until well blended, about 2 minutes. Do not overmix.
3. Fill tins half full. Bake for 25 minutes, or until a toothpick comes out clean.

Cal. **79** *Carb.* **16g** *Protein* **2g** *Chol.* **3mg** *Fat* **1g/13%**

Banana Muffins

YIELD: 12 MUFFINS
3 ripe bananas, mashed
1 cup sugar
1 egg
¼ cup canola oil
½ cup applesauce
2 cups all-purpose flour
2 teaspoons baking soda
3 tablespoons low-fat buttermilk
2 tablespoons vanilla extract

1. Preheat the oven to 300°.
2. In a large mixing bowl, mix the bananas, sugar, egg, oil, and applesauce. Add the flour and baking soda, and mix until just blended; add the buttermilk and vanilla, and blend again; do not overmix.
3. Lightly spray or wipe the muffin tins with vegetable oil. Using an ice cream scoop to measure, drop the dough into the muffin tins, filling them two-thirds full.
4. Bake for 25 to 30 minutes, or until a toothpick comes out clean.

Cal. **218** *Carb.* **41g** *Protein* **3g** *Chol.* **15mg** *Fat* **5g/21%**

Vanilla Granola

We've baked granola golden with apple juice instead of oil. Now, the only fat is in the coconut.

SERVES 10

2 cups old-fashioned oats
⅓ cup frozen apple juice concentrate, thawed
2 tablespoons light brown sugar
1 tablespoon ground cinnamon
1 cup unsweetened flaked coconut
1 vanilla bean, split and seeds removed
1 cup dried sour cherries
1 cup golden raisins

Preheat the oven to 300°. In a large bowl, place the first four ingredients, and toss well. Spread the granola onto a large cookie sheet and bake for 25 minutes, stirring occasionally. Stir in the coconut and vanilla seeds, and bake for another 20 to 25 minutes, until lightly browned. Stir in the cherries and raisins. Cool and store in an airtight container for up to 1 month.

*Cal. **212** Carb. **43g** Protein **4g** Chol. **0mg** Fat **4g/17%***

Morning Müesli

Our version of that favorite European cereal.

SERVES 4

2 cups corn flakes
½ cup bran flakes
½ cup quick-cooking oats
⅓ cup frozen apple juice concentrate, thawed
1 teaspoon ground cinnamon
1 teaspoon light brown sugar
½ cup golden raisins
½ cup dried cranberries, cherries, or blueberries

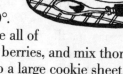

1. Preheat the oven to 300°.
2. In a large bowl, combine all of the ingredients except the berries, and mix thoroughly.
3. Spread the mixture onto a large cookie sheet and bake for 30 minutes, or until lightly browned. Add the dried berries and combine. Cool and store in an airtight tin.

*Cal. **194** Carb. **44g** Protein **4g** Chol. **0mg** Fat **1g/5%***

Skipping Breakfast to Save Calories?

Don't. Missing one meal only makes you hungrier for the next. So hungry, you might consume twice the calories you thought you saved. Worse, this bad habit can depress your metabolic rate and everything you eat could be burned more slowly. You need carbohydrates to encourage calorie-burning.

Big Breakfast Cookies

Family on the run? Send along one of these. They're packed with carbohydrates. And they store well, too.

YIELD: 64 MEDIUM COOKIES

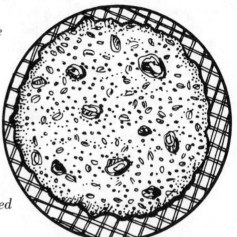

½ cup canola oil
½ cup unsweetened applesauce
2 egg whites
½ cup frozen apple juice concentrate, thawed
1 cup seven-grain cereal
½ cup all-purpose flour
⅓ cup whole-wheat flour
1 teaspoon ground cinnamon
1 teaspoon ground allspice
1 teaspoon ground ginger
1 tablespoon minced crystallized ginger
½ teaspoon ground cloves
1 cup golden raisins
¾ cup light brown sugar
2 tablespoons fresh orange juice
2 tablespoons fresh lemon juice
½ cup unsweetened shredded coconut
½ cup canned or homemade mincemeat
3 cups "quick" oatmeal
1 teaspoon baking soda
3 teaspoons vanilla extract

1. Preheat the oven to 350°. Lightly spray or wipe a large cookie sheet with vegetable oil.
2. In a large mixing bowl, combine all of the ingredients in the order listed and mix well.
3. Place ¼-cup measures of the cookie dough on the sheet, 2 inches apart. Press the dough into large circles and bake for 15 minutes, or until golden. Remove the cookies from the sheet immediately and cool completely. These are fragile and soft when still warm and firm up as they cool.

*Cal. **68** Carb. **10g** Protein **1g** Chol. **0mg** Fat **2g/29%** (analyzed per cookie)*

Hot Cross Buns

Since the Middle Ages, these traditional Good Friday buns have been marked with a cross to ward off evil spirits.

YIELD: 30 BUNS

½ cup golden raisins
½ cup dried cherries
½ cup dried cranberries, currants, or strawberries
2 tablespoons frozen orange juice concentrate, thawed
Zest of 1 lemon, chopped
2 cups plus 2 tablespoons skim milk
2 tablespoons unsalted butter
2 tablespoons canola oil
¾ cup sugar
½ teaspoon ground cinnamon
¼ teaspoon ground nutmeg
½ teaspoon salt
2 packages active dry yeast
2 large eggs
4 egg whites
5½ cups all-purpose flour
1 cup confectioners' sugar
½ teaspoon vanilla extract
4 tablespoons fresh lemon juice

1. In a saucepan over low heat, macerate the dried fruits with the orange juice and ¼ cup of water for 20 minutes. Add the lemon zest and cool.
2. In a separate pan, scald the 2 cups of milk. Add the butter, oil, sugar, spices, and salt. Set aside to cool.
3. In a small bowl, sprinkle the yeast over 4 tablespoons of warm water, and stir until dissolved. Set aside until foamy, about 5 minutes.
4. In a large mixing bowl, combine the cooled fruit and the milk mixture. Add the eggs, egg whites, and yeast mixture, and mix well, using a dough hook. Slowly add the flour, until the dough is smooth and elastic. Turn the dough out onto a lightly floured surface, cover with plastic wrap, and let rise until doubled in size, about 1 hour. Preheat the oven to 375°.

How Many Eggs?
Medical science has yet to resolve the egg question. Some nutritionists think 6 eggs a week is okay, while others put the limit at 2. An egg is one of the cheapest and most accessible sources of protein, and one egg averages only 88 calories. About half the protein is found in the yolk—along with vitamins A and B, some minerals, and lecithin. Of course, the yolk also has an enormous amount of cholesterol: 275 mg. in one large egg. A little more than half the protein is in the white, but none of the other nutrients. And none of the cholesterol. More whites and fewer yolks can be a reasonable compromise.

When you monitor your egg consumption, don't forget the ones that are hidden in baked goods and other cooked dishes.

Sage Sausage Patties

YIELD: TWENTY-FOUR
2-INCH PATTIES

*3 pounds ground turkey
(99% fat free)*
*1 medium onion, coarsely
chopped*
*½ cup finely chopped Italian
parsley*
*2 tablespoons finely chopped
fresh sage, or 2 teaspoons
dried sage*
6 garlic cloves, finely minced
2 teaspoons ground ginger
*2 teaspoons crushed red pep-
per flakes*
1 teaspoon ground cloves
*1 teaspoon freshly ground
pepper*

1. In a large mixing bowl, thoroughly combine the turkey using fingers or two forks, and the onion, parsley, sage, garlic, ginger, pepper flakes, cloves, and black pepper. Mix well.

2. By hand, form the meat mixture into 24 patties, 2 inches in diameter and ¾ to 1 inch thick. Arrange the patties in two very large skillets.

3. Cook over medium heat, turning once, for 12 to 17 minutes, until cooked through in the center.

Cal. **42** *Carb.* **1g** *Protein* **8g**
Chol. **3mg** *Fat* **.3g/7%**
(analyzed per patty)

5. Lightly spray or wipe two baking sheets with vegetable oil. Divide the dough into about thirty equal pieces. Roll each piece into a round ball and place on the sheets. Cover with dish towels and place in a warm spot to rise again until doubled in size.

6. Lightly brush the dough with the remaining milk. Place in the oven and bake for 30 to 40 minutes, until the buns are browned. Remove from the pan and cool on racks.

7. In a small bowl, combine the confectioners' sugar, 2 teaspoons hot water, the vanilla, and the lemon juice. Using a knife, make a cross on the top of each bun with this glaze.

Cal. **172** *Carb.* **33g** *Protein* **4g** *Chol.* **17mg** *Fat* **3g/13%**
(analyzed per bun)

White Frittata

Lots of vegetables held together by egg whites is a classic Italian peasant dish. Historically, it was the noblemen who got the yolks . . . along with all the cholesterol.

SERVES 4

½ teaspoon olive oil
6 large egg whites
Salt to taste
Ground black pepper
*4 scant cups lightly steamed mixed veg-
etables such as: chopped broccoli, thinly
sliced carrots, chopped string beans,
thinly sliced onions, roasted peppers,
peeled, seeded, and julienned*
1 teaspoon fresh garlic, minced finely
*1 tablespoon finely minced sun-
dried tomatoes*
2 tablespoons minced chives

1. Preheat the oven to 350°. Lightly wipe an 11-inch glass pie pan with oil.

2. In a large bowl, whisk by hand the egg whites, salt, and pepper until foamy, approximately 1 minute. Add the vegetables, garlic, and sun-dried tomatoes until well combined. Pour into the pie pan and bake until the egg whites are set, about 14 to 16 minutes. Remove from the oven; loosen edges with a spatula. Sprinkle with chives, cut into wedges, and serve.

Cal. **79** *Carb.* **10g** *Protein* **10g** *Chol.* **0mg** *Fat* **1g/12%**

Peasant Tortilla

cinnamon & brown sugar   or   vanilla sugar & mint

SERVES 6

3 eggs
4 egg whites
2 tablespoons olive oil (less if using a nonstick skillet)
1 large potato (about ³/₄ pound), preferably Yukon Gold,
  scrubbed, halved lengthwise, and sliced very thin
½ cup thinly sliced onion
2 tablespoons finely minced fresh garlic
2 ounces finely chopped prosciutto
1 cup frozen peas, thawed
½ cup chopped fresh tomato
Salt and freshly ground pepper
2 tablespoons finely chopped fresh Italian parsley

1. Preheat the oven to 500°.
2. In a medium-size bowl, combine the eggs and egg whites.
With a fork, break the yolks and whisk them into the whites,
leaving the mixture streaky, with some of the yolk showing in
the white. Set aside.
3. In a 12-inch ovenproof skillet with slanted sides, preferably nonstick, heat 1⅓ tablespoons (or less) oil over medium-
high heat. Layer the potatoes in a concentric circular pattern
in the bottom of the skillet. Drizzle with the remaining ⅔
tablespoon oil, and fry the potatoes until they are crisp and
golden brown on the bottom. Do not turn.
4. Remove the skillet from the heat and sprinkle the potatoes
evenly with the onion, garlic, prosciutto, peas, and tomatoes.
Pour the egg mixture over all, tilting the skillet to cover the
eggs evenly. Season with salt and pepper to taste.
5. Bake the tortilla for 6 minutes, or until just
set. (Cook for up to 1 minute longer if not
quite done.) Remove the skillet from the
oven, and carefully loosen the tortilla
from the bottom and sides with a
long spatula. Invert onto a heated
platter. Sprinkle with the parsley
and serve immediately.

Cal. **143** *Carb.* **13g** *Protein* **9g**
Chol. **100mg** *Fat* **6g/37%**

Tortillas for Breakfast

Season flour tortillas with
your favorite wake-up flavors. Brush mint oil on both
sides and sprinkle lightly
with vanilla sugar and mint.
Or brush lightly with canola
oil and shake on brown sugar
and cinnamon. You can also
brush the tortillas with oil
and top them with raspberries or sliced bananas and
vanilla sugar. Heat them in a
toaster oven for 6 to 8 minutes and they will pop out
hot, bubbly, and brown.

Asparagus Omelette

SERVES 4

1 tablespoon olive oil
2 teaspoons finely minced fresh garlic
16 pencil-thin fresh asparagus stalks, washed, trimmed, and
*   cut into 3-inch julienne strips (1 cup)*
½ large red bell pepper, roasted, peeled, and cut into very
*   thin strips (½ cup)*
1 egg
4 egg whites
1 tablespoon minced fresh chives
Salt and freshly ground pepper
2 tablespoons finely minced fresh Italian parsley

1. Preheat the oven to 500°.

2. In a 12-inch ovenproof skillet with slanted sides (prefer-ably nonstick), combine the oil and garlic. Tip the skillet so that the oil coats the bottom and halfway up the sides. Place the skillet in the oven, and bake until the garlic begins to brown, 40 to 60 seconds. With a slotted spoon, remove the garlic and reserve.

3. Add the asparagus to the skillet, turning to coat with oil; roast for 2 minutes. Add the pepper strips and roast for 1 minute more.

4. Meanwhile, in a medium-size bowl, combine the eggs, egg whites, chives, reserved garlic, and salt and pepper to taste. With a fork, break the yolks and whisk slightly, leav-ing some yolk showing in the white. Pour the egg mixture over the asparagus, tilting the skillet to cover the vegeta-bles evenly.

5. Bake for 2 minutes, or until the eggs are just set. (If the eggs are still runny, bake for another 30 seconds.) Remove the skillet from the oven, and with a long spatula, loosen the bottom and sides. Invert onto a warm serving platter and roll up as you would a crepe. Garnish with the parsley and serve immediately.

*Cal. **75** Carb. **3g** Protein **6g** Chol. **45mg** Fat **5g/53%*** 🅥

Tortillas

Spanish culinary historians maintain that the French learned to make omelettes after Louis XIV married the daughter of Philip IV of Spain in 1658. Egg tortillas, they say, began to appear at the court following that union. The Romans dispute the claim, citing the ancient classic "Ona mellita," a much older dish of beaten eggs with honey cooked on a flat clay dish.

CITRUS BURSTS OF SUNSHINE

Basics

Ripe, juicy citrus was once so rare it was a symbol of wealth, especially in cold seasons. Today citrus fruits are so available they might be taken for granted. But the accent they give everyday cooking makes them a real gem.

In the Market

✪ Choose fruit that feels heavy for its size; the heavier, the juicier.

✪ The fruit should be firm and resilient to the touch, with no soft spots.

✪ Look for fruit with smooth, shiny skin, and no wrinkles or bruises.

✪ Green on the skin is a natural occurrence caused by warm weather, not a sign that the fruit is unripe. By law, citrus must be ripe before it is picked.

✪ Refrigerate citrus you plan to keep for a week or longer.

Using the Zest

Citrus skin is loaded with aromatic oils. Use a zester to scrape only the fruit's colored surface, skimming the flavorful peel and leaving the bitter white pith behind. Zesting enlivens other flavors in everything—soups, salads, grilled foods, and desserts.

I prefer the fine threads produced by a zester to grated zest, which seems to dry out in the process. A vegetable peeler gouges too deeply and is wasteful. With a zester you can zest directly over the dish to capture the oil spray. Zest into the thinnest strands or mince according to the texture you want.

Using the Juice

✪ If you are going to grate, zest, or strip the rind, do it before juicing. (Figure one tablespoon of zest per lemon or orange, 2 teaspoons per lime).

✪ To get more juice, press down on the fruit and roll it several times back and forth over a hard surface before cutting it. Your juicing fruit should be at room temperature, or you can microwave it on high for 20 to 30 seconds.

✪ Refrigerated, juice will retain most of its vitamin C for up to a week. Always keep it covered to keep out refrigerator odors.

✪ Freeze freshly squeezed juice for up to 4 months.

★ GOOD FOR YOU ★

Citrus is packed with vitamin C, an essential component in healing. Research suggests that vitamin C, an antioxidant, may have a role in protecting against certain types of cancer, particularly of the stomach, lungs, throat, and digestive tract.

Oranges and grapefruits have a pectin that slows the absorption of fats, which lowers dietary cholesterol.

Pink and red grapefruit contain a healthy portion of beta-carotene, which converts to vitamin A, another cancer–fighting nutrient.

Grapefruit has lots of potassium; oranges, lemons, and limes deliver potassium and calcium.

VARIETIES

Fruit	Nutrition
Grapefruit Ugli Fruit Sweet-tart fruit with yellow to blush-yellow skin. Types include white, pink, seedless, Florida, ruby, and star ruby. Year-round.	An average-size ruby has 41 mg. of vitamin C, plus A and beta-carotene. The pink varieties have lots of potassium. One medium grapefruit has 76 calories and is low in fiber and fat.
Citron The oldest cultivated citrus fruit—very large and heavy. Most often candied. February and March.	
Kumquat Tiny orange fruit the size of a large grape; sweet skin and tart pulp—eat the skin and pulp in one bite. December to February.	1 medium kumquat has 12 calories, is moderate in fiber, and high in vitamins A and C, and calcium and potassium.
Lemon Sunny yellow, sour-tart fruit with high acidity. Year-round.	An ounce of lemon juice has 13 mg. of vitamin C. Low in fat and fiber, high in potassium, with 38 calories.
Lime Green to yellow-green, sour fruit with high acidity. Year-round.	An ounce of lime juice has 8.4 mg. of vitamin C. Limes are nutritionally similar to lemons.
Blood Oranges Sweet oranges with red flesh. November to March.	A single orange has 32 calories, 53 mg. of vitamin C (88% RDA for a hearty adult). A good source of potassium and vitamin A.

TYPES OF ORANGES

Clementine
Tiny, with a honey-sweet flavor.

Mandarin
A tangerine; mild and sweet with some seeds.

Navel
Seedless, best for eating—large, very sweet and juicy.

Royal Mandarin
Red-orange skin, sweet orange flavor.

Seville
Sour Mediterranean orange for marmalade.

Temple
Sweet and juicy, for eating and juicing.

Valencia
Thin-skinned, sweet and juicy with few seeds. Best for juicing.

Pomelo
The largest of all citrus fruit. Pear-shaped with orange-yellow rind.

Tangelo
Cross between grapefruit and tangerine. Tart mandarin taste.

Tangerine
Small, bright orange fruit with loose skin and sweet flavor.

The Lunch Crunch

No time to say hello, goodbye, it's late, it's late, it's late! There never seems to be enough time for lunch. But with a little planning, you can avoid the high-fat, fast-food habit and have a good, nutritious lunch.

Besides the always-popular salads and sandwiches, there's soup. Not only satisfying, but good for you. Make soups the night before for a quick warming at home or at the office. (Most soups just get better after a night in the refrigerator, anyway). There's hardly an office anymore without a refrigerator and microwave oven on the premises. You won't even need a thermos to eat lunch at your desk.

SUPER SOUPS (...and sandwiches)

"Creamy" Asparagus Tip Soup

I crave pure, intense asparagus flavor, without the classic cream that usually masks it. Here, I've kept it simple and added the crunchy tips.

SERVES 4

1 pound asparagus
4 cups chicken broth (see Basics)
1½ cups tightly packed spinach, cleaned and stems removed

*"Five minutes—
Zounds! I have
been five minutes
too late all my
lifetime."*

Hannah Cowley

22

Great Good Sandwiches

★ Steamed veggies in a pita, topped with Lemon Dip

★ Sliced cucumbers and Tomato Tapenade on whole-wheat bread

★ Roasted eggplant, tomato, chèvre, and Broccoli Pesto on a fresh baguette

★ Roast beef shavings smothered in Hellfire Barbecue Sauce, sautéed onions, and roasted peppers on sourdough

★ Smoked turkey, aged Monterey Jack, sliced red onions, and mustard on whole wheat

★ Bagelwich with alfalfa sprouts, sliced tomato, Lemon Dip, fresh basil, cucumber slices, and red onions

★ Sliced tomato, alfalfa sprouts, provolone cheese, fresh basil, red onions, roasted red pepper, and watercress on seven-grain bread

★ Spinach leaves, Lime Chicken, Rosy Beet Dip, red onions, and sliced tomatoes on pita bread

★ Sliced Granny Smith apples, smoked turkey breast, tomato, Maple Cream, and romaine lettuce on oat bread

★ Cucumber slices on pumpernickel spread with Spinach Dill Dip

(See Index for recipes)

½ cup minced fresh dill
Pinch cayenne
Pinch ground nutmeg

1. Trim the tips from the asparagus and cut the stalks into 1-inch pieces. Set the tips aside.

2. Place the chicken broth and pieces of asparagus stalks in a large pot and bring to a boil. Reduce the heat and simmer, covered, for 25 minutes. Add the spinach, dill, cayenne, and nutmeg, and simmer, uncovered, for 5 minutes.

3. Remove the soup from the heat. Process in batches in a blender or food processor until smooth.

4. Return the soup to the pot, add the asparagus tips, and simmer over medium heat until the tips are just tender, about 5 minutes. Taste and adjust the seasoning. To make ahead, cool to room temperature and store in the refrigerator.

*Cal. **41** Carb. **5g** Protein **4g** Chol. **0mg** Fat **.3g/7%***

Tomato Consommé

Its delicious taste belies its simplicity.

SERVES 4
2 cups tomato juice
2 cups chicken broth
  (see Basics)
¼ cup chopped celery leaves
3 sprigs fresh parsley
2 onion slices
5 peppercorns
3 whole cloves
½ bay leaf, crumbled
1 teaspoon chopped fresh basil
¼ teaspoon salt
Lemon slices

1. In a saucepan, combine all of the ingredients except the lemon slices. Bring to a boil and cover; reduce the heat and simmer for 30 minutes. The consommé can be cooled to room temperature and then refrigerated overnight.

2. Strain the soup and reheat. Serve garnished with lemon slices.

*Cal. **48** Carb. **10g** Protein **2g** Chol. **0mg** Fat **1g/17%***

Spring Onion Soup

There's something magical in the sun, soil, and water of Vidalia, Georgia, that makes the onions there so sweet. Balanced with a hint of sage, this is light and luscious.

SERVES 4

6 cups chicken broth (see Basics)
¼ cup dried mushrooms (half morels and half shiitakes or cèpes)
1 teaspoon olive oil
2 cups thinly sliced Vidalia onion
½ cup finely minced fresh sage
1 cup dry white wine
2 tablespoons minced fresh Italian parsley
Freshly ground black pepper

1. Heat 1 cup of chicken broth and pour over the dried mushrooms in a small bowl. Soak the mushrooms for 30 minutes. Strain and reserve the liquid. Finely mince the mushrooms.
2. Heat the olive oil in a large soup pot. Add the sage and onion and cook, covered, over low heat until the onion is soft, about 20 minutes.
3. Add the reserved liquid, minced mushrooms, remaining chicken broth, wine, parsley, and pepper to taste. Cover and simmer for 40 minutes. Taste and adjust the seasoning.

*Cal. **78** Carb. **11g** Protein **3g** Chol. **0mg** Fat **1g/22%***

"The best kind of onion soup is the simplest kind."

Ambrose Bierce

Sorrel-Lentil Soup

Sorrel's lemony-fresh taste awakens lentils with a whole new flavor dimension.

SERVES 4

1 teaspoon olive oil
1 cup finely chopped red onion
½ cup dry lentils
5 cups chicken broth (see Basics)
2 tablespoons tomato paste
⅛ teaspoon ground cloves
Freshly ground black pepper
2 cups tightly packed slivered fresh sorrel

1. In a soup pot over medium-high heat, heat the olive oil

★ **GOOD FOR YOU** ★
Onions

Onions possess an oil that helps lower LDL cholesterol levels and raise HDL cholesterol levels significantly. The most dramatic effect occurs with raw onions, but cooked onions help, too. Onions thin the blood, have a lot of vitamin C, A, and B complex, fiber, calcium, and potassium. One cup (raw) of all of this flavor, fiber, and vitamins has only 60 calories and .3 grams of fat.

Sorrel in the Garden . . .

Sorrel is a hardy perennial. In mild climates, it remains green all winter but grows little. Full sun and rich, well-drained soil are best; partial shade will achieve only moderately good growth. But take care: Warm weather turns leaves bitter, so harvest them small, before the season heats up much. Use sorrel fresh; its thin leaves don't dry or freeze well.

. . . and at the Table

In the spring, the French eat one of the most elegant of all soups—sorrel—under the guise of "spring tonic," to quicken the blood and stimulate the appetite.

Sorrel is slightly sour, with a lemony zest. For a spark for salads and palates like no other, add young leaves by the handful, and cut the vinegar and lemon juice way down or out.

Most cooks are familiar with two French classics: sorrel soup and sorrel sauce. In the classic manner, these preparations often involve cream, but that isn't necessary to enjoy sporrel's special taste.

and sauté the onion for 10 minutes. Add the lentils, chicken broth, tomato paste, and cloves. Season with pepper to taste.

2. Slowly bring the soup to a boil, cover, and simmer for 30 to 45 minutes, until the lentils are soft.

3. In individual soup bowls, place ½ cup sorrel and ladle hot soup over it. Serve.

Cal. **222** *Carb.* **37g** *Protein* **13g** *Chol.* **0mg** *Fat* **3g/11%**

"Creamy" Minted Pea Soup

The spring flavors you love—liberated from cream.

SERVES 8

1 teaspoon canola oil
4 large scallions, finely chopped, white and green parts separated
1 large yellow onion, finely chopped
2 stalks celery, finely diced
Salt and finely ground pepper
5 cups chicken broth (see Basics)
5 cups freshly shelled peas, or 2 packages (16 ounces each)
   frozen peas
½ cup coarsely chopped fresh mint
Fresh mint leaves

1. In a large pot over low heat, place the canola oil, scallion, onion, celery, and salt and pepper to taste. Cook, covered, until the onion is transparent, about 30 minutes. Add the chicken broth and simmer for 30 minutes longer.

2. Increase the heat to medium-high and add the peas. Cook until the peas are just tender, about 5 minutes. Remove from the heat, add the mint, and let cool for 20 minutes.

3. In a blender, purée the soup in batches. Reheat, taste, and adjust the seasonings; add additional broth if the soup seems too thick. Garnish with mint leaves.

NOTE: The soup can be chilled and reheated if made ahead.

Cal. **71** *Carb.* **11g** *Protein* **4g**

Chol. **0mg**

Fat **2g/19%**

Broccoli & Sorrel Soup

Creamy, but without cholesterol, and sorrel makes broccoli springier.

SERVES 6

6 cups chicken broth (see Basics)
4 cups coarsely chopped broccoli (about ¾ pound)
2 tablespoons minced lemon zest
Pinch cayenne
3 cups tightly packed sorrel
¼ cup Low-Fat Blend (see Basics)

1. In a large stockpot, combine the chicken broth, broccoli, lemon zest, and cayenne, and bring to a boil. Reduce the heat and simmer, covered, for 20 minutes, until the broccoli is tender. Add the sorrel and simmer for 3 to 5 minutes.
2. Remove the soup from the heat. Process in batches in a blender or food processor until smooth.
3. Return the puréed soup to the stockpot. Stir in the Low-Fat Blend. Warm over low heat but do not boil. Serve immediately.

Cal. 95 Carb. 13g Protein 8g Chol. .3mg Fat 1g/10%

Garlic & Watercress Soup

Slowly simmered garlic sweetens the broth and infuses it with a deep, rich flavor. Watercress adds a soft, peppery bite.

SERVES 4

2 heads garlic, cloves peeled and left whole
2 bay leaves
1 teaspoon dried thyme
2 sprigs fresh parsley, coarsely chopped
3 potatoes, peeled and diced
3 teaspoons tarragon vinegar
1 tablespoon Dijon mustard
1 cup skim milk
2½ cups coarsely chopped watercress
2 scallions, minced

1. Place 6 cups of water, garlic, bay leaves, thyme, parsley, and potato in a soup pot. Bring to a boil, lower the heat, and simmer, covered, for 1 hour.
2. Remove from the heat and strain, reserving the broth.

"I live on good soup, not fine words."

Molière

... More Sandwiches
★ Watercress, sliced scallions, turkey, Apple Salad Spray, black olives, and tomato slices on wheat or oat bread
★ Softened chèvre and orange marmalade on cut-out hearts of wheat bread
★ Tuna, chopped arugula, roasted red peppers, and low-fat mozzarella
★ Sliced tomato, feta or low-fat mozzarella cheese, and chopped fresh basil open-face on a bagel or other bread, broiled or toasted
★ Tomato Tapenade, sliced tomatoes, arugula, and Pesto Dip on sourdough bread
★ Maple Cream, currants, and chopped cress on raisin pumpernickel
★ Hot pastrami and Creamy Coleslaw with Green Tomato Chutney on black bread
(See Index for recipes)

. . . And More

★ Asparagus Omelette, Canadian bacon, and Lemon Dip on toasted rye bread
★ Sardines, watercress, and Lemon Dip on whole-wheat
★ Sliced ripe summer tomatoes with Guacamole Dip on fresh white bread with crusts removed
★ Monterey Jack cheese and Lebanese Yogurt Dip on toasted sourdough bread
★ Everyday Garlic Chicken, arugula, and caponata in a pita
★ Dilled Shrimp Salad, watercress, and diced tomato on a toasted sourdough baguette
★ Sliced tomatoes, Canadian bacon, red onion, and Cucumber Mousse in a pita
★ Cajun Meat Loaf, Cool Tomato Salsa, and arugula in a pita
★ Smoked salmon, Lemon Dip, red onions, and capers in a pita
★ Ratatouille Meat Loaf, Pesto Dip, and sliced tomatoes on multigrain bread
★ Tuna, Lime Dip, lettuce, and tomato on rye bread
★ Roasted red and yellow peppers with sliced ham and Red Pepper Dip on a thin baguette
★ Sliced cucumbers, tomatoes, beets, Rosy Beet Dip, and watercress in a pita
★ Sliced Roast Lamb, sliced tomatoes, Tahini Dip, and cucumber in a pita
(See Index for recipes)

Remove and discard the bay leaves. Mash the potato mixture, return it to the soup pot, and pour in 3½ cups of broth. Stir over medium heat until combined.
3. Stir in the vinegar, mustard, milk, watercress, and scallion. Simmer just until the watercress has wilted, about 30 seconds.
4. Taste and adjust the seasoning. Serve immediately. Garnish each serving with a dollop of yogurt, if desired.

Cal. ***106*** *Carb.* ***21g*** *Protein* ***5g*** *Chol.* ***1mg*** *Fat* ***1g/8%***

Spring Lentil Soup

Point, counterpoint! The trick is to balance the emphatic flavor of lentils.

SERVES 8

1 teaspoon canola oil
1 cup finely chopped onion
1 cup finely chopped celery
1 cup lentils
1 can (16 ounces) plum tomatoes, coarsely chopped
6 cups chicken broth (see Basics)
2 teaspoons curry powder
6 whole cloves
½ cup fresh lime juice
½ cup minced fresh cilantro

1. Heat the oil in a soup pot. Add the onion and celery, and sauté over low heat until the vegetables are soft and translucent, 10 to 15 minutes.
2. Stir in the lentils, tomatoes, broth, curry, cloves, ¼ cup lime juice, and ¼ cup cilantro. Bring to a boil, lower the heat, and simmer, covered, until the lentils are tender, 30 to 45 minutes.
3. Stir in the remaining lime juice and cilantro. Taste and adjust seasonings. Serve.

Cal. ***138*** *Carb.* ***23g*** *Protein* ***9g*** *Chol.* ***0mg***
Fat ***2g/12%***

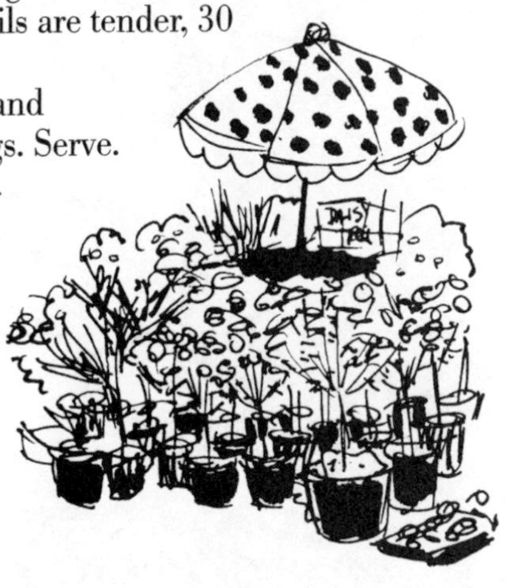

"Hark to a lettuce lover. I consider lettuce a blessing. And

Who perished by Romulus, who monkeys with this, the most sacred of formulas?"—Ogden Nash

I place my Trust in oil and vinegar. May I perish as Remus

amaranth

peppery, lemony mizuna

red grenoble

lollo bionde

frisée endive

sugarloaf chicory

hot pepper cress

spinach – savoy

Turn Over

A New Leaf

red salad bowl

tat soi mustard greens

Russian kale

mesclun

arugula or rocket

Red Riding Hood

soft, tender mauwel

what do I want on my lettuce? Simply a simple dressing...

New Leaf O Turn

It's oil and vinegar, dears; No need to tiddle and toil; Just salt and pepper and vinegar and oil... I'm not an effort, Just a vinegar. But

lollo rossa

ruben romaine

ruby Swiss chard

chervil

radicchio chicory

rossa di Trento

frisée

mache

green-salad-bowl

piquant sorrel

orache

loose leaf garnet lettuce

purple ruffles basil

full-heart endive

saka or purple mustard

romaine

LETTUCES & GREENS

GREEN, GREENER, GREENEST!

The darker the greens in your salad bowl, the better. With the wonderful fresh variety of greens available every day, you can mix and match at will—a long way from the days of iceberg and romaine. Just remember: the younger, the more tender; the darker in color, the better for you. Dark greens have the most beta-carotene, a potent cancer fighter (the orange color is masked by chlorophyll). Popeye was right about his spinach—not to mention chard, collards, mustards, watercress, and dandelions. Just one cup of any provides 100 percent of the USRDA for vitamin A. And only 10 calories.

Tender young greens can be mixed with lettuces as you wish. More and more of these crisp, emerald gems are available year-round. The only danger: drowning greens with an oil-based salad dressing. If you splash on something tart, the taste of the greens comes shining through.

GREEN

Belgian Endive	 White, yellow-edged crunchy leaves with a bitter bite.
Bibb Lettuce	 Small heads with pale-to-medium green tender leaves that have a sweet, subtle taste.
Boston Lettuce	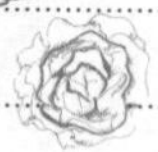 A loose head with soft, pale green leaves that have a buttery flavor.
Cabbage	
Green	Pale green, crisp leaves with a bite.
Chinese	Very light green, crinkly leaves on an elongated head; this is the most delicate of all cabbages.
Chicory	 (Also known as curly endive) Curly and crisp green leaves with pale center.

Escarole		Green leaves with a pale heart; the crisp, light-colored leaves are best for salads. The dark leaves are good to cook.
Frisée		The sweetest in the chicory family, with pale green to almost white curly leaves; mildly bitter.
Iceberg		Crisp, cool leaves; very mild flavor, not high in nutrients.

GREENER

Arugula/Rocket		Dark greens with a peppery taste; small leaves are mildest.
Dandelion		For salads, pale young leaves are best, while the larger, darker, more pungent leaves are good cooked.
Loose-Leaf Lettuce		Young, soft red or green leaves are sweetest.
Mâche		(Also known as lamb's lettuce, corn salad, field lettuce) Sweet-nutty taste; best when young.
Mesclun		Mixture of very young tender greens; may include arugula, nasturtium, mâche, chervil, dandelion, Oakleaf lettuce, and herbs.
Romaine		Long, crisp, succulent medium green or red leaves with a fresh, sweet, nutty flavor.

GREENEST

Red Cabbage		Crisp, purple leaves.
Cress		Grows wild or cultivated and has a hot, peppery taste.
Kale		Dark red or green robust leaf; young and small are good for salads, others great braised.
Radicchio		Brilliant, ruby-colored leaves with a cabbagelike tender head; slightly bitter, peppery-tasting.
Spinach		Long, heart-shaped smooth leaves with a spicy taste.
Watercress		Tiny round, dark green, glossy leaves; spicy, peppery flavor.

SALAD SPRAYS, SPRITZES,

Dressing Greens

Drowning a wonderful fresh salad of greens with a heavy oil-based vinaigrette is a big mistake.

Over the years, I've evolved to the point where I like my dressings made with more acid and far less oil. Sometimes I use just a squeeze of straight lemon or lime juice. I think this brings the kind of intense flavor that really wakes up the greens. Splash on a tablespoon per portion and toss your salad like mad.

The recipes on these pages can be made by placing all of the ingredients in a bottle and shaking well to blend. Some of the fat percentages may look high. But check the grams; they're quite low. And remember, you're tossing the dressing over lots of great things.

These dressings are analyzed by the tablespoon, which is all you really need to dress one serving of salad. The flavors are so intense, you just have to spray or splash them on.

And more . . .
There are flavored vinegars, oils, and more vinegar-based dressings on pages 288-291.

Lime Spritz

YIELD: ¾ CUP

1/4 cup nonfat plain yogurt
6 tablespoons fresh lime juice
2 teaspoons minced fresh
  lime zest
2 teaspoons horseradish
2 teaspoons Dijon mustard
2 tablespoons white wine
  vinegar
Freshly ground pepper
Cal. 7 Carb. 1g Protein .3g
Chol. 0mg Fat .1/14%*

Apple Salad Spray

YIELD: ¾ CUP

1/2 cup apple juice
1/4 cup cider vinegar
2 tablespoons finely minced
  fresh chives
2 tablespoons finely minced
  fresh mint
1/2 teaspoon ground cinnamon
Cal. 6 Carb. 2g Protein 0g
  Chol. 0mg Fat 0g/0%*

Citrus Spray

YIELD: ¾ CUP

6 tablespoons fresh orange
  juice
4 tablespoons fresh lime juice
2 tablespoons finely minced
  fresh cilantro
2 tablespoons finely minced
  fresh mint
4 teaspoons cumin seeds
Pinch cayenne
Cal. 9 Carb. 2g Protein .2g
Chol. 0mg Fat .2g/19%*

Sherry Salad Spray

YIELD: ¾ CUP

1/4 cup fresh orange juice
1/4 cup sherry vinegar
2 teaspoons Dijon mustard
2 tablespoons capers, drained
2 tablespoons finely minced
  shallot
2 tablespoons finely minced
  fresh parsley
2 tablespoons finely minced
  fresh chives
Cal. 7 Carb. 1g Protein .1g
Chol. 0mg Fat .2g/22%*

Balsamic Vinaigrette

YIELD: 1 CUP

6 tablespoons minced shallot

1/2 cup balsamic vinegar

2 tablespoons sugar

1/2 teaspoon salt

1/4 teaspoon freshly ground
pepper

1/2 cup chicken broth
(see Basics)

2 teaspoons minced garlic

1/2 cup chopped fresh Italian
parsley

2 teaspoons Dijon mustard

2 tablespoons fresh orange
juice

Cal. **15** Carb. **2g** Protein **.3g**

Chol. **0mg** Fat **.1g/33%***

Sweet-and-Sour Splash

YIELD: 3/4 CUP

1/4 cup fresh carrot or orange
juice

6 tablespoons cider vinegar

2 tablespoons sugar

2 tablespoons toasted sesame
seeds

1/4 cup finely sliced scallion

Dash Tabasco

Cal. **19** Carb. **3g** Protein **.4g**

Chol. **0mg** Fat **.7g/33%***

Champagne Spritz

YIELD: 1 CUP

2 tablespoons nonfat plain
yogurt

1/4 cup champagne vinegar

1/4 cup sparkling mineral
water

3 tablespoons fresh lime juice

2 teaspoons Dijon mustard

2 tablespoons finely minced
garlic

2 tablespoons chopped
scallion

Freshly ground pepper

Cal. **7** Carb. **1g** Protein **.3g**

Chol. **0mg** Fat **.1g/14%***

*Nutrition information
analyzed per tablespoon

Roquefort Dressing

YIELD: 1 1/2 CUPS

1 cup Low-Fat Blend
(see Basics)

6 tablespoons low-fat buttermilk

1/4 cup crumbled Roquefort
cheese

Freshly ground pepper

In a blender, process the
Low-Fat Blend, buttermilk,
and cheese until smooth.
Add pepper to taste. Transfer
to a jar with a tight lid and
refrigerate. This keeps well
for up to 1 week.

Cal. **18** Carb. **.7g** Protein **2g**

Chol. **3mg** Fat **1g/49%***

THE SALAD BOWL

EAT YOUR GREENS They're the food of the hour, high in fiber, and practically calorie-free, helpful in lowering cholesterol and controlling diabetes. And of course, they are anti-carcinogens.

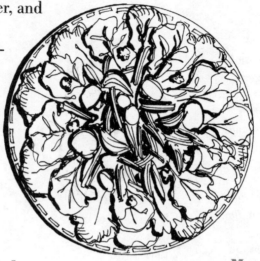

A Big Chef's Salad

Fewer calories and a lot less fat than the traditional dish.
SERVES 4

4 cups spinach leaves, washed
4 cups red-leaf lettuce, washed
1 tablespoon finely minced fresh oregano
1/4 cup coarsely chopped fresh basil
1 small red onion, thinly sliced
2 cups cleaned and chunked button mushrooms
1 cup julienned prosciutto or Canadian bacon, trimmed
2 cups frozen artichoke hearts, defrosted
1 cup shredded smoked chicken
1/4 cup julienned Havarti cheese
1/2 cup crumbled feta cheese
1/4 cup Balsamic Vinaigrette (page 33)

Place the greens and herbs in a bowl and toss well. Divide the greens among four dinner plates and top with the onion and mushrooms. Divide the bacon, artichokes, chicken, and cheeses on top. Serve with the dressing on the side.

*Cal. **296** Carb. **20g** Protein **29g** Chol. **70mg** Fat **11g/33%***

Mesclun

The classic green salad favored in the south of France is now finding its way into American gardens and greengroceries. Mesclun is a blend of a variety of tender greens, each grown in its own row. For correct flavor and texture, only the youngest, most tender shoots make their way into the mix. They are picked early in the morning, tossed together in more or less equal proportions, and plunged directly into a water bath. A typical mix: green-tipped Oakleaf lettuce, rocket or arugula, romaine, chervil, two endives—one slightly curly white and one very curly green variety—escarole, and dandelion.

"Nasturtium Salad — Put a plate of flowers of the nasturtium in a salad-bowl, with a table-spoonful of chopped chervil; sprinkle over with your fingers half a teaspoonful of salt, two or three tablespoonsful of olive oil, and the juice of a lemon; turn the salad in the bowl with a spoon and a fork until well mixed, and serve."

Turabi Efendi, _Turkish Cookery Book_, 1864

Edible Flowers

A strange idea at first, eating flowers, but a practice that is centuries old. Try peppery nasturtiums, cinnamony cottage pinks and carnations, mild-tasting pansies, pea-flavored tulips. The taste of lilac resembles its fragrance; blue borage reminds us of cucumber. Velvety rose petals are sweet and so are violets. Chive flowers have the delicate taste of onion, while marigolds are nutty. Bold hollyhock blooms are the best of all. Toss them in to brighten green salads; strew them on plates. Choose monochromatic pink or use the garden's whole edible spectrum to astonish and delight.

Warning: Please be aware that some flowers are poisonous. If you're not sure one's safe, don't try it!

Spinach Salad

A smidgen of smoky bacon's taste goes a long way.

SERVES 4

12 ounces spinach, washed, dried, and trimmed
1 can (8 ounces) water chestnuts
1 pound mushrooms, cleaned and sliced
1 cup fresh bean sprouts, rinsed and drained
3 slices bacon, cooked until crisp and finely crumbled
1 small red onion, thinly sliced

Dressing:
2 tablespoons canola oil
2 tablespoons sugar
1 tablespoon catsup
½ cup cider vinegar
2 tablespoons Worcestershire sauce

1. Layer the spinach, water chestnuts, mushrooms, bean sprouts, bacon, and onion in a large salad bowl. Cover with plastic wrap and refrigerate until ready to use.
2. In a glass bowl, whisk together the dressing ingredients and refrigerate.
3. When ready to serve, toss the salad with the desired amount of dressing (about ¼ cup for the quantity here) and serve immediately. The remaining dressing can be kept refrigerated for up to 2 weeks.

Cal. **150** Carb. **21g** Protein **8g** Chol. **4mg** Fat **5g/28%**

Easy Caesar Salad

The best salads are made with the smaller, crunchier inner romaine leaves.

SERVES 4

1 teaspoon salt
1/2 teaspoon freshly ground pepper
3 large garlic cloves, minced
1 teaspoon Dijon mustard
1 teaspoon Worcestershire sauce
2 tablespoons chicken broth (see Basics)
2 tablespoons olive oil
1/2 cup fresh lemon juice
1/4 cup grated imported Parmesan
2 large heads romaine, washed, trimmed, patted dry, and well chilled
1 small can anchovies

1. In a blender, combine the salt, pepper, garlic, mustard, Worcestershire, broth, and oil. Add the lemon juice and Parmesan. Pulse the blender on and off several times to combine. The dressing will be very thick. Cover and refrigerate until ready to use.
2. Tear the romaine into pieces and place in a large salad bowl. Add dressing to taste. Toss and divide the salad among four chilled plates. Garnish with anchovies. Add croutons if desired.

Cal. **126** *Carb.* **10g** *Protein* **8g** *Chol.* **5mg** *Fat* **7g/37%**

Mango Chicken Salad

I could eat this every day for lunch—and have!

SERVES 6

4 skinless and boneless chicken breast halves
1 cup chicken broth (see Basics)
1/2 cup golden raisins
1 mango, peeled, and cut into 1/2-inch cubes
2 cups seedless green grapes
3/4 cup Low-Fat Blend (see Basics)
1/4 cup mango chutney
2 tablespoons low-fat sour cream
2 1/2 teaspoons curry powder

Parmesan Toast

Crisp, crunchy, habit-forming, and perfect with salads. Go as spicy as you dare.

YIELD: 24 SLICES

24 slices 1/4-inch-thick Italian or French bread
2 tablespoons canola oil
Crushed red pepper flakes
1 1/2 cups fresh Parmesan shards, made with a potato peeler

1. Set the bread out overnight to dry.
2. Preheat the oven to 500°.
3. Place the bread on a piece of aluminum foil. Lightly brush each piece with oil. Place in the oven and bake for 2 minutes, until it just begins to brown.
4. Turn the bread over and lightly brush with oil. Sprinkle with red pepper to taste, and cover the bread completely with cheese; bake for 1 minute.
5. Remove from the oven, smooth the cheese with a knife, and bake for 1 minute more, or until it just begins to bubble. Cool before serving.

Cal. **77** *Carb.* **8g** *Protein* **4g** *Chol.* **5mg** *Fat* **3g/39%** (analyzed per slice)

36

Parmesan-Chive Popovers

Crisp, flaky, towering popovers.

SERVES 4

¼ cup grated Parmesan
1 egg
3 egg whites
1 cup skim milk
1 cup all-purpose flour
¼ teaspoon salt
Pinch cayenne
½ cup snipped fresh chives

1. Preheat the oven to 425°.
2. Lightly spray or coat four 1-cup ramekins or custard cups with vegetable oil. Make 4-inch-tall foil collars, coat with oil, and place inside the ramekins. Place 1 teaspoon of Parmesan in each ramekin.
3. In a large bowl, using an electric mixer, beat the egg, egg whites, and milk. Add the flour, salt, and cayenne, and mix well. Fold in the chives.
4. Divide the batter evenly, filling the cups about three-quarters full. Bake for 30 minutes. Do not peek or the popovers will fall. The popovers should be golden brown. Serve immediately, piping-hot from the oven.

*Cal. 62 Carb. 8g Protein 4g
Chol. 18mg Fat 2g/19%*

¼ cup minced fresh Italian parsley
1 cup coarsely chopped fresh pineapple

1. Preheat the oven to 350°. Arrange the chicken breasts in a baking pan and cover with chicken broth. Bake for 25 to 30 minutes, or until the chicken is tender and the juices run clear when it is pierced with a knife. Remove the chicken from the oven and set aside to cool.
2. In a large bowl, shred the chicken into bite-size pieces. Add the raisins, mango, and grapes, and mix well.
3. In a small bowl, whisk the Low-Fat Blend, chutney, sour cream, curry powder, and parsley together. Combine with the chicken and chill for at least 3 hours. Just before serving, stir in the pineapple. Serve on a bed of mixed greens.

Cal. 227 Carb. 25g Protein 21g Chol. 4mg Fat 6g/23%

Dilled Shrimp Salad

SERVES 4

1½ pounds medium shrimp, shelled and
    deveined
½ cup Low-Fat Blend (see Basics)
2 tablespoons low-fat buttermilk
½ cup minced fresh dill
Tabasco or other pepper sauce
Freshly ground pepper
2 cups peeled, seeded, and diced
    cucumber
4 cups watercress, stemmed, washed,
    and patted dry
1 lemon, cut into wedges

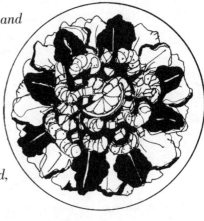

1. Bring a large pot of water to a boil; add the shrimp and boil for 1 minute. Drain immediately and refresh under cold water. When cool, transfer the shrimp to a large bowl.
2. In a blender, place the Low-Fat Blend and buttermilk, and blend until smooth. Add the dill, Tabasco, and pepper to taste; blend for 10 seconds.
3. Pour the mixture over the shrimp and toss to coat. Cover and refrigerate for at least 1 hour.
4. Just before serving, stir in the cucumber and adjust the seasonings if necessary. Arrange 1 cup of the watercress on each of 4 plates; top with the shrimp and garnish with lemon.

Cal. 158 Carb. 3g Protein 32g Chol. 259mg Fat 2g/10%

Tomato Aspic

SERVES 4

2 cups tomato juice

3 ounces lemon-flavored gelatin

2 tablespoons horseradish (more if desired)

2 tablespoons grated onion (more if desired)

1 tablespoon fresh lemon juice

1/4 teaspoon celery seeds

2 cups watercress, trimmed, rinsed,
   drained, and patted dry

Balsamic Vinaigrette (page 33; optional)

watercress bed   *full of flavor aspic*

1. In a medium-size saucepan, bring 1 cup of tomato juice to a boil. Add the gelatin and stir until dissolved. Add the remaining cup of juice, horseradish, onion, lemon juice, and celery seeds. Add more horseradish and onion if desired, keeping in mind that the flavor will be less sharp when cold.

2. Pour the aspic into four 6-ounce molds. Chill for several hours, until firm, or place in the freezer for 30 minutes and then in the refrigerator until ready to serve.

3. Divide the watercress among four pretty salad plates. Unmold the aspic onto the watercress. Serve with Balsamic Vinaigrette, if desired.

Cal. **107** *Carb.* **26g** *Protein* **3g** *Chol.* **0mg** *Fat* **.1g/1%**

Perfect Aspic

For years, aspic has been considered old-fashioned. Now something old seems new again. Especially when it's really loaded with flavor, like this tomato aspic.

Cucumber Mousse

SERVES 4

2 1/2 cups well-packed, grated cucumber

2 garlic cloves, minced

2 tablespoons minced fresh mint

1/3 cup minced fresh dill

2 cups Low-Fat Blend (see Basics)

1 1/2 teaspoons unflavored gelatin

1 egg white, at room temperature

1. Place the grated cucumber in a strainer. Set aside for 10 minutes to drain, then squeeze out excess liquid.

2. Place the drained cucumber, garlic, mint, and dill in a food processor. Process until just puréed. Add the Low-Fat Blend and process until just combined; do not overmix.

3. In a small saucepan, add the gelatin to the cold water, and set it aside to soften for 1 minute. Stir the

Salad Bar Smarts

Oh, what a tempting array the salad bar offers! Greens, fresh fruits, sliced vegetables—side by side with red potatoes in sour-cream dressing. Bacon pieces lurk in the apple salad. Mayonnaise salad has a little cabbage mixed in. There are cold-cut strips and olives marinated in oil, and extra dressings, loaded with fat calories. A little bit of this, a little bit of that . . . you've exceeded your fat budget three times over! Unless you're prepared to carefully select only the fruit or vegetables with little or no dressing, skip the salad bar—it can sabotage the healthiest intentions.

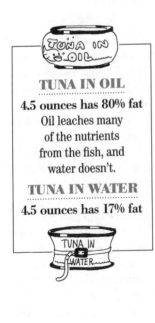

TUNA IN OIL

4.5 ounces has 80% fat
Oil leaches many of the nutrients from the fish, and water doesn't.

TUNA IN WATER

4.5 ounces has 17% fat

gelatin over low heat, until it is completely dissolved. Transfer to a large bowl and whisk until it is just warm to the touch.

4. Slowly whisk the puréed mixture into the gelatin. Make sure the mixture is well incorporated. Refrigerate until thick, about 20 to 30 minutes, whisking occasionally to prevent lumps from forming.

5. In another bowl, beat the egg white until stiff. Gently fold the egg into the cucumber mixture. Blend well, making sure there are no lumps. Transfer to a serving bowl; cover, and refrigerate for at least 3 hours before serving.

*Cal. **102** Carb. **12g** Protein **12g** Chol. **3mg** Fat **1g/9%***

Spanish Tuna Salad

I first enjoyed this on a veranda on Ibiza.

SERVES 4

2 cups fresh orange sections, all pith removed
4 ounces white tuna packed in water, drained and flaked
1 red bell pepper, halved, seeded, and thinly sliced
1 cup halved and thinly sliced red onion
2 teaspoons minced garlic
1 tablespoon anchovies, drained on a paper towel
1 tablespoon red wine vinegar
2 tablespoons fresh orange juice
Chopped zest of one orange
2 tablespoons canola oil
Salt and freshly ground pepper
Crisp lettuce leaves (about 2 cups)
1/4 cup chopped fresh Italian parsley
1/4 cup sliced and toasted almonds
4 green olives, pitted and minced

1. In a large bowl, combine the orange, tuna, red pepper, and onion. Toss gently and set aside.

2. Pound the garlic and anchovies together with a pestle. Whisk in the vinegar, orange juice, zest, oil, salt, and pepper.

3. Pour the dressing over the tuna mixture, toss, and cover with plastic wrap. Let marinate for 1 hour.

4. When ready to serve, line 4 plates with lettuce leaves. Divide the tuna mixture equally among the plates, and garnish with parsley, almonds, and olives. Serve immediately.

*Cal. **243** Carb. **22g** Protein **12g** Chol. **2mg** Fat **13g/46%***

Shrimp & Lobster Ring

Summery and elegant. A wonderful luncheon served with sun-ripened tomato slices, niçoise olives, and a crusty peasant bread.

SERVES 4

1½ tablespoons unflavored gelatin
2 cups chicken broth (see Basics)
½ cup thinly sliced cucumber
1 cup cooked lobster meat, cut into chunks, chilled
1 cup cooked shrimp, halved if large, chilled
½ cup finely diced celery
1 tablespoon horseradish
1 tablespoon fresh lemon juice
½ teaspoon grated onion
½ teaspoon dry mustard
Salt and freshly ground pepper
4 cups washed and stemmed watercress

1. Lightly spray or wipe a 6-cup ring mold with canola or vegetable oil and place in the refrigerator.
2. In a small bowl, sprinkle the gelatin over ¼ cup of the chicken broth and set aside to soften for 5 minutes.
3. In a medium saucepan over medium heat, bring the remaining chicken broth to a boil. Turn the heat off and add the softened gelatin, stirring constantly until the gelatin has completely dissolved. Transfer the mixture to a large bowl and refrigerate until it becomes syrupy.
4. Spoon 3 to 4 tablespoons of the thickened chicken broth into the mold. Place the cucumber slices around the bottom, overlapping slightly; reserve any remaining slices. Refrigerate the mold until the gelatin is set.
5. Meanwhile, fold the lobster, shrimp, celery, horseradish, lemon juice, onion, dry mustard, salt and pepper into the remaining gelatin mixture. Taste and correct seasonings carefully. Pour the mixture into the mold, taking care not to disturb the cucumber slices. If there are any cucumber slices left, place them around the top. Refrigerate the mold until firm. When ready to serve, make a bed of watercress on a large serving dish. Dip the mold into hot water for a few seconds, then invert onto the watercress. Great with dressing.

*Cal. **104** Carb. **6g** Protein **12g** Chol. **89mg** Fat **1g/12%***

Lobster: The Inside Story

Your lobster has probably dined better than you have. He indulged in a seafood diet of clams and crabs, mussels and urchins, starfish and small fish—even other lobsters.

Inside your lobster look for the green matter called *tomalley;* it's a delicacy.

Gray, light blue, orange, green, or light pink fluids are lobster blood. Cooked, they become colorless juices.

Salmon-colored sacs are female ovaries, full of roe and very tasty.

Discard anything blackish or dark green.

Mussels in Artichoke Cups

SERVES 4

4 medium artichokes
Juice of 1 lemon
Zest of 1 lemon
1 bay leaf
1 teaspoon salt
1 pound fresh mussels
1 cup dry white wine
½ cup finely chopped onion
2 tablespoons finely minced garlic
¼ teaspoon crushed red pepper flakes
4 cups curly endive, washed and dried
4 teaspoons Anchovy Vinaigrette (page 226)
¼ cup finely chopped fresh Italian parsley

Zesting

Citrus skin is loaded with aromatic oils that bring flavor to dishes. Remove it with a zester, just scraping off the fruit's colored surface and leaving the bitter white pith behind. If possible, zest over the dish you are preparing in order to capture the oil spray, too. Then use the zest in long strands or mince to achieve the texture you want.

1. Wash the artichokes and cut ½ inch from the tops with a sharp knife. With scissors, clip off the sharp tips from each leaf. Trim the stems. Rub all cut surfaces with lemon.

2. In a large saucepan, stand the artichokes upright, snugly and in one layer. Cover with water. Add the juice, zest, bay leaf, and salt to the saucepan. Cover, and simmer for 30 to 35 minutes, or until an outside leaf pulls off easily.

3. Drain the artichokes upside down until cool. Carefully spread the center leaves apart, and use a spoon to scrape out the fuzzy chokes. Chill the artichokes until ready to serve.

4. Meanwhile, rinse the mussels in several changes of water to wash out all the sand. Just before cooking, scrub and debeard the mussels.

5. In a large kettle or skillet with deep sides, combine the mussels, wine, onion, garlic, and pepper flakes. Cook over high heat, covered, shaking the pan from time to time, until the mussels open, 6 to 8 minutes. Discard any mussels that have not opened.

6. With a slotted spoon, remove the mussels from the pot. When they are cool enough to handle, remove them from their shells; discard the shells and cooking liquid. Refrigerate the mussels until ready to serve.

7. When ready to serve, place 1 cup of the endive on each of 4 plates, and top with a chilled artichoke. Carefully fill the artichoke cavities with mussels. Drizzle 1 generous teaspoon of Anchovy Vinaigrette over each serving of mussels and garnish with chopped parsley.

*Cal. **147** Carb. **25g** Protein **10g** Chol. **12mg** Fat **2g/10%***

GREAT GARLIC

Basics

In many ways, it's become one of our greatest comfort foods—nourishment for the body, as well as heart and soul.

People either love garlic or they don't. Those who love it seem curiously unable to get enough. With every passing year, I'm astonished at the increasing impact garlic has on my cooking.

In the millennia since the first large-scale cultivation began in Mesopotamia in 3000 B.C., garlic has made its mark in the world's cuisines.

A member of the lily family, garlic grows below ground in the form of a bulb, or head. Each bulb is made up of 12 to 24 cloves held together by an outer skin. The flavor is best in the spring, when the new crop of plump, succulent bulbs first appears.

Varieties

Garlic varies in color, size, and taste around the world. Pink garlic, *ail rosé*, from Lautrec in southwest France is even labeled with a guarantee of its provenance and quality. The most common varieties are California white, Mexican pink, and Argentinian purple. I think the purple-skinned variety has the most flavor and punch, without any bitterness. Elephant garlic, which has enjoyed a moment in food fashion, is actually an ancient ancestor of the leek and not a true garlic. As far as I can tell, its large size is its greatest feature, for its flavor, while very delicate, is often bitter in the aftertaste. I avoid it altogether.

In cooking, I use only fresh garlic. Not dried, pre-minced, or flaked, and no garlic powder or salt. Ever.

Growing Garlic

Once you grow your own plump, crispy garlic, bursting with flavor, you'll never think about buying garlic again!

It's remarkably easy:
• In the fall, break a head of garlic into cloves.
• Choose a sunny site with rich, moist soil; in heavy clay, loosen the soil with some sand first.
• Plant each clove flat end down, 2 inches deep and 5 inches apart.
• Mulch and overwinter.
• Pull garlic before it flowers. Freshly harvested, the "wet" garlic is tender and mild. Hang heads up to cure; the flavor will intensify and the garlic will last for months.

In the Market

Freshness is the most important consideration. Heads should be firm and compact, with no brown spots or sprouting. Loose heads, not those packed in boxes, tend to be freshest. For best flavor, the peeled cloves should be bright white with no green core.

At Home

Store garlic in a cool, dry, dark, well-ventilated place. Don't refrigerate. Use it within two weeks.

In Cooking

The more you mince, slice, dice, or crush garlic, releasing its juices (diallyl sulfides), the more pungent it tastes. The mildest, then, is whole cloves; the most pungent, garlic crushed with a mortar and pestle.

The power of garlic, however, is subdued by cooking. If burned, it becomes bitter. Roasted, it's sweeter. One method is to take a cut, peeled clove and rub it on grilled bread, a salad bowl, or poultry or meat to infuse its flavor. Use the thick green stalk and juicy cloves of mild "wet" garlic (just harvested) to lightly flavor summer vegetables and salads. In Spain, fried fresh garlic shoots are a delicacy served as tapas. Classic dishes in France, Italy, and Spain often begin with a simple sauté of oil and garlic with onions to begin a soup, stew, or sauce. I still find myself beginning many dishes this way. And I often add a tablespoon or two of freshly minced garlic at the end of cooking for extra zing.

Roasted Garlic Cloves

Peel 4 to 6 heads of garlic and spread them on a baking sheet pan. Drizzle or spray with 1 tablespoon of olive oil. Pour over 1 cup of chicken broth. Roast 45 minutes to 1¼ hours, basting and stirring every 15 minutes, until the cloves are golden. Serve at once or store in plastic in the refrigerator to use within 10 days.

Braised Garlic

Peel 3 heads of garlic. Place 1 tablespoon of canola oil in a medium-sized skillet over medium-high heat. Add the garlic and 1 cup of chicken broth, cover and braise 12-15 minutes. Uncover, add the remaining broth, and stir frequently until the liquid has evaporated and the cloves become golden.

GOOD FOR YOU

In the second century, the Greek physician Galen first identified garlic as an effective antibiotic, but only when eaten raw. The odor-producing ingredient allicin is what kills viruses, fungi, bacteria, and protozoa. Cooking not only makes garlic milder; it reduces its potency as an antibiotic.

In the body, garlic works to lower the "bad" LDL-cholesterol while raising the level of HDL or "good" cholesterol. Garlic also lowers triglyceride levels and thins the blood, which helps prevent blood, which can lead to stroke and heart attack. Garlic capsules with parsley are an effective way to take your daily dose and still have some non-garlic-loving friends.

Spicy Scallop Pasta

Don't overcook scallops—ever—or they will get tough.

SERVES 4

8 ounces cooked linguine
1 pound fresh sea scallops, rinsed and patted dry
2 tablespoons olive oil
2 tablespoons finely chopped garlic
1/2 cup finely chopped fresh parsley
1/4 teaspoon chopped fresh or dried hot red pepper
Salt
1/2 cup unflavored bread crumbs

1. While the pasta is cooking, prepare the scallops. If they are large, cut them in half horizontally.
2. Pour the oil into a saucepan and place over medium heat. Add the garlic and cook until lightly golden. Add the parsley and hot pepper and stir once or twice. Add the scallops with a pinch or two of salt. Increase the heat to high, and cook for 1 minute. Turn off the heat.
3. In a large bowl, pour the scallops over the pasta, add the bread crumbs, and toss well. Serve immediately on heated plates.

*Cal. **431** Carb. **57g** Protein **28g** Chol. **38mg** Fat **4g/19%***

Garlic & Herb Pasta

SERVES 4

2 tablespoons olive oil
20 garlic cloves, peeled
1 1/2 cups chicken broth (see Basics)
1/4 teaspoon freshly ground pepper
1/2 cup minced fresh chives
1/2 cup minced fresh chervil or Italian parsley
1/4 cup minced fresh basil
1/4 cup minced fresh dill
2 tablespoons minced fresh tarragon
8 ounces cooked fettuccine

1. In a large skillet over medium heat, heat the oil. Add the garlic and sauté for 3 minutes. Reduce the heat to low and

PARMESAN PRECAUTION

True, Parmesan is one of the cheeses lowest in fat and cholesterol. But you should still be aware that it has 28 calories per tablespoon and 1.8 grams of fat. In other words, it's 61% fat. Our recommendation: Buy the very best, well-aged for taste, and use it sparingly.

★ Italian cooks have an unshakable rule: Never leave the kitchen while pasta's in the pot. Timing is crucial.

★ Bring a large pot of water to a boil, then add about 1½ tablespoons coarse salt. Slide the pasta into the boiling water. Stir with a wooden fork or spoon to separate. Cover the pot and bring back to a boil as quickly as possible. Then set the cover askew and cook until al dente: When you bite into a cross-section, it will still have a chalky white core.

★ Drain and toss immediately with sauce. Or, depending on the dish, add the pasta to the sauce and heat for a moment, stirring to coat every nook and cranny.

★ I do as they do in Naples, home of spaghetti. I lift long pasta from the water with a long fork or tongs instead of draining it in a colander.

★ However you drain your pasta, *never* rinse it.

★ Don't overdo the sauce. More pasta, less sauce: that's the Italian way and the most healthful.

add ½ cup broth; cover and cook for 15 to 20 minutes. Remove the cover and cook until the garlic is soft and the liquid has evaporated. Crush half the garlic with the back of a wooden spoon, and stir in the remaining broth, pepper, chives, chervil, basil, dill, and tarragon. Mix well and keep warm over low heat.

2. Place the fettuccine in a large pasta bowl; add the garlic sauce and toss well. Serve immediately.

Cal. 311 Carb. 49g Protein 9g Chol. 0mg Fat 8g/24%

Spring Green Pasta

Asparagus, sugar snaps, and artichokes sing spring's song.

SERVES 4

1 cup Low-Fat Blend (see Basics)
1 cup chicken broth (see Basics)
Pinch ground nutmeg
⅛ teaspoon freshly ground pepper
1 box (9 ounces) frozen artichoke hearts, defrosted
1 cup frozen peas, defrosted
½ cup minced fresh basil
1 cup sugar snap peas
2 cups fresh asparagus tips
8 ounces cooked fettuccine
½ cup minced fresh Italian parsley

1. In a saucepan, place the Low-Fat Blend, broth, nutmeg, and pepper; warm over low heat, stirring constantly. Stir in the artichoke hearts, frozen peas, and basil. Keep the sauce warm over low heat.

2. Bring a pot of water to a boil. Drop in the sugar snaps; blanch until tender, about 1 minute. Remove and drain well. Drop in the asparagus and boil until tender, about 2 minutes. Remove and drain well.

3. Place the fettuccine, sugar snaps, and asparagus in a large pasta bowl, and toss well. Add the sauce and toss again. Garnish with the parsley. Serve immediately.

Cal. 330 Carb. 60g Protein 19g Chol. 1mg Fat 2g/6%

East-West Pasta Primavera

Sweet spring peas, snow peas, and red and yellow peppers create a lively dish.

SERVES 6

1 pound fresh snow peas
12 ounces cooked dry fettuccine
2 tablespoons sesame oil
¼ teaspoon chili oil
2 tablespoons rice vinegar
3 tablespoons soy sauce
3 cups fresh peas
2 cups finely julienned red bell pepper
2 cups finely julienned yellow bell pepper
1 cup diagonally cut scallions (¼-inch pieces)
¾ cup minced fresh parsley
Zest of 2 limes, chopped
2 tablespoons toasted sesame seeds
Freshly ground pepper

1. Bring a small pot of water to a full boil. Stir in the snow peas and blanch for 30 seconds, until they are tender but still crisp and bright green. Drain immediately.

2. Bring a large stockpot of water to a full boil. Stir in the fettuccine and cook until tender but still firm.

3. While the pasta is cooking, combine the sesame oil, chili oil, rice vinegar, and soy sauce in a large bowl. Add the snow peas, fresh peas, red and yellow pepper, scallion, parsley, lime zest, sesame seeds, and pepper. Add the pasta, toss to distribute the vegetables and sauce, and serve at once.

*Cal. **404** Carb. **65g** Protein **16g** Chol. **58mg** Fat **9g/20%***

Tuscan Pasta

SERVES 4

1 teaspoon olive oil
3 garlic cloves, minced
⅓ cup sun-dried tomatoes
2 cups fava beans, shelled and skinned
¼ cup pine nuts, toasted
1 cup Broccoli Pesto (page 48)
1 pound fresh spinach, trimmed and washed, with water still clinging to leaves

Fava Beans

They're also known as broad beans. Part of Mediterranean cooking for centuries, favas are newly popular here. Fresh, they have a robust, earthy flavor, a taste as bright as their color . . . a bean like no other.

Watch for them now at farmers' markets, Italian greengrocers, or specialty markets. Look for bright, shiny pods filled with beans of even size. Once the pods are opened, the beans should be nestled in a white bunting. Bean skins shouldn't be leathery; but even if they are, the beans will taste fresh after the skins have been removed.

Some cooks like to slip off the skins before cooking. It's easier after. A fiddly job, but relaxing, and a chore that adds to the anticipation. Blanch or steam the beans for 1 minute, then break the skins with your fingernail, and squeeze the beans between thumb and forefinger. They'll pop right out.

Favas make a glorious soup; puréed, steamed, or buttered, a great side dish. Or toss them with other vegetables in a ragoût or stir-fry.

"...with some fava beans and a nice Chianti."

Hannibal Lecter
Silence of the Lambs

8 ounces cooked linguine
Freshly ground pepper

1. In a large skillet over medium heat, heat the oil. Add the garlic, sun-dried tomatoes, fava beans, and pine nuts, and sauté for 3 minutes. Reduce the heat, add the pesto, and keep the sauce warm.
2. Place the spinach in a large heavy skillet, and cook, covered, over medium heat, shaking the pan once or twice, until the leaves are wilted. Remove from the heat.
3. Place the linguine and pesto sauce in a large pasta bowl; toss well. Add the cooked spinach and toss again. Add a generous amount of fresh pepper, and serve immediately.

Cal. **426** *Carb.* **65g** *Protein* **20g** *Chol.* **2mg** *Fat* **12g/24%**

Tarragon Shrimp Pasta

Vary the herbs: tarragon, dill, basil, chives, or chervil in spring and summer, sage or thyme in fall, rosemary in winter. Limit the rosemary and sage to just one tablespoon.

SERVES 4
2¼ cups bottled clam juice
¾ cup dry white wine
3 tablespoons finely minced garlic
¼ cup finely minced fresh tarragon
1 tablespoon cognac
1 tablespoon unsalted butter
1½ pounds shrimp, peeled and deveined,
  tail shells on
8 ounces spinach linguine

1. In a large saucepan, combine the clam juice, wine, garlic, and tarragon. Bring to a simmer. Add the cognac and butter, and continue to simmer until the sauce is reduced by half.
2. Add the shrimp to the sauce. Stir well and cook for 2 to 4 minutes, or just until the shrimp are cooked through.
3. Meanwhile, bring a large pot of water to a boil. Add the pasta to the water and cook according to directions.
4. Drain the pasta and divide it evenly among four large shallow soup or pasta plates. Arrange the shrimp on top of the pasta and spoon the sauce over. Serve immediately.

Cal. **325** *Carb.* **41g** *Protein* **27g** *Chol.* **207mg** *Fat* **5g/14%**

★ **GOOD FOR YOU** ★
Shellfish

Eating shrimp, crab, oysters, mussels, scallops, and clams helps increase levels of HDL, the good cholesterol, which blocks the absorption of bad cholesterol (LDL). All shellfish contain Omega-3 fatty acids, lots of protein, and minimal fat. Of course, if you bread and fry, dip in butter, or use tartar sauce, you undermine those advantages by adding fat.

Instead, broil, grill, or steam seafood. Squeeze on lemon juice or vinegar. or dip in a Great Good Pesto (pages 48–49) or salsa.

5 GREAT GOOD PESTOS

SPRING

Broccoli Pesto

YIELD: 2¼ CUPS

4 cups chopped broccoli florets
1 cup chicken broth (see Basics)
4 garlic cloves, peeled
1 cup tightly packed fresh basil leaves
¼ cup lightly toasted almonds
¼ cup grated Parmesan
⅛ teaspoon salt

1. In a large pot, steam the broccoli over the broth for 5 minutes, until tender. To the remaining liquid add broth to measure 6 tablespoons.
2. With the food processor motor running, drop the garlic into the work bowl. Process until the garlic is minced. Scrape down the sides. Add the basil and almonds and process until finely chopped. Add 2 tablespoons of the cooking liquid and process until smooth. Add the broccoli, Parmesan, salt, and remaining cooking liquid. Process until very smooth, scraping the sides frequently.
3. Store in a covered container in the refrigerator until ready to use.

Cal. 13 Carb. 1g Protein 1g Chol. .5mg
Fat .8g/48%*

Creamy Pesto

For every 2 ounces of dried fettuccine, I use 2 tablespoons of Basil Pesto. Or if I want a creamy pesto, I mix 1 tablespoon of Basil Pesto with 1 tablespoon of low-fat buttermilk. The traditional method uses ricotta, but with reduced oil in the pesto, ricotta tends to make it too dry. This satisfies very nicely.

SUMMER

Basil Pesto

YIELD: 1 CUP

6 garlic cloves, peeled
2 cups fresh basil leaves, packed, washed, dried, and stemmed
¼ cup toasted pine nuts
¼ cup coarsely grated Parmesan
1 tablespoon extra-virgin olive oil

1. With food processor motor running, drop garlic into working bowl. Process until finely chopped, scraping down sides twice. Add the basil and process until smooth. Add pine nuts and cheese and process until smooth.
2. With motor running, slowly drizzle in olive oil.
3. With a spatula, scrape the pesto into a container, cover and refrigerate or freeze until needed.

Cal. 70 Carb. 8g Protein 3g Chol. 2mg
Fat 4g/42%*

Pesto Fat Facts

• Great Good Pestos are all much lower in fat grams than a classic pesto of basil, olive oil, garlic, pine nuts, and Parmesan. Those would have approximately 11g. fat, with 90% of the calories for each portion coming from fat.
• A serving of 2 tablespoons of classic pesto on a 2-ounce portion of fettucine would add up to 416 calories, 45g. carbohydrate, 11g. protein, and 14g. cholesterol, for a total fat content of 22g., or 47% fat.
• For example, with Great Good Broccoli Pesto, the same portion results in 237 calories, 44g. carbohydrate, 9g. protein, 1g. cholesterol, and 2.5g. fat. In other words, 10% fat per serving.

FALL

Pumpkin Seed Pesto

YIELD: 1½ CUPS

1 cup raw pumpkin seeds
1 cup fresh Italian parsley
8 garlic cloves, peeled
5 tablespoons fresh lemon juice
Zest of one lemon, grated
1 teaspoon freshly ground pepper
½ teaspoon salt
2 tablespoons extra-virgin olive oil
6 tablespoons chicken broth (see Basics)

1. In a sauté pan over low heat, dry-roast the pumpkin seeds, stirring constantly, for 5 minutes or until they finish popping. Remove the seeds from the heat and let cool.

2. In a blender, place the seeds, parsley, garlic, lemon juice, zest, pepper, and salt. Blend to a paste. Slowly add the oil and broth and blend until smooth.

3. Transfer to a covered container and refrigerate until needed.

Cal. **42** *Carb.* **2g** *Protein* **0g** *Chol.* **3mg**
Fat **3g/48%***

HOLIDAY

Potato Pesto

YIELD: 1½ CUPS

1 medium potato, peeled and thinly sliced
½ cup chicken broth (see Basics)
12 garlic cloves, peeled and roughly chopped
Juice of one lemon
2 cups firmly packed fresh basil
1 cup fresh Italian parsley
¼ cup grated Parmesan
Salt
Freshly ground pepper

1. In a small saucepan over medium heat, simmer the potato, garlic, and broth, covered, for 10 minutes. Remove the cover, increase the heat to medium-high, and continue to cook until any remaining broth evaporates, about 1 minute.

2. Place the hot potato mixture in a blender or food processor, and blend until smooth. Add the lemon juice and combine. Let the mixture cool slightly before adding the basil, parsley, and Parmesan, and pulse to the desired texture. Season with salt and pepper.

Cal. **13** *Carb.* **2g** *Protein* **1g** *Chol.* **1mg**
Fat **.4g/24%***

WINTER

Hot Parsley Pesto

YIELD: 1½ CUPS

2 cups tightly packed fresh Italian parsley
1 cup fresh basil, tightly packed
½ cup fresh mint
2 tablespoons olive oil
2 tablespoons chicken broth (see Basics)
2 small jalapeno peppers, seeded
2 tablespoons grated fresh ginger
6 garlic cloves
4 tablespoons fresh lemon juice
Freshly ground pepper

In a blender or food processor, purée the herbs with a little oil. Add the remaining ingredients and blend to a smooth paste.

Cal. **16** *Carb.* **1g** *Protein* **.3g** *Chol.* **0mg**
Fat **1g/64%***

*Nutrition information analyzed per tablespoon

MOTHER'S DAY TEA

Mother's Day Tea. A cozy time to catch up. Make it pretty and leisurely, an affair that makes her feel special. Sink into chairs on the porch and enjoy each other's company. Invite those who consider any time teatime—the Mad Hatter, Eloise, Winnie-the-Pooh, Christopher Robin.

Teatime's catching on around the globe from Britain to Japan. The French seem to linger longer, perhaps because the gossip's so good. Tea salons have popped up all over Paris, with menus broadened to include spiced fruit and vegetable juices, hot chocolate with whipped-cream roses, and coffee.

"Love and scandal are the best sweeteners of Tea."

Henry Fielding

Currant Scones

YIELD: 24 SCONES

1 cup currants
¼ cup fresh orange juice
2 cups all-purpose flour
1 cup low-fat buttermilk
1 tablespoon baking powder
1 teaspoon baking soda
3 tablespoons canola oil
¼ cup sugar
1 tablespoon vanilla extract

1. Soak the currants in the orange juice for 1 hour.
2. Preheat oven to 350°. Lightly spray or wipe 2 baking sheets with vegetable oil.
3. In a medium-size bowl, place all of the remaining ingredients and stir with a fork until just blended; do not overmix. Add the soaked currants and juice.
4. Drop the dough in 2 tablespoon measures spaced about 1½ inches apart, on the sheets. You should have 24 scones.
5. Bake for 10 to 12 minutes, until golden brown.

Cal. **69** *Carb.* **12g** *Protein* **2g** *Chol.* **0mg** *Fat* **2g/24%**
(analyzed per scone)

Warm Ginger Tea

SERVES 4

4 teaspoons loose English Breakfast tea
1 teaspoon chopped fresh ginger
4 orange slices, ¼ inch thick
8 whole cloves

1. Fill a kettle with water and bring to a boil. Rinse the inside of a teapot with 2 cups of hot water and drain. Put the tea leaves and ginger in the teapot and add 6 cups of boiling water. Cover the teapot with a tea towel and steep for 5 minutes.
2. Stud each orange slice with 2 cloves and place at the bottom of a teacup. Stir the tea, then strain into the cups.

Cal. **24** *Carb.* **4g** *Protein* **.36g** *Chol.* **0mg** *Fat* **1g/33%**

Iced Mint Tea

SERVES 4

$1\frac{1}{4}$ tablespoons green Chinese tea, or 4 tea bags
1 orange, thinly sliced
1 lemon, thinly sliced
$\frac{1}{4}$ cup granulated sugar
$\frac{1}{2}$ cup fresh chopped mint
4 short mint sprigs

1. In a teapot, place the tea leaves or bags with four cups of boiling water and let steep for 5 minutes.
2. Meanwhile, place the orange and lemon in a heat-resistant pitcher. Pour the tea through a strainer into the pitcher. Add the sugar and mint. Chill for 1 hour.
3. Serve in tall chilled glasses filled with ice and garnish with mint sprigs.

Cal. 48 Carb. 12g Protein 0g Chol. 0mg Fat 0g/0%

Sugar Straws

YIELD: FORTY 12-INCH STRAWS

1 pound frozen puff pastry, defrosted according to package
  directions
1 egg white, lightly beaten with 2 tablespoons water
4 tablespoons raw sugar

1. Preheat the oven to 400°. Line a 12 x 16-inch baking sheet with parchment paper, leaving 1 inch of metal exposed on both long sides.
2. Cut each sheet of pastry dough in half, and return two sheets to the refrigerator. On a lightly floured surface, roll the dough out to a 10 x 16-inch rectangle, about $\frac{1}{16}$-inch thick.
3. Brush the dough lightly with the egg wash. Sprinkle the surface with 1 tablespoon sugar. Fold the dough in half to form an 8 x 10-inch rectangle. Brush the surface with egg wash and sprinkle with $\frac{1}{2}$ tablespoon sugar. Turn the dough over and repeat.
4. With a long sharp knife, using a ruler as a guide if necessary, slice the folded dough into $\frac{1}{2}$ x 8-inch strips. Carefully unfold each strip and place on the parchment paper, pressing the ends down onto the exposed metal, to prevent the straws from curling while baking. Place in the freezer and repeat with the remaining pastry.
5. When all are prepared, place in the oven and bake for 10

Smoky Tea

I enjoy the flavor of a smoky Lapsong Souchong. Or a scented orange pekoe. Or a flower-flecked jasmine tea. But I now know there's nothing that calms me faster than a strong, freshly brewed Darjeeling with milk in my favorite cup.

What is tea? Simply an infusion made with the leaves from an evergreen plant, *Camellia sinensis*, which grows in India, Ceylon, and East Africa as well as in its native China. It's the same plant wherever it grows, but the flavor varies with location and processing. "Teas" such as jasmine, chamomile, and mint don't come from the tea plant; they are infusions of flowers or herbs. Teas come in a spectrum of flavors, from robust and pungent to fragile and flowery.

★ Start with a glass or porcelain teapot.

★ Put on a kettle of fresh cold water to boil.

★ As the water heats, keep your teapot nearby to warm. Swish a little water from the kettle into the teapot as it nears the boil to warm it, then pour it out.

★ Measure tea leaves into the pot. Figure one heaping teaspoon per cup and one for the pot.

★ As soon as the water boils, pour it over the tea. Stir quickly, cover the pot, and put it under a tea cozy or in a warm spot to steep for 5 to 7 minutes.

★ To be properly English, pour a little whole milk in the bottom of each teacup. Not cream, not half-and-half, not even skim. It really does make the tea taste just right.

★ Stir the tea to blend the stronger settled tea with the weaker tea at the top.

★ Warm the cups first by swirling hot water in them and pouring it out.

★ Pour the tea through a fine strainer into the cups.

minutes, until puffed and golden brown. Store in an airtight container.

NOTE: The dough can be kept, well wrapped, and frozen, for up to 2 weeks before baking.

*Cal. **32** Carb. **3g** Protein **1g** Chol. **5mg** Fat **2g/53%***

Berry Strawberry Shortcake

Childhood memories are made of strawberries, juicy red and sweet. But my new shortcake makes berries taste better than ever. I purée some and use the purée to glaze the berries—a method that takes less time and sugar for the berries to become juicy. Then I add part of the purée to nonfat yogurt to create a creamy berry topping. The result is astonishing.

SERVES 8

*3 quarts strawberries, cleaned and left whole if small, halved
    or quartered if very large*
Juice of 1 orange
Juice of 2 lemons
³⁄₄ cup plus 2 tablespoons sugar
1 cup nonfat plain yogurt
2 tablespoons vanilla extract
1 recipe Buttermilk Biscuits (see Basics)

1. Place 2 cups strawberries, the orange and lemon juices, and ³⁄₄ cup sugar in a blender; process until smooth. Pour all but ½ cup of the purée over the rest of the berries. Taste and adjust the sugar. Set aside at room temperature.

2. In a small bowl, place the yogurt, 2 tablespoons sugar, remaining ½ cup berry purée, and vanilla, and blend well. Taste and adjust the sugar; refrigerate.

3. Preheat the oven to 350°. Make the biscuits and bake them.

4. While the biscuits are still warm, place them on individual plates and split in half horizontally. Generously spoon berries between the layers and over the top. Top with a dollop of the strawberry cream. Serve immediately.

*Cal. **307** Carb. **62g***

*Protein **5g** Chol. **1mg** Fat **5g/13%***

A spot of tea

TEA	TASTE
Assam	Robust and malty. Most Assam is blended with Ceylon tea for Irish Breakfast tea.
Ceylon	Delicate and sweet. Most important for its blends–Irish and English Breakfast teas.
Chamomile	Dried leaves and flowers make a mild, grassy, slightly appley tea.
Darjeeling	Delicate and slightly winey.
Earl Grey	Mild and slightly smokey. A blend of fermented black tea.
Formosa Oolong	Semifermented tea with the depth of black tea and the tang of green.
Ginger	Warm, spicy, with wonderful aroma.
Hibiscus	Strong and lemony.
Japanese	Delicate, fresh, and unfermented.
Jasmine	Flowery and light, good aroma.
Keemun	Winey and strong.
Lapsong Souchong	Strong and smoky.
Lemon Verbena	Very lemony herb tea.
Mint	Cool and refreshing, like the herb.
Raspberry Leaf	Delicate and grassy, slightly berry.
Rose Hips	Light and citrusy.
Yunnan	Mild and slightly sweet.

"Pray, Mary, fill the teapot up, And do not make it strong." Barry Pain

"I am glad I was not born before tea

Orange Tea

SERVES 4

4 teaspoons loose orange pekoe tea
2 teaspoons minced fresh ginger
2 cups orange, pear, peach, or apricot juice
4 slices of orange, pear, peach, or apricot
4 sprigs mint

Bring a large saucepan containing 6 cups of water to a boil. Add the tea and ginger, cover, and steep for 5 minutes. Strain into a pitcher and cool to room temperature. Add the fruit juice. For each serving, pour 1 cup of tea-juice mixture over ice in a glass. Garnish with a slice of fruit and a sprig of mint.

Cal. **28** *Carb.* **6g** *Protein* **.4g** *Chol.* **0mg** *Fat* **.1g/4%**

Caffeine Content of Brewed Teas

(5-oz. cup)

Tea bags (black tea)

5-min. brew	47 mg.
1-min. brew	29 mg.

Loose tea

Black

5-min. brew	41 mg.

Green

5-min. brew	36 mg.

Green (Japanese)

5-min. brew	21 mg.

Drip-brewed coffee

139 mg.

Source: The American Dietetic Association, *Handbook of Clinical Dietetics*

★ GOOD FOR YOU ★

Nutritionally, not all teas are created equal. But they start out that way.

Green, black, and oolong tea all come from the same plant. The difference is in the way they are processed. Green tea is made from leaves dried right after harvesting, black tea from leaves allowed to ferment after harvesting, and oolong in between, its brownish-green leaves allowed to ferment only a short time.

Teas are rich in flourides for healthy teeth and bones. They also provide some magnesium and potassium, and are a good source of the B vitamin folacin. The green tea of China and Japan has a delicate flavor and is the one most filled with nutritional tannis, helping fend off some carcinogens, perhaps the reason Chinese sages believed green tea bestowed long life and wisdom, while the ancient Greeks found it beneficial for asthma and colds.

Black tea is next best, with a more intense flavor. Souchong, pekoe, and orange pekoe refer to grades of black-tea leaves. Souchong has round leaves; orange pekoe has thin wiry ones; and pekoe has leaves that are similar, but shorter and rounder. In taste, oolong falls somewhere in the middle.

ev. Sydney Smith

AT TWILIGHT TIME

Day is done. The sun descends. In the lingering magic of dusk, friends and family gather to ease into evening. To take the edge off hunger but not dull the appetite, light foods appeal most.

Spicy Shrimp

Shrimp with a nice bite, to be shelled around a newspaper-covered table.

SERVES 4

1½ pounds large shrimp, shells left on
*1 cup ripe Roma (plum) tomatoes, seeded and
   cut into large chunks*
1 medium onion, cut into large chunks
½ cup minced fresh cilantro
2 teaspoons ground cumin
Pinch cayenne
Pinch crushed red pepper flakes
Dash Tabasco
Freshly ground pepper

Salmon

Salmon, native to both Atlantic and Pacific waters spawn in cold rivers, spend most of their lives downstream in the ocean, and return to their natal river to reproduce and finish the life cycle.

Wild salmon is about 17 percent fat, which protects it from the chill of northern waters—and the inexactitude of the cook. You can cook salmon longer without drying it out. But slightly medium-rare is usually best.

In Scandinavia and the Pacific Northwest, salmon are raised on farms. These are far more delicate than their wild cousins. Their flesh is lighter pink, their flavor less fishy, and their texture finer. They also have more HDL cholesterol.

Salmon's flavor is nutty, woodsy, almost gamy. Treat it like meat: best quickly sautéed, steamed, or broiled. When roasted, braised, or grilled, salmon shines.

1. Bring 3 cups of water to a boil in a large stockpot.
2. In a large mixing bowl, toss all of the ingredients together until the shrimp are coated.
3. Transfer the shrimp to a metal steamer inserted over the boiling water in the stockpot. Cover and steam for 3 to 5 minutes. Remove and serve immediately.

Cal. 115 Carb. 5g Protein 20g Chol. 179mg Fat 1.5g/12%

Salmon Mousse

My favorite cocktail fare dolloped on pumpernickel or scooped onto endive. Every time I taste this, it's like the first. Now it's better than ever, with no heavy cream.

YIELD: 1 QUART
1 envelope unflavored gelatin
½ cup low-fat buttermilk
2 cups Low-Fat Blend (see Basics)
2 tablespoons fresh lime juice
Zest of 1 lime, minced
⅛ teaspoon cayenne
1 tablespoon minced fresh chervil or
* parsley*
¼ cup minced fresh dill
2 tablespoons minced fresh cilantro
2 cups finely flaked fresh poached salmon, or canned
* salmon*
1 egg white, at room temperature

1. In a small saucepan over low heat, soften the gelatin in ¼ cup of water; let the mixture stand for 1 minute. Transfer the dissolved gelatin to a large mixing bowl and cool slightly, but do not jell.
2. Slowly whisk in the buttermilk, Low-Fat Blend, lime juice and zest, cayenne, chervil, dill, and cilantro, and mix well. Gently fold in the salmon and refrigerate the mixture for 20 minutes, or until it thickens.
3. In another bowl, beat the egg white until stiff, then gently fold it into the salmon mixture, blending well to make sure there are no lumps.
4. Transfer the mixture to a 6- to 8-cup bowl or decorative mold. Cover and chill for at least 2 hours before serving.

Cal. 14 Carb. 1g Protein 2g Chol. 4mg Fat .4g/29%
(analyzed per tablespoon)

Snappy Green Beans

These spicy beans were inspired by a bar treat served at Chin Chin, a New York Chinese restaurant. We serve them often at the inn I own with my husband, and at our home.

SERVES 4
1/2 cup sugar
1/2 cup white wine vinegar
1/4 teaspoon crushed red pepper flakes
1 garlic clove, minced
1 pound green beans, ends snipped

1. In a small bowl, whisk the sugar and vinegar together until the sugar has dissolved. Stir in the crushed red pepper and garlic. Set the mixture aside and let the flavors mellow for 4 hours or longer.
2. Thirty minutes before you are ready to serve the beans, blanch them in boiling water for 1 minute, or until tender but still crisp. Drain. Run the beans under cold water and drain again.
3. Mix the beans with the marinade and let the flavors blend for 1/2 hour. Serve.

Cal. **137** *Carb.* **35g** *Protein* **2g** *Chol.* **0mg** *Fat* **.1g/1%**

Popping Beans

SERVES 12
3 cups giant white or brown beans, sorted and soaked in
   water overnight
6 sprigs fresh thyme
3 tablespoons olive oil
1/2 teaspoon salt
1/4 teaspoon white pepper
1/4 cup chopped Italian parsley
1 cup Poetic Aïoli (page 316) or Red Pepper Aïoli (page 218)

1. Drain the beans and put them in a large heavy saucepan. Cover with water to 1 inch over the beans, and add the thyme. Bring to a boil, and boil for 10 minutes, skimming off any foam. Reduce the heat and simmer for 1 to 1 1/2 hours, until the beans are just tender. Drain and transfer to a large bowl.
2. In a small bowl, mix together the oil, salt, pepper, and parsley. Pour the mixture over the warm beans and toss well.

Cover and chill for several hours, then serve at room temperature with the aïoli.

*Cal. **231** Carb. **34g** Protein **12g** Chol.**0mg** Fat **6g/22%***

Spicy Chinese Riblettes

Glistening with spicy sauce. Supply plenty of dampened napkins!

SERVES 12
1 cup hoisin sauce
6 tablespoons rice wine or white wine
½ cup soy sauce
1 cup sugar
½ cup tomato paste
¼ cup finely minced garlic
2 tablespoons Tabasco
2 pounds pork ribs, cut into 1-inch riblettes

1. Preheat the oven to 350°.
2. In a medium-size mixing bowl, mix all of the ingredients, except the riblettes, until smooth. Taste and set aside.
3. Place the riblettes in a large roasting pan, and bake, uncovered, for 45 minutes.
4. Remove the pan from the oven, pour the sauce over the riblettes, and toss to coat. Return the pan to the oven, uncovered, and bake for another 45 minutes. Toss every 10 minutes so that the riblettes stay well coated with sauce.

*Cal. **194** Carb. **27g** Protein **11g** Chol. **26mg** Fat **5g/21%***

Spring Herbs

Herbs crave frequent picking. Snip chives often for a lush, sturdy plant that quickly shoots out fresh, tender leaves. Pick parsley and chervil from the outside in; new green sprigs start from the middle. Basil needs its tops picked continually to prevent early flowering and to encourage a sturdy, aromatic bush.

Savory Cheese Straws

These foot-long straws quickly become everyone's favorite nibble.

YIELD: EIGHTY 12-INCH STRAWS

1 pound frozen puff pastry, defrosted
2 egg whites, lightly beaten with 4 teaspoons water
2 cups plus 2 tablespoons freshly grated Parmesan or Romano
½ cup finely chopped fresh herbs (chives, dill, rosemary, or sage)

1. Preheat the oven to 400°. Line the bottom of a 12 x 16-inch baking sheet with the parchment paper, leaving 1 inch of the pan exposed on both long sides.
2. Cut each sheet of pastry dough in half (there are two sheets per package), and keep the dough chilled until you are ready to work with it. On a lightly floured surface, roll the dough into a 10 x 12-inch rectangle about ¹⁄₁₆ inch thick.
3. Brush the dough lightly with the egg wash. Sprinkle the surface with ½ cup of cheese and 2 tablespoons of herbs. Using a rolling pin, lightly press the cheese and herbs into the dough. Fold the dough in half to enclose the cheese, forming a 6 x 10-inch rectangle. Brush with egg wash and sprinkle with 1½ teaspoons of cheese. Turn the dough over and repeat.
4. With a long sharp knife, using a ruler as a guide if necessary, slice the folded dough into ½ x 6-inch strips. Carefully unfold each strip and place on the parchment paper, pressing the ends down onto the exposed edge of the baking sheet, to prevent the cheese straws from curling while baking. Place in the freezer and repeat with the remaining pastry.
5. When all are prepared, place in the oven and bake for 10 minutes, until puffed and golden brown. Store in an airtight container.

*Cal. **34** Carb. **2g** Protein **1g** Chol. **6mg** Fat **2g/60%***
(analyzed per straw)

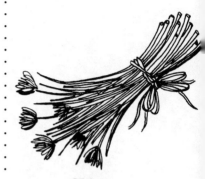

Chives

Chives' thin, grassy spikes are the first rumors of fine weather. A member of the onion, leek, garlic, and shallot tribe, chives impart a delicate onion taste.

Chives create a lush, green border to the garden, punctuated with flowers—little mauve pom-poms—that are charming when added to mixed posies or simply left to nod in the breeze. Better still, pick the flowers along with the leaves—both are edible. The chive plant only gets stronger, the flavor better, as you pick.

Chicken & Vegetable Strudel

YIELD: 2 STRUDELS (24 SLICES)

1 whole chicken breast, boned and skinned
1 teaspoon olive oil
1 cup chopped celery
1 medium onion, chopped
½ cup chopped fresh Italian parsley

- ½ cup chopped fresh dill
- 1 cup Low-Fat Blend (see Basics)
- ¼ cup Dijon mustard
- 2 ounces Gruyère cheese, grated
- 2 large carrots, peeled and cut lengthwise into ⅛-inch strips
- 12 thin asparagus, trimmed to 7 inches
- 6 sheets phyllo dough

1. Heat the oil in a medium-size skillet, and sauté the chicken pieces for 2 minutes on each side. Remove to a large mixing bowl, and set aside.

2. Add the celery and onion to the skillet, and cook for 10 to 12 minutes, stirring frequently, until tender. Stir in the parsley and dill and immediately add the mixture to the chicken.

3. Reduce the heat to low, add the Low-Fat Blend and the mustard to the skillet, and heat through. Add the cheese and simmer for 6 to 8 minutes to thicken slightly. Combine the sauce with the chicken, mix well, and set aside.

4. In a pot of boiling water, blanch the carrots and asparagus for 1 minute, and immediately rinse with cold water to stop the cooking process. Drain and pat dry.

5. Preheat the oven to 325°. Place a 3-inch square piece of waxed paper on a flat work surface. Unfold 1 sheet of phyllo dough onto the paper and spray with the oil; top with another and spray; repeat the process with a third sheet.

6. Lightly wipe a 9 x 9-inch baking sheet with the spray.

7. With the long side of the sheet nearest you, arrange in the lower quarter: three asparagus stalks and three carrot strips, end to end. Place half of the chicken mixture over the strips, laying the chicken strips in the same direction as the asparagus. Place two more asparagus stalks and one carrot on either side, and one of each on top of the chicken strips.

8. With the help of the waxed paper, lift the edge of the dough closest to you; roll up the dough, tightly, away from you. Spray the edge to seal; tuck in the ends and spray again. Place the strudel on the baking sheet. Repeat the process with the remaining ingredients to make a second strudel.

9. Bake for 20 to 25 minutes, until golden brown. Let cool before serving.

*Cal. **59** Carb. **6g** Protein **5g***
*Chol. **10mg** Fat **1.8g/26%***
(analyzed per slice)

Peppered Potatoes

A cocktail-time variation of my favorite Herb-Roasted Potatoes. This time, they have more pepper to spark everyone's wits.

SERVES 20

1 tablespoon salt
1 tablespoon sugar
2 tablespoons freshly ground
  pepper
2 pounds smallest new red
  potatoes
¼ cup very finely chopped
  fresh mint

1. Preheat the oven to 400°.
2. In a small bowl, combine the salt, sugar, and pepper. Wash the potatoes and leave them damp; sprinkle with the seasonings. Place in a roasting pan and bake for 40 minutes to 1 hour, until tender. Toss with the mint and serve warm as finger or toothpick food.

*Cal. **41** Carb. **9g***
*Protein **1g** Chol. **0mg***
*Fat **1g/2%***

Chicken Spring Rolls

YIELD: 8 ROLLS

½ cup chicken broth (see Basics)
1 half chicken breast, boneless, skinned
1 cup peeled, cored, and coarsely chopped Granny Smith
  apple
2 cups mung bean sprouts, rinsed and drained
1 cup julienned jícama
¼ cup sliced scallion, green part only
3 to 4 tablespoons Pang-Pang Sauce (page 509)
8 spring-roll wrappers, defrosted, or lettuce leaves
Canola oil for deep-frying

1. Preheat the oven to 350°.
2. Pour enough chicken broth into a small baking dish to cover the bottom. Place the chicken in the dish; cover and bake for 30 minutes. Remove from the oven and cool. Shred the meat into small pieces.
3. In a large mixing bowl, combine the chicken, apple, beans, jícama, scallion, and Pang-Pang Sauce to taste. Mix well.
4. If you are using spring-roll wrappers, place a wrapper on a flat surface, with a point facing you. Place ⅓ cup of the filling diagonally across the lower third of the wrapper. Bring the tip of the lower corner over the filling and roll once. Bring the left and right flaps together to make an envelope, and wet each tip to seal. Continue rolling to form a nice tight roll. Seal the last tip. Place on a plate, seam-side down, and repeat the procedure with the remaining wraps and filling. Pour oil into a skillet or a wok to a depth of about 1 inch, and bring to medium-high heat. Place four spring rolls in the skillet and fry, turning constantly, until golden brown and crisp, about 4 to 5 minutes. Remove the rolls, place them on a paper towel to drain, and cover to keep warm. Fry the remaining spring rolls and serve immediately. If you are using leaf wrappers, spray a skillet or wok with vegetable oil. Heat well, add the stuffing, and stir-fry for 2 to 3 minutes; do not overcook. Wrap tightly in lettuce leaves and refrigerate until ready to serve.

*Cal. **208** Carb. **23g** Protein **9g** Chol. **34mg** Fat **9g/39%***
(wrapper & oil)
*Cal. **50** Carb. **6g** Protein **6g** Chol. **11mg** Fat **1g/7%***
(leaves)

It's a Wrap

Vegetable leaves provide a wonderful low-fat, low-calorie way to enclose certain foods. They can keep fragile foods from falling apart, or can sometimes replace a crust in, say, a vegetable tart.

Here are some swell choices:

◆ Iceberg lettuce
◆ Romaine lettuce
◆ Spinach
◆ Cabbage
◆ Grape leaves
◆ Banana leaves
◆ Steamed corn husks
◆ Sorrel

Spicy Sauce

YIELD: ½ CUP

¼ cup sugar
½ cup sherry vinegar
¼ teaspoon crushed red
  pepper flakes
1 teaspoon soy sauce
2 garlic cloves, finely minced

In a small bowl, whisk the sugar and sherry together until the sugar has completely dissolved. Whisk in the remaining ingredients. Transfer to a small dipping bowl.

Cal. 9 Carb. 2g Protein 0g Chol. 0mg Fat 0g/0% (analyzed per teaspoon)

Mint Sauce

YIELD: 1 CUP

1¼ cups fresh mint leaves
1 cup white vinegar
6 tablespoons sugar
3 tablespoons finely minced
  fresh lemon grass

1. In a food processor, place 1 cup of the mint leaves and purée for 30 seconds. Add the vinegar and process for another 6 seconds. Scrape into a small saucepan.
2. Add the sugar and lemon grass. Heat over medium heat, stirring constantly, until the sugar has dissolved. Reduce the heat to a simmer; cover and steep for 20 minutes.
3. Strain the sauce into a small serving bowl and let it cool. Finely mince the remaining mint and stir into the dipping sauce.

Cal. 9 Carb. 2g Protein 0g Chol. 0mg Fat 0g/0% (analyzed per teaspoon)

Spicy Shrimp Spring Rolls

YIELD: 8 ROLLS

8 fresh large shrimp, shelled and deveined
2 cups mung bean sprouts, rinsed and dried
1 cup julienned red bell pepper
1 cup julienned yellow bell pepper
½ cup water chestnuts
2 tablespoons horseradish
2 teaspoons finely minced fresh jalapeño pepper
1 teaspoon Dijon mustard
8 spring-roll wrappers or lettuce leaves

1. Bring a small pot of water to a boil. Cook the shrimp for 1 minute, drain, rinse under cold water, and cool.
2. In a large mixing bowl, combine the shrimp, beans, peppers, water chestnuts, horseradish, jalapeño pepper, and mustard. Mix well.
3. Proceed with step 4 in the recipe for Chicken Spring Rolls on the previous page.

Cal. 170 Carb. 20g Protein 5g Chol. 30mg Fat 8g/40% (wrapper & oil)
Cal. 22 Carb. 3g Protein 2g Chol. 8mg Fat .2g/9% (leaves)

Vegetable Spring Rolls

YIELD: 8 ROLLS

½ cup rice vinegar
½ cup sugar
½ teaspoon crushed red pepper flakes
4 garlic cloves, minced
2 cups mung bean sprouts, rinsed and drained
2 cups coarsely shredded Chinese cabbage
1 cup julienned carrot
½ cup slivered water chestnuts
8 spring-roll wrappers or lettuce leaves

1. In a large mixing bowl, whisk the rice vinegar and sugar until the sugar has completely dissolved. Add the remaining ingredients (except the spring-roll wrappers) and combine well.
2. Let the mixture sit for 1 hour at room temperature, stirring occasionally. Drain the mixture in a colander for 15 minutes.
3. Proceed with step 4 in the recipe for Chicken Spring Rolls on the previous page.

Cal. 228 Carb. 42g Protein 10g Chol. 23mg Fat 8g/23% (wrapper & oil)
Cal. 69 Carb. 17g Protein 1g Chol. 0mg Fat 1g/2% (leaves)

ENCHANTED EVENINGS

Spring Vegetable Stew

Bright and fresh, perfect for a light spring supper. So satisfying, you won't miss the classic chicken or beef.

SERVES 6

1 large lemon, thinly sliced
2 tablespoons sugar
6 garlic cloves, peeled, roasted, and mashed into a paste (page 43)
1 tablespoon canola oil
1 teaspoon freshly ground pepper
2 quarts chicken broth (see Basics)
8 red potatoes, 1½ inches in diameter, scrubbed and cut into quarters
4 small leeks, white parts only, rinsed, trimmed, and split
1 pound fresh green beans, trimmed
8 small carrots, scraped and cut into 2-inch pieces
1 pound sugar snap peas
2 cups spinach, slivered and stems removed
½ cup finely minced fresh dill, Italian parsley, or chervil

Menu

*Salmon Mousse
on Endive*

*Spring
Vegetable Stew*

*Lemon Rice
with Leeks*

*Young Greens
with Citrus Spray*

Strawberry Fool

64

French Onion Bread

The variations are limitless:
Stuff the loaves with shallots,
roasted garlic, or onion marmalade, basil, dill, or thyme.

YIELD: 24 SLICES
*¼ cup finely chopped red
   onion*
2 tablespoons olive oil
2 tablespoons canola oil
*2 tablespoons finely chopped
   fresh dill, basil, or thyme*
*1 loaf French bread
   (24 inches long)*
*3 tablespoons slivered
   Monterey Jack cheese*

1. Place the onion, oils, and
dill in a covered container
and let sit for 3 hours at room
temperature. Preheat the
oven to 300°. Slice the bread
in half lengthwise.
2. Cover the bottom half of
the loaf with the onion mixture. Cover with the top half;
sprinkle the cheese over.
Place the bread on a cookie
sheet and bake for 10 minutes. Slice the loaf and serve
immediately.

*Cal. **88** Carb. **12g** Protein **2g**
Chol. **1mg** Fat **3g/32%***
(analyzed per slice)

"'Tis an old
maxim in the
schools,
That flattery's
the food of fools."

Jonathan Swift

1. In a small sauté pan, place the lemon slices, sugar, and 1
cup of water, and simmer until the lemon is tender, 10 to 15
minutes. Remove the lemon slices and reserve the liquid.
When the lemon is cool, coarsely chop it. Place the lemon,
garlic, and oil in a blender and blend until smooth. Season
with pepper and set aside.
2. Pour the chicken broth into a large stockpot, and bring to a
simmer over medium-high heat. Add the potatoes and leeks,
and simmer for 10 minutes. Add the green beans and carrots,
and simmer until they are tender. Add the sugar snaps and
simmer 1 minute longer. With a slotted spoon, remove all the
vegetables and place them in a bowl. Set aside.
3. Bring the broth back to a boil. Lower the heat and simmer
about 15 minutes, until reduced to about 4 cups. Remove
the broth from the heat and whisk in the lemon mixture.
4. Place one-fourth of the spinach in the bottom of each of
four soup bowls in the shape of a wreath; place the vegetables in the center.
5. Strain the broth through a sieve and season to taste with
pepper and reserved lemon liquid. Gently ladle the broth over
the vegetables and sprinkle with the minced herbs.

*Cal. **269** Carb. **51g** Protein **11g** Chol. **11mg** Fat **4g/13%***

Strawberry Fool

For every sweet tooth, a dream fulfilled.

SERVES 8
1 quart fresh strawberries, cleaned
1 cup low-fat cottage cheese
2 cups nonfat plain yogurt
4 tablespoons honey
2 teaspoons vanilla extract
1 vanilla bean, split, seeds removed
½ cup strawberry preserves

1. In a blender, purée the strawberries and cottage cheese.
2. Place the yogurt in a medium bowl, and fold in the strawberry mixture. Add the honey, vanilla extract, and vanilla
seeds, and mix gently but thoroughly. Chill.
3. When ready to serve, place equal amounts of the yogurt
mixture into six dishes and swirl a teaspoon of the preserves
into each.

*Cal. **122** Carb. **22g** Protein **7g** Chol. **1mg** Fat **1g/6%***

Spring Lamb with Mint Salsa

A Tuscan treasure, lightened with a velvety sauce.

SERVES 12

1 cup wild rice
2¼ cups chicken broth (see Basics)
3 cups button or cremini mushrooms, cleaned and stemmed
1 teaspoon canola oil
1 cup raisins
3 tablespoons finely minced fresh sage
Zest of 2 lemons, chopped
6 minced garlic cloves
2 slivered garlic cloves
6 scallions, green parts only, chopped
1 cup coarsely chopped fresh Italian parsley
Freshly ground pepper
1 butterflied leg of lamb (7 to 7½ pounds)
2 cups red wine
2 cups beef broth (see Basics)

1. In a small saucepan, place the wild rice and 1¾ cups chicken broth. Cook over medium-high heat for 30 minutes, or until just before the rice starts to bloom.
2. Quarter the mushrooms. In a medium-size skillet, heat the canola oil over high heat. Add the mushrooms and ½ cup chicken broth, and sauté for 6 to 8 minutes.
3. Place the rice in a large bowl; add the mushrooms, raisins, sage, lemon zest, minced garlic, scallion, parsley, and pepper.
4. Preheat the oven to 400°. Make small slits evenly spaced into the meat and insert the slivered garlic. Spread the rice mixture over the leg; roll and tie the lamb.
5. Place any extra stuffing in the bottom of a shallow baking pan, and place the lamb in the pan. Bake for 30 minutes. Add 1 cup wine and 1 cup beef broth. Baste every 10 minutes for 30 minutes. Add the remaining wine and broth, and continue basting for 20 to 30 minutes for a pink roast, or until it reaches an internal temperature of 135°.
6. Place the lamb on a platter and let it rest for 10 minutes before slicing. Defat the juices and pass them at the table. Serve with Mint Salsa (at right) on the side.

Cal. 348 Carb. 23g Protein 40g Chol. 136mg Fat 11g/28%

Menu

Cheese Straws

Spring Lamb with Mint Salsa

Cinnamon Rice & Lentils

Sautéed Spinach with Ginger

Venetian Country Cake

Mint Salsa

YIELD: 1 CUP
½ cup sugar
⅓ cup cider vinegar
⅓ cup fresh lime juice
2 packed cups fresh mint leaves
2 kiwis, peeled and diced
1 tablespoon minced lime zest

1. In a heavy skillet, over medium heat, place the sugar, vinegar, and lime juice. Bring to a boil, reduce the heat to low, and simmer for 5 minutes.
2. Meanwhile, place the mint in a blender or food processor, and pulse until very finely chopped.
3. Remove the liquid from the heat and let cool to room temperature. When cool, add the mint, kiwi, and zest to the vinegar mixture and refrigerate until ready to use.

Cal. 34 Carb. 9g
Protein .3g Chol. 0mg
Fat .1g/2%
(analyzed per tablespoon)

Tricolor Streamers

A fiesta of fresh color and crunch.

SERVES 6

1½ cups peeled and grated carrot
1 cup peeled and grated jícama
1 cup peeled and grated parsnip
1 cup fresh orange juice
Zest of 1 orange, minced
½ cup minced fresh mint

1. In a large sauté pan, place the carrot, jícama, parsnip, orange juice, and orange zest. Sauté over high heat for 2 to 5 minutes, tossing frequently. Remove from the heat.
2. Toss the vegetables with the mint. Taste and adjust seasoning.

Cal. 61 Carb. 14g
Protein 1g Chol. .3mg
Fat 1g/3%

"At morn the cherry-blooms will be white, And the Easter bells be ringing!"

Edna D. Proctor

Cinnamon Rice & Lentils

SERVES 6

¼ cup golden raisins
1 tablespoon applejack, Calvados, or Grand Marnier
1½ cups chicken broth (see Basics)
4 canela sticks (Mexican cinnamon) or 1 cinnamon stick
½ cup lentils
½ cup brown basmati rice
1 tablespoon canola oil
2 teaspoons minced orange zest
¼ cup fresh orange juice
¼ cup chopped fresh mint

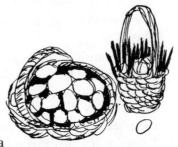

1. Combine the raisins with the applejack. Set aside to plump.
2. Place the broth and cinnamon in a heavy saucepan and bring to a boil. Stir in the lentils, rice, oil, and raisins, and return to a boil. Reduce the heat to low and cover tightly. Let the rice simmer, undisturbed, for about 35 minutes.
3. Uncover the pan and toss the rice with the remaining ingredients. Adjust seasoning to taste.

Cal. 169 Carb.30g Protein 7g Chol. 0mg Fat 3g/16%

Sautéed Spinach with Ginger

SERVES 4

1½ cups fresh orange juice
2 tablespoons peeled and minced fresh ginger
1 tablespoon fresh lemon juice
1 pound fresh spinach, trimmed and washed (leave water clinging to leaves)
Freshly ground pepper

1. In a skillet, bring the orange juice and ginger to a boil over medium-high heat. Boil until the liquid is reduced to approximately ½ cup. Stir in the lemon juice and set aside.
2. Place the spinach in a large, heavy pot. Cover and cook over medium heat, tossing once or twice, until wilted, about 3 minutes. Drain and return to the pot. Add the orange sauce and sauté for 30 seconds.
3. Transfer to a serving plate and season with fresh pepper to taste. Serve immediately.

Cal. 63 Carb. 13g Protein 3g Chol.0mg Fat .5g/6%

Cozy Chicken Pot Pie

My Grandma Drechsler always topped her chicken pot pie with a biscuit crust. Somewhere along the way, we began using double crusts and puff pastry—only to add more fat. Now the old way seems new again.

SERVES 6

2 whole chicken breasts, skinless
3 cups chicken broth (see Basics)
1 teaspoon salt
2 sprigs fresh thyme
2 carrots, trimmed and sliced
1 stalk celery, cleaned and diced
1 small onion, chopped
4 sprigs fresh Italian parsley
1 cup peeled pearl onions

1 pound sugar snap peas, trimmed
1 pound baby carrots, cleaned and halved
8 baby kohlrabi, peeled and halved
½ pound asparagus, cleaned and cut
into 1½-inch lengths
1 turnip, halved and sliced
1 leek, cleaned and sliced, including
about 2 inches of the green part
2 large garlic cloves, peeled and sliced
1 teaspoon chopped fresh thyme
½ cup chopped fresh dill
Salt and freshly ground pepper
2 tablespoons chopped fresh Italian parsley
½ recipe Buttermilk Biscuits (see Basics)

1. Place the chicken in a Dutch oven with 3 cups of chicken broth. Add the salt, thyme, carrot, celery, onion, and parsley. Bring to a boil and cover; reduce the heat and simmer for 30 minutes. Turn the heat off and cool to room temperature. Remove the chicken from the broth. Remove the meat from the bone and shred it into bite-size pieces. Strain and reserve the broth. Set aside.

2. Cook the pearl onions in boiling water for 10 to 12 minutes. Drain and set aside.

Menu

Cozy Chicken
Pot Pie

Mesclun
with Balsamic
Vinaigrette

Sweet Pea Shoots

Strawberry Sorbet

Free-Range Chicken

There's been a lot of talk about the advantages of free-range poultry, and even more confusion about just what "free range" means. Finally, the organic farming industry is about to be covered by labeling laws that will standardize practices.

Here's what you can expect from poultry labeled "free range":

• That the animal was fed organic grains

• That growth medication was not used

• That the animal was raised uncaged, allowed to roam inside and out.

• Leaner, tastier chicken

3. Blanch the vegetables as follows, and transfer to bowl of cold water to cool and drain; set aside:

  sugar snaps: 30 seconds; carrots: $1\frac{1}{2}$ to 2 minutes; kohlrabi: 2 minutes; asparagus: $1\frac{1}{2}$ minutes

4. In a medium-size saucepan, combine the turnip, leek, garlic, chopped thyme, and 2 cups of the remaining chicken broth. Bring to a boil, lower the heat slightly, and cook the vegetables until very tender, about 20 minutes. Cool slightly, then purée in a blender or food processor.

5. In a large bowl, combine the chicken, onions, blanched vegetables, and vegetable purée, tossing gently. Fold in the dill and salt and pepper to taste. Pour into a 2-quart casserole dish.

6. Preheat the oven to 375°. Make the Biscuit Dough; dot the top of the casserole with the dough, covering the chicken mixture completely. Bake for 25 to 30 minutes, until the biscuit topping is golden.

7. Garnish with parsley and serve immediately.

*Cal. **350** Carb. **41g** Protein **25g** Chol. **53mg** Fat **9g/23%***

Carrots

Once cooked, young spring carrots pulled fresh from the ground can be intensely flavorful. Or highly disappointing. My secret: Don't peel them. Wash them well and cook with the skins on. When soft enough to penetrate with a fork, plunge the carrots into cold water—the skins will rub right off, leaving behind a most distinctive sweet flavor.

★ **GOOD FOR YOU** ★

Carrots are rich in beta-carotene, a naturally occurring, cancer-preventing form of vitamin A.

Sweet Pea Shoots

Tender new sweet pea shoots, with the very freshest taste of spring inside, quickly wilted with minced garlic. Be sure and buy plenty, both because they "melt" and because everyone will want more!

SERVES 4

1 tablespoon olive oil
24 garlic cloves, minced
$\frac{1}{2}$ cup chicken or beef broth (see Basics)
6 cups sweet pea shoots, washed and patted dry

1. In one large skillet or two medium skillets, heat the olive oil over medium heat. Add the garlic cloves and toss well to coat. Add the broth; cover and cook, stirring occasionally for 5 to 6 minutes until garlic begins to soften. Remove the cover and turn up the heat.

2. Increase the heat from medium to high and add the pea shoots. Cover and let the shoots wilt for 5 to 7 minutes, stirring frequently and adding one tablespoon of broth at a time to maintain moisture. Remove the cover and turn up the heat so that all juices are completely absorbed.

*Cal. **63** Carb. **7g** Protein **1g** Chol. **0mg** Fat **3g/49%***

Salmon with Fava Beans

Luscious pink salmon presented on a bed of dark-green ruffled spinach, dotted with soft green favas, lemon zest, and dill.

SERVES 6

1 cup shelled fresh fava beans (from about 2 pounds)
10 ounces cleaned and steamed fresh spinach
2 pounds fillet of salmon, trimmed of
  fat and skinned
1 teaspoon unsalted butter, melted
1 tablespoon minced lemon zest
1/2 cup chopped fresh dill
1/4 cup dry white wine

1. Preheat the oven to 375°.
2. Steam the fava beans over boiling water until tender, about 3 minutes. Remove from the heat, cool slightly, and gently slip the skins off the beans.
3. Form a bed of spinach on a piece of foil large enough to wrap around the fillet. Place the fillet on the bed of spinach, brush with butter, and sprinkle with lemon zest, dill, wine, and the fava beans.
4. Close the package by folding the foil over the fillet and sealing the edges tightly.
5. Set the package on a baking sheet and bake for 25 to 35 minutes. Remove from the oven, and serve immediately.

Cal. **249** *Carb.* **4g** *Protein* **35g** *Chol.* **64mg** *Fat* **10g/36%**

Asparagus with Orange Glaze

Marinades infuse flavor, so why not use one with vegetables? A lingering taste of orange makes these special.

SERVES 6

1/2 cup fresh orange juice
Zest of 1 orange
1 tablespoon sugar
1 tablespoon minced fresh ginger
2 teaspoons soy sauce
2 pounds fresh asparagus, trimmed

"He that plants trees loves others besides himself."

English proverb

Asparagus

Here's a surefire way to cook asparagus when they have slightly thicker stems. No fussing, no draining, and all the juices stay in the spears, ready to release their spring-like perfume when the dish is uncovered:

Preheat the oven to 350°. Place 2 pounds of asparagus two layers deep in a covered casserole or earthenware dish. Season lightly with salt and pepper. Drizzle with olive oil. Add 2 tablespoons water and cover tightly. Place in the preheated oven. For medium asparagus, bake for 14 minutes; larger, 17 minutes. Uncover the dish at the table.

FISH

Plain, unadulterated fish: the perfect choice for a healthful meal, with a variety and range of flavors that defy boredom. And hardly any fat.

UP TO 9% CALORIES FROM FAT

raw cod ★ mahi-mahi
haddock ★ lobster
pollock ★ scallops
★ sunfish ★

9–15% CALORIES FROM FAT

flounder ★ grouper ★ tuna
pike ★ snapper ★ sole
★ shrimp ★

OVER 15% CALORIES FROM FAT

monkfish ★ rockfish
ocean perch ★ mackerel
herring ★ salmon ★ trout
★ orange roughy ★

Seafood leaves plenty of room in the fat budget for other choices.

Lean fish is no lean dish if deep-fried or drowned in butter or tartar sauce. Bake, broil, poach, or grill, and use little or no fat. Add flavor with herbs, citrus juices and zest, and salsas.

1. In a medium-size mixing bowl, combine all of the ingredients except the asparagus, and mix well.
2. Place the asparagus in a shallow dish, cover with the marinade, and refrigerate for at least 2 hours, turning occasionally.
3. Preheat the broiler.
4. Drain the asparagus and reserve the marinade. Place the asparagus on a baking sheet underneath the broiler and broil for 5 minutes, or until tender; do not overcook. Meanwhile, transfer the marinade to a saucepan and reduce by half over high heat.
5. Transfer the cooked asparagus to a serving dish and pour the reduced marinade over the asparagus. Serve immediately.

Cal. 40 Carb. 8g Protein 3g Chol. 0mg Fat .2g/4%

A Ring of Green Rice

SERVES 6
½ teaspoon salt
1 cup white rice
1 tablespoon unsalted butter
4 scallions, white and green parts, chopped
1 cup finely chopped fresh Italian parsley
Freshly ground pepper

1. Preheat the oven to 350°.
2. In a medium-size saucepan, bring 2¼ cups of water and the salt to a boil. Add the rice and stir once. Cover, reduce the heat, and simmer for 15 minutes.
3. Meanwhile, in a medium-size skillet, heat the butter and and sauté the scallion until wilted, about 5 minutes. Combine the scallion with the cooked rice and stir in the remaining ingredients.
4. Lightly spray or wipe a 1-quart ring mold, or four 1-cup molds, with vegetable oil. Pack the rice into the mold and place it in a baking pan with enough hot water to come 2 to 3 inches up the sides of the mold. Bake for 20 minutes, or until well heated. To serve, carefully run a spatula around the mold and invert onto a heated platter. Serve immediately.

Cal. 138 Carb. 26g Protein 2g Chol. 5mg Fat 2g/16%

green Earth

GONE SMELTING

Spicy Smelt Tempura

The lightest of batters, with just enough fireworks! Best of all, only ¼ cup of oil is absorbed in the frying.

SERVES 8
5 tablespoons all-purpose unbleached flour
5 tablespoons cornstarch
3 teaspoons cayenne
½ teaspoon freshly ground black pepper
3 cups canola oil, for deep-frying
2½ pounds fresh smelts
Lemon wedges
Salt and pepper

1. In a mixing bowl, combine the flour, cornstarch, cayenne, pepper, and ⅔ cup water. Refrigerate for 20 minutes.
2. Preheat the oven to 350°. In a deep-fryer or a high-sided heavy pan, heat the oil to 350°.
3. Dip the fish in the batter, draining off any excess. Fry the fish in the hot oil until crisp and golden, about ½ to 1 minute on each side. Place the fried fish on a baking sheet lined with paper towels, and place in the oven to keep warm until all the fish is finished.

Cal. **257** *Carb.* **9g** *Protein* **26g** *Chol.* **100mg** *Fat* **13g/45%**

Ginger Sugar Snap Peas

SERVES 8
2 pounds sugar snap peas, ends trimmed
3 tablespoons finely minced fresh ginger
2 teaspoons canola oil

1. Place 1 inch of water in a stockpot and bring to a boil.
2. Arrange the sugar snap peas and ginger on top of a steamer, and place over the boiling water. Cover and steam until the sugar snaps are tender yet still crisp, 4 to 6 minutes. Transfer to a serving bowl and mist with oil; mix well. Serve immediately.

Cal. **60** *Carb.* **9g** *Protein* **3g** *Chol.* **0mg** *Fat* **1g/20%**

The Smelt Run

Last spring, my friend Brownie's husband, Al, took us smelt-dipping. At midnight, under a full, bright moon, we waded out to Lake Michigan's second sandbar, with cold water swirling around our thighs like liquid silver.

Turning back toward shore, we were dumbstruck at another sight: Across the inky water, the shoreline shimmered with the reflected light of hundreds of hand-held lanterns and candles. It looked like the skyline of Chicago in our own backyard.

FLOUR TIP

A method that's easy and light: Mix all-purpose flour, salt, and pepper with either herbs, cayenne, or lemon or lime zest in a plastic bag. Shake a few well-dried small fish in the bag to coat lightly. Fry in small batches. Drain very well and serve with sea salt and lemon wedges.

Menu

Spicy Smelt Tempura

Spinach Salad

Ginger Sugar
Snap Peas

Risi e Bisi

Berry Strawberry
Shortcake

Sweet Peas

The doges of Venice started a craze in the fourteenth century for early spring peas. Every year on April 25, the feast day of St. Mark, they served them in a rich broth with rice called *risi e bisi.*

Thomas Jefferson's contemporaries considered young, fresh garden peas an exotic luxury—something like truffles today. Jefferson himself cultivated some thirty varieties in his pea patch, among them the sugar snap pea. Today, it is my hands-down favorite: Sugar Snap—also called Sugar Daddy, Sugar Ann, or Sugar Rae.

As any gardener knows, the sugar in vegetables quickly turns to starch. The shorter the trip from garden to table, the better the taste. And so with peas.

When young and extremely fine, peas are fit to be briefly sweated, with only the smallest bit of defatted chicken stock and plenty of fresh mint.

Risi e Bisi

SERVES 8

1 tablespoon minced garlic
1 teaspoon olive oil
2 cups Arborio rice
5½ cups beef broth (see Basics)
1 package (9 ounces) artichoke hearts, defrosted
10 ounces fresh or frozen peas
2 cups chopped arugula
½ cup snipped fresh chives
1 tablespoon chopped fresh thyme leaves
Salt and freshly ground pepper

1. In a large saucepan over low heat, sauté the garlic in the oil for 5 minutes. Add the rice, stir, and cook for 3 minutes longer, or until the rice just begins to turn brown.

2. Slowly add 1 cup of the broth, stirring constantly. Continue to stir until the liquid has been absorbed. Then add another ½ cup broth; allow it to simmer, stirring constantly, until this liquid is absorbed. Repeat this process two more times, using ½ cup each time. Add the artichokes, and continue to add broth until the rice is tender.

3. Add the peas, arugula, chives, and thyme. Continue to cook until the peas are tender and the arugula is wilted. Add more broth if needed. Altogether, the rice should cook for 20 to 25 minutes.

4. Add the salt and pepper to taste. Serve immediately.

*Cal. **203** Carb. **40g** Protein **8g** Chol. **0mg** Fat **2g/9%***

Sage Clouds

Monday is gnocchi day all over Rome. Made from Sunday's leftover potatoes, these are the lightest dumplings I know how to make, due to the amazingly small amount of flour added to the potatoes. They're as easy as pie. Without the sauce, they have only 210 calories and .4 grams of fat per serving.

SERVES 8

8 large Idaho or russet potatoes
Salt
1½ cups all-purpose flour
⅛ teaspoon freshly grated nutmeg
5 tablespoons finely minced fresh sage
2 cups nonfat cottage cheese
½ cup nonfat plain yogurt
¼ cup skim milk
2 cups freshly grated Parmesan
Freshly ground pepper

1. Preheat the oven to 400°.
2. Bake the potatoes until tender, crisp, and dry (1 to 1½ hours). While the potatoes are still hot, scoop the flesh from the skins and put it through a ricer into a bowl. Season with salt to taste.
3. While the flesh is still hot, sprinkle it with flour, ¼ cup at a time; work the flour into the potato with a fork. Continue to add the flour, working as quickly as possible, until the dough holds together and is no longer sticky. Add the nutmeg and 1 tablespoon sage. Do not overmix—the longer the dough is worked, the more flour will be needed, and the heavier the gnocchi will become.
4. On a lightly floured surface, with lightly floured hands, roll the dough out into five or six ropes, each about ½ inch in diameter. Slice the ropes at ½-inch intervals, and indent each dumpling with a thumbprint or the tongs of a fork to produce a ribbed effect.
5. To cook, heat a large pot of water (about 6 quarts). When the water comes to a boil, add 2 tablespoons salt, return to a boil, and drop the gnocchi in a few at a time, stirring gently with a wooden spoon. Cook for 2 to 3 minutes. As the gnocchi rise to the surface, remove them with a slotted

Menu

Sage Clouds

Mélange of Baby Vegetables

Mesclun with Lime Spritz

Strawberries and Lemon-Ginger Squares

Lucky May

Since the Middle Ages, Europeans have heralded the first day in May by dancing around the maypole, a high pole fluttering with streamers and garlands of fresh flowers. The custom seems inexplicable without another seasonal celebration—the hearty consumption of May wine.

spoon and place them in a 9 x 13 x 2-inch baking dish. Repeat until all the gnocchi are done.

6. Preheat the oven to 375°.

7. Process the cottage cheese until smooth. Pour into a medium bowl and add the remaining sage, the yogurt, the skim milk, and 1 cup Parmesan, and blend well. Season sauce with sage, nutmeg, and pepper to taste.

8. Drain any water from the baking dish. Spread the gnocchi out in a single layer, and cover evenly with the cottage-cheese mixture. Sprinkle with the remaining Parmesan. Place in the oven and bake for 20 minutes.

*Cal. **352** Carb. **50g** Protein **21g** Chol. **21mg** Fat **8g/20%***

Mélange of Baby Vegetables

A vivid fanfare of colors and flavors.

SERVES 8

2 pounds mixed baby vegetables (zucchini, yellow crookneck squash, patty pan squash, trimmed)
2 cups sugar snap peas
1 red bell pepper, julienned
1 yellow bell pepper, julienned
1 medium red onion, halved and thinly sliced
4 scallions, cut diagonally into ½-inch slices
1 tablespoon Dijon mustard
¼ cup rice wine vinegar
½ teaspoon celery seeds
Freshly ground pepper
2 tablespoons canola oil
2 tablespoons chopped fresh cilantro
2 tablespoons chopped fresh chervil or Italian parsley
2 tablespoons chopped fresh dill

1. In a large pot of boiling water, blanch the baby vegetables and sugar snaps until tender (1 to 2 minutes for the zucchini, crooknecks, and sugar snaps; 2 to 3 minutes for the patty pans). Refresh under cold water and drain well.

2. In a large bowl, combine all of the vegetables.

3. In a small bowl, combine the mustard, vinegar, celery seeds, pepper to taste, and oil; whisk until well combined. Add the cilantro, chervil, and dill. Pour over the vegetables and toss until evenly coated. Serve well chilled.

*Cal. **89** Carb. **12g** Protein **3g** Chol. **0mg** Fat **4g/39%***

"*Earth laughs in flowers.*"

Ralph Waldo Emerson

TEENY WEENY ZUCCHINI

PATTY PAN

When it's soft-shell crab time, we can barely satisfy our craving for them. I used to think that their sweet flavor was totally dependent on soaking them in milk or buttermilk, dredging them in flour, sautéing them in vats of butter, and topping them with sautéed sliced almonds. How wrong I was. Acidic marinades—orange, lime, balsamic vinegar—accent the crabs' natural sweetness and give them a taste that is fresh and interesting.

Here are four fabulous recipes that are low in fat and cholesterol and high in protein, and couldn't be tastier. For a real feast, invite a crowd into the kitchen and prepare a sampling of all of these.

Soft-Shell Crabs with Lime Marinade

Ginger and lime add pizzazz, and honey softens a silky sauce.

SERVES 4

Juice and chopped zest of 2 limes
1 garlic clove, minced
1 teaspoon chopped fresh ginger
1 jalapeño pepper, finely chopped
1 cup chicken broth (see Basics)
8 soft-shell crabs, cleaned, rinsed, and patted dry
1 tablespoon sesame oil
1 tablespoon olive oil
2 tablespoons honey
1/2 cup chopped fresh cilantro

1. In a large bowl, combine the juice, zest, garlic, ginger, jalapeño pepper, and chicken broth, and mix well. Add the crabs and marinate, covered, in the refrigerator for at least 1 hour and up to 3 hours.
2. In a large skillet, heat the sesame and olive oils over medium-high heat. Remove the crabs from the marinade; reserve

Seafood Fest

Spicy Shrimp

*Mesclun with
Sherry Salad Spray*

*Soft-Shell Crabs with
Lime Marinade*

*Risotto with Mint and
Wild Mushrooms*

*Floating Islands with
Vanilla Custard Sauce*

the marinade, and allow any excess to drip off. Sauté the crabs in the oil for 2 to 3 minutes on each side, or until the shells turn red. Remove to a platter and keep warm.

3. Add the reserved marinade to the skillet and bring to a boil, scraping up any bits from the bottom; reduce by half. Stir in the honey.

4. Place two crabs on each of four plates. Drizzle the crabs with sauce and garnish with cilantro.

*Cal. **293** Carb. **11g** Protein **40g** Chol. **169mg** Fat **9g/29%***

Balsamic Soft-Shell Crabs

Garlic, capers, and balsamic vinegar, with an inkling of butter.

SERVES 4

*8 soft-shell crabs, cleaned, rinsed,
and patted dry*
*¼ cup plus 1 tablespoon
balsamic vinegar*
Salt and freshly ground pepper
1 tablespoon olive oil
1 tablespoon unsalted butter
2 garlic cloves, minced
1 cup chicken broth (see Basics)
1 tablespoon capers, drained
4 tablespoons chopped fresh Italian parsley

1. Place the crabs on a plate. Sprinkle both sides with vinegar and salt and pepper to taste. Cover tightly with plastic wrap and refrigerate for 20 to 30 minutes.

2. In a large skillet, heat the olive oil and 1 teaspoon of the butter over medium-high heat. Add the garlic and sauté for 30 seconds. Remove the crabs from the vinegar, allowing any excess vinegar to drip off, and sauté for 2 minutes per side, or until the shells have turned red. Remove and place on a heated platter; keep warm.

3. Add the chicken broth to the skillet. Bring to a boil and reduce to ¼ cup, scraping up any bits from the bottom. Stir in the remaining vinegar, capers, and butter if desired.

4. Place two crabs on each of four plates. Pour the sauce over the crabs and garnish with parsley.

*Cal. **257** Carb. **2g** Protein **40g** Chol. **177mg** Fat **9g/33%***

Cleaning Soft-Shell Crabs

The soft-shell crabs have arrived, glistening in the sink. Uncleaned. Alive. And—take a deep breath—briny fresh. First, using thumb and forefinger, pinch off the crab's eyes. Second, lift the pointed ends of the shell and pinch out the gills—the spongy, saclike organs on either side. Third, turn the crab on its back. Pry up and pull off the flap, or apron. The crab is now fully cleaned, completely edible, and ready to cook.

If you want the fishmonger to do the job, order your crabs "pan ready," but plan to cook them within a few hours.

Soft-Shell Crabs with Orange Relish

A zesty orange relish freshened with ginger, cilantro, and scallions crowns these crab pairs.

SERVES 4

1 cup skim milk
1 teaspoon Tabasco
   or other pepper sauce
8 soft-shell crabs, cleaned,
   rinsed, and patted dry
1 tablespoon sesame oil
1 tablespoon olive or canola oil
3 tablespoons chopped scallion, white and green parts
2 teaspoons minced garlic
2/3 cup fresh orange juice
1 tablespoon red wine vinegar
2 tablespoons minced orange zest
1 tablespoon minced fresh ginger
Fresh cilantro, chopped

1. In a baking dish, combine the milk and Tabasco. Add the crabs and marinate for 15 minutes, turning once or twice.
2. Heat the sesame oil in a large skillet over medium-high heat. Drain the crabs, allowing any excess marinade to drip off. Sauté the crabs for 2 to 3 minutes per side, or until the shells turn red. Remove to a heated platter and keep warm.
3. Add the olive oil to the skillet. Sauté the scallion and garlic for 1 minute. Add the orange juice, vinegar, orange zest, and ginger. Bring the sauce to a boil, scraping up any bits off the bottom. Cook until the sauce is reduced and resembles relish.
4. Place two crabs on each of four plates. Top each crab with orange relish and garnish with cilantro.

*Cal. **315** Carb. **10g** Protein **42g** Chol. **177mg** Fat **11g/33%***

Spicy Soft-Shell Crabs

Spiced hard blue crabs are a Chesapeake specialty. Here we've applied the same premise to the soft-shell variety.

SERVES 4

1/4 teaspoon crushed red pepper flakes
1/2 teaspoon freshly ground pepper
1 teaspoon chopped fresh thyme or 1/2 teaspoon dried

A Longer Season

Once, soft-shell crabs were available for just one all-too-brief month each spring. That hardly satisfied our craving.

Happily, today soft-shells are part of the ever-growing aquafarming industry. As a result, the season is dramatically extended and there's little need to fall back on the frozen soft-shells, which always fall short of our expectations. Instead, they arrive full of life on a bed of straw, ensuring absolute freshness and fullest flavor.

Spring Fling
Summertime Bruschetta
Spicy Soft-Shell Crabs
Spring Green Pasta
Blackberry Frozen Yogurt
Chocolate Chip Bites

Early Garden Supper

Snappy Green Beans

*Soft-Shell Crabs
with Orange Relish*

Cinnamon Rice with Lentils

*Mesclun with White Wine
Vinegar Dressing*

Chocolate Coffee Torte

- *½ tablespoon chopped fresh oregano or ½ teaspoon dried*
- *1 tablespoon unsalted butter*
- *2 garlic cloves, minced*
- *½ teaspoon Worcestershire sauce*
- *8 soft-shell crabs, cleaned, rinsed, and patted dry*
- *1 cup clam juice*
- *Freshly chopped Italian parsley*

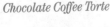

1. In a small bowl, combine the pepper flakes, pepper, thyme, and oregano.

2. In a large skillet, heat the butter over medium-high heat; add the spices, garlic, and Worcestershire sauce, and cook for 1 to 2 minutes. Add the crabs and sauté for 2 to 3 minutes per side, or until the shells turn red. Remove to a heated platter and keep warm.

3. Add the clam juice to the skillet and bring to a boil, scraping bits from the bottom of the pan, for 2 minutes, or until reduced to ¼ cup.

4. Return the crabs to the skillet briefly, to coat each piece with sauce. Place two crabs on each of four plates, napping each with a little sauce. Garnish with parsley.

Cal. 223 Carb. 2g Protein 40g Chol. 177mg Fat 5g/24%

The Way of the Crab

Twenty times in a life span of three years, the Atlantic blue crab sheds its shell. Hidden in a protected spot, the limp crab emerges, bigger by a third. It grows by a quarter to a third of its size within the hour. Six hours later, it's a "papershell," still officially soft and vulnerable to any predator—often its brethren. This is a short-lived gastronomic opportunity for those who appreciate soft-shell crabs.

Native to the Atlantic coast from Maine to Argentina, the blue crab thrives in greatest profusion in the largely unspoiled waters of Chesapeake Bay, where it is pursued by the nation's largest concentration of watermen—people who follow the long and unflinching tradition of making a livelihood from the Bay.

The spring crab run starts in April around Cape Charles, Virginia, and ends in September. The biggest run, according to lore, occurs on the first full moon in May.

As the water warms, crabs migrate from the depths into the shallow waters of the bay. The watermen wait, with trot-lines baited with eel, pots of heavy chicken wire, and chicken-wire traps running out from the shoreline.

Caught, the crabs' claws are "nicked"—broken to prevent them from pinching—then the crabs are sorted by size and sex. Females—called "Sallies"—are identified by their red-tipped claws and triangular aprons, males—"Jimmies"—by their T-shaped aprons.

I find the very best way to entertain is to serve your guests what you would your family. Not only will you be cooking some of your favorites, you'll pull it off with great aplomb.

Light Salmon Cakes

Mashed potatoes and egg whites lighten these nicely. You can use fresh cooked salmon, of course. But nobody would ever know they're made with canned.

SERVES 4

3 medium Idaho potatoes
Juice of 1 lemon
Zest of 1 lemon, finely minced
½ cup chopped fresh dill
2 tablespoons minced fresh Italian parsley
12 ounces cooked fresh or canned salmon, skin and bones removed
2 egg whites, stiffly beaten
Mustard-Dill Sauce (at right; optional)

1. Preheat the oven to 350°.
2. Bake the potatoes for 1 to 1½ hours. Cool slightly. Scoop the flesh from the skins; place in a bowl and mash. Let cool completely.
3. Mix the potato with the lemon juice, lemon zest, dill, and parsley. Gently mix in the salmon. Fold in the egg whites.
4. Form the mixture into twelve salmon patties, 2 inches in diameter and ½ inch thick.
5. Heat a large sauté pan over medium-high heat. Spray or wipe with canola oil. Fry the salmon cakes for 5 minutes on each side, until golden brown. Serve immediately with lemon wedges or Mustard-Dill Sauce on the side.

Cal. **199** *Carb.* **10g** *Protein* **20g** *Chol.* **38mg** *Fat* **8g/39%**

Chow Chow Bok Choy

Bok choy, that pale, crisp Chinese lettuce, and smoky shi-itakes, with a wisp of a chow chow—sweet-and-sour—glaze.

SERVES 4

2 tablespoons peanut oil
2 garlic cloves, thinly sliced

Mustard-Dill Sauce

The classic Scandinavian sauce for gravlax, lightened with canola oil.

YIELD: 1½ CUPS

4 tablespoons Dijon
  mustard
1 tablespoon sugar
2 tablespoons white
  vinegar
¼ cup canola oil
1 tablespoon minced fresh
  dill

Combine all of the ingredients in a small bowl. May be served cold or warm.

Cal. **8** *Carb.* **.2g**
Protein **0g** *Chol.* **0mg**
Fat **.8g/91%**

(analyzed per teaspoon)

Menu

*Spinach Dill Dip with
Herbed Fresh Pita Toasts*

Light Salmon Cakes

Mustard-Dill Sauce

Chow Chow Bok Choy

*Braised
Artichokes*

*The Berriest Bombe
with Fruit Sauce*

- *8 heads baby bok choy, washed to remove all traces of sand, split in half if large*
- *6 shiitake mushrooms, thinly sliced*
- *½ teaspoon light brown sugar*
- *1 teaspoon sesame oil*
- *1 tablespoon soy sauce*
- *1 tablespoon sherry*

1. In a very large skillet or wok, heat the oil with the garlic over medium-high heat. Add the bok choy and sauté for 1 minute on all sides. Push the bok choy aside and add the mushrooms. Stir-fry for 30 seconds, then reduce the heat slightly.

2. In a small bowl, combine the brown sugar, sesame oil, soy sauce, and sherry. Add this mixture to the skillet and turn the bok choy several times, until well coated and heated through. Serve immediately, dividing the bok choy and sauce among four plates.

*Cal. **179** Carb. **18g** Protein **12g** Chol. **0mg** Fat **9g/41%***

Braised Artichokes

Tender baby artichokes are infused with slow-roasted garlic.

SERVES 4
*24 baby artichokes, tops, bases, and
outer leaves trimmed*
36 garlic cloves, peeled
1¾ cups chicken broth (see Basics)
1 tablespoon olive oil
2 sprigs fresh rosemary
Juice of 1 lemon
Freshly ground pepper

1. Place the artichokes, garlic, 1¼ cups chicken broth, olive oil, and rosemary in a medium sauté pan over medium-high heat, and cover. Let braise for 10 to 12 minutes, until the artichokes are tender when pierced with a fork. Toss occasionally.

2. Remove the cover and add the remaining chicken broth. Cook, tossing frequently, until the liquid has evaporated. When the garlic turns golden, add the lemon juice, season with pepper to taste, toss, and serve immediately.

*Cal. **275** Carb. **48g** Protein **14g** Chol. **0mg** Fat **5g/15%***

Bok Choy

Short, long, or baby bok choy. It is sometimes known as Peking Cabbage and often labeled "Chinese cabbage" in the supermarket. This is the most popular of the Chinese cabbages, compact and barrel-shaped with white crunchy stalks and crinkled pale green or yellow leaves. Bok choy is available year-round in two sizes: long and narrow (12–18 inches long, about 4 inches in diameter), or short and thicker (10–12 inches long, about 6 inches in diameter). Use the short one to stuff, the long one for salads or shredding. Shanghai bok choy, in the same family, looks like a large flower with paler green leaves.

Everyday Garlic Chicken

SERVES 4

1 whole chicken (about 3 pounds)
2 teaspoons ground ginger
1 whole lemon, pricked several times
24 garlic cloves, peeled
3 cups chicken broth (see Basics)
Freshly ground pepper

1. Preheat the oven to 400°.
2. Wash the chicken and pat it dry inside and out. Place the lemon in the cavity and place the chicken in a small roasting pan. Cut one clove of garlic in half and rub over the breast skin.
3. Place the chicken in the oven and bake for 20 minutes; add 1½ cups of broth and bake for another 20 minutes. Reduce the heat to 375°; add the remaining broth and garlic, and cook for 30 to 40 minutes, basting every 10 minutes. Remove the chicken from the pan and place it on a platter, breast side down, to rest for 10 to 15 minutes.
4. Pour the collected juices into a fat-skimming cup and defat. With a fork, mash the garlic. Place the garlic and defatted juices back in the roasting pan. Over medium-high heat, reduce the liquid by half, stirring frequently. Strain if you desire a smoother sauce. Carve the chicken and pass the sauce at the table.

NOTE: For a "leftover luncheon," shred the chicken and warm it with the remaining sauce. Serve it over toasted English muffins.

Cal. 289 Carb. 12g Protein 38g Chol. 109mg

Fat 9g/30%

Herb-Roasted Potatoes

A basic in our house. I make them at least once a week.

SERVES 4

2 pounds russet new potatoes, quartered or left whole
2 tablespoons olive oil
1 head garlic, cloves peeled and left whole

Menu

Snappy Green Beans

Everyday Garlic Chicken

Herb-Roasted Potatoes

*Red Pepper
Confetti Asparagus*

Raspberry-Almond Parfait

THE SKINNY
ON CHICKEN

Remove the skin from poultry before eating, not before cooking. Skin seals in moisture during cooking, and may actually help conserve heat-sensitive vitamins, such as the B's. What's more, there's little evidence that fat migrates from skin to meat during cooking.

After is another story. The skin on a roasted half chicken breast has about 50 calories and a teaspoon of fat. More good news: While frying, marinating, and basting with fat raise total fat content, if you don't eat the skin, the amount is insignificant.

2 cups minced mixed fresh herbs (such as parsley, basil, sage, chives, oregano, mint)
Salt and freshly ground pepper

1. Preheat the oven to 350°.
2. Combine the potatoes, oil, garlic, and ½ cup mixed herbs in a shallow baking dish.
3. Place in the oven and roast until golden brown, stirring occasionally, 45 minutes to 1 hour. Remove from the oven and toss with the remaining herbs. Taste and season with salt and pepper. Serve warm or at room temperature.

Cal. 255 Carb. 45g Protein 5g Chol. 0mg Fat 7g/25%

Red Pepper Confetti Asparagus

Red peppers are roasted to magnify their flavors, then sprinkled on pencil-thin asparagus.

SERVES 4
1 red bell pepper
1 tablespoon olive oil
2 tablespoons fresh lemon juice
1 pound asparagus
Salt and freshly ground pepper

1. Preheat the broiler.
2. Place the red pepper on a baking sheet and place underneath the broiler, about 2 inches from the flame. Turn until the skin is charred on all sides. Remove and place in a heavy brown bag. Seal and let steam for 30 minutes. Remove the pepper from the bag; peel and finely chop.
3. Mix the oil and lemon juice in a small bowl. Place the asparagus on a baking sheet and brush with the oil mixture. Sprinkle the chopped pepper over the asparagus.
4. Place the sheet under the broiler. Broil for 3 to 5 minutes, taking care that the asparagus does not burn. Remove from the oven; taste and adjust the seasoning.

Cal. 55 Carb. 5g Protein 2g Chol. 0mg Fat 4g/52%

Lamb Chops with Ginger and Mint

Lamb chops are by far my favorite red meat. And they're an occasional treat at our house. I trim as much fat as possible, then I like to vary their flavor ever so slightly, never masking their natural taste.

SERVES 4

8 lamb chops, 1 inch thick, trimmed of fat
1 cup chicken broth (see Basics)
2 tablespoons finely minced fresh ginger
4 garlic cloves, finely chopped
Freshly ground pepper
¼ cup cider vinegar
1 tablespoon unsalted butter
4 tablespoons finely chopped fresh mint leaves

1. Prepare the grill for grilling or preheat the broiler.
2. Place the lamb on the rack and grill for 4 to 5 minutes per side for medium-rare.
3. Meanwhile, in a small saucepan over medium-high heat, combine the broth, ginger, garlic, pepper, and vinegar. Reduce the sauce by two-thirds. Whisk in the butter, remove from the heat, and add the mint. Taste and adjust the seasoning. Serve the sauce at the table, on the side.

Cal. **247** *Carb.* **4g** *Protein* **29g** *Chol.* **96mg** *Fat* **12g/46%**

> **Never Too Minty**
>
> Scatter mint across the dining table to stimulate appetite, as was once the custom. Fresh mint is nothing to be shy about; it's hard to use too much.

Baby Carrots with Mint

Tender spring carrots, steamed and laced with ginger and mint.

SERVES 4

4 cups baby carrots
¼ cup minced fresh mint
1 tablespoon minced fresh
  ginger

1. Steam the carrots over boiling water until tender, 3 to 5 minutes. Remove from the heat and reserve 2 tablespoons of the cooking liquid.

Menu

Lamb Chops with
Ginger and Mint

Baby Carrots with Mint

Herbed Breadsticks

Green Beans with
Sweet-and-Sour Splash

Spring Hash Browns

Honeydew Sorbet

The Potato Scoop

South American Indians ate them raw or baked them in the ashes of their campfires. The French took to frying thin wafers cut into fancy shapes.

Blame the Founding Fathers for America's 5-billion-pounds-a-year French-fry habit. Franklin and Jefferson discovered the potato (which had come from the New World in the first place) in Paris and planted it in their own American gardens.

Now the diet myth has been dashed, and the word is out: Eating potatoes, baked, boiled, or broiled, can actually help you lose weight. Fill them with nonfat yogurt or flavor them with a dash of herbed olive oil or mustard. Or just eat them plain.

★ **GOOD FOR YOU** ★

Potatoes are fat-free and high in vitamin C, thiamine, niacin, and iron.

---

2. In a medium-size serving bowl, while they're still warm, toss the carrots with the cooking broth, mint, and ginger, and serve immediately.

Cal. 50 Carb. 12g Protein 1g Chol. 0mg Fat .2g/4%

Spring Hash Browns

Zucchini lightens this hashed medley.

SERVES 4

2 medium zucchini, scrubbed
1 teaspoon salt
2 medium potatoes, scrubbed
2 parsnips (or turnips or rutabaga)
1 tablespoon olive oil
2 medium onions, finely chopped
6 garlic cloves, finely minced
2 tablespoons minced fresh sage (or rosemary, dill, or tarragon)
Freshly ground pepper

1. Coarsely grate the zucchini and place in a colander. Sprinkle with the salt and let stand in the sink to drain for about 20 minutes. Squeeze out the excess moisture by hand.
2. Coarsely grate the potatoes and squeeze out the moisture by hand. Coarsely grate the parsnip.
3. In an ovenproof skillet, heat the oil over medium-high heat. Add the onion, garlic, and sage, and sauté until the onion wilts. Add the potato, zucchini, and parsnip, and continue to cook for 10 minutes, stirring occasionally. Season with pepper to taste, and reduce the heat to moderate. Cook for 10 minutes more, stirring often to prevent sticking. Preheat the broiler while the mixture is cooking.
4. When the mixture is done, remove from the heat and place under the broiler just long enough to brown the top of the vegetables. Taste and adjust the seasoning.

Cal. 163 Carb. 33g Protein 5g Chol. 0mg Fat 2g/12%

On the first perfect spring day in Michigan, my husband, Wills, and I take to the skies.

Monkfish Medallions

These look and taste like pearly treasures from the sea. They couldn't be simpler.

SERVES 4

12 scallions, green stalks only
24 paper-thin lemon slices, cut in half
Twelve $\frac{1}{4}$-inch-thick monkfish medallions ($1\frac{1}{2}$ pounds)
1 teaspoon canola oil
2 cups white wine
1 tablespoon fresh lemon juice
2 tablespoons unsalted butter
3 tablespoons capers, drained

1. Split the scallion stalks in half lengthwise; unroll and flatten. Place four lemon-slice halves around the circumference of each medallion, and use the scallion stalks to hold them in place like a string. Tie the scallion ends in a knot.
2. In a large skillet, heat the oil until very hot. Add the medallions and quickly sear them on both sides. Add $\frac{1}{2}$ cup of wine. Cover the skillet, and cook for 1 to 3 minutes, until the medallions are just cooked through; do not overcook or the fish will toughen. Remove the medallions from the skillet and keep warm.
3. Add the remaining wine and the lemon juice to the skillet. Bring to a brisk boil, stirring and scraping up any browned bits from the bottom of the skillet. When the mixture is reduced by half, stir in the butter and capers. Remove from the heat, taste, and adjust the seasoning. Serve the pan sauce over the medallions.

Cal. **212** *Carb.* **27g** *Protein* **12g** *Chol.* **59mg**
Fat **9g/26%**

Menu

Herbed Bruschetta
Monkfish Medallions
Baby Zucchini with Pesto
Red-Hot Radishes
Strawberry Sorbet

" Nobody can be uncheered with a balloon."

Winnie-the-Pooh

Radishes

The pepper's in the peel, fired by an enzyme. To get the full effect, some Chinese cooks use the mouth-searing peels alone as a braised vegetable. Peel the radish and you peel away the spicy temperature.

Americans consume 400 million pounds of radishes a year, most of which go into salads. The most popular varieties are Cherry Belle, Easter Egg, China Rose, Round Black Spanish, White Icicle, Red Button, Daikon, and French Breakfast. Each has its own distinctive color, size, and degree of heat.

Radishes can be found in the market year-round. Look for firm, smooth-skinned radishes with bright green, fresh-looking tops. To store, clip the tops, wrap in plastic, and refrigerate for up to one week. Daikons will keep well for up to two weeks.

★ **GOOD FOR YOU** ★

Radishes are a good source of vitamin C, with a meager 20 calories per cup. Use chives, parsley, and chervil as flavor enhancers.

Baby Zucchini with Pesto

Fingerling summer squash, with the sparkle of pesto and Parmesan.

SERVES 4

4 cups baby zucchini, rinsed and ends trimmed
¼ cup Broccoli Pesto (page 48)

1. Steam the zucchini over boiling water until tender, about 5 minutes. Remove from the heat.
2. In a medium-size serving dish, toss the warm zucchini with the pesto. Sprinkle with Parmesan if desired. Serve immediately.

*Cal. **43** Carb. **5g** Protein **3g** Chol. **1mg** Fat **2g/32%***

Red-Hot Radishes

Red and white radishes, roasted in foil. Tossed with pepper to turn up the heat, mint to cool them down. A real eye-opener.

SERVES 4

1½ cups red radishes, cleaned
1½ cups baby daikon radishes, cleaned, or 1 large daikon, cut into pieces
1 tablespoon olive oil
⅓ cup minced fresh mint
2 tablespoons minced fresh Italian parsley
Freshly ground pepper

1. Preheat the oven to 350°.
2. On a baking sheet, place a piece of aluminum foil large enough to hold all the radishes and to enfold them completely; place the radishes at the center of the foil.
3. Sprinkle the radishes with olive oil, mint, and Italian parsley. Season with freshly ground pepper.
4. Fold the ends of the foil over the radishes, and seal all the edges tightly by crimping them together.
5. Set the package on a baking sheet and bake for 15 to 20 minutes. Serve immediately.

*Cal. **45** Carb. **3g** Protein **.6g** Chol. **0mg** Fat **4g/68%***

In Michigan, the first spring day flies in on a whim. It might be early—a mild day in March—or tardy—a late-May breath of warmth. Suddenly, it's here. Propelled by gravity and joy, the dogs, Black Jack and Kelly, Wills, and I bound down the dunes to the beach. We draw in a first big breath, shedding winter's cocoon. Free at last!

Life is suddenly simpler, narrowed to a search for treasures: a bit of cobalt beach glass or one of pale sea-foam green, a pebble polished by waves.

Glazed Spicy Shrimp

Inspired by a visit to Jean-Georges Vongerichten's Jo Jo in Manhattan. The freshness of the orange juice counterbalances the nutmeg, cloves, and cayenne to accent the prawns.

SERVES 4

3 cups shredded carrot
2 cups fresh orange juice
1 tablespoon minced orange zest
$\frac{1}{8}$ teaspoon freshly grated nutmeg
2 tablespoons Grand Marnier or other
   orange-flavored liqueur
$\frac{1}{8}$ teaspoon cayenne
$\frac{1}{8}$ teaspoon ground cloves
$1\frac{1}{4}$ pounds large shrimp, shelled and
   deveined, tails left on

1. In a large sauté pan over high heat, sauté the carrot, orange juice, orange zest, and nutmeg over high heat for 2 to 4 minutes, tossing frequently. Remove from the heat. Strain, and reserve liquid. Cover the carrots and keep them warm.
2. Pour the reserved liquid back into the sauté pan; add the Grand Marnier, cayenne, and cloves. Over high heat, reduce the liquid to a rich golden glaze (about ¾ cup). Add the shrimp, and cook over high heat for 2 to 3 minutes. Remove from the heat.
3. Mound the carrots on four dinner plates and fan the shrimp around the carrot mounds.

*Cal. **244** Carb. **25g** Protein **31g** Chol. **216mg** Fat **3g/10%***

Our freshwater ocean

Menu

Glazed Spicy Shrimp

Five-Spice Rice

Very Green Beans

*Champagne Spritz
on Watercress*

Peanut Butter Bites

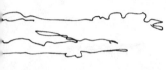

Five-Spice Rice

One taste, and the rest is history.

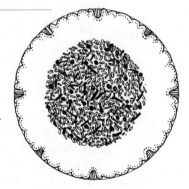

SERVES 6
1 tablespoon sesame oil
1 cup extra-long white rice
1 tablespoon five-spice powder
1 tablespoon finely minced fresh ginger
¼ cup dry sherry
1¼ cups chicken broth (see Basics)
⅓ cup julienned red bell pepper
½ cup chopped scallion
1 cup frozen peas, defrosted
2 tablespoons soy sauce
Chopped zest of 1 lime

1. Preheat the oven to 350°.
2. In a heavy flameproof casserole, heat the oil over medium-high heat. Add the rice, five-spice powder, and ginger, and cook for 3 minutes, stirring constantly. Add the sherry, chicken broth, and red pepper. Cover the casserole with aluminum foil and bake for 30 minutes.
3. Remove the casserole from the oven. Stir in the scallion, peas, soy sauce, and lime zest. Serve immediately.

Cal. 98 Carb. 16g Protein 3g Chol. 0mg Fat 2.8g/22%

Very Green Beans

Parsley seems to make green beans taste greener.

SERVES 4
1 pound young string beans, trimmed
1 tablespoon unsalted butter, softened
½ cup finely chopped Italian parsley
Salt and freshly ground pepper

Steam the beans for 4 to 6 minutes, until tender but still crisp. Drain and toss with butter, parsley, and salt and pepper to taste. Serve immediately.

Cal. 64 Carb. 8g Protein 2g Chol. 8mg

Fat 3g/40%

Salmon in Pink Sauce

An extraordinary, easy-to-make sauce sets the stage for an elegant salmon dish.

SERVES 8

1 fresh salmon fillet (2 pounds), trimmed of fat
2 tablespoons unsweetened coconut milk
2 tablespoons skim milk
1 cup chicken broth (see Basics)
1 teaspoon red curry paste*
1 tablespoon fresh lime juice
2 tablespoons dry sherry
2 tablespoons minced fresh cilantro
2 teaspoons potato starch, mixed with 1 tablespoon cold water

1. Preheat the oven to 375°.
2. Lightly coat a piece of aluminum foil, large enough to form a package around the fillet, with vegetable oil. Place the fillet on the foil, and close the package by folding the foil over the salmon and tightly sealing the edges. Set the package on a baking sheet and bake for 30 to 35 minutes.
3. Meanwhile, in a medium-size saucepan, combine all of the remaining ingredients except the potato-starch mixture, and simmer for 5 minutes. Increase the heat and whisk in the dissolved potato starch, stirring constantly until the sauce is slightly thickened.
4. Taste and adjust the seasoning with additional lime juice and sherry as desired. Keep the sauce warm until ready to serve over the salmon fillet.

Found at Chinese or Thai markets.

Cal. **217** Carb. **2g** Protein **25g** Chol. **77mg** Fat **12g/48%**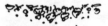

Menu
Mâche with Lime Dressing
Salmon in Pink Sauce
Herbed Spätzle
Asparagus Roasted in Foil
Crème Brûlée

Herbed Spätzle

These light, tiny dumpling ribbons are a cinch to make.

SERVES 8

3 cups all-purpose flour
½ teaspoon salt
¼ teaspoon finely ground pepper
Pinch cayenne

4 large eggs
1 cup skim milk
6 tablespoons very finely minced mixed fresh herbs such as tarragon, cilantro, basil, and Italian parsley
Basil Oil (page 289)

1. Bring a large pot of salted water to a rolling boil.
2. In a large bowl, combine the flour, salt, pepper, and cayenne. Make a well in the center of the mixture, place the eggs, milk, and herbs in the well, and beat with a wooden spoon until the dough is just smooth.
3. Place one-quarter of the dough in a colander. Hold the colander over the water, and with a spoon, press the dough through the holes, allowing it to drop into the water. When the spaetzle float to the surface, they are done. Remove with a slotted spoon to a warm bowl; cover to keep warm. Repeat. Serve with the oil.

*Cal. **220** Carb. **38g** Protein **9g** Chol. **106mg** Fat **3g/13%***

Asparagus Roasted in Foil

SERVES 8

2 pounds asparagus
2 tablespoons olive oil
4 tablespoons fresh lemon juice
1/2 cup chopped fresh dill
Freshly ground pepper

1. Preheat the oven to 350°.
2. Place the asparagus on a piece of aluminum foil large enough to hold the asparagus in a single layer and to fold over and seal.
3. Sprinkle the asparagus with olive oil, lemon juice, and dill. Season with pepper.
4. Wrap the foil around the asparagus (snugly but not tightly), and tightly seal by folding the edges together.
5. Set the package on a baking tray and bake for 10 to 15 minutes, depending on the thickness of the asparagus. Serve immediately.

*Cal. **46** Carb. **3g** Protein **2g** Chol. **0mg** Fat **4g/61%*** ⊘

Grilled Tarragon Tenderloin

The taste we love with far less fat.

SERVES 8

3 pounds beef tenderloin
2 tablespoons black pep-
    percorns, coarsely
    crushed
4 tablespoons finely minced
    fresh tarragon
Béarnaise Sauce
    (see Basics; optional)

1. Prepare the grill for
cooking, or preheat the
broiler.
2. Roll the beef in the crushed pepper and then the tarragon.
Place the tenderloin about 4 inches from the heat and grill,
covered with foil, turning frequently with tongs, for 25 minutes. Let rest for 5 minutes before slicing. Then serve immediately. Serve with Béarnaise Sauce if you like.

Cal. 219 Carb. 2g Protein 27g Chol. 79mg Fat 11g/45%

Garlic Potatoes

SERVES 8

2½ pounds baby potatoes, scrubbed
2 teaspoons canola oil
6 garlic cloves, minced
1 cup diced onion
2 jalapeño peppers, stemmed, seeded, and minced
1 teaspoon ground coriander
1½ cups Low-Fat Blend (see Basics)
½ cup chopped fresh cilantro
2 tablespoons crumbled blue cheese
1 teaspoon celery seeds

1. Preheat the oven to 250°.
2. Bring a large pot of water to a boil. Drop in the potatoes
and boil until tender, about 10 minutes. Drain and place in a
large ovenproof bowl; keep warm while preparing the sauce.

Menu

*Grilled Tarragon
Tenderloin with
Béarnaise Sauce*

Garlic Potatoes

*Arugula with
Roquefort Dressing*

Oven-Roasted Veggies

*Raspberry-Almond
Parfaits*

Baby Potatoes

Spring is the chance to enjoy choice little new potatoes. They are so moist, sweet, and dense, larger potatoes pale beside them; seek them out when they're dime-size, even if it means picking them out one by one from a pile at the farmers' market. (In any case, they'll cook evenly if they're similar in size.) Be sure to use them quickly. Once potatoes are liberated from the ground, starchiness sets in.

New potatoes are best steamed, boiled, or braised; the lightest gilding of butter, olive oil, or a splash of sweet cream and herbs makes them glorious. You will like them crusty, too. Roast them in a medium oven for an hour or so, tossed with olive oil (a little), minced garlic (lots), fresh herbs—minced Italian parsley, dill, mint, sage, or rosemary—and freshly ground black pepper, and salt. Serve warm or at room temperature.

3. In a medium-size skillet, heat the oil over medium-low heat. Add the garlic and onion, and sauté for 5 minutes. Stir in the jalapeño and coriander, and sauté for another 3 minutes. Remove from the heat.

4. Place the Low-Fat Blend in a small saucepan, and heat over low heat until just warm, stirring constantly. Stir in the onion mixture and mix well.

5. Add the sauce to the warm potatoes and mix gently. Add the cilantro and toss well. Transfer to serving plates and garnish with blue cheese and celery seeds.

*Cal. **173** Carb. **31g** Protein **8g** Chol. **3mg** Fat **2g/12%***

Oven-Roasted Veggies

Vividly colored vegetables, thinly sliced, spritzed with a wisp of olive oil, laced with pesto, and roasted at a high heat to intensify their natural flavors.

SERVES 8

4 medium tomatoes, sliced very thin
4 medium zucchini, sliced thin
4 medium red onions, sliced thin
2 medium eggplants, sliced thin
4 tablespoons Broccoli Pesto (page 48)
4 tablespoons finely minced garlic
Freshly ground pepper
4 tablespoons chopped fresh thyme
1 cup chopped fresh Italian parsley
Olive or canola oil

1. Preheat the oven to 400°.

2. On two baking sheets, arrange the sliced vegetables in rows. In a mixing bowl, combine the pesto, garlic, and pepper to taste. Dab the mixture onto the vegetables, so each has a hint of pesto.

3. Sprinkle with the thyme and parsley, and lightly spray with oil.

4. Bake for 35 to 40 minutes, then place under the broiler until slightly charred. Serve immediately.

NOTE: Other vegetables that work well here are leeks, scallion, and peppers.

*Cal. **35** Carb. **7g** Protein **2g** Chol. **0mg** Fat **1g/11%***

The Rice of Life

In Cooking

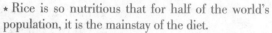

✳ With some exceptions, any rice can be used in any preparation.

✳ Always measure the rice and liquid accurately.

✳ Don't stir rice while it is cooking, unless the recipe says to. Stirring releases the starch, which makes rice sticky.

✳ Fluff the rice with a fork before serving. This allows the steam to escape and helps keep the grains separated.

✳ Cook rice just before serving. If you must delay serving for a short time, place a tea towel over the pot, then cover it to keep the rice from getting gummy.

✳ Rice that has been stored in a dry area for a long time may need to be cooked longer.

✳ Cooking rice in high concentrations of acid, such as tomatoes or orange juice, inhibits its ability to take in water, so extra liquid, and possibly extra cooking time, may be needed.

✳ You can pack flavor into rice while it is cooking. Vegetable, chicken, or beef broths can be substituted for water; wine can replace some of the water or other liquid; sprigs of thyme or rosemary or a few garlic cloves can be added.

RICE	DESCRIPTION	COOK/YIELD	BEST
Long-grain rice, Indian or Pakistani basmati, aromatic Jasmine, Texmati, Wild Pecan, Lundburg Royal, Wehani, Gourmet, O Della, Delta Rose	Slender long grains colored white, tan, or deep brown; fragrant, delicate taste and light, fluffy texture. The aromatic properties improve with age.	Rinse, then simmer, covered. 1 cup rice to 1¾ cups salted water, 15–20 min. Yield: 3 cups.	All-purpose, but especially as a side dish.
Long-grain rice, white and brown	White has a bland flavor and firm texture; brown has a nuttier flavor and even firmer texture, and may really be various shades of red or black.	Boil in plenty of salted water or simmer covered. 1 cup rice to 2 cups salted water 15–20 min. Add 2 t. olive oil to prevent sticking. Brown rice takes 15–30 min. longer. Yield: 3 cups.	For side dishes, casseroles, pilaf, salads.
Medium-grain rice, white and brown	Slightly longer than short-grain rice.	Boil in salted water. 1 cup rice to 1½ cups water, 15 min. Yield: 3 cups.	All-purpose.
Glutenous rice (sweet, waxy, or sticky rice)	Polished white Asian rice even shorter than Arborio; slightly sweet, very sticky.	Soak overnight, then simmer, covered. 1 cup rice to 1 cup salted water, 15 min. Yield: 2½ cups.	For dim sum, sushi, and dessert puddings.
Italian short-grained rice (Arborio)	Polished white kernels a little longer than wide; bland taste and soft, creamy texture; firm to the bite.	Never rinse. Sauté in 1 t. olive oil, then simmer 1 cup rice to 2½ cups water or broth (liquid added gradually), 20 min. Yield: 3 cups.	For risotto.
Parboiled rice (converted)	"Converted" by a process of steaming and pressurizing to force the nutrients from the bran to the center; converting also hardens the grain.	Same as for long-grain. Cooked rice grains that have been converted stay separate even when kept warm for 20–30 min.	Same as for long-grain.
Blended rice	Combined rices; may include black, orange, red, brown, and wild.	Same as parboiled.	Same as parboiled.
Wild rice	Not a true rice, but the grain of an aquatic grass native to North America.	Rinse well; simmer, covered. 1 cup rice to 3 cups water, 45 min. to 1 hr. Yield: 2 cups.	Use alone or combine with other rices and ingredients for stuffings, salads, and side dishes.

sweet nothings

Floating Islands

Sometimes, it's fun to make these airy puffs in miniature; other times, make them softball-sized, as they do at the Ritz. Contrary to their appearance, they're not hard to make at all. If you want to splurge, sprinkle Floating Islands with toasted almonds.

SERVES 4
4 egg whites, at room temperature
¼ cup sugar
Vanilla Custard Sauce (recipe opposite)

1. In a large shallow skillet, bring ½ inch of water to a simmer. Line a baking sheet with a damp towel and set aside.
2. In a bowl, beat the egg whites until they just begin to hold their shape. Add the

wonderful Vanilla custard sauce

"Things are seldom what they seem, Skim milk masquerades as cream."

H. M. S. Pinafore
Sir Wm. Gilbert

96

Vanilla Custard Sauce

I cut down the quantity of egg yolks in a classic crème anglaise dramatically, and substituted skim milk for classic heavy cream. Not the taste of supreme sacrifice—just fresher! This is terrific with fresh or baked fruits.

YIELD: 2 CUPS
2 cups skim milk
1 whole vanilla bean
4 egg yolks
4 tablespoons sugar
2 teaspoons vanilla extract

1. In a saucepan over high heat, scald the milk with the vanilla bean. Set aside for 20 to 30 minutes, until cool. Remove and split the bean, and scrape the seeds back into the milk; discard the bean and reheat the mixture until hot but not boiling.
2. In a small mixing bowl, whisk the egg yolks and sugar. Slowly add the hot milk, whisking constantly. Return the custard to the saucepan over medium-low heat. Cook until slightly thickened, stirring constantly, 5 to 6 minutes. Stir in the vanilla extract. Transfer to a glass bowl, and cool to room temperature. Cover with plastic wrap and refrigerate until cold.

*Cal. **19** Carb. **2g***
*Protein **.8g** Chol. **23mg***
*Fat **.6g/28%***

(analyzed by the tablespoon)

sugar, beating in 1 tablespoon at a time. (This will help them retain their peaks and make them satiny.)
3. Shape four meringues with serving spoons to the desired size, rounding off the tops to form ball shapes.
4. Gently place the meringues in the simmering water. Poach gently for 2 minutes, turning once. When the meringues are firm to the touch, lift them out and place them on the damp towel.
5. To serve, ladle ½ cup of the Vanilla Custard Sauce on four dessert plates, and top each plate with a meringue.

*Cal. **210** Carb. **32g** Protein **10g** Chol. **184mg** Fat **5g/20%***

Zabaglione

The classic Italian custard, made with melted marshmallows, of all things. But it works! Drizzle over fresh fruits.

SERVES 8
2 egg yolks
½ cup sugar
½ vanilla bean, split, seeds removed
⅓ cup plus 2 tablespoons Marsala
1½ cups miniature marshmallows
¼ cup soda water

1. Lightly spray the top of a double boiler with vegetable oil. Add the egg yolks, sugar, vanilla seeds, and wine. Fill the bottom of the double boiler with just enough water so that the top won't touch water when it is inserted. Bring the water to a rolling boil. Using a whisk, beat the egg mixture until smooth and thick.
2. When the mixture is thick, add the marshmallows and soda water, and continue to whisk until a thick sauce is formed. Serve immediately, or cool to room temperature and refrigerate overnight. Can be reheated in a microwave oven for 1 minute on high. Serve over fresh fruit.

*Cal. **142** Carb. **29g** Protein **1g** Chol. **46mg** Fat **1g/8%***

Sky-High Angel Food Cake

A classic reaches new heights.

SERVES 16

15 egg whites, at room temperature
1¼ cups sugar
1 cup all-purpose flour
½ teaspoon salt
1 teaspoon cream of tartar
1 teaspoon vanilla extract

1. Preheat the oven to 350°.
2. Place an aluminum foil collar in a 10-inch tube pan, extending it 4 inches above the top of the pan. Do not grease or spray.
3. Place the egg whites in a large mixing bowl; set aside.
4. In a separate bowl, sift together 1 cup of the sugar, the flour, and the salt; set aside.
5. Whip the egg whites until foamy. Add the cream of tartar and vanilla, and continue to whip until stiff peaks form. Slowly add the remaining sugar. The peaks will appear glossy. With a rubber spatula, fold the flour mixture into the whites until combined.
6. Spoon the batter evenly into the pan. Place in the oven and bake for 50 minutes, or until the cake springs back when touched.
7. Remove the cake from the oven and invert, placing the opening over a wine bottle to hold the pan off the surface. Let stand for several hours, or until cool.
8. To remove the cake from the pan, run a knife around the edge of the pan and invert again.

*Cal. **103** Carb. **22g** Protein **4g** Chol. **0mg** Fat **.1g/1%***

Variations:
1. Add 2 cups fresh raspberries or blackberries to the batter just before spooning it into the pan.
2. Chop four chocolate-covered toffee bars into small chunks, and add to the batter just before spooning it into the pan.
3. Substitute 1 teaspoon mint extract for vanilla extract, and add 2 cups fresh chopped mint to the batter just before spooning it into the pan.

Cooking Naturally

My cooking has always been based on using fresh, natural products. I like to know precisely the ingredients I'm using—and be able to pronounce them.

When challenged to limit the fats in foods, I didn't suddenly start using square eggs and synthetic sugar, or tomatoes with chicken genes—just good, natural ingredients. A few years from now, I don't want to hear about the hazards of what I've been eating on the six o'clock news.

Crème Brûlée

For years, I searched for the richest, creamiest crème brûlée, which I found at Joel Robuchon's Jamin in Paris. Here's that wonderful vanilla flavor, lightened to permit more frequent indulgence.

SERVES 8
2 cups skim milk
1 whole vanilla bean
4 whole eggs
8 egg whites
³⁄₄ cup sugar
2 teaspoons potato starch
1 tablespoon vanilla extract
½ cup light brown sugar

1. Preheat the oven to 300°.
2. In a heavy saucepan, slowly heat the milk with the vanilla bean; do not boil or the milk will curdle. Remove and split the bean, scrape out the seeds, and return them to the milk.
3. Meanwhile, whisk the eggs, egg yolks, sugar, potato starch, and vanilla. Slowly whisk this mixture into the hot milk.
4. Cook over low heat, stirring with a wooden spoon, until the custard coats the back of the spoon. Divide the custard into six 6-ounce ramekins.
5. Place the ramekins in a baking dish with 2-inch sides. Pour hot water into the baking dish, until the water comes halfway up the sides of the ramekins. Place the baking dish in the oven and bake for 35 to 40 minutes, or until a knife inserted in the center comes out clean. Remove the ramekins from the dish and place them on a rack to cool. Refrigerate until well chilled, about 2 hours.
6. Preheat the broiler. Sprinkle each custard lightly with brown sugar, spreading it evenly to the edges. Place the ramekins on a baking sheet and broil for about 1½ minutes, until the sugar is melted and bubbly. Watch carefully. Remove and serve immediately, or chill until served.

*Cal. **219** Carb. **36g** Protein **10g** Chol. **122mg** Fat **3g/13%***

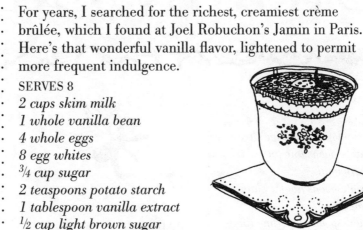

Vanilla bean

Vanilla sugar

vanilla seeds

Dreamy Creams

Vanilla Cream

YIELD: 1 CUP
3/4 cup low-fat cottage cheese
3 tablespoons low-fat
 buttermilk
3 tablespoons nonfat plain
 yogurt
3 tablespoons superfine sugar
1/2 vanilla bean, split, seeds
 scraped from the pod
1/4 teaspoon vanilla extract

Process all of the ingredients in
a blender until smooth.
*Cal. 16 Carb. 2g Protein 2g
Chol. .6mg Fat .1g/8%**

Passionfruit Cream

YIELD: 2/3 CUP
3 ripe passionfruits
1/2 cup Low-Fat Blend
 (see Basics)
2 tablespoons honey
Slice the passionfruit in half,
discard the seeds, and scoop
out the pulp. Place in a
blender or food processor, and
purée. Add the Low-Fat Blend
and honey and blend until
just combined.
*Cal. 21 Carb. 4g Protein 1g
Chol. 0mg Fat .1g/4%**

Mint Cream

YIELD: 1 CUP
1 cup low-fat plain yogurt
2 tablespoons fresh lemon
 juice
1/4 cup minced fresh mint
Salt
Combine all of the ingredients in a small bowl and
cover with plastic wrap. Place
in the refrigerator for 1 hour
to allow the flavors to blend.
*Cal. 8 Carb .1g Protein 8g
Chol. 0mg Fat .1g/12%**

Raspberry Cream

YIELD: 2⅓ CUPS
2 cups fresh or frozen raspberries
1 cup nonfat plain yogurt
2 tablespoons honey
1 tablespoon vanilla extract
Juice of 1 orange
Place the berries in a blender
and purée. Transfer to a bowl
and add the remaining ingredients, mixing well by hand.
Chill until ready to serve.
*Cal. 29 Carb. 6g Protein 1g
Chol. .3mg Fat 1g/3%**

Coffee Cream

YIELD: 1 CUP
1 cup Low-Fat Blend
 (see Basics)
2 tablespoons honey
1 teaspoon ground espresso
Process all of the ingredients in
a blender until just combined.
Transfer to a bowl, cover, and
refrigerate until needed.
*Cal. 14 Carb. 2g
 Protein 1g Chol. .2mg
 Fat .1g/6%**

Maple Cream

YIELD: 1 CUP

1 cup Low-Fat Blend
(see Basics)
3 tablespoons maple syrup
Pinch ground cinnamon

Process all of the ingredients in a blender until just combined. Transfer to a bowl, cover, and refrigerate until needed.

Cal. 18 Carb. 3g Protein 1g
*Chol. .3mg Fat .1g/6%**

Orange Cream

YIELD: 1 CUP

1 cup Low-Fat Blend
(see Basics)
2 tablespoons frozen orange
juice concentrate, defrosted
1 tablespoon honey
1 tablespoon Grand Marnier
1 teaspoon grated orange zest

Process all of the ingredients in a blender until just combined. Transfer to a bowl, cover, and refrigerate until needed.

Cal. 16 Carb. 2g Protein 1g
*Chol. .3mg Fat .1g/6%**

Mango Cream

YIELD: 1¼ CUPS

¾ cup skinned and coarsely
chopped fresh ripe mango
1 cup Low-Fat Blend
(see Basics)
¼ cup fresh orange juice
1 tablespoon honey

Purée the mango in a blender or food processor. Transfer to a small bowl, add the remaining ingredients, and mix well. Cover and refrigerate until needed.

Cal. 19 Carb. 3g Protein 1g
*Chol. 0mg Fat .4g/4%**

Ginger Cream

YIELD: 1 CUP

1 cup Low-Fat Blend
(see Basics)
2 tablespoons finely minced
crystallized ginger
1 tablespoon honey

Process all of the ingredients in a blender until just combined. Transfer to a bowl, cover, and refrigerate until needed.

Cal. 14 Carb. 2g Protein 1g
*Chol. .2mg Fat .1g/6%**

** Nutrition information
analyzed per tablespoon*

Citrus Cream

YIELD: 1 CUP

1 cup Low-Fat Blend
(see Basics)
3 tablespoons frozen lemon
or lime juice concentrate,
defrosted
1 tablespoon honey
1 tablespoon finely minced
fresh mint
1 teaspoon grated lemon or
lime zest

Process all of the ingredients in a blender until just combined. Transfer to a bowl, cover, and refrigerate until needed.

Cal. 15 Carb. 2g Protein 1g
*Chol. .3mg Fat .1g/8%**

★ GOOD FOR YOU ★
Fruit

Fresh fruit is an elegant present as well as a great source of fiber, ellagic acid, beta-carotene, and vitamin C. Add fruit drizzled with Dreamy Cream after a meal and your sweet tooth will be satisfied.

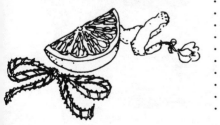

Raspberry Mousse

SERVES 4

2 ½ cups fresh raspberries (or blackberries)
1 cup Low-Fat Blend (see Basics)
1 teaspoon unflavored gelatin
½ cup plus 1 tablespoon sugar
1 egg white, at room temperature

1. Place 2 cups of the raspberries in a food processor. Process until just puréed. Add the Low-Fat Blend and process until just combined; do not overmix. Set aside.
2. In a small saucepan, soften the gelatin in ¼ cup cold water, and let it stand for 1 minute. Place the pan over low heat, and stir until the gelatin has completely dissolved. Add ½ cup sugar, and stir until completely dissolved. Transfer the mixture to a large bowl and whisk until it is just warm to the touch.
3. Slowly whisk the puréed mixture into the gelatin; mix well. Place in the freezer for 30 to 40 minutes, until the mixture is quite thick, whisking occasionally to prevent lumps.
4. In another bowl, beat the egg white to soft peaks. Add the remaining 1 tablespoon sugar and beat until stiff. Gently fold the egg white into the raspberry mixture and blend well, making sure there are no lumps. Gently fold in the remaining raspberries. Transfer to a serving bowl, cover, and refrigerate for at least 8 hours before serving.

*Cal. **187** Carb. **40g** Protein **7g** Chol. **1mg** Fat **1g/4%***

"Raspberries are best not washed. After all, one must have faith in something."

Ann Batchelder

Strawberry Mousse

SERVES 4

2 heaping cups fresh strawberries
2 tablespoons fresh orange juice
2 tablespoons fresh lemon juice
1 teaspoon unflavored gelatin
⅓ cup plus 1 tablespoon sugar
1 cup Low-Fat Blend (see Basics)
1 egg white, at room temperature

1. Purée the strawberries, orange juice, and lemon juice in a blender or food processor until smooth. Set aside.

Magic Mousses

Luscious, creamy mousses are usually made with flavor added to a base of heavy cream lightened with egg whites. My tastes tend toward mousses with very vibrant flavorings, those generally in need of even more whipped cream to lighten them. We were ecstatic that using our Low-Fat Blend cut the fat dramatically while magnifying the fruit's true flavor.

2. In a small saucepan, soften the gelatin in ¼ cup cold water; let stand for 1 minute. Dissolve the gelatin over low heat, stirring constantly. Add the ⅓ cup sugar, stirring until the sugar has dissolved completely and the mixture has thickened slightly. Transfer to a large bowl and whisk until just warm to the touch. Do not allow the gelatin to jell.

3. Slowly whisk the Low-Fat Blend and strawberry purée into the gelatin mixture. Place in the freezer for 30 to 40 minutes, until the mixture is quite thick but not set. Whisk the mixture occasionally to prevent lumps from forming.

4. Beat the egg white to soft peaks. Add the remaining 1 tablespoon of sugar and beat until stiff. Gently fold the egg white into the gelatin mixture, blending well and making sure there are no lumps.

5. Transfer to a serving bowl and cover. Chill for 8 hours.

*Cal. **145** Carb. **30g** Protein **6g** Chol. **1mg** Fat .7g/4%*

Lemon Mousse

SERVES 6

1 teaspoon unflavored gelatin
¾ cup lemon (or lime) juice
¾ cup plus 1 tablespoon sugar
Zest of 2 lemons (or limes), minced
2 cups Low-Fat Blend (see Basics)
1 egg white, at room temperature

1. In a small saucepan, soften the gelatin in ¼ cup of the juice and let stand for 1 minute. Dissolve the gelatin over low heat, stirring constantly. Add the remaining juice, ¾ cup sugar, and zest, stirring until the sugar has dissolved completely and the mixture has thickened slightly. Transfer the mixture to a large bowl and whisk until just warm to the touch; do not allow the gelatin to jell.

2. Slowly whisk the Low-Fat Blend into the gelatin mixture. Place in the freezer for 30 to 40 minutes, until the mixture is quite thick but not set. Whisk the mixture occasionally to prevent lumps.

3. Beat the egg white to soft peaks. Add the remaining 1 tablespoon of sugar, and beat until stiff. Gently fold the egg whites into the lemon mixture and blend well.

4. Spoon into individual dessert glasses or a large serving bowl. Chill for at least 8 hours before serving.

*Cal. **164** Carb. **34g** Protein **7g** Chol. **2mg** Fat .6g/3%*

Peach Mousse

I love the fresh peach flavor of this mousse. To further emphasize the flavor, remember to reserve the juice as you peel and chop the peaches.

SERVES 4

2 cups peeled and coarsely chopped fresh peaches
2 tablespoons minced crystallized ginger
2 tablespoons fresh lemon juice
1 cup Low-Fat Blend (see Basics)
1 teaspoon unflavored gelatin
¼ cup peach juice
⅓ cup plus 1 tablespoon sugar
1 egg white, at room temperature

1. Place the peaches, ginger, and lemon juice in a food processor; process until just puréed. Add the Low-Fat Blend and process until just combined; do not overmix. Set aside.
2. In a small saucepan, soften the gelatin in ¼ cup cold water and let it stand for 1 minute. Place the pan over low heat, and stir until the gelatin has completely dissolved. Add the peach juice and ⅓ cup sugar, and stir until the sugar has completely dissolved. Transfer to a large bowl and whisk until the mixture is just warm to the touch.
3. Slowly whisk the puréed mixture into the gelatin; mix well. Place the mixture in the freezer for 30 to 40 minutes until it is quite thick, whisking occasionally to prevent lumps.
4. In another bowl, beat the egg white to soft peaks. Add the remaining 1 tablespoon sugar, and beat until stiff. Gently fold the egg white into the peach mixture and blend well, making sure there are no lumps. Transfer to a serving bowl, cover, and refrigerate for at least 8 hours before serving.

Cal. **181** *Carb.* **40g** *Protein* **7g** *Chol.* **1mg**
Fat **.5g/3%**

At the market, fresh apricots are a rare jewel—exceedingly delicate, both in taste and "travelability." In most places the local crop will have a short season—two to three weeks in July. The most common types grown are Royal and Blenheim. California apricots are in season May through July, when our fleeting Michigan season begins.

★ **GOOD FOR YOU** ★

Apricots are rich in beta-carotene and iron.

Great Grapes

. . . And here's a great way to eat Thompson seedless grapes, and it's so simple, you don't need a recipe: Stem a bowl of grapes. Add enough low-fat plain yogurt to barely cover. Squeeze on lemon juice and sprinkle lightly with brown sugar to taste. Stir to dissolve the sugar. Chill to let the flavors blend.

Apricot Mousse

SERVES 4

$1\frac{1}{2}$ cups skinned and coarsely chopped fresh apricots
2 tablespoons fresh lemon juice
1 cup Low-Fat Blend (see Basics)
1 teaspoon unflavored gelatin
$\frac{1}{4}$ cup canned apricot nectar
2 tablespoons Amaretto liqueur
$\frac{1}{3}$ cup plus 1 tablespoon sugar
1 egg white, at room temperature

1. Place the apricots and lemon juice in a food processor; process until just puréed. Add the Low-Fat Blend and process until just combined; do not overmix. Set aside.
2. In a small saucepan, soften the gelatin in $\frac{1}{4}$ cup cold water and let it stand for 1 minute. Place the pan over low heat, and stir until the gelatin has completely dissolved. Add the apricot nectar, amaretto, and $\frac{1}{3}$ cup sugar, and stir until the sugar has completely dissolved. Transfer to a large bowl and whisk until just warm to the touch.
3. Slowly whisk the puréed mixture into the gelatin; mix well. Place in the freezer for 30 to 40 minutes, until the mixture is quite thick, whisking occasionally to prevent lumps.
4. In another bowl, beat the egg white to soft peaks. Add the remaining 1 tablespoon of sugar and beat until stiff. Gently fold the egg white into the apricot mixture and blend well, making sure there are no lumps. Transfer to a serving bowl, cover, and refrigerate for at least 8 hours before serving.

*Cal. **168** Carb. **35g** Protein **7g** Chol. **.1mg** Fat **1g/4%***

Dark Chocolate Mousse

Dense and satisfying, but the egg yolks and cream are gone.

SERVES 12

16 ounces semisweet chocolate chips
1 tablespoon unflavored gelatin
4 tablespoons double-strength brewed coffee
4 to 6 tablespoons Grand Marnier or Frangelico
1 cup Low-Fat Blend (see Basics)
4 egg whites, at room temperature
¼ cup sugar

1. Melt the chocolate chips in the top of a double boiler set over simmering water. Stir until smooth and completely melted. Cool slightly.

2. In a small saucepan, soften the gelatin in ¼ cup cold water, then dissolve over medium-high heat. Add the coffee and Grand Marnier, and slowly whisk until the gelatin mixture thickens slightly—enough to glaze a spoon but not to jell. Transfer to a large mixing bowl. Cool to room temperature.

3. Whisk in the melted chocolate and Low-Fat Blend. Stir until well blended. Allow the mixture to thicken slightly at room temperature (10 to 20 minutes).

4. Beat the egg whites to soft peaks. Beat in the sugar, 1 tablespoon at a time. Gently fold the egg whites into the chocolate mixture and blend well.

5. Spoon into individual dessert glasses or a large serving bowl. Chill for at least 2 hours before serving.

Cal. **230** *Carb.* **29g** *Protein* **4g** *Chol.* **.42mg**

Fat **13g/46%**

Tiramisu Cake

SERVES 24

1 recipe Sky-High Angel Food Cake (page 98)
1 cup cold espresso coffee
$^3/_4$ cup Amaretto liqueur
$1^1/_2$ cups nonfat ricotta cheese
1 cup mascarpone
3 tablespoons skim milk
$^1/_4$ cup plus 1 tablespoon confectioners' sugar
$1^1/_2$ cups sliced almonds, toasted
1 ounce shaved bittersweet chocolate

1. Cut the angel food cake into three equal layers.
2. In a small bowl, combine the coffee and $^1/_2$ cup of the amaretto. Spoon one-third of the mixture evenly over each layer of cake.
3. In a medium-size bowl, whisk together $^1/_4$ cup amaretto, 1 cup ricotta, $^1/_2$ cup mascarpone, skim milk, and $^1/_4$ cup sugar.
4. Place one of the layers on a plate, and spread half of the mascarpone mixture on top. Add the second layer and repeat. Place the remaining layer on top.
5. In a medium-size mixing bowl, whisk together the remaining ricotta, mascarpone, amaretto, and sugar until well blended.
6. Cover the entire cake with the second mascarpone mixture. Press the almonds onto the sides of the cake. Grate the chocolate onto the top of the cake. Cover loosely with plastic wrap. Refrigerate at least 24 hours before serving.

*Cal. **201** Carb. **25g** Protein **8g***
*Chol. **7mg** Fat **7g/32%***

VANILLA

Basics

The fruit of a rare species of climbing orchid, vanilla originated in Mexico with the Aztecs. Today, it is grown in many parts of the tropical world.

The vanilla bean is picked when it is only partially ripened (and practically scentless), then immediately dropped into boiling water to halt its growth. After six to nine months of curing in the sun, the subtle chemical changes take place that give vanilla its robust, intriguing aroma and flavor.

Vanilla extract is an invention born of American ingenuity, a flavoring comprised of several ingredients, mostly vanillin. Vanilla extract must be carefully aged for three to six months in order to develop a full, rounded flavor. Artificial extract just doesn't compare.

Varieties

Most modern vanilla is grown in Madagascar, Indonesia, Bali, Tonga, Fiji, and Tahiti. Each offers its own nuance of sweetness, pungency, complexity, and perfume. All fall into three types: Mexican, Bourbon, and Tahitian, the latter being a fatter, thicker-skinned bean with a more intensely flowered scent.

In the Market

Look for beans that are plump, supple, and dark brown. Vanilla is very expensive, so if you use it often, try to buy from a wholesale source.

At Home

Store vanilla in an airtight container in a dark, cool place. Use the beans before they dry out. Vanilla extract should also be kept in a cool, dark place.

In Cooking

Vanilla brings a gentle sweetness to tropical fruits, coffee, custards, cakes, cookies, ice cream, soups, and puddings. It seems to both accent and mellow flavors, even making chocolate choclatier.

I split the beans and add the seeds to everything from frozen yogurt and oatmeal to fruit salad, rice pudding, and buttermilk biscuits—even to lobster sauce.

Place the empty pod in a canister of sugar, a jar of honey, a tin of cocoa, granola, or your coffee beans.

On Just One Day

The blossoms of the vanilla plant last but a day. This once meant that all depended on a bee or hummingbird to pollinate at just the right moment for the pod to develop. In the 1840s a former slave developed a method of artificial pollination, which left matters much less to chance.

GINGER

Basics

In ancient China, ginger was much more revered as a medicine than as a food flavoring. It was recommended for cleansing the body, as a blood thinner, and as an aid in digestion and lowering cholesterol. In time, of course, it also became essential to the taste of many dishes.

The biggest and best ginger comes from Hawaii. Young baby Hawaiian ginger is available early summer to early fall. A more mature grade follows, which is available the rest of the year. Most of the ginger in U.S. markets is Hawaiian.

Ginger's clean, fresh spring flavor is used in both savory and sweet dishes. It is essential to most Asian cuisines, and increasingly to contemporary cookery around the world. In Chinese cooking, it is what is called a yang, a hot ingredient—pungent, creating a warming sensation on the palate and in the stomach. It comes in many forms: fresh, dried, pickled, preserved in syrup, crystallized, and ground.

In the Market

Look for fresh ginger that is rock hard, heavy, unwrinkled, and without a speck of mold. The older and more shriveled, the more fibrous it will be. A more mature root will have longer "fingers" and taste hotter.

At Home

Store fresh ginger wrapped in paper towels tightly enclosed in plastic wrap. Refrigerate for up to a week.

In Cooking

Ginger makes fresh foods taste fresher. It works in harmony with lemon, garlic, and herbs. And as our American palates crave hotter foods, ginger plays a major role in creating levels of flavor.

❖ In using fresh ginger, it's up to you and the dish you're preparing whether to peel or not. The skin is paper thin and practically disappears during cooking or when sliced or minced. Or use a very fine grater (available in Japanese specialty-food stores).

❖ Sliced ginger can be pounded with a mortar and pestle to combine it with other spices.

❖ To create ginger juice, grate the ginger onto cheesecloth. Tighten and twist, squeezing the juice into a measuring spoon or cup.

❖ Ground ginger is most often used in baking. In stews, ragoûts, and soups it cuts the fattiness of meats. I often rub the skin of a chicken or the outside of a pork roast with ground ginger.

❖ Large pieces of crystallized ginger are great as after-dinner palate cleansers, and are especially delicious if dipped in bittersweet chocolate.

SPANISH SUNSHINE

TAPAS TIME

Red Pepper Bites

YIELD: 8 PIECES
4 red bell peppers
2 tablespoons olive oil
6 garlic cloves, slivered
¼ cup niçoise olives, drained
1 sprig fresh summer savory
Freshly ground pepper
8 slices of baguette, 2 inches wide, toasted

1. Slice the peppers into ¾-inch strips.
2. In a medium-size skillet, heat the olive oil over medium heat. Add garlic and pepper strips, and sauté for 2 minutes. Reduce the heat to moderately low, and sauté, tossing occasionally, for 20 to 25 minutes. Remove from the heat and cool.
3. In a glass bowl, combine the pepper, olives, and savory, and season to taste with pepper. Cover and refrigerate for several hours. Serve on the sliced toast. This keeps well, refrigerated, for up to a week.

*Cal. **127** Carb. **17g** Protein **3g** Chol. **.6mg** Fat **6g/38%** %*
(analyzed per piece)

Uncovering Tapas
It was early-twentieth-century Seville, the gastronomic capital of Andalusia. Lacking a bar, thirsty members of the men's club Círculo de Labradores sent the waiter to the bar across the street. He returned, bearing tall glasses of sherry. Each glass was protected by a *tapa*, or cover, made of ham or cheese. A tradition was born. Today, the Círculo still stands. And snacking on tapas while sipping sherry is a national habit.

There cannot be said to be one single Spanish cuisine. Rather, it is a patchwork from many regions. They have in common a passion for olive oil, garlic, bread, legumes, and pork. They also share a straightforwardness, simplicity, and lack of pretense—and a high regard for tastes that are natural and uncontrived.

Spain can be divided into three regions: the Mediterranean, Central, and Atlantic. The influences of the Romans, the French, and the Moors can be seen in the cooking.

Luscious olive oil is a key ingredient all around the Mediterranean—with often quite a bit of it called for in classic dishes. Spain is no exception. Most sofregit, samfaina, and Romesco recipes call for at least one cup, sometimes two, with the other ingredients in about the same proportions as here. The fat in the versions of those dishes in this section is decreased, with the flavor, I think, still very reminiscent of those classic sauces.

Olive-Basil Sauce

YIELD: 1 CUP

1/2 cup pitted Kalamata olives
1 packed cup fresh basil leaves
1 packed cup fresh spinach leaves
1/4 cup toasted almonds
6 garlic cloves
2 tablespoons fresh lemon juice
2 tablespoons olive oil
Fresh Italian parsley

1. In a blender or food processor, purée the olives, basil, spinach, almonds, garlic, and lemon juice. With the machine running, add the oil gradually.
2. Refrigerate until ready to serve. Garnish with parsley.

*Cal. **11** Carb **.5g** Protein **.3g** Chol. **0mg** Fat **1g/72%** (analyzed per teaspoon)*

Pequeño Lamb Chops

SERVES 6

12 small loin lamb chops, about 3/4 inch thick (about 1 1/2 pounds)
Salt and freshly ground pepper
1 cup coarse bread crumbs, preferably from day-old French bread
1 tablespoon paprika
1 tablespoon finely chopped fresh rosemary
1 teaspoon olive oil
2 garlic cloves
Minced fresh mint

1. Pat the lamb chops dry with a paper towel. Season with salt and pepper on both sides, and set aside.
2. Combine the bread crumbs, paprika, and rosemary, and spread out on a plate. Coat both sides of the chops with the bread-crumb mixture.
3. Heat the oil in a large skillet over medium-high heat. Add the garlic and mash it into the oil as it heats. Discard the garlic.
4. Sauté the lamb chops for 2 to 3 minutes per side, until nicely browned and at desired doneness. Remove the chops, place on serving plates, and garnish with mint.

*Cal. **142** Carb. **7g** Protein **14g** Chol. **42mg** Fat **6g/40%***

Sofregit

A good sofregit can be made in 10 minutes, but a really good one takes much longer. Ours takes an hour of simmering. In Spain, it's the first thing into the pot to build a foundation for many recipes.

YIELD: 1½ CUPS

2 tablespoons olive oil

3 cups chopped onion

16 plum tomatoes, peeled, seeded, chopped or 2 cans (15 ounces), drained

1. Place the oil in a heavy pot over medium heat. When the oil is hot, but not near the smoking point, add the onion. Reduce the heat and simmer, covered, until the onion is wilted and starting to caramelize, stirring occasionally. Do not allow the onion to burn.

2. Add the tomato and cook until the liquid has evaporated and the tomato has begun to "melt" into the onion (about 1 hour). NOTE: Sofregit can be kept in the refrigerator.

Cal. **15** Carb. **2g** Protein **.3g** Chol. **0mg** Fat **.7g/42%**
(analyzed per tablespoon)

Rosemary & Anchovy Tart

SERVES 8

1 sheet puff pastry, defrosted according to package directions

1 teaspoon olive oil

4 large garlic cloves, minced

1 cup Sofregit (above), or Onion Marmalade (see Basics)

1 tablespoon chopped fresh rosemary

2 fresh tomatoes, sliced into ¼-inch slices

8 anchovy fillets, rinsed and patted dry

4 tablespoons freshly grated Manchego or Parmesan

Fresh rosemary sprigs

1. Preheat the oven to 425°. On a lightly floured surface, roll out the pastry dough to a 13-inch square. Fit the pastry into a floured 11-inch tart tin with a removable rim. Trim the excess dough and place in the freezer until ready to use.

2. Heat the oil in a medium-large skillet over medium-high heat. Add the oil and garlic, and sauté until the garlic becomes soft, about 3 minutes. Lower the heat and add

More Tapas

The art of eating standing up is well defined across Spain, particularly in Andalusia, where it all began. A group of friends begins the slow, quiet walk along certain streets, perhaps through an entire neighborhood where tapas bars beckon. They talk, sip, and nibble, delighting in the extravagant array of tiny, exquisite morsels, hot and cold. This is *tapadera*, in its finest form.

Go north, they say, and the portions get larger, the crowds noisier. But the mix is the same from one Spanish horizon to the other: tapas, a little wine or sherry, and people from every walk of life, mixing and munching, talking politics, and laughing.

Tapas can be as simple and hearty as chorizo sausage, or as elegant and dainty as caviar canapés. The variety is endless. Most are served quickly and in small portions—little bites to quell the appetite while enjoying wine and lively conversation.

In fact, *tapas* refers both to a range of little snacks served in tapas bars and restaurants throughout Spain, and to a convivial, relaxed eating style—a social ritual performed in the company of friends. Or while making new ones. It goes like this: Stand around the bar sipping beer, wine, or sherry. Select small portions from huge, bright platters heaped with boiled shrimp, marinated anchovies, vegetables, olives, salads, and more. Talk, argue, flirt. Don't stop eating, drinking, and socializing until satisfied. The tapas ritual is best if adopted with the Spanish eating schedule.

the sofregit and chopped rosemary. Simmer for 5 minutes. Set aside and let cool slightly.

4. Remove the tart shell from the freezer. Spread the sofregit mixture into the shell. Arrange tomato slices on top, followed by the anchovies, dividing the tart into eighths. Sprinkle the cheese over the top, and place the rosemary sprigs decoratively in the center.

5. Bake the tart for 20 to 25 minutes, or until it is brown and crispy. Serve immediately.

Cal. **260** *Carb.* **22g** *Protein* **5g** *Chol.* **37mg** *Fat* **17g/59%**

Shrimp Sofregit

SERVES 8

1 tablespoon olive oil
6 garlic cloves, slivered
1 cup Sofregit (opposite)
¼ cup chopped fresh basil
Salt
¼ teaspoon crushed red pepper flakes
16 jumbo shrimp, shelled and deveined

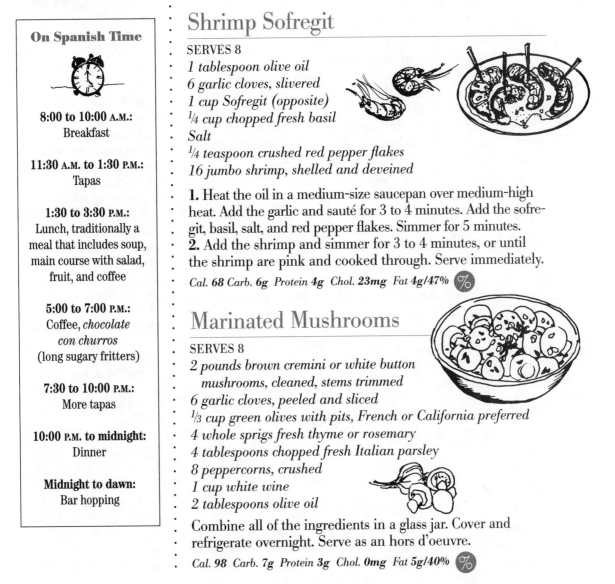

1. Heat the oil in a medium-size saucepan over medium-high heat. Add the garlic and sauté for 3 to 4 minutes. Add the sofregit, basil, salt, and red pepper flakes. Simmer for 5 minutes.

2. Add the shrimp and simmer for 3 to 4 minutes, or until the shrimp are pink and cooked through. Serve immediately.

Cal. **68** *Carb.* **6g** *Protein* **4g** *Chol.* **23mg** *Fat* **4g/47%**

Marinated Mushrooms

SERVES 8

2 pounds brown cremini or white button
  mushrooms, cleaned, stems trimmed
6 garlic cloves, peeled and sliced
⅓ cup green olives with pits, French or California preferred
4 whole sprigs fresh thyme or rosemary
4 tablespoons chopped fresh Italian parsley
8 peppercorns, crushed
1 cup white wine
2 tablespoons olive oil

Combine all of the ingredients in a glass jar. Cover and refrigerate overnight. Serve as an hors d'oeuvre.

Cal. **98** *Carb.* **7g** *Protein* **3g** *Chol.* **0mg** *Fat* **5g/40%**

Samfaina

YIELD: 8 CUPS

2 tablespoons olive oil
8 garlic cloves, minced
2½ pounds onions, halved and thinly sliced
1½ pounds eggplant, skinned and cut into 1-inch chunks
1 pound zucchini, cut into 1-inch chunks
10 plum tomatoes, peeled, seeded, and chopped
1½ pounds red or green bell peppers, roasted, peeled, and cut
*   into strips (page 240)*
Salt and freshly ground pepper

1. Heat the oil in a stockpot. Add the garlic, onion, eggplant, and zucchini. Stir to coat the vegetables with oil; cover and cook for 10 minutes over low heat. Uncover and cook over medium to medium-high heat until the liquid has evaporated, stirring occasionally.

2. Reduce the heat, add the tomato and bell pepper, and simmer until the vegetables are soft and the liquid has again evaporated. Season with salt and pepper to taste.

Cal. 95 Carb. 20g Protein .4g Chol. 0mg Fat 1g/12%
(analyzed per ¼ cup)

Samfaina Pizzas

SERVES 8

1 sheet frozen puff pastry, defrosted according to package
*   directions*
1 teaspoon olive oil
2 garlic cloves, slivered
1 cup Samfaina (above)
¼ cup finely chopped fresh Italian parsley
2 tablespoons capers
¼ cup chopped and pitted French green olives
¼ teaspoon crushed red pepper flakes
Salt
1 tablespoon balsamic vinegar
Pinch sugar
2 tablespoons Parmesan shards, made with a potato peeler

1. Preheat the oven to 375°.

2. On a lightly floured surface, roll out the pastry into a 13-inch square. Cut the square into four equal parts. Fit the pas-

Catalonia

Four basic sauces anchor this regional style:

★ Samfaina, made from onion, tomato, pepper, zucchini, and eggplant.

★ Picada, made from crushed garlic, parsley, almonds, hazelnuts, pine nuts, and bread crumbs. It can be fried, toasted, or mashed to a paste to enrich another dish.

★ Sofrito, made by gently sautéing chopped onion, garlic, parsley, and a bit of tomato.

★ Aïoli, made from garlic and olive oil. It is eaten with grilled meat, fish, or artichokes.

Even Spaniards from other parts agree that Catalonia is home to some of the country's best food, particularly in the Ampurdán area, the extreme northeast. As in the Basque country, the cooking here is influenced by close proximity to France and Italy.

try into four floured 4-inch tartlet tins, and trim off the excess. Place them in the freezer until ready to use.

3. Heat the oil in a medium-size saucepan over medium heat. Add the garlic and sauté for 3 minutes, or until softened. Remove from the heat and stir in the samfaina, parsley, capers, olives, and red pepper flakes. Salt to taste.

4. Remove the tartlet tins from the freezer, and divide the filling equally, about ½ cup per tartlet. Sprinkle each tartlet with vinegar and dust lightly with sugar. Sprinkle each tartlet with ½ tablespoon Parmesan.

5. Bake for 20 to 25 minutes, or until nicely browned.

Cal. 251 Carb. 25g Protein 5g Chol. 33mg Fat 15g/53%

Romesco Sauce

YIELD: 1½ CUPS
3 dried ancho chilies
2 tablespoons olive oil
3 pieces coarse French bread, about
  3 x 2 x ½-inch thick, crusts removed
3 tablespoons blanched and roughly chopped almonds
4 garlic cloves, chopped
3 plum tomatoes, peeled, seeded, and chopped
Pinch cayenne
Freshly ground pepper

1. Stem and seed the chilies and break them into pieces. Place the chilies in a bowl, and pour 2 cups of boiling water over them. Set aside.

2. In a skillet, heat half of the oil over medium heat. When the oil is hot, sauté the bread on both sides until brown and crisp, about 3 minutes. Drain on a paper towel. Remove the softened chilies from the water and pat dry. Sauté the chilies in the skillet for 2 minutes.

3. In a blender or food processor, purée the almonds and garlic, scraping down the sides several times. Add the bread, tomatoes, and chilies, and purée. With the machine running, slowly add the remaining oil. Season the sauce with the cayenne and fresh pepper.

Cal. 29 Carb. 3g Protein 1g Chol. 0mg Fat 2g/52%
(analyzed per tablespoon)

What to Do with Romesco Sauce

Often called the Queen of Catalan sauces, this is one of the region's classics. It is based on pulverized almonds, sweet nyora peppers, and tomatoes. My version calls for ancho peppers, which are more widely available here. Romesco sauce seems to keep forever and offers a myriad of uses:

★ Add it to stews

★ Serve it as a condiment with lamb, potatoes, beef, or grilled fish

★ Put it onto a tart with onions.

Garlic Garbanzos

Loaded with fiber and nutrition.

SERVES 12

2 cans (16 ounces each) garbanzo beans
2 tablespoons olive oil
2 tablespoons finely minced fresh garlic
12 sprigs fresh thyme
Salt and freshly ground pepper

1. Preheat the oven to 450°.
2. Drain the beans and place them in a glass baking dish in a single layer. Drizzle with the oil, and toss with your fingers to coat each bean. Sprinkle evenly with the garlic, and place the thyme evenly over. Roast for 15 minutes. Season with salt and pepper to taste. Serve with toothpicks to spear the beans.

Cal. 91 Carb. 14g Protein 3g Chol. 0mg Fat 3g/29%

Catalan Meatballs

SERVES 8

Meatballs:
1 pound freshly ground lean turkey (99% fat free)
6 garlic cloves, minced
1 small onion, chopped fine
4 tablespoons minced fresh parsley
1 egg, lightly beaten
½ cup fresh bread crumbs, preferably from a coarse-textured
    peasant bread
2 tablespoons skim milk
2 teaspoons finely minced fresh thyme
1 teaspoon finely minced fresh rosemary
Salt and freshly ground pepper
1 tablespoon olive oil

Sauce:
2 garlic cloves, chopped fine
1 small onion, chopped fine
2 plum tomatoes, peeled, seeded, and chopped
1 cup chicken broth (see Basics)
¼ cup sherry
½ cup slivered and toasted almonds
Freshly chopped parsley

1. In a large bowl, combine all of the meatball ingredients

Chick-Peas

Charlemagne loved chick-peas, which were brought to Spain from Central Asia by the Phoenicians. An egalitarian pleasure, they have continued to appeal to rich and poor. With their high fiber content, they are as healthful as they are delicious. Add them to stews, soups, purées, and salads; boil them, fry them, roast them, purée them—or eat them raw. In Spain, they make a fine dessert with quince. In some regions, they are toasted, ground, and made into delicious, eye-opening coffeelike drinks.

Choose from several varieties, but the most current crop will be consistently best. Castilian chick-peas are considered especially good. Two traditional tricks: Add a teaspoon of bicarbonate of soda to the water. When done, don't drain immediately or the skins will peel.

★ GOOD FOR YOU ★

One cup of chick-peas has 270 calories, 45 grams of carbohydrates, and 4 grams of fat—or 13% from calories—which makes them somewhat higher in fat than most beans.

except the olive oil, and blend completely. Shape into meatballs 1½ inches in diameter.

2. In a large skillet, heat the oil. Add the meatballs and brown on all sides. Remove and set aside.

3. In the oil remaining in the skillet, sauté the garlic and onion until slightly soft, 2 to 3 minutes. Stir in the tomatoes, broth, and sherry. Bring to a boil, scraping up the bits from the bottom. Return the meatballs to the pan and cover. Simmer the meatballs for 15 to 20 minutes. Just before serving, add the almonds and sprinkle with parsley.

*Cal. **184** Carb. **8g** Protein **21g** Chol. **45mg** Fat **8g/39%***

THE SPANISH PANTRY

The Spanish pantry is a rich one, with today's local cooking based on the ingredients that have been used for centuries: olives and olive oil, seafood, sausages, port, rice, capers, sherry, beef, cheeses, grains, saffron. Many Spanish products have become a part of our own everyday cooking.

Olive Oil

Spain is the world's largest producer of olive oil. Italy is a close second.

Olives are grown and oil made virtually all over the country. But the northern region of Catalonia, specifically around the town of Lérida, stands out. There, a number of small producers are making oil from the tiny but juicy Arbequina olive that has a distinctly herbal flavor.

The olives are hand-picked, often from trees that are cen-turies old. The olives are then rushed to be crushed before fermentation begins. By keeping fermentation at bay, the acid level also is kept low, no higher in fact than 0.5 percent.

Capers

They're unopened flower buds, really, picked by hand from a wild Mediterranean shrub, then cured in either a salty vinegar solution or plain salt to develop the pungent flavor of capers. If you're used to only the pickled version you'll find dry-salted capers an eye opener. They're plumper, firmer in texture, and intensely flavored—in fact, almost like nutmeats, and nearly as addicting. I can hardly resist eating them straight from the container. Capers come in all sizes. Small ones are most familiar, with the larger kinds now available at specialty shops.

Pimientos

A far cry from the supermarket version in a jar; the true Spanish pimiento is a flavorful, deliciously smoky red, fantastic fire-roasted pepper. Serve them straight from the jar, stuffed with goat cheese and broiled, or tossed into rices, salads, or sandwiches.

Jerez Sherry Vinegar

Made in Jerez de la Frontera, in southern Spain. Jerez sherry vinegar begins with the juice of a single grape, the Spanish Palomino, and is aged in American white oak. The result: a rich and complex flavor, almost almondy. The process of making Jerez sherry vinegar is not unlike the process of making fine balsamic vinegar, and the sweet-aged flavors that result are likewise similar. They can often be used in place of each other.

Haddock Picada

Picada, while a classic Catalan sauce, often refers to the delightful flavor of sweet and sour.

SERVES 12

3 Anaheim peppers, halved, seeded, and chopped (1 cup)
1 pound tomatoes, peeled, seeded, and chopped (2 cups)
2 cups finely chopped onion
1 tablespoon minced fresh garlic
1 tablespoon olive oil
2 pounds haddock fillets, skinned and cut into 12 pieces
Paprika
Turmeric
Salt and freshly ground pepper
½ cup drained large Spanish capers
½ cup golden raisins

1. In a large bowl, combine the pepper, tomato, onion, and garlic.
2. Preheat the oven to 325°.
3. Drizzle the bottom of a 9 x 9-inch baking dish with 1 teaspoon olive oil. Spread half the pepper mixture over the bottom of the dish. Place the haddock on top of the pepper mixture, and sprinkle liberally with the seasonings. Sprinkle the capers and raisins over the fish. Drizzle with 1 teaspoon olive oil, and cover with the remaining pepper mixture. Season again with the salt and spices, and drizzle with the last teaspoon of oil.
4. Cover tightly with foil and bake for 10 minutes. Lower the heat to 275°, and bake for 2 hours. Serve immediately.

Cal. 119 Carb. 10g Protein 15g Chol. 21mg Fat 2g/13%

Sangria

Each region of Spain has its own variation of this cooling wine and fruit drink. It begins with red or white wine. Sherry, brandy, champagne, soda, and/or lemonade may be added, then peaches, grapes, lemons, oranges, apples, or even berries, with a pinch of cinnamon and cloves to give it a bite. The flavors are allowed to blend for an hour before ice is added. Then the celebration begins.

Roasted Asparagus

SERVES 4

1 tablespoon olive oil
1 tablespoon slivered fresh garlic
1 pound fresh asparagus, washed and trimmed
1 tablespoon red wine vinegar
Salt and freshly ground pepper
½ cup bread crumbs, preferably from toasted French bread
Pinch crushed red pepper flakes
2 tablespoons toasted and chopped almonds

2 tablespoons finely minced fresh Italian parsley
¼ cup thin strips roasted red pepper (optional)

1. Preheat the oven to 500°.
2. In a large ovenproof skillet or baking dish, combine the oil and garlic. Place in the oven and roast until the garlic begins to brown slightly, 40 to 60 seconds; be careful not to burn the garlic. Remove the garlic with a slotted spoon and reserve.
3. Add the asparagus to the skillet, tipping the skillet to coat the asparagus evenly with oil. Roast the asparagus until tender and crisp, about 5 minutes (longer if asparagus are thick).
4. With a slotted spoon, transfer the asparagus and reserved garlic to a serving platter. Drizzle with vinegar, add salt and pepper to taste, and keep warm. Add the bread crumbs, red pepper flakes, and almonds to the skillet and stir.
5. Return the skillet to the oven for 2 minutes, stirring once. Spoon the toasted crumbs over the asparagus, and toss to coat completely. Garnish with the parsley and red pepper, if desired, and serve immediately.

*Cal. **100** Carb. **9g** Protein **4g** Chol. **0mg** Fat **6g/53%*** %

Glazed Garlic Prawns

This is a staple of the tapas bar.

SERVES 4

1 pound prawns or jumbo shrimp, peeled and deveined
1 tablespoon olive oil
¼ cup coarse sea salt
¾ cup chicken broth (see Basics)
2 tablespoons finely minced fresh garlic
3 tablespoons fresh lemon juice
¼ cup finely chopped fresh Italian parsley

1. Rinse the prawns, pat dry, and brush with the olive oil.
2. Spread the salt on a large plate and roll the prawns in the salt to cover completely. Preheat the broiler.
3. Place the prawns directly on a rack, and broil 4 inches from the heat for 2 minutes per side.
4. Meanwhile, heat the chicken broth in a small saucepan over medium heat. Add the garlic, and cook for 2 minutes, stirring constantly. Add the lemon juice and parsley, and cook for 1 minute. Transfer the sauce to a serving bowl. Serve the prawns and dipping sauce immediately.

*Cal. **162** Carb. **3g** Protein **24g** Chol. **172mg** Fat **6g/32%***

Basque Seafood Stew

SERVES 4

1 teaspoon olive oil
12 garlic cloves, minced
$\frac{1}{2}$ cup chopped scallion, white and green parts
$1\frac{1}{2}$ cups clam juice
1 cup white wine
2 tablespoons chopped fresh sage
$1\frac{1}{2}$ teaspoons dried oregano
2 tablespoons chopped lime, rind included
$1\frac{1}{2}$ pounds cod fillet or other firm white fish, cut into
    2-inch chunks
12 littleneck clams, scrubbed
24 mussels, scrubbed and debearded just before cooking
Salt and freshly ground pepper
1 cup chopped fresh Italian parsley

1. In a large skillet with 3-inch sides, heat the oil over medium-high heat. Add the garlic and scallion and sauté for 2 to 3 minutes, stirring constantly. Add the clam juice, wine, sage, oregano, and lime, and simmer for 5 minutes. Add the fish and poach for 5 minutes; the broth should be barely simmering. Remove the fish with a slotted spoon and set aside.
2. Increase the heat to medium-high. When the broth begins to boil, add the shellfish. Cover and cook until the shells open, about 8 minutes (clams may take longer). Discard all unopened shells.
3. Return the cod to the skillet and heat through. Taste and season with salt and pepper. Transfer the stew to a serving dish and garnish with parsley.

*Cal. **279** Carb. **11g** Protein **48g** Chol. **111mg** Fat **6g/8%***

Chicken Madeira

SERVES 4

2 whole chicken breasts, boned, skinned, and split in half
Salt and freshly ground pepper
1 tablespoon olive oil
1 pound thinly sliced mushrooms
$\frac{1}{2}$ cup thinly sliced onion
2 garlic cloves, minced
$\frac{1}{4}$ cup Madeira
$\frac{1}{4}$ cup low-fat sour cream

Those Basque Culinarians

The northeastern Basque country is markedly sophisticated, thanks to the proximity of France and the rest of Europe. Add to that the vitality of the region's renowned gastronomic societies—numbering in the hundreds, the men-only *confradias* meet regularly all over the region.

1 tablespoon unsalted butter
½ cup bread crumbs

1. Preheat the oven to 350°.

2. Sprinkle both sides of the breasts with salt and pepper. Lightly coat the bottom of a 8 x 8-inch baking dish with vegetable or canola oil. Place the breasts in the dish in one layer.

3. In a medium skillet over medium heat, place ½ tablespoon olive oil. Add the mushrooms and sauté for 2 to 4 minutes. Remove the mushrooms with a slotted spoon, and distribute evenly over the chicken. Add the remaining oil to the skillet; sauté the onion and garlic until transparent, about 4 minutes, and place over the mushrooms.

4. Combine the wine and sour cream; pour over the chicken.

5. Discard the oil and wipe the skillet clean with a paper towel. Melt the butter in the skillet; add the crumbs and toss to coat. Sprinkle the crumbs over the chicken breasts. Cover the dish with foil, and bake for exactly 1 hour. Serve immediately.

*Cal. **382** Carb. **19g** Protein **38g** Chol. **116mg** Fat **17g/40%***

Garlic-Fried Greens

SERVES 6

½ cup golden raisins
2 tablespoons sherry
1 teaspoon olive oil
10 garlic cloves, slivered
3 pounds tender young greens (such as arugula, spinach, dandelion, or young turnip tops, or a combination), washed and trimmed
Freshly ground pepper
¼ cup toasted pine nuts or slivered almonds

1. In a small skillet, heat the raisins in the sherry, and plump for 30 minutes.

2. In a very large skillet, heat the oil over medium heat. Add the garlic and sauté for 1 minute. Turn the heat to medium-high. Add the greens and cover; cook for 30 to 40 seconds. Remove the lid, toss the greens with a fork, replace the lid, and cook for 1 minute, tossing several times. Some greens may take longer to cook.

4. Pour the raisins and sherry over the greens. Season generously with pepper. Add the pine nuts and toss. Serve immediately.

*Cal. **131** Carb. **18g** Protein **6g** Chol. **0mg** Fat **6g/36%***

Chicken & Sausage Paella

The traditional paella evolved from early rice dishes, and is as old as the plains-dwelling Gypsies of Spain. Paella is named for the pan in which it is cooked and is created for large groups of friends who participate in its preparation. Some build the fire, a rosy circle of coals ignited from grapevine shoots built to the size of the paella pan. The group gathers around to watch the paella cook, then eats directly out of the pan. Each consumes only his share, as if guided by imaginary boundaries.

SERVES 10

3 heads garlic, cloves peeled, heads intact
2 tablespoons olive oil
6 cups chicken broth (see Basics)
2 whole boneless and skinless chicken breasts,
  cut into 2 x ½-inch strips
2 tablespoons paprika
1 pound turkey sausage, cut into 2-inch pieces
2 large onions, chopped
2 large red bell peppers, cored, seeded, and cut into 2-inch pieces
4 medium zucchini, yellow squash, or eggplant, sliced

Spanish Rice

The earliest Spanish rices appeared in Arab cooking in the thirteenth century. The now-classic rice with almonds was enjoyed by Saint Louis, king of France, as he set out for the Crusades.

Today, every region enjoys its own specialty. The most authentic paella in Valencia includes lightly fried garlic, parsley, rice, and eels from the local rice fields. Elsewhere this classic dish includes duck, monkfish, squid and its ink, prawns, pork chops, sausages, clams, red and green peppers, potatoes, sardines, mullet, grouper, chick-peas and white beans. In some parts, even game goes into paella.

The Spanish Rose

Saffron is one of Spain's oldest treasures. Living gold, it grew wild until its value prompted cultivation. Today it is grown primarily in La Mancha and Lower Graza, Spain's two main saffron-producing regions.

A member of the crocus family, saffron thrives in dry soil, remaining underground until autumn rains wake its sleeping buds. On a day in early November, the saffron fields erupt into a lush carpet of velvety purple blooms with stamens of gold, red, and orange; it's a breathtaking sight. Soon, the women will begin moving across this brilliant tapestry, gathering their "roses."

When adding saffron to a dish, grind it in a mortar with a little stock until it colors the liquid.

10 large garlic cloves, sliced
3 cups long-grain white rice
12 plum tomatoes, cored and sliced lengthwise
4 sun-dried tomatoes packed in oil, drained and julienned
½ cup unpitted whole green olives (French or Californian)
1 cup chopped fresh Italian parsley
½ teaspoon saffron threads
½ teaspoon salt
½ teaspoon crushed red pepper flakes
4 ears fresh corn, husked and cut into 2-inch pieces

1. Trim the tops off the garlic heads with a sharp knife. Place the garlic, 1 tablespoon olive oil, and ½ cup of chicken broth in a small saucepan. Bring to a boil over medium-high heat. Reduce the heat and simmer for 30 minutes, basting frequently or until the garlic is soft. Set aside.

2. Preheat the oven to 350°.

3. Season the chicken on all sides with paprika. In a very large ovenproof skillet with 3-inch sides, heat the remaining olive oil over medium-high heat. Brown the chicken on all sides, about 5 minutes altogether. Remove the chicken to a large plate and drain off the oil.

4. Brown the sausage on all sides in the skillet, about 8 minutes. Drain off the oil. Add to the chicken.

5. In the oil remaining in the skillet, sauté the onion, pepper, zucchini, and garlic until the vegetables start to brown slightly. Add the rice and stir until the rice starts to brown, about 5 minutes.

6. Add the plum tomatoes, sun-dried tomatoes, olives, and ½ cup parsley to the rice mixture.

7. Combine the saffron, salt, and red pepper flakes with the remaining chicken broth, and pour over the rice. Stir to combine and turn the heat to high.

8. Return the chicken and sausage to the skillet. Bury the whole garlic heads in the middle of the skillet, along with any chicken broth left in the saucepan. Bring to a boil.

9. Place the skillet immediately into the oven, uncovered, and bake for 30 minutes. Remove the skillet; add the corn, pushing the pieces into the rice mixture. Return to the oven and bake for another 30 minutes.

10. Remove the skillet, sprinkle with remaining parsley, and serve immediately, directly from the skillet.

NOTE: Carefully lift the whole garlic heads and pass them at the table to spread on French bread.

*Cal. **490** Carb. **70g** Protein **3g** Chol. **44mg** Fat **2g/25%***

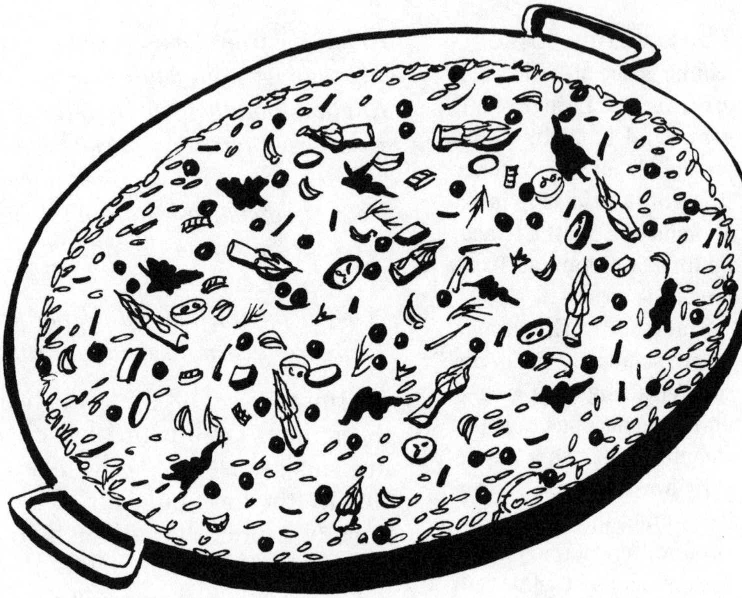

Vegetable Paella

SERVES 10

1 tablespoon olive oil
3 heads garlic cloves,
    peeled and chopped
2 cups long-grain white rice
6 cups chicken broth
    (see Basics)
2 red onions, coarsely
    chopped
1/4 teaspoon saffron threads
1 teaspoon paprika
2 tablespoons marjoram
2 yellow peppers, diced
16 asparagus stalks, washed, trimmed and cut into 2-inch pieces
16 scallions, chopped, green part only
4 medium zucchini or yellow squash or 1 medium eggplant
1/2 pound spinach, cleaned and trimmed
1 cup chopped fresh Italian parsley
2 cups fresh green peas, shelled, or 16 ounces frozen peas
1/2 cup chopped fresh dill
1/2 teaspoon salt
1/2 teaspoon crushed red pepper flakes

1. Preheat the oven to 350°.
2. In a big paella pan or ovenproof skillet, place the oil and garlic and cook over medium heat until the garlic softens, approximately 4 minutes. Add the rice and sauté for 3 to 4 minutes longer, stirring frequently. Add 2 cups of broth, the onion, saffron, paprika, marjoram, and yellow peppers.
3. Cover the pan and bake for 20 minutes. Add 2 cups of broth and allow to bake another 10 minutes before adding the asparagus, scallion, zucchini, spinach, parsley, and remaining 2 cups of broth. Return the pan, uncovered, to the oven and bake for 30 minutes. Stir in the peas, dill, salt, and red pepper to taste. Bake for 5 more minutes. Serve from the pan.

*Cal. **252** Carb. **49g** Protein **10g** Chol. **0mg** Fat **3g/11%***

124

Rice and beans. The perfect
union of flavor and nutrition.
A partnership so intimate,
we say it as one word:
"ricenbeans." And it can be
found all over the world.

- In Latin America, it's
moros y cristianos.
- The Lebanese combine
lentils and rice or bulghur.
- An ancient Jewish dish
called *cholent* is made with
barley and lima or kidney
beans.
- Africans blend pigeon peas
with rice.
- The Japanese mix adzuki
beans with their glutenous
rice.
- Italian *minestra all
Mialses* combines fresh
green beans with risotto.
- Native American succo-
tash combines lima beans
and fresh corn.

Black Rice

Black runner beans not only blacken the rice in a stunning
way, but the combination makes a "complete" protein. And
black rice is delicious.

SERVES 4

1 cup black runner or black beans
5 cups chicken broth (see Basics)
½ teaspoon olive oil
1 small onion, finely chopped
4 garlic cloves, minced
1 ounce finely chopped Canadian bacon
½ cup short-grain white rice
¼ cup white wine
1 tomato, coarsely chopped
½ teaspoon ground cumin
Pinch cayenne
Salt and freshly ground pepper
½ cup finely chopped fresh cilantro

1. Soak the beans in 1 quart of cold water overnight. Drain
and rinse.
2. Place 3 cups of broth and the beans in a stockpot, and
bring to a boil. Reduce the heat and simmer for 2 to 2½
hours, or until tender. Drain the beans and reserve the broth
and the beans. Set aside.
3. Place 1½ cups of the bean broth in a small saucepan.
(If there isn't enough bean broth, add chicken broth to make
1½ cups.) Place over low heat to keep warm.
4. In a stockpot over high heat, heat the oil. Add the onion,
garlic, and Canadian bacon, and sauté until the onion is softened, about 5 minutes. Add the rice and stir constantly for 1
minute. Add the wine and cook for 2 minutes. Add the tomato and cook for 2 minutes.
5. Gradually add the bean broth, ½ cup at a time, stirring
until the liquid is absorbed before adding more
broth. This will take 20 to 25 minutes. Add the beans and the remaining broth. Season with cumin,
cayenne, and salt and pepper to taste.
Remove from the heat and stir in the
cilantro; serve immediately.

*Cal. **152** Carb. **26g** Protein **7g** Chol. **4mg** Fat **2g/10%***

Catalan Lamb Stew

SERVES 6

1 teaspoon olive oil

1½ pounds leg or shoulder of lamb, well
 trimmed and cut into 1½-inch cubes

4 heads whole garlic

2 heads garlic, cloves separated and peeled

2 cups peeled pearl onions

1 pound new potatoes

4 carrots, peeled and cut into 1-inch pieces

½ cup finely chopped fresh Italian parsley

2 tablespoons finely chopped fresh thyme leaves

2 tablespoons finely chopped fresh rosemary

2 bay leaves

1 bottle (750 milliliters) dry sherry

¼ cup red wine vinegar

2 tablespoons tomato paste

2 cups beef broth (see Basics)

1 teaspoon salt

1 teaspoon freshly ground pepper

1. Preheat the oven to 325°.

2. In a large skillet over high heat, heat the oil. Add the lamb and sauté until brown on all sides, 5 to 7 minutes. Do not overcrowd the pan. (You may have to do this in batches.) Transfer the lamb to a covered 4-quart casserole. Add the whole garlic heads, garlic cloves, onions, potatoes, and carrot. Lightly spray or brush the vegetables with vegetable or olive oil. Sprinkle in ¼ cup of the parsley, and the thyme, rosemary, and bay leaves. Toss to combine.

3. Deglaze the skillet with the sherry, scraping up the brown bits from the bottom. Add the vinegar and simmer for 5 minutes. Stir in the tomato paste, beef broth, salt, and pepper, and simmer for 10 minutes more, until thickened and reduced slightly. Pour over the lamb and vegetables, cover, and place in the preheated oven. Bake for 15 minutes; remove the cover and bake for 1 hour.

4. With a slotted spoon, remove the whole heads of garlic and set them aside. Remove and separate the meat and vegetables and set aside in bowls, reserving three pieces of carrot. Strain the broth and add any remaining vegetables to the vegetables in the bowl. Place the strained sauce back into the casserole—there should be about 3 cups—and simmer until reduced by half, about 15 minutes. Place the sauce in a blender with the

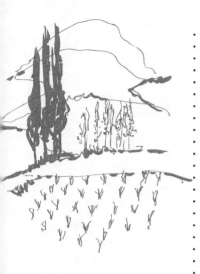

reserved carrot, and blend until smooth. Pour the sauce back into the casserole. Add the reserved meat and vegetables, and reheat briefly. Serve over cooked rice or cracked wheat.

5. Sprinkle 1 tablespoon of the remaining parsley on top. Serve with fresh bread; the whole garlic cloves should be passed at the table and used as a spread for the bread.

*Cal. **297** Carb. **8g** Protein **25g** Chol. **50mg** Fat **6g/23%***

Caldo Verde

SERVES 6

1½ cups cannellini beans
2 large Spanish onions, sliced
10 garlic cloves, unpeeled
10 cups chicken broth (see Basics)
6 ounces Italian turkey sausage
4 large sweet new potatoes (about 2 pounds), diced
6 whole cloves
2 tablespoons chopped fresh sage
8 cups coarsely shredded fresh spinach or collard greens
  (about 1 pound)
Salt
½ teaspoon coarsely ground pepper

1. Soak the beans in 1 quart of cold water overnight. Drain and rinse. Preheat the oven to 450°.

2. Lightly spray or wipe a baking sheet with olive oil. Arrange the onion and garlic on the sheet, and roast for 8 minutes. Turn the onion and garlic over, and roast for another 6 minutes. Coarsely chop the onion and peel and mince the garlic.

3. Place the onion and garlic in a large stockpot; cover with the chicken broth. Add the beans and bring to a boil. Reduce the heat and simmer for 1 hour, until the beans are almost tender.

4. Meanwhile, in a small skillet, cook the sausage through, 8 to 12 minutes, depending on the thickness. Cool and slice into ¼-inch slices. Set aside.

5. When the beans are almost tender, add the potato, cloves, and sage, and simmer for 15 to 20 minutes, until the potato is tender. Add the spinach and sausage and simmer for 10 to 15 minutes. Season with salt and pepper.

*Cal. **348** Carb. **53g** Protein **23g** Chol. **30mg** Fat **6g/14%***

Pamplona Bullfight Party

Roasted Asparagus

Garlic Garbanzos

Red Pepper Bites

Glazed Garlic Prawns

Catalan Lamb Stew

Caldo Verde

Orange Flan

Pole Bean Casserole

Fresh broad beans and tomatoes simmer with sherry, thyme, marjoram, onions, and just enough bacon to provide a smoky flavor to a hearty vegetable dish or a terrific entrée on its own.

SERVES 4

1 teaspoon olive oil
1½ tablespoons slivered fresh garlic
1 medium onion, cut in half lengthwise and thinly sliced
1 ounce smoked bacon (about one slice), finely chopped
1½ pounds broad beans, such as pole beans or wonder beans,
  rinsed, trimmed, and cut diagonally into 2-inch lengths
2 cups peeled, seeded, and cubed fresh tomatoes
¾ cup sherry
½ teaspoon dried thyme
1 bay leaf
Salt and freshly ground pepper
2 tablespoons finely minced fresh
  Italian parsley
2 tablespoons bread crumbs, preferably from toasted French bread
1 teaspoon dried marjoram

1. Preheat the oven to 350°.
2. In a large oval flameproof baking dish, heat the oil over medium heat. Add the garlic, onion, and bacon, and cook, stirring, for 5 minutes. Add the beans, tomato, sherry, ½ cup water, thyme, bay leaf, and salt and pepper to taste. Cover tightly with foil and bake for 1 hour, stirring once or twice. Remove the foil and bake for 15 to 20 minutes longer, or until the beans are very tender.
3. In a small bowl, combine the parsley, crumbs, and marjoram. When ready to serve, remove and discard the bay leaf, sprinkle the crumb mixture over the beans, and serve immediately.

*Cal. **210** Carb. **35g** Protein **12g** Chol. **2mg** Fat **4g/11%***

A Hen and a Hare

A dark, rich ruby sauce envelops the chicken and rabbit. A green salad and rice make this a real feast.

SERVES 8

3 boneless, skinless chicken breasts, cut into 1-inch cubes
1 rabbit (about 3 pounds), cut into serving pieces
1 teaspoon olive oil
6 ounces prosciutto, cut into $\frac{1}{2}$-inch cubes
2 green bell peppers, halved, seeded, and cut into strips
2 cups coarsely chopped onion
12 garlic cloves, peeled
1 cup chicken broth (see Basics)
1 cup ruby port
1 bay leaf
$\frac{1}{2}$ teaspoon fresh thyme
$\frac{3}{4}$ cup white rice
Salt and freshly ground pepper
$\frac{1}{2}$ cup coarsely chopped fresh Italian parsley
$\frac{1}{2}$ cup whole green olives, preferably imported

1. Preheat the broiler.
2. Lightly spray the chicken and rabbit with olive oil. Broil the meat until lightly browned on both sides, about 15 minutes altogether.
3. Meanwhile, in a large skillet or sauté pan with 3-inch sides, heat the teaspoon of oil over medium heat. Add the prosciutto, pepper, onion, and garlic. Sauté for 8 minutes, until the prosciutto and onion begin to brown. Stir in the broth, port, bay leaf, and thyme, and bring to a boil. Add the browned chicken and rabbit; cover and lower the heat. Simmer for 40 minutes. Add the rice, cover, and simmer for 20 minutes more. Add salt and pepper to taste.
4. When ready to serve, stir in the parsley and green olives. Transfer to a serving platter and serve immediately.

Cal. **554** *Carb.* **30g** *Protein* **62g**
Chol. **175mg** *Fat* **19g/30%**

"Every child is an artist. The problem is how to remain an artist once he grows up."

Pablo Picasso

A Most Perfect Little Spanish Cake

A real honest-to-goodness indulgence—with flavors straight out of classic Catalan cooking that I've chosen *not* to make low-fat: chocolate, almonds, butter, and port. The reduced port makes the chocolate taste awesome. But after a piece, I'd watch my fat grams for at least a week.

SERVES 8

2 tablespoons all-purpose flour
1 cup ruby port
1¼ cups semisweet chocolate (7 ounces)
4 tablespoons (½ stick) unsalted butter
⅓ cup toasted and ground hazelnuts
2 tablespoons plus 2 teaspoons cocoa powder
1 jumbo egg
⅓ cup sugar
1 teaspoon vanilla extract
1 tablespoon light corn syrup
6 whole hazelnuts

1. Preheat the oven to 350°.
2. Lightly spray or wipe a 5 x 5-inch square cake pan with vegetable oil, and dust with 1 tablespoon flour, tapping out the excess.
3. In a small heavy saucepan over medium-high heat, reduce the port to 3 tablespoons (10 to 15 minutes).
4. In another small saucepan, combine ½ cup chocolate with the butter and stir over low heat until melted; do not let the mixture burn. Remove from the heat and cool slightly. Stir in 2 tablespoons of the port, the ground hazelnuts, the cocoa, and the remaining tablespoon of flour. Set aside.
5. In a medium-size bowl, beat the egg and sugar with an electric mixer until tripled in volume, about 5 minutes.
6. Fold the egg mixture into the chocolate mixture thoroughly, and pour into the prepared pan. Bake for 35 to 40 minutes, or until a toothpick inserted in the center comes out with moist crumbs. Place the pan on a wire rack to cool for 5 minutes. Run a knife around the sides to loosen. Continue to cool for 1 hour, then invert the pan onto a serving plate.
7. In a small heavy saucepan over very low heat, melt the remaining ¾ cup of chocolate. Stir in the remaining port, and add the vanilla and corn syrup. Remove from the heat and cool until the icing reaches a good spreading consistency. Spread the icing over the sides and top of the cake,

Indulge Yourself

A smidgen of this luscious chocolate cake satisfies your chocolate cravings. Pile a slice high with mixed berries or other fresh fruit, and drizzle a Dreamy Cream (see pages 100-101) atop.

Figs

Figs are the sweetest fruit of all—55 percent sugar. From a botanical perspective, a fig is like an inside-out strawberry: seedlike fruit surrounded by thick flesh.

Figs have been cultivated for 6,000 years. They reached England from Italy during the Renaissance and were first cultivated in this country in the eighteenth century, when Franciscan friars planted them at California missions.

Hence the Mission fig, purple-to-black, a fairly large variety that we buy fresh and dried. Also grown in California: the Calimyra fig, a variation on the ancient Smyrna fig, black-skinned with pinkish flesh, like the Brunswick and the Brown Turkey. Smaller and less sweet is the Adriatic, marketed both fresh and dried. The yellow-green-fleshed Kadota, with thick green skin, is available fresh or canned. Fresh figs are in season July through September.

★ **GOOD FOR YOU** ★

Figs are a good source of natural sugar and iron, with 50 calories per large fig. Choose those with blemish-free skins that are not split; refrigerate and use as soon as possible.

---

garnish with the whole hazelnuts, and refrigerate until ready to serve.

*Cal. **298** Carb. **32g** Protein **4g***
*Chol. **13mg** Fat **20g/50%***

Chocolate-Mint Figs

YIELD: 48 HALVES
½ cup mini semisweet chocolate chips
4 tablespoons finely chopped fresh mint leaves
48 almonds, toasted and coarsely chopped
24 fresh figs, halved

1. Preheat the oven to 350°.
2. In a small mixing bowl, combine the chocolate chips, mint, and almonds, stirring well. Press a little of this mixture into each fig half.
3. Lightly spray or wipe a baking sheet with vegetable oil. Place the figs on the baking sheet and bake for 15 minutes. Serve warm or at room temperature.

*Cal. **37** Carb. **6g** Protein **.6g** Chol. **0mg** Fat **1g/32%***
(analyzed per piece)

Heavenly Meringue Kisses

Adding toasted almonds to meringues is a classic Andalusian trick. A delicious sleight of hand in these bite-sized kisses.

YIELD: 36 KISSES
2 egg whites, at room temperature
½ cup plus 2 tablespoons sugar
½ cup toasted and finely ground almonds
1 teaspoon finely grated lemon zest

1. Preheat the oven to 300°. In a bowl, beat the egg whites until they hold a soft peak. Gradually beat in the sugar to make a stiff meringue. Fold in the almonds and lemon zest.
2. Line a baking sheet with parchment paper. Transfer the meringue to a pastry bag fitted with a number-2 plain tip. Pipe about 1½ teaspoons of meringue onto the paper, lifting up quickly to shape the "kisses." Bake for 1 hour, or until very lightly browned and dry to the touch. Cool a little longer if not crisp. Store in an airtight container.

*Cal. **26** Carb. **4g** Protein **1g** Chol. **0mg** Fat **1g/35%***
(analyzed per piece)

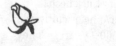

Summer, the Season of Plenty

SAUGATUCK FARMERS MARKET

WE SELL ONLY WHAT WE GROW

"Time has fallen asleep in the afternoon sunshine."
Alexander Smith

Summary Journal

July

1   FINISH GARDEN KITCHEN!   Work in the garden EVERYDAY!

4   Invite folks for fireworks.

8   Take Mother to the Blueberry Festival

12   Tennis anyone?

15   Play golf – Special Olympics Scramble
         – with Bill, Sue & Sharon

20   Condition flowers for Garden Club Flower Show
21   Arrangement to Flower Show by 8:45 a.m.

24   Water!
26   Decorate boat for Harbor Days.

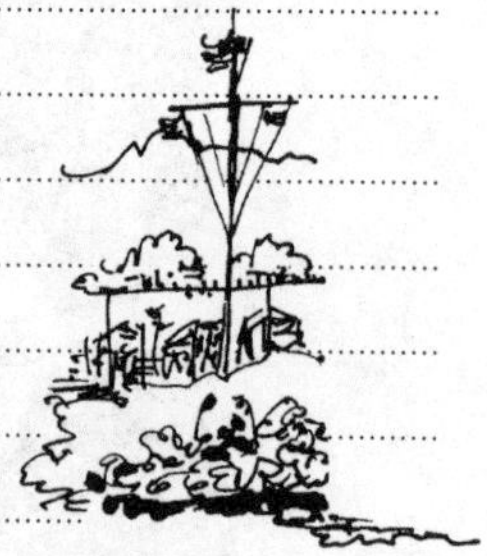

27   Gallery opening

29   Stake foxgloves. WEED!!!

31   Bike trip to Kalamazoo on the new Trail

August

1 STAKE THE TOMATOES! Make green Tomato Mincemeat

2 Freeze vegetables and herbs.

3 Corn should be ready!

8 Ice cream social — chez moi?

11 SHOOTING STAR NIGHT! Picnic on beach? in boat?

13 Trim herbs and use trimmings to flavor oil or vinegar.

14 Make pesto — lots! Start drying herbs.

16 Walk in the garden every day.

18 Bake a fruit tart.

19 Chamber Music Concert
at the Women's Club

20 Dry the hydrangeas.

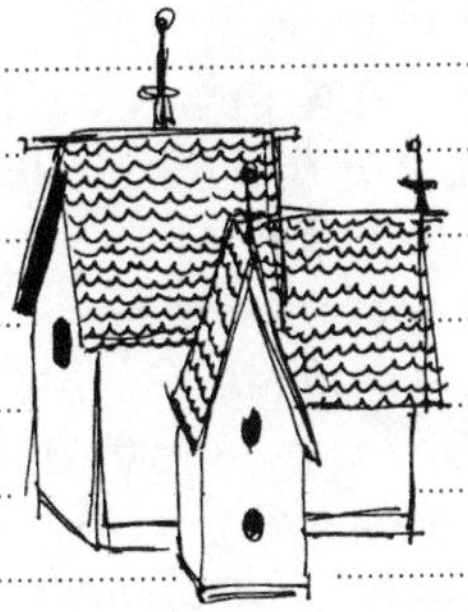

23 Antiquing with Christa

24 Paint bird houses.

26 Order spring bulbs.

29 Cocktails after Commodore's Regatta

Lazy Summer Mornings

This is the season of lush abundance; days grow longer, the deep color of the leaves on the trees reflects their maturing powers. Early in the cool green of a summer's morning, before anyone else is awake, I walk through the garden alone, reveling in its still, sheer perfection.

Vanilla Waffle Hearts

The Low-Fat Blend eliminates all need for fattier dairy ingredients in these rich-tasting waffles. Top with Strawberry-Rhubarb Compote (opposite).

YIELD: SIXTEEN 3-INCH WAFFLES

1 cup Low-Fat Blend (see Basics)
1¼ cups white flour
1 cup low-fat buttermilk
2 tablespoons sugar
1 tablespoon vanilla extract
1 vanilla bean, split, seeds removed from the pod
2¼ teaspoons baking powder
2 egg whites

1. Preheat a waffle iron, and lightly spray it with vegetable oil.
2. In a large mixing bowl, blend all the ingredients except the egg whites.

Strawberry-Rhubarb Compote

The very taste of spring served atop waffles, angel food cake, or frozen yogurt.

YIELD: ABOUT 3 1/2 CUPS

2 cups diced rhubarb
2 cups cleaned and quartered strawberries
1 cup sugar
One 2-inch vanilla bean, split, seeds removed
1 tablespoon coarsely chopped crystallized ginger

In a medium-size saucepan over medium heat, place the first three ingredients. Cook until tender, 8 to 10 minutes. Add the vanilla seeds and ginger. Serve warm or cool.

Cal. 59 Carb. 15g
Protein .3g Chol. 0mg
Fat .1g/1%
(analyzed per 1/4 cup)

Take Time for Nature

At the beginning of each day, as you sip your morning coffee:

• Find something in Nature that catches your eye and study it for an entire hour.
• Observe the patterns and textures of leaves in the garden.
• Walk the beach, experiencing the scrunch of every footstep.
• Listen with your heart to the sounds of birds.
• Watch as dawn shrugs off its silver cloak of fog.

3. Whip the egg whites to soft peaks and fold them into the batter.

4. Pour the batter into the waffle iron, and cook until golden brown. Continue until the batter is used up, spraying or wiping the waffle iron with oil as needed.

Cal. 61 Carb. 11g Protein 3g Chol. 1mg Fat 1g/5%

Spicy Sausage Patties

SERVES 6

1 poblano chili, roasted, stemmed, and seeded
1/2 cup tightly packed fresh cilantro
1/2 cup tightly packed fresh Italian parsley
1/2 cup tightly packed romaine lettuce
1 bay leaf
2 teaspoons crushed dried oregano
1/2 teaspoon salt
1/8 teaspoon freshly ground pepper
1/8 teaspoon ground cumin
1/8 teaspoon ground cloves
1 pound lean ground turkey (99% fat free)

1. In a food processor, place all of the ingredients except the turkey, and process until smooth. Scrape the mixture into a medium-size bowl. Add the turkey and combine well with your hands until the spice mixture is evenly distributed. Cover and refrigerate for at least 4 hours to let the flavors meld.

2. Heat a nonstick skillet over medium heat. Form the sausage into 3-inch patties. Fry the patties for 3 to 5 minutes, turning once, until lightly browned. Serve immediately.

Cal. 108 Carb. 1g Protein 23g Chol. 57mg Fat 1g/8%

Sunday Scrambled Eggs

Analyzed nutritionally, my once-a-week egg treat was a shocker. I knew I was splurging on cholesterol—but the ridiculously high amount of calories and fat percentages was something I hadn't really considered.

SERVES 1

3 jumbo eggs
2 tablespoons unsalted butter
1 tablespoon fresh chives, dill, chervil, or parsley
Salt and freshly ground pepper

1. In a small bowl, break the eggs and blend well with a fork.
2. In a small skillet, melt the butter over medium-high heat until it bubbles but doesn't brown. Add the eggs, cooking very quickly, swirling them with a fork. Repeatedly allow them to almost set, then swirl them again. While still wet, remove from the heat, add the chives, and blend well. Serve immediately.

A Note About Eggs

If you really want to eat eggs, how you do it is your choice. The yolk has most of the nutrients, including a bit more than half of the protein—but all of the cholesterol. The white, with no cholesterol, has nearly half the protein and fewer other nutrients. You can change the proportions of white to yolk in your scrambled eggs in order to get the most nutrition and pleasure along with less fat and cholesterol. Here's what happens as whites are added to whole eggs and the butter is decreased:

3 whole eggs, plus 2 tablespoons butter
Cal. **513** *Carb.* **3g** *Protein* **25g** *Chol.* **879mg** *Fat* **45g/81%**

2 whole eggs plus 2 egg whites in 1 tablespoon butter
Cal. **262** *Carb.* **2g** *Protein* **22g** *Chol.* **553mg** *Fat* **18g/62%**

1 whole egg plus 3 egg whites in 1 tablespoon butter
Cal. **177** *Carb.* **8g** *Protein* **17g** *Chol.* **271mg** *Fat* **11g/55%**

1 whole egg plus 3 egg whites, oil spray/nonstick pan
Cal. **143** *Carb.* **2g** *Protein* **17g** *Chol.* **271mg** *Fat* **7g/45%**

Egg Safety

Raw or undercooked eggs pose a very real risk of salmonella poisoning. Infants, the elderly, and those with weakened immune systems are particularly sensitive to this bacteria, which can be fatal. To be safe, I never serve my younger and older friends anything containing raw or undercooked eggs.

Some other safeguards you can follow are:

• Buy small quantities of eggs at a time—no more than you expect to use in a week or two. Make a mental or physical note of when you bought the eggs. And buy from a market that seems to have a brisk turnover.

• Refrigerate eggs as soon as you get them home. Turn them occasionally.

• Keep your eggs in the box they come in, and keep the cover closed. Use the egg tray in your refrigerator for something else, like cut lemons!

• Don't use eggs with cracked shells for dishes in which eggs aren't completely cooked. Save them for baked goods.

• Always refrigerate egg dishes like flan or custard.

Herbed Eggs in a Basket

SERVES 12

1 cup all-purpose flour
⅛ teaspoon freshly ground white pepper
¼ teaspoon salt
½ cup skim milk
15 eggs
3 tablespoons unsalted butter, melted
2 tablespoons chopped fresh dill, or 2 teaspoons dried
  dill or summer savory
Salt and freshly ground pepper
Sprigs of fresh dill or savory

1. In a blender or food processor, combine the flour, white pepper, and salt to blend. With the motor running, add the milk, ½ cup plus 2 tablespoons water, 3 eggs, and 2 tablespoons of the melted butter; blend until smooth. Stir in the dill. Let the batter rest for 1 hour.

2. Heat a 7-inch crepe pan or a nonstick skillet over medium-high heat. Brush very lightly with some of the remaining butter. Pour in 2 tablespoons of the batter, quickly tipping the pan back and forth to spread the batter evenly over the bottom of the pan. Cook until lightly browned, 15 to 25 seconds. Using a spatula, flip the crepe and cook on the other side for 15 seconds more.

3. Repeat with the remaining batter, brushing the pan with additional butter as needed. As you finish the crepes, stack them between sheets of waxed paper to prevent them from sticking to each other. You should have at least twelve crepes.

4. Preheat the oven to 350°. Spray or wipe twelve standard-size muffin tins with vegetable oil. Gently ease one crepe into each muffin opening, ruffling the edges. Bake for 8 minutes, then remove from the oven.

5. Break one egg into each crepe basket, season with salt and pepper, and return to the oven. Bake for 7 to 9 minutes, or until the eggs are set but the yolks are still runny and the crêpes are golden.

6. Remove the tin from the oven. Carefully lift out the egg baskets and place them onto plates. Garnish with dill sprigs and serve immediately.

NOTE: The crepes can be kept, wrapped in plastic wrap in the refrigerator, for up to 2 days or in the freezer for up to 1 month.

Cal. **140** *Carb.* **8g** *Protein* **8g** *Chol.* **227mg** *Fat* **9g/54%** %

Toast Cups

These large, crunchy cups are great for containing scrambled or poached eggs, fruit salads, and countless other breakfast or luncheon dishes. Tiny ones can stand in as pastry cups for hors d'oeuvres.

Preheat the oven to 400°. Lightly wipe or spray large or miniature muffin cups with oil. Trim crusts from slices of white or whole-grain bread. Gently press each slice into a muffin cup to conform to its shape. Brush or spray the surface of the bread with oil. Bake for 10 to 15 minutes, until golden. Try these once, and you'll find a zillion uses for them.

Oven Puff with Fruit

SERVES 4

2 eggs
3 egg whites
½ cup skim milk
1 tablespoon vanilla extract
½ cup all-purpose flour
Dash salt
1 tablespoon fresh lemon juice
Confectioners' sugar
4 cups mixed fresh fruit, such as raspber-
    ries, sliced strawberries, blueberries,
    sliced nectarines, peaches, or bananas

1. Preheat the oven to 425°.
2. Spray or wipe a heavy 10-inch skillet with
vegetable oil and place the skillet in the oven.
3. In a large bowl, whisk the eggs, egg whites, milk, and
vanilla. Add the flour and salt, and stir to combine.
4. Remove the skillet from the oven. Pour the batter into the
skillet and return it to the oven. Bake for 15 to 20 minutes,
until it is puffed and the edges are browned and crisp.
5. Remove from the oven, sprinkle with lemon juice, and sift
over confectioners' sugar to taste. Fill the center with fresh
fruit and serve immediately.

*Cal. **208** Carb. **36g** Protein **10g** Chol. **90mg** Fat **3g/13%***

Corn Cakes & Corn Syrup

During corn season, I cut the kernels off leftover ears and
make corn cakes for Sunday breakfast. I load the batter with
more corn than it looks like the cake could possibly hold. Add
even more fresh corn to heated maple syrup, to pour on top.

SERVES 8

2 cups maple syrup
2 cups fresh corn kernels
½ cup cornmeal
2 tablespoons all-purpose flour
½ teaspoon baking soda
¼ teaspoon salt
1½ teaspoons canola oil
¾ cup low-fat buttermilk
1 egg

*"Light tomorrow
with today!"*

*Elizabeth Barrett
Browning*

Honey Syrup

YIELD: 3 CUPS

1 cup sugar
2 cups honey
2 tablespoons finely grated
* lemon zest*
Two 2-inch pieces cinnamon
* stick*
2 whole cloves
1 vanilla bean
¼ cup fresh lemon juice

1. In a large saucepan, combine all of the ingredients except the lemon juice, and add 1 cup of water. Bring to a boil, reduce the heat, and simmer for 10 minutes.
2. Add the lemon juice; stir to combine. Remove the cinnamon, cloves, and vanilla bean. Serve warm.

*Cal. **59** Carb. **16g***
*Protein **1g** Chol. **0mg***
*Fat **0g/0%***

(analyzed per tablespoon)

1. In a small saucepan, heat the syrup and 1 cup of the corn kernels over low heat, until the corn is tender and the mixture is heated through, 10 to 15 minutes.
2. In a medium-size bowl, combine the cornmeal, flour, baking soda, and salt. Stir in the oil, buttermilk, and egg until just combined.
3. Gently fold in the remaining corn kernels.
4. Onto a nonstick skillet lightly coated with vegetable oil, drop 1 tablespoon of the batter for each cake. Cook for 1 minute per side, or until lightly golden. Top with the maple syrup and corn.

*Cal. **197** Carb. **43g** Protein **4g** Chol. **23mg** Fat **2g/10%***

Lemon Pancakes

YIELD: SIXTEEN 2-INCH CAKES

½ cup all-purpose flour
3 teaspoons baking powder
3 tablespoons sugar
¼ teaspoon salt
¼ cup skim milk
½ cup club soda
1 egg yolk
2 tablespoons minced lemon zest
1 teaspoon vanilla extract
1 tablespoon canola oil
2 egg whites

1. In a large bowl, combine the dry ingredients. Add the milk, club soda, egg yolk, lemon zest, vanilla, and oil, and beat well.
2. In a separate bowl, beat the egg whites on high speed until stiff peaks form. Carefully fold the egg whites into the batter.
3. Lightly spray or wipe a large regular or nonstick skillet with vegetable oil. Place the skillet over medium-high heat; drop the batter into the pan by tablespoonfuls to form 2-inch pancakes, and cook until they are golden brown on both sides.

*Cal. **39** Carb. **6g** Protein **1g** Chol. **11mg** Fat **1g/28%***
(analyzed per pancake)

Variations: Omit the lemon zest and add one of the following to the batter:
2 tablespoons minced lime zest
1½ cups fresh raspberries
1½ cups fresh blueberries
Seeds from 1 vanilla bean

Sunday Pecan Coffee Cake

A classic sour-cream coffee cake that I've loved for ages.
With Low-Fat Blend, the fat is reduced dramatically.

YIELD: 24 SLICES
2 cups sugar
¼ cup canola oil
1 tablespoon minced lemon zest
1 egg, lightly beaten
2 egg whites, lightly beaten
1 cup Low-Fat Blend (see Basics)
2½ teaspoons vanilla extract
2 teaspoons fresh lemon juice
2 cups all-purpose flour
1 tablespoon baking powder
½ cup coarsely chopped pecans
4 tablespoons light brown sugar
1½ teaspoons ground cinnamon

1. Preheat the oven to 350°.
2. In a large bowl, cream the sugar, oil, and zest. Add the egg
and egg whites and mix completely. Blend in the Low-Fat
Blend. Add the vanilla and lemon juice and combine.
3. Slowly add the flour and baking powder, stirring until
completely blended.
4. Lightly spray or wipe a 10-inch Bundt pan with vegetable
oil, then lightly dust with flour. Pour two-thirds of the batter
into the pan.
5. In a small bowl, combine the nuts, brown sugar, and cinnamon. Sprinkle the nut mixture evenly over the batter,
then gently pour in the remaining batter. Place in the oven
and bake for 40 to 45 minutes, or until a
toothpick inserted into the cake
comes out clean.

Cal. **155** *Carb.* **27g** *Protein* **3g**

Chol. **8mg** *Fat* **4g/24%**

(analyzed per slice)

"I am one who eats breakfast gazing at morning glories."

Matsuo Basho

MORNING GLORY
HEAVENLY BLUE

Savory Breakfast Loaf

Mr. Webster defines *savory* as "a pleasant or agreeable taste," and this breakfast loaf surely has just that.

SERVES 24

¼ *pound Canadian bacon, trimmed of fat*
    and very finely diced
1 teaspoon olive oil
1 yellow bell pepper, cored, seeded, and finely diced
1 red bell pepper, cored, seeded, and finely diced
1 orange bell pepper, cored, seeded, and finely diced
½ *cup finely chopped onion*
1 cup fresh corn kernels
1 tablespoon chopped fresh thyme
1 tablespoon finely chopped fresh sage
1 tablespoon finely chopped fresh summer savory or tarragon
½ *cup finely chopped fresh Italian parsley*
½ *teaspoon salt*
2 cups all-purpose flour
1 tablespoon baking powder
1 teaspoon baking soda
Pinch cayenne
¾ *cup low-fat buttermilk*
1 egg, lightly beaten
¼ *cup hand-grated Parmesan*

1. Preheat the oven to 375°. Lightly spray or wipe an 8 x 11-inch, 2-quart baking dish with vegetable oil.
2. In a large skillet, cook the bacon for 5 minutes, until lightly browned. Add the olive oil, all the peppers, and onion. Sauté until soft, about 7 minutes. Stir in the corn, thyme, sage, savory, parsley, and salt. Set aside.
3. In a large bowl, sift together the flour, baking powder, baking soda, and cayenne. Slowly whisk in the buttermilk and egg until just combined. Fold in the vegetables and spread the dough into the prepared pan.
4. Place in the oven and bake for 15 minutes. Sprinkle the top with the cheese and bake for another 20 to 25 minutes, or until a toothpick inserted in the center comes out clean. Remove from the oven and place the dish on a wire rack to cool. Remove the loaf from the pan, divide down the center, and cut into ¼-inch slices.

Cal. **67** *Carb.* **11g** *Protein* **3g** *Chol.* **10mg** *Fat* **1g/18%**

Fruit Clafouti

In *Outlaw Cooking*, John and Matt Lewis Thorne pioneered the notion of *clafouti*—that wonderful French dessert pancake made with cherries—for breakfast. So why not custard for breakfast? This dish actually falls somewhere between a clafouti and a custard, and it's loaded with fruit and then topped with even more.

While the custard is baking, mix or match the fruit to top it off.

SERVES 4

1 cup raspberries, blackberries, or blueberries, or 2 peaches or
  nectarines, cut into thick slices
½ vanilla bean, split, seeds removed
6 tablespoons sugar
⅛ teaspoon ground cinnamon
½ cup skim milk
1 cup Low-Fat Blend
  (see Basics)
1 egg
¼ teaspoon minced lemon
  zest
¼ cup all-purpose flour
¼ teaspoon salt
Fruit Topping (at right)

1. Preheat the oven to 425°.
2. Lightly spray or wipe four 6-ounce custard cups with vegetable oil. Arrange the fruit in the cups.
3. Place the vanilla seeds in a small bowl with the sugar and cinnamon. Combine and set aside.
4. In a blender, combine the milk and Low-Fat Blend until smooth. Add the egg and lemon zest and blend. Add the flour, salt, and the sugar mixture; blend until smooth. Divide the mixture over the fruit in the cups. Bake for 20 to 25 minutes, until set and lightly golden.
5. Run a knife around the edges of the custard cups; invert and unmold the individual *clafouti* onto plates. Top with Fruit Topping. Serve warm.

*Cal. **176** Carb. **34g** Protein **8g** Chol. **47mg** Fat **2g/10%***

Fruit Topping

Select your favorite fruit combination—1 cup each of raspberries and blueberries; 1 cup each of raspberries and blackberries; 1 cup of blueberries and 2 cups sliced peaches; or 4 cups peaches—and combine with 1 tablespoon of sugar and 1 tablespoon of lemon juice.

Raspberry Loaves

This moist coffee cake is also delicious with blackberries, blueberries, or peach slices.

YIELD: 4 LITTLE LOAVES (32 SLICES)

2 cups all-purpose flour
1 tablespoon baking powder
1 teaspoon baking soda
1/4 teaspoon salt
1/8 teaspoon ground cinnamon
1 cup light brown sugar
1/4 cup canola oil
1/2 cup low-fat buttermilk
4 tablespoons Low-Fat Blend (see Basics)
1 egg
2 egg whites
Zest of 2 lemons, minced
2 pints raspberries
1 cup confectioners' sugar
1/4 cup fresh lemon juice

1. Preheat the oven to 325°.
2. Spray or wipe four 5¾ x 3 x 2-inch loaf pans with vegetable oil and dust lightly with flour.
3. In a medium bowl, sift together the flour, baking powder, baking soda, salt, and cinnamon.
4. In another medium bowl, combine the sugar and oil, breaking up any lumps.
5. In a blender, process the buttermilk and Low-Fat Blend until smooth. Add the buttermilk mixture to the sugar mixture, and stir to combine; stir in the egg, egg whites, and half the lemon zest. Gradually add in the dry mixture, stirring until just combined. Gently fold in the raspberries, being careful not to break them up. Pour into the prepared pans and smooth the tops. Bake for 50 minutes, or until a toothpick inserted in the center comes out clean and the loaves are golden.
6. Place the pans on wire racks and cool for 20 minutes. Run a thin knife around the edges to free the loaves. Cool the loaves on wire racks.
7. In a small bowl, place the confectioners' sugar, lemon juice, and remaining lemon zest, and blend. Drizzle the glaze over the tops of the loaves.

Cal. **76** Carb. **13g** Protein **1g** Chol. **12mg** Fat **2g/25%**
(analyzed per slice)

" I came across excellent blackberries — ate of them heartily. It was midday, and when I left the brambles, I found I had a sufficient meal so there was no need to go to an inn. "

George Chandler Harris

Family Reunions

Rum-Glazed Country Ham

A succulent slice of the tropics.

SERVES 30

1 country ham (10 pounds), trimmed of fat
24 whole cloves
2 tablespoons ground ginger
1 can (12 ounces) frozen orange juice concentrate, defrosted
1 can (12 ounces) frozen lime juice concentrate, defrosted
2 cups light rum
2 mangoes, cut into wedges

1. Preheat the oven to 375°.

2. Place the ham in a roasting pan and score the top in a diamond pattern. Stud the ham with the cloves at the crossing point of each diamond. Rub the ham with the ginger. Bake for 45 minutes.

3. In a large bowl, combine the juices and rum and blend well. Remove the ham from the oven after 45 minutes, and secure the mango wedges to the top of the ham with toothpicks. Pour the juice mixture over the ham, return to the oven, and begin basting well every 15 minutes for the next hour and 15 minutes.

4. Transfer the ham to a serving platter and let it rest for 10

Getting Together

Summertime inspires the Big Family Celebration. Usually, it is planned around a significant birthday or anniversary that must not pass unheralded, or one of our three high-spirited patriotic summer holidays, marked by picnics, parades, softball, and sparklers. Of course, these may just be good excuses for three-legged races, pickin' 'n fiddlin' contests, fly- and big-fishing competitions, inner-tube and swim meets, or a good golf scramble. Whatever the occasion, a family reunion should be a joyous gathering that lasts well into the lingering dusk, buoyed by love, laughter, and multigenerational fun under the sun.

Ham Gets a Bad Wrap

In the past two decades, pigs have gradually been bred to have less fat—50% less, in fact. Well-trimmed pork can now compete with chicken for leanness. With ham, it's important to buy the best (generally, the leanest) and trim all fat possible.

☆ ☆ 🖐🖐 ☆ ☆

Summer Celebrations

Memorial Day Picnic
✷
Father's Day Lunch
✷
Launching the Sailboat
✷
A Housewarming Party
✷
Joe's Graduation
✷
The Pool Is Open!
✷
The Kids' Wedding
✷
Mom's Birthday Party
✷
Grandma and Grandpa's Fiftieth Wedding Anniversary
✷
Fourth of July Fireworks
✷
Big Fish Catches
✷
Football Practice Begins
✷
Labor Day Parade
✷
Susan Goes to College
✷
Back-to-School Party

☆☆ 🖐 🖐 ☆ ☆

minutes. Slice the ham into ¼-inch slices. Remove the fat from the collected juices and pour into a sauceboat. Accompany the ham with mustard, chutney, and pan juices.

*Cal. **246** Carb. **13g** Protein **30g** Chol. **71mg** Fat **8g/30%***

BBQ Baked Beans

SERVES 12
2 cans (15½ ounces each) black beans, drained
2 cans (15½ ounces each) kidney beans, drained
2 cups Hellfire and Damnation Barbecue Sauce (page 236)

1. Preheat the oven to 350°.
2. Place all of the ingredients in a 2-quart casserole dish and mix well. Bake, covered, for 2 hours.

*Cal. **218** Carb. **44g** Protein **14g** Chol. **0mg** Fat **2g/6%***

Roasted Turkey with Mint

Mint gently awakens the wonderful taste of turkey.

SERVES 12
2 cups minced fresh mint
2 cups chicken broth (see Basics)
½ cup frozen apple juice concentrate, defrosted
½ cup dry white wine
1 whole turkey breast with bone (about 6 pounds)
24 ounces fresh mushrooms, thickly sliced
1 medium onion, diced
Salt and freshly ground pepper
8 fresh mint sprigs

1. Preheat the oven to 375°.
2. Combine the mint, broth, juice, and wine in a mixing bowl. Set aside.
3. Rinse the turkey inside and out and pat dry. Place the turkey in a roasting pan with the mushrooms and onion. Season with salt and pepper. Spread the mint sprigs over the breast. Add the mint mixture to the roasting pan.
4. Place the turkey in the oven and bake for 1½ hours, uncovered. Baste the turkey every 15 minutes.
5. Remove the turkey from the pan and let it rest for 15 minutes before carving. Serve the sliced turkey with roasted mushrooms, onions, and basting sauce.

*Cal. **233** Carb. **9g** Protein **44g** Chol. **117mg** Fat **1g/5%***

Chicken Salad with Tarragon

SERVES 10

6 whole chicken breasts, split in half (about 3 pounds)
2 cups chicken broth (see Basics)
1 cup Low-Fat Blend (see Basics)
4 celery ribs, cut into 1-inch julienne
½ cup shelled walnuts
½ cup minced fresh tarragon
Salt and freshly ground pepper

1. Preheat the oven to 350°.
2. In a large baking pan, place the chicken in a single layer. Pour the broth over the chicken and bake for 30 minutes; turn and bake 30 minutes longer. Remove and cool for 30 minutes.
3. Remove the skin and bones from the breasts. Shred the meat into bite-size pieces and place in a large bowl.
4. Pour the Low-Fat Blend over the chicken; add the celery and walnuts and toss well. Sprinkle the tarragon over, toss well, and season with salt and pepper to taste; toss. Cover with plastic wrap and refrigerate for 2 hours. Taste before serving and adjust seasoning.

*Cal. **224** Carb. **3g** Protein **34g** Chol. **85mg** Fat **7g/32%***

Summer Vegetable Salad

A pretty jumble of potatoes, sugar snaps, tomatoes, and fennel, with no oil at all!

SERVES 6

1 pound new potatoes, quartered
½ pound carrots, cleaned and cut diagonally into 2-inch pieces
½ pound green beans, trimmed and cut into 2-inch pieces
½ pound sugar snap peas, trimmed
⅓ cup dry white wine
1 cup julienned fennel
1 red onion, peeled and cut in half vertically, then thinly sliced
3 tablespoons black-currant wine or raspberry vinegar
½ cup black olives (oil-cured preferred)
1 pint cherry tomatoes, halved
2 tablespoons chopped fennel fronds
¼ cup chopped fresh Italian parsley
Salt and freshly ground pepper

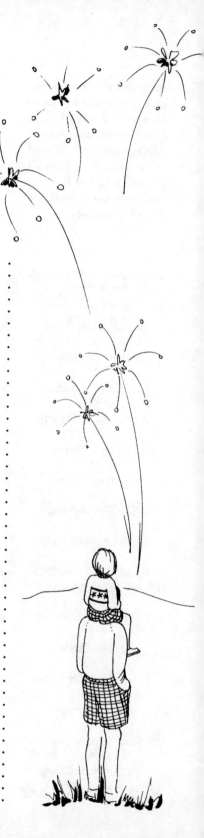

1. Separately steam the potatoes, carrots, beans, and sugar snaps until just tender. Place the steamed vegetables in a large bowl. Pour the wine over the vegetables and toss gently.
2. Add the julienned fennel and the onion; sprinkle with the vinegar and toss gently. Add the olives, tomatoes, fennel fronds, parsley, and salt and pepper to taste. Toss gently and serve.

*Cal. **150** Carb. **28g** Protein **5g** Chol. **0mg** Fat **2g/9%***

Grilled Herb Chicken

SERVES 6

2 whole broiling chickens (about 2½ pounds each)
2 cups chicken broth (see Basics)
5 tablespoons chopped garlic
1 Anaheim pepper, halved, seeded, and coarsely chopped
½ cup coarsely chopped onion
1 cup fresh orange juice
2 tablespoons fresh thyme
2 tablespoons fresh marjoram
2 tablespoons fresh oregano
Salt
Freshly ground pepper
1 teaspoon finely chopped orange zest

1. The day before cooking, cut the chickens in half lengthwise; rinse and pat dry. In a large nonreactive baking dish, place the chicken, skin side up.
2. In a small saucepan, place the broth and garlic. Reduce over medium-high heat to ⅓ cup.
3. In a food processor, place the pepper and onion, and pulse until finely chopped. With the motor running, add the broth, garlic, and orange juice. Process for 30 seconds. Add the herbs, salt and pepper, and the zest; process for 10 seconds longer. Pour the marinade over the chicken, turn to coat, cover with plastic wrap, and refrigerate for 6 to 8 hours, basting occasionally.
4. Prepare the grill for cooking.
5. When the grill is very hot, place the chicken, skin side up, on the rack and grill for 30 to 35 minutes. Turn the chicken every 6 to 7 minutes and baste frequently. When the juices run clear, serve immediately.

*Cal. **299** Carb. **9g** Protein **41g** Chol. **121mg** Fat **10g/32%***

Poached Chicken Express

Poach chicken breasts lickety-split: Place two whole chicken breasts—skinless, boneless, and split—on a plate, pinwheel fashion. Sprinkle on ½ cup chicken broth or skim milk. Add a few sprigs of fresh herbs. Cover tightly with plastic wrap. Cook in a microwave oven at full power for 8 minutes. Serve on a bed of rice, shred into a salad, or add to a stew or pot pie.

Curried Chicken Salad

Chicken, wild and brown rice, and a sparkle of red and green pepper, very lightly laced with curry.

SERVES 8

2 pounds whole chicken breasts, split in half
1½ cups or more chicken broth (see Basics)
1¼ cups cooked wild rice
½ cup cooked brown rice
½ cup water chestnuts
½ cup julienned green bell pepper
½ cup julienned yellow bell pepper
Zest of 1 lemon, grated
Zest of 1 orange, grated
½ cup fresh orange juice
1 tablespoon canola oil
1 tablespoon curry powder
⅛ teaspoon freshly ground pepper
¼ cup finely minced fresh Italian parsley

1. Preheat the oven to 350°.
2. In a large baking dish, place the chicken in a single layer and pour the broth over; bake for 30 minutes.
3. Discard the skin and bone. Shred the chicken into bite-size pieces and transfer to a large bowl.
4. Add the wild and brown rice, water chestnuts, peppers, and zest, and toss well to combine.
5. In a small covered container, combine the orange juice, oil, curry powder, pepper, and parsley; shake well.
6. Pour the dressing over the salad, toss to coat, and cover. Refrigerate until needed.

Cal. 215 Carb. 13g Protein 28g Chol. 94mg Fat 5g/21%

Cucumber Salad

SERVES 4

2 pounds cucumbers
4 tablespoons fresh lemon juice
¼ cup minced fresh mint leaves

Peel the cucumbers, cut them in half lengthwise, and remove the seeds. Grate the cucumbers and place them in a medium-size bowl. Add the lemon juice and mint, and toss well. Cover and refrigerate until needed.

Cal. 34 Carb. 8g Protein 1g Chol. 0mg Fat .3g/7%

150

Palm Tree - leaves bursting off the trail of a trunk

Stars in the Sky

The Chinese invented the "spear of fire" to frighten away evil spirits. Queen Elizabeth I loved fireworks so much she was called the Fire Martin of England.

The best we've ever seen were during the 1976 Bicentennial. Standing high above New York Harbor at Windows on the World restaurant, we watched fireworks shoot into the sky in perfect synchrony with the *1812 Overture.* The music soared, the shells exploded, then they dwindled to sparks above the twinkling lights of thousands of boats floating in the harbor. Ahhh!

Chrysanthemum—perfectly symmetrical in a round flower-like shape

Split Comet—successive explosions split as they fall from the sky

Custom designs—from heart and star shapes to letters forming words

Deb's Ratatouille

Debbie Hudgins—a friend and cooking-school instructor—took the fat out of ratatouille and made the flavors shine through.

SERVES 12

1 eggplant (2 pounds), trimmed, cut into four 1-inch-thick
*   lengthwise slices*
1 tablespoon olive oil
1 pound onions, peeled, cut in half lengthwise, and sliced
*   (about 3 cups)*
2 tablespoons chopped fresh garlic
1 cup ¼-inch-thick zucchini slices
1 cup ¼-inch-thick summer squash slices
1 large red bell pepper, cut in half, seeded, and cut into ½-inch
*   slices*
1 large green bell pepper, cut in half, seeded, and cut into ½-inch
*   slices*
2 Anaheim peppers, cut in half, seeded, and cut into 1½-inch
*   pieces*
5 fresh tomatoes, peeled and cut into eight wedges each
Salt and freshly ground pepper
2 tablespoons capers, drained
2 cups finely chopped fresh Italian parsley

1. Preheat the broiler. Lightly brush both sides of the eggplant slices with half of the olive oil and place on a wire rack. Broil until nicely browned on both sides, 10 to 12 minutes. Set aside.
2. In a large Dutch oven, heat the remaining oil over medium heat. Add the onion and sauté until translucent, 6 to 8 minutes. Add the garlic and cook for 2 to 3 minutes.
3. Add the squash and peppers and sauté for 6 to 8 minutes, until just tender; don't overcook.
4. Cut the eggplant slices into 1-inch cubes and add them to the vegetables. Cover, with the lid askew, and simmer gently for 1 hour, stirring occasionally.
5. Stir in the tomatoes and salt and a generous grinding of pepper to taste, and simmer until thick, about 20 minutes.
6. Add the parsley and capers; cook for 15 minutes. Serve warm or at room temperature.

*Cal. **42** Carb. **8g** Protein **1g** Chol. **0mg** Fat **1g/17%***

Sassy Baked Beans

Boston baked beans at their best.

SERVES 10

1 pound giant or regular pinto beans
1 teaspoon olive oil
1/4 pound Canadian bacon, cut into 1/4-inch dice
1 3/4 cups finely chopped onion
2 tablespoons finely minced garlic
2 tablespoons finely minced fresh ginger
3 tablespoons seeded and finely minced jalapeño pepper
2 cups apple cider
1 cup cider vinegar
1 cup apple juice or water
1/4 cup (or more) molasses
1/4 cup light brown sugar
1 tablespoon dry mustard
1 tablespoon Dijon mustard
2 bay leaves
1 teaspoon dried thyme
1/4 teaspoon ground allspice
1/8 teaspoon ground cloves
Salt and freshly ground pepper

1. Pick through the beans and remove any twigs and stones. Wash the beans well and soak them overnight in cold water to cover.
2. Drain the beans. In a skillet, heat the oil over medium heat. Add the bacon, onion, garlic, and ginger, and sauté until golden brown, 4 to 5 minutes.
3. Preheat the oven to 350°.
4. Transfer the onion mixture to a bean pot or casserole dish. Add the beans to the pot and stir in the remaining ingredients. Place the pot in the oven and bake for 3 hours, or until the beans are very tender; stir occasionally.

Cal. 272 Carb. 52g Protein 13g Chol. 7mg Fat 3g/8%

Creamy Coleslaw

SERVES 4

4 cups thinly sliced green cabbage
2 tablespoons cider vinegar
1/4 cup apple juice
1/2 cup nonfat plain yogurt
Freshly ground white pepper

1. Crisp the sliced cabbage in ice water for 15 minutes. Drain thoroughly.
2. In a large mixing bowl, combine the vinegar, apple juice, yogurt, and pepper. Stir well and refrigerate for 2 hours to combine flavors. Add the cabbage and toss well to combine.

Cal. 33 Carb. 7g Protein 2g Chol. 0mg Fat .1g/3%

Garlic Potato Salad

SERVES 4

1 pound new potatoes, well
   rinsed
1/2 to 3/4 cup Low-Fat Blend
   (see Basics)
1 tablespoon low-fat sour
   cream
2 tablespoons minced fresh
   Italian parsley
1 tablespoon finely minced
   garlic
Salt and freshly ground pepper

1. Place the potatoes in a large
stockpot and cover with water.
Bring to a boil, and boil until
tender but still firm, 5 to 7
minutes. Drain the potatoes
and rinse under cold water.
Let them cool in a strainer.
2. In a large bowl, combine
the remaining ingredients and
blend well. Add the potatoes
and gently toss to combine.
Taste and adjust the seasoning
as necessary.
3. Serve at room temperature
or chilled. If chilled, you may
need to add moisture with up
to 1/4 cup Low-Fat Blend just
before serving.

*Cal. **122** Carb. **23g***
*Protein **5g** Chol. **2mg***
*Fat **1g/7%***

Colorado Pasta Salad

When she has time to cook, my longtime friend Beth Grif-
fiths, owner of Kazoo & Company in Denver (the best toy
store in the world), makes a big batch of this.

SERVES 12

1 pound fettuccine, cooked, drained, and cooled
2 cups peas
1 cup chopped scallion
3 cups halved cherry tomatoes
1 cup quartered artichoke hearts
3 cups cooked shrimp
3 tablespoons finely chopped onion
4 garlic cloves, finely minced
1 1/2 teaspoons Dijon mustard
1 1/2 teaspoons salt
3 tablespoons sugar
1 teaspoon Tabasco
3/4 cup Broccoli Pesto (page 48)
1/2 cup chicken broth (see Basics)
1/4 cup olive oil
1/4 cup cider vinegar
1/2 cup coarsely minced fresh Italian
   parsley
2 tablespoons finely minced oregano
Freshly ground pepper

1. Place the fettuccine, vegetables,
and shrimp in a very large bowl and
toss to combine.
2. In a large mixing bowl or food
processor, combine the remaining
ingredients and mix well. Taste and
adjust the seasoning. Pour the
dressing over the noodles,
seafood, and vegetables and
toss to coat evenly. Serve at room
temperature.

*Cal. **279** Carb. **40g** Protein **15g***
*Chol. **63mg** Fat **7g/23%***

A FRENCH FAMILY FEAST

Bastille Day

*Crudités with
Spinach-Dill Dip*

*Mâche with Herbed Chèvre
and Citrus Spray*

Vegetable Bouillabaisse

Country French Baguettes

Vin Ordinaire

Peaches with Mint

Vegetable Bouillabaisse

Bouillabaisse always brings back the taste of warm sun on a terrace in Provence. My version has a tomato stock laced with saffron. Alongside, a slice of crusty bread topped with saffron-, garlic-, and cayenne-flavored Poetic Rouille is a must.

SERVES 6

1 teaspoon olive oil
2 cups coarsely chopped onion
6 garlic cloves, minced
3 cups Lindsay's Tomato Juice
  (page 286) or canned tomato juice
6 cups chicken broth (see Basics)
2 bay leaves
Scant $\frac{1}{2}$ teaspoon saffron
1 teaspoon minced fresh thyme
$\frac{1}{2}$ pound new potatoes, left whole or quartered, according to size
$1\frac{1}{2}$ cups baby carrots, peeled and left whole
$1\frac{1}{2}$ cups baby zucchini, scrubbed and left whole
$\frac{1}{2}$ cup coarsely chopped fresh Italian parsley
$\frac{1}{4}$ cup coarsely chopped fresh tarragon
1 cup sugar snap peas, trimmed and left whole
$1\frac{1}{2}$ cups haricots verts, trimmed and left whole

baby carrots

baby zucchini

"... they drank the bottle of wine while a faint wind rocked the pine needles and the sensual heat of early afternoon made blinding freckles on the checkered luncheon cloth."

*F. Scott Fitzgerald
Tender is the Night*

Poetic Rouille

Rouille is traditionally made with olive oil mixed with egg yolk and flavored with saffron. Here, we've replaced that mayonnaise-like emulsion with puréed waxy russet potatoes (as in the great Greek garlic dip *skordalia*), adding *rouille* flavor with saffron, cayenne, and garlic—the same thick, shiny consistency, but a fraction of the fat.

YIELD: 1²/₃ CUPS
1 pound potatoes (new or russets), peeled and thinly sliced
1²/₃ cups chicken broth (see Basics)
Scant ¹/₄ teaspoon cayenne
Pinch saffron
8 to 12 garlic cloves, peeled and coarsely chopped
¹/₃ cup extra-virgin olive oil
Salt and freshly ground white pepper

1. In a medium saucepan, place the potatoes, broth, cayenne, and saffron. Cook, covered, over medium heat for 15 minutes. Remove the cover and cook until the broth evaporates, 5 to 8 minutes more.
2. While the potatoes are still hot, place them in a blender or processor, and gradually add the garlic and olive oil to taste. Purée thoroughly. Add pepper to taste and salt if desired, or additional saffron or cayenne to taste. Cool to room temperature or refrigerate, covered, to prevent a skin from forming. Will keep well for 5 days under refrigeration.

*Cal. **40** Carb. **4g** Protein **1g***
*Chol. **0mg** Fat **3g/60%***
(analyzed per tablespoon)

1 cup fresh or frozen peas
Freshly ground pepper
Ten ¹/₄-inch slices French or Italian bread, toasted
Poetic Rouille (at left)

1. Heat the olive oil in a large stockpot. Add the onion and cook over low heat until tender, about 10 minutes. Add the garlic and cook for 1 minute. Add the tomato juice, chicken broth, bay leaves, saffron, and thyme. Add the potatoes and bring just to a boil. Reduce the heat and simmer, covered, for 30 minutes.
2. Add the carrots, zucchini, parsley, and tarragon; simmer for 15 minutes. Add the sugar snap peas, *haricots verts*, and peas. Simmer an additional 3 to 5 minutes, or until all the vegetables are tender but still a bit crisp. Season with pepper. Taste and adjust seasoning.
3. Serve with the *rouille* on the side or with the toasted bread spread with the *rouille* and floated on top.

*Cal. **287** Carb. **54g** Protein **10g** Chol. **1mg** Fat **3g/9%***

Country French Baguettes

YIELD: 6 LOAVES (72 SLICES)
1¹/₂ teaspoons salt
1 teaspoon active dry yeast
¹/₂ cup Sourdough Starter (see Basics)
7 cups bread flour
2 tablespoons rye flour

1. In the bowl of a mixer fitted with a dough hook, place all of the ingredients, except the rye flour, plus 2 cups of water, and mix for 8 minutes. Remove the dough to a lightly oiled glass bowl and cover with plastic wrap or a damp towel and place in a warm place, until the dough has doubled in size, about 2 hours.
2. Punch down the dough and shape into six 24-inch-long baguettes, about 1 inch in diameter. Place onto an oiled baking sheet and put in a warm place. Allow to double in size.
3. Preheat the oven to 400°. Brush the baguettes lightly with water and sprinkle with rye flour. Bake for 20 to 25 minutes, until golden brown.

*Cal. **48** Carb. **10g** Protein **1g** Chol. **0mg** Fat **.1g/4%***
(analyzed per slice)

Raspberry-Almond Parfait

Luxuriously elegant, and so easy!

SERVES 4

1/2 recipe Raspberry Cream (page 100)
12 Amaretto cookies, coarsely crumbled
1 quart fresh red or black raspberries
4 sprigs fresh mint

1. Prepare the Raspberry Cream; set aside.
2. Into each of four balloon-type wine glasses or dessert dishes, layer 1 tablespoon of the crumbled cookie, one quarter of the berries, and 3 tablespoons of the Raspberry Cream. Garnish with sprigs of mint. Serve immediately.

*Cal. **210** Carb. **39g** Protein **4g** Chol. **22mg** Fat **6g/22%***

Chocolate and Coffee Torte

Fluffy ribbons of layered Coffee Cream and chocolate meringues.

SERVES 16

6 egg whites, at room temperature
1 cup superfine granulated sugar
9 tablespoons Coffee Cream (page 100)
6 tablespoons Chocolate Ganache (see Basics)
2 ounces semisweet chocolate shavings

1. Preheat the oven to 225°.
2. Line two baking sheets with parchment paper. Draw two circles, 7 inches in diameter, on each.
3. Beat the egg whites until soft peaks form. Continue to beat, and gradually add the sugar until it is completely incorporated and the mixture is smooth.
4. Divide the mixture equally among the four circles and spread to cover the circles evenly.
5. Place the baking sheets in the oven and bake for 1 hour, or until the meringues are crisp to the touch and very lightly colored. Turn the oven off. Leave the meringues in the oven for 1 hour. Remove the meringues and carefully set them on racks to cool completely.
6. Place one meringue layer on a plate. Spread the top with 3 tablespoons of Coffee

Cream. Spread the underside of the second layer with 2 tablespoons of Chocolate Ganache and place it, chocolate side down, on the first layer. Repeat with the remaining meringues.
7. Sprinkle the top of the torte with the chocolate shavings. Cover loosely with plastic wrap and place in the refrigerator for at least 5 hours. The torte will hold for several days in the refrigerator.

Cal. **55** *Carb.* **11g** *Protein* **2g** *Chol.* **.4mg** *Fat* **.7g/12%**

Lemon-Ginger Squares

YIELD: 120 MINI SQUARES
1 recipe Snappy Ginger Cookies (page 434)
½ cup fresh lemon juice
2 tablespoons grated lemon zest
⅓ cup canola oil
2 eggs
4 egg whites, slightly beaten
1 cup sugar

1. Preheat the oven to 350°.
2. Lightly spray or wipe an 11 x 14-inch baking pan with vegetable oil. Press the dough into the bottom and ½ inch up the sides of the pan. Bake for 15 minutes; cool. Raise the oven temperature to 400°.
3. In a medium mixing bowl, beat together the lemon juice, zest, and oil. Add the eggs, egg whites, and sugar, and mix well.
4. Gently pour the lemon mixture over the cooled crust.
5. Bake for 20 minutes, or until golden brown. Cool before cutting into 1 x 1-inch squares.

Cal. **43** *Carb.* **6g** *Protein* **1g** *Chol.* **8mg** *Fat* **2g/42%**

THE HERB GARDEN

DELICATE HERBS

Angelica

Fresh, bright green leaves with a sweet, pungent smell. Can be added to tart fruit drinks, drinks, homemade jellies and jams, custards, seafood, vegetables, and grain and bean salads. The seeds are dried and the stems are crystallized.
♣ Grows outdoors.

Borage

Leafy; tastes faintly of cucumbers. Use young leaves in green or fruit salads, with string beans, or in fruit drinks and teas. The blue flowers are sweet-tasting and make a pretty garnish. Pick young and small leaves; older leaves are tougher and hairy. Chop the leaves before using. When using the flowers for salad, add them at the last minute.
♣ Grows indoors and out.

Chervil

Delicate, with a subtle celery-licorice taste. Should never be cooked—add only at the last minute. Excellent in green salads, with fish, shellfish, chicken, eggs, cream, peas, string beans, and tomatoes. Essential for *fines herbes*.
♣ Grows indoors and out. Available as fresh sprigs and crumbled dried.

Chives

Decorative as well as useful, with a light onion or garlic taste. Use chopped, or cut with scissors, added at the last minute. Excellent in cream soups and sauces, with fish and shellfish, cheese and eggs.
♣ Grows indoors and out. Available as fresh stalks; frozen and freeze-dried, minced or chopped.

Sweet Cicely

Fernlike pale green leaves with a sweetness and delicate anise taste. It will reduce the need for sugar when added to a sour fruit or rice pudding; also good for salsas, soups, stews, yogurt or any dessert, and berries.
♣ Grows indoors; occasionally found in specialty markets.

Cilantro

Tastes minty and fresh, somewhat like anise. The root has an intense flavor. Fresh cilantro should be used immediately and added at the last minute. Essential in Mexican, Latin American, and Asian cooking. Use with rice, dried beans, fish, shellfish, poultry, vegetables, salsas, and salads. Available fresh and crumbled dried, but the dried is rarely satisfactory.
♣ Grows outdoors.

Dill

Has a delicate caraway taste. Fresh dill should be very fresh and added just before serving.
Used, along with seeds, for pickles. Use leaves with eggs, fresh cheeses, yogurt, seafood, chicken, cucumbers, green beans, potatoes, tomatoes, and beets.
✤ Grows outdoors. Available fresh and crumbled dried (sometimes labeled "dillweed").

Lemon Verbena

Long, pointed leaves with a rough texture that grow on a shrub. The leaves have a strong lemon scent, and can be added to fruit drinks, herb teas, fruit salads, peaches, strawberries, or rice puddings. Use as a substitute for lemongrass.
✤ Grows outdoors.

Parsley

Crisp herb with faint celery flavor. Of two common varieties—Italian flat leaf and curly leaf—flat leaf has the stronger flavor. Use curly parsley for garnishing. Flat-leaf parsley stands up well to heat and is excellent in soups, stocks, cream and tomato sauces, salads, salad dressings, and pesto; with poultry, game, meats, fish and shellfish, dried beans, and vegetables—from artichokes to zucchini.
✤ Grows indoors and out. Readily available fresh. Dried whole and crumbled leaves are available but seem pale and dusty in comparison.

Mint

Refreshing scent and cool taste. Peppermint and spearmint are best known of more than 30 varieties. Lemon, orange, and apple mint have distinctive fruit tastes. Use in Middle Eastern yogurt and grain dishes (tabbouleh), salads, with peas, beans, corn, and potatoes, in jellies, fruit salads, desserts and iced tea.
✤ Grows indoors and out. Available as fresh sprigs (look for bright green, unblemished leaves), dried whole leaves, and crumbled dried.

Salad Burnet

Lacy-leaved herb with a fresh cucumber taste. Use young small leaves in salads and with fresh cheeses (should not be cooked).
✤ Grows outdoors. Available as fresh sprigs in specialty markets.

Lemon Balm

Has a sweet lemon flavor and citrusy scent. Excellent in summer soups, salads, jellies and jams, especially fruit.
✤ Grows indoors and out. Available fresh in specialty markets.

ROBUST HERBS

Basil

Has a sweet, clovelike taste. Varieties include sweet basil, small-leaved bush basil, lemon basil, and opal basil, which has a gingerlike flavor. Fresh leaves are best torn and cut or pounded to release flavor. The leaves at the top of the plant are sweetest. Essential for Italian cooking, especially with eggs, tomatoes, pasta, chicken, fish, and shellfish.
❖ Grows indoors and out. Available fresh, in bunches or pots.

Bay Leaf

Pungent, woodsy herb with sturdy leaves and faint cinnamon taste. Strong, spicy flavor intensifies with drying. Whole leaves dispense more flavor. Remove bay leaves from dishes before serving. Essential for *bouquet garni*. Good with meat and/or bean stews, game, pot roasts.
❖ A perennial, bay leaves grow indoors and out, but won't overwinter in harsh climates. Available mostly dried, but also fresh.

Fennel

Slight licorice flavor, similar to dill and anise. Interchangeable with fronds from Florence fennel. Used in raw and cooked dishes. Add fresh fronds at the end of cooking. Favorite for Scandinavian breads, cakes, and cookies. Also good to cut the oiliness of some fish; especially good in fish soup, salads and salad dressings, and with vegetables.
❖ Grows outdoors.

Hyssop

Pungent, with a minty taste. Flower buds have a more delicate taste than the leaves and can be sprinkled in salads. Use flowers for garnish and young leaves in both fresh and fruit salads.
❖ Grows outdoors and is also a decorative garden plant. Fresh sprigs are available in some specialty markets.

Lavender

Has a fresh, clean scent excellent for sachets and potpourris. Also good added judiciously to *herbes de Provence*, fruit, fruit drinks, and iced tea.
❖ Best grown outdoors, but will grow indoors. Fresh sprigs and dried whole leaves available in specialty markets.

Lovage

Has a sharp celery taste. Use sparingly in salads, stock, or soup.
❖ Grows outdoors. Fresh sprigs available in specialty markets.

Marjoram

First cousin to oregano, with a similar but more delicate taste. Use in almost any fish, meat, poultry, egg, or vegetable dish, and in tomato sauce. Add fresh at the end of cooking.
❖ Grows indoors and out. Available as fresh sprigs, dried whole or crumbled leaves.

Oregano

Herb with a pungent, more intense marjoram taste; often used in pizza and some tomato sauces. An essential herb for Italian, Greek, and Mediterranean cooking. Use with fish, meat, poultry, dried beans, cheese, eggs, tomatoes, mushrooms, peppers, summer squash, and eggplant and in vegetable soup.

❧ Grows indoors and out. Available as fresh sprigs, dried whole leaves, crumbled dried and ground.

Rosemary

Needlelike leaves with strong piny scent and flavor. To release the flavor, finely chop fresh leaves and crush dry ones. Best with game, poultry, and meats, especially grilled. Add judiciously to mushrooms, roasted potatoes, stuffing, olive oil, breads and buns, and ripe melon.

❧ Best grown outdoors, but will grow indoors. Available as fresh sprigs, whole dried, and crumbled dried.

Sage

Herb with a musky, slightly mentholated flavor. Dried sage has a more powerful flavor than fresh. Aids digestion when mixed with fatty foods.

Excellent and best known for poultry stuffing. Use judiciously with chicken, duck, goose, pork, sausages, cheese, eggplant, and dried bean stews and soups.

❧ Outdoors, silver-green leaves make it a decorative garden plant; also grows indoors. Available as fresh sprigs, dried whole leaves, crumbled, dried, and ground.

Tarragon

Herb with a mild licorice flavor. French tarragon is the subtlest, with anise flavor. Best with chicken, veal, fish, shellfish, and eggs, with tomatoes, mushrooms, and carrots, and in mayonnaise and salad dressings.

❧ Grows indoors and out. Look for fresh sprigs, dried whole leaves and crumbled dried.

Thyme

Herb with tiny leaves and minty, tealike flavor. Many varieties include lemon, orange, English, and French thyme. Essential herb of the *bouquet garni*. Excellent with fish and shellfish, poultry, tomatoes, beans, eggplant, mushrooms, potatoes, and summer squash.

❧ Grows indoors and out. Available as fresh sprigs, dried whole leaves, and crumbled dried.

Winter Savory

A peppery herb with two varieties—winter and summer. Summer is more delicate and best suited for most cooking; winter is stronger and spicier. It is also excellent in meat loaf, meatballs, and sausages; with poultry, cheese, eggs, cauliflower, tomatoes, and onion.

❧ Summer savory grows indoors and out; winter, outdoors. Available as fresh sprigs, dried whole leaves and crumbled dried.

tarragon · fennel · borage · chives · rosemary · sage · oregano · bay · peppermint · cinnamon mint · spearmint · opal basil · applemint · basil · thyme · lemon thyme · summer savory · chervil

Planting an Herb Garden

An herb garden is magic. It stimulates and soothes, quickening the senses while quieting the world. Most of all, fresh herbs have become such an integral part of our cooking we can't imagine doing without the silvery patchwork of scents, tastes, and textures just outside the back door.

Herbs are the most undemanding of plants. In most of the world they grow wild and, without care, literally like weeds.

In your own garden, they're easy to grow; they're not terribly fussy about soil and need infrequent watering. They'll repay your minimal efforts with great pleasure, both in adding beauty to the landscape and in the serendipity of snipping herbs from your own garden as you cook.

While herbs can withstand casual neglect, the more care and attention they are given, the more they will flourish.

With their origins in warmer climes, most herbs need the maximum of sunshine during the growing season, approximately 7 hours a day. A wall, hedge, or natural slope will provide good shelter from cold winds.

The more you pinch, the sturdier and fuller your herb plants will be. And there are those who insist a little pleasant conversation doesn't hurt either.

Tips for Cooking with Herbs

❖ Pick early in the day, just after the dew dries, for juicier, more aromatic and more nutritious herbs.

❖ Buy fresh herbs in small quantities unless you're planning to freeze or preserve them in oil.

❖ Always snip herbs with scissors.

❖ Gently wash herbs and pat them dry, or let them drip dry.

❖ Strip the leaves from the stems of thickly stemmed herbs. Mince, snip, chop, pound, tear, chiffonade, or use whole.

❖ Don't combine too many different herbs and spices in one dish or you will confuse the palate.

❖ Use fresh herbs by the handful. Forget herb flavor charts—trust your own taste.

❖ If while cooking you're uncertain about what or how much herbs to use, separate a bit of your dish and add the herb a little at a time. Taste, and proceed accordingly.

❖ Place clean herb sprigs or edible flowers in ice trays and add distilled water. Freeze and serve with sangria, iced tea, lemonade, spritzers, or just your favorite mineral water.

❖ Make herbed oils and vinegars when you have a good harvest. You'll be happy to have them in the fall and winter.

❖ Herbs are decorative in baskets, pots, and pitchers. Use them as table decorations, and their aromas will waft throughout the house.

❖ Use herbs in your recipe as you cook or marinate. Then add fresh herbs at the last minute for added dimension.

❖ Rub herbs into meat, fish and poultry before cooking.

❖ Vary a pesto recipe with herb and nut combinations. Tarragon with pecans, shallots, and hazelnuts; dill, garlic, and almonds; rosemary, parsley, garlic, and pecans; oregano, parsley, and walnuts.

❖ The flavor of the herb is in the stem as well as the leaves. Use fresh herb stems in preparing soups, stocks, and long-simmering sauces. The stems will deliver flavor, but because they have less chlorophyll, they won't tint the dish green.

Drying Herbs

❖ To dry fresh herbs in a microwave oven, first wash and air-dry them. Then place them on paper towels and cook at 100° for 4 minutes. If they are still moist, turn them and cook to dry a few more minutes. This is an excellent method to retain color and flavor.

❖ Buy dried herbs in small quantities and store them in small opaque or green glass jars in a dark, cool spot for 4 to 6 months.

❖ Dried and fresh herbs may be used interchangeably in most recipes, but dried are more intense than fresh. Use 3 to 5 times more fresh herbs than dried, depending on the natural strength of the herb.

❖ Let dried herbs soak in salad dressing for 15 minutes to an hour before tossing with your greens.

❖ Tie bunches of herbs and name tags together with raffia to use as place cards.

Out of the garden

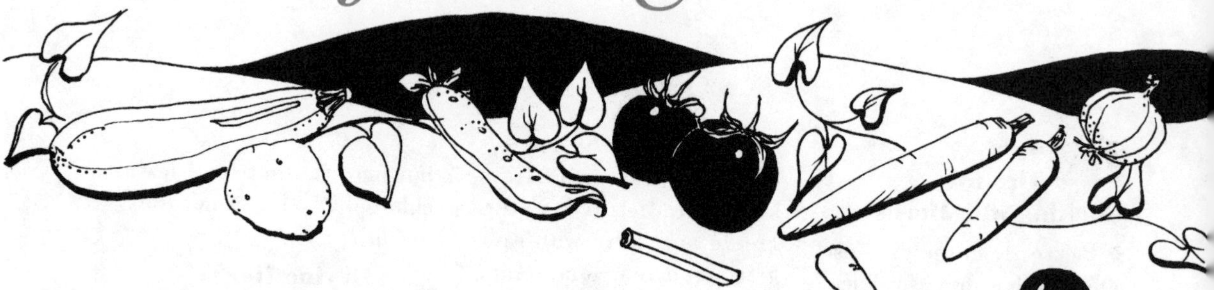

Glazed Vegetable Wreath

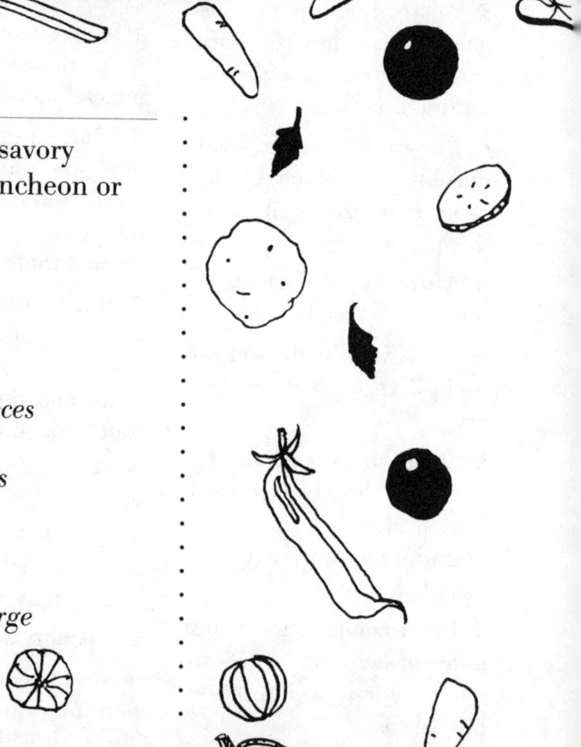

The best of summer's vegetables atop a ring of savory choux (cream puff pastry). This is a fabulous luncheon or light supper dish.

SERVES 6

$\frac{1}{2}$ cup plus $1\frac{1}{2}$ tablespoons all-purpose flour
$\frac{1}{8}$ teaspoon salt
$\frac{3}{4}$ teaspoon freshly ground pepper
4 tablespoons ($\frac{1}{2}$ stick) unsalted butter, cut in pieces
2 eggs
$\frac{1}{2}$ cup plus 1 tablespoon finely minced fresh chives
2 cups chicken broth (see Basics)
1 tablespoon olive oil
1 cup small pearl onions, peeled
2 cups baby carrots, scrubbed and cut in half if large
1 cup tiny new potatoes, scrubbed
1 pound young string beans, cut in 2-inch lengths
2 small zucchini, scrubbed and thinly sliced
1 pound sugar snap peas or 1 pound fresh peas, shelled
1 pint perfectly ripe cherry tomatoes, washed and stemmed
2 tablespoons shredded fresh basil
Salt and freshly ground pepper
Additional basil leaves

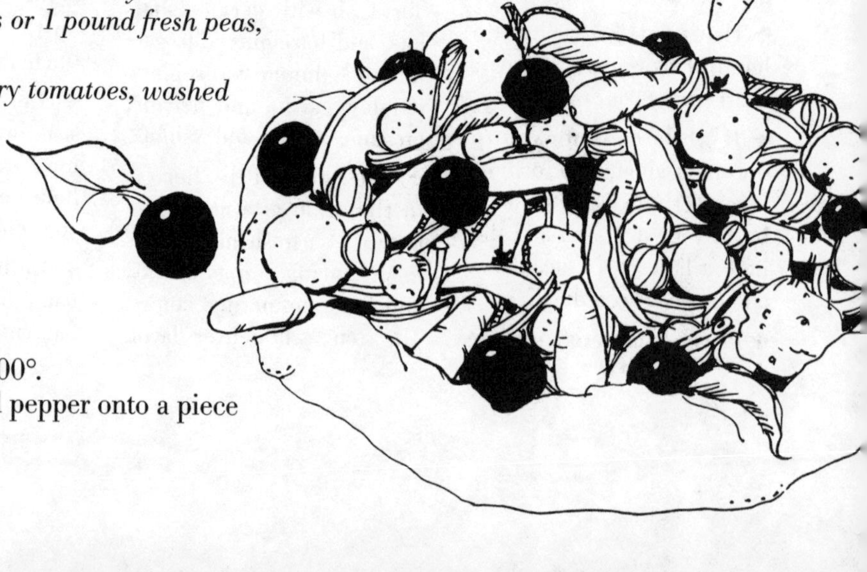

1. Preheat the oven to 400°.
2. Sift the flour, salt, and pepper onto a piece of waxed paper.

164

3. In a medium saucepan with a heavy bottom, combine ⅔ cup of boiling water and the butter. Stir until the butter melts, and return to a boil.

4. Remove the saucepan from the heat and immediately beat in the flour mixture all at once, using a wooden spoon. Return the pan to medium-high heat and stir constantly until the mixture leaves the sides of the saucepan and a thin film of flour forms on the bottom of the pan.

5. Remove the saucepan from the heat and beat in the eggs, one at a time, making sure the first egg is well incorporated before adding the second. Stir in the chives.

6. Lightly spray or wipe a baking sheet with vegetable oil. Place spoonfuls of pastry, ¾ to 1 teaspoon each, onto the greased baking sheet to form six 3-inch circles, or one large 10-inch circle. The spoonfuls should just touch each other so that they bake into a neat ring. Bake for about 35 minutes, or until the pastry is well risen and golden brown. Don't peek during the first 20 minutes or the pastry might sink. Remove from the oven and transfer to a wire rack to cool.

7. In a large skillet, bring the chicken broth and olive oil to a boil. Cook each vegetable in order until tender, beginning with the onions and carrots, which need the most cooking time, and ending with the sugar snaps and tomatoes, which only need about 30 seconds. As each vegetable is cooked, re-move it with a slotted spoon to a heated bowl and keep warm. If there is any chicken broth remaining, reduce it to 1 table-spoon and add it to the vegetables. Fold in the 1 tablespoon of chives, basil, salt, and freshly ground pepper to taste.

8. To serve, place a ring on each of six plates, and spoon the vegetables into the centers; the rings should appear to be bountifully overflowing with vegetables. Garnish with addi-tional basil leaves and serve immediately.

*Cal. **290** Carb. **36g** Protein **9g** Chol. **82mg** Fat **13g/39%***

By law, "Certified Organic" on a label means the farm of origin has used no chemicals for a year or more. Such a claim must be verified by state agricultural officials or private inspectors.

When you choose organic produce, you help to reduce pesticides and fungicides in the ecosystem.

AND THE BEET GOES ON

Orange Beets

Beets' robust color and taste, with the sweet-tart tang of orange dressing.

SERVES 4

1 pound baby beets, trimmed, leaving 1 inch of stem, and rinsed
$1/2$ cup fresh orange juice
2 tablespoons fresh lemon juice
1 tablespoon extra-virgin olive oil
$1/8$ teaspoon ground cloves
Freshly ground pepper

1. Place the beets in a medium-size saucepan; cover with water and bring to a boil. Reduce the heat and simmer until the beets are tender, 20 to 25 minutes. Rinse the beets under cold water, drain, and slip off the skins. Slice the beets into $1/4$-inch-thick rounds and place in a medium bowl.

2. In a small bowl, combine the remaining ingredients. Pour over the beets and refrigerate for at least 3 hours.

Cal. 95 Carb. 15g Protein 2g Chol. 0mg Fat 4g/33%

Mustard Beets

SERVES 4

1 pound baby beets, trimmed, leaving 1 inch of stem, and rinsed
1 cup plain nonfat yogurt
1 tablespoon low-fat sour cream
3 teaspoons Dijon mustard

1. Prepare the beets according to the instructions in step 1 of Orange Beets (left).

2. In a small bowl, combine the remaining ingredients; cover and refrigerate for at least 2 hours.

3. Just before serving, gently stir the yogurt mixture into the beets, just until soft pink swirls form. Do not overmix.

Cal. 75 Carb. 12g Protein 4g Chol. 1mg Fat 2g/19%

Honey-Pepper Beets

SERVES 4

1 pound baby beets, trimmed, leaving 1 inch of stem, and rinsed
$1/4$ cup cider vinegar
$1/4$ cup honey
1 tablespoon mustard seeds
$1/4$ teaspoon crushed red pepper flakes
1 cup thinly sliced onion

1. Prepare the beets according to the instructions in step 1 of Orange Beets (left).

2. In a small bowl, combine the remaining ingredients except the onion. Pour over the beets and onion and toss thoroughly. Refrigerate for at least 3 hours before serving.

Cal. 127 Carb. 30g Protein 2g Chol. 0mg Fat 1g/6%

Cassis Beets

SERVES 4

1 pound baby beets, trimmed leaving 1 inch of stem, and rinsed

$\frac{1}{2}$ cup fresh orange juice

3 tablespoons white wine vinegar

2 tablespoons currant jelly

1 tablespoon light brown sugar

1 tablespoon crème de cassis (optional)

1 teaspoon poppy seeds

1. Prepare the beets according to the instructions in step 1 of Orange Beets (page 166).

2. In a large saucepan, combine the orange juice, vinegar, jelly, and sugar. Place over medium-low heat and stir until the jelly and sugar are completely dissolved. Increase the heat, bring the sauce to a boil, and reduce to $\frac{1}{4}$ cup. Remove the sauce from the heat and stir in the cassis, poppy seeds, and beets. Serve immediately or cool to room temperature.

*Cal. **94** Carb. **21g** Protein **2g** Chol. **0mg** Fat **1g/5%***

Baby Beets with Caraway

SERVES 4

1 pound baby beets, trimmed, leaving 1 inch of stem, and rinsed

1 teaspoon horseradish

1 tablespoon caraway seeds

$1\frac{1}{4}$ cups Low-Fat Blend (see Basics)

1. Prepare the beets according to the instructions in step 1 of Orange Beets (page 166).

2. Place the whole beets in a medium-size bowl. Add the horseradish, caraway seeds, and Low-Fat Blend; mix thoroughly. Cover and refrigerate for 1 to 4 hours.

*Cal. **75** Carb. **12g** Protein **4g** Chol. **1mg** Fat **2g/19%***

The Beet Goes On... and On...and On...

With a bit of:

Orange juice & zest

Minced tarragon

Ground cloves

Lemon juice & zest

Sliced red onion

Chopped walnuts

Minced dill

Caraway seeds

Balsamic vinegar

Ginger

Grainy mustard

Cardamom

White-wine dressing

Honey mustard

Maple syrup

Chopped pecans

Minced thyme

Chopped fennel & fronds

Raspberry vinegar

Coriander & cilantro

Lemon juice & cloves

Crumbled chèvre

Horseradish & cider vinegar

Red onion & Rosy Beet Dip

Balsamico Beets and Greens

SERVES 4

1/4 cup balsamic vinegar

1 tablespoon extra-virgin olive oil

2 teaspoons sugar

1/4 teaspoon Dijon mustard

12 ounces baby beets, trimmed, peeled, and thinly sliced

1 teaspoon canola oil

2 garlic cloves, minced

8 cups loosely packed beet greens, washed and drained, with
water left clinging to the leaves

2 tablespoons fresh lemon juice

Freshly ground sea salt

Freshly ground pepper

1. In a small bowl, whisk the vinegar, olive oil, sugar, and mustard. Toss with the beets and marinate at room temperature for at least 1 hour.

2. In a large skillet, heat the oil over medium heat. Add the garlic and sauté for 1 minute. Add the greens, lemon juice, and salt and pepper to taste. Cook for 2 to 3 minutes, stirring well. Cover and cook until the greens are wilted, about 5 minutes.

3. Divide the hot greens among four salad plates and top with the beets and vinaigrette. Serve immediately.

Cal. **108** *Carb.* **16g** *Protein* **3g** *Chol.* **0mg** *Fat* **5g/36%**

Snappy Beets and Greens

SERVES 4

1 1/2 pounds very young, tiny beets, greens attached

1 teaspoon olive oil

4 garlic cloves, slivered

3 tablespoons minced red onion

1 tablespoon balsamic vinegar

1/2 cup chicken broth (see Basics)

1/3 cup nonfat plain yogurt

2 tablespoons horseradish

Freshly ground pink, black, or white peppercorns

1. Wash the beets and greens carefully to remove all traces of sand and dirt, but do not separate them. Set aside to drain.

2. Heat the oil in a very large skillet over medium-high heat.

Beets come in robust shapes, from squat to ovoid to long and turnip-shaped. They range in size—from as big as a baseball to petitely quarter-sized—and colors: red, golden-yellow, white, and the cherry-red-skinned Chioggia, which has a candy-striped inner core.

Cook beets separately from other vegetables and from each other when mixing varieties. The red dye—betacyanin—leaches into cooking water, but a dash of vinegar or lemon juice in the water may help.

Look for beets year-round, with the peak from June through October. In the market, choose firm beets with smooth skins and deep green leaves that aren't wilted.

To store, remove the tops—the leaves and most of the stem. Refrigerate, unwashed, in a plastic bag for up to a week. Cook the greens or use very young ones in salads.

> ★ **GOOD FOR YOU** ★
>
> Beets are a good source of potassium and vitamins C and A, and deliver about 55 calories per cup.

Add the garlic and onion and sauté until they begin to soften. Add the vinegar and chicken broth and bring to a boil.

3. Add the beet greens; cover the skillet and cook for 3 to 4 minutes, shaking the pan, until the greens are wilted and the beets are tender-crisp when pierced with the tip of a sharp knife.

4. Meanwhile, in a small bowl, whisk the yogurt and horseradish. Add a liberal grinding of peppercorns to taste. Whisk in 1 to 2 tablespoons of the cooking juices from the beets; adjust all seasonings to taste.

5. To serve, divide the greens and beets on individual plates. Spoon on a little sauce and serve immediately.

*Cal. **52** Carb. **8g** Protein **3g** Chol. **1mg** Fat **1g/21%***

ROASTING BEETS

Roasting beets in the oven intensifies their flavor and sweetens them beautifully, retaining more of their nutrients. In French markets you can buy them fully roasted, ready to eat.

Baby Beets with Ginger

SERVES 4

1½ pounds baby beets, peeled and trimmed
1 sprig fresh lemon thyme or regular thyme
1 sprig fresh Italian parsley
Three 2-inch strips orange peel
¼ cup plus 1 teaspoon red wine vinegar
¼ cup sugar
3 tablespoons coarsely chopped crystallized ginger
Salt and freshly ground pepper

1. Cut any larger beets in half, so that all the beets are of uniform size.

2. Tie the thyme, parsley, and orange peel together with a string or in a piece of cheesecloth to make a *bouquet garni*.

3. In a medium-size saucepan, place the beets, 2 cups of water, ¼ cup vinegar, sugar, *bouquet garni*, and crystallized ginger. Bring to a boil over high heat. Reduce the heat and simmer until the beets are tender, about 1 hour, stirring occasionally. Remove the *bouquet garni* and discard.

4. Remove the beets with a slotted spoon to a serving dish, leaving the sauce in the pan. Add the remaining vinegar to the pan to deglaze it, scraping down the sides. Taste and adjust seasoning with salt and pepper. Spoon the sauce over the beets and serve immediately.

*Cal. **128** Carb. **32g** Protein **2g** Chol. **0mg** Fat **.2g/1%***

Farm Stand

Buy direct from local farmers for the freshest, tastiest, and cheapest produce available. But be careful: Some stands hawk the same nonlocal produce you'll find in the supermarket. And some may be as exclusive—and expensive— as the fanciest in-city specialty food store.

BUNCHES OF BEANS

Farmers' Market Beans

When these three summer beans appear in the market at the same time, I can't resist roasting them together. Yet each retains a nutty flavor all its own.

SERVES 12

2 pounds fresh green beans
2 pounds fresh yellow wax beans
1 pound fresh cranberry beans, shelled
2 tablespoons olive oil
2 tablespoons balsamic vinegar
1 teaspoon coarse salt
Freshly ground pepper
4 tablespoons finely minced garlic
¼ cup coarsely chopped fresh tarragon

1. Preheat the oven to 400°.
2. Snap the ends off the green and wax beans. Wash all the beans and pat them dry.
3. In a shallow roasting pan, place the beans in a single layer. Sprinkle with the oil, vinegar, and salt and pepper to taste, and bake for 15 to 20 minutes, until the beans are tender and lightly browned. Remove the beans to a large bowl and toss with the garlic and tarragon; adjust seasoning. Serve warm or at room temperature.

Cal. **198** *Carb.* **35g** *Protein* **12g** *Chol.* **0mg** *Fat* **3g/12%**

Three-Bean Salad

SERVES 4

½ pound fresh green beans, rinsed and trimmed
½ pound fresh yellow beans, rinsed and trimmed
½ pound fresh purple beans, rinsed and trimmed
12 fresh thyme sprigs
½ cup champagne vinegar
2 tablespoons extra-virgin olive oil
1 tablespoon minced fresh Italian parsley
1 tablespoon Dijon mustard
2 teaspoons sugar

**Beans Show
Their Colors**
★
Green "String"
Beans
★
Kentucky Wonder
★
Blue Lake
★
Yellow Wax
★
Broad Beans
★
Fava Beans
★
Cranberry Beans

170

1 teaspoon cracked black pepper
1 garlic clove, minced

1. In a large pot over high heat, bring 2 quarts of water to a boil. Add all of the beans and blanch for 1 to 2 minutes, or until the beans are tender yet crisp. Drain the beans in a colander and rinse immediately under cold water. Drain again.

2. Place the beans and thyme in a shallow serving dish.

3. In a small bowl, whisk the remaining ingredients together. Pour the vinaigrette over the beans and toss to coat the beans evenly. Cover and marinate at room temperature for 1 hour before serving. (The beans will lose some of the vibrancy of their color the longer they marinate.)

Cal. 84 Carb. 16g Protein 4g Chol. 0mg Fat 2g/18%

Green Beans & Roasted Peppers

SERVES 4
8 ounces red, yellow, or purple bell peppers
1½ pounds green beans
1 tablespoon olive oil
2 tablespoons fresh lemon juice
2 teaspoons Dijon mustard
1 tablespoon minced fresh basil
1 tablespoon minced fresh chives
1 tablespoon minced fresh parsley

1. Preheat the broiler.

2. Place the bell peppers on a baking sheet under the broiler. Broil about 2 inches from the burner, turning until the skins are blistered and charred all over, 2 to 4 minutes. Remove the peppers from the oven, place them in a brown paper bag, and seal tightly. Allow the peppers to steam in the bags for 20 to 30 minutes. Remove from the bag, peel away the skins, and discard the seeds. Slice the peppers into long thin strips. Cover and refrigerate.

3. Steam the green beans until tender but still crisp, 3 to 5 minutes. Remove from the heat and run under cold water. Drain and set aside.

4. In a small bowl, whisk the olive oil, lemon juice, mustard, basil, chives, and parsley. Pour over the beans, toss well, and let marinate for 1 to 4 hours in the refrigerator.

5. Divide the peppers among four salad plates. Place the marinated green beans over the peppers and serve.

Cal. 80 Carb. 16g Protein 4g Chol. 0mg Fat 1g/11%

Lima Beans
★
Haricots Verts
★
Pole Beans
★
Scarlet Runner
Beans
★
French Beans
★
Wax Beans
★
Snap Beans
★
Romano
★
Chinese Long Beans

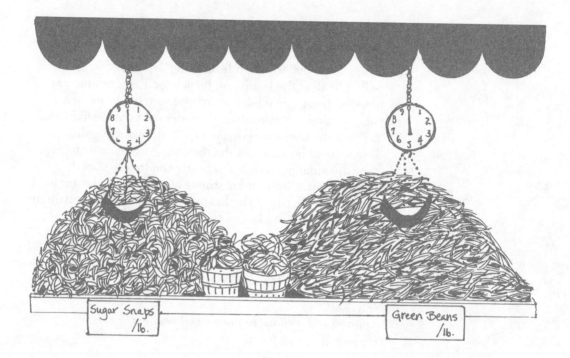

Walnut Haricots Verts

SERVES 4

12 ounces haricots verts *or young, thin green beans, trimmed*
2 teaspoons walnut oil
¼ cup toasted and finely chopped walnuts
2 teaspoons fresh lemon juice
Freshly ground pepper

1. To cook the beans follow step 2 in Pesto Haricots Verts (page 173).
2. In a medium-size serving dish, combine the warm *haricots verts* with the reserved water, walnut oil, walnuts, and lemon juice. Season with pepper and serve immediately.
Cal. **96** *Carb.* **8g** *Protein* **3g** *Chol.* **0mg** *Fat* **7g/60%** ℀

Blue Haricots Verts

SERVES 4

1 pound haricots verts *or young, thin green beans, trimmed*
2 tablespoons blue cheese or Roquefort, crumbled
Freshly ground pepper

1. To cook the beans follow step 2 in Pesto Haricots Verts (page 173).
2. In a medium-size serving dish, combine the warm *haricots verts* with the reserved water and the blue cheese. Toss gently. Season with the pepper and serve immediately.
Cal. **57** *Carb.* **6g** *Protein* **3g** *Chol.* **6mg** *Fat* **3g/37%** ℀

Chèvre Haricots Verts

SERVES 4

1 pound haricots verts *or young, thin green beans, trimmed*
1 tablespoon minced fresh dill
2 tablespoons fresh lemon juice
3 tablespoons goat cheese
Freshly ground pepper

1. To cook the beans follow step 2 in Pesto Haricots Verts (page 173).
2. In a medium-size serving bowl, combine the reserved water, dill, lemon juice, goat cheese, and pepper. Stir in the *haricots verts* and toss. Serve immediately.
Cal. **61** *Carb.* **7g** *Protein* **4g** *Chol.* **7mg** *Fat* **3g/36%** ℀

172

Pesto Haricots Verts

SERVES 4

1/4 cup Broccoli Pesto
(page 48)
3 tablespoons balsamic
vinegar
1 pound haricots verts or
young, thin green beans,
trimmed

1. In a food processor, process the Broccoli Pesto and balsamic vinegar until smooth. Scrape the pesto into a small bowl and set aside.
2. Pour 1 inch of water into a large stockpot; place a collapsible steamer into the pot. Cover and bring the water to a boil over medium-high heat. Place the beans in the steamer, cover, and steam for 5 minutes, or until tender-crisp.
3. Transfer the cooked beans to a shallow serving bowl. Add the pesto and toss to coat the beans evenly. Serve hot or at room temperature.

*Cal. 53 Carb. 9g Protein 3g
Chol. .6mg Fat 1g/21%*

Tricolor Beans

SERVES 4

1/2 pound green beans
1/2 pound yellow beans
1/2 pound purple beans
1 tablespoon canola oil
1 teaspoon minced fresh
rosemary
1 tablespoon minced fresh
sage
1/2 cup minced fresh Italian
parsley
1 tablespoon minced lemon
zest
4 garlic cloves, finely minced
Freshly ground pepper

1. In a large skillet over medium heat, place about 1/2-inch of water. If the beans are large, snap them in half. Place all the beans in the skillet and steam for 2 to 3 minutes, until just tender. Drain and refresh under cold water.
2. In a small bowl, combine the remaining ingredients and mix well.
3. In a large bowl, place the beans and pour the dressing over; toss to coat evenly. Serve warm or at room temperature.

*Cal. 93 Carb. 14g Protein 4g
Chol. 0mg Fat 4g/32%*

★ GOOD FOR YOU ★

Green beans are a good source of iron, vitamin C, potassium, fiber, and carbohydrates. Hidden by their green chlorophyll is a healthy dose of beta-carotene, making them a good source of vitamin A. Serve raw, or steam just until crisp to preserve most of their benefits.

Eggplant Parmesan

A summer event, boldly topped with basil, garlic, and Parmesan.

SERVES 4

2 small eggplants (about 1¼ pounds each)
Freshly ground sea salt
Freshly ground pepper
⅓ cup seasoned bread crumbs
¼ cup freshly grated Parmesan
3 tablespoons finely minced fresh basil
2 tablespoons finely minced fresh parsley
3 garlic cloves, finely minced
2 teaspoons unsalted butter

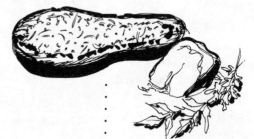

1. Preheat the oven to 500°. Lightly spray or wipe a baking sheet with vegetable oil.
2. Trim the tops of each eggplant and slice in half lengthwise. Make two deep lengthwise slashes into the flesh of each half, being careful not to cut through the skin. Season with salt and pepper to taste. Place the halves on the baking sheet, flesh sides down. Bake for 15 to 20 minutes, until the eggplants are tender and the skin is shriveled.
3. Meanwhile, in a small bowl, combine the bread crumbs, cheese, basil, and parsley. Set aside.
4. Remove the eggplant from the oven, and turn flesh sides up. Sprinkle each half first with garlic and then with the bread-crumb mixture. Dot with butter.
5. Place under the broiler for 1 to 2 minutes, until golden and bubbly. Remove and serve immediately.

*Cal. **160** Carb. **25g** Protein **7g** Chol. **10mg** Fat **5g/25%***

> ### ★ GOOD FOR YOU ★
> Anyone who has ever cooked with eggplant knows this: It soaks up fat and oil very quickly. Fortunately, it does the same thing in your body, which helps to eliminate cholesterol before it gets to the bloodstream. Eggplant's also one of the foods eaten most often by populations with a low rate of stomach cancer.

Eggplant Balsamico

Eggplant topped with the vivid flavors of tomato paste, balsamic vinegar, and basil.

SERVES 4

2 small eggplants (about 1¼ pounds each)
Freshly ground sea salt
Freshly ground pepper

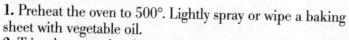

Eggplant

Round, oblong, big, small, white, purple, green; streaked with pink, orange, lavender; mottled or black.

Cooks know that beneath their skin, most eggplants taste pretty much the same. When choosing eggplants, the most important consideration is freshness.

Eggplant hails from India, a member of the deadly nightshade family and kin to potatoes, bell peppers, tomatoes, tobacco, and any number of poisonous plants.

Once exposed to the air, eggplant flesh tends to discolor. Cut eggplants with a stainless-steel blade and mash them when cooked with a wooden utensil. Raw eggplant is spongy and can absorb enormous amounts of oil in cooking. But the best texture and taste are achieved with just a touch of fat. Spray or wipe eggplant slices very lightly with oil and cook at a high heat, rather than putting more oil than is needed into the pan first.

As to the conventional wisdom that salting draws out bitterness and excess moisture from eggplants—don't bother, I say. Eggplant has changed over the years through hybridization, and excessive bitterness seems to have been bred out. I roast, grill, or pan-cook it right away and usually include the skin for added color and flavor.

¹/₃ cup tomato paste
¹/₃ cup balsamic vinegar
1¹/₂ tablespoons sugar
¹/₄ cup finely minced fresh basil
4 sprigs fresh thyme

1. Roast eggplant as in Eggplant Parmesan (opposite), following steps 1 and 2.
2. Meanwhile, in a small bowl, combine the tomato paste, vinegar, sugar, and basil, stirring until the sugar has dissolved. Set aside.
3. Remove the eggplant from the oven, and turn flesh side up. Spread each half with the mixture and top each with a sprig of thyme.
4. Place under the broiler for 1 to 2 minutes until golden and bubbly. Serve immediately.

Cal. 105 Carb. 26g Protein 4g Chol. 0mg Fat .6g/5%

Pesto Eggplant

SERVES 4
2 small eggplants (about 1¹/₄ pounds each)
Freshly ground sea salt
Freshly ground pepper
5 tablespoons Broccoli Pesto (page 48)
3 tablespoons minced sun-dried tomato
3 tablespoons freshly grated Parmesan

1. Roast the eggplant as in Eggplant Parmesan (opposite), following steps 1 and 2.
2. Remove the eggplant from the oven and turn flesh side up. Spread each half with pesto and sprinkle with sun-dried tomato and Parmesan.
3. Place under the broiler for 1 to 2 minutes, until bubbly. Remove and serve immediately.

Cal. 108 Carb. 17g Protein 6g Chol. 4mg Fat 3g/22%

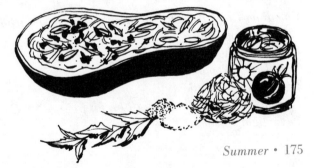

Zucchini Blossom Pasta

Delicate zucchini and zucchini blossoms melt into a wonderful and most beautiful pasta sauce.

SERVES 6

36 zucchini blossoms, of various sizes
1 pound linguine
2 tablespoons olive oil or chicken broth
2 teaspoons unsalted butter
2 ounces prosciutto, or Canadian bacon trimmed of fat
1 cup ½-inch zucchini, chunks
6 garlic cloves, minced
½ cup finely chopped fresh Italian parsley
2 tablespoons finely minced fresh chives
Pinch saffron
Salt and freshly ground pepper

1. Carefully detach the pistils and stamen from inside the blossoms; remove the stems. Wash the blossoms in cold water and pat dry. Cook the linguine according to the package directions.

2. In a large skillet over medium heat, melt the oil and butter. Add the prosciutto, zucchini, garlic, parsley, and chives, and sauté for 2 minutes.

3. In a small bowl, place 2 tablespoons of the juices from the skillet, and add the saffron. Add to the skillet with the blossoms, and cook until the juices reduce, 3 to 5 minutes. Season with salt and pepper and serve over the hot pasta.

*Cal. **419** Carb. **70g** Protein **16g** Chol. **13mg** Fat **9g/20%***

Stuffed Zucchini Boats

SERVES 4

4 medium (6- to 8- inch) zucchini, scrubbed and trimmed
1 teaspoon olive oil
4 scallions, chopped
6 garlic cloves, minced
3 garlic cloves, crushed
1 pound lean ground turkey (99% fat free)
1 egg, lightly beaten

Zucchini Blossoms

These mild orange-yellow blossoms have a subtle flavor that's hard to describe. They're best when captured young and tender.

Female blossoms grow at the end of the baby squash, open briefly, and then stay closed. The more showy male blossoms grow directly from the stem. Use both. I like to mix them.

Pick zucchini blossoms as soon as they open, while still dewy and fresh. (Separate them carefully from the squash and it will continue to grow.) Handling them gently, trim away the green stem and pinch out the stamen and pistils. Rinse gently with cool water and drain upside down. If you're not using the blossoms right away, wrap them in paper towels and refrigerate immediately. They'll keep a day or two. Can't find any in your own garden? Many local farmers' markets have them. You may also find tiny blossoms still attached to small zucchinis.

Zucchini Fritters

Frying is an occasional indulgence, and such dishes should always be monitored. In this case, the fat percentage is skewed even higher because the calories are so low.

SERVES 8

2 cups shredded zucchini
1/2 cup shredded leek
2 tablespoons grated imported Parmesan
1/2 cup fresh bread crumbs, lightly toasted
1/4 cup finely chopped fresh Italian parsley
2 tablespoons finely chopped fresh mint
1 egg
1 egg white
Salt and freshly ground pepper
1 tablespoon olive oil

1. In a medium-size bowl, combine all of the ingredients except the olive oil. Shape into twenty-four 2-inch patties.
2. In a large nonstick skillet, heat the oil over medium-high heat. Sauté as many patties as fit comfortably into the skillet at a time; do not crowd them. Cook until nicely browned. Turn and brown the second side, about 4 minutes altogether. Remove to a heated platter and keep warm until the remaining fritters are cooked. Serve immediately.

Cal. 45 Carb. 3g

Protein 2g

Chol. 24mg

Fat 3g/56%

- 1/2 cup bread crumbs
- 2 tablespoons chopped fresh oregano
- 1/2 cup chopped fresh basil
- 2 tablespoons freshly grated imported Parmesan
- Salt and freshly ground pepper
- 3 1/2 cups Old-Fashioned Tomato Sauce (page 287) or other tomato sauce
- 1/2 teaspoon crushed red pepper flakes
- 1/4 cup coarsely chopped fresh Italian parsley

1. Slice the top third, lengthwise, from the zucchini and scoop out the pulp. Chop the pulp and set aside.
2. In a large skillet, heat 1 teaspoon of oil over medium-high heat. Add the scallion and minced garlic, and sauté for 3 minutes, stirring, until softened. Add the zucchini pulp and sauté 3 minutes longer. Drain the mixture in a colander. Preheat the oven to 350°.
3. In the same skillet, add the ground turkey. Sauté the turkey, breaking it up with a fork, until it is no longer pink. Add the turkey to the colander to drain.
4. In a large bowl, combine the zucchini mixture, the turkey, the egg, the bread crumbs, oregano, half the basil, and salt and pepper to taste; mix well. Spoon the stuffing into the zucchini boats.
5. In a heat- and ovenproof pan large enough to hold the zucchini boats, combine the sauce, crushed garlic, remaining basil, pepper flakes, parsley, and salt and pepper to taste.
6. Place the boats on the sauce and sprinkle with the Parmesan. Cover the pan tightly with foil and bake for 30 minutes. Uncover and bake for 20 minutes. Serve immediately.

Cal. 392 Carb. 41g Protein 47g Chol. 120mg Fat 7g/15%

Crackling Corn Bread

SERVES 12

1 cup coarsely ground yellow cornmeal
½ teaspoon salt
½ teaspoon baking soda
1 cup low-fat buttermilk
1 egg
1 cup fresh or frozen, thawed corn kernels
2 teaspoons olive oil
18 whole fresh sage leaves, or 1 to 2 tablespoons fresh rosemary

1. Preheat the oven to 450°.
2. In a medium-size bowl, combine the cornmeal, salt, and soda. In a small bowl, beat together the buttermilk and egg. Combine the buttermilk mixture with the cornmeal mixture with a few swift strokes; do not overbeat. Gently stir in the corn kernels.
3. Heat a 10-inch cast-iron skillet for 5 minutes in the oven. When the skillet is hot, add the oil and swirl to cover the bottom. Spread the sage leaves decoratively—to resemble sage leaves growing—in the bottom of the skillet, with the faces of the leaves facing down. Carefully spoon the batter into the pan, taking care not to disturb the leaves. Bake for 10 minutes, or until a knife inserted into the center comes out clean. Cool for 5 minutes in the pan. Place a rack over the skillet, turn the skillet over, and invert the bread onto the rack. Serve warm or at room temperature.

*Cal. **42** Carb. **6g** Protein **2g** Chol. **15mg** Fat **1g/28%***

Corn and Wild Rice Sauté

SERVES 4

1 ounce sun-dried tomatoes
1 teaspoon olive oil
2 garlic cloves, minced
2 shallots, minced
½ cup chicken broth (see Basics)
1 cup fresh corn kernels (about 2 ears)
2 cups cooked wild rice

"You may stroll to the garden to cut the corn... But you had darn well better run back to the kitchen to make it."

New England adage

Corn

Corn is *the* American grain, the very salvation of our earliest settlers, a gift of survival from Native Americans. So vital was it to the native peoples that the beginning of their year was set by its planting, the greatest feasts by its harvest. By some estimations, corn was the New World's most important contribution to the human diet.

4 plum tomatoes, chopped
3 tablespoons or more balsamic vinegar
Salt and freshly ground pepper
¼ cup coarsely chopped opal or regular basil

1. Steep the sun-dried tomatoes in 1 cup boiling water for 10 minutes. Drain, squeeze dry, and coarsely chop.

2. In a medium-size skillet, heat the oil over medium-high heat. Sauté the garlic and shallot until softened, about 2 minutes. Add the broth and corn and simmer for 2 minutes. Add the rice and tomatoes and heat through, about 4 minutes. Add 3 tablespoons of vinegar and salt and pepper to taste. Stir in the basil.

3. Serve warm or at room temperature. If serving at room temperature, taste after the dish sets, as additional vinegar may be needed; add it 1 teaspoon at a time.

*Cal. **161** Carb. **32g** Protein **6g** Chol. **1mg** Fat **3g/13%***

HOW SWEET IT IS: COOKING WITH CORN

How do you know when corn is done? When it's bright yellow and the juices are no longer milky if the kernels are pierced with a knife.

In a pot:

To boil, fill a large stockpot with 6 quarts of water; add a splash of skim milk and bring to a rapid boil. Add the cleaned ears, and when the water returns to a rapid boil, cover the pot and turn off the heat. Drain and serve after 5 minutes.

To steam, place a basket over boiling water in a pot. Place the cleaned ears in the basket; cover tightly. Cook for 10 to 15 minutes.

On the grill:

Pull back the husks and remove the silk. Replace the husks and tie closed with twine. Soak the ears in salted water for 15 minutes. Place the ears on the grill and cook until the husks are brown and the kernels are bright yellow, 15 to 20 minutes, depending on the size of the kernels, the freshness of the ears, and the intensity of the fire. Use the pulled-back husks as handles to hold on to the hot ears.

In the microwave oven:

Wrap the husks in wet paper towels. Cook for 4 minutes on high or according to the manu-facturer's directions. If the husks have not fallen off during cooking, let them cool for several minutes before husking. You will see that it is easier to remove the silk after the corn is cooked by this method.

An alternative: Wrap 4 husked ears of corn in plastic wrap. Cook for 4 minutes on high or according to the manufacturer's directions.

In the oven:

Preheat to 425°. Prepare the corn as for grilling. After soaking, place the ears in the oven and roast for about 20 minutes; the husks should be charred.

Black Bean and Corn Salad

SERVES 6

2 cups black beans, picked over and soaked overnight
1 green bell pepper, roasted, peeled, and sliced
1 red bell pepper, roasted, peeled, and sliced
2 cups chopped plum tomato
1 cup sliced scallion, green and white parts
1 cup fresh or frozen, thawed corn kernels
2 teaspoons cumin seeds
1 teaspoon coriander seeds
2 tablespoons sherry wine vinegar
½ tablespoon olive oil
2 tablespoons fresh lime juice
1 tablespoon grated lime zest
¼ teaspoon crushed red pepper flakes
Salt and freshly ground pepper
½ cup chopped fresh cilantro

1. Drain the beans and place them in a large stockpot; cover with water and bring to a boil. Cover and reduce the heat to a simmer. Cook the beans for 45 minutes to an hour and 15 minutes, or until just tender; do not overcook or they will be mushy. Drain and rinse in cold water. Place in a large bowl.
2. Add the peppers, tomato, scallion, and corn, and cover.
3. In a small cast-iron skillet, toast the cumin and coriander seeds over medium-high heat until fragrant. Pulverize the seeds to a powder in a spice grinder.
4. In a small bowl, whisk the vinegar and oil. Add the cumin, coriander, lime juice, lime zest, red pepper flakes, and salt and pepper to taste.
5. Pour the dressing over the beans and vegetables and stir to combine. Fold in the cilantro, cover, and set aside for 1 hour. Serve at room temperature.

Cal. **199** *Carb.* **37g** *Protein* **11g** *Chol.* **0mg** *Fat* **2g/9%**

Turkey-Corn Hash

SERVES 8

½ pound lean ground turkey (99% fat free)
2 garlic cloves, finely minced
2 teaspoons ground cumin
Cayenne
Salt and freshly ground pepper

Corn Is Bursting Out

Corn comes in fashion colors: white, yellow, red, purple, blue, brown, black, calico. Cobs range from 2-inch miniatures with tender edible cores to 2-foot giants. Historically, corn was important as a sustenance crop that could keep the human machine running.

Most contemporary corn lovers crave sweetness. The low-starch, high-sugar varieties popular today have been achieved through modern breeding. But remember that sugar converts rapidly to starch once the corn is picked; it is sweetest minutes after picking. Trying to capture that sweetness before it turns to starch endears us to the local farmers who grow Peaches 'N Cream—it has just the right sweetness, with a good corny taste. Some of the new super-sweet varieties offer twice the sugar and a slower sugar-to-starch conversion rate. Still, it makes me wonder: If corn is bred to be any sweeter, will it taste like corn anymore?

3 cups fresh corn kernels
¼ cup seeded and minced jalapeño pepper
3 tablespoons cornmeal
4 egg whites
½ cup finely chopped scallion
Tabasco or other pepper sauce

1. Preheat the oven to 425°.
2. Lightly wipe a 10-inch cast-iron skillet with vegetable oil. Place the skillet in the oven and heat for 20 minutes.
3. Meanwhile, in a large skillet over medium heat, sauté the turkey, breaking it up with a fork; add the garlic, cumin, cayenne, and salt and pepper to taste. Sauté until the turkey is no longer pink, 5 to 6 minutes. If there seems to be any excess fat at all, drain the mixture on paper towels. In a mixing bowl, combine the turkey mixture, corn, jalapeño pepper, cornmeal, egg whites, scallion, and Tabasco to taste.
4. Carefully remove the skillet from the oven. Carefully wipe away any burned oil, and oil again if necessary. Pour the turkey mixture into the pan, flatten it with a spatula, and bake for 15 minutes, or until set.
5. Gently run a flexible spatula around the edges to loosen the cake, and invert it onto a serving platter. Cut into wedges and serve immediately.

Cal. **115** *Carb.* **15g** *Protein* **12g** *Chol.* **22mg** *Fat* **1g/9%**

CORN TIP
Try not to store corn, but if you must, refrigerate it, in its husk, wrapped in plastic, and use it within 2 days.

Corn Custard

SERVES 4
2 cups fresh corn kernels
2 egg whites
½ cup low-fat buttermilk
1 tablespoon seeded and finely chopped jalapeño pepper
1 ounce grated white cheddar cheese
Salt and freshly ground pepper

1. Preheat the oven to 350°. Lightly wipe four 6-inch ramekins with vegetable oil.
2. In a blender, purée 1 cup of corn kernels, the egg whites, and the buttermilk until smooth. Transfer to a medium mixing bowl.
3. Add the remaining corn, jalapeño pepper, and cheese. Season with salt and pepper to taste.
4. Pour the mixture into the ramekins and bake for 30 minutes, or until the centers are set. Serve warm.

Cal. **114** *Carb.* **16g** *Protein* **7g** *Chol.* **7mg** *Fat* **3g/24%**

Fried Green Tomatoes

I think it was the movie that finally made me try these. Now I'm crazy for them. When the oil is good and hot, the cold milk keeps the tomatoes from absorbing oil and getting soggy.

SERVES 8

½ cup all-purpose flour
½ teaspoon freshly ground sea salt
½ teaspoon freshly ground pepper
2 tablespoons cold skim milk
3 tablespoons olive oil
4 green tomatoes, sliced ¼ inch thick
¼ cup minced fresh dill, chives, or basil
2 lemons, cut into wedges

1. In a small bowl, combine the flour, salt, and pepper. Pour the skim milk into another small bowl.
2. In a large skillet, heat the oil over medium heat.
3. Dip each tomato slice into the milk and then the flour. Fry the slices in the hot oil until golden, about 5 minutes, turning once or twice. Drain on paper towels.
4. Garnish with the dill and serve immediately with lemon.

Cal. **90** *Carb.* **9g** *Protein* **2g** *Chol.* **0mg** *Fat* **5g/52%** %

Green Tomato Mincemeat

YIELD: 9½ CUPS

3 pounds green tomatoes, coarsely chopped
1½ pounds tart apples, coarsely chopped, with skin
3⅓ packed cups light brown sugar
10 ounces currants
6 ounces dried cherries
1 cup cider vinegar
½ cup chopped crystallized ginger
2 oranges, sliced into ¼-inch-thick rounds, seeds removed
2 cinnamon sticks
1 teaspoon ground mace
1 teaspoon ground cloves

Green Tomatoes

The taste of green tomatoes is lovely, but let's not fool ourselves about their nutrition. Tomatoes allowed to ripen fully on the vine have more than twice the vitamins A and C than they do when they are young and green. (Yet a green tomato grown outdoors still has twice the vitamin C of a hothouse tomato.) But for a tart, crunchy treat early in the season or later, when early frost is coming—and at only 40 calories per medium tomato—why not?

1 teaspoon grated nutmeg
2 juniper berries, cracked

1. Place the tomatoes in a large stockpot and cover with water. Bring to a boil and blanch for 4 to 5 minutes. Drain.
2. Add all of the remaining ingredients. Mix well; bring to a boil over medium heat. Reduce the heat and simmer for 1½ hours, stirring occasionally.
3. Let the mincemeat cool. Remove the orange slices and cinnamon sticks and transfer to a covered container. Store in the refrigerator for up to 1 week.
NOTE: The mincemeat can be preserved in sterilized jars. Leave ¼ inch of headspace; seal and process according to the manufacturer's directions.

Cal. **96** *Carb.* **24g** *Protein* **1g** *Chol.* **0mg** *Fat* **.3g/3%**
(analyzed per ¼ cup)

Green Tomato Chutney

The sharp, clear flavor makes this one of my favorites. It's neither too cloying, nor too spicy—just the right condiment.

YIELD: 4 CUPS
5 juniper berries
4 whole cloves
4 cups coarsely diced green tomatoes
2 cups thinly sliced onion
2 cups coarsely chopped tart apples,
*   with skin*
¾ packed cup light brown sugar
½ cup golden raisins
¼ cup cider vinegar
2 tablespoons minced fresh ginger
1 garlic clove, minced

1. Tie the juniper berries and cloves together in a piece of cheesecloth. Place in a large stockpot with all of the remaining ingredients and ½ cup of water, and bring to a boil over medium heat. Reduce the heat and simmer until thick, about 1½ hours. Remove and discard the spice bag; taste and adjust the seasoning.
2. Cool the chutney at room temperature; cover and refrigerate. Serve warm or cold.

Cal. **67** *Carb.* **17g** *Protein* **1g** *Chol.* **0mg** *Fat* **.2g/2%**
(analyzed per ¼ cup)

...AND RED TOMATOES, TOO!

Tomato Tapenade

YIELD: 1 CUP

1 jar (8½ ounces) sun-dried tomatoes in oil, drained, oil reserved
12 anchovies, drained and patted dry
4 teaspoons finely chopped garlic
1 tablespoon capers, drained
2 teaspoons fresh lemon juice
4 tablespoons finely chopped fresh Italian parsley

1. Place the tomatoes, anchovies, garlic, capers, and lemon juice in a food processor, and process until smooth. With the machine running, add 4 tablespoons of the reserved oil in a slow, thin stream. Transfer to a mixing bowl, cover with plastic wrap, and refrigerate for at least 1 hour.
2. To serve, bring the tapenade to room temperature. Sprinkle with parsley and serve with toasted French bread.

Cal. 23 Carb. 1g Protein 1g Chol. 1mg Fat 2g/69% %
(analyzed per teaspoon)

Summer Tomato Pasta

SERVES 4

1 pound very ripe vine-ripened tomatoes, diced, skin on
6 large garlic cloves, finely minced
¼ cup finely minced fresh basil
2 tablespoons extra-virgin olive oil
Salt and freshly ground pepper
Pinch crushed red pepper flakes
½ pound linguine or cappelletti

1. Place the tomatoes in a large bowl and add the remaining ingredients except the linguine. Mix well and set aside for 3 hours at room temperature.
2. In a large stockpot of boiling water, cook the linguine until al dente. Remove the pasta from the pot with tongs and add it to the tomato sauce. Toss very well and serve immediately.

Variations: Shallots, anchovies, jalapeño peppers, bell peppers, fresh sage, or balsamic vinegar may be added to the sauce.

Cal. 312 Carb. 50g Protein 9g Chol. 0mg Fat 8g/23%

TOMATO MYTH

You'll only know they're vine-ripened if you've grown them yourself. It's not difficult. After the last frost, plant young plants in well-turned, compost-rich soil. Make sure it's your sunniest spot. And if you're a traditionalist, plant heirloom varieties.

The staking of tomatoes has long been a source of controversy among gardeners. New evidence shows that trench-growing actually brings about a much better and earlier tomato. Allowing the vine to grow in a trench keeps the tomato far more open to the sun and less likely to be overshadowed by its own leaves. The result: a redder, more nutritious tomato.

Roasting Tomatoes

Slowly roasting tomatoes results in almost a tomato pudding. Only one-quarter of the oil is absorbed and the remainder can be used as a flavored oil.

★ **GOOD FOR YOU** ★

Fresh, vine-ripened tomatoes are loaded with credentials. At only 40 calories per medium tomato, they may seem unlikely prospects, but the National Cancer Society puts them near the top of the list of cancer preventatives. They're loaded with vitamins C and A and fiber, are rich in natural sugar and potassium, and have little protein, only a trace of fat, and of course, no cholesterol. Most of the stuff that's good for you is found in the "jelly" around each seed.

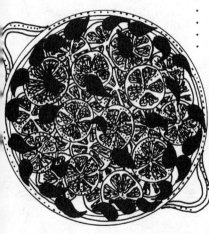

Tomatoes Provençale

SERVES 8

2 cups minced, mixed fresh herbs, such as sage, basil, chives, or chervil

4 sprigs fresh thyme

4 sprigs fresh oregano

12 garlic cloves, minced

1 cup olive oil

1 cup chicken broth (see Basics)

8 large ripe tomatoes

1. Preheat the oven to 250°.

2. In a large baking dish, combine the mixed herbs, thyme, oregano, and garlic. Pour the oil and broth over the herbs. Place the tomatoes, stem sides down, in the baking dish. Place in the oven and bake for 10 hours. Remove the tomatoes from the oil and let the excess oil drain off. Serv hot or at room temperature.

NOTE: The remaining 1¾ cups of oil and broth can be strained and kept refrigerated to use as a flavored oil.

Cal. **77** *Carb.* **10g** *Protein* **2g** *Chol.* **0mg** *Fat* **4g/44%**

Tomatoes and Roasted Onions

SERVES 4

1½ pounds red and yellow tomatoes (about 4), cut into wedges

¼ cup Balsamic Vinaigrette (page 33)

1½ pounds sweet onions, such as Vidalia, Maui, or red, cut into wedges

6 cups mixed greens, such as red leaf, mâche, or arugula

¼ cup snipped fresh basil

Freshly ground pepper

1. In a medium-size bowl, toss the tomatoes with the vinaigrette. Set aside for at least 1 hour.

2. Preheat the oven to 500°. Lightly wipe a baking sheet with olive oil. Place the onion wedges on their sides on the baking sheet and lightly spray with olive oil. Bake for 10 minutes, turn, spray lightly again, and bake for 8 to 10 minutes more. The onions should be slightly caramelized.

3. Arrange the greens on four salad plates; top with the tomatoes and onions. Drizzle the vinaigrette remaining in the bowl over the salad. Season with the basil and pepper to taste.

Cal. **144** *Carb.* **27g** *Protein* **5g** *Chol.* **0mg** *Fat* **3g/19%**

Tomatoes have been subjected to intense hybridization in recent decades, and the focus has been on those that ship well—never mind the taste. This led to the development of "square" tomatoes, most of which are shipped hard and unripe to keep damage to them minimal. They are gassed with ethylene to promote ripening en route or in local storehouses. This process actually re-creates what would happen naturally if the tomatoes were let be—that is, on the vine. Now, biogenetic tomatoes loom on the horizon.

If you find all this techno-farming unnerving, look for vine-ripened tomatoes at the local farmers' market from early summer to early fall, depending on where you are. Keep in mind that real tomatoes are seasonal. The consumers' demand for tomatoes year-round has helped to create the market for those lovely-to-look-at but tasteless specimens.

Or grow your own. According to the National Gardening Association, 85% of America's gardening households do just that. Raising America's most popular home-grown vegetable is extremely easy, even for weekend gardeners with only a small patch or a pot. Choose the most flavorful varieties: beefsteak for salads, Roma (plum) for sauces. Other familiar varieties: VSF by Burpee, Jet Star, Moreton Hybrid, Celebrity, Caruso, Bonnie Best, Rutgers, Sweet 100, Marmande.

To plant, choose the sunniest spot in the garden. Add lots of compost to the soil. After the danger of frost, set out the largest, stockiest plants you can find that haven't flowered. Avoid any chemical fertilizers.

Water your tomatoes generously all season, but let the ground dry out between waterings—this method has worked best for me. About a week before harvest, I stop watering altogether, which seems to intensify the flavor.

Goat Cheese in Tomatoes

SERVES 4

⅓ cup low-fat goat cheese
2 tablespoons Basil Pesto (page 48)
4 medium-size ripe tomatoes
2 teaspoons olive oil
Salt and freshly ground pepper
1 tablespoon minced fresh basil

1. Preheat the oven to 350°.
2. In a small bowl, mix the goat cheese and pesto; set aside.
3. Cut a thin slice off the top of each tomato and discard. Drizzle the exposed top of each tomato with olive oil. Season with salt and pepper.
4. Place the tomatoes on a baking sheet and bake for 45 to 60 minutes, until they are soft but not collapsed. Remove from the oven.
5. Spread a spoonful of the goat-cheese mixture over the top of each tomato. Sprinkle with basil and place under the broiler for 2 to 3 minutes, until bubbly. Remove and serve immediately.

*Cal. **132** Carb. **14g** Protein **7g** Chol. **8mg** Fat **7g/42%***

Tomatoes Pure and Simple

At the peak of tomato time:
★ Sprinkle with 100-year-old balsamic vinegar ★ Season with salt, pepper, a sprinkle of sugar, and a dash of vinegar; steep for 15 minutes ★ Combine with basil, balsamic vinegar, sun-dried tomatoes, and fresh mozzarella ★ Toss with minced tarragon and tarragon vinegar ★ Add red wine vinegar and chopped red onion ★ Drizzle with black-currant vinegar and chopped chervil ★

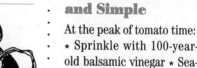

A cardinal rule: Never, NEVER store tomatoes in the refrigerator, and don't buy from a refrigerated case, either. Below 55° a tomato loses its ability to keep ripening off the vine. Low temperatures damage delicate aroma-producing compounds as well. Nothing can repair this damage. Store tomatoes at room temperature to maintain their vine-ripened peak.

• If you must buy in advance, choose firm, well-colored tomatoes not yet soft and ripe, and keep them in a cool, dark, well-ventilated place.

• Green tomatoes bought in the winter will never ripen. Buy the salmon-pink ones instead and hope for the best.

• Cut a tomato open, and its aroma disappears in about 15 minutes. Eat it right away to absorb its full flavor impact.

• If you want to dress a tomato, drizzle on just a touch of oil and vinegar.

• Restraint is the rule: Don't overpower the singular taste of tomatoes in season.

• Tomatoes ripen at home fastest not on the windowsill, but in a brown bag in a closet or pantry.

Tomato Antipasto

The dish to make when tomatoes are at their juicy best. Sliced tomatoes, a spicy salsa, broiled mozzarella, olives, basil, arugula, and Parmesan Toast—you'll feel like you're in Portofino.

SERVES 4

1 pound Italian plum tomatoes, cored and chopped
1 tablespoon minced jalapeño pepper
2 teaspoons chopped fresh summer savory
4 teaspoons fresh lime juice
Salt and freshly ground pepper
1/2 cup tomato juice
2 tablespoons rice vinegar
1/4 cup finely chopped fresh chervil or Italian parsley
1 teaspoon minced lime zest
2 large tomatoes (about 1/2 pound)
4 ounces fresh low-fat mozzarella
1 tablespoon coarsely snipped fresh basil
8 niçoise olives
6 cups arugula
1 medium-size tomato, diced

1. Preheat the broiler. Lightly spray or wipe a baking sheet with olive oil.
2. In a small bowl, combine the plum tomatoes, jalapeño, savory, and lime juice. Toss well and season with salt and pepper to taste. Set aside.
3. In a small bowl, combine the tomato juice, rice vinegar, chervil, and lime zest. Season with pepper to taste.
4. Slice the large tomatoes into six slices each. Season with salt and pepper to taste.
5. Slice the mozzarella into twelve slices. Arrange the slices on the baking sheet. Season with pepper to taste. Place under the broiler for 2 to 3 minutes, until bubbly and lightly colored.
6. On each of four dinner plates, place three tomato slices and three mozzarella slices; confine the tomatoes and mozzarella to one-third of the plate; sprinkle with basil. Arrange two olives next to the slices. Arrange 1 cup of the tomato mixture on the second third of each plate.
7. In a large bowl, toss the arugula, diced tomato, and tomato vinaigrette, and place on the remaining third of the plate. Serve immediately with slices of Parmesan Toast (page 36).

Cal. **170** *Carb.* **18g** *Protein* **20g** *Chol.* **33mg** *Fat* **7g/28%**

The VEGETABLE PATCH

Vegetables are one of the best food categories for us, generally low in calories and fat, and packed with carbohydrates, fiber, vitamins, and minerals. Many offer great benefits as anticarcinogens and cholesterol- and blood pressure-lowerers. All are most nutritious if only steamed or blanched to crisp tenderness. The longer you cook them, the less the benefits.

Avocado
360 calories*
High in fiber (and fat), vitamins A, B complex, C, and E, and potassium

Beets
55 calories*
Low in fiber and fat,
High in vitamins A and C, and potassium
The best source of quick, nonfattening energy

Broccoli
40 calories*
Low in fat
High in calcium and cancer-preventive vitamin A; more vitamin C than orange juice

Artichoke
35 calories*
High in carbohydrates, vitamins A and C, potassium, and calcium

Cabbage
20 calories*
High in carbohydrates, vitamins A, B complex, C, and K, calcium, potassium, and magnesium
Helps guard against cancer

Carrots
35 calories*
High in fiber and carbohydrates, vitamin A, and potassium
Appears to block cancer development
Pectin helps lower cholesterol
More healthful crisp-cooked than raw

Asparagus
35 calories*
High in vitamins A, B, and C, potassium, and iron
Best cooked just until tender

Brussels Sprouts
35 calories*
High in fiber, carbohydrates, cancer-fighting vitamins A and C, also potassium, and iron

Cauliflower
30 calories*
High in fiber and carbohydrates, cancer-preventive vitamins A and C, also B complex and E, potassium, calcium, phosphorus, and magnesium

had been sown with lettuces)." Beatrix Potter
The Tale of Benjamin Bunny

Celery
8 calories*
High in carbohydrates,
vitamins A, B, C, and E,
potassium, and phosphorus

Celery Root
45 calories*
High in fiber, starch,
vitamins A, B, and C,
and iron
As much protein as potatoes,
but far fewer calories (also 5
times the fiber and calcium)

Corn
75 calories per ear
137 calories per cup
High in carbohydrates,
vitamins A, B, and C (yellow
corn), and potassium
Corn oil works better than
any other vegetable oil to
lower cholesterol levels

Eggplant
38 calories*
High in fiber and
carbohydrates,
vitamins A, B complex, and
C, phosphorus, potassium,
and calcium
Absorbs fat and
cholesterol before it reaches
the bloodstream

Fennel
30 calories*
High in fiber and
carbohydrates,
vitamin C, calcium, and iron
The ancient diet food—high
in protein, it breaks down
fats and aids in digestion

Green Beans
40 calories*
High in fiber, carbohydrates,
vitamins A and C, iron,
and potassium
Help prevent colon cancer

Jícama
50 calories*
High in vitamin C
and potassium
Best raw or slightly steamed

Kohlrabi
40 calories*
High in carbohydrates, fiber,
protein, and
vitamin C
Best steamed only to blanch

Mushrooms
20 calories*
High in fiber, carbohydrates,
vitamin B, riboflavin,
vitamin D, and potassium;
low in fat
Dried, they are 44% protein
Shiitake, oyster, enoki, and
black strengthen the
immune system;
mushrooms help guard
against colds and flu.

Okra
45 calories*
High in fiber, carbohydrates,
vitamins A and C, and
potassium; low in fat

* Per cup

Onions
36 calories*
High in fiber, carbohydrates, vitamin C, iron, and calcium
Raw onion oil helps lower cholesterol significantly and helps prevent heart attacks
Contains blood-thinning elements

Parsnips
90 calories*
High in fiber, carbohydrates, and protein
Exceptionally high in vitamin C and potassium; some calcium

Peas
95 calories*
High in protein and carbohydrates, vitamins A, B complex, and C, iron, calcium, potassium, and phosphorus
Lots of fiber to lower cholesterol, helps prevent cancer

* Per cup

Peppers (Bell)
35 calories*
High in fiber and carbohydrates
Packed with vitamins C and A, iron, and potassium
Best raw

Potatoes
114 calories*
High in carbohydrates and fiber
Jam-packed with vitamins C and B_6, and potassium
Skins contain anti-carcinogenic vitamin C and fiber

Radishes
20 calories*
High in carbohydrates, vitamin C, iron, and potassium
Low in fiber

Rutabagas
60 calories*
High in vitamin A and potassium

Spinach
60 calories*
High in protein, vitamins A and C, and potassium
Beta-carotene (masked by chlorophyll) makes it a great anti carcinogen.
Moderate in carbohydrates, low in fiber

Sugar Snap Peas
60 calories*
High in fiber, protein, carbohydrates, vitamins A and C, and iron

Sweet Potatoes
165 calories*
High in carbohydrates,
Exceptionally high in vitamin A, a good cancer-preventive (the darker, the better)
Also have potassium
Low in fiber and fat

Tomatoes
40 calories*
High in carbohydrates, vitamin C, potassium, and beta-carotene, which makes it a great cancer fighter; can help lower blood pressure

Turnips
28 calories*
High in carbohydrates,
vitamins A and C, potassium, iron, and calcium
Roots and greens are
anticarcinogenic

Winter Squash
100 calories*
High in vitamin A—the
darker the squash,
the higher the content

Zucchini/Summer Squash
25 calories*
High in carbohydrates,
vitamin A
(an anticarcinogen)
masked by chlorophyll;
also C and potassium
Low in fiber
Best eaten raw

THE KITCHEN GARDEN

"We must cultivate our garden," said Voltaire. A French senti-ment, indeed, typical of a people long convinced of the benefits of using fresh, seasonal ingredi-ents. Thriving for centuries with their *potagers*, or kitchen gar-dens, and open markets held on special market days. French cooks hold that the best ingredi-ents are no more than half a day out of the garden. This philoso-phy makes them the experts in everyday shopping.

Kitchen Garden Tips

* Think of the kitchen garden as a garden kitchen. Add an outside sink for cleaning vege-tables and potting plants. Con-sider a work counter or table nearby, too. (How logical!)
* Use natural, carefree materi-als in the kitchen garden. Con-sider wood, fireslate, terra-cotta, wooden half-tubs, and timbers.
* Choose a variety of containers for a variety of plants and give each its appropriate mix of soil and fertilizer.
* Pots dry out quickly. At plant-ing time, mix water-absorbent polymer granules (Water Grab-ber or Soil Moist) into soil.

* When filling containers, bank the soil right up to the rims, leav-ing a shallow depression in the center of the pot. Water will flow to the center, not down the sides.
* Use perennials in the herb garden, herb annuals in the veg-etable garden—perhaps even with a flower color theme.
* Don't grow herbs in the house unless you have a greenhouse or grow lights and great air circu-lation. Without these assets, your herbs never will develop full taste.
* Mulch *after* it gets cold to maintain an even ground tem-perature.

Feed Your Garden

Most plants need supplemen-tary nutrition for maximum growth and an abundant har-vest. Fertilizer is available in many forms, from organic fish emulsion, bone and blood meal to chemical time-release com-pounds and balanced liquid for-mulas. Feed at prescribed regular intervals throughout the growing season. Plants in sandy soils especially need a constant, adequate supply.

Sunset sips...

In summer, we often have a special drink of the evening. It helps create a more festive mood, from the moment guests arrive. We also offer special nonalcoholic "cocktails" to friends who don't indulge and are bored to tears with mineral water. They're so good, some of the real drinkers like them on occasion.

Strawberry Margarita

SERVES 2

3/4 cup fresh strawberries, cleaned and hulled
    (reserve 2 whole berries for garnish)
1 tablespoon superfine sugar
1 cup ice cubes
1/3 cup tequila
3 tablespoons orange liqueur, such as Triple Sec
1/3 cup liquid sour mix (store-bought)
1/4 cup fresh lime juice

Place the berries and sugar in a blender and process until almost smooth. Add the remaining ingredients and blend until smooth. Serve immediately, garnished with whole berries.
Cal. 220 Carb. 27g Protein 1g
Chol. 0mg Fat .3g/1%

Piña Colada Sip

SERVES 6

2 cups coarsely chopped fresh pineapple
1 cup fresh orange juice
1 banana, coarsely chopped
1/4 cup skim milk
2 tablespoons honey
2 cups ice cubes

Place all of the ingredients in a blender and process until smooth. Serve immediately.
Cal. 105 Carb. 25g
Protein 1g Chol. .2mg
Fat 1g/4%

Raspberry Daiquiri

SERVES 2

1½ cups fresh raspberries
6 tablespoons frozen limeade concentrate
1 cup ice cubes
2 sprigs fresh mint

Place the raspberries, limeade, and ice in a blender. Process until smooth. Pour into two glasses, garnish with mint, and serve.
Cal. **110** Carb. **28g** Protein **1g** Chol. **0mg** Fat **.4g/3%**

Mint Limeade

SERVES 4

½ cup fresh lime juice
½ cup Sugar Syrup (see Basics)
¼ cup chopped fresh mint
1 cup cold water or club soda
Mint sprigs

1. In a small pitcher, combine the lime juice, sugar syrup, and chopped mint. Stir briskly until well mixed. Pour into a container, cover, and refrigerate until needed.
2. For each serving, pour ½ cup limeade and ½ cup cold water or soda over ice and garnish with mint sprigs
Cal. **105** Carb. **27g** Protein **.2g** Chol. **0mg** Fat **0g/0%**

Citrus Cocktail

SERVES 2

¾ cup fresh orange juice
½ cup fresh grapefruit juice
½ cup Sugar Syrup
    (see Basics)
¼ cup fresh lime juice
¼ cup fresh lemon juice
¼ cup club soda
½ cup ice cubes
Citrus slices

In a pitcher, combine all of the ingredients except the citrus slices; mix well. Garnish each serving with a slice of citrus.
Cal. **91** Carb. **24g** Protein **.4g** Chol. **0mg** Fat **.1g/1%**

Pineapple Zinger

SERVES 3

1 cup fresh orange juice
2 cups peeled, cored, and coarsely chopped
    fresh pineapple
1 banana, coarsely chopped
¼ cup skim milk
2 tablespoons honey
2 cups ice cubes

Place the all of the ingredients in a blender. Process until smooth. Serve immediately.
Cal. **127** Carb. **29g** Protein **.1g** Chol. **0mg** Fat **1g/1%**

...and dips

Guacamole

YIELD: 2½ CUPS

¼ cup Low-Fat Blend
    (see Basics)
1 large avocado, diced
½ cup finely chopped red
    onion
2 cups finely chopped tomato
1 jalapeño pepper, seeded
    and chopped
4 garlic cloves, finely minced
1 tablespoon fresh lemon juice
Dash Tabasco or other pepper
    sauce
¼ cup chopped fresh cilantro

Blend all of the ingredients
well. Cover with plastic wrap
and refrigerate for at least 1
hour before serving.
Cal. 14 Carb. 1g Protein .4g
Chol. 1mg Fat 1g/58%*

Pesto Dip

YIELD: 1½ CUPS

1¼ cups Low-Fat Blend
    (see Basics)
½ cup Broccoli Pesto
    (page 48)
¼ cup low-fat sour cream
Tabasco or other pepper
    sauce

Whisk all of the ingredients
until well blended. Chill and
use as a dip for vegetables.
Cal. 7 Carb. .5g Protein 1g
Chol. 0mg Fat .4g/43%*

Lemon Dip

YIELD: 2⅓ CUPS

2 cups Low-Fat Blend
    (see Basics)
2 tablespoons minced lemon
    zest
2 teaspoons ground coriander
4 tablespoons fresh lemon juice
½ cup chopped fresh dill

Combine all of the ingredients
in a small mixing bowl; stir
until well blended. Taste and
adjust seasoning. Cover and
refrigerate until needed.
Cal. 3 Carb. 0g Protein 0g
    Chol. 0mg Fat .01g/11%*

Spinach-Dill Dip

YIELD: 2 CUPS

1½ cups Low-Fat Blend
   (see Basics)
2 cups cleaned and chopped
   spinach
4 garlic cloves, minced
Pinch nutmeg
Freshly ground pepper
½ cup chopped fresh dill

Place all of the ingredients in
a blender or food processor
and blend until smooth. Correct the seasonings and blend
again. Transfer to a bowl,
cover, and chill.
Cal. **4** Carb. **.4g** Protein **.5g**
Chol. **.3mg** Fat **.04g/29%***

Red Pepper Dip

YIELD: 1¾ CUPS

2 red bell peppers, roasted,
   skinned, and seeded
1½ cups nonfat plain yogurt
¼ cup minced fresh basil
1 garlic clove, finely minced
Freshly ground pepper
2 tablespoons finely minced
   fresh cilantro or Italian
   parsley

1. Cut the roasted pepper
into large chunks. Place
in a blender or food
processor and pulse until
just puréed; do not overpurée.
2. Transfer the purée to a
small bowl. Add the yogurt,
basil, and garlic, and mix well.
Taste and add pepper to taste.
Transfer to a serving bowl,
cover, and refrigerate until

ready to serve. Sprinkle with
the cilantro and serve.
Cal. **2** Carb. **.6g** Protein **.3g**
Chol. **0mg** Fat **1g/8%***

Tahini Dip

YIELD: 1 CUP

1 cup Low-Fat Blend
   (see Basics)
3 tablespoons tahini
3 tablespoons fresh orange
   juice
1 tablespoon frozen orange
   juice concentrate, defrosted
1 tablespoon honey
Pinch cayenne
Zest of 1 orange, grated

Place all of the ingredients in a
blender and process until just
combined. Transfer to a bowl,
cover, and refrigerate until
needed.
Cal. **13** Carb. **1g** Protein **.7g**
Chol. **0mg** Fat **.7g/46%***

Lime Dip

YIELD: 2 CUPS

2 cups Low-Fat Blend
   (see Basics)
1 tablespoon minced lime zest
1 tablespoon chopped fresh
   ginger or 1 jalapeño pepper,
   seeded and chopped
2 tablespoons fresh lime juice
¼ cup minced fresh cilantro

Combine all of the ingredients
in a small mixing bowl. Stir
until well blended. Taste and
adjust seasoning. Cover and
refrigerate until needed.
Cal. **3** Carb. **.3g** Protein **.4g**
Chol. **.1mg** Fat **.1g/11%***

Rosy Beet Dip

YIELD: 2 CUPS

2 cans beets
   (8¼ ounces each)
2 red onions, coarsely
   chopped
1 cup nonfat plain yogurt
½ cup chopped fresh dill

Place the beets and onion in
the bowl of a food processor
and process until smooth.
Transfer to a medium-size
bowl; add the yogurt and dill
and blend well by hand. Chill
until ready to serve.
Cal. **3** Carb. **.7g** Protein **.2g**
Chol. **0mg** Fat **.03g/5%***

*The nutrition for all dips on
these pages was analyzed per
teaspoon.

Roquefort Dip

YIELD: 1⅓ CUPS

1 cup Low-Fat Blend
(see Basics)
¼ cup crumbled Roquefort
cheese
Freshly ground pepper

Combine the ingredients in a
blender and blend until
smooth. Transfer the dip to a
bowl and chill.

Cal. 5 Carb. .2g Protein .5g
Chol. .6mg Fat .2g/45%*

%

Lebanese Yogurt Dip

YIELD: 2½ CUPS

2 cups Yogurt Cheese
(see Basics)
4 tablespoons bulghur
(cracked wheat)
¼ cup finely chopped scallion
1 tablespoon finely minced
garlic
¼ cup finely minced fresh mint
2 tablespoons finely minced
fresh Italian parsley
1 tablespoon finely grated
lemon zest
2 tablespoons fresh lemon juice
Salt and freshly ground pepper
Fresh Italian parsley

1. Place the yogurt cheese in a
small bowl and stir in the bulghur; cover and refrigerate
overnight.
2. Place the yogurt mixture in
a large bowl. Stir in the
remaining ingredients, except
the parsley, and transfer to a
serving dish. Garnish with
parsley. Serve with fresh

vegetables or pita chips.

Cal. 4 Carb. .5g Protein .4g
Chol. 0mg Fat 0g/0%*

Black Bean Dip

YIELD: 2½ CUPS

2 cans black beans
(19 ounces each), rinsed
and drained
3 tablespoons fresh lime juice
3 tablespoons chopped lime
zest
½ cup chicken broth
(see Basics)
1 teaspoon ground cumin
½ teaspoon cayenne
4 jalapeño peppers, coarsely
chopped
1 red bell pepper, stem, seeds,
and ribs removed
½ cup chopped fresh cilantro

1. Place the first six ingredients in the bowl of a food
processor and pulse until just
chunky.
2. Transfer to a medium-size
bowl and add the remaining
ingredients; mix well. Taste
and adjust seasoning with
more lime juice or cayenne.

Cal. 5 Carb. 1g Protein .3g
Chol. 0mg Fat .02g/20%*

**The nutrition for all
dips on these pages
was analyzed per
teaspoon.*

Dips in Summer

Low-Fat Blend and…
Salsa
Honey mustard
Chutney
Handfuls of minced herbs
Lemon juice & zest
Horseradish
Sesame oil
Tomato Tapenade
Garlic Pesto
Guacamole
Black Bean Dip
Minced sun-dried tomatoes
Lentil Tapenade
Roquefort cheese
Caviar
Tomatoes, basil, & garlic
Orange juice and zest
Raspberries &
raspberry vinegar
Spinach
Artichoke hearts
Chinese ginger &
balsamic vinegar
Capers
Tapenade
Beet purée
Tahini & sesame seeds
Minced scallions
Roasted pepper purée
Pesto
Salmon Rillettes
(See Index for recipes)

THE YOGURT CULTURE

Is it yogurt that keeps so many of the Georgians of Eastern Europe going strong past the century mark? Perhaps. In any case, this nutritious food is certainly a wonderful ally in healthful cooking.

A Great Pinch Hitter

Yogurt and yogurt cheese substitute readily for sour cream, mayonnaise, heavy cream, and cream cheese. If your yogurt is too tart or acidic for your tastes, tame it with a little fruit juice or honey and olive oil or round it out with chicken broth for sauces.

A Word of Warning

Don't give yourself carte blanche just because it's yogurt. Read the labels. Some brands contain cream and whole milk. For instance, one brand of standard plain yogurt has 163 calories and 8 grams of fat and is approximately 48% fat.

Plain low-fat yogurt has 127 calories and 3 grams of fat and is approximately 22% fat. Nonfat yogurt has 106 calories and approximately 1 gram of fat, and is about 10% fat.

The Low-Fat Cheese Connection

Like low-fat yogurt, low-fat cheese requires extra care in selection and cooking:

❂ Read labels carefully. "Light" may be used to describe low fat, or it might just refer to taste. The real low-fat cheeses we've noticed include ricotta, goat, mozzarella, and cream.

❂ Low-fat cheeses melt in the same way as mild cheeses but tend to toughen if a toaster, broiler, or direct heat are used.

❂ Melt low-fat cheese over low heat, stirring slowly in one direction. It will take about 25% longer than regular cheeses.

❂ Add flour, cornstarch, or arrowroot to shredded low-fat cheese to make a smooth sauce.

★ GOOD FOR YOU ★

A cup of low-fat yogurt has 52% of the adult daily requirement of calcium in a 1-cup serving. In nonfat yogurt, the percentage jumps to 57%. An equal portion of milk has only 37%. Yogurt is high in potassium, riboflavin, and vitamin B_1, too. Besides having little or no fat, yogurt is very low in cholesterol.

Summertime Bruschetta

YIELD: 32 SLICES

16 fresh ripe plum tomatoes, very finely diced
4 tablespoons finely minced garlic
1 cup coarsely chopped fresh basil
1/2 cup finely chopped fresh Italian parsley
2 tablespoons fresh lemon juice
Pinch crushed red pepper flakes
Salt and freshly ground pepper
Thirty-two 1/4-inch-thick slices French or Italian baguette
6 garlic cloves, cut in half

1. In a large mixing bowl, combine the tomato, minced garlic, basil, parsley, lemon juice, red pepper flakes, and salt and pepper to taste. Toss very well and set aside for at least 3 hours.
2. Just before serving, toast the bread and rub on one side with the cut sides of the garlic cloves. Place a small bowl in the center of a serving platter. Fill the bowl with the tomato mixture and arrange the toast around the bowl. Serve immediately.

Cal. 63 Carb. 13g Protein 2g Chol. .4mg Fat .7g/9%

Herbed Bruschetta

The Italian classic you can create.

YIELD: 24 SLICES

1/2 cup finely chopped fresh Italian parsley
1/2 cup drained capers, chopped
1 tablespoon finely minced fresh tarragon
Salt and freshly ground pepper
1/4 cup extra-virgin olive oil
2 large, very ripe tomatoes
3 tablespoons finely minced fresh mint
Twenty-four 1/4-inch-thick slices peasant bread or French baguette

1. In a medium-size bowl, place the parsley, capers, tarragon, and salt and pepper to taste. Add the oil and toss well.
2. Dice the tomatoes very fine, but do not peel or seed them. Place the tomato in another bowl. Season with salt and pepper to taste, and add the mint. Let everything stand at room temperature for at least 1 hour.

Bruschetta

From the Italian *bruscare*, "to toast." This is an annual tradition that began in celebration of the newly pressed olive oil. The most important component: bread grilled over an open fire. The second: the spicy fresh-pressed virgin olive oil of the late fall season. Ancient Romans were the first to brush crusty grilled bread with olive oil, a custom that spread throughout central Italy, gathering other ingredients—tomatoes, garlic, herbs—as it traveled.

3. Toast or grill the bread. Spread it with the herb mixture. Top with the tomato.

*Cal. **69** Carb. **9g** Protein **2g** Chol. **.4mg** Fat **3g/37%*** %

Usually, we love it pure and simple. But occasionally, an unconventional twist appeals. To the basic recipe, try adding one or more of the following:

Balsamic vinegar
•
Kalamata olives
•
Fresh mint, tarragon, chives
•
Sun-dried tomatoes
•
Capers
•
Shallots or scallions
•
Red or yellow peppers, roasted or raw
•
Jalapeño peppers
•
Tabasco
•
Fresh sweet corn
•
Black beans
•
Cucumbers
•
Prosciutto
•
Grilled tuna

Lentil Tapenade

A gutsy classic French spread of olives, capers, and anchovies that I've "lightened" with lentils. It's still robust but has far less fat because far fewer olives are included.

YIELD: 1 QUART
1 cup lentils, preferably French Le Puy, rinsed and sorted
2½ cups chicken broth (see Basics)
2 tablespoons chopped garlic
2 tablespoons sun-dried tomatoes packed in oil, drained and patted dry, slivered
1 tablespoon anchovy oil or olive oil
3 tablespoons drained capers
½ cup Kalamata olives, pitted and coarsely chopped
2 tablespoons fresh lemon juice
Salt and freshly ground pepper
½ cup finely chopped fresh Italian parsley
Additional chopped fresh Italian parsley
1 thin lemon slice

1. Drain and rinse the lentils.
2. In a large saucepan over medium heat, combine the lentils, broth, garlic, and tomatoes. Simmer until the lentils are cooked, 30 to 45 minutes; set aside to cool.
3. Place all of the ingredients from the saucepan in a food processor, and process for 30 seconds, scraping down the sides several times. Add the oil, capers, chopped olives, lemon juice, and salt and pepper to taste. Process until smooth, scraping down the sides several times. Add the ½ cup parsley and pulse several times to blend.
4. Transfer the tapenade to a serving dish. Garnish with lemon slices, and parsley around the lemon. Serve with toasted French bread, fresh pita bread, or pita chips.

*Cal. **18** Carb. **2g** Protein **1g**
Chol. **0mg** Fat **.6g/32%*** %
(analyzed per tablespoon)*

Mushroom Caviar

YIELD: 1 CUP

1 tablespoon olive oil
4 scallions, green parts only, minced
1/2 pound Portobello mushrooms, cut into 1 1/2-inch cubes,
    or cremini mushrooms, halved
4 garlic cloves, roughly chopped
1/2 teaspoon chopped fresh thyme leaves
2 teaspoons fresh lemon juice
4 teaspoons balsamic vinegar
1/4 teaspoon coarsely ground pepper

1. In a large saucepan over medium heat, heat 1 teaspoon of olive oil and sauté the scallion for 2 minutes. Set aside.
2. Heat the remaining oil. Add the mushrooms, garlic, and thyme, and sauté until tender. Do not overcrowd the pan, or the mushrooms will be poached. Work in two batches.
3. Transfer the scallion and mushrooms to a food processor fitted with a steel blade. Using the pulse button, process until coarsely chopped, not mushy; do not overprocess.
4. Return the mushrooms to the saucepan. Add the lemon juice, vinegar, and pepper. Sauté over medium-high heat until the liquid has evaporated, 1 to 2 minutes.
5. Serve in a small crock or dish as a spread for toast, zucchini rounds, or Belgian endive.

*Cal. **14** Carb. **1g** Protein **1g** Chol. **0mg** Fat **1g/50%*** %
(analyzed per tablespoon)

Middle Eastern "Bruschetta"

Spread a thin layer of Yogurt Cheese (see Basics) on grilled or toasted bread. Then layer it with very thin slices of the juiciest tomatoes, a drizzle of olive oil, and finally, chopped fresh mint.

Summer Hummus

YIELD: 2 1/2 CUPS

1 cup dried chick-peas or Rachael beans, rinsed, sorted, and
    soaked in water to cover overnight
3 cups chicken broth (see Basics), plus additional if needed
3 whole garlic cloves
1 garlic clove, chopped
6 tablespoons fresh lemon juice
1 1/2 teaspoons cumin seeds, toasted and ground
1 teaspoon salt, or to taste
Generous grinding of pepper
2 tablespoons finely chopped fresh cilantro
1 to 2 thin lemon slices

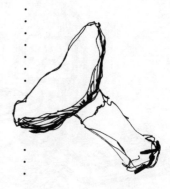

Herbed Fresh Pita Toasts

YIELD: 64 TRIANGLES

½ teaspoon dried basil
½ teaspoon dried thyme
½ teaspoon dried dill
½ teaspoon dried tarragon
Four 8-inch nonfat pita breads

1. Preheat the oven to 300°.
2. Combine the herbs in a small bowl.
3. Cut the pita breads in half and split them apart to make sixteen pieces. Cut each into four triangles.
4. Place the triangles on a baking sheet. Brush or spray a few triangles at a time with olive or canola oil and sprinkle each with a pinch of herbs. Continue until all of the herbs and triangles have been used.
5. Bake until the triangles are crisp and lightly browned, 8 to 10 minutes. Serve at once or store in an airtight container.

Cal. 10 Carb. .3g Protein .4g Chol. 0mg Fat .1g/5% (analyzed per piece)

1. Drain and rinse the chick-peas. In a medium saucepan, combine the chick-peas, chicken broth, and the whole garlic cloves. Simmer over low heat until the chick-peas are tender, about 45 minutes or longer, depending on their dryness. Set aside to cool.
2. Drain the chick-peas and reserve the broth—there should be about ¼ cup; if not, add chicken broth to measure ¼ cup. Place the chick-peas and the chopped garlic in a food processor. With the machine running, add the reserved broth. Scrape down the sides several times. Add the lemon juice, cumin, and salt and pepper to taste, and process until the mixture is smooth. Taste and correct seasonings, adding more lemon juice, cumin, salt, or pepper if necessary.
3. Transfer the hummus to a serving bowl and garnish with chopped cilantro and lemon slices. Serve with wedges of fresh pita bread or pita chips.

Cal. 21 Carb. 4g Protein 1g Chol. 0mg Fat .4g/17% (analyzed per tablespoon)

Caponata

YIELD: 2¼ CUPS

1 large eggplant, cut in half lengthwise
2 cups Old-Fashioned Tomato Sauce (page 287)
3 ounces capers, drained
¼ cup pitted and coarsely chopped Kalamata olives

1. Preheat the oven to 500°. Lightly spray or wipe a large baking sheet with vegetable oil.
2. Make three diagonal slashes in each eggplant half on the flesh side, and place the halves, flesh sides down, on the baking sheet; bake for 20 minutes. Remove the eggplant from the oven and set it aside to cool. Scoop out the pulp and place it in a medium-size bowl.
3. Add the remaining ingredients, mix, and serve.

Cal. 10 Carb. 2g Protein .3g Chol. 0mg Fat .4g/30% (analyzed per tablespoon)

Ratatouille Tart

SERVES 8

1 recipe Flaky Pie Crust (see Basics)
½ pound onions, sliced
4 whole garlic cloves, peeled
2 garlic cloves, peeled and finely minced
2 teaspoons olive oil
½ pound eggplant, coarsely diced
½ pound tomato, coarsely chopped
1 ounce sun-dried tomatoes, plumped in boiling water,
  drained, and coarsely chopped
1 tablespoon chopped fresh thyme leaves
Salt and freshly ground pepper
1 tablespoon balsamic vinegar
2 ounces Parmesan, cut into shards with a vegetable peeler
4 large tomato slices

1. Preheat the oven to 400°.
2. Prepare Flaky Pie Crust.
3. Between two sheets of waxed paper, roll out the dough to fit an 8-inch round tart pan. Place the dough in the pan and trim the edges; refrigerate for 15 minutes.
4. Line the tart shell with foil, fill with pie weights or dried beans, and bake until the crust is lightly golden, about 10 minutes. Remove the foil and pie weights and spray the crust with olive oil.
5. Lightly coat a baking sheet with olive oil. Place the onion and whole garlic on the sheet, and lightly spray them. Roast for 14 to 16 minutes, turning once after the first 10 minutes; the vegetables should take on a golden caramel color. Do not let them burn.
6. In a large skillet, heat 1 teaspoon of olive oil over medium heat. Add the eggplant and sauté for 4 minutes. Add the minced garlic and sauté for 1 minute. Add the chopped tomatoes, sun-dried tomatoes, thyme, and salt and pepper to taste, and simmer for 10 minutes; stir in the vinegar.
7. Arrange the onion slices on the crust, and top with the eggplant filling. Arrange half the Parmesan shards over the eggplant, and top with the sliced tomatoes and whole garlic cloves. Drizzle the remaining olive oil over and scatter on the remaining Parmesan shards. Bake for 25 minutes, or until bubbly and golden.

*Cal. **175** Carb. **20g** Protein **6g** Chol. **5mg** Fat **9g/43%*** %

Avocados

In Mexico, they're often called "the poor man's butter." No wonder—they're up to 22% fat. The good news is, avocado oil is 71% monounsaturated and 13% polyunsaturated. But it's fat, just the same. And at 360 calories per medium avocado, you should use them very sparingly.

There's more good news: The fiber in avocados helps fight cancer, and their high potassium level (twice that of bananas) helps lower blood pressure. They also have protein, vitamins A, B complex, C, and E, calcium, iron, potassium, magnesium, and phosphorus. Still . . . if you indulge in an avocado, remember to monitor the rest of your diet.

Great Green Vegetable Tart

SERVES 6

$1/4$ pound green beans, trimmed, blanched for 4 minutes, and cut into $1/2$-inch pieces (about 1 cup)

4 cups $1/2$-inch-diced zucchini

2 cups trimmed, peeled, chopped broccoli, blanched for 2 minutes

$1/4$ pound (about 2 packed cups) fresh spinach, washed, trimmed, and finely chopped

$1/4$ cup finely chopped scallion, white parts with some green

$1/4$ cup finely chopped fresh Italian parsley

$1/4$ cup finely chopped fresh mint

$1/4$ cup finely chopped fresh dill

2 eggs

4 egg whites

$1/4$ pound crumbled feta cheese

$1/2$ cup imported grated Parmesan

$1/4$ teaspoon freshly grated nutmeg

Salt and freshly ground pepper

8 sheets phyllo dough, thawed according to package directions

1. Preheat the oven to 400°.

2. In a large bowl, toss all the vegetables and fresh herbs.

3. In another bowl, whisk the eggs and whites. Stir in the feta, Parmesan, and nutmeg. Pour the egg mixture over the vegetables and stir until well combined; season with salt and pepper.

4. Lightly coat or wipe a 9-inch springform pan with olive oil.

5. Lightly coat or wipe six sheets of phyllo dough with oil. Working with one sheet at a time, line the prepared pan with the sheets, allowing the excess to hang over the sides. Pour the filling into the pan and fold the overlapping edges over the filling. Cut four 9-inch circles out of the remaining sheets. Lightly spray or wipe each circle with oil, and stack them on top of the filling. Lightly spray or wipe the top again.

6. Place the pan on a baking sheet and bake for 40 to 45 minutes, or until the crust is puffed and golden brown. Remove and cool in the pan for 10 minutes.

7. To serve, remove the sides and cut the pie with a sharp knife.

*Cal. **208** Carb. **28g** Protein **15g** Chol. **71mg** Fat **6g/23%***

Regatta Stripes

YIELD: 40 PIECES

2 pounds boneless and skinless chicken breasts
½ cup nonfat plain yogurt
3 tablespoons fresh lemon juice
1 tablespoon Dijon mustard
3 garlic cloves, minced
2 tablespoons chopped fresh oregano
1 tablespoon chopped fresh sage
Salt and freshly ground pepper
½ cup grated Parmesan
½ cup bread crumbs
½ cup minced fresh Italian parsley
Cayenne

1. Cut the chicken into ½ x 1½-inch strips. In a large bowl, combine the yogurt, lemon juice, mustard, garlic, oregano, sage, and salt and pepper to taste. Add the chicken and toss to coat. Cover and refrigerate for at least 2 hours or overnight.

2. Preheat the oven to 400°.

3. In a bowl, combine the cheese, bread crumbs, parsley, salt, pepper, and cayenne to taste. Remove the chicken from the marinade, allowing the excess to drip off, and roll in the bread-crumb mixture to coat evenly.

4. Lightly spray or wipe a baking sheet with vegetable oil. Arrange the chicken in a single layer on the sheet and bake for 30 minutes, or until golden brown. Serve hot or cold.

*Cal. **31** Carb. **1g** Protein **4g** Chol. **5mg** Fat **1g/26%***
(analyzed per piece)

Lime Chicken Strips

YIELD: 60 PIECES

3 pounds boneless and skinless chicken breasts
6 ounces frozen limeade concentrate, defrosted
3 ounces tequila
2 tablespoons minced lime zest
6 garlic cloves, minced

1. Cut the chicken into ½ x 1½-inch strips. In a large mixing bowl, combine all of the ingredients and refrigerate. Marinate overnight.

2. Preheat the oven to 350°. Pour the marinade into a bowl and set aside. Place the chicken in a shallow baking dish and bake for 45 minutes.

"Against the background of the sky the white riggings of the sailing-boats criss-cross like pathways."

Colette

Regatta Stripes and Lime Strips are adapted from what once were my favorite ways to cook chicken wings for snacking. But then I realized that 1 pound of baked chicken wings has almost 500 calories, 144 mgs. of cholesterol, and 3.3 grams, or 62%, fat. One pound of skinless, boneless chicken breast, by comparison, has 355 calories, 72 mg. cholesterol, and 8 grams, or 20%, fat.

3. Pour the marinade over the chicken and bake for another 45 minutes, tossing every 10 minutes to coat thoroughly. Cook until golden brown. Serve hot.

Cal. **24** *Carb.* **2g** *Protein* **3g** *Chol.* **6mg** *Fat* **.4g/13%** *(analyzed per piece)*

Baby Burgers

YIELD: 16 BABY BURGERS

8 ounces lean ground sirloin
8 ounces lean ground turkey (99% fat free)
10 ounces frozen spinach, defrosted and chopped
2 tablespoons minced fresh parsley
1 teaspoon minced fresh sage
1 teaspoon minced fresh thyme
½ teaspoon minced fresh rosemary
Freshly ground pepper

1. In a large bowl, thoroughly combine all of the ingredients. Shape the mixture into sixteen patties. Place on a plate and refrigerate for at least 1 hour to allow the flavors to meld.
2. Heat a skillet over medium-high heat. Add the burgers and cook to desired degree of doneness. Serve on toast rounds.

Cal. **52** *Carb.* **1g** *Protein* **7g** *Chol.* **18mg** *Fat* **2g/34%** ⦰
(analyzed per burger)

OLIVES

Kalamata, Niçoise, Picholine, Sicilian, Lugano, Nyons, Gaeta, Royal, Manzanilla. I love the flavors of olives from all around the world, and at every stage of development, from green, picked before they are ripe, to black, picked at their juicy peak.

Olives so easily perk up a salad, a sauce, a stew, or cocktail time. One bite has the taste of the sun and soil that a 400-year-old olive tree thrives on. It's the taste of antiquity.

Olives may not seem fatty . . . but remember where olive oil comes from. Besides being filled with oil, however, olives are high in fiber, vitamin A, iron, and sodium. And their flavor is so deep and rich that a few go a long way.

Green Olives
cal. 45 ★ 98% fat
....

Black Olives
cal. 5 ★ 72% fat
....

Greek Olives
cal. 65 ★ 95% fat
....

(Values given are for one medium-size olive)

PIZZA! TOSS-UP!

*mozzarella
crumbled chèvre
broccoli florets
new peas
artichoke hearts
scallions
roasted garlic
Parmesan shards*

*tomato sauce
slices of mozzarella
sliced vine-ripened tomatoes
slivers of basil
shards of Parmesan*

*onion marmalade
wilted spinach
roasted garlic
pine nuts
golden raisins
fig quarters
lemon zest
drizzle of olive oil*

Semolina Pizza Crusts

YIELD: FOUR 10-INCH CRUSTS, 8 SLICES EACH

1 package (¼ ounce) active dry yeast
½ teaspoon sugar
1 cup semolina flour
1¾ cups all-purpose flour
1 teaspoon salt
Olive oil

1. Place 1 cup of warm (110° to 115°) water in a small mixing bowl, and sprinkle in the yeast and sugar; stir to combine. Set the mixture aside for 5 minutes, or until foamy.
2. In the large mixing bowl of an electric mixer fitted with a dough hook, combine the flours, salt, and yeast mixture, and mix until the dough is relatively smooth.
3. Lightly flour a flat surface. Remove the dough from the bowl, place on the surface, and knead by hand for 10 minutes. If the dough is too wet, add small amounts of flour; if too dry, add drops of water. The dough should be smooth and elastic.
4. Very lightly wipe a large bowl with olive oil. Place the dough in the bowl, and turn it to coat it with oil; cover with plastic wrap and set aside in a warm place to rise for 45 minutes, or until doubled in bulk. Preheat the oven to 450°. Lightly spray or wipe individual pizza pans or large baking sheets.

Pizza Power

Breads were first baked in the sun, then in ovens on stone slabs. Focaccia and pizza—flat breads with toppings—evolved from these early types.

Over the years, pizza's popularity has grown. Once considered a fattening food, it is now regarded as a snack that can be healthful. It all depends on what goes on the crust; keep the carbs up and the calories and fat down.

5. Punch down the dough, transfer it to a lightly floured surface, and knead for 2 minutes. Let the dough rest for 20 minutes. On a floured surface, flatten it into four 10-inch discs, using your fingertips. Place on a pizza pan. Top with sauce and toppings and bake for 15 to 20 minutes, or until crisp.

*Cal. **47** Carb. **2g** Protein **2g** Chol. **0mg** Fat **.14g/3%*** *(analyzed per slice)*

Quick Tomato Sauce

YIELD: 2 CUPS

1 teaspoon olive oil
2 tablespoons slivered garlic
1 can (28 ounces) plum tomatoes
3 tablespoons finely chopped fresh basil
Salt and freshly ground pepper

1. In a medium-size skillet, heat the oil over medium heat. Add the garlic and sauté until lightly browned. Do not overcook or the sauce will be bitter.

2. Add the tomatoes, breaking them up with a wooden spoon. Add the basil. Reduce the heat and simmer gently for 20 to 30 minutes, or until reduced to about 2 cups. Season with salt and pepper to taste.

*Cal. **8** Carb. **1g** Protein **.3g** Chol. **0mg** Fat **.2g/25%*** *(analyzed per tablespoon)*

Herbed Pizza Cheese

YIELD: 1 CUP

1 cup low-fat ricotta cheese
2 tablespoons nonfat plain yogurt
1 tablespoon finely minced garlic
4 tablespoons chopped fresh chives
4 tablespoons chopped fresh basil
4 tablespoons finely chopped fresh Italian parsley
Freshly ground pepper

In a small bowl, place all of the ingredients and mix until well combined.

*Cal. **25** Carb. **1g** Protein **2g** Chol. **4mg** Fat **1g/45%*** *(analyzed per tablespoon)*

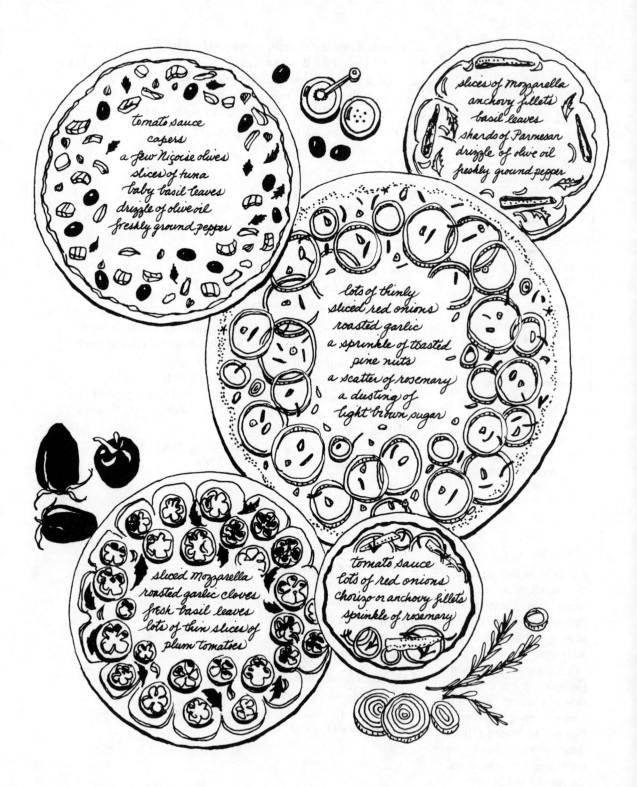

tomato sauce
capers
a few Niçoise olives
slices of tuna
baby basil leaves
drizzle of olive oil
freshly ground pepper

slices of Mozzarella
anchovy fillets
basil leaves
shards of Parmesan
drizzle of olive oil
freshly ground pepper

lots of thinly
sliced red onions
roasted garlic
a sprinkle of toasted
pine nuts
a scatter of rosemary
a dusting of
light brown sugar

sliced Mozzarella
roasted garlic cloves
fresh basil leaves
lots of thin slices of
plum tomatoes

tomato sauce
lots of red onions
chorizo or anchovy fillets
sprinkle of rosemary

tomato sauce
dots of herb cheese
bay scallops
shrimp
roasted garlic cloves
lemon zest
drizzle of olive oil

onion marmalade
wild mushrooms
fresh thyme
Pecorino shards

tomato slices
onion marmalade
thin slices of eggplant
brushed with balsamico
drizzle of olive oil
Parmesan shavings

crumbled chèvre
scallions
slices of grilled salmon
scattering of capers
fresh dill
drizzle of olive oil

tomato sauce
slices of Mozzarella
carrot rounds
broccoli florets
tomato chunks
artichoke hearts
sprinkle of fresh dill
drizzle of olive oil
fresh pepper

tomato sauce
roasted peppers
slices of red onion
shards of Romano
bits of basil

fish TALES

Catfish Niçoise

So often we limit catfish to grilling, blackening, or sautéing—but this is fabulous.

SERVES 4

2 large fresh catfish fillets (about 1½ pounds), skinned and boned
3 tablespoons fresh lime juice
1 teaspoon olive oil
1 tablespoon thinly sliced garlic
2 cups halved and thinly sliced onion
1 can (28 ounces) plum tomatoes, coarsely chopped, with juice
2 bay leaves
1 tablespoon chopped fresh marjoram
One 2-inch cinnamon stick
2 tablespoons canned pickled jalapeño peppers, sliced
1 tablespoon juice from canned jalapeños
Salt and freshly ground pepper
½ cup green olives, with pits
¼ cup capers, drained

1. Rinse the fish and pat dry. Place the fish in a nonreactive dish, and sprinkle with 2 tablespoons of the lime juice. Cover with plastic wrap and refrigerate for 1 hour.
2. In a large heavy skillet over medium heat, combine the oil and garlic. Sauté until the garlic begins to brown. Remove it

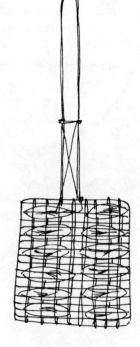

with a slotted spoon and set it aside in a small bowl. Add the onion to the skillet and sauté until softened, about 5 minutes. Return the garlic to the skillet. Add the tomato and reserved juice, bay leaves, marjoram, cinnamon, jalapeño peppers and juice, and salt and pepper to taste. Simmer for 10 minutes. Add the olives, capers, and remaining lime juice, and simmer for 5 minutes. Remove from the heat.

3. Preheat the oven to 350°.

4. Carefully transfer the fish, in one layer, to a baking dish. Pour the tomato sauce over the fish, and cover the dish tightly with aluminum foil. Bake for 10 to 15 minutes, until the fish is opaque and flakes when pierced with a fork. Serve immediately.

*Cal. **312** Carb. **21g** Protein **34g** Chol. **99mg** Fat **11g/30%***

Red Snapper and Black Bean Salsa

SERVES 4

1½ cups diced tomato
1 cup cooked black beans or black-eyed peas
¾ cup coarsely chopped fresh cilantro
3 tablespoons red wine vinegar
1 jalapeño pepper, stem and seeds removed, finely minced
Dash Tabasco or similar pepper sauce
Salt and freshly ground pepper
2 pounds red snapper fillets
3 tablespoons fresh lime juice
Grated zest of 2 limes

1. In a medium-size mixing bowl, combine the tomato, black beans, cilantro, vinegar, jalapeño, Tabasco, and salt and pepper to taste. Mix well. Set aside at room temperature for 30 minutes, stirring once or twice.

2. Preheat the oven to 375°.

3. Place each red snapper fillet on a piece of aluminum foil large enough to enclose it. Sprinkle each fillet with lime juice and lime zest. Season with pepper to taste.

4. Close the packages by folding the foil over the fish and tightly sealing the edges. Set the packages on a baking sheet and bake for 25 to 35 minutes. Open the packet to see that the fish is opaque and flakes when pierced with a fork. If so, remove from the oven.

5. Place each fillet on a dinner plate and top with a generous portion of the salsa.

*Cal. **306** Carb. **16g** Protein **51g** Chol. **83mg** Fat **4g/11%***

Whitefish with Capers

The icy waters of Lake Superior reward us with whitefish, one of the best freshwater fish to be found. In cooking, we try to keep it simple. Here, its fresh taste is complemented with a delicate greens-and-tomato salad.

SERVES 4

1 cup ¼-inch sliced cucumber
1 cup ¼-inch diced fresh tomato
¼ cup capers
2 tablespoons minced fresh parsley
2 tablespoons minced fresh chives
4 to 6 tablespoons Champagne Spritz (page 33)
2 whitefish fillets (1 pound each)
2 cups mâche or mixed greens, trimmed, rinsed, and patted dry
Freshly ground pepper

1. In a small bowl, combine the cucumber, tomato, capers, parsley, and chives. Add the vinaigrette and toss well. Cover and marinate at room temperature for 30 minutes to 2 hours, stirring occasionally.
2. Preheat the oven to 375°.
3. Place each fish fillet on a piece of aluminum foil large enough to enclose it. Season the fillets with pepper. Close the packages by folding the foil over and sealing the edges tightly. Set the packages on a baking sheet and bake for 25 to 35 minutes, until the fish is no longer transluscent.
4. Remove the packages from the oven; open, and cut each fillet in half. Place the pieces on four dinner plates. Spread ½ cup of mâche over each fillet, and spoon a generous portion of the marinade mixture over the mâche. Serve immediately.

*Cal. **247** Carb. **4g** Protein **44g** Chol. **131mg** Fat **5g/19%***

Herbed Walleye

The prize of our fly fishermen, baked instead of the traditional pan-fry in butter.

SERVES 4

2 pounds fresh walleye fillets
1 tablespoon fresh lemon juice
Freshly ground pepper

Buying Fresh Fish

Our fish-buying rule of thumb: Buy it whole, with bones and gills intact. That way, you can really tell if it's fresh. Look for clear, shiny, slightly bulging eyes; bright-scaled plump flesh that bounces back when touched and doesn't feel slimy. Check for a sweet—never fishy—smell, the scent of the sea. Gills should be bright pink or red, not dry and brown. Once you've chosen, have the fishmonger clean and fillet your fish.

Buying prefilleted fish? Select moist, firm flesh that looks bright and almost translucent. Skip any with dark, bruised spots or browning or yellowing around the edges. Make sure the fish is firm, not spongy or watery, and not harboring any fishy odors.

Whether displayed on ice or prepackaged, fish shouldn't be sitting in water. Since you can't always poke or prod, buy at a fish market where you can trust the quality to be good.

6 tablespoons malt vinegar
½ cup finely minced fresh chives
½ cup finely minced fresh chervil
2 tablespoons finely minced fresh dill
2 tablespoons finely minced fresh Italian parsley

1. Preheat the oven to 375°.
2. Place each fillet on a piece of aluminum foil large enough to enclose it. Splash the fillets with the lemon juice; season with the pepper. Sprinkle the vinegar and herbs evenly over the fillets. Close the packages by folding the foil over the fillets and tightly sealing the edges.
3. Place the packages on a baking sheet and bake for 25 to 35 minutes, until the fish is opaque and flakes when pierced with a fork. Serve immediately.

Cal. 216 Carb. 2g Protein 44g Chol. 203mg Fat 2g/10%

Walleye with Green Tomato Chutney

SERVES 4

2 pounds fresh walleye fillets
3 tablespoons fresh lime juice
1 tablespoon extra-virgin olive oil
½ teaspoon crush dried oregano
¼ teaspoon sea salt
¼ teaspoon cracked pepper
1 cup Green Tomato Chutney (page 183)

1. Place the fillets in a large baking dish. In a small bowl, combine the lime juice, oil, oregano, and salt and pepper. Pour the marinade over the fillets, and turn to coat. Refrigerate for 1 hour.
2. Preheat the oven to 375°.
3. On a work surface, lay out a piece of aluminum foil large enough to enclose the fillets. Place the fillets in the center of the foil, fold over the ends, and tightly seal the edges.
4. Place the package on a baking sheet and bake for 25 to 35 minutes, until the fish is opaque and flakes when pierced with a fork.
5. In a small saucepan over low heat, warm the chutney.
6. Remove the fillets from the package and divide among four dinner plates. Top each piece with ¼ cup of the warm chutney. Serve immediately.

Cal. 309 Carb. 18g Protein 45g Chol. 204mg Fat 6g/17%

Trout in an Almond Coat

SERVES 4

8 rainbow trout fillets (about 3 ounces each)
Juice of 1 lemon
Salt
2 egg whites
½ cup bread crumbs
½ cup sliced almonds

1. Preheat the oven to 400°.
2. Brush the fillets on the fleshy sides with the lemon juice. Sprinkle with salt to taste.
3. Dip the fleshy sides into the egg whites, then into the bread crumbs mixed with almonds; they should be evenly coated. Place the fish in a baking dish, skin side down, in a single layer, and bake for 10 minutes, or until the fish is opaque and flakes when pierced with a fork. Serve immediately.

Cal. **387** *Carb.* **15g** *Protein* **43g** *Chol.* **98mg** *Fat* **18g/41%**

Chervil Yellow Flounder

This method and sauce are great for any mild white fish.

SERVES 4

1½ pounds yellow flounder fillets, skinned
2 tablespoons all-purpose flour
Salt and freshly ground pepper
1 tablespoon hazelnut or walnut oil
½ cup chicken broth (see Basics)
2 tablespoons fresh lemon juice
2 tablespoons drained capers
2 tablespoons finely chopped fresh chervil
Whole chervil leaves
4 lemon wedges

1. Rinse the fillets and pat dry. Combine the flour and salt and pepper to taste on a plate. Dredge the fillets in the flour and shake off the excess; set aside.
2. Preheat the oven to 300°. In a large heavy skillet, heat the oil over medium-high heat. Sauté the fillets, two at a time, for 1 to 2 minutes per side, until lightly browned and just cooked. Do not overcook. Check periodically with a fork to see if the fish is flaky. Repeat with the remaining fish and

Saugatuck Fishing Boat - Kenosha

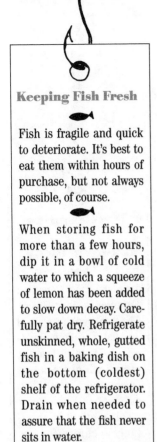

When storing fish for more than a few hours, dip it in a bowl of cold water to which a squeeze of lemon has been added to slow down decay. Carefully pat dry. Refrigerate unskinned, whole, gutted fish in a baking dish on the bottom (coldest) shelf of the refrigerator. Drain when needed to assure that the fish never sits in water.

Steaks and fillets can be wrapped in plastic wrap or waxed paper and refrigerated on the bottom shelf in an ice-filled colander set in a bowl to catch the melting water. Or surround them with ice packs and refrigerate in a baking dish. Use within 4 days.

keep warm in the oven until ready to serve. Pour off any oil remaining in the skillet.

3. Add the broth and lemon juice to the skillet. Bring to a boil for 2 minutes, scraping up any brown bits on the bottom of the pan. Stir in the capers and chopped chervil, and cook for 1 minute more. Return the fillet to the skillet, and turn to coat with sauce.

4. To serve, place the fillets and sauce on a serving plate and garnish with the chervil leaves and lemon wedges.

*Cal. **210** Carb. **4g** Protein **33g** Chol. **91mg** Fat **6g/27%***

Cod with Garlic

SERVES 4

1½ pounds fresh cod fillets, or other meaty fish fillets, such as
* bass or snapper*
¼ cup plus 1 tablespoon fresh lime juice
1 teaspoon olive oil
1 tablespoon unsalted butter
5 tablespoons thinly sliced garlic
3 tablespoons all-purpose flour
4 tablespoons coarsely chopped fresh cilantro
Salt and freshly ground pepper

1. Rinse the fillets and pat dry. Place the fillets in a glass or enamel-coated dish with 2-inch sides, and sprinkle with the lime juice. Cover with plastic wrap and refrigerate for 1 hour.

2. In a large heavy skillet, combine the oil and butter, and heat over medium heat. Add the garlic and sauté only until lightly brown; be careful not to burn or the dish will be bitter. Using a slotted spoon, remove the garlic and set aside; remove the pan from the heat, but hold for cooking the fish.

3. Remove the fish from the dish, reserving the lime juice, and pat dry with a paper towel. Dust it lightly with the flour and shake off the excess.

4. Warm the skillet over medium-high heat, and quickly fry the fish for 2 to 3 minutes per side, or until brown and crisp outside and just done on the inside. Remove the fish to a heated platter and keep warm while you finish the dish.

5. Return the garlic to the skillet to reheat. Stir in the reserved lime juice, cilantro, and salt and pepper to taste. Heat just until the cilantro begins to wilt. Pour the sauce over the fish and serve immediately

*Cal. **231** Carb. **13g** Protein **32g** Chol. **81mg** Fat **6g/22%***

Nantucket Cioppino

SERVES 12

1 teaspoon olive oil
1 pound carrots, scraped and coarsely chopped
3 cups coarsely chopped onion
3 cups coarsely chopped green bell pepper
3 tablespoons finely chopped garlic
1½ pounds mushrooms, sliced
8 cups peeled and coarsely chopped plum tomatoes, or 2 cans
(28 ounces each) plum tomatoes with basil, chopped
1 can (6 ounces) tomato paste
2 cups dry red wine or 1 cup red and 1 cup marsala wine
3 cups beef broth (see Basics)
1 lemon, thinly sliced (about ½ cup)
1½ cups finely chopped fresh Italian parsley
¼ cup shredded fresh basil
1 tablespoon dried oregano
Salt and freshly ground pepper
1 pound swordfish, cut into 2-inch chunks
3 live lobsters (about 1½ pounds each), cut into pieces
24 hard-shell clams, scrubbed
1 pound mussels, scrubbed and debearded
1½ pounds fresh cod, cut into 2-inch pieces
1 pound large shrimp, shelled and deveined

1. In a very large kettle, heat the oil over medium heat. Add the carrot, onion, pepper, and garlic, and cook, stirring occasionally, for 10 minutes.

2. Add the mushrooms, tomato (and any accumulated juices), tomato paste, wine, bouillon, lemon slices, 1 cup of the parsley, basil, oregano, and salt and pepper to taste. Bring to a boil, reduce the heat, cover, and simmer for 20 to 25 minutes.

3. Add the swordfish and lobster pieces and simmer, covered, for 15 minutes.

4. Add the clams, mussels, cod, and shrimp, and simmer, covered, for 10 more minutes, or until all the clams and mussels have opened and the fish is cooked.

5. Serve the cioppino in large bowls; sprinkle with the remaining parsley.

*Cal. **289** Carb. **23g** Protein **41g** Chol. **135mg** Fat **4g/13%***

The Canadian Fisheries Cooking Theory

I swear by the Canadian Fisheries Cooking Theory: The total cooking time of any fish can be estimated at 10 minutes for every inch of thickness (measured at the thickest part).

This method is amazingly accurate for any fish subjected to any cooking method—whole fish, steaks, or fillets, whether grilled, broiled, fried, poached, or baked.

How can you tell when your fish is cooked just right? Fish flesh turns opaque when done. Test by inserting the tip of a knife into the thickest part. White-fleshed fish should be milky white and fully cooked at the bone, and the juices should run clear when the flesh is pierced with a fork at the thickest part.

Little Fishes Sandwiches

SERVES 12

24 fresh sardines, anchovies, mackerel, perch, smelts, or herrings, 6 to 7 inches long, cleaned and filleted, tails left on
2 tablespoons all-purpose flour
Salt and freshly ground pepper
2 pounds spinach or Swiss chard tops
1 teaspoon olive oil
1 medium onion, finely chopped
4 garlic cloves, finely minced
1 teaspoon ground nutmeg
1 tablespoon finely minced fresh thyme
3 ounces white bread crumbs, soaked in ¼ cup skim milk
3 tablespoons finely minced fresh chervil
3 tablespoons finely minced fresh chives
1 egg white, lightly beaten

1. Preheat the oven to 450°.
2. Place the fish fillets on a work surface, skin sides up, and sprinkle lightly with the flour and salt and pepper to taste. Wash the spinach very well and pat it dry.
3. In a saucepan over medium heat, wilt the spinach until tender, 3 to 5 minutes. Drain, refresh under cold water, and squeeze out the excess moisture; finely chop the spinach.
4. In a skillet, warm the olive oil and sauté the onion and garlic until softened. Add the spinach, nutmeg, and thyme, and cook for 5 minutes. Cool.
5. By hand, squeeze out the moisture from the bread crumbs. In a large mixing bowl, combine the spinach mixture, bread crumbs, chervil, chives, and egg white, and mix well.
6. Very lightly wipe a large baking dish with olive oil. Place half the fillets, skin sides down, in the dish. With a spoon, evenly divide the spinach mixture onto the fillets, and top with the remaining fillets. Place in the oven and bake for 10 minutes, or until brown and tender. Serve immediately.

Cal. 86 Carb. 8g Protein 10g Chol. 27mg Fat 2g/19

Nantucket Mussels and Broth

SERVES 4

4 pounds fresh mussels, scrubbed and debearded just before
   cooking
1 cup dry white wine
1 cup chicken broth (see Basics) or water
1 cup shredded leeks, rinsed well, white parts with some green
$\frac{1}{2}$ cup chopped fresh tarragon
10 whole black peppercorns
5 whole garlic cloves
$\frac{1}{2}$ teaspoon salt
2 ounces salicornia, washed and drained (optional)
$\frac{1}{4}$ cup finely chopped fresh Italian parsley

1. Discard any mussels that do not close completely during
cleaning. Drain the mussels in a colander.
2. In a large heavy saucepan, combine the remaining ingredients, except the salicornia and parsley, and bring to a boil.
Lower the heat and simmer for 5 minutes. Add the mussels,
cover tightly, and return the heat to high. Cook the mussels
for 3 minutes, shaking the pan occasionally. Remove the pan
from the heat, add the salicornia, and let stand for 3 minutes,
or until the mussels are open.
3. Line a large colander with several layers of cheesecloth,
and pour the mussels in. Discard any unopened mussels.
Place the mussels in a large tureen, pour the strained juice
over, and garnish with the parsley. Serve immediately.

Cal. **187** *Carb.* **14g** *Protein* **22g** *Chol.* **51mg** *Fat* **5g/20%**

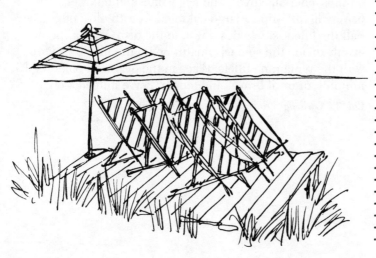

Red Pepper Aïoli

YIELD: $3\frac{1}{3}$ CUPS

1 pound new or russet potatoes, peeled and thinly sliced
$1\frac{2}{3}$ cups chicken broth
   (see Basics)
3 red bell peppers, roasted,
   skin, seeds, and stems
   removed, coarsely chopped
8 to 12 cloves garlic, peeled
   and coarsely chopped
Juice of 2 lemons
$\frac{1}{3}$ cup extra-virgin olive oil
Cayenne
Salt

1. Place the potatoes and
chicken broth in a saucepan.
Cook over medium heat, covered, for 15 minutes. Remove
the cover and cook for 20
minutes, or until all the broth
evaporates.
2. Place the roasted red peppers in a blender or food
processor and process until
smooth.
3. While the potatoes are still
hot, add them to the puréed
pepper; gradually add the garlic, lemon juice, and olive oil,
tasting periodically, until the
desired flavor is achieved and
the ingredients are puréed.
Add cayenne and salt to taste.
Cool, covered (to avoid a skin
forming), at room temperature. Refrigerate if not using
immediately.

Cal. **22** *Carb.* **2g** *Protein* **.3g**
Chol. **0mg** *Fat* **1g/57%**

Tarragon Lobsters

SERVES 2

2 live lobsters (about 1½ pounds each)
6 tablespoons dry sherry
2 tablespoons minced fresh tarragon
2 tablespoons minced fresh Italian parsley
1 tablespoon unsalted butter, melted
½ teaspoon grated lemon zest
1 lemon, cut into wedges

1. Insert the tip of a sharp knife into the flesh between the head and the body of each lobster, to sever the spinal cords. Set aside for 2 minutes.

2. Crack the claws and remove any loose bits of shell.

3. With the lobsters belly side up, using kitchen shears or a sharp knife, make a lengthwise slit in the lobsters' bellies.

4. Preheat the broiler. Arrange the lobsters, belly side up, on a baking sheet.

5. In a small bowl, combine the remaining ingredients except the lemon wedges, and mix well. Brush each lobster with the herb mixture.

6. Place the lobsters under the broiler for 6 to 8 minutes, or until the meat is tender and the shells are red. Garnish with lemon wedges and serve immediately with Red Pepper Aïoli (opposite) if desired.

*Cal. **206** Carb. **6g** Protein **29g** Chol. **116mg** Fat **7g/25%***

Spicy Boiled Lobsters

SERVES 4

4 tablespoons sea salt
2 tablespoons coriander seeds
1 tablespoon cayenne
1 tablespoon crushed red pepper flakes
20 black peppercorns
3 bay leaves
4 live lobsters (about 1½ pounds each)

1. Bring a large pot of water to a boil. Add the salt, coriander seeds, cayenne, red pepper flakes, peppercorns, and bay leaves.

2. Lower the lobsters carefully into the pot of boiling water. Return to a boil and cook for 6 minutes. Transfer the lobsters to a large bowl, and pour 6 cups of the cooking liquid over them. Allow to cool slightly before serving.

*Cal. **135** Carb. **2g** Protein **28g** Chol. **99mg** Fat **.8g/7%***

Salicornia

A delicate, dark green, jointed sea plant that grows wild on the "saltings" or mudflats along the eastern seaboard. Salicornia, which is sometimes called "glasswort," tastes of the sea—salty and a little briny—and is crunchy to the bite. It is said to be traditionally eaten on the longest day of the year in some places.

GRILL *of my* DREAMS

Grilled Chicken with Arugula Salad

SERVES 4

1 whole chicken (3½ to 4 pounds), butterflied
Juice of 4 lemons
3 tablespoons chicken broth (see Basics)
1 tablespoon olive oil
4 garlic cloves, peeled and finely chopped
Salt and freshly ground pepper
3 cups arugula leaves
2 vine-ripened tomatoes, diced
¼ cup chopped red onion
1 lemon, cut into wedges

1. Place the chicken in a glass baking dish. In a mixing bowl, combine half the lemon juice, the chicken broth, half the oil, half the garlic, and salt and pepper to taste. Pour over the chicken and refrigerate for 2 hours, basting several times.
2. Prepare the grill for cooking.
3. When the coals are hot, remove the chicken from the marinade and grill for 40 minutes, basting with the marinade and turning six times.
4. Meanwhile, cut the arugula into chiffonade and place it in a glass bowl. In another bowl, combine the remaining lemon juice, garlic, olive oil, and salt and pepper to taste, and mix well. When mixed, add the tomato and onion, and toss well. Let stand at room temperature until the chicken is ready to

Backyard Cooking

Summer. Time to move outdoors to our garden kitchen. Next to the grill are a sink, a fridge, and a big chopping block. We wash garden soil off the vegetables outdoors, sparing the kitchen sink. We're in the middle of the herb garden, so we can grab a handful of this or that, making it up as we go along. Better yet, one of us isn't indoors chopping while the other's outdoor grilling. And when there's a party, we're all together. Meals are simpler, the living's easy. There's more time for the really important things . . . building sand castles, meandering through the meadow, collecting beach glass, taking boat rides to the lagoon at midnight, catching lightning bugs, watching shooting stars, singing around a beach bonfire . . .

A Cut Above

Paillards, scallops, tender-loins. Across the country, these flat slices of chicken or turkey breast, veal loin, or other meats are known by a variety of names. Whichever is familiar to you, make sure you and your butcher are speaking the same language. Once home, whether you choose to pound your meat even thin-ner or not, sauté, broil, or grill it quickly—these are lean cuts and you want them to be nice and moist. Garnish with salsas or a salad on top; a dab of mus-tard or chutney on the side adds interest.

THE MATERIAL GRILL

Long-handled fork, tongs, and basting brush

★

To-the-elbow mitt

★

Assorted fruitwood chips

★

Herbs for basting and flavoring the fire

★

Grilling baskets in various sizes

★

Extra-long matches

★

Charcoal starter

★

Fire extinguisher

serve. Cut the chicken into portions, and serve each topped with the arugula salad and lemon wedges.

*Cal. **335** Carb. **14g** Protein **44g** Chol. **127mg** Fat **15g/36%***

Veal Chops with Greens

SERVES 4
4 veal chops (8 ounces each), about ¹/₂ inch thick
1 whole lemon
2 garlic cloves, smashed
4 sprigs fresh rosemary, slightly bruised
1 tablespoon olive oil
Salt and freshly ground pepper
1¹/₃ cups shredded radicchio
1¹/₂ cups shredded dandelion greens
1¹/₂ cups shredded arugula or watercress

1. Prepare the grill for cooking or preheat the broiler.
2. Remove all traces of fat from the veal chops and trim around the edges to remove any sinew. Place on a plate in one layer and set aside.
3. Remove the zest of the lemon with a zester and place it in a small bowl. In another small bowl, squeeze the juice from the lemon. Place 2 teaspoons of the juice with the zest, and reserve the remaining juice. To the bowl with the zest, add the garlic, rosemary, 1 teaspoon olive oil, and salt and pepper to taste. Stirring with a wooden spoon, smash and bruise all of the ingredients to release their flavors. Pour over the chops and let marinate for 20 minutes.
4. When ready to grill, remove the chops from the marinade and place on a grilling rack. Grill for 2 minutes per side, basting every time you turn the chops. These may also be cooked under the broiler or in a skillet.
5. Just before serving, in a small bowl, whisk the remaining oil and reserved lemon juice (about 2¹/₂ tablespoons) and salt and pepper to taste. Place the greens in a large bowl, pour the oil over them, and toss to coat evenly. Divide the greens among four dinner plates, top with the chops, and serve immediately.

*Cal. **256** Carb. **11g** Protein **29g** Chol.**99mg***

*Fat **12g/39%***

Spicy Grilled Chicken

SERVES 4

1 chicken (2$\frac{1}{2}$ to 3 pounds), quartered
4 lemon wedges
2 teaspoons mustard seeds
1$\frac{1}{2}$ teaspoons ground turmeric
1 teaspoon ground coriander
$\frac{1}{2}$ teaspoon ground allspice
$\frac{1}{2}$ teaspoon ground cloves
$\frac{1}{2}$ teaspoon cayenne
$\frac{1}{2}$ teaspoon cracked black pepper
2 tablespoons paprika
Grated zest of 1 orange
$\frac{1}{2}$ cup fresh orange juice
$\frac{1}{2}$ cup white wine
$\frac{1}{4}$ cup chicken broth (see Basics)

1. Rinse the chicken and pat it dry. Rub the chicken with lemon wedges and place it in a shallow dish.
2. In a blender or food processor, blend all the remaining ingredients. Pour the marinade over the chicken. Cover and refrigerate for 24 hours.
3. Preheat the oven to 325°. Prepare a grill for cooking.
4. Bring the chicken and marinade to room temperature. Bake in the oven for 30 to 40 minutes. Remove the chicken from the marinade, and reserve the marinade.
5. Place the chicken on the prepared grill and cook for 5 to 6 minutes on each side, until tender, basting with the reserved marinade. Serve immediately.

*Cal. **243** Carb. **11g** Protein **31g** Chol. **91mg** Fat **9g/30%***

Grilled Lime Chicken

SERVES 4

1 whole chicken (2$\frac{1}{2}$ pounds)
3 tablespoons honey
$\frac{1}{4}$ cup chicken broth (see Basics)
$\frac{1}{2}$ cup fresh lime juice
$\frac{1}{2}$ cup minced fresh cilantro
1$\frac{1}{2}$ teaspoons ground coriander
Zest of 4 limes, grated
4 Serrano chiles, seeded and minced

> ## GRILLED GOODNESS
>
> To increase the flavor of grilled foods:
> • Marinate and baste.
> • Serve with tasty—but not overwhelming—sauces.
> • Do as the Greeks, Spaniards, and Italians do: Drizzle on some great olive oil.
> • Match the food and the intensity of its flavor with the intensity of the oil. Grilled fish may take a light, mild oil. Grilled vegetables can vary: a light, mild oil for zucchini, but a rich, intense oil for sweet, viscous red peppers. Meats run the gamut, too; for thin veal paillards, light oils, and dark, peppery, full-bodied and fragrant oils for the most robust beefs.

1. Rinse the chicken and pat dry. Arrange the chicken in a shallow baking dish.
2. In a medium-size bowl, combine the remaining ingredients and mix well. Pour the marinade over the chicken, cover, and refrigerate for at least 24 hours, turning occasionally.
3. Preheat the oven to 325°. Prepare a grill for cooking.
4. Follow steps 4 and 5 of Spicy Grilled Chicken (opposite) to complete this recipe.

Cal. **244** *Carb.* **15g** *Protein* **34g** *Chol.* **92mg** *Fat* **4g/14%**

Grilled Balsamic Chicken

SERVES 4
1 chicken (2½ to 3 pounds), quartered
¼ cup chicken broth
½ cup balsamic vinegar
⅓ cup chopped scallion
2 tablespoons Dijon mustard
1 tablespoon minced garlic
1 tablespoon sugar
2 teaspoons Worcestershire sauce
1 teaspoon dry mustard
1 teaspoon cracked black pepper

1. Rinse the chicken pieces and pat them dry. Arrange the chicken in a shallow baking dish.
2. In a small bowl, combine the remaining ingredients and whisk to blend well. Pour the marinade over the chicken, cover, and refrigerate for at least 24 hours, turning occasionally.
3. Preheat the oven to 325°. Prepare a grill for cooking.
4. Follow steps 4 and 5 of Spicy Grilled Chicken (opposite) to complete this recipe.

Cal. **235** *Carb.* **8g** *Protein* **30g** *Chol.* **91mg** *Fat* **9g/34%**

"The wonderful world of home appliances now makes it possible to cook indoors with charcoal and outdoors with gas."

Bill Vaughan

Big Beef Burgers

SERVES 8

1 pound lean ground sirloin
1 pound lean ground turkey (99% fat free)
2 tablespoons nonfat plain yogurt
Freshly ground pepper

1. In a medium-size bowl, combine the sirloin, turkey, and yogurt, and mix thoroughly by hand. Cover and chill for at least 1 hour.
2. Prepare the grill or broiler for cooking.
3. Remove the meat from the refrigerator and shape into eight 1-inch patties. When the fire is ready, place the patties on the grill or broiler, 4 inches from the heat, and cook for 4 to 6 minutes per side. Serve the burgers on toasted buns.

*Cal. **188** Carb. **3g** Protein **27g** Chol. **70mg** Fat **8g/38%***

Bill's Beef Roast

SERVES 8

4 pounds prime rib of beef, with bone
1 head garlic, cloves separated and peeled
8 juniper berries
3 cups beef broth (see Basics)
Salt and freshly ground pepper
1 cup mesquite wood chips

1. Prepare a kettle-type or other covered grill for cooking.
2. Sliver four garlic cloves. With a sharp knife, make slits on all sides of the beef; push the garlic slivers into the slits.
3. Place the remaining garlic, juniper berries, and broth in a baking pan. Place the beef in the pan and baste well. Season with salt and pepper to taste
4. When the grill is very hot, sprinkle the wood chips over the coals. Remove the beef from the pan and place it on the grill. Cover immediately. Grill for 40 minutes, turning every 5 minutes, to sear all sides, basting every other time. Close the lid as soon as possible each time.
5. Remove the beef from the grill, and put it back into the baking pan. Baste the beef with the marinade, cover the pan with aluminum foil. Place the pan on the grill and close the lid. Cook for 25 minutes more for rare, basting every 10 minutes, or until the internal temperature reaches 155° on a meat thermometer. Let the beef rest for 10 minutes before carving.

*Cal. **241** Carb. **2g** Protein **27g** Chol. **74mg** Fat **13g/51%***

Sage and chive blossoms

Stuff a Burger

Love burgers? Try different ones. Stuff with just a tablespoon of:
- Sliced Monterey Jack
- Red-Hot Salsa
- Barbeque sauce
- Minced herbs
- Onion
- Lemon zest
- Honey mustard
- Sautéed mushrooms
- Prosciutto
- Parmesan
- Chopped olives

Parsley   *Marjoram*
Rosemary

Grilling

Herb bunches make great basters for food on the grill. When you're finished basting, toss the sprigs onto the fire for added flavor.

Rowdy's Best Beef

Our friends Al and Linda Rowder perfected a traditional Dutch beef marinade. We always look forward to summertime invitations for dinner at their home.

SERVES 8

2 London broil or top round roasts (1½ pounds each), 2½ to 3½ inches thick
Salt and freshly ground pepper
2 cloves garlic, minced
¼ cup soy sauce
¼ cup light brown sugar
1 cup good whiskey
4 tablespoons fresh lemon juice
1 teaspoon salt
3 tablespoons Worcestershire sauce
2 tablespoons canola oil

1. Place the meat in a glass baking dish large enough to hold it in a single layer. Season with the salt and pepper to taste. Combine all the remaining ingredients with 1 cup of water and pour over the meat. Place the meat in the refrigerator for 24 hours, turning and basting several times.
2. Preheat the grill.
3. Remove the meat from the refrigerator an hour before grilling. Place the meat over the hot coals and grill for 6 to 7 minutes per side, turning several times and basting each time. Pierce the meat with a fork or make a small cut to test the doneness. Cut into ¼-inch slices diagonally against the grain, and serve immediately.

Cal. 252 Carb. 2g Protein 26g Chol. 66mg Fat 12g/45%

Beefsteak Florentine

SERVES 8

3 porterhouse steaks (1¾ to 2 pounds each and 3 inches thick)
Coarse salt
2 tablespoons balsamic vinegar
Freshly ground pepper
2 lemons, cut into wedges

1. Prepare the grill for cooking.
2. When the coals are white, place the steaks on the grill and cook on one side for 5 minutes to sear. Season lightly with salt, brush with ⅓ tablespoon vinegar, and flip with two spatulas—never pierce with a fork. Cook for 5 minutes. Season lightly with salt and brush each with ⅓ tablespoon vinegar; flip and cook for 5 minutes more.
3. Transfer to a platter, grind pepper over, and cut into eight portions. Serve with lemon wedges.

Cal. 384 Carb. 3g Protein 51g Chol. 150mg Fat 18g/43%

Here's the Beef

Beef is a complete protein. It has no food fiber or carbohydrates; it's an excellent source of B vitamins, vitamin C, iron, niacin, and zinc. Beef fat is saturated, but much of today's beef is bred to be leaner, and of course, some cuts are leaner than others in any case. The human need for protein is not great, and there are many nonanimal sources, so 9 ounces or so of red meat a week is probably all any of us should have.

Chuck ★ 65% fat
Short Ribs ★ 55% fat
Skirt Steak ★ 55% fat
Corned Beef ★ 54% fat
Standing Rib ★ 53% fat
Blade Roast ★ 51% fat
Pot Roast ★ 51% fat
London Broil ★ 49% fat
Rib-Eye Steak ★ 48% fat
Porterhouse ★ 45% fat

T-Bone Steak ★ 44% fat
Tenderloin ★ 44% fat
Flank ★ 43% fat
Brisket ★ 41% fat
Arm Roast ★ 37% fat
Bottom Round ★ 37% fat
Sirloin ★ 36% fat
Round Steak/Eye ★ 33% fat
Rump Roast ★ 26% fat
Top Round ★ 20% fat

Figures indicate the percentage of calories from fat (meat trimmed of fat and cooked).

Grilled Bluefish

SERVES 4

2 skinned bluefish fillets (about 2 pounds, total, after skinning)
1 clove garlic, cut in half
1 tablespoon olive oil
2 tablespoons soy sauce
2 teaspoons Dijon mustard
Generous amount of freshly ground pepper
1 lemon, cut into wedges

1. Rinse the fillets and pat dry. Rub each side with the cut sides of the garlic and place in an oiled glass baking dish. Drizzle the fillets with ½ tablespoon olive oil and the soy sauce. Cover with plastic wrap and refrigerate for several hours.
2. Prepare a charcoal fire. When the coals have ashed over, rub ½ teaspoon Dijon mustard atop each fillet. Place the fillets in a wire fish basket and grill about 4 minutes per side, or until just cooked through. Serve immediately with fresh lemon.

Cal. **328** *Carb.* **4g** *Protein* **47g** *Chol.* **124mg** *Fat* **13g/36%**

Nantucket Seafood Grill

SERVES 6

6 lobster tails (4 ounces each), thawed if frozen, uncooked, shells split and meat carefully removed
1 pound swordfish steak, cut into six pieces
12 large sea scallops (about ¾ pound)
4 tablespoons Anchovy Vinaigrette (at right)
2 pounds baby red potatoes, steamed and sliced ¼ inch thick
8 cups assorted young salad greens, such as romaine, Oakleaf, Bibb lettuce, arugula, watercress
2 pound haricots verts or young string beans, trimmed, steamed for 2 minutes, drained, and cooled
1 red bell pepper, seeded and thinly sliced
2 small red onions, peeled and thinly sliced
1 pint perfectly ripe cherry tomatoes, halved and chilled
¼ cup drained capers
¼ cup drained niçoise olives
1 cup finely chopped fresh Italian parsley

1. Place all the fish in a large baking dish. Brush on all sides with 2⅔ tablespoons of the Anchovy Vinaigrette. Cover with plastic wrap and refrigerate for 2 hours.

Anchovy Vinaigrette

YIELD: ABOUT ⅔ CUP

1 tablespoon chopped garlic
1 tablespoon anchovy fillets, drained, 1 tablespoon anchovy oil reserved
¼ cup red wine vinegar
1 teaspoon Dijon mustard
¼ cup chicken broth (see Basics)
Salt and freshly ground pepper

1. In the bowl of a food processor, with the machine running, drop the garlic. Add the anchovies and process until smooth, scraping down the sides of the bowl once or twice.
2. With the motor still running, add the vinegar and mustard. Very slowly, add the broth and anchovy oil, drop by drop at first, then gradually in a thin stream, until a thick emulsion forms. Add salt and pepper to taste. Refrigerate until ready to serve.

Cal. **29** *Carb.* **1g** *Protein* **.4g** *Chol.* **.4mg** *Fat* **1.4g/65%**

(analyzed per tablespoon)

2. In a medium bowl, combine the warm sliced potatoes and remaining vinaigrette, and toss to coat. Cover and chill. Wash the greens and tear them into bite-size pieces.

3. Prepare a charcoal grill. When the coals have ashed over, grill the swordfish and lobster for 4 to 5 minutes per side; place on a warm platter. Grill the scallops for 2 minutes per side, or until slightly firm and just opaque. Transfer to the platter.

4. When ready to serve, divide the greens among four plates. Place a lobster tail, a piece of swordfish, and two scallops on each plate. Arrange the potatoes, *haricots verts*, red pepper, and onion on the plates. Garnish each plate with tomato, capers, olives, and parsley. Serve immediately, passing additional vinaigrette if desired.

*Cal. **503** Carb. **54g** Protein **52g** Chol. **105mg** Fat **9g/16%***

Perch on the Grill

SERVES 6

3 pounds perch fillets
2 tablespoons unsalted butter
2 tablespoons canola oil
1/2 cup finely minced fresh dill or Italian parsley
1/4 cup fresh lemon juice
Salt and freshly ground pepper
2 lemons, cut into wedges

1. Preheat the grill or broiler. Preheat the oven to 300°.

2. Rinse the fillets, pat dry, and place them on a baking sheet. In a small saucepan, melt the butter with the oil and brush one side of each fillet with the mixture. Sprinkle with the dill and lemon juice.

3. Carefully place the perch in a grilling basket and grill, herb side down, for 3 minutes. Remove the basket from the grill; brush the other side of the fillets with oil, and sprinkle with dill and lemon juice. Place back on the grill and grill for 2 to 3 minutes, until just opaque; continue with the remaining fillets, keeping the grilled fish warm in the oven or wrapped in foil. Serve with lemon wedges.

*Cal. **287** Carb. **1g** Protein **44g** Chol. **215mg** Fat **11g/35%***

Salmon on Salsa

SERVES 4

4 garlic cloves, minced
6 scallions, chopped, green parts only
1 medium red onion, chopped
12 ripe plum tomatoes, diced
4 tablespoons fresh lime juice
2 jalapeño peppers, seeded and chopped
1/2 cup chopped fresh cilantro
1/8 teaspoon ground cumin
Salt and freshly ground pepper
4 salmon fillets (about 6 ounces each), skinned and boned
2 tablespoons grainy mustard
3/4 to 1 teaspoon coarsely ground fresh pepper
1 teaspoon olive oil
4 cilantro sprigs
4 limes, cut into wedges

1. In a large bowl, combine the garlic, scallion, onion, tomato, lime juice, jalapeño, cilantro, cumin, and salt and pepper to taste. Cover and set aside.
2. Rinse the fillets and pat dry. Brush each side with the grainy mustard and sprinkle with coarsely ground pepper.
3. Heat a large skillet over medium-high heat. Add the oil. Sauté the fillets for 2 to 3 minutes on each side; do not overcook—the fish should be a little pink inside and very moist.
4. Spoon some salsa on each plate and top with a salmon fillet. Garnish with cilantro and lime wedges.

Cal. **302** *Carb.* **8g** *Protein* **38g** *Chol.* **66mg** *Fat* **13g/37%**

Grilled Salmon and Green Lentils

SERVES 4

1 salmon fillet (1 1/2 to 1 3/4 pounds), skinned and boned
2 garlic cloves, smashed
2 tablespoons honey
1 tablespoon light soy sauce
1/8 teaspoon crushed red pepper flakes
Lemon wedges

1. Prepare a charcoal grill and place a rack 4 inches above the coals.
2. Meanwhile, rinse the salmon and pat dry. Rub with garlic on all sides. Place in a glass dish.

Papa John's Planked Fish

In the summertime at my house, we most often cook fish the way my husband learned from Papa John, a Native American friend who's a terrific cook. Planking fish means cooking it on a piece of fruitwood over the fire. It's fabulous, virtually effortless, and a great way to cook and serve fish to a crowd. Our favorite fish for planking are whitefish, trout, salmon, bass, and walleye. Planked salmon is a style that prevails, from its Native American roots, throughout the Pacific Northwest.

Whatever your choice, have the fish filleted but its skin left on. Then find a new fruitwood board. Wild cherry is our choice, especially if it has a little sap still in it. Peach, apple, or pear are good, too. Cut the board so that it's 2 inches larger than your fillets but of a size that will fit on your grill.

Prepare the coals for grilling, then let them burn down to white ash. Brush one side of the board with olive or canola oil and place it, oiled side down, on the grill. When it's charred well, flip it over, brush it with oil again and place the fish fillets, skin side down, on the charred side. Place the board on the grill. Close the hood or cover the grill with heavy-duty foil, and cook the fish for 10 minutes for every inch of thickness, measured at the thickest part.

When it's done, sprinkle the fish with lemon juice and some freshly chopped herbs. Bring the fish, board and all, to the table to serve. Use a spatula to lift the fish gently from its skin. It will have a delicate, smoky, woodsy flavor that simply can't be beat.

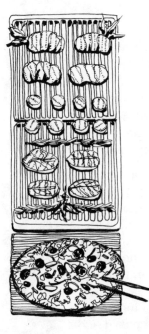

Grilled Salmon

Gravlax, that wonderful Scandinavian dill-cured salmon, is usually served cold. Try drizzling it with a teaspoon or two of olive oil and placing it on a hot grill. Grill 4 minutes per side, just enough to heat it through and char it a bit.

3. Whisk the honey, soy sauce, and pepper flakes. Pour over the fish and turn to coat evenly on both sides. Let marinate for 15 minutes at room temperature; most of the marinade should be absorbed by the fish.

4. Remove the fish from the marinade, and place in a fish basket. Grill for 4 to 5 minutes per side, according to its thickness; do not overcook. (It should flake when pierced with a fork.) Serve immediately, garnished with lemon wedges.

NOTE: The salmon can also be grilled under the broiler, about 3 to 4 inches from the heat, on a sheet of foil. When it's time to flip the fish, place another sheet of foil over it and turn it over.

*Cal. **284** Carb. **14g** Protein **37g** Chol. **66mg** Fat **10g/33%***

Bed of Green Lentils

SERVES 6
1 teaspoon olive oil
1 cup diced onion
2 tablespoons chopped garlic
2 cups diced carrot
4 cups dried green lentils, preferably Le Puy
2 sprigs fresh thyme
1 bay leaf
⅛ teaspoon ground cloves
Salt and freshly ground pepper

1. Heat the oil in a large skillet over medium heat. Add the onion and garlic, and sauté until tender and translucent. Add the carrot and continue to cook, stirring frequently, until lightly caramelized.

2. Add the lentils, thyme, bay leaf, and cloves, and cover with 1 inch of water. Reduce the heat and simmer for 15 to 20 minutes, until tender. Add more water as needed.

3. Remove from the heat. Season with salt and pepper to taste. Serve immediately.

*Cal. **355** Carb. **61g** Protein **28g** Chol. **0mg** Fat **2g/4%***

Bay Scallops on a Branch

SERVES 4

1 pound bay scallops (about 1
    inch in diameter)
Juice of 1 lemon
1 teaspoon olive oil
Freshly ground pepper
8 fresh rosemary sprigs (8 to
    10 inches long), leaves
    removed, or skewers
24 large garlic cloves,
    peeled
4 plum tomatoes, quartered
2 small limes, sliced into
    16 slices

1. Light the charcoal grill.
2. In a large bowl, combine
the scallops, lemon juice, oil,
and pepper. Marinate for 30
minutes.
3. Remove the scallops from
the marinade, letting the
excess drip off; reserve the
marinade. Thread each
rosemary sprig alternately
with four scallops, three
garlic cloves, four tomato
quarters, and four lime
slices.
4. Place the branches in a
grilling basket. Grill for 2 to
3 minutes per side, or until
the scallops are cooked through,
basting once or twice with the
marinade. Serve two sprigs per
person, on a bed of rice.

Cal. **150** Carb. **12g** Protein **20g**
Chol. **37mg** Fat **3g/17%**

Vegetable Kebabs

SERVES 4

1 eggplant, cut into cubes
1 red bell pepper, cut into 1-inch strips
8 small onions, trimmed and peeled
16 mushrooms, untrimmed
8 cherry tomatoes
1 medium cucumber, cut into
    8 slices
1 celery stalk, cut into 1-inch
    pieces
1/2 cup fresh lemon juice
Zest of 2 lemons
1 tablespoon olive oil
2 garlic cloves, finely minced
1 tablespoon chopped fresh
    thyme
1 cup chopped fresh mixed
    herbs, such as fennel, tar-
    ragon, chives, oregano, thyme,
    summer savory, or parsley

1. Thread the vegetables onto
skewers, alternating according
to color. Place the skewers in a
large glass dish. Sprinkle the
vegetables with the lemon juice
and zest, oil, garlic, and thyme.
Marinate for 1 hour, turning
frequently.
2. Prepare the grill for cooking.
3. Place the cup of mixed herbs
on a plate. Remove the skewers
from the marinade and roll each
one in the herbs.
4. Place the skewers directly on
the grill, about 4 inches from
the coals, and roast for 15 to 20
minutes, turning several times,
until the vegetables are tender
and browned. Serve immediately.

Cal. **192** Carb. **37g** Protein **7g**
Chol. **0mg** Fat **4.5g/19%**

Lime Prawns

SERVES 4

16 prawns or jumbo shrimp, in
  the shell
  Juice and zest of 3 limes
4 garlic cloves, finely
  minced
1 tablespoon olive oil
Freshly ground pepper
4 limes, cut into wedges
Lime Dip (page 195;
  optional)

1. In a shallow glass dish,
place the prawns, juice, zest,
garlic, oil, and pepper.
Baste the prawns and
marinate for 2 hours.
2. Prepare the grill.
3. Thread the prawns on
skewers. Place the skewers
on the grill and grill for 10
minutes, turning and basting once, or until pink.
Serve with Lime Dip if
desired.

Cal. **118** *Carb.* **2g** *Protein* **19g**
Chol. **140 mg** *Fat* **3g/26%**

Steak on a Stick

SERVES 4

1 pound beef tenderloin, cut into 1-inch
  cubes
16 large garlic cloves
8 cherry tomatoes
12 new potatoes
4 red onions, quartered
2 zucchini, each cut into 6
  slices
1 cup red wine
½ cup fresh herbs such as tarragon, fennel, oregano, parsley
2 tablespoons olive oil
4 large garlic cloves, chopped
Freshly ground pepper
8 long sprigs rosemary

1. Thread the meat and vegetables onto skewers, alternating colors and textures.
Place in a shallow glass dish.
2. Sprinkle the wine, herbs,
oil, garlic, and pepper over
the skewers and marinate
for 2 hours, turning every 20
minutes.
3. Prepare the grill for cooking.
4. Wind the rosemary around
the skewers securely. Place
the skewers on the grill and
baste. Cook for 8 to 10
minutes, turning to cook
evenly and basting as you
turn.

Cal. **475** *Carb.* **90g** *Protein* **33g**
Chol. **60mg** *Fat* **16g/22%**

THE MOST BEAUTIFUL

Grilled vegetables are also a fabulous antipasto or main dish.

VEGETABLE	GRILL STYLE
Artichokes	Parboil. Cut into halves or wedges and marinate before grilling over hot direct heat, 10 to 15 minutes.
Asparagus	Grill over hot direct heat 10 minutes, then move away from the coals to the outer edge of the grill for 10 minutes.
Broccoli	Cut stalks lengthwise in half. Grill over medium-direct heat 10 minutes per side.
Carrots	Parboil thick slices or sticks; then foil-wrap or cover, and cook over medium-hot heat 5 to 7 minutes.
Corn	Foil-wrap and cook 20 minutes over medium-hot direct heat; or husk and roast on the grill or in the embers for 15 minutes.
Eggplants	Grill whole in its skin until it blisters, blackens, and becomes limp. Scoop out the flesh, mash with a fork, and season with olive oil, lemon juice, and garlic.
Endive	Cook halved or whole 4 minutes per side over medium-hot direct heat.
Fennel	Blanch and grill halves or slices over medium-hot direct heat, 4 minutes per side.
Garlic	Grill a large head on the outer grill edge, over indirect heat, for 30 to 40 minutes, basting with oil or butter.
Green Beans	Cook, tossing occasionally, on foil or directly on grill over hot indirect heat.
Jícama/Kohlrabi	Slice and cook 3 minutes per side over hot direct heat.
Mushrooms	Cook cultivated types on a skewer over hot direct heat 4 to 8 minutes, rotating. Cook wild caps over hot direct heat 4 to 8 minutes per side, basting with broth.
Onions, white and red	Ember-cook in coals 45 to 50 minutes to caramelize. Or cook whole, halved, or sliced on grill over medium-direct heat 15 to 30 minutes.
Peppers	Foil-wrap whole peppers (or cook with cover down) over hot or medium-hot direct heat for 15 to 20 minutes, until the skin is slightly blackened.
Potatoes	Rub whole new potatoes, or halved or quartered larger ones, with butter or oil. Cook over medium-hot direct heat 45 to 55 minutes.

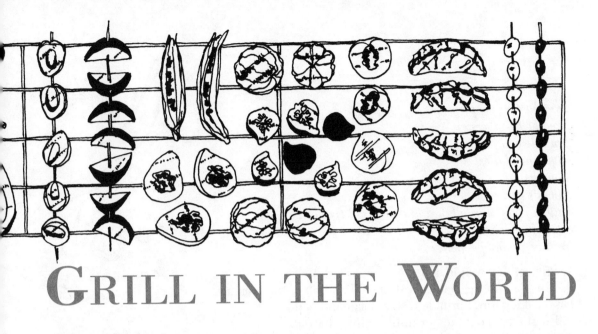

GRILL IN THE WORLD

Radishes, red and white	Brush with olive oil, season with salt and pepper. If very large, cut into thick slices. Cook over direct heat 10 to 12 minutes.
Squash	Grill summer squash over hot direct heat, 4 minutes per side. Grill winter squash over medium-direct heat, 45 to 55 minutes.
Sweet Potatoes	Wrap in foil; cook for 1½ hours over medium-direct heat.
Tomatoes	Grill whole cherry tomatoes 2 minutes per side over hot direct heat. Cook tomatoes 8 to 10 minutes over the same heat. Can be cooked covered.
Turnips	Slice, brush with oil and tarragon, and cook in foil 30 minutes over direct heat; turn once, and cook over direct heat 5 minutes.
Zucchini	Grill small ones whole, basting with oil until tender. Season with salt and pepper. Cook over direct heat 8 to 15 minutes, depending on size.

Grilled fruits, over the embers, keep the party aglow.

FRUIT	GRILL STYLE
Peaches, Apricots, Nectarines, Oranges, Mangoes, Papaya, Passionfruit, Star Fruit, Melons, Guava, Figs	Sprinkle with lemon juice and a bit of brown sugar and grill over indirect heat until golden caramel, about 7 to 9 minutes.
Apples	Granny Smiths: Place wedges on the end of a skewer; turn over the fire until skins blister, about 8 to 10 minutes. Roll in sugar and relish.
Bananas	Slit skins open; add a tablespoon of rum and some cinnamon. Close up and roast on grill 10 to 12 minutes.
Oranges	Peel and remove pith. Sprinkle with light brown sugar and cinnamon, then rum. Wrap in foil, roast 10 to 15 minutes.
Pears	Core; stuff with chopped almonds, brown sugar, Poire William. Wrap in foil. Or layer in slices, baste with honey-mustard glaze, and grill for 12 to 15 minutes.

Roasted Peppers

SERVES 6

2 yellow bell peppers
2 red bell peppers
2 purple bell peppers
6 banana chilies
3 onions
3 heads garlic
1 tablespoon olive oil or a Flavored Oil (pages 288–89)
Sea salt
Freshly ground pepper

1. Preheat the oven to 375°.
2. Brush all the vegetables with the oil and place them on a large baking tray. Sprinkle with sea salt and pepper.
3. Roast for 45 minutes, or until slightly charred.
4. Arrange the vegetables on a large platter. Serve immediately or at room temperature.

Cal. **117** *Carb.* **21g** *Protein* **3g** *Chol.* **0mg** *Fat* **3g/20%**

Grilled Summer Vegetables

SERVES 4

1½ cups chicken broth (see Basics)
1 tablespoon sliced garlic
2 pieces lemon zest, about 3 x ½ inch
½ teaspoon dried marjoram
1 cup peeled pearl onions
1 cup 1-inch-thick zucchini slices
1 cup 1-inch-thick summer squash slices
1 cup fennel pieces (about half of a small bulb, quartered)
1 cup cherry tomatoes
1 cup mushroom caps

1. Prepare a charcoal grill. In a medium saucepan, bring the chicken broth, garlic, lemon zest, and marjoram to a boil. Reduce the heat slightly and simmer for 10 minutes.
2. Add the onions to the liquid and simmer for 3 minutes. Add the zucchini and summer squash and simmer for 2 minutes. Add the fennel and simmer for 1 minute. Drain the vegetables.
3. Thread the vegetables, including the tomato and mushrooms, on four metal skewers, alternating them.
4. When the coals are ashed over, cook the vegetables, turning the skewers frequently, until the tomatoes are heated through

cherry twigs

charcoal briquets

hickory log

maple branch

cherry chips

grapevine root

and the other vegetables are beginning to char. Remove and serve at once with Poetic Aïoli (page 316) if desired.

*Cal. **67** Carb. **13g** Protein **3g** Chol. **0mg** Fat **1g/12%***

Grilled Potatoes

SERVES 4

4 long, slender baking potatoes, scrubbed and cut in half lengthwise
½ teaspoon coarse salt
4 garlic cloves
1 tablespoon chopped fresh rosemary or thyme leaves
1 teaspoon coarsely ground pepper
1 tablespoon olive oil

1. Prepare the grill for cooking. Cook the potatoes in a large pot of boiling water until just tender, about 15 minutes.
2. Meanwhile, using a mortar and pestle or small bowl, work the garlic into the salt until a paste is formed. Add the herbs and pepper, and stir in the oil.
3. Drain the potatoes and pat off excess water. Brush each potato with the herb mixture.
4. Grill the potatoes, turning occasionally and brushing with the remaining herb mixture, until they are cooked through and slightly charred, about 15 minutes. Serve immediately.

*Cal. **312** Carb. **64g** Protein **7g** Chol. **0mg** Fat **4g/19%***

Grilled Eggplant

SERVES 4

3 tablespoons hoisin sauce
1 tablespoon olive oil
2 tablespoons sugar
4 tablespoons balsamic vinegar
1 eggplant, cut lengthwise into ¼-inch slices

1. Prepare the grill. In a large bowl, combine the hoisin sauce, oil, sugar, and vinegar, and whisk to blend well.
2. Lay the eggplant on a baking sheet, and brush the top side of each slice with the sauce. Place the slices, brushed sides down, on the grill, 2 inches from the flame, and cook just until they start to blacken. Brush with the sauce, flip, using a spatula, and cook until the second side is blackened slightly.

*Cal. **68** Carb. **17g** Protein **1g** Chol. **0mg** Fat **.4g/12%***

mesquite logs

pecan chips

apple or

crabapple twigs

apple log

Hellfire-and-Damnation Barbecue Sauce

Best for beef, pork, and chicken.

YIELD: 4½ CUPS

1 tablespoon canola oil
1 cup finely chopped onion
6 garlic cloves, finely minced
4 cups tomato catsup
¼ cup cider vinegar
½ cup dark molasses or light
    brown sugar
½ cup Worcestershire sauce
½ cup beer
2 tablespoons Dijon mustard
¼ teaspoon Tabasco
Freshly ground pepper
1 tablespoon finely minced jalapeño pepper

In a medium-size saucepan, heat the oil over medium heat. Add the onion and garlic and sweat until transparent. Add the remaining ingredients, reduce the heat, and simmer for 30 minutes.
Cal. **25** Carb. **6g** Protein **.4g** Chol. **0mg**
Fat **.2g/8%***

Fresh Herb Marinade

To use on fish, shellfish, chicken, lamb, or vegetables.

YIELD: 1 CUP

1 cup finely chopped fresh herbs
1 tablespoon minced fresh garlic
¼ cup fresh lemon juice
Zest of 1 lemon
2 tablespoons olive oil
Salt and freshly ground pepper

Combine all of the ingredients well and mound over fish or chicken. Marinate for 1 hour.
Cal. **18** Carb. **.8g** Protein **.1g** Chol. **0mg**
Fat **1.7g/80%*** 🔘

Yogurt Marinade

Adds a nice warm zip to meat, poultry, and game.

YIELD: 1¼ CUPS

1 cup plain nonfat yogurt
4 cloves garlic, minced
¼ cup minced fresh ginger
¼ teaspoon ground cinnamon
¼ teaspoon ground all-spice
¼ teaspoon ground cumin
¼ cup finely minced fresh cilantro

Place all of the ingredients in a blender. Process until well mixed.
Cal. **11** Carb. **1.8g** Protein **1g** Chol. **0mg**
Fat **.1g/10%***

Beer Marinade

Great for beef, shrimp, crab, pork, lamb, or duck.

YIELD: 2¼ CUPS

½ cup Dijon mustard
½ cup white wine vinegar
1 cup beer
¼ cup light brown sugar
2 tablespoons chopped fresh tarragon
Freshly ground pepper

In a medium-size saucepan over medium heat, place all of the ingredients and cook until blended, stirring occasionally. Remove from the heat, cool, and use as a basting liquid.
Cal. **9** Carb. **1.4g** Protein **0g**
Chol. **0mg** Fat **.5g/36%*** 🔘

Honey-Pepper Sauce

Wonderful with chicken, pork, duck, whitefish, swordfish, salmon, trrout, shrimp or vegetables.

YIELD: 1 CUP

4 tablespoons white wine
4 tablespoons soy sauce
3 tablespoons honey
4 garlic cloves, very finely
    minced
1/4 teaspoon crushed red
    pepper flakes
Freshly ground pepper

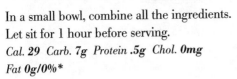

In a small bowl, combine all the ingredients. Let sit for 1 hour before serving.

Cal. 29 Carb. 7g Protein .5g Chol. 0mg Fat 0g/0%*

Mopping Sauce

For basting poultry, pork, lamb, or vegetables while grilling.

YIELD: 2½ CUPS

2 cups cider vinegar
2 tablespoons Dijon mustard
2 teaspoons cayenne
2 tablespoons Worcestershire
    sauce
2 tablespoons canola oil

In a medium-size saucepan over low heat, combine all of the ingredients and heat well, stirring to combine. Remove from the heat and cool.

Cal. 10 Carb. 1g Protein .0g Chol. 0mg Fat .8g/67%*

* The nutrition for the sauces on these pages was analyzed per tablespoon.

Chimichurri Sauce

The sauce of the Argentinian gauchos, ideal for basting pork ribs, sausage, or beef.

YIELD: 2 CUPS

1 cup coarsely chopped garlic
1/2 cup coarsely chopped fresh oregano
1/2 cup chopped fresh Italian parsely
4 anchovy fillets, mashed
2 red Serrano chilies, finely chopped
1/3 cup sherry vinegar
1/4 cup olive oil
3/4 cup chicken broth (see Basics)

In a glass jar, combine all of the ingredients. Cover and refrigerate for 2 weeks.

Cal. 18 Carb. 1g Protein .2g Chol. .3mg Fat 2g/83%*

★ Marinades ★

Usually combine an acid, oil, flavorings, and often a sweetener. Acids (vinegar, wine, or citrus juice) tenderize. Oil moisturizes. Garlic, mustard, herbs, and spices flavor. And sweeteners like honey or sugar take the edge off the acid and provide a rich, crusty surface. The marinade time depends on the food. Generally, porous flesh and delicate flavor—like that of fish—need the shortest time. Beef and game can take the longest. For additional flavor, also use marinades to baste while grilling.

★ Salsas ★

Mostly served with cooked food, they also can be used as marinades.

★ Dry Rub Marinades ★

Before grilling: rub food with garlic, cracked peppercorns, dry mustard or ginger, spices, and/or fresh herbs.

Salsa of the Tropics

YIELD: 1 QUART

2 ripe mangoes, diced
1 cup diced fresh tomato
1 cup diced red bell pepper
1 cup diced red onion
2 tablespoons minced garlic
1 jalapeño pepper, minced
2 teaspoons ground cumin
2 tablespoons olive oil
4 tablespoons red wine vinegar or sherry vinegar
½ cup fresh lime juice
Zest of 2 limes
Freshly ground pepper
Dash Tabasco or other pepper sauce
1 cup coarsely chopped fresh cilantro

Place all of the ingredients in a glass bowl and mix very well. Marinate for 2 to 3 hours in the refrigerator before serving.

*Cal. **34** Carb. **8g** Protein **13g** Chol. **0mg** Fat **.3g/6%***

Cool Tomato Salsa

YIELD: 2 CUPS

1½ cups finely diced or chopped plum tomatoes
½ cup finely diced white onion
½ cup finely chopped fresh cilantro
2 tablespoons cider vinegar
1 teaspoon sugar

Place all of the ingredients in a small bowl and mix well. Set aside for 1 hour to let the flavors meld.

*Cal. **13** Carb. **3g** Protein **.4g** Chol. **0mg** Fat **.1g/9****

Corn Salsa

YIELD: 6 CUPS

3 cups fresh corn kernels, blanched for 3 minutes
1 can (15 ounces) black beans, rinsed and drained
5 scallions, thinly sliced
1 medium red bell pepper, cored, seeded, and diced
1 medium jalapeño pepper, cored, seeded, and finely diced
⅓ cup rice wine vinegar
1 tablespoon Dijon mustard

*The nutrition for the salsas on these pages has been analyzed per ¼ cup

1 tablespoon olive oil
⅔ cup finely chopped fresh cilantro
Tabasco or other pepper sauce
Pinch cayenne
Salt and freshly ground pepper

1. In a large bowl, combine the corn, beans, scallion, red pepper, and jalapeño pepper. Set aside.
2. In a small bowl, whisk the vinegar and mustard. Pour in the oil by drops, whisking constantly. Add the cilantro and season with Tabasco, cayenne, and salt and pepper to taste. Whisk until well combined.
3. Drizzle the vinaigrette over the corn salad and toss until well combined. Refrigerate for at least 2 hours before serving.

Cal. 39 Carb. 8g Protein 2g Chol. 0mg Fat .8g/14%*

SALSA

It simply means "sauce" in Spanish. But sometimes salsa is a hot sauce, laced with chili peppers that ignite upon contact with the tongue and go on to warm the whole body. Other times, salsa is sweet and sour and gently titillates the palate. A salsa can be a fruit, herb, or vegetable mixture that brightens a piece of grilled meat, fish, or poultry. Generally speaking, though, you should expect some chili fire. Consider salsa's hot-blooded origins: Spain and Latin America.

Billy's Bad Salsa

YIELD: 3 CUPS

6 jalapeño peppers, seeded and sliced
12 whole garlic cloves
12 fresh ripe tomatoes, cut into wedges
2 tablespoons olive oil
1 tablespoon honey
1 teaspoon ground cumin
1 teaspoon salt
8 scallions, cut into 1-inch lengths
2 cups coarsely chopped fresh cilantro
¼ cup fresh lime juice
Zest of 4 limes
Freshly ground pepper

1. Preheat the broiler. Place the jalapeño, garlic, and four tomatoes on a baking sheet, and broil until the garlic is tender and the tomatoes are slightly blackened.
3. Place the broiled ingredients in a blender or food processor, and purée slightly. Add the oil, honey, cumin, and salt, and pulse until almost puréed. Add the scallion and process just until the scallion still has some texture. Transfer the purée to a bowl.
4. Dice the remaining tomatoes and add to the salsa. Add the cilantro, lime juice, and zest, and season with pepper. Set aside for 2 to 4 hours, at room temperature before serving.

Cal. 76 Carb. 13g Protein 2g Chol. 0mg Fat 3g/28%*

A **PECK** OF PEPPERS

Basics

Peppers come in an endless variety of appearance and taste: fiery red, cool white, and royal purple; from sweet and mild to incendiary. Experts count more than 1,000 types.

Latin American and Asian cuisines have brought an explosion of peppers into our cooking. There's confusion as well, particularly when it comes to pepper nomenclature.

Capsicum is the botanical classification of all peppers. But *chile* is the Mexican word for both hot and sweet peppers. In the U.S., chile or chile pepper always refers to hot. *Pimiento* is the generic Spanish name for pepper, but we use it for a particular sweet red pepper mostly found roasted and packed in jars.

For our purposes the categories are "sweet" and "chile."

SWEET PEPPERS

These include the familiar bell peppers and the tasty, elongated light green Italian "frying" peppers. All bell peppers start out green and all ripen to the characteristic color for which they are named—red, yellow, orange, ivory, purple, and black or chocolate brown—becoming sweeter in the process. True green peppers, of course, simply remain as they began. Except for some red and green, most types are imported principally from the Netherlands. They are far sweeter—and far more expensive.

Sweet peppers are prized for both color and flavor. They are roasted, skinned, and bathed in olive oil; essential for ratatouille and Hungarian goulash; sliced into salads; minced for relishes; pickled and stuffed.

The Italian or "frying" peppers are usually sautéed in olive oil.

In Cooking

Preparation depends on how you intend to use them. Before slicing or dicing, cut the pepper in half through the stem end. Cut the stem away, shake out the seeds and trim the pithy ribs on the inside with a small paring knife.

Roasted peppers have a velvety texture and a rich, soft but intense flavor.

To roast: preheat the broiler. Place on a broiler pan and broil 2 to 3 inches from the heat. Turn the peppers until the skins are blackened all over. Using tongs, transfer the peppers to a brown or plastic bag and close well with a twist tie. Let the peppers sweat in the bag 15 to 20 minutes, then remove them and peel away the skin.

CHILE PEPPERS

Chile peppers are a matter of regional and individual taste. Some people go for the burn. I prefer deep flavor that develops by layering various levels of warmth. My best advice: Always taste peppers and the dish you are adding them to. Two peppers, even from the same plant, can have radically different levels of heat. Generally, the longer and thinner the pepper, the hotter it is. Cutting out the pithy ribs and seeds can help turn down the heat. Most of the flavor, but less of the heat, is in the fleshy outer wall, while the heat concentrates in the ribs.

In Cooking

I use fresh chiles primarily for flavor accents, taking into account their heat, texture, and color. Fresh chiles vary widely in heat, acidity, and citrus quality.

In many cuisines (including Southwestern and Mexican)

chiles are roasted or grilled before they are used in a dish. The skin, which can be bitter, is easily removed after roasting, which also tends to bring out a fuller, distinctively earthy and smoky flavor.

Roast chiles quickly and evenly on a rack over an open gas flame, under a broiler (see roasting instructions for sweet peppers, above), or on a grill. The skin should blacken and blister all over, but the flesh should not burn.

Don't wash roasted chiles under running water or the natural oils will be diluted and the wonderful smoky flavor reduced. Split open and scoop out the seeds and pith with the tip of a knife; remove the stem. Chiles can be roasted and kept in the refrigerator for a day or two before using.

When using roasted chiles in a sauce, try a blend of two or three compatible types rather than just one.

Dried Chiles

Ounce for ounce, they pack a lot more punch than fresh. Drying intensifies and magnifies the flavors and concentrates sugar. The result is much more flavor distinction and dimension.

Dried peppers that are dusty, faded, or have white spots have been improperly dried and stored. Check for the powerful fresh aroma all well-dried spices have.

To release the flavor of dried chiles for cooking, first dry-roast them in a skillet or a 250° oven for 3 to 4 minutes. Shake them so they don't scorch, which will make them bitter. Then soak in hot (not boiling) water for 30 minutes or so until they are soft. Purée them in a blender, adding some of the soaking water as needed.

There are only two ways to truly enjoy and understand how to cook with dried chiles: by meticulously following recipes, or by trial and error in testing and tasting.

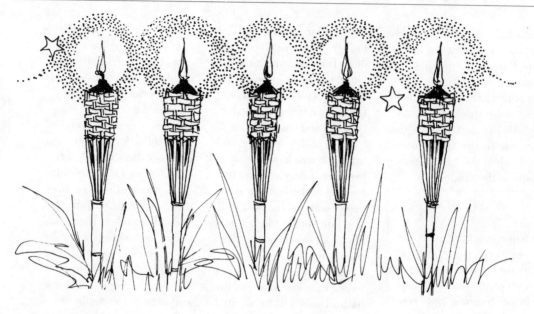

Minted Monkfish Fillet

The lobsterlike taste of monkfish is gently infused with mint and lime in an easy oven-roasting method that keeps the juices sweet and the monkfish moist.

SERVES 4

1 monkfish fillet (2 pounds), trimmed of fat
1 tablespoon unsalted butter, melted
2 tablespoons minced fresh Italian parsley
2 tablespoons minced lime zest
½ cup minced fresh mint
¼ cup dry vermouth
Freshly ground pepper

1. Preheat the oven to 375°.
2. Place the monkfish on a piece of aluminum foil large enough to enclose it.
3. Brush the melted butter on the fillet and sprinkle with parsley, lime zest, mint, vermouth, and pepper to taste.
4. Form a package by folding the foil over the fillet and tightly sealing the edges.
5. Set the package on a baking sheet and bake for 25 to 35 minutes. Remove from the oven, open the foil, and check to see

To Light the Night

★ Votives flicker along a railing or are hung like captured stars in the branches of a tree
★ Citronella candle lanterns cast pools of light and scent the cool dock
★ Torches of bamboo spin into flame
★ Luminarias made with votives and paper bags are weighted with sand, curving along a softly shimmering pathway.

Summer Nights

Minted Monkfish Fillets

Veggies in a Skillet

Honeydew Sorbet

that the fish is opaque and flakes easily when pierced with a fork. Place the fish and juice on a platter. Serve immediately.

Cal. **202** *Carb.* **1g** *Protein* **33g** *Chol.* **65mg** *Fat* **6.5g/28%**

Veggies in a Skillet

SERVES 8

1 teaspoon olive oil
1 potato (about ¾ pound), cut into 1-inch cubes
1 bunch baby turnips (about ¾ cup), peeled
1 cup peeled and cubed eggplant
1 cup trimmed and bias-cut (to 2 inches) string beans or pole beans
1 cup sliced zucchini
1 cup sliced yellow squash
1 cup cut-up broccoli, florets and stems
1 cup bias-cut (to 1 inch) celery
½ cup pearl onions
1 cup bias-cut (to 2 inches) asparagus
1 cup peas, thawed if frozen
1 cup julienned green or red bell pepper
1 cup cherry or yellow plum tomatoes
1 tablespoon olive oil
1½ cups beef broth (see Basics)
1 bay leaf
4 whole garlic cloves, smashed
½ teaspoon dried savory
½ teaspoon dried tarragon
Salt and freshly ground pepper

In a large skillet with 3-inch sides, heat the oil over medium heat. Add the potato and turnip and cook for 5 minutes, stirring occasionally. Add the remaining vegetables, except the tomatoes, and stir to mix. Add the beef broth, bay leaf, garlic, savory, tarragon, and salt and pepper to taste. Bring to a boil, cover, lower the heat, and simmer for 15 minutes. Add the tomatoes and cook for 10 minutes. Serve immediately.

Cal. **83** *Carb.* **16g** *Protein* **4g** *Chol.* **0mg** *Fat* **1g/11%**

Peach Soup

SERVES 4

½ cantaloupe, peeled and cut into chunks
4 ripe peaches
½ cup Low-Fat Blend (see Basics)
2 tablespoons Grand Marnier
2 tablespoons minced fresh mint

In a blender or food processor, combine the cantaloupe and peaches, and blend until smooth. Add the Low-Fat Blend and Grand Marnier, and mix well. Transfer to a bowl and stir in the mint. Cover and chill until needed.

Cal. 86 Carb. 15g Protein 4g Chol. .6mg Fat .7g/7%

Grilled Tuna

SERVES 4

Four 1-inch-thick tuna steaks (7 ounces each)
¼ cup fresh lemon juice
1 tablespoon extra-virgin olive oil
2 small garlic cloves, minced
2 teaspoons chopped fresh oregano
1 tablespoon grated lemon zest
¼ teaspoon salt
Freshly ground pepper

1. Prepare a charcoal grill.
2. Meanwhile, rinse the tuna, pat dry, and place in a shallow glass or ceramic dish.
3. In a small bowl, whisk the remaining ingredients. Pour over the fish and cover with plastic wrap; marinate for 30 to 45 minutes in the refrigerator.
4. When the fire is ready, drain the tuna and place it in a fish or meat basket. Grill the steaks 4 inches from the fire, 3 minutes per side for rare or approximately 5 minutes per side to cook through. Pierce with a fork to see if the tuna is flaky and done. Baste with the remaining marinade if desired.
NOTE: You can substitute lime juice and zest for the lemon.

Cal. 210 Carb. 2g Protein 38g Chol. 80mg Fat 5g/23%

Crisp Herb Toast

YIELD 24 SLICES

24 slices French bread, ½ inch thick
2 tablespoons extra-virgin olive oil
4 tablespoons chopped fresh dill, sage, tarragon, basil, summer savory, or mint, or a combination
4 tablespoons finely minced fresh Italian parsley
2 tablespoons cracked black peppercorns

1. Preheat the oven to 500°.
2. Place the bread slices on a cookie sheet, and lightly brush them with about 1 tablespoon of the oil. Place in the oven and toast for 3 to 4 minutes, until golden brown.
3. Remove the toast from the oven, turn it over, and lightly brush with the remaining oil. Evenly sprinkle the bread with the herbs and pepper, and toast for another 3 to 4 minutes.

Cal. 97 Carb. 17g
Protein 3g Chol. .9mg
Fat 2g/20%
(analyzed per slice)

Fire and Ice Salad

SERVES 6

2 English cucumbers or regular cucumbers
¼ cup salt
¼ cup nonfat plain yogurt
Juice of 1 lemon
Dash Tabasco
2 ripe tomatoes, cut into wedges
Freshly ground pepper
½ cup finely chopped fresh cilantro

1. If desired, peel the cucumbers and slice them into paper-thin circles. Place in a bowl and toss with the salt. Refrigerate for 30 minutes.
2. In a small bowl, whisk the yogurt, lemon juice, and Tabasco. Drain the cucumber of all collected juices and squeeze to release as much liquid as possible. Stir the cucumber and sauce together and add the tomato, pepper, and cilantro. Refrigerate for 30 minutes before serving.

Cal. 32 Carb. 7g Protein 2g Chol. 0mg Fat .4g/9%

Peppered Long Beans

SERVES 4

2 cups chicken broth (see Basics)
2 tablespoons distilled white vinegar
1 tablespoon soy sauce
2 tablespoons sesame oil
1 tablespoon Szechuan peppercorns, slightly crushed
⅛ teaspoon freshly ground pepper
Dash Tabasco
1 pound Chinese long beans, rinsed and ends trimmed

1. In a large skillet, bring all of the ingredients, except the beans, to a boil; continue to boil until reduced by half. Add the beans, cover, and cook for 2 minutes. Remove the cover; continue to cook over medium heat, stirring occasionally, until the beans are tender yet still crisp, about 5 minutes.
2. Transfer the cooked beans to a serving dish. Continue to cook the liquid in the skillet until it is reduced to ⅓ cup. Pour the sauce over the beans and serve immediately.

Cal. 80 Carb. 12g Protein 4g Chol. 0mg Fat 3g/31%

Chinese Long Beans

They are really long—1 to 3 feet—and taste like green beans without strings. They're sold year-round in approximately 1-pound bunches, either light or dark green. I like the dark green ones, the more tender of the two. Cook as you would green beans.

Shooting-star night

Artichoke Spread

YIELD: 4 CUPS

3 jars (6 ounces each) marinated artichoke
  hearts, well drained
1/2 teaspoon finely grated lemon zest
1/2 cup mild, soft low-fat goat cheese
1/2 cup nonfat plain yogurt
2 cups finely chopped Italian parsley
1 1/2 teaspoons coarsely ground pepper
Dash Tabasco or other pepper sauce

1. In a food processor, pulse the artichoke hearts until coarsely chopped. Transfer to a bowl and toss with the lemon zest.
2. Place the goat cheese and yogurt in the food processor and
purée until smooth. Gently fold the cheese into the artichokes,
along with the parsley and pepper. Add Tabasco to taste; stir to
combine. Cover and refrigerate for at least 2 hours.

*Cal. **14** Carb. **2g** Protein **1g** Chol. **2mg** Fat **.4g/28%***
(analyzed per tablespoon)

Cool Cucumber Soup

SERVES 4

3 cups English hothouse cucumbers, cut in chunks
1/4 cup chopped scallion, white and green parts
4 garlic cloves, minced
1/2 cup chicken broth (see Basics)
2 cups Low-Fat Blend (see Basics)

The Night Beach

On a summer's night, the
beach is black magic:

★ Fireflies twinkle and dart.
★ Crabs scrabble across the
shore, fleeing night hunters.
★ Gulls and sandpipers skit-
ter and settle into the dark.
★ Stars shoot across the sky.
★ Faraway running lights
bob and twinkle.
★ Minnows, guppies, elvers,
and chubs streak silver
under water.
★ Fireworms and tiny, glow-
ing protozoans shimmer as
"star phosphorescence."
★ Blue-tailed flies and tree
swallows swarm.
★ Cottonwood fluff and
will-o'-the-wisps wander.

AUGUST 11

Sky watchers have observed it since A.D. 830: An annual meteor shower, thought to originate in the constellation Perseus. Its peak arrives so punctually every year, many consider this "The Night of the Shooting Stars." It's a great night for a party.

Menu

Strawberry Margaritas

Artichoke Spread on Endive

Cool Cucumber Soup

Moroccan Chicken Salad

Five-Grain Pilaf

Black Raspberry Sorbet

1 tablespoon fresh lemon juice
2 tablespoons finely chopped fresh mint
1 tablespoon minced fresh chives
Cayenne
Salt
Fresh mint leaves and lemon slices

1. In a blender or food processor, purée the cucumber, scallion, garlic, and chicken broth until smooth. Transfer to a bowl.
2. Whisk in the remaining ingredients, except the mint leaves and lemon slices, until well combined; refrigerate.
3. Serve very cold. Whisk well, then ladle into bowls and garnish with the mint leaves and lemon slices.

Cal. 93 Carb. 10g Protein 11g Chol. 3mg Fat 1g/10%

Moroccan Chicken Salad

SERVES 6

2 whole chicken breasts (1³/4 pounds)
1 large red bell pepper, cored, seeded, and thinly sliced
1 red onion, peeled and thinly sliced
1 tablespoon toasted and ground cumin seeds
¹/2 teaspoon cayenne
1 teaspoon paprika
2 tablespoons finely minced garlic
¹/4 cup fresh lemon juice
¹/4 cup red wine vinegar
1 cup chicken broth (see Basics)
2 tablespoons olive oil
¹/2 cup finely minced fresh cilantro
¹/2 cup finely minced fresh Italian parsley
Salt and freshly ground pepper
¹/4 cup niçoise or Kalamata olives

1. Roast, broil, or poach the chicken. When it is cool, bone and skin it, and shred the meat into bite-size pieces.
2. In a large bowl, combine the chicken, pepper, and onion. Refrigerate, covered.
3. Combine the cumin, cayenne, paprika, and garlic. Whisk in the lemon juice, vinegar, chicken broth, and olive oil. Stir in the cilantro, parsley, and salt and pepper to taste.
4. Remove the chicken from the refrigerator; pour the vinaigrette over and toss. Garnish with the olives.

Cal. 310 Carb. 8g Protein 40g Chol. 118mg Fat 13g/38%

Shrimp Risotto

SERVES 4

1 cup clam broth
5 cups chicken broth (see Basics)
1 pound jumbo shrimp
1 teaspoon olive oil
1 cup halved and thinly sliced onion
2 teaspoons minced garlic
2 cups Arborio rice
¾ cup white wine
3 cups coarsely chopped mixed greens,
   such as watercress, arugula, or spinach
1 cup peeled, seeded, and coarsely
   chopped tomato
1 package (10 ounces) frozen peas, defrosted
½ cup green olives, with pits
Salt and freshly ground pepper
½ cup coarsely chopped fresh Italian parsley

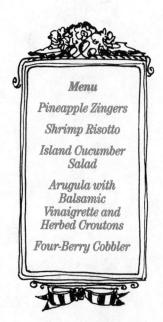

1. In a large pot, bring the clam broth and chicken broth to a boil. Add the shrimp; lower the heat to medium and cook for 3 to 4 minutes, or until just cooked through. Do not overcook.
2. Remove the shrimp with a slotted spoon and place in a colander; rinse with water to stop cooking, and set aside. Strain the cooking liquid into another pot and keep it warm over a low flame. Peel, devein, and coarsely chop the shrimp, and set aside.
3. In a large heavy skillet with 3-inch sides, heat the oil over medium heat. Add the onion and garlic, and sauté for 4 to 6 minutes. Add the rice and stir to coat; cook for 3 minutes, stirring constantly. Add the wine and cook until it evaporates.
4. Add enough of the shrimp cooking liquid to cover the rice. Stir constantly with a wooden spoon until most of the liquid is absorbed and the risotto is creamy and tender, about 20 minutes. It may not be necessary to use all the liquid.
5. About 5 minutes before the risotto is finished, stir in the chopped shrimp, greens, tomato, peas, olives, and salt and pepper to taste. Add the parsley and serve immediately.

*Cal. **230** Carb. **41g** Protein **13g** Chol. **119mg** Fat **2g/7%***

Menu

Pineapple Zingers

Shrimp Risotto

Island Cucumber
Salad

Arugula with
Balsamic
Vinaigrette and
Herbed Croutons

Four-Berry Cobbler

Island Cucumber Salad

SERVES 4

1/4 pound low-fat goat cheese, crumbled
1 cucumber, thinly sliced
1 small red onion, thinly sliced
1 cup thin strips of fennel
2 scallions, chopped
8 Greek olives, quartered
6 tablespoons white wine vinegar
1½ tablespoons sugar
Salt and freshly ground pepper

1. In a serving bowl, combine the cheese, cucumber, red onion, fennel, scallion, and olives. In a small bowl, combine the vinegar and sugar; stir until the sugar has dissolved.
2. Pour the dressing over the salad and season with salt and pepper. Toss well until evenly coated. Let the salad sit at room temperature for 1 hour to let the flavors blend.

*Cal. **80** Carb. **13g** Protein **3g** Chol. **25mg** Fat **3g/26%***

Herbed Croutons

SERVES 4

8 slices seven-grain bread, cubed
1 tablespoon olive oil
Salt and freshly ground pepper
4 garlic cloves, very finely minced
3 tablespoons finely minced fresh Italian parsley
2 tablespoons finely minced fresh basil
1 tablespoon finely minced fresh oregano
2 teaspoons finely minced fresh thyme

1. Preheat the oven to 375°. Lightly coat a baking sheet with olive oil.
2. Lightly brush each side of the bread with oil. Cut the slices into 1/4-inch cubes. Spread the cubes in a single layer on the prepared sheet. Sprinkle with the salt, pepper, and garlic. Bake for 10 to 14 minutes, or until toasted.
3. In a small bowl, combine the parsley, basil, oregano, thyme, and 2 teaspoons of water, and mix well. Sprinkle over the toasted croutons. Bake 2 to 4 minutes more, stirring to coat each crouton evenly. Cool completely on a rack.

*Cal. **74** Carb. **8g** Protein **2g** Chol. **0mg** Fat **4g/49%***
(analyzed per 1/4 cup)

Tuna and White Bean Salad

SERVES 4

1 pound cannellini beans, rinsed and sorted
1 teaspoon salt
1 cup chopped fresh Italian parsley
1 cup coarsely chopped scallion, green and white parts
1 can (6½ ounces) tuna packed in water
4 tablespoons fresh lemon juice
2 tablespoons red wine vinegar
3 tablespoons olive oil
Salt and freshly ground pepper

1. Two days before serving, soak the beans in a large bowl of water.
2. The next day, drain the beans and place them in a large saucepan. Cover with water, add the salt, and bring to a boil. Reduce the heat, cover, and simmer gently until the beans are tender, 1 to 1½ hours. Drain.
3. In a large bowl, combine the beans, parsley, and scallion. Flake the tuna with a fork and fold into the beans.
4. In a small bowl, whisk the lemon juice, vinegar, and oil. Pour over the beans and stir gently to combine. Season with salt and pepper to taste. Refrigerate for 8 hours or overnight. Serve over mixed greens.

*Cal. **340** Carb. **48g** Protein **22g** Chol. **5mg** Fat **8g/20%***

Black Angus & Black Beans

SERVES 4

1 tablespoon olive oil
1 pound sirloin steak, trimmed of all fat and cut into 1/2-inch strips
2 cups coarsely chopped onion
5 garlic cloves, finely chopped
4 jalapeño peppers, seeded and minced
2 cups chopped fresh plum tomato
1 1/2 cups beef broth (see Basics)
1/2 pound black beans, cooked
3 tablespoons chili powder, or to taste
2 teaspoons ground cumin
2 teaspoons dried oregano
1/4 teaspoon cayenne
1/2 teaspoon salt
Freshly ground pepper
1/2 cup chopped scallion, green and white parts

1. In a large stockpot or very large skillet, heat the oil over medium-high heat. Sauté the sirloin just until no longer pink; do not overcook. Remove the meat with a slotted spoon to a bowl and set aside.
2. Add the onion and garlic to the pot and sauté over medium heat until tender, about 8 minutes.
3. Stir in the jalapeño pepper, tomato, broth, beans, spices, and salt. Lower the heat to a simmer, cover, and simmer for 30 to 45 minutes. Add the sirloin and simmer for 15 minutes; taste and adjust the seasoning. Serve immediately, garnished with chopped scallion.

Cal. 349 Carb. 34g Protein 32g Chol.64mg Fat 11g/29%

West Coast Seafood Salad

SERVES 6

1 pound shrimp
One live lobster (1 to 1½ pounds)
½ pound lump crabmeat
½ pound bay scallops
Flour for dredging
1 tablespoon canola oil
1 cup white wine
1 cup clam juice
1 tablespoon chopped shallot
One salmon fillet (1 pound), skinned and boned
1 pound mussels, in their shells
1 pound peas, shelled, steamed, and chilled
½ pound new potatoes, steamed, chilled, and quartered
1 jar (16 ounces) pickled beets, drained and julienned, juice
  reserved
2 stalks celery, diced
1 sweet onion, sliced thin
1 apple, peeled, cored, and chopped
Boston lettuce
Lemon slices
Dill sprigs
Dill Dressing (opposite)

Midsummer Night's Supper

On the west coast of Norway, this salad is traditionally eaten to celebrate both the longest day of the year and the sea's bounty. We've kept it simple so that the shrimp, lobster, crab, and scallops can speak for themselves. Of course, you can always limit the kinds of seafood or substitute a variety of grilled fish for one or more of the kinds of seafood. But when you are feeling very festive, invite your favorite folks over and indulge.

The Solstice

The longest day of the year. The Land of the Midnight Sun. Together, an experience like no other. Feasting till all hours on dilled crayfish and cucumbers. Tossing back golden jiggers of brisk, bracing aquavit. At 2 A.M., the sky's still aglow, as yesterday melds into today. Like the sun, you give no thought to rest. What, and miss all the fun?

1. Bring a large pot of salted water to a boil. Add the shrimp and cook until just pink, about 3 minutes. Remove the shrimp with a slotted spoon. Rinse under cold water and cool. Peel, devein, and refrigerate in a large bowl.

2. Bring the water back to a boil and add the lobster, head first. Cover the pot and cook for 13 to 15 minutes. Remove and cool. Remove the meat from the shell and cut into bite-size pieces.

3. Pick through the crabmeat to remove any cartilage. Refrigerate with the shrimp.

4. Dust the scallops with flour. Heat the oil in a large skillet over medium-high heat. Sauté the scallops for 1 to 2 minutes on each side, or until brown and cooked through. Remove and cool. Refrigerate with the shrimp.

5. In a Dutch oven, bring the wine, clam juice, shallot, and 2 cups of water to a boil. Add the salmon, lower the heat, and poach for 8 minutes. Remove and cool. Break into large pieces. Refrigerate.

6. Bring the poaching liquid back to a boil. Add the mussels, cover, and steam until the shells open, about 3 minutes. Remove the mussels. Discard any unopened shells, and cool the remaining shells. Remove the mussels from their shells. Refrigerate.

7. In a very large bowl, combine all the seafood. Being very gentle, fold in the peas, potatoes, beets, celery, onion, and apple. Line a large platter with Boston lettuce. Place the seafood on the lettuce and garnish with lemon and dill. Serve with Dill Dressing on the side.

*Cal. **416** Carb. **30g** Protein **53g***

*Chol.**184mg** Fat **9g/19%***

Dill Dressing

YIELD: 2 CUPS
*1 pint nonfat plain yogurt
Pinch white pepper
2 tablespoons chopped scallion
1 teaspoon white vinegar
¼ cup chopped fresh dill
1 tablespoon fresh horseradish*

Combine all of the ingredients; cover and chill. Serve with seafood salad.

*Cal. **8** Carb. **1g** Protein **.7g** Chol. **0mg** Fat **.1g/12%**
(analyzed per tablespoon)*

ON A GREEK ISLAND

The light in Greece is extraordinary. I first saw it as I sailed through the islands on an early summer morning. I was stunned—literally—by the piercing blue sky, the deeper azure waters below. Nothing I've seen before or since has come close.

Souvlaki

SERVES 4

6 garlic cloves, sliced in half
1 cup chicken broth (see Basics)
1 tablespoon olive oil
1 sprig fresh thyme
4 sprigs fresh rosemary
4 tablespoons fresh lemon juice
Salt and freshly ground pepper
1 pound lamb shoulder, trimmed of all fat, cut into 1-inch cubes
Bamboo skewers (4 to 8), soaked in water for 1 hour
4 pita breads, cut in half to form pockets
1 medium red onion, coarsely chopped
2 ripe tomatoes, coarsely chopped
2 cups shredded romaine

1. In a large bowl, combine the garlic, broth, oil, thyme, rosemary, lemon juice, and salt and pepper to taste. Stir well. Add the lamb and marinate for several hours or overnight, covered, in the refrigerator.
2. Prepare a charcoal fire or broiler. Divide the meat evenly and thread on four skewers, alternating with pieces of garlic. Wind the sprigs of herbs around the skewers. Reserve the marinade.
3. Grill or broil for 6 to 8 minutes, basting with the marinade and turning frequently.
4. To serve, warm the pita halves and place two on each plate. Place the skewered meat alongside and pass the onion, tomatoes, and lettuce so that guests can fill their pitas as they like. Serve with Yogurt Sauce (opposite), if desired.

Cal. 337 Carb. 36g Protein 21g Chol. 51mg Fat 12g/31%

"An artist lives everywhere."

Greek proverb

Yogurt Sauce

YIELD: 1 GENEROUS CUP

1 cup nonfat plain yogurt
2 tablespoons fresh lemon juice
2 large garlic cloves, finely minced
¼ cup minced fresh mint
Salt

Combine all of the ingredients in a small bowl and cover with plastic wrap until ready to serve.

*Cal. **9** Carb. **1g** Protein **1g** Chol. **1mg** Fat **.1g/11%***
(analyzed per tablespoon)

Spinach Pie

SERVES 8

2 eggs, lightly beaten
1 cup low-fat cottage cheese
1 cup shredded low-fat mozzarella
1 tablespoon minced fresh Italian parsley
1 teaspoon canola oil
8 ounces fresh mushrooms, thinly sliced
2 teaspoons fresh lemon juice
¼ teaspoon freshly ground pepper
10 ounces fresh spinach, chopped
⅛ teaspoon grated fresh nutmeg
1 tablespoon minced fresh chives
¼ cup minced fresh dill

1. Preheat the oven to 350°.
2. In a large mixing bowl, combine the eggs, cottage cheese, mozzarella, and parsley. Mix well; set aside.
3. In a large skillet, heat the oil over medium heat. Add the mushrooms, lemon juice, and pepper, and sauté until the mushrooms are tender and the liquid has evaporated. Add the spinach and nutmeg; cover and sauté for 1 minute. Remove the cover and sauté another 2 minutes, or until the spinach is cooked. Remove from the heat and stir in the chives and dill. Cool slightly.
4. Combine the vegetables with the egg mixture and pour into a 9-inch pie pan.
5. Bake for 25 to 35 minutes, until lightly browned on top. Remove from the oven and let cool for 5 minutes before serving. Cut into wedges.

*Cal. **96** Carb. **4g** Protein **9g** Chol. **58mg** Fat **5g/48%***

The Greek Diet

Greece has the lowest incidence of heart disease in Europe. Traditionally, Greeks do not eat red meat in great quantity, in spite of their wonderful lamb. The daily Greek diet still consists largely of grains and beans, vegetables, fresh herbs, fruit, fish, goat and sheep cheeses, yogurt, and olive oil.

Greek Sandwiches

YEILD: 32 SANDWICHES

2 recipes Basic Bread (see Basics)
1 cup Onion Marmalade (see Basics)
1 green bell pepper, roasted, seeded, and cut into 2-inch strips
2 tablespoons crumbled feta cheese
2 tablespoons finely chopped fresh dill
2 tablespoons finely chopped fresh Italian parsley
⅓ cup pitted and chopped Greek olives
Salt and freshly ground pepper
1 tablespoon cornmeal
1 egg white, lightly beaten
1 tablespoon caraway seeds

1. Make the bread according to the directions through the first rising.

2. Place the marmalade in a medium-size bowl. Add the pepper strips, cheese, dill, parsley, olives, and salt and pepper to taste, and toss to combine thoroughly.

3. Lightly spray or wipe a large baking sheet with olive oil and dust with cornmeal; set aside.

4. Punch down the bread dough and knead for 1 minute on a lightly floured board. Divide the dough into sixteen equal pieces. Working with one piece at a time, divide each piece in half and flatten into a 2½-inch disc. Place 1½ to 2 teaspoons of filling in the center of one disc. Moisten the edge of the filling with water and place the second disc over, stretching it gently to cover the filling. Press the edges together to seal, then fold the edges under to make a neat, round roll. Place the roll on the baking sheet and make two or three small slashes on top to serve as air vents. Repeat with the remaining pieces of dough, placing the rolls 2 inches apart. Cover the rolls with a kitchen towel and let rise in a warm place until doubled in bulk, about 40 minutes.

5. Preheat the oven to 400°.

6. In a small bowl, whisk the egg white until frothy. Brush the tops of the rolls with the glaze, and sprinkle each with a few caraway seeds.

7. Bake for 25 minutes, or until the rolls are nicely browned and sound hollow when tapped on the bottom. Cool slightly and serve.

*Cal. **124** Carb. **21g** Protein **4g** Chol. **15mg** Fat **3g/20%***

Greek Time

Routine didn't vary much during our lazy summer days on Mykonos. Under the grape arbor of our pension, we started the day with a leisurely breakfast of melons and coffee. Then, a quick sprint to the shops, followed by a rumbling autobus ride to the beach. Across a farmer's field, up over a crumbling stone wall, we discovered our own very private beach. With a paperback novel in my teeth, I'd swim out to a huge rock—my own private Greek island! There I spent the mornings reading and taking dips in the sea.

Around one o'clock, we had lunch at the farmer's house, a simple meal prepared by his wife. I'll never forget the taste of those sun-warmed, juicy, perfectly ripened tomatoes. She served them dressed in salads, sometimes roasted. Most often, we ate them like apples.

Lamb & Green Peppercorn Pasta

SERVES 6

1 teaspoon olive oil
1½ pounds lamb (from the shoulder or leg), well trimmed and cut
    into 1½-inch cubes
8 garlic cloves
2 medium onions, coarsely chopped (about 3 cups)
1½ cups red wine
3 cups beef broth (see Basics)
2 to 3 medium new potatoes
1 teaspoon fresh thyme
2 bay leaves
1 can (2 ounces) green peppercorns in brine, drained
Salt and freshly ground pepper
¾ pound dry fettuccine

1. In a nonstick skillet over high heat, heat ½ teaspoon of the oil. Add the lamb and sauté until brown on all sides. Do not overcrowd the pan; do this in batches if necessary. Transfer the lamb to a stockpot.
2. Heat the remaining oil in the skillet. Add the garlic and onion, and sauté until soft, about 3 to 4 minutes. Remove to the stockpot.
3. Pour the wine into the skillet, scraping up any brown bits from the bottom; add the lamb.
4. Add the beef broth, potatoes, thyme, and bay leaves to the stockpot. Bring to a boil, reduce the heat to a simmer, and cover. Simmer for 1½ hours, until the lamb is tender.
5. Bring a pot of water to a boil for the fettuccine. Remove the lamb and the potatoes to a bowl, using a slotted spoon. Increase the heat to medium-high. Add the peppercorns and cook for 8 to 10 minutes, until the sauce is reduced slightly. You should have about 1½ cups. Strain the sauce, and add the peppercorns and onion to the lamb. Discard the bay leaves. Place the broth and potatoes in a blender and purée. Season with salt and pepper to taste, and pour over the lamb. Cook the fettuccine according to the package directions while you are finishing the sauce. Serve the lamb over the fettuccine.

Cal. **480** *Carb.* **64g** *Protein* **30g** *Chol.* **68mg** *Fat* **12g/21%**

Oil of Antiquity

Greece has one of the world's oldest olive-growing traditions, and ranks third among olive-oil-producing nations. To be sure, it offers oils of gutsy flavor and drama.

Dilled Peach Swordfish

SERVES 4

Four 1½-inch-thick swordfish steaks (about 1½ pounds),
  skins removed
1 teaspoon fresh lemon juice
Salt and freshly ground pepper
1 teaspoon olive oil
2 cups thinly sliced onion
2 teaspoons slivered garlic
1 teaspoon honey
1½ pounds fresh peaches, peeled and cut lengthwise into
  ½-inch-thick slices
½ cup finely chopped fresh dill
1 lemon, cut into wedges
Fresh dill sprigs

1. Rinse the swordfish and pat it dry. Lightly coat a roasting pan with vegetable oil and arrange the fish in the pan. Sprinkle with lemon juice and salt and pepper to taste. Turn the fish to coat; cover and refrigerate until ready to bake.
2. Preheat the oven to 350°.
3. In a large skillet, heat the oil over medium-high heat. Add the onion and garlic, and sauté until translucent, about 5 minutes. Reduce the heat to medium, add the honey, and stir well. Cook until the onion begins to caramelize, 3 to 5 minutes.
4. Gently stir in the peaches and simmer for 5 minutes. Stir in the dill and remove from the heat. Spoon the peach mixture around—not over—the fish, and bake for 20 minutes, uncovered. The swordfish is done when it turns opaque and is firm to the touch. Be careful not to overcook.
5. To serve, transfer the fish to a warm serving platter or individual plates. Spoon the peach mixture over the fish. Garnish with lemon wedges and sprigs of dill, and serve immediately.

Cal. 340 Carb. 26g Protein 36g Chol. 66mg Fat 11g/28%

Garlic Shrimp and Scallops

SERVES 4

1 teaspoon olive oil
2 tablespoons slivered garlic
½ teaspoon crushed red pepper flakes
½ pound large shrimp, peeled and deveined
½ pound bay scallops

The Greek Pantry

The Greeks have as long and distinguished a reputation for cooking as they have for art, politics, and literature. Influenced by the Venetians as well as the Turks, theirs is the epitome of the Mediterranean diet.

Greek staples include olive oil (which lies at the heart of the cooking), garlic, lemon, mint, dill, oregano, cinnamon, lamb, seafood, eggplant, tomatoes, grapes, all sorts of breads, phyllo, rice, goat and sheep cheeses and yogurt, and honey.

½ teaspoon paprika
4 tablespoons chicken broth
1 teaspoon fresh lime juice
½ cup finely chopped fresh Italian parsley
Salt and freshly ground pepper

1. In a large heavy skillet, heat the oil over medium heat. Add the garlic and sauté until it begins to brown. Remove the garlic with a slotted spoon and set aside.
2. Add the red pepper flakes to the skillet and increase the heat to medium-high. Add the garlic, shrimp, scallops, and paprika. Sauté for 1 to 2 minutes, stirring constantly.
3. Add the chicken broth and cook for 1 minute. Remove the shrimp and scallops with a slotted spoon. Place on a platter; set aside and keep warm. Add the lime juice, parsley, and salt and pepper to taste to the pan, and just warm through. Pour the sauce over the shrimp and scallops, and serve immediately.

Cal. **137** *Carb.* **5g** *Protein* **22g** *Chol.* **105mg** *Fat* **3g/19%**

Greek Leg of Lamb

SERVES 16
1 leg of lamb (9 to 10 pounds)
3 heads garlic, cloves peeled, 6 cloves slivered
Salt and freshly ground pepper
2 cups beef broth
2 cups very good red wine
8 sprigs fresh rosemary

1. Preheat the oven to 375°.
2. Trim the lamb of extra fat and place it in a shallow roasting pan. With a sharp knife, make small slits all around the lamb and insert the slivered garlic. Season with salt and pepper, and place the remaining garlic around the lamb. Pour 1 cup of the broth and 1 cup of the wine into the pan, and place the rosemary sprigs on top of the leg.
3. Place the lamb in the oven and bake for 18 minutes per pound—about 2½ to 3 hours for medium; baste occasionally. After 1 hour add the remaining broth and wine, and continue to baste until done. Remove the lamb from the roaster and let it rest for 10 minutes before carving. Discard the rosemary.
4. Meanwhile, place the roaster over medium-high heat, and reduce the liquid by half. Mash the garlic into the liquid with a fork while it is reducing. Serve the juice on the side.

Cal. **248** *Carb.* **3g** *Protein* **36g** *Chol.* **109mg** *Fat* **10g/36%**

Lemon Rice with Leeks

SERVES 4

*1 tablespoon slivered sun-dried tomatoes packed in oil, well
    drained, and 1 teaspoon oil reserved*
2 cups shredded leek (3 to 4 medium leeks)
½ teaspoon sugar
⅛ teaspoon ground cinnamon
½ teaspoon salt
Freshly ground pepper
1 cup Arborio rice
1½ teaspoons grated lemon zest
3¼ cups chicken broth (see Basics)
1 cup finely chopped fresh parsley

1. In a very large skillet, heat the oil over medium heat. Add
the leek and sugar, and sauté until the leek begins to soften,
6 to 8 minutes. Add the tomatoes, cinnamon, salt, pepper, and
rice. Cook for 2 minutes, stirring. Stir in the lemon zest, chick-
en broth, and parsley. Cover and simmer for 10 minutes.
2. Remove the skillet from the heat and remove the lid;
quickly place a piece of cheesecloth or a clean dish towel
over the skillet and replace the lid. Let the rice steam in a
warm place for 15 to 20 minutes. When all the liquid has
been absorbed, the rice is ready to serve.

*Cal. **210** Carb. **42g** Protein **5g** Chol. **0mg** Fat **3g/11%***

Petros the Pelican

Years ago, Petros the pelican
was a fixture on Mykonos,
sauntering among the café
tables that rimmed the harbor. I can still feel the
warmth of the afternoon sun,
and taste those olives with
rosemary that we enjoyed as
we leaned back to sip ouzo
and watch Petros startle the
latest visitors to Mykonos.

Turnips with Swiss Chard

SERVES 4

1 teaspoon olive oil
1 tablespoon slivered garlic
1 pound turnips, peeled, halved, and very thinly sliced
*1 pound Swiss chard, washed, stemmed, and
    roughly chopped*
1 teaspoon chopped lemon zest
3 tablespoons fresh lemon juice
Salt and freshly ground pepper

1. In a large heavy skillet, heat the oil over
medium heat. Add the garlic and sauté, stirring, until it starts to brown. Remove with a
slotted spoon.
2. Add the sliced turnip to the pan and sauté for 5
minutes, stirring, until it is just cooked and begins to brown.

3. Turn the heat to medium-high and return the garlic to the skillet. Stir in the chard and zest; sauté for 1 to 2 minutes. Turn the heat off, cover, and steam for 5 minutes. Season with lemon juice and salt and pepper to taste. Serve immediately.

Cal. **69** *Carb.* **12g** *Protein* **3g** *Chol.* **0mg** *Fat* **1g/17%**

Ancient Honey Cakes

YIELD: 3 DOZEN LITTLE CAKES
3¹/₂ cups unbleached flour
³/₄ teaspoon baking soda
Pinch salt
³/₄ cup plus 2 tablespoons olive oil
¹/₂ cup plus 3 tablespoons sugar
¹/₄ cup ruby port
1 tablespoon finely grated orange zest
¹/₄ cup fresh orange juice
2 tablespoons plus 1 teaspoon ground cinnamon
³/₄ teaspoon ground cloves
¹/₂ teaspoon grated fresh nutmeg
Honey Syrup (page 141)
¹/₂ cup finely chopped toasted almonds

1. Preheat the oven to 400°. Lightly coat a baking sheet with vegetable oil; set aside.
2. Sift the flour, soda, and salt into a medium bowl.
3. In a large bowl, beat together with a wooden spoon the oil and ¹/₂ cup plus 2 tablespoons sugar. Beat in the wine, zest, juice, 2 tablespoons of cinnamon, the cloves, and the nutmeg until well combined. Slowly beat in the flour mixture.
4. Place the dough on a lightly floured surface and knead until very smooth, about 15 minutes. Add more flour if necessary. Pinch off small pieces of the dough, about 2 teaspoons each, and form little balls. Flatten the balls slightly and place on the baking sheet about 2 inches apart. Bake for 12 to 15 minutes, or until brown. Cool slightly.
5. Pour the Honey Syrup into a pie plate or similar flat dish, such as a baking dish. When cool enough to handle, carefully set the cakes into the Honey Syrup. After 1 minute, remove the cakes with a slotted spoon to a tray to cool.
6. In a small bowl, combine the almonds, and the remaining sugar and cinnamon; sprinkle over the cakes.

Cal. **199** *Carb.* **35g** *Protein* **2g** *Chol.* **0mg** *Fat* **7g/28%**
(analyzed per cake)

"To eat figs off the tree in the very early morning, when they have been barely touched by the sun, is one of the exquisite pleasures of the Mediterranean."

Elizabeth David

B·E·R·R·Y
PICKING TIME

Very Berry Salad

Raspberries, blackberries, blueberries...when the berry season
is in full swing, can we ever get enough? Just served in a bowl
with skim milk, yogurt, or a Dreamy Cream (pages 100-101),
they're sweet. But this is also the time of the year when we
pine for a warm pie from the oven, a crisp cobbler, or a
moist cake loaded with the very best berry flavor.

SERVES 12
6 cups strawberries, hulled
1 tablespoon minced fresh mint
1 tablespoon fresh lemon juice
½ cup sugar
1 pint blackberries
1 pint blueberries
1 pint raspberries

1. Purée 2 cups of strawberries in a food processor. Pour
into a small mixing bowl. Stir in the mint, lemon juice, and

Those sweet, luscious, elegant raspberries we love are low in calories and very high in vitamin C. They're also packed with fiber, carbohydrates, and potassium, and have just a trace of fat. All this, and only 45 calories per cup. They're so delicious!

sugar; taste and adjust the seasoning.

2. In a large mixing bowl, combine all the berries. Pour the purée over the berries and gently stir to combine. Transfer to a large glass serving bowl.

Cal. 110 Carb. 27g Protein 1g Chol. 0mg Fat 1g/5%

Deep-Dish Berry Pie

SERVES 8

3 cups fresh blueberries, washed and drained
2 cups fresh red raspberries
1 cup fresh black raspberries
2 cups fresh strawberries, washed, hulled, and halved if large
2 tablespoons fresh lemon juice
1 teaspoon finely minced lemon zest
1/3 cup blackberry brandy
2 tablespoons all-purpose flour
1/4 cup tapioca
3/4 cup sugar
1 sheet frozen puff pastry, thawed according to package directions
1 egg, beaten with 1 tablespoon water

1. In a large bowl, combine all of the berries. Sprinkle with the lemon juice, zest, and brandy. Toss gently to coat.

2. In a small bowl, combine the flour, tapioca, and sugar, and toss the mixture gently with the fruit. Pour the berry mixture into a 1½-quart ovenproof baking dish, and set it aside.

3. Meanwhile, on a lightly floured surface, roll out the pastry to ⅛ inch thick. Use a sharp knife to cut out a circle about 2 inches larger than the baking dish. Brush the circle lightly with the egg wash. Place the pastry, wash side down, over the dish, and stretch it tight, like the head of a drum. Press the overhanging dough against the sides of the dish; it should adhere all around. Cover and refrigerate for 1 hour.

4. Preheat the oven to 450°.

5. When ready to bake, brush the top with egg wash and bake for 15 minutes; reduce the heat to 375° and bake for 25 minutes longer, or until the crust is golden. Do not open the oven door for the first 20 minutes or the pastry may fall. Remove the dish from the oven and place it on a wire rack to cool slightly. Serve warm or at room temperature.

NOTE: The combination of berries can vary according to taste and availability, but in any case should equal 8 cups.

Cal. 241 Carb. 47g Protein 3g Chol. 35mg Fat 6g/20%

Four-Berry Cobbler

SERVES 12

1 recipe Buttermilk Biscuits (see Basics)
1 quart plus 1 pint (6 cups) strawberries,
  cleaned and hulled
1 pint raspberries
1 pint blackberries
1 pint blueberries
1²/₃ cups sugar
¼ cup all-purpose flour
2 tablespoons vanilla extract
1 tablespoon cinnamon-sugar

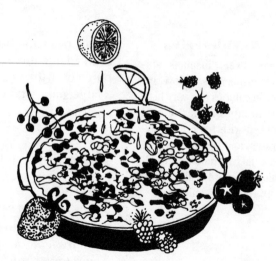

1. Preheat the oven to 425°. Reserve 1 pint of strawberries. Place the rest in a Dutch oven and sprinkle with ²/₃ cup of sugar and the flour. Set aside.
2. In a food processor, purée the reserved strawberries with 1 cup sugar and the vanilla. Pour the purée over the berry mixture and bring to a boil over medium-high heat, stirring.
3. Turn the hot fruit into a 9 x 13 x 2-inch baking dish. Drop the prepared biscuit dough by spoonfuls on top of the hot fruit until it is almost covered. Sprinkle the cinnamon-sugar over the dough. Bake for 35 to 40 minutes, or until the topping is light golden brown. Remove from the oven and cool slightly. Serve with Raspberry Cream (page 100) if desired.

*Cal. **138** Carb. **20g** Protein **3g** Chol. **0mg** Fat **4g/38%***

Rosy Summer Pudding

SERVES 12

12 to 16 slices good-quality commercial white bread, crusts
  removed
2 tablespoons frozen cran-raspberry juice concentrate, defrosted
1 envelope unflavored gelatin
2 pounds raspberries
2 cups fresh red currants or blackberries
³/₄ cup sugar
2 tablespoons Framboise or crème de cassis

1. Line the bottom and sides of a 2-quart soufflé dish with plastic wrap, carefully smoothing the wrap to conform to the dish and allowing some overhang. Line the dish with overlapping bread slices; the bread should be even with the top of the dish.

Blueberries

Blueberries grow best on land where almost nothing else will because they require a high water table that would damage the roots of most crops—blueberries are about 84% water. They like sandy soil, long cold winters, and summers long enough to mature. That's a fitting description of the southwestern shores of Lake Michigan.

Native Americans greeted the Pilgrims with dried wild blueberries. Lewis and Clark noted that Pacific tribes pounded dried blueberries into venison when preparing to preserve it for winter.

The cultivated blueberry commonly found in today's markets comes mostly from high-bush blueberries, which grow up to 10 feet tall.

A good blueberry for fresh consumption is plump and luscious, azure blue with a waxy whitish-gray glaze that resembles frost on a glass. Eat them fresh and raw out of hand, with just a little skim milk and sugar, tossed into pancake batter, in tiny fluted blueberry muffins at teatime, or chilled, with blueberry sauce.

2. Place the cranberry juice in a small bowl, and sprinkle with the gelatin. Let soften for 5 minutes.

3. In a large saucepan over low heat, combine the raspberries, currants, and sugar. Simmer, stirring occasionally, until the sugar has dissolved and the raspberries break down. Stir in the softened gelatin until dissolved. Stir in the Framboise.

4. Pour the hot mixture into the prepared dish and completely cover the top with additional slices of bread. Place a weighted saucer on top of the bread. Cover the mold with plastic wrap over the saucer and weight. Refrigerate for 48 hours.

5. To serve, remove the weight, plastic wrap and the saucer from the top of the dish. Holding the edges of the plastic wrap, invert the pudding onto a serving platter. Serve with Fruit Sauce (page 281) or Raspberry Cream (page 100).

*Cal. **230** Carb. **49g** Protein **5g** Chol. **1mg** Fat **2g/7%***

Razzle-Dazzle Raspberry Pie

SERVES 8

6 cups raspberries, half red, half black if
  possible, or all red
1 tablespoon fresh lemon juice
1/2 cup Grand Marnier or Framboise
1/4 cup all-purpose flour
1 cup plus 1 tablespoon sugar
2 teaspoons ground cinnamon
1 recipe Flaky Pie Crust (see Basics)
1 tablespoon skim milk
1 teaspoon plus a pinch cinnamon-sugar

1. Preheat the oven to 375°. Place the berries in a bowl and sprinkle with the lemon juice and Grand Marnier.

2. In a small bowl, combine the flour, 1 cup of sugar, and 1 teaspoon of cinnamon, and sprinkle over the fruit. Toss lightly to combine.

3. Roll out half the dough and use it to line a 9-inch pie tin. Gently transfer the fruit into the pie shell. Roll out the remaining dough and place it on top. Trim off the excess and crimp the edges decoratively.

4. Place in the oven and bake for 40 minutes. Remove the pie, brush with the milk, and sprinkle with the cinnamon-sugar. Bake 10 minutes longer, or until the pie is brown and the filling is bubbling. Place the pie on a wire rack to cool.

*Cal. **478** Carb. **83g** Protein **6g** Chol. **.06mg** Fat **15g/26%***

Peach and Blueberry Tart

SERVES 8

1 recipe Flaky Pie Crust (see Basics)
1 cup pitted, peeled, and thinly sliced fresh peaches
1 cup fresh blueberries, washed and drained
1 tablespoon tapioca
³⁄₄ cup sugar
2 tablespoons fresh lemon juice
¹⁄₄ teaspoon freshly ground nutmeg
Pinch salt

1. Preheat the oven to 425°. Roll out the pastry on a lightly floured surface to a 17 x 17-inch square. Fit the pastry into a 12-inch round tart pan with a removable bottom. Trim and reserve the scraps. Place the pan in the freezer.
2. Cut the remaining pastry into ten to twelve ½-inch-wide strips. Place on a plate on top of waxed paper, cover with a second sheet, and refrigerate.
3. In a small bowl, combine the remaining ingredients. Stir gently and let stand for 15 minutes.
4. Remove the tart pan from the freezer, and pour the fruit into the shell. Spread the fruit out evenly. Weave the pastry strips into a lattice pattern over the fruit. Trim the ends and crimp the edges together with your fingers.
5. Bake the tart for 35 to 40 minutes, or until the pastry is crisp and well browned. Cool slightly before serving.

*Cal. **244** Carb. **44g** Protein **2g** Chol. **.02mg** Fat **7g/26%***

Michigan Blueberry Pie

SERVES 8

¹⁄₂ cup plus 1 teaspoon sugar
2 tablespoons all-purpose flour
¹⁄₂ teaspoon ground cinnamon
¹⁄₈ teaspoon ground allspice
¹⁄₈ teaspoon ground cloves
Pinch freshly grated nutmeg
¹⁄₂ teaspoon grated orange zest
4 cups blueberries, washed and drained
2 tablespoons fresh orange juice
1 tablespoon light rum
1 recipe Flaky Pie Crust (see Basics)
1 tablespoon skim milk

Peaches

On his travels in China, Marco Polo encountered peaches that weighed as much as several pounds.

Far more modest, today's peaches are categorized according to the ease with which the flesh separates from the pit: freestones and clings. Thirty-five states grow peaches; California, South Carolina, Pennsylvania, and Georgia lead in the quality and quantity of their commercial crops.

But peaches don't sweeten once they are harvested, and cold storage gives them a wooly texture—two good reasons to seek out locally grown, tree-ripened fruits. Their season may be short and their harvest small, but these will always be best.

The peach harvest peaks in August, though they're available June through October. You can tell the variety by its indent: Rio Oso has a deep suture and bumps; the Cadillac of peaches—the Fay

266

Alberta—is pretty and smooth; a rosy dent means it's a Red Haven, the juiciest and best-tasting of all.

Look—don't feel—to choose a perfect peach. Squeezing only bruises. Observe the stem end. It should be clear, greenless yellow all around. Avoid green, hard peaches: They aren't ripe and never will be.

Keep peaches at room temperature for 2 to 3 days to ripen; refrigerate for up to a week, covered in plastic wrap.

Cinnamon, nutmeg, ground coriander, and mint bring out the flavor of peaches. Peaches are rich in vitamin A, with about 50 calories per medium fruit.

"I remember his showing me how to eat a peach by building a little white mountain of sugar and then dipping the peach into it."

Mary McCarthy

1. Preheat the oven to 400°. In a large mixing bowl, combine well the ½ cup sugar, flour, cinnamon, allspice, cloves, nutmeg, and orange zest. Add the berries, juice, and rum, and toss gently until the berries are well coated.

2. Roll half the pastry to fit a 9-inch pie plate; fit the pastry into the plate. Pour the berry mixture into the shell. Roll out the second crust and use it to cover the berries. Seal the pie by crimping the edges with your fingers; make a few slits in the top to allow steam to escape while baking. Brush with the milk, and sprinkle with the remaining teaspoon of sugar.

3. Bake the pie for 10 minutes; reduce the heat to 350° and bake for an additional 25 minutes, or until golden brown.

*Cal. **397** Carb. **63g** Protein **5g** Chol. **.01mg** Fat **14g/32%***

Blueberry Cake

SERVES 16

2 tablespoons cornmeal
2 cups all-purpose flour
1½ teaspoons baking powder
1½ teaspoons baking soda
¼ teaspoon salt
1½ cups sugar
1 teaspoon ground cinnamon
1 teaspoon ground cloves
½ cup port wine
¼ cup canola oil
1 egg
2 egg whites
⅔ cup low-fat buttermilk
1 tablespoon vanilla extract
3 cups blueberries

1. Preheat the oven to 350°. In a large mixing bowl, combine all the dry ingredients and set aside.

2. In a small saucepan, reduce the port over medium heat to ¼ cup. Cool to room temperature.

3. Add the port and remaining ingredients, except the blueberries, to the dry mixture, one at a time, stirring constantly, until combined and smooth. Gently fold in the blueberries.

4. Lightly spray or wipe a 7 x 11-inch glass baking pan with vegetable oil. Pour the batter into the pan and bake for 45 minutes, or until a toothpick inserted in the center comes out clean. Serve warm from the oven or cool to room temperature.

*Cal. **196** Carb. **37g** Protein **3g** Chol. **12mg** Fat **4g/18%***

Perfect Peach Pie

SERVES 12

4 cups peeled and sliced perfectly ripened peaches
¼ cup all-purpose flour
½ cup light brown sugar
Zest and juice of 1 lemon
1 recipe Flaky Pie Crust (see Basics)
4 tablespoons toasted and finely
  chopped pecans
2 teaspoons skim milk

1. Preheat the oven to 425°.
2. Toss the peaches in a bowl with the flour, sugar, and lemon juice and let them stand.
3. Prepare the Flaky Pie Crust, replacing granulated sugar with light brown sugar. Add the chopped pecans and mix just to combine. Roll out the bottom crust and place in a pie plate. Add the peaches, mounding them toward the center of the pie. Roll out the second crust and place over the pie. Roll out the second crust and place over the pie; crimp the edges together. Slash the top in a few places. Brush the top crust with milk. Bake for 1 hour, or until golden brown. Serve topped with Vanilla Frozen Yogurt (page 275) if desired.
4. Pour the batter over the peaches, and bake for 50 minutes to 1 hour, until a toothpick inserted in the center comes out clean. Cool, cut into wedges and serve warm or cold.

*Cal. **384** Carb. **60g** Protein **6g** Chol. **.1mg** Fat **14g/31%***

Upside-Down Peach Cake

SERVES 12

¼ cup light brown sugar
2 cups sliced fresh peaches (about 3 peaches)
½ teaspoon freshly ground nutmeg or 1 tablespoon finely
  chopped crystallized ginger
1 cup all-purpose flour
¾ cup granulated sugar
2 teaspoons baking powder
¼ teaspoon baking soda
¼ teaspoon salt
1 tablespoon unsalted butter, softened

The Paradox of the Perfect Peach

The prettier the fruits or vegetables, the greater the chance they're bad for you. Man—not Nature—produces that sort of perfection. Consider citrus fruits: More than 60% of the chemicals sprayed on them are only for cosmetic purposes. Learn to live with produce shaped only by Nature's hand. You'll be rewarded with terrific taste.

The real fruit of the Garden of Eden? Some scholars think it may have been the apricot. Probably of Chinese origin, apricots came to Europe during the reign of Alexander the Great and were called Armenian plums by the Romans.

From mid-May to early August, most of the commercial apricot crop comes from California. There's one major drawback: They're harvested before their flavor reaches its true ripeness.

So, we seek out the handful of stubborn local farmers still willing to grow this temperamental fruit, waiting out the good old-fashioned winter needed to "set" the fruit and the spring frosts that can snuff out early blooms. After all that, humid or very hot weather can cause rot just before the July harvest. Not to mention the deer who rub their antlers on tree branches and knock off the fruit.

When buying, look for velvety-skinned fruit with a sweet fragrance and rich blush; it should give a little to the touch. Sometimes the smaller ones are the most flavorful. The most common varieties are Royal and Blenheim.

★ **GOOD FOR YOU** ★

Apricots are rich in beta-carotene and iron, with about 20 calories per fruit.

½ cup low-fat buttermilk
1 teaspoon vanilla extract

1. Preheat the oven to 350°. Lightly wipe the bottom of an 8-inch cake pan with 2-inch sides with vegetable oil.
2. Sprinkle the bottom of the cake pan evenly with the brown sugar. Arrange the peaches in the pan in a tight pinwheel pattern. Sprinkle with nutmeg or ginger. Set aside.
3. In a mixing bowl, sift togther the flour, sugar, baking powder, soda, and salt. Add the softened butter, buttermilk, and vanilla, and beat with an electric mixer until smooth.
4. Pour the batter over the peaches, and bake for 50 minutes to 1 hour, until a toothpick inserted in the center comes out clean. Cool, cut into wedges, and serve warm or cold.

Cal. 177 Carb. 26g Protein 2g Chol. 15mg Fat 7g/31%

Apricot-Amaretto Pie

SERVES 8
½ cup plus 1 teaspoon sugar
2 tablespoons all-purpose flour
1 teaspoon grated lemon zest
Pinch nutmeg
4 cups sliced apricots (about 1½ pounds), skins on
2 tablespoons Amaretto
1 recipe Flaky Pie Crust (see Basics)
1 tablespoon skim milk

1. Preheat the oven to 400°.
2. In a large mixing bowl, combine the ½ cup sugar, flour, lemon zest, and nutmeg; mix well. Add the apricots and Amaretto, and toss gently until the apricots are evenly coated.
3. Roll half the pastry out to fit a 9-inch pie plate. Line the plate and pour in the apricot filling. Roll the second crust and cover the pie; crimp the edges by pinching them together, and make a few slits in the top to allow steam to escape. Brush with the skim milk and sprinkle with the teaspoon of sugar.
4. Place the pie in the oven and bake for 10 minutes. Reduce the heat to 350° and bake for an additional 30 to 40 minutes, or until the filling is bubbling and the crust is golden.

Cal. 396 Carb. 62g Protein 6g Chol. .1mg Fat 14g/31%

Cool Gin Honeydew

SERVES 4

1 perfectly ripened honeydew melon, quartered
  and seeded
2 tablespoons fresh lime juice
2 tablespoons gin
2 tablespoons finely chopped fresh mint
Zest of 1 lime, minced
4 lime wedges
4 sprigs fresh mint

Place a piece of melon on each of four plates. Sprinkle each
with lime juice, gin, chopped mint, and lime zest. Garnish
with wedges of lime and sprigs of mint. Serve immediately.

*Cal. **137** Carb. **31g** Protein **2g** Chol. **0mg** Fat **.4g/2%***

Peaches with Mint

SERVES 12

Coarse salt
12 perfectly ripe peaches
5 cups dry white wine
³⁄₄ cup brandy
¹⁄₄ cup sugar
¹⁄₄ cup very coarsely chopped fresh mint leaves
12 sprigs fresh mint

1. Place a large stockpot filled with water over medium heat.
When the water starts to boil, add a pinch of salt, and with a
spoon, drop each peach into the pot for 3 minutes. Remove
the peaches with a slotted spoon and immediately place them
in a bowl of cold water to stop the cooking process.
2. In a large bowl, combine the wine, brandy, sugar, and
chopped mint, and stir well. Remove the skin from each
peach, and place the peaches in the wine mixture. When
all the peaches are in the bowl, cover and refrigerate for at
least 8 hours. Serve each peach with a sprig of mint.

*Cal. **155** Carb. **15g** Protein **.7g** Chol. **0mg** Fat **.1g/1%***

*"In cooking, as
in all the arts,
simplicity is
the sign of
perfection."*

Curnonsky

Anytime Apricot Soufflé

SERVES 8

½ cup plus 3 tablespoons sugar
2 cans (16 ounces each) apricot halves in light syrup
14 dried apricot halves
2½ teaspoons cornstarch
2 tablespoons fresh lemon juice
Zest of one lemon, chopped
½ cup low-fat plain yogurt
8 large egg whites
Salt
¼ teaspoon cream of tartar

1. Place the rack in the lower third of the oven; preheat to 425°. Lightly spray or wipe the sides and edges of a 2½-quart soufflé dish with vegetable oil. Coat the dish with 2 tablespoons of the sugar. Knock out any excess.

2. Place ½ cup sugar, the canned apricots and syrup, and the dried apricots in a heavy saucepan. Simmer, uncovered, stirring occasionally, until the dried apricots are tender and the mixture is slightly thickened, about 20 minutes.

3. Meanwhile, in a small bowl, dissolve the cornstarch in 2½ teaspoons of water.

4. In a food processor or blender, pureé the cooked apricot mixture with the cornstarch mixture. Return the mixture to the saucepan, and heat gently until thickened to the consistency of a cake batter, stirring constantly to avoid burning; transfer to a mixing bowl. Stir in the lemon juice and zest. Measure 1½ cups of the mixture into a small saucepan and reserve the rest, adding the yogurt to it. Over low heat, gently warm the 1½ cups of mixture; do not boil.

5. In a large mixing bowl, beat the egg whites until foamy. Add the salt and cream of tartar and continue beating until the egg whites hold their shape but are not dry. Fold in the remaining sugar.

6. Transfer the warm mixture to a medium bowl and whisk in one-quarter of the egg whites, blending thoroughly. Fold in the remaining whites. Spoon the mixture into the dish; it should come to the top. Spread to even with a spatula.

7. Bake until very brown, 16 to 18 minutes. To serve, spoon onto dessert plates. Pass the reserved mixture, at room temperature, to use as a separate sauce.

*Cal. **139** Carb. **30g** Protein **4g** Chol. **0mg** Fat **0g/0%***

FABULOUS FRUIT

Fruit's the perfect way to begin and end the day—and to snack your way through the middle. Few of us eat the 4 to 5 fruits a day the Basic Pyramid suggests. But take a gander at the great nutritional benefits and low calories of fruit, and you'll see that fruit's a great way to satisfy a sweet tooth many times every day.

Fruit's a good source of fiber (the insoluble kind), vitamins A, B, C, and D, potassium, iron, calcium, boron, magnesium, natural sugar, and ellagic acid (a natural anticarcinogen). Pectin, found in many fruits, is a soluble fiber that helps lower blood cholesterol levels. And fruit does it all with very few calories.

Select fruit ripe off a tree or bush. Nurture it at home to full ripeness. And eat it raw with its skin for the most nutritious benefits.

Apples
Calories 77*
Fiber high
Boron, other minerals
When harvested mature, will get sweeter.

Blackberries
Calories 45*
Fiber high
Vitamin C
Must ripen before harvest.

Apricots
Calories 100*
Fiber low
Vitamins A & C
Harvested mature, will ripen but not sweeten.

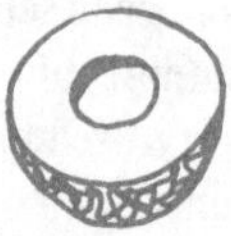

Cantaloupe
Calories 40*
Fiber low
Vitamins A & C
Harvested when mature, will ripen but not sweeten.

Bananas
Calories 300*
Fiber low
Potassium
Will ripen and sweeten after harvest.

Cherries
Calories 65*
Fiber low
Vitamins A & C
Must ripen before harvest.

Figs
Calories 150*
Fiber high
Vitamin B, iron
Harvested when mature, will ripen but not sweeten.

Peaches
Calories 50*
Fiber low
Vitamin A
Harvested when mature, will ripen but not sweeten.

Plums
Calories 125*
Fiber low
Vitamin A
Harvested when mature, will ripen but not sweeten.

Strawberries
Calories 55*
Fiber high
Vitamin C
Must ripen before harvest.

Grapes
Calories 70*
Fiber low
Vitamins A, C, & potassium
Must ripen before harvest.

Pears
Calories 150*
Fiber high
Vitamin C, phosophorus, potassium
Harvested when mature, will get sweeter.

Raspberries
Calories 45*
Fiber high
Vitamin C
Must ripen before harvest.

Watermelon
Calories 110*
Fiber low
Vitamins A & C
Harvested when mature, will ripen but not sweeten.

Mango
Calories 125*
Fiber low
Vitamins A & C
Harvested when mature, will ripen but not sweeten.

Pineapple
Calories 52*
Fiber low
Vitamin C
Must ripen before harvest.

Rhubarb
Calories 20*
Fiber low
Calcium, potassium
Must ripen before harvest.

Per cup

THE SODA FOUNTAIN

There's nothing better than ice cream on a hot day. Or any day, come to think of it. Our little village alone boasts an old-fashioned ice cream parlor, several ice cream stores, and a soda fountain at Oval Beach.

We all love our ice cream. But after making sorbets and frozen yogurts at home, I'm convinced: The ice cream we've known and loved isn't worth the fat calories! These even taste better.

274

Frozen Yogurt

Vanilla

SERVES 8

2 cups Yogurt Cheese
  (see Basics)
3/4 cup sugar
1 1/4 cups skim milk
1/4 cup heavy cream
1/2 teaspoon vanilla extract
1 vanilla bean

1. In a mixing bowl, combine the yogurt cheese, sugar, milk, cream, and vanilla extract. Whisk until well combined.
2. Split the vanilla bean in half lengthwise, and scrape the seeds into the bowl; stir to combine.
3. Transfer the mixture to an ice cream machine and freeze according to the manufacturer's directions.

Cal. **167** *Carb.* **29g** *Protein* **7g**
Chol. **13mg** *Fat* **3g/15%**

Chocolate-Chunk

SERVES 8

2 ounces semisweet chocolate
2 ounces unsweetened chocolate
2 cups Yogurt Cheese
  (see Basics)
2 cups skim milk
1 cup sugar
1/3 cup unsweetened cocoa

1. Coarsely chop the semisweet chocolate; put it into a covered container and place in the freezer.
2. Melt the unsweetened chocolate in a heavy saucepan over very low heat. Transfer to a mixing bowl and cool to room temperature.

3. Add the yogurt cheese, skim milk, sugar, and cocoa to the melted chocolate. Whisk until thoroughly combined.
4. Transfer the mixture to an ice cream machine and freeze according to the manufacturer's directions. When the mixture is almost frozen but still soft, add the chilled chocolate chunks.

Cal. **252** *Carb.* **44g** *Protein* **10g**
Chol. **4mg** *Fat* **6g/21%**

Cappuccino

SERVES 8

1 1/2 cups skim
  milk
4 tablespoons
  ground coffee
  beans
2 cups Yogurt
  Cheese
  (see Basics)
3/4 cup sugar
1/4 cup heavy
  cream

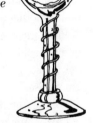

1. In a small saucepan, combine the milk and ground coffee. Place over low heat for 10 minutes. Remove from the heat, cover, and let steep for 30 minutes. Transfer to a covered container and refrigerate for at least 4 hours. Strain the coffee grounds from the milk: reserve 1 1/4 cups of the milk.
2. In a mixing bowl, combine the reserved milk, yogurt cheese, sugar, and cream. Whisk until well combined.
3. Follow step 3 in the Vanilla Frozen Yogurt recipe.

Cal. **170** *Carb.* **35g** *Protein* **7g**
Chol. **13mg** *Fat* **3g/13%**

Mint-Chip

SERVES 6

1 3/4 cups skim milk
1 1/2 cups loosely packed fresh
  mint leaves
2 ounces semisweet
  chocolate
2 cups Yogurt Cheese
  (see Basics)
1 cup sugar

1. In a small saucepan, combine the milk and mint leaves. Place over low heat for 10 minutes. Remove from the heat, cover, and let steep for 30 minutes. Transfer to a covered container and refrigerate for at least 4 hours. Strain the mint from the milk. Reserve 1 1/2 cups of the milk.
2. Chill the chocolate in the refrigerator. With a sharp knife, shave the chocolate into flakes. Place the flaked chocolate in a covered container, and place it in the freezer.
3. In a mixing bowl, combine the reserved milk, yogurt cheese, and sugar. Whisk until well combined.
4. Follow step 3 in the Vanilla Frozen Yogurt recipe.

Cal. **202** *Carb.* **40g** *Protein* **8g**
Chol. **3mg** *Fat* **3g/11%**

Frozen Yogurt

Lemon-Mint
SERVES 8

1 cup skim milk

*Peel of 1 lemon, cut into 1-
   inch strips*

*2 cups Yogurt Cheese
   (see Basics)*

1½ cups sugar

¼ cup heavy cream

3 teaspoons minced lemon zest

1 cup minced fresh mint leaves

1. In a small saucepan over low heat, combine the milk and lemon peel. Simmer for 10 minutes. Remove from the heat, cover, and let steep for 30 minutes. Transfer to a covered container and chill in the refrigerator for at least 4 hours. Strain and reserve the milk.
2. In a large mixing bowl, whisk well the reserved milk, yogurt cheese, sugar, cream, and lemon zest.
3. Follow step 3 in the Vanilla Frozen Yogurt recipe.
Cal. **244** *Carb.* **49g** *Protein* **9g** *Chol.* **14mg** *Fat* **3g/10%**

Strawberry-Amaretto
SERVES 8

*2 cups coarsely chopped
   fresh strawberries*

1 cup sugar

2½ cups nonfat plain yogurt

¼ cup Amaretto

1. Place the strawberries in a food processor, and purée for 1 minute. Add the sugar and purée another 30 seconds.
2. Place the strawberry mix-

ture in a medium-size mixing bowl. Fold in the yogurt and Amaretto and mix well. Chill for 1 hour.
3. Follow step 3 in the Vanilla Frozen Yogurt recipe.
Cal. **191** *Carb.* **36g** *Protein* **4g** *Chol.* **0mg** *Fat* **.6g/4%**

Raspberry
SERVES 8

2 cups fresh raspberries

1½ cups sugar

2½ cups plain nonfat yogurt

¼ cup Framboise

1. Place the raspberries in a food processor, and purée for 1 minute. Add the sugar and purée another 30 seconds.
2. Place the raspberry mixture into a medium-size mixing bowl. Fold in the yogurt and Framboise.
3. Follow step 3 in the Vanilla Frozen Yogurt recipe.
Cal. **225** *Carb.* **50g**
Protein **4g** *Chol.* **0mg**
Fat **.7g/3%**

Very Berry
SERVES 10

2 cups strawberries, hulled

2 cups blueberries

2 cups raspberrires

1 cup sugar

Seeds of 1 vanilla bean

*2½ cups low-fat plain
   yogurt*

1. Place the berries in a blender and blend until smooth. Transfer to a large bowl.
2. Stir in the sugar and vanilla

Easy Freeze

I thought making frozen yogurt would be hard. Certainly, it seemed to present one challenge—to replace the custard base of ice cream.

As it turned out, there was nothing to it. Just purée fruit, add a little sugar and other flavorings, if you like—liqueurs, herbs, spices, vanilla, etc.—and fold in nonfat plain yogurt. Use less yogurt for a more intense taste, more for a creamier texture, and use Yogurt Cheese with acidic flavors. Chill first to speed the process, then put it in the ice cream maker. Before long, it's ready, vibrant in flavor and color, and best enjoyed sooner rather than later.

seeds until well blended. Then fold in the yogurt until completely integrated.

3. Follow step 3 in the Vanilla Frozen Yogurt recipe.

Cal. 192 Carb. 43g Protein 4g Chol. 4mg Fat 1g/6%

Peach Brandy

SERVES 8

2 cups pitted coarsely chopped fresh peaches, with skin
2 tablespoons fresh lemon juice
1 cup packed light brown sugar
2 cups nonfat plain yogurt
3 tablespoons brandy

1. Place the peaches and lemon juice in a food processor, and purée for 1 minute. Add the sugar and purée another 30 seconds.
2. Pour the peach mixture into a medium-size mixing bowl. Fold in the yogurt and brandy and mix well. Chill for 1 hour.
3. Follow step 3 in the Vanilla Frozen Yogurt recipe.
NOTE: Leaving the skin on the peaches will produce a deeper and richer color, with flecks. If you prefer a smoother, lighter color, remove the skin.

Cal. 148 Carb. 31g Protein 4g Chol. 0mg Fat .4g/3%

Apricot-Almond

SERVES 8

2 cups pitted, skinned, and coarsely chopped fresh apricots
1¼ cups sugar

3 cups nonfat plain yogurt
½ teaspoon almond extract

1. Place the apricots in a food processor, and purée for 1 minute. Add the sugar and purée another 30 seconds.
2. Pour the apricot mixture into a medium-size mixing bowl. Fold in the yogurt and almond extract and mix well. Chill for 1 hour.
3. Follow step 3 in the Vanilla Frozen Yogurt recipe.

Cal. 184 Carb. 42g Protein 5g Chol. 0mg Fat .7g/3%

Blueberry

SERVES 8

2 cups fresh blueberries
1 cup sugar
3 cups nonfat plain yogurt

1. Place the blueberries in a food processor, and purée for 1 minute. Add the sugar and purée another 30 seconds.
2. Place the blueberry mixture in a medium-size mixing bowl. Fold in the yogurt and mix well. Chill for 1 hour.
3. Follow step 3 in the Vanilla Frozen Yogurt recipe.

Cal. 162 Carb. 36g Protein 5g Chol. 0mg Fat .6g/3%

Blackberry

SERVES 10

1 pint blackberries
1 cup sugar
2 tablespoons Triple Sec
2 tablespoons frozen orange juice concentrate
Zest of 2 oranges
1½ cups nonfat plain yogurt

1. Place the berries and sugar in a blender and purée. Remove to a large bowl.
2. Stir in the Triple Sec, orange juice, and zest; blend thoroughly. Fold in the yogurt until completely blended.
3. Follow step 3 in the Vanilla Frozen Yogurt recipe.

Cal. 135 Carb. 28g Protein 2g Chol. 3mg Fat .7g/4%

Banana Daiquiri

SERVES 8

1 ripe banana (about 4 ounces)
¾ cup sugar
½ cup pineapple juice
1¼ cups skim milk
2 cups Yogurt Cheese (see Basics)
Zest of 1 orange, grated

1. Place the banana in a blender or food processor and purée.
2. Transfer the purée to a large mixing bowl. Add the sugar, pineapple juice, milk, yogurt cheese, and zest. Mix well.
3. Follow step 3 in the Vanilla Frozen Yogurt recipe.

Cal. 164 Carb. 35g Protein 8g Chol. 3mg Fat .2g/1%

Fruit Sorbets

Peach

SERVES 8

4 cups peeled, pitted, and
  coarsely chopped fresh
  peaches
3/4 cup fresh lemon juice
1 cup sugar
5 tablespoons Amaretto

1. In a blender or food processor, purée the peaches. Add
the remaining ingredients.
Pulse to combine, and refrigerate until very cold.
2. Place the mixture in an ice
cream machine and freeze
according to the manufacturer's directions.

*Cal. **164** Carb. **40g** Protein **.7g***
*Chol. **0mg** Fat **0g/0%***

Blueberry

SERVES 8

2 quarts fresh blueberries,
  washed and stemmed
1 cup sugar
3/4 cup fresh lemon juice
1/2 cup fresh orange juice

1. In a blender or food processor, combine all of the ingredients and purée. Strain the
purée if desired, and place in
the refrigerator until very cold.
2. Follow the directions in step
2 for Peach Sorbet.

*Cal. **167** Carb. **42g** Protein **2g***
*Chol. **0mg** Fat **.44g/2%***

Orange and
Purple Basil

SERVES 6

3 cups fresh orange juice,
  strained if desired
1 cup fresh lemon juice,
  strained if desired
1 cup sugar
2 tablespoons finely chopped
  fresh purple basil

1. In a blender or food processor, blend the juices and sugar
for 30 seconds. Transfer to a
medium-size bowl and cover
with plastic wrap; refrigerate
until very cold.
2. When the mixture is cold,
stir in the basil. Follow the
directions in step 2 for Peach
Sorbet.

*Cal. **195** Carb. **50g** Protein*
*1g Chol. **0mg** Fat **.25g/1%***

Strawberry Sorbet

Strawberry-sweet, with an
inkling of tart. Watch out--
it's addictive!

SERVES 6

1 1/2 quarts fresh strawberries, hulled
1 cup sugar
3/4 cup fresh lemon juice
1/2 cup fresh orange juice

1. In a blender or food
processor, combine all of
the ingredients and purée. Strain the purée
if desired, and chill in the
refrigerator until very cold.
2. Follow the directions in step
2 for Peach Sorbet.

*Cal. **190** Carb. **48g** Protein **1g***
*Chol. **0mg** Fat **.9g/2%***

Fresh Mango

SERVES 6

2 large ripe mangoes, pitted
  and chopped
1 cup canned mango nectar
1/2 cup fresh lime juice
3/4 cup sugar

1. In a food processor, combine all of the ingredients and
purée. Transfer the mixture to
a medium-size bowl, cover
with plastic wrap, and refrigerate until very cold.
2. Follow the directions in step
2 for Peach Sorbet.

*Cal. **161** Carb. **42g** Protein*
*.43g Chol. **0mg** Fat **.2g/1%***

Black Raspberry

SERVES 8

1½ quarts black raspberries,
rinsed and dried
1 cup sugar
¾ cup fresh lemon juice
¼ cup crème de cassis

1. In a blender or food processor, combine all of the ingredients and blend until smooth..

2. Strain the purée to remove the seeds, and chill until very cold.

2. Follow the directions in step 2 for Peach Sorbet.

*Cal. **195** Carb. **45g** Protein **2g***
*Chol. **0mg** Fat **.7g/2%***

Very Berry Sorbet

A symphony of summer berries, together for a limited run.

SERVES 8

1 quart fresh strawberries,
hulled
1 quart fresh raspberries
1 quart fresh blackberries
1 quart fresh blueberries
1 cup sugar
¾ cup fresh lemon juice
¾ cup fresh orange juice
Mint leaves for garnish

1. Place the berries in a large mixing bowl and toss well. Reserve 1 cup of mixed berries for garnish. Purée the fruit in batches in a food processor or blender. Add the sugar and juices and blend until smooth.

2. Strain the purée to remove seeds, and chill. Place the chilled purée in an ice cream machine and freeze according to the manufacturer's directions.

3. Scoop the sorbet into bowls and garnish with the reserved berries and mint leaves.

NOTE: For best results, use seasonal fruit.

*Cal. **145** Carb. **37g** Protein **1g***
*Chol. **0mg** Fat **.3g/2%***

BIG CHILL TIPS

We All Scream . . .

On sweltering days, ice cream reigns supreme. Too bad the Good Humor man doesn't stop on my corner anymore.

The solution: Get yourself a good, quick ice cream maker. True, some are expensive. But what better investment in yourself than knowing exactly what's going into your favorite sweet?

Sweet and Salty

I like frozen desserts a bit on the tart side. Yet one of the secrets in making frozen yogurt and sorbets is to make them a touch sweeter before freezing. I add a pinch of kosher salt to intensify both the sweet and the tart. Why? Because flavors are dulled by freezing. This way they're just right when served.

Ice Cream Machines

Today's home ice cream makers do most of the work for you, freezing the flavored cream-and-sugar mixture while blending in air with an agitating blade. The least expensive? Traditional electric crank models that chill the mixture with salt and ice. There's another version, the prefrozen canister of artificial coolant, which is cranked by hand. Hand-cranking is best suited to making basic ice creams, while water-based treats such as ices, slushes, and sorbets require the even churning only an electrically operated machine can guarantee.

Just Keep It Cool

Pack just-churned ice cream into a container (no bubbles, please). To avoid cyrstallization, smooth the top, spread plastic wrap directly on the frozen dessert, and replace the container top.

Red, White, and Blue Celebration Cake

Sky-high baked Alaska seems the perfect celebration cake for our patriotic holidays—Flag Day, Memorial Day, the Fourth of July, and Labor Day. Made fashionable by the Hôtel de Paris in Monaco as Omelette Norveginne, it is actually Chinese in origin, and was renamed in America to celebrate Alaska's addition as a U.S. territory. Let the fireworks last forever!

SERVES 16

½ recipe White Wine Cake (page 455)
1½ cups Blueberry Sorbet (page 278)
2 cups Raspberry Frozen Yogurt (page 276)
5 egg whites
½ teaspoon vanilla extract
1 tablespoon sugar

1. Preheat the oven to 450°.
2. Place the cooled cake on a baking sheet. Place the sorbet in the center of the cake, and shape it into a mound. Coat the mound with a 2-inch layer of the frozen yogurt.
3. Working quickly, beat the egg whites and vanilla in a large bowl, until soft peaks form. Sprinkle in the sugar and beat until stiff.
4. Using a spatula, coat the entire cake with a 3-inch layer of meringue; extend the meringue to the baking sheet to seal the bottom.
5. Bake the cake for 5 minutes, or until golden brown. Transfer to a cake plate and decorate with flags or crystallized flowers. Serve immediately.

Cal. **197** Carb. **38g** Protein **3g**

Chol. **6mg** Fat **4g/16%**

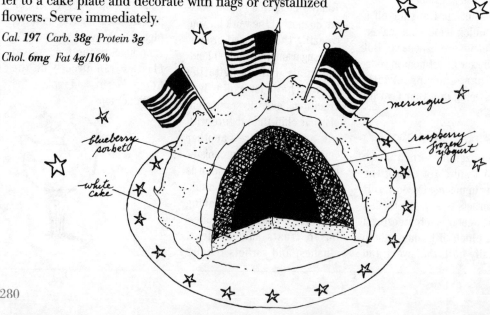

blueberry sorbet

white cake

meringue

raspberry frozen yogurt

The Berriest Bombe

SERVES 12

*1 recipe Black Raspberry
  Sorbet (page 279)*
*1 recipe Blackberry
  Frozen Yogurt
  (page 277)*

1. Line a 1½-quart Pyrex bowl
with heavy foil. Press the foil against the bowl snugly, leaving
no gaps or loose spots. Let the ends hang over the bowl.
Place the bowl in the freezer for 2 hours.
2. Spoon the sorbet into the prepared bowl. Using the back
of a spoon, spread the sorbet over the bottom and up the
sides of the mold, forming a 1¼-inch-thick layer. Freeze until
firm, about 2 hours.
3. Spoon the yogurt into the center of the sorbet layer and
smooth the top. Freeze the bombe until firm, 3 to 4 hours.
4. To serve, remove the bombe from the freezer. Using the
edges of the foil, carefully lift the bombe out of the bowl and
invert it onto a serving dish. Peel off the foil. Serve with
Bombe Fruit Sauce (below).

*Cal. **177** Carb. **38g** Protein **3g** Chol. **2mg** Fat **2g/7%***

Bombe Fruit Sauce

YIELD: TWELVE ¼-CUP SERVINGS

½ cup frozen cran-raspberry juice concentrate, thawed
¼ cup Framboise
3 cups blueberries
2 cups raspberries

1. In a medium-size saucepan lightly sprayed or wiped with
vegetable oil, place the juice and Framboise. Over medium
heat, reduce the liquid to ¼ cup.
2. Add the berries and cook for 10 to 15 minutes. Remove
from the heat and allow to cool before placing atop bombe.

*Cal. **14** Carb. **4g** Protein **0g** Chol. **0mg** Fat **.1g/4%***
(analyzed per ¼ cup)

COUNTRY FARE

Blueberry Chutney

YIELD: 3 CUPS

1/2 cup red wine vinegar
1/3 cup light brown sugar
1/4 cup finely chopped crystallized ginger
Zest of 2 lemons, minced
Juice of 2 lemons
1/4 teaspoon ground cinnamon
1/8 teaspoon crushed red pepper flakes
4 whole cloves
Pinch ground mace
4 cups blueberries, fresh or frozen

1. In a medium-size nonreactive saucepan, heat the vinegar and sugar over low heat. Simmer for 6 minutes, until slightly reduced. Add the ginger, lemon zest and juice, cinnamon, red pepper flakes, cloves, and mace, and simmer for 4 minutes. Stir in the blueberries and simmer for 2 minutes only.

2. Remove from the heat and allow to cool. Cover tightly and refrigerate. This will keep for 1 week in the refrigerator.

Cal. 15 Carb. 4g Protein 1g Chol. 0mg Fat 1g/6%
(analyzed per tablespoon)

Five-Fruit Chutney

YIELD: 2 QUARTS

4 cups rice wine vinegar
2 cups light brown sugar
1 large onion, finely chopped
1 large bell pepper, seeded and finely chopped
4 garlic cloves, minced
3 tablespoons crystallized ginger
2 tablespoons minced orange zest
1 tablespoon mustard seeds

Putting By

Summer canning used to occupy the better part of late August and early September all across the country. As farmers' markets multiply, canning is coming back.

Canning is a true science. Each food has its own requirements, depending on the balance of natural preservatives, including such factors as acidity, pectin, and sugar.

Always use a candy thermometer when canning, and read the instructions on pectin and canning jars carefully. Store preserved foods in a cool, dry place.

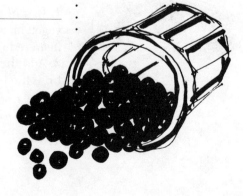

A sweet-tart and sometimes hot combination of fruits and/or vegetables, honey, vinegar, and spice, a chutney is best described as a condiment or relish.

Chutneys can be served with grilled, roasted, or smoked meats, poultry, or fish. They can make leftovers special. Dab a bit on a sandwich or use some as a wonderful ingredient in stews or braised meats. Keep a variety on hand, store-bought or homemade.

½ tablespoon salt
1 teaspoon ground cinnamon
¼ teaspoon cayenne
2 pounds firm pears, cored and finely chopped
1 pound plums, pitted and finely chopped
1 pound peaches, pitted and finely chopped
2 cups blueberries, rinsed and sorted
1 cup dried currants

1. In a stockpot, combine the vinegar, sugar, onion, bell pepper, garlic, ginger, zest, mustard seeds, salt, cinnamon, and cayenne. Bring to a boil, reduce the heat, and simmer for 15 minutes.

2. Stir in the pears, plums, and peaches, and simmer for 1 hour and 15 minutes, stirring occasionally.

3. Add the blueberries and currants and cook for an additional 15 minutes, until thickened, stirring occasionally. The mixture will continue to thicken as it cools.

4. Spoon the hot chutney into sterilized jars and seal, or refrigerate for up to 1 month.

*Cal. **21** Carb. **5g** Protein **.2g** Chol.**0mg** Fat **.1g/4%***
(analyzed per tablespoon)

Apple-Sage Chutney

YIELD: 4 CUPS

⅓ cup thinly sliced onion
2½ pounds tart apples, coarsely chopped, with skin
1 cup apple cider or apple juice
½ cup packed light brown sugar
⅓ cup dried cherries
½ cup golden raisins
⅓ cup chopped dates
6 tablespoons white wine vinegar
2 garlic cloves, minced
½ cup chopped fresh sage

1. In a large stockpot, combine all of the ingredients except the sage, and bring to a boil over medium heat. Reduce the heat and simmer until thick, about 1 hour. Stir in the sage and simmer for 5 minutes.

2. Allow the chutney to cool to room temperature, then cover and refrigerate. Serve warm or at room temperature.

*Cal. **24** Carb. **6g** Protein **.2g** Chol.**0mg** Fat **.1g/3%***
(analyzed per tablespoon)

Green Jalapeño Jelly

YIELD: 5½ CUPS

2 pounds medium green bell peppers (6 to 7), seeded and
   roughly chopped
4 jalapeño peppers, seeded and roughly chopped
1 cup cider vinegar
1 cup apple juice
½ teaspoon salt
1 package (1¾ ounces) natural fruit pectin
5 cups sugar
2 to 3 drops green vegetable food coloring

1. Purée half the bell and jalapeño peppers with half the
vinegar in a food processor. Transfer to a noncorrosive bowl.
Repeat with the remaining peppers and vinegar. Add the apple
juice and marinate, covered, overnight in the refrigerator.
2. Strain the liquid through cheesecloth, pressing down gently,
and discard the peppers. Measure exactly 3 cups of strained
liquid into a large stockpot or preserving pan; stir in the salt
and pectin. Bring to a boil. Add the sugar and return to a boil.
Boil for 1 minute, stirring constantly, until the jelly reaches
220° on a candy thermometer. You can test the "set" by dropping a spoonful of jelly into a cold metal bowl and placing it in
the freezer for a few minutes. Return the jelly to a boil for an
additional moment or two if the set is too loose.
3. Skim any bubbles off the jelly, and add green food coloring.
Pour into sterilized jelly jars, leaving ¼ inch headspace. Place
two-part lids on the jars. Process for 5 minutes in a boiling-
water bath. Remove the jars from the canner. Cool for 24
hours and check lids for seal.

*Cal. **46** Carb. **12g** Protein **0g** Chol. **0mg** Fat **0g/0%***
(analyzed per tablespoon)

Red Pepper Jelly

YIELD: 6 CUPS

2 pounds red bell peppers (about 6), seeded and roughly chopped
¼ cup seeded and roughly chopped red Hungarian peppers
   (about 4)
½ pound seeded and roughly chopped small hot red
   chili peppers (about 8)
1½ cups white vinegar
1 cup apple juice

Use
Pepper Jelly On...

Low-Fat Blend on crackers

✳

Smoked meats or fish

✳

Grilled chicken,
lamb, or beef

✳

Roasted duck, pheasant,
or goose

✳

Leftover meat loaf

✳

Roast turkey sandwich

✳

Cottage cheese

✳

Veggies in a pita

Dr. Pepper

My friend Dr. Lois Murphy
has perfected Red Pepper
Jelly. It has just the right
heat and just enough sweet.
Best of all, it's bright red.
Her trick is seeking out the
deepest red peppers, ripened
on the vine, not in the hothouse. Thanks for sharing
this, Dr. Murphy.

- *1 jar (2 ounces) red-hot candies*
- *7 cups sugar*
- *1 pouch (3 ounces) liquid fruit pectin*

1. Purée half the bell, Hungarian, and chili peppers with half the white vinegar in a food processor. Transfer to a non-corrosive bowl. Repeat with the remaining peppers and vinegar. Add the juice and the red-hots. Marinate, covered, for 4 hours.

2. Strain the liquid through cheesecloth, pressing down gently, and discard the peppers. Measure exactly 2½ cups of strained liquid; stir the sugar into the liquid. Bring to a rolling boil in a large stockpot or preserving pan. Add the pectin and boil for 2 to 3 minutes more, stirring constantly; it is important to maintain a rolling boil. The jelly mixture should reach 220° on a candy thermometer.

3. Skim any bubbles off the jelly, pour into sterilized jelly jars, leaving ¼ inch headspace, and process for canning, or cool and refrigerate until ready to use. Remove the jars from the canner. Cool for 24 hours; check lids for seal.

Cal. **64** *Carb.* **16g** *Protein* **.1g** *Chol.* **0mg** *Fat* **0g/0%**
(analyzed per tablespoon)

Tart Lemon Curd

YIELD: ¾ CUP

- *½ cup sugar*
- *2 eggs*
- *1 egg yolk*
- *2 tablespoons fresh lemon juice*
- *4 tablespoons (½ stick) unsalted butter, melted*
- *2 tablespoons minced lemon zest*

1. In a small mixing bowl, combine the sugar, eggs, and egg yolk. Beat with an electric mixer until frothy. Slowly add the lemon juice.

2. In a heavy saucepan over medium heat, pour in the egg mixture and gently simmer for 12 minutes, stirring constantly.

3. Return the curd to the mixing bowl. Beat for 1 minute, slowly adding the melted butter and then the lemon zest. Place a piece of plastic wrap directly onto the surface of the curd, and refrigerate until well chilled.

Cal. **84** *Carb.* **9g** *Protein* **1g** *Chol.* **56mg** *Fat* **5g/54%**
(analyzed per tablespoon)

Just a Smidge of Lemon Curd on...

Buttermilk Biscuits

✳

Lemon tarts

✳

Gingerbread

✳

Vanilla Waffles

✳

Lemon Pancakes

✳

Whole-wheat toast

✳

Currant Scones

Lindsay's Tomato Juice

YIELD: 8 QUARTS

2 pounds very ripe tomatoes, stemmed, cored, and cut into chunks
1 pound celery, cleaned and cut into 1-inch chunks
1 pound green beans, trimmed
1 pound fresh spinach, washed and patted dry
1 pound carrots, cleaned and cut into chunks
1 pound red onions, peeled and cut into chunks
3 large garlic cloves, chopped
½ pound beets, well scrubbed and quartered, greens removed
2 medium green bell peppers, cored and seeded
1 tablespoon freshly ground pepper
2 tablespoons salt
3 tablespoons Worcestershire sauce
½ teaspoon crushed red pepper flakes
3 tablespoons light brown sugar

1. Place all of the ingredients, in batches, in a blender or food processor and purée. Pour the purée into a large stockpot.
2. Bring to a boil over medium-high heat. Reduce the heat and simmer for 40 minutes, covered. Pass through a strainer, pressing down on the pulp to squeeze out any juices. Reheat, pour into jars, and process according to canning manufacturer's directions.

*Cal. **25** Carb. **6g** Protein **1g** Chol. **0mg** Fat **.1g/4%***
(analyzed per cup)

Spicy Catsup

YIELD: ABOUT 2½ CUPS

1 teaspoon canola oil
2 garlic cloves, minced
1 cup minced onion
1 jalapeño pepper, minced
¼ teaspoon cayenne
Pinch crushed red pepper flakes
3 dashes Tabasco
3 tablespoons tomato paste
1 can (15 ounces) concentrated crushed tomatoes

1. In a medium-size saucepan over low heat, heat the oil. Add the garlic, onion, and jalapeño pepper, and cook until the onion is tender, stirring occasionally, about 10 minutes. Stir in the remaining ingredients and cook, partially covered, stirring occa-

Bill's Best Bloody

SERVES 1

1 cup Lindsay's Tomato Juice (at left), or canned tomato juice
2 tablespoons fresh lime juice
2 tablespoons dill sauce (Milani's)
Dash Tabasco
1 teaspoon fresh chopped dill
Salt and freshly ground pepper
Sprig of dill
1¼ tablespoons Aquavit

Place all the ingredients except the sprig of dill in a 12-ounce glass. Stir very well. Add six ice cubes, and garnish with the dill sprig.

*Cal. **102** Carb. **19g** Protein **2g** Chol. **0mg** Fat **.2g/2%** (analyzed per cup)*

Old-Fashioned Tomato Sauce

YIELD: 2 QUARTS

1 tablespoon canola oil
1 cup coarsely chopped onion
12 garlic cloves, coarsely
    chopped
4 cups eggplant, (1-inch slices)
8 cups cored and coarsely
    chopped tomato
2 cups red wine
Salt and freshly ground pepper
6 bay leaves
1 dried Mexican green sandias
    pepper, or 2 tablespoons
    fresh jalapeño pepper
½ cup balsamic vinegar
½ cup Madeira

In a medium-size stockpot, heat the oil over medium heat. Sauté the onion and garlic until transparent. Add the remaining ingredients. Bring to a boil, reduce the heat, and simmer, uncovered, for 4 hours. Taste and adjust the seasoning.

Cal. **82** Carb. **17g**
Protein **3g** Chol. **0mg**
Fat **2g/22%**
(analyzed per cup)

sionally, until the catsup has thickened slightly, about 10 minutes. Transfer to a container, cool to room temperature, cover, and chill until serving.

Cal. **26** Carb. **5g** Protein **1g** Chol. **0mg** Fat **.3g/12%**
(analyzed per tablespoon)

Tomato-Carrot Broth

I use this tomato broth for soups, poaching, braising, and steaming.

YIELD: 11 CUPS
3 pounds ripe tomatoes
3 pounds carrots, cut into 1-inch slices
2 large white onions, sliced
Six ¼-inch slices fresh ginger
4 ribs celery, with leaves
6 cloves garlic, finely minced
2 bay leaves
12 black peppercorns
6 whole cloves
4 cups canned tomato juice or Lindsay's Tomato Juice (opposite)
1 cup fresh chopped dill

1. In a large pot filled with 2½ quarts of water, combine all of the ingredients except the tomato juice and place over very low heat. Simmer, uncovered, for 3 hours.
2. Remove from the heat, cool to room temperature, and purée in a food processor, returning purée to pot. Add the tomato juice, stirring, until well combined, and place over medium heat, covered, for 20 minutes. Add dill, remove from heat, and cool. The broth keeps 1 week refrigerated or 3 months frozen.

Cal. **59** Carb. **3g** Protein **1g** Chol. **0mg**
Fat **.8g/5%**
(analyzed per cup)

Flavored Oils

Each flavored oil can be made by first placing the herbs and/or spices in the bottle, then adding the oil. The bottle should be kept in a cool, dark place to season for two weeks, then strained and rebottled. It is best to refrigerate until needed and then bring back to room temperature before using.

Cinnamon Oil
YIELD: 1 CUP
4 cinnamon sticks
8 whole cloves
1 cup canola oil

Herbs de Provence Oil
YIELD: 1 PINT
2 sprigs fresh rosemary
1 sprig fresh thyme
2 garlic cloves
2 sprigs fresh oregano
2 sprigs fresh marjorom
2 bay leaves
6 black peppercorns
1 pint olive or
    canola oil

Spicy Herbed Oil
YIELD: 1 PINT
1/2 tablespoon peppercorns
1/2 tablespoon coriander seeds
2 bay leaves
2 sprigs fresh rosemary
3 red chilies
1/2 teaspoon fennel seeds
1 pint olive oil

Thai Oil
YIELD: 1 PINT
Three 6-inch blades lemon
    grass
2 sprigs fresh basil
1/4 cup finely chopped fresh
    cilantro
2 sprigs fresh mint
2 garlic cloves
2 thin slices fresh ginger
1 pint peanut or canola oil

Red-Hot Stuff
YIELD: 1 PINT
4 dried hot red chili peppers
2 garlic cloves
1 cup coarsely chopped fresh
    cilantro leaves
2 teaspoons cumin seeds
6 sprigs fresh oregano
1 quart olive or canola oil

Hot Chili Oil
YIELD: 1 CUP
4 fresh jalapeño peppers,
    with seeds, sliced in half
    lengthwise
Zest of 2 limes
1 cup extra-virgin olive oil

Sage Oil
YIELD: 1 CUP
1/2 cup whole fresh sage leaves
1 cup extra-virgin olive oil

Orange Spice Oil
YIELD: 1 PINT

1/2 teaspoon coriander seeds
2 garlic cloves
3 thin slices fresh ginger
1/2 teaspoon ground cloves
1/2 tablespoon ground allspice
Zest of 1 orange
One 4-inch cinnamon stick
1 pint olive oil

Fennel Oil
YIELD: 1 PINT

2 dried fennel stalks
2 sprigs fresh dill
Zest of 1 lemon
2 sprigs fresh lemon thyme
1 teaspoons coriander seeds
1 pint olive or canola oil

Basil Oil
YIELD: 1 PINT

1 cup tightly packed fresh
basil leaves
1 cup best-quality olive oil

1. Bring a medium-size saucepan of water to a boil. Add the basil and blanch for 2 minutes. Remove the leaves and squeeze dry.
2. In a blender, place the leaves and half of the oil; blend until smooth. With the motor running, gradually add the remaining oil. Pour the oil into a glass jar, cover, and allow to steep for at least a day at room temperature strain and rebottle. Refrigerate until ready to use.

THE OIL PANTRY
A Spray of Oil. . . A Drizzle of Oil

As Americans move away from butter and its saturated fat, two oils have become popular for their monounsaturates: olive oil, long a staple of the Mediterranean diet; and canola (rapeseed) oil, a staple of Canada, Japan, India, and China—they are very close in composition. I generally choose one over the other based on the flavor I want—the fruitiness of a good olive oil, or the neutral taste of canola.

One of the best ways to make their flavor even more effective (and more powerful, so you can use less) is to infuse oils with additional flavor. Herbs, peppers, garlic, and spices can all excite a basic oil, so that they can impart more flavor.

Flavored oils can be kept in a bottle to drizzle or in a spray bottle to spritz over salads, steamed or roasted vegetables, potatoes, bread, pizza, grilled fish, or poultry, or in a wok for stir-frying. Use sparingly. Remember, their taste is magnified, so you don't need very much.

vibrant vinegars

Provençale Vinegar
YIELD: 1 PINT
1 sprig fresh rosemary
2 bay leaves
1 sprig fresh thyme
1 sprig fresh savory
1 sprig fresh lavender
1 sprig fresh marjorom
4 garlic cloves
1 hot red pepper
1 pint white wine vinegar
Cal. **4** Carb. **1g** Protein **.1g**
Chol. **0mg** Fat **0g/0%***

Salad Greens Vinegar
YIELD: 1 PINT
1 sprig salad burnet
1 sprig fresh thyme
1 sprig fresh tarragon
1 sprig fresh Italian parsley
3 chive blades
1 tablespoon black
  peppercorns
1 pint white wine vinegar
Cal. **3** Carb. **1g** Protein **.1g**
Chol. **0mg**
Fat **0g/0%***

Tuscan Vinegar
YIELD: 1 PINT
2 sprigs fresh rosemary
2 sprigs fresh oregano
1 sprig fresh sage
2 sprigs fresh basil
1 garlic clove
1 tablespoon black
  peppercorns
1 pint red wine vinegar
Cal. **4** Carb. **1g** Protein **.1g**
Chol. **0mg** Fat **0g/0%***

Summer Vinegar
YIELD: 1 PINT
4 sprigs fresh dill
1 dill blossom
Zest of 1 lemon
1 garlic clove
$1/2$ tablespoon mustard seed
1 pint white wine vinegar
Cal. **3** Carb. **.9g** Protein **.1g**
Chol. **0mg** Fat **0g/0%***

Cider Dressing
YIELD: 1 PINT
$1/8$ teaspoon ground
  cloves
$1/8$ teaspoon freshly
  ground pepper
$1/2$ teaspoon ground
  ginger
One 3-inch cinnamon
  stick
1 cup apple juice

1 cup cider vinegar
2 tablespoons superfine sugar
Cal. **8** Carb. **2g** Protein **0g**
Chol. **0mg** Fat **0g/0%***

Red Wine Dressing
YIELD: 1 PINT
$1/4$ teaspoon mustard
$1/4$ teaspoon freshly ground
  pepper
12 fresh basil, sage, rosemary, thyme, marjoram,
  or oregano leaves
2 tablespoons finely minced
  garlic
$1/8$ teaspoon salt
3 tablespoons sugar
2 cups red wine vinegar
Cal. **8** Carb. **2g** Protein **.1g**
Chol. **0mg** Fat **0g/0%**

Lime Dressing
YIELD: 1 PINT
3 sprigs fresh mint
1 garlic cloves
Zest of 1 lime
$1/2$ tablespoon coriander seeds
2 tablespoons sugar
1 pint white wine vinegar
Cal. **5** Carb. **2g** Protein **0g**
Chol. **0mg** Fat **0g/0%***

White Wine Dressing

YIELD: 1 PINT

2 tablespoons fresh garlic
  finely minced

6 sprigs tarragon, rosemary,
  or sage

Zest of 1 lime or lemon

3 tablespoons superfine sugar

2 cups white wine vinegar

Cal. **8** *Carb.* **2g** *Protein* **.1g**

Chol. **0mg** *Fat* **0g/0%***

Herb Dressing

YIELD: 1 PINT

1/2 cup fresh tarragon

1/2 cup watercress

1/2 cup fresh chervil

1/3 cup fresh salad burnet

1 garlic clove, crushed

1 jalapeño pepper, finely
  chopped

1 teaspoon peppercorns

2 tablespoons superfine sugar

2 cups white wine vinegar

Cal. **6** *Carb.* **2g** *Protein* **.1g**

Chol. **0mg** *Fat* **0g/0%***

Spiced Vinegar Dressing

YIELD: 1 PINT

1/2 tablespoon peppercorns

1 teaspoon celery seeds

1 teaspoon mustard seeds

1/2 tablespoon chopped ginger

1 cinnamon stick

2 jalapeño peppers

2 garlic cloves

2 cups white wine vinegar

2 tablespoons superfine sugar

Cal. **7** *Carb.* **2g** *Protein* **.1g**

Chol. **0mg** *Fat* **.1g/6%***

Berry Dressing

YIELD: 1 PINT

2 cups white wine vinegar

1/2 cup raspberries, blueberries,
  blackberries, or cranberries

2 tablespoons honey

One 6-inch cinnamon stick

Cal. **7** *Carb.* **2g** *Protein* **0g**

Chol. **0mg** *Fat* **0g/0%***

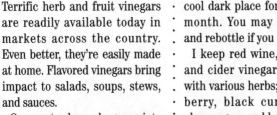

THE VINEGAR PANTRY

Terrific herb and fruit vinegars are readily available today in markets across the country. Even better, they're easily made at home. Flavored vinegars bring impact to salads, soups, stews, and sauces.

Our pantry has a large variety of vinegars, with more aging on the back shelves all the time. They're easily made with endless flavor combinations and merely require steeping in a cool dark place for at least one month. You may strain them and rebottle if you desire.

I keep red wine, white wine, and cider vinegars—pure and with various herbs; sherry, raspberry, black currant, malt, champagne, and balsamic—one for everyday use and an aged one for special dishes. If those bottles weren't there, I'd feel as if I were cooking with my hands tied behind my back.

And because I love tart tastes, it's often vinegar alone that I sprinkle on a salad. That's why I created the vinegar dressings here. (Beware: They're highly addictive!) Just a dash of sugar softens the acidic edge, while the herbs and spices bring sparkle to any salad!

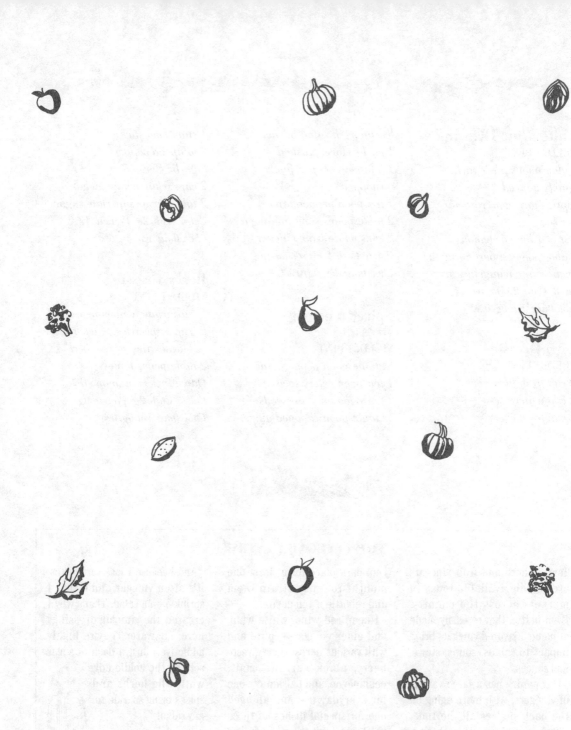

Autumn Leaves

ORCHARD FARM MARKET

"Live within your harvest." Persian proverb

Fall Journal

September

1

3 Labor Day weekend
Potluck — bring salad.

6 Organize hayride.

8 Mushroom hunting

15 Football game —
tailgate picnic

19 Make green
tomato chutney.

23 Plant new tree.
County Fair!!

25 Shut down the pool.

29 Pick apples in orchard.

October

1 Pancake supper

4 Stone boat.

6 GOOSE FEST WEEKEND!

9 J and J's birthdays!

10 Unpack sweaters.

12 ANNIVERSARY!
Northern color trip

14 Rake, rake, rake and
compost.

16 Gallery Stroll

17 Octoberfest Party

18 Divide perennials—
transplant and give.

19 Dig up herbs and pot
for kitchen.

20 Buy pumpkins at the
Farmer's Market.

25 Dig up tender bulbs.
Plant bulbs.

26 make costumes.

28 Carve pumpkins—
buy treats.

31 HALLOWEEN!

November

2 Start amaryllis and
paperwhites.

6 Fill bird
feeders.

11 MIDNIGHT MADNESS!
12 Plan for Thanksgiving.

17 Wills goes deer hunting.
Julee to Paris

23 Beaujolais
Nouveau
today

30 Last walk on the beach

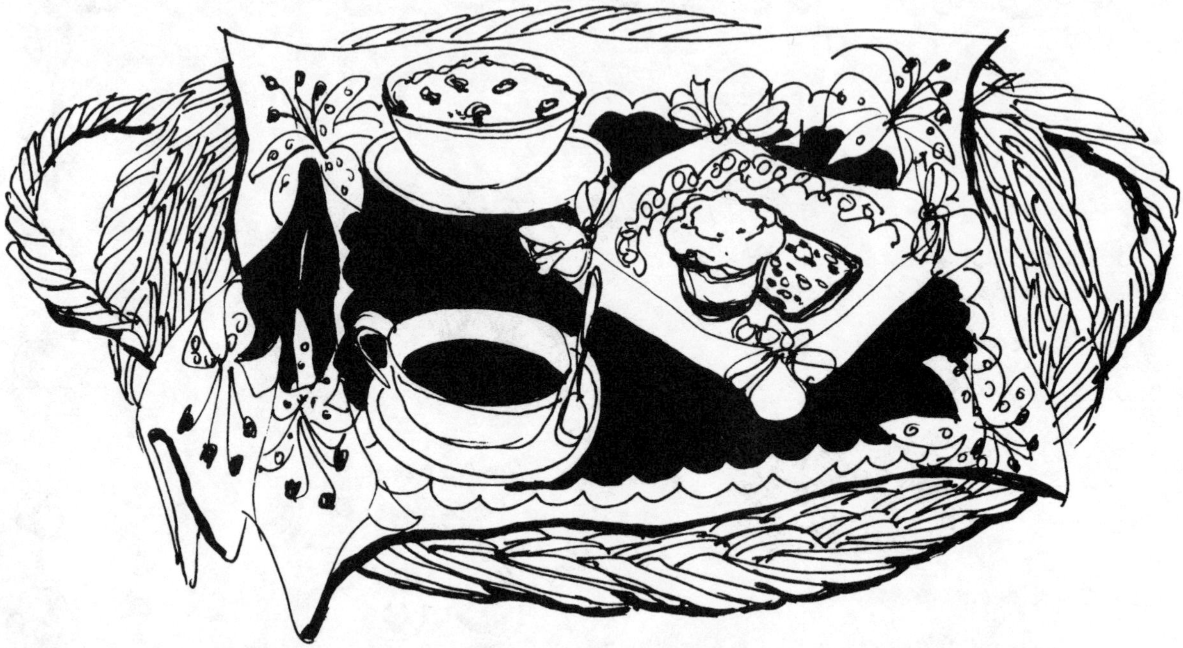

Cinnamon Mornings

Old-Fashioned Irish Soda Bread

Grandma Clark taught me how she made this in the Old Country for special occasions. I know she'd like the taste of this one, even without the amount of butter she used.

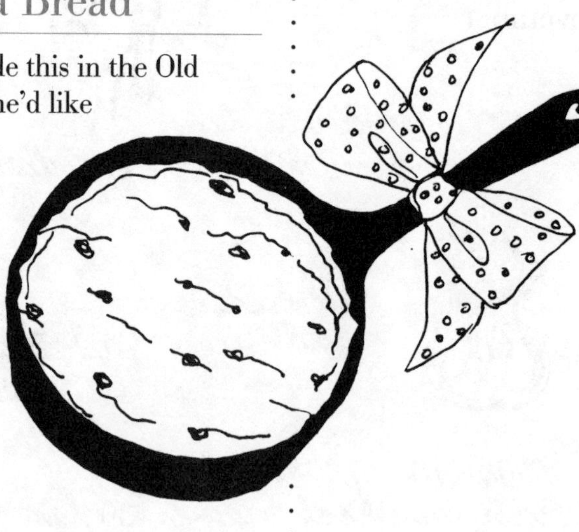

YIELD: 24 SLICES
1½ cups golden raisins
Juice of 2 oranges
3 cups all-purpose flour
1½ teaspoons salt
1 tablespoon baking powder
1 teaspoon baking soda
¾ cup sugar
¼ cup canola oil
1¾ cups low-fat buttermilk
1 medium egg, well beaten
2 egg whites

Autumn

The first warm days of fall could surely pass for summer's last. But the brightness and clarity of Indian summer subtly signal change, preparing us for cold to come. One day is crisp, the next mellow, as familiar scenes ignite with vibrant hues of auburn and scarlet.

The market, too, undergoes transformation. Deep-orange persimmons and red pomegranates mirror the blazing vistas. Suddenly, rosy banks of apples replace summer's mounds of ripe tomatoes. Fennel and celeriac bulbs appear alongside cranberry beans, gourds, pumpkins, and clusters of grapes of every flavor and dusky hue. Bunches of sturdy root vegetables mingle with heads of purple kale and large-leafed chard. Out in the woods, wild mushrooms send tender frills through the forest floor, and hunting season begins.

With the waning of summer's light and warmth, our cooking becomes robust, earthy, and heartwarming.

¼ cup applesauce
2 tablespoons unsalted butter, melted

1. Preheat the oven to 350°.
2. Lightly spray or wipe a 12- to 14-inch cast-iron skillet with vegetable oil. Line the pan with waxed paper and set aside.
3. In a small saucepan over low heat, place the raisins and orange juice, and macerate until the raisins are plump.
4. Meanwhile, in a large bowl, combine all the dry ingredients and mix well. Drain the raisins, add them to the dry ingredients, and toss to coat.
5. In a small bowl, combine the oil, buttermilk, egg, egg whites, and applesauce, and add to the dry ingredients; mix well. Pour the batter into the prepared skillet and smooth the top with a spatula. Drizzle the melted butter over the dough. Bake for 1 hour, or until golden and a toothpick inserted in the center comes out clean. Serve warm, or cool and wrap in plastic wrap. It will stay fresh for 3 days.

*Cal. **153** Carb. **27g** Protein **3g** Chol. **11mg** Fat **4g/22%***
(analyzed per slice)

Apples and Cracked Wheat

SERVES 6
2 teaspoons canola oil
1 cup cracked wheat
3½ cups apple juice
2 Granny Smith apples (about ¾ pound), peeled and diced
1½ teaspoons ground cinnamon
¼ teaspoon ground cardamom
⅛ teaspoon ground cloves
2 tablespoons finely minced orange zest

1. In a medium saucepan over medium heat, heat the oil. Add the cracked wheat and toast until golden, about 3 to 4 minutes, stirring constantly. Bring the apple juice to a boil and carefully add it to the wheat—it will splatter. Stir in the apples, cinnamon, cardamom, and cloves. Lower the heat, cover, and simmer for 15 to 20 minutes, or until the liquid is absorbed. Remove from the heat and let stand, covered, for 5 minutes.
2. Stir in the orange zest. Serve with skim milk.

*Cal. **204** Carb. **43g** Protein **4g** Chol. **0mg** Fat **2g/9%***

Breakfast Crepes

Light crepes, laced with a hint of orange.

YIELD: SIXTEEN 7-INCH CREPES

1 cup all-purpose flour
¼ teaspoon salt
½ cup skim milk
3 eggs
2 teaspoons finely grated orange zest, or 2 tablespoons
  finely chopped fresh mint
2 tablespoons unsalted butter, melted

1. Lightly wipe a 7-inch nonstick skillet with vegetable oil.
2. In a food processor, combine all of the ingredients and process until smooth, scraping down the sides once. Transfer the batter to a glass bowl, cover with plastic wrap, and refrigerate for 1 hour.
3. Heat the prepared skillet over medium-high heat. Add 2 tablespoons of the batter. Quickly tilt the pan back and forth so the batter spreads evenly over the bottom of the skillet. Cook until lightly browned, 30 to 45 seconds. Then turn and cook on the other side for 15 to 20 seconds. Repeat with the remaining batter, stacking the crepes between sheets of waxed paper to prevent them from sticking together. If you are not using the crepes immediately, wrap them in plastic wrap and refrigerate for up to 2 days or freeze them for a month. Serve with fresh fruit or Plum Compote (opposite).

Cal. 57 Carb. 6g Protein 2g Chol. 38mg Fat 2g/38%

Oats

The Scots and the Welsh have their brewis (oatmeal broth) and siot (oatcakes in buttermilk), the Swiss, their muesli, the Irish, their marvelous steel-cut oats. In whatever form, oats are terrific. Cooked oats have always been a great morning starter in winter; for most oatmeal eaters, brown sugar, maple syrup, and warm skim milk are the garnishes of choice.

Baked French Toast

This is a delicious way to enjoy French toast—without frying it in butter.

SERVES 8

1 cup maple syrup
1 loaf French bread
3 eggs
3 egg whites
1½ cups skim milk
2 teaspoons vanilla extract
¾ teaspoon ground nutmeg

1. Lightly spray or wipe a large baking dish with vegetable oil. Pour the syrup into the dish. Slice the French bread into

Cereal Toppings

Per tablespoon:

Sugar
cal. 45 ★ fat 0gm.

Honey
cal. 63 ★ fat 0gm.

Molasses
cal. 54 ★ fat 0gm.

Maple Syrup
cal. 51 ★ fat 0gm.

Raisins
cal. 27 ★ fat 0gm.

Almonds
cal. 48 ★ fat 4.3gm.

Walnuts
cal. 52 ★ fat 5.1gm.

Coconut
cal. 26 ★ fat 2.5gm.

Wheat Germ
cal. 27 ★ fat .8gm.

Blueberries
cal. 5 ★ fat .03gm.

Strawberries
cal. 3 ★ fat .03gm.

Bananas
cal. 6.5 ★ fat .03gm.

Raspberries
cal. 4 ★ fat .04gm.

Dried Figs
cal. 30 ★ fat .13gm.

eight 2-inch-thick slices and place them over the syrup.

2. In a separate bowl, combine the eggs, egg whites, milk, vanilla, and ¼ teaspoon nutmeg, and beat until well mixed. Pour the egg mixture over the bread, pressing the bread down gently so it soaks up the batter. Cover and refrigerate overnight.

3. Preheat the oven to 350°. Remove the pan from the refrigerator and sprinkle the remaining ½ teaspoon nutmeg over the bread; bake for 40 to 45 minutes, or until golden brown. Serve with fresh fruit, if desired.

Cal. 232 Carb. 44g Protein 7g Chol. 69mg Fat 3g/10%

Plum Compote

Plums warmed with cinnamon, spice, and everything nice.

YIELD: 4 CUPS

2 pounds assorted plums, washed, dried, pitted, and quartered
1½ cups apple juice or apple cider
Zest of 1 orange
Zest of 1 lime
Zest of 1 lemon
1 vanilla bean, split
4 whole cloves
2 pieces cinnamon (2 inches each)
1 cup light brown sugar
1 tablespoon fresh lemon juice

1. In a large saucepan over low heat, combine the plums, apple juice, zests, vanilla bean, cloves, and cinnamon. Stir in the sugar and lemon juice and simmer for 20 minutes, until the plums are cooked. Remove the plums with a slotted spoon and set aside.

2. Reduce the juices by half, to about 2 cups. Place the plums in a 1-quart jar. Pour the juice and spices over the plums, cool to room temperature, cover, and refrigerate for several days. Remove the vanilla bean, cloves, and cinnamon. Serve over waffles or angel food cake.

Cal. 82 Carb. 20g Protein 1g
Chol. 0mg Fat 1g/6%
(analyzed per ¼ cup)

Pumpkin-Ginger Muffins

YIELD: 20 MUFFINS

1½ cups fresh or canned pumpkin purée
2 cups light brown sugar
2 tablespoons canola oil
3 tablespoons applesauce
1 egg
1 egg white
½ cup apple juice concentrate
1½ cups all-purpose flour
2 teaspoons baking soda
2 teaspoons baking powder
1 teaspoon salt
4½ teaspoons ground ginger
1 teaspoon ground nutmeg
⅓ cup finely chopped crystallized ginger
1 cup Green Tomato Mincemeat (page 182), or canned mincemeat

1. Preheat the oven to 350°. Lightly spray or wipe muffin tins with vegetable oil.
2. In a large bowl, combine the pumpkin, sugar, oil, and applesauce. Add the egg and egg white; beat until smooth. Stir in the juice. In another bowl, mix the dry ingredients together.
3. Gradually stir the dry mixture into the wet mixture and mix well, but do not overbeat. Fold in the crystallized ginger and mincemeat.
4. Use an ice cream scoop to fill the muffin tins generously with batter (about two-thirds full). Bake for 25 minutes, or until a toothpick inserted in the center comes out clean.

Cal. **145** *Carb.* **31g** *Protein* **2g** *Chol.* **0mg** *Fat* **2g/11%**
(analyzed per muffin)

Scarborough Fair Sausage

YIELD: 24 PATTIES

2 pounds freshly lean ground turkey (99% fat free)
4 jalapeño peppers, seeded and finely minced
2 garlic cloves, finely minced
4 slices white bread, broken into ½-inch pieces
½ cup chicken broth (see Basics)
1 cup finely minced fresh parsley
2 tablespoons finely minced fresh sage
1 tablespoon finely minced fresh rosemary

1 tablespoon finely minced fresh thyme
1 teaspoon ground ginger
1 teaspoon crushed red pepper flakes
1 tablespoon horseradish
1 teaspoon ground cloves

In a large mixing bowl, blend all of the ingredients very well. Shape into 2-inch patties. In a large skillet, sauté until well browned, turning frequently, about 8 to 10 minutes altogether.

*Cal. **68** Carb. **4g** Protein **11g** Chol. **42mg** Fat **.6g/8%***
(analyzed per patty)

Baby Schnecken

YIELD: 30 MINI ROLLS

½ cup light brown sugar
1 teaspoon ground cinnamon
8 tablespoons (1 stick) unsalted butter
1 cup Yogurt Cheese (see Basics)
2 cups all-purpose flour
½ teaspoon salt
2 tablespoons honey
1 cup finely chopped pecans

1. Preheat the oven to 350°. Combine the brown sugar and cinnamon and set aside. In a medium bowl, cream the butter and yogurt cheese until almost smooth.
2. Add the flour and salt; with a pastry blender or fork, cut the cheese mixture into the flour until the pieces are the size of small peas. Add 2 to 4 tablespoons of water, until the mixture starts to form a ball. Shape the dough into a ball.
3. On a lightly floured surface, roll the dough out to a 9 x 12-inch rectangle.
4. Spray or brush the dough lightly with vegetable oil. Spread the sugar-and-cinnamon mixture evenly over the top two-thirds of the dough. Roll the dough tightly toward you.
5. With a serrated knife, slice the roll into 2-inch lengths.
6. Lightly spray or wipe an 8-inch cake pan with vegetable oil. Tuck the tail of each roll under and push up slightly on the bottom to dome slightly. Place in the cake pan.
7. In a small bowl, mix the honey and pecans. Place ½ teaspoon of the mixture on top of each roll.
8. Bake for 25 to 30 minutes, or until golden brown.

*Cal. **104** Carb. **12g** Protein **2g** Chol. **9mg** Fat **6g/39%***
(analyzed per roll)

"Good communication is as stimulating as black coffee, and just as hard to sleep after."

Anne Morrow Lindbergh

Harvest Strata

This tastes much cleaner than stratas made with
heavy cream. I've loaded it with vegetables.

SERVES 12

8 slices white bread, crusts removed
5 eggs
3 egg whites
5 cups skim milk
1 teaspoon dry mustard
1 cup Low-Fat Blend (see Basics)
$\frac{1}{2}$ cup grated Parmesan
2 garlic cloves, chopped
Freshly ground pepper
1 cup chopped fresh Italian parsley
1 tablespoon chopped fresh rosemary
$\frac{1}{2}$ cup chopped scallion, green part only
1 cup broccoli florets
2 medium zucchini, quartered lengthwise and sliced
1 cup slivered fresh spinach
$\frac{1}{2}$ cup Parmesan shards

1. Arrange the bread on the bottom of a 9 x 13-inch casserole dish, overlapping the slices slightly.
2. In a large mixing bowl, combine the eggs, egg whites, milk,
and mustard. Blend well and set aside.
3. In a food processor blend the Low-Fat Blend, Parmesan,
garlic, pepper, parsley, and rosemary. Pour into the egg mixture and stir until well combined. Pour over the bread and
press the bread down, as it tends to float. Cover with plastic
wrap, and place in the refrigerator for 6 to 8 hours or overnight;
the bread should be completely soaked with the mixture.
4. Preheat the oven to 375°. Remove the strata from the
refrigerator; place the vegetables on the surface, then push
them into the egg mixture; they should be covered. Top with
the Parmesan shards.
5. Bake the strata for 1 hour, or until it is browned and a
knife inserted in the center comes out clean. Serve hot.

*Cal. **155** Carb. **17g** Protein **12g** Chol. **81mg** Fat **4g/23%***

STRUT YOUR STRATA

Fresh herbs

❖

Asparagus

❖

Ground turkey
(99% fat free)

❖

Broccoli

❖

Zucchini

❖

Tomatoes

❖

Low-fat goat cheese

❖

Spinach

❖

Canadian bacon

❖

Leeks

❖

Scallions

❖

Roasted garlic

❖

Artichoke hearts

❖

Nasturtium leaves

❖

Zucchini blossoms

❖

Prosciutto, pancetta

❖

Sun-dried tomatoes

❖

Red onions

❖

Carrot slices

COTTAGE CHEESE

The diet food of the seventies is now the darling of the nineties, thanks to the growing concern about health. Cottage cheese comes in an array of curd sizes and ranges from creamy to dry. Closely related are pot cheese, a skim-milk form of cottage cheese with a larger, drier curd, and farmer cheese, which is similar to skim-milk cottage cheese, but is pressed into a block.

Cottage cheese ranges dramatically in its nutrient composition. For instance, creamed may have 109 calories, 5 fat grams, and 63 mg. of calcium, while nonfat has only 70 calories, no fat, and 100 mg. calcium. Farmer's cheese has the most calories—160—and the most calcium—120 mg. The only way to really know is to read labels carefully.

Use cottage cheese:
- In our Low-Fat Blend
- As a topping for pizza
- In an omelette
- As "cream" for salad dressings
- In baked goods
- In dips
- On fruit salad
- With tomatoes

Lemon–Poppy Seed Bread

YIELD: 2 LARGE LOAVES (36 SLICES)

3 cups all-purpose flour
1 egg
4 egg whites
1 1/2 cups skim milk
2 1/4 cups sugar
1/2 teaspoon salt
1 1/2 teaspoons baking powder
1/2 cup canola oil
1/2 cup applesauce
2 tablespoons poppy seeds
1 teaspoon vanilla extract
4 tablespoons chopped lemon zest
1 teaspoon fresh lemon juice

Glaze:
1/3 cup confectioners' sugar
2 teaspoons fresh lemon juice
1/2 teaspoon skim milk
2 teaspoons chopped lemon zest

1. Preheat the oven to 350°. Lightly spray or wipe two 10 x 5-inch loaf pans with vegetable oil.

2. In a large mixing bowl, place the flour, egg, egg whites, milk, sugar, salt, baking powder, oil, and applesauce. Mix until well blended.

3. Add the poppy seeds, vanilla, zest, and lemon juice, and mix.

4. Divide the dough between the pans and bake for 40 minutes, or until a toothpick inserted in the center comes out clean.

5. Whisk the ingredients for the glaze until smooth; spoon the mixture over the loaves while they are still warm and in the pan. Cool and, using a knife to loosen the sides, unmold and wrap in foil until ready to serve.

Cal. **129** *Carb.* **23g** *Protein* **2g** *Chol.* **5mg** *Fat* **3g/23%** (analyzed per slice)

GOING WITH THE GRAINS

Basics

The ripened seed or fruits of cultivated grasses, grains, and rices are the world's most important staple foods. Wholesome, delicious, and nourishing, they are proteins that, when mixed with other complementary seeds, nuts, legumes, or dairy products, become a "complete" protein.

In the Market

More and more grains are readily available in the supermarket. If organically grown produce is important to you, shop for grains at a health-food store for a broader assortment.

At Home

Hulled grains such as barley, bulghur, wheat, and cornmeal will keep for as long as a year in tightly sealed containers if stored in a cool, dry place.

Cereals

No food in history has been more vital in providing nourishment than grains: oats, wheat, bulghur, corn, kasha, farina, barley, rye, and rice. Milled for flour or coarsely ground as bread, a part of every culture. The goddess of grain, Ceres, honors the ancient women who scattered and harvested the seed. Hence, the name "cereal."

Cereals are carbohydrates. Good, filling, stick-to-your-ribs food. They're grains that have been milled to remove the outer covering so that humans can digest them better. Cereals with the bran plus the germ intact are called whole-grain cereals. They spoil more quickly than "degermed" cereals because the germ is high in fat. Wheat cereals provide B vitamins, iron, and potassium. Eaten with milk, cheese, beans, or meat, they become a "complete" protein.

★ GOOD FOR YOU ★

Grains are high in complex carbohydrates, protein, and fiber (both soluble and insoluble). They have B vitamins, iron, and potassium. Corn is the only grain that provides vitamin A, which helps lower cholesterol levels. Wheat germ makes up only 3% of a wheat berry, but it contains 23 nutrients, including B complex vitamins, calcium, iron, potassium, and phosphorus. Wheat bran is loaded with fiber, a leading cancer fighter. Semolina and couscous offer protein, carbohydrates, B vitamins, and fiber. Oatmeal and oat bran are outstanding in cutting cholesterol because of their beta glucan.

Grain	Description	Liquid per 1 c. dry	Cooking (min.)	Yield
Amaranth	Nutty flavor	2 c.	20–25	2 c.
Barley Hulled	Whole-grain cereal; or unground	3 c.	90	3¾ c.
Pearl	Bland flavor, soft texture	2 c.	45	2 c.
Job's Tears	A form of barley	2½ c.	50	3 c.
Buckwheat	Mild, nutty flavor; kasha is roasted buckwheat and tastes nuttier	2 c.	12–15	2 c.

Grain	Description	Liquid per 1 c. dry	Cooking (min.)	Yield
Corn				
Cornmeal (polenta)	Sweet taste, soft texture	4 c.	30	2 c.
Hominy (posole)	Slightly sweet, firm texture	3 c.	2½ hrs.	2 c.
Hominy grits	Ground hominy	4 c.	15–20	4 c.
Millet	Chewy, slightly nutty	2½ c.	25–30	3½ c.
Oats				
Oatmeal (rolled oats)	Slightly nutty, soft texture	2¾ c.	10	2½ c.
Steel-cut (Irish, Scottish)	Nutty flavor, firm texture	3½ c.	15–20	3 c.
Quinoa	Sweet flavor, soft texture	2 c.	15	3 c.
Rice				
White	Bland, soft texture	2 c.	20	3 c.
Brown	Nutty flavor, soft texture	1½ c.	30	3 c.
Wild	Intense nutty, earthy flavor; thicker than oats	2½ c.	50–55	4 c.
Rye				
Rye berries	A bit thicker than oats	3 c.	2 hrs.	2½ c.
Rye groats (rolled or flakes)	Thicker than oats	3 c.	25–30	2⅔ c.
Triticale	Nutty flavor, crunchy texture	3 c.	75	2¼ c.
Wheat				
Cracked wheat	Flavor like wheat berries	2 c.	30–35	2½ c.
Bulghur	Nutty flavor, soft texture	2 c.	20–25	2 c.
Bulghur, fine grind	Nutty flavor, light	3 c.	5	1½ c.
Bran	Outer coating of the wheat seed or germ	1½ c.	5	2⅔ c.
Wheat germ	Seed of the wheat kernel			
Couscous (quick-cooking)	Ground durum wheat	2 c.	3	3 c.
Wheat berries (soft)	Crunchy, healthy addition to soups, breads, etc.	3 c.	30	2¼ c.
Wheat berries (hard)	Same as above	3 c.	2 hrs.	2¼ c.

SATURDAY LUNCHES

Autumn Vegetable Soup

YIELD: 20 SERVINGS

3 pounds veal shank, cut 1½ inches thick
6 pounds beef shank, cut 1½ inches thick
2 pounds soup bones, sawed in half
4 cups coarsely chopped onion
2 cups coarsely chopped carrot
3 cups coarsely chopped celery
5 cloves garlic, minced
Bouquet garni: *2 sprigs thyme, 1 bay leaf, 8 sprigs fresh*
    Italian parsley, tied together
2 cups finely shredded leek
4 cups peeled and diced fresh tomato
3 cups tomato juice
2 cups shredded cabbage
4 cups peeled and diced potato
1 bag (32 ounces) frozen mixed vegetables
Salt and freshly ground pepper

1. Preheat the oven to 425°.
2. Wipe the meat and bones with paper towels and place them in a large roasting pan. Add the onion, carrot, and celery. Place the roasting pan in the oven and roast for 30 to 45 minutes, stirring frequently, until the meat browns and the vegetables begin to caramelize.
3. Transfer the meat and vegetables to a large stockpot. Add the garlic, *bouquet garni*, and 6 quarts of water.

Trust Your Own Tastes

This is one of the most difficult things to impart to my students in cooking classes. Taste as you go along; recipes may give specific amounts, but ingredients vary in taste. Try tasting ingredients individually, then after they've been added, and you'll see. Oil helps anchor and transport flavor; so do salt and sugar when you sprinkle just a little over such ingredients as garlic, citrus fruits, or ginger, which are meant to flavor dishes. The flavors are captured in the salt or sugar crystals and melt into the dish.

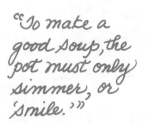

4. Add 1 cup of water to the roasting pan and bring to a boil over high heat on top of the stove. Boil for 1 minute, scraping up all the brown bits. Transfer the bones and liquid to the stockpot.

5. Bring the soup to a boil over medium-high heat. Skim off every bit of foam. Lower the heat and simmer the soup for 4 hours.

6. Increase the heat to medium and add the leek, tomato, tomato juice, cabbage, and potatoes. Cook for 50 minutes.

7. Add the frozen vegetables and cook for 20 minutes.

8. Just before serving, remove the meat and bones from the soup. Shred the meat and return to the stockpot. Skim any fat from the surface; season with salt and pepper to taste. Serve immediately.

Cal. 165 Carb. 16g Protein 17g Chol. 40mg Fat 4g/21%

"Creamy" Pumpkin-Sherry Soup

Smoky and silky-smooth with buttermilk.

SERVES 8

1 pumpkin (3½ pounds), peeled, seeded, and roughly
*   chopped, seeds reserved*
1 teaspoon canola oil
1 medium onion, coarsely chopped
3½ cups chicken broth (see Basics)
¾ cup low-fat buttermilk
⅛ teaspoon white pepper
¼ cup dry sherry

1. Preheat the oven to 400°. Place the pumpkin seeds on a sheet pan and lightly spray or drizzle with vegetable oil; toss well. Toast the seeds until golden, about 12 minutes.

2. Heat the oil in a large stockpot. Add the onion and sauté 4 to 5 minutes, until soft and lightly golden. Add the pumpkin and chicken broth. Cover and simmer for 40 to 45 minutes, or until the pumpkin is tender. Transfer to a food processor and purée. Return the purée to the stockpot and whisk in the buttermilk, pepper, and sherry. Heat through, about 5 minutes.

3. Serve immediately, sprinkled with the toasted pumpkin seeds.

Cal. 68 Carb. 13g Protein 3g Chol. 4mg Fat 1g/14%

Honeybunch Soup

Individual sweet squash tureens.

SERVES 4

2 honeybunch or acorn squash
2 tablespoons minced Canadian bacon, trimmed
8 tablespoons Gruyère cheese
Salt and freshly ground pepper
2 cups skim milk (approximately)
Freshly grated nutmeg

1. Preheat the oven to 350°.
2. Remove the tops from the squash and reserve.
Scoop out the seeds and discard.
3. Place ½ tablespoon of the bacon, 2 tablespoons Gruyère,
and salt and pepper to taste in each squash. Add up to ½ cup
skim milk for each squash; it should come to within ½ inch
of the top. Season with grated nutmeg to taste.
4. Replace the lids and place the squash in a 2-inch-deep
baking dish. Add 1 inch of water and place the baking dish
in the oven. Bake for 1 to 1½ hours or until the flesh is easily
pierced with a fork.
5. To serve, place the squash in individual small serving bowls.

Cal. **201** *Carb.* **25g** *Protein* **13g** *Chol.* **24mg** *Fat* **7g/28%**

More Peas Please Soup

SERVES 12

1 pound dried peas, sorted and rinsed
2 quarts chicken broth (see Basics)
1½ pounds ham hocks
2 cups chopped onion
2 cups chopped carrot
2 cups chopped celery
1 bay leaf
1 package (10 ounces) frozen petit peas, thawed
Salt and freshly ground pepper
½ cup finely chopped fresh Italian parsley

1. In a large stockpot, combine the dried peas, broth, and
ham hocks. Bring to a boil and skim off any scum that comes
to the surface.
2. Add the onion, carrot, celery, and bay leaf. Cover, lower
the heat, and simmer for 2½ to 3 hours, until the peas are

Winter Squash

It's a bit of a lottery, select-
ing squash. Quality depends
on ripeness when picked,
how long it's been stored,
and where.

Try the traditional test: If
you hear a dull thud when
you knock on a squash, it's
probably good. A hollow
sound means it might be
drying out.

Look for clear, bold color
and weight. A squash should
seem heavy for its size.
Avoid bruised, moldy, or
shriveled specimens.

Acorn

Dark green, deeply ribbed, acorn-shaped. Best freshly harvested. I love them cut in half and baked; they turn out moist, rich, sweet, and tender.

Blue Hubbard

An elongated, bumpy blue-green-gray teardrop. Blue Hubbard is often sold in chunks, since a whole one can weigh 10 to 15 pounds. It's very good baked or steamed.

Buttercup

A knobbed turban squash. Buttercups vary from 1½-pound miniatures to 4- to 6-pounders. Sweet and moist, this is the most reliably good squash.

Delicata

A creamy green football with dark green stripes. Delicata is sweet and smooth, with an exquisite taste.

Golden Nugget

Looks like a miniature pumpkin and has a pumpkinlike taste.

Red Kuri

Shaped like Blue Hubbard, but bright orange and smaller (5 to 7 pounds). Glorious looking and tasting.

Spaghetti

A small to medium, yellow squash with moist, tender flesh that looks like pale orange spaghetti strands when cooked.

Turban

Small to medium-sized, and turban-shaped. These are principally grown as fall ornaments but can be cooked.

cooked and the soup thickens slightly. Remove the bay leaf. Remove the meat from the bone, chop it into small pieces, and return it to the pot.

3. Add the thawed peas to the pot and simmer for 5 minutes. Season with salt and pepper to taste.

4. To serve, ladle the soup into serving bowls and garnish with the parsley. Serve with croutons if desired.

Cal. 193 Carb. 32g Protein 14g Chol. 3mg Fat 2g/8%

Acorn Squash and Lentil Soup

Salad and crusty bread make this hearty autumn warmer a meal.

SERVES 12

1 tablespoon unsalted butter
½ cup finely chopped onion
½ cup finely chopped carrot
½ cup finely chopped celery
5 cups chicken broth
(see Basics)
2 cups red or green lentils
4 medium acorn
squash, halved,
seeded, peeled, and
cut into 1-inch chunks
½ to 1 teaspoon dried thyme
Salt and freshly ground pepper
1 ounce lean bacon (about 2 slices), cooked crisp, drained,
and crumbled

1. In a large stockpot, heat the butter over medium heat. Add the onion, carrot, and celery, and sauté for 7 to 8 minutes. The vegetables should be soft but not browned.

2. Add them to the stockpot with 4 cups of chicken broth and the lentils. Bring to a boil, cover, lower the heat, and simmer for 1 hour.

3. Add the squash and ½ teaspoon dried thyme and simmer for 30 to 45 minutes, or until the squash and lentils are thoroughly cooked. Add the remaining cup of broth if the soup seems too thick. Season to taste with additional thyme, salt, and pepper.

4. To serve, ladle into warm soup bowls and garnish with the bacon.

Cal. 163 Carb. 25g Protein 10g Chol. 4mg Fat 3g/15%

Ratatouille Soup

SERVES 4

1 medium eggplant (about 1½ pounds)
Freshly ground sea salt
Freshly ground pepper
1 teaspoon canola oil
2 garlic cloves, minced
1 cup thinly sliced onion
1 can (16 ounces) plum tomatoes, coarsely chopped,
   with their juice
2 cups coarsely chopped zucchini
2 sprigs oregano or 1 teaspoon dried
¼ teaspoon crushed red pepper flakes
4 cups chicken broth (see Basics)
¼ cup minced fresh Italian parsley
½ cup minced fresh basil

1. Preheat the oven to 500°. Wipe a baking sheet with vegetable oil. Set aside.
2. Trim the top off the eggplant and cut it in half lengthwise. Cut two deep lengthwise slits in each half on the cut sides, being careful not to cut through the skin. Season each half with sea salt and pepper. Place on the prepared baking sheet, cut sides down, and bake for 15 to 20 minutes, or until the eggplant is tender and the skin shriveled. Scoop out the pulp, place it in a blender or food processor, and purée. Set aside.
3. Meanwhile, in a stockpot, heat the oil over medium-low heat. Add the garlic and onion, and sauté until the onion is tender, about 10 minutes. Stir in the tomatoes and their juice, the zucchini, oregano, and red pepper until the liquid is absorbed and reduced, stirring frequently.
4. Add the chicken broth and puréed eggplant. Reduce the heat to low and simmer, partially covered, for 45 minutes. Stir in the parsley, basil, and pepper to taste. Simmer for 5 minutes; taste and adjust seasoning. Serve immediately.

*Cal. **124** Carb. **23g** Protein **6g** Chol. **0mg** Fat **3g/17%***

To Nibble or Not

Which is better: the three-large-meals-a-day tradition dictates? Or several small meals at shorter intervals?

Large meals seem to boost an enzyme that triggers cholesterol production and high insulin levels, which may directly encourage the thickening of artery walls with fat and muscle cells.

Frequent, small meals seem not to have this effect. In fact, a University of Toronto study found both insulin and cholesterol levels *dropped* sharply when subjects consumed their normal calorie intake in numerous small meals throughout the day. This suggests that increasing meal frequency—but not calories—could keep cholesterol levels in check and aid in preventing heart disease.

Root Chips

Baked vegetable chips are a great replacement for potato chips. The trick is to make them crisp without too much oil. (They have not been analyzed because of the various sizes of vegetables.)

YIELD: 30 CHIPS

Choose four of the following:
medium sweet potato,
rutabaga, new potato,
turnip, celery root, taro,
lotus, parsnip, fennel bulb,
carrot, batata, yuca, or beet;
use very fresh vegetables
Olive oil spray
Salt

1. Preheat the oven to 325°.
2. Peel the vegetables and slice, using a mandolin, in paper-thin slices, about ¹⁄₃₂-inch thick. Lightly spray a baking sheet with olive oil. Arrange the vegetable slices on the sheet, keeping like vegetables together in sections. Spray the vegetables with olive oil. Bake for 8 minutes, turn once, and bake for 7 to 15 minutes more, until very crisp. The baking time will vary slightly for different vegetables and because of their level of freshness.
3. Remove the chips from the oven when they are dry and crisp and toss them lightly with salt. Serve warm or cooled.

Cream of Flageolet Soup

The secret to cooking bean soup is to surround the beans with flavor, which they absorb as they plump. In this case, the flavors are those of herbs and lemon.

SERVES 6

1 cup dried flageolets, rinsed, sorted, and soaked overnight
1 teaspoon olive oil
1 cup shredded leek
1 cup finely chopped onion
1 cup finely chopped celery
1 cup finely chopped carrot
1½ tablespoons finely minced garlic
6 cups chicken broth (see Basics)
2 sprigs fresh thyme
½ cup skim milk
1 tablespoon unsalted butter, softened
1 tablespoon all-purpose flour
1 tablespoon finely minced fresh Italian parsley
1 tablespoon finely minced fresh thyme
1 tablespoon finely minced fresh basil
1 tablespoon finely minced fresh tarragon
3 tablespoons fresh lemon juice
Salt and freshly ground white pepper
Paper-thin lemon slices

1. Drain and rinse the beans and set aside.
2. In a large Dutch oven, heat the oil over medium-high heat. Add the leek, onion, celery, carrot, and garlic, and sauté for 6 to 8 minutes, until softened. Add the chicken broth, flageolets, and thyme, and bring to a boil. Cover, lower the heat, and simmer for 1 to 1½ hours, until the flageolets are cooked through. Remove the thyme sprigs.
3. In a food processor or blender, purée the soup in batches; return it to the Dutch oven. Add the milk and reheat slowly.
4. In a small bowl, beat the butter and flour with a wooden spoon to make a *beurre manié*. Whisk the *beurre manié* into the hot soup, stirring constantly, until the soup comes to a boil and thickens. Simmer for 3 minutes.
5. Just before serving, stir in the lemon juice, remaining herbs, and salt and pepper to taste. Serve immediately with thin slices of fresh lemon.

*Cal. **201** Carb. **32g** Protein **11g** Chol. **6mg** Fat **5g/19%***

The Best of Bistro

Salmon Rillettes

YIELD: 3 CUPS

1 salmon fillet (12 ounces)
½ cup bottled clam juice
½ cup dry white wine
2 tablespoons unsalted butter, at room temperature
¼ cup finely minced shallot
½ pound cold smoked salmon, cut into thin strips
2 tablespoons fresh lemon juice
2 tablespoons drained capers
3 lemons, cut in wedges

1. Rinse the salmon and pat dry.
2. In a medium skillet (large enough to hold the salmon in one piece), combine the clam juice and white wine over medium-high heat. Bring to a boil, add the salmon, cover, lower the heat, and poach for 6 to 8 minutes, until opaque and flaky when pierced with a fork. Remove the fish from the liquid; remove the skin and flake the flesh. Set aside.
3. Discard the poaching liquid and wipe the skillet dry. Heat 1 tablespoon of butter over medium heat. Add the shallot and sauté until softened, about 4 minutes. Add the cold smoked salmon and sauté for 3 minutes, mashing with the back of a wooden spoon. Add the flaked salmon and remove from the heat. Continue to mash and combine the fish.
4. Beat in the remaining butter and season with the lemon juice. Pack the mixture into a crock, cover, and refrigerate.
5. To serve, garnish with the capers and lemon wedges. Spread on sliced French bread.

Cal. 7 Carb. .5g Protein .8g Chol. 2mg Fat .4g/28% (per teaspoon)

To Start . . .

Salmon rillettes and Coquille St. Jacques are bistro classics for the first course. The rillettes are traditionally full of butter; here, I've used just enough to bind the fresh and smoked salmon into a paste. This deserves its crown as a classical French hors d'oeuvre. The taste is so full, you can spread it thinly.

In the Coquille St. Jacques, sweet bay scallops are tossed with mushrooms and brought to perfection with white wine, lemon, and Gruyère.

Bistro

The word comes from the French *bistrouille*, denoting a mixture of coffee and eau-de-vie.

The name was applied to the multitude of small bohemian establishments that once peppered Paris's Left Bank. They served their neighborhood as message centers, mail drops, and hotbeds of local gossip. The Lost Generation discovered, idolized, and idealized them in the twenties.

Today, the bistro is an earthy, homey, relatively inexpensive institution lacking in pretense or formality. Bistros usually stock a wide variety of liquors and wines: eaux-de-vie, marcs, Calvados, Armagnacs, ports, sherries, Madeiras, cordials, and most important of all, Muscat de Beaumes de Venise and pastis. Generally a bistro is distinguished by a zinc-topped bar, nicotine-stained walls, stamped tin ceilings, coarse lacey curtains, house wines in squat pitchers, pale butcher-paper "tablecloths," hefty china, thick drinking glasses, and Piaf on the record player. But above all is the aroma that blends the fragrances of lusty, robust cooking (garlic and mountains of herbs) with the scents of strong fruit brandy, black coffee, black pepper, and black tobacco. It's a formula that should not be tampered with.

Coquilles St. Jacques

SERVES 4

1 teaspoon olive oil
1 pound scallops, rinsed and drained
1 teaspoon minced garlic
1 teaspoon finely minced lemon zest
1/4 cup dry white wine
2/3 cup chicken broth (see Basics)
1 tablespoon unsalted butter, softened
1 tablespoon all-purpose flour
1 cup sliced mushrooms
4 teaspoons Scotch or Irish whiskey
Freshly ground pepper
4 tablespoons finely grated Gruyère
   cheese

1. In a large heavy skillet, heat 2/3 teaspoon of oil over medium-high heat. Add the scallops, garlic, and lemon zest. Sauté quickly, stirring and shaking the pan, until the scallops turn opaque and begin to brown. Add the wine, bring to a boil, and remove from the heat. Let cool 10 minutes. Drain the scallops and reserve the cooking liquid (about 1/3 cup). Add enough chicken broth to make 1 cup.
2. In a small bowl, blend the butter and flour with a wooden spoon to make a *beurre manié*.
3. In a small saucepan, bring the chicken broth mixture to a boil over medium-high heat. Add the *beurre manié* by bits, and whisk until thickened and smooth. Lower the heat slightly and simmer for 5 to 6 minutes. Add the sauce to the scallops and set aside.
4. In a small skillet, heat the remaining oil over medium heat. Add the mushrooms and sauté for 2 to 3 minutes. Set aside.
5. Lightly spray or wipe four 4-inch baking shells or gratin dishes with vegetable oil. Preheat the broiler.
6. Combine the mushrooms and scallops. Divide the mixture among the baking shells. Splash each with 1 teaspoon of whiskey and top with 1 tablespoon of the cheese. Place the shells on a baking sheet.
7. Broil the scallops 6 to 8 inches from the heat, until the cheese is melted and begins to brown around the edges.

*Cal. **184** Carb. **6g** Protein **22g** Chol. **54mg** Fat **8g/37%***

Green Lentil Soup

An earthy lentil soup, made with tiny green French lentils.
We've added a bit of quince and mint to wake things up.

SERVES 8

10 ounces lentils, preferably green French lentils, washed and
   picked through
2 ounces finely chopped Canadian bacon, trimmed of fat
5 cups chicken broth (see Basics)
4 garlic cloves, peeled and smashed
2 ripe quince (about 4 ounces each), quartered, seeded, and
   finely chopped
1/2 cup finely chopped Italian parsley
1 small bay leaf
1/2 teaspoon paprika
1/4 teaspoon cayenne
1/2 teaspoon dried marjoram
1/4 cup chopped fresh mint
Salt

In a large, heavy saucepan, combine all of the ingredients
except the mint and salt. Bring to a boil, cover, reduce the
heat to low, and simmer for 1 hour, stirring occasionally; add
more broth as necessary. Cook for 30 minutes more, or until
the lentils are soft. Taste and add mint, salt if needed.

*Cal. **168** Carb. **27g** Protein **13g** Chol. **4mg** Fat **2g/15%***

Classic Onion Soup

There's nothing better to take off the chill after an early-morn-
ing trip to the markets than the soup made famous in the cob-
blestone streets of Paris's Les Halles.

SERVES 4

1 pound sweet Spanish onions, thinly sliced (about
   2 cups)
2 cups dry white wine
1 tablespoon unsalted butter
4 cups beef broth (see Basics)
4 slices day-old French bread, sliced 1/3 inch thick
1/2 cup freshly grated Parmesan

1. Preheat the oven to 425°.
2. In a 9 x 13-inch Pyrex dish, combine the onion,

Le Puy Lentils

The little slate-colored
Lentilles de Puy from the
Auvergne in France possess
an extraordinary flavor,
earthy and rich. Their supe-
riority may be due to the
volcanic soil in which they
are grown.

Le Puys are very light, cook
quickly, don't require soaking, and don't get mushy.
Simmer slowly until tender,
20 to 25 minutes.

LENTIL TIP

Green, red, yellow, brown,
or Le Puy lentils need no
soaking and cook rapid-
ly compared to other
legumes—sometimes,
faster than you expect,
depending on how re-
cently they've been dried.
Pay attention when cook-
ing lentils—they may be
done in as little as 10 to
12 minutes or take as
long as 25 to 30.

The variations of great onion soup extend around the globe. In the French countryside, wild mushrooms and sherry are added, and in Normandy, Calvados, of course. A tomato purée is added in Bordeaux; garlic, herbs, and Madeira in Lyons. In Burgundy, onion soup is topped with a poached egg.

Spain enhances onion soup with almonds; in Portugal, it's sweet wine and raisins, while Middle Eastern countries serve it sparked with lentils, yogurt, or meat. The English add Stilton; the Moroccans, minced chicken. Germans put their dark beer to good use in onion soup. And in Latin America, it's transformed with coconut milk, peppers, and local cheeses.

wine, and butter. Bake in the oven, uncovered, until most of the liquid has evaporated, stirring occasionally, about 1 hour. Remove from the oven and keep warm.

3. Preheat the broiler; place the rack about 6 inches from the heat.

4. In a medium-size saucepan, bring the beef broth and ¾ cup of water to a boil, then reduce the heat to a simmer. Divide the onion into four ovenproof soup bowls and place the bowls on a baking sheet. Ladle the broth over the onion and top each bowl with a slice of French bread. Sprinkle the bread evenly with the cheese.

5. Place the baking sheet under the broiler and broil for 2 to 3 minutes, or until the cheese is melted and lightly browned. Serve immediately.

Cal. 226 Carb. 27g Protein 10g Chol. 19mg Fat 8g/26%

Potato-Leek Soup

For a long time, the evening meal in France consisted solely of soup. In some households, this is still true. Add a salad, some bread, a glass of wine, and you're set.

SERVES 6

½ teaspoon olive oil
1 medium onion, finely chopped
½ pound leeks, well cleaned and finely chopped
1 shallot, finely minced
1 ounce Canadian bacon, finely diced
1¼ pound potatoes, peeled and quartered
3½ cups chicken broth (see Basics)
2 tablespoons finely chopped fresh dill
Salt and freshly ground pepper

1. Heat the oil in a large stockpot over medium heat. Add the onion, leek, shallot, and Canadian bacon, and cover. Sweat for 10 minutes, stirring once or twice.

2. Add the potato, chicken broth, and dill; cover and simmer for 30 minutes, or until the potato is tender.

3. Remove the potato and place in a blender or food processor with 1 cup of the hot broth. Purée, then whisk back into the remaining soup to thicken. Season with salt and pepper to taste.

Cal. 86 Carb. 15g Protein 4g Chol. 3mg Fat 1.6g/16%

Vegetable Bourride

A wintery stew, filled with robust, heart-warming flavors, that's as comforting as the much-richer French classic. Stir in the aïoli at the table, and the stew takes on an even deeper dimension of flavor.

SERVES 8

1 teaspoon olive oil
1 cup coarsely chopped onion
2 leeks, cleaned and coarsely chopped
4 garlic cloves, minced
8 cups chicken broth
2 tablespoons minced fresh rosemary
2 teaspoons fennel seeds
1 teaspoon minced fresh thyme
1 teaspoon green peppercorns
1 pound new potatoes
1½ cups baby turnips, cleaned and trimmed
1 fennel bulb, coarsely chopped
1½ cups haricots verts, *trimmed*
1 cup fresh or frozen peas
Ten ¼-inch slices French or Italian bread
1 teaspoon fennel fronds or fresh tarragon
2 tablespoons Broccoli Pesto (page 48) or Basil Pesto (page 48)
Freshly ground pepper
Poetic Aïoli (at right)

1. Heat the oil in a large soup pot. Add the onion and leek and cook over medium heat until the vegetables are tender and translucent, about 20 minutes, stirring occasionally. Add the garlic and cook for 1 minute.
2. Add the chicken broth, rosemary, fennel seeds, thyme, peppercorns, and potatoes. Bring just to a boil, then reduce the heat and simmer, covered, for 30 minutes. Add the turnips and fennel and simmer for 15 minutes. Add the *haricots verts* and peas, and simmer for 3 to 5 minutes, or until all the vegetables are just tender.
3. Toast the bread. Stir in the fennel fronds, pesto, and pepper to taste; adjust all the seasonings.
4. Serve with toasted bread thinly spread with Poetic Aïoli floating in the soup, and/or Poetic Aïoli on the side.

*Cal. **341** Carb. **63g** Protein **11g** Chol. **2mg** Fat **4g/11%***

Poetic Aïoli

YIELD: 2 CUPS

1 pound new potatoes, peeled
  and thinly sliced
1⅔ cups chicken broth
  (see Basics)
8 to 10 garlic cloves, peeled
  and coarsely chopped
Juice of 2 lemons
⅓ cup low-fat buttermilk
Salt and freshly ground
  white pepper

1. Place the potatoes and chicken broth in a medium-size saucepan, and cook, covered, over medium heat for 15 minutes. Remove the cover and continue to cook until the broth evaporates, 5 to 8 minutes.
2. While the potatoes are still hot, place them in a blender. Gradually add the garlic, lemon juice, and buttermilk, tasting until the desired flavor is achieved and the ingredients are puréed. Add pepper to taste and salt if desired. Cool to room temperature or refrigerate, covered, to prevent a skin from forming on the surface. Will keep well for 5 days under refrigeration.

*Cal. **16** Carb. **3g** Protein .6g*
Chol. 0mg Fat 0g/0%
(analyzed per tablespoon)

Poetic Aïoli

Bourride doesn't seem quite complete without aïoli, which is to say, the taste of garlic. The great Greek garlic dip *skordalia*, the staple in every taverna, inspired this low-fat version. *Skordalia* is built on potatoes, bread, or walnuts and flavored with good olive oil and garlic. Here, chicken broth smooths the waxy, shiny, puréed russet potatoes, which simulate bourride's mayonnaise base.

Pastis

A French anise-flavored liqueur, pastis is the successor to the outlawed absinthe. Pernod and Ricard are the most widely recognized brands. The traditional way to drink pastis is simple—mix with water and perhaps 1 or 2 ice cubes. Occasionally, a drop of grenadine may be added, which turns the drink into *tomates*, a hugely popular drink of the twenties.

Pot au Feu

Leeks, carrots, fennel, and lamb shanks simmered into a wonderful boiled dinner. This classic is sometimes made with beef and chicken; other times, with oxtails. Traditionally, sea salt, pickles, horseradish, and mustard are put on the table.

SERVES 4

1 teaspoon canola oil
4 lamb shanks (about 3 pounds), outer membranes removed
12 cloves
2 onions, peeled
2 carrots, thickly sliced
1 rib celery, thickly sliced
6 garlic cloves, smashed
Bouquet garni of 2 bay leaves, 2 sprigs of thyme, 12 pepper-
*   corns, 8 sprigs of parsley, tied with cheesecloth*
7 cups beef broth (see Basics)
4 carrots, peeled, quartered lengthwise, and cut into 4-inch lengths
4 leeks, white parts only, quartered lengthwise, cut in 4-inch
*   lengths and washed*
4 ribs celery, quartered lengthwise and cut in 4-inch lengths
1 large turnip, cut into 4-inch-long julienne
2 fennel bulbs, julienned
¹⁄₂ cup finely chopped fennel fronds
Salt and freshly ground pepper

1. In a large stockpot, heat the oil. Add the lamb shanks and brown on all sides, about 5 minutes. Stick the cloves into the onions and add them to the pot with the carrots, celery, garlic, *bouquet garni*, and broth. Cover partially and simmer for 2½ hours, skimming as necessary.
2. Transfer the meat to a bowl and strain the broth, discarding the *bouquet garni* and vegetables. Degrease the broth; you should have about 5 cups.
3. Return the shanks and the strained liquid to the stockpot. Divide the carrot, leek, celery, turnip, and fennel into four piles. Tie them into bunches with the green part of a scallion or kitchen string. Add the bunches to the stockpot. Bring to a boil, then reduce to a simmer. Cover partially and simmer for 30 minutes. Stir in the fennel fronds, reserving 2 tablespoons. Season to taste with salt and freshly ground pepper. Serve in soup plates—place one shank and one vegetable bunch into each and divide the broth among the bowls. Garnish with the reserved fennel fronds.
Cal. 399 Carb. 47g Protein 37g Chol. 100mg Fat 8g/18%

Apple Coleslaw

A great coleslaw for the best of autumn's apples. Remember that cabbage is part of the family of vegetables that helps protect against cancer, and raw is best.

SERVES 6

¼ cup Low-Fat Blend (see Basics)
2 tablespoons cider vinegar
1 tablespoon "light" mayonnaise
1 tablespoon sugar
1 teaspoon celery salt
½ pound Granny Smith apples, cored and thinly sliced
½ pound red apples, cored and thinly sliced
½ pound green apples, cored and grated
1 tablespoon fresh lemon juice
1½ cups thinly sliced green cabbage

1. In a small bowl, whisk the Low-Fat Blend, vinegar, mayonnaise, sugar, and celery salt.
2. In a large bowl, toss the sliced and grated apples with the lemon juice. Add the cabbage and toss. Add the dressing and toss again. Serve immediately.

*Cal. **103** Carb. **21g** Protein **1g** Chol. **1mg** Total Fat **2g/19%***

Celery Rémoulade

SERVES 8

1 tablespoon sherry vinegar
½ cup low-fat buttermilk
2 tablespoons "light" mayonnaise
6 tablespoons nonfat plain yogurt
2 teaspoons Dijon mustard
Salt and freshly ground pepper
1½ pounds celeriac (celery root), peeled and grated
  (about 4 cups)
4 tablespoons drained capers

Place the vinegar, buttermilk, mayonnaise, yogurt, mustard, and salt and pepper to taste in the blender. Purée. Pour the dressing over the grated celery root and toss to combine. Sprinkle with capers.

*Cal. **59** Carb. **10g** Protein **3g** Chol. **2mg** Fat **2g/25%***

Celeriac

Celeriac, a root vegetable, has a crunchy texture and a flavor similar to that of a sweet cauliflower. To prepare, scrub vigorously, cut off the top and bottom knobs, and peel. Drop it into water with a bit of lemon juice added to keep it from discoloring. Celery rémoulade is the best-known celeriac dish, but it also can be used raw in salads, steamed, or added to soups and stews.

★ **GOOD FOR YOU** ★

Celeriac has about 62 calories per cup, with 2.3 grams of protein, 14.4 grams of carbohydrate, .5 grams of fat, zero cholesterol, and 2 grams of fiber.

Carrot Râpée

SERVES 6

1 pound carrots, peeled and finely shredded
¼ cup fresh orange or carrot juice
¼ cup balsamic vinegar
2 teaspoons Dijon mustard
1 tablespoon chopped fresh ginger
2 tablespoons canola oil
¼ cup chopped fresh Italian parsley
1 cup currants

1. Place the carrots in a colander to drain for ½ hour.
2. Meanwhile, in a small mixing bowl, whisk the juice, vinegar, mustard, and ginger. Drizzle in the oil.
3. Transfer the carrots to a medium mixing bowl, add the dressing, and toss well. Add the parsley and currants and toss well. Cover and chill until ready to serve.

Cal. **93** *Carb.* **12g** *Protein* **1g** *Chol.* **0mg** *Fat* **5g/46%** %

Bacon and Leek Quiche

SERVES 8

1 bunch fresh spinach, well rinsed and trimmed
Salt and freshly ground pepper
1 teaspoon canola oil
2 pounds leeks, quartered, washed, and finely chopped
2 ounces Canadian bacon, trimmed of fat and finely minced
1 egg, lightly beaten
½ cup skim milk
1 teaspoon Dijon mustard
2 ounces low-fat goat cheese
⅓ cup Parmesan shards
2 teaspoons unsalted butter

1. Preheat the oven to 375°. Lightly spray or wipe a 9-inch pie plate with vegetable oil. Place the spinach leaves in a vegetable steamer over low heat and steam until just wilted, about 1 minute. Line the pie plate with the spinach leaves. Season with salt and freshly ground pepper to taste.
2. Heat the oil in a saucepan. Add the leek, cover, and sweat for 5 minutes.
3. Whisk the Canadian bacon, egg, skim milk, mustard, and goat cheese, and add the leek. Pour the mixture carefully over the spinach, top with the Parmesan, and dot with the butter. Bake for 45 minutes, or until set. Serve warm.

Cal. **130** *Carb.* **14g** *Protein* **10g** *Chol.* **34mg** *Fat* **5g/32%** FAT MONITOR

Nouveau Cassoulet

Traditionally made with bacon or goose fat, duck confit, pork rind, and olive oil. Not here. The meats are leaner, too.

SERVES 16

2 pounds dried beans (a combination of Esther's Swedish, roquil, cannellini, or great Northern beans), rinsed, sorted, and soaked overnight

8 cloves

2 whole onions

3 bay leaves

2 garlic heads, outside skin removed, tips cut to expose the flesh

6 cups beef broth (see Basics)

1 pound lamb shoulder, cut into 2-inch chunks, bones reserved

1 pound boneless, skinless duck breast, cut into 1-inch chunks

3 cups red wine

1 pound lean turkey sausage (99% fat free), in casings

1 pound venison sausage

5 tablespoons tomato paste

1½ teaspoons dried thyme

4 sprigs fresh rosemary

16 pearl onions (1 inch in diameter), peeled

1 cup julienned Canadian bacon

Freshly ground pepper

2 cups fresh bread crumbs, preferably made from French bread

½ cup finely minced fresh Italian parsley

1. Drain and rinse the beans and drain again.

2. Transfer the beans to a large ovenproof casserole. Stick

"A dinner invitation, once accepted, is a sacred obligation. If you die before the dinner takes place, your executor must attend."

Ward McAllister

320

THE COLORS
OF BEANS

White
Boston
Great Northern
Haricot
Navy
Lima

Tan
Broad/Fava
Cannellini
Pinto

Brown
Swedish Brown
Mung

Green
Pea/Split Pea
Flageolet

Red
Adzuki
Kidney
Jacob's Cattle

Black
Turtle
Kidney

Pretty Beans
Painted
Christmas Lima

four cloves into each of the onions and add them to the casserole with the bay leaves, garlic, 5 cups of beef broth, and 2 cups of water. Simmer, partially covered, until the beans are tender, 50 minutes to 1 hour. Drain and reserve about 2 cups of the cooking liquid. Discard the onions and bay leaves. Squeeze the softened garlic from its skin and reserve; set the beans aside. Preheat the oven to 350°.

3. While the beans are cooking, place the lamb, lamb bones, and duck in a roasting pan. Add 2 cups of the wine and roast for 1 to 1¼ hours, basting frequently. Drain the meat, reserve the cooking liquid, and set aside. Discard the bones.

4. Simmer the sausages for 5 minutes in water to cover. Drain, cut into 1½-inch pieces, and set aside.

5. In a mixing bowl, mash the softened garlic with a wooden spoon to make a paste. Stir in the tomato paste, thyme, and reserved meat and bean-cooking liquid, the remaining wine and beef broth, and 1 cup water.

6. In the casserole, place a layer of one-third of the beans, half the lamb and duck pieces, half the sausages, the sprig of rosemary, and the pearl onions. Cover with another third of the beans, the remaining lamb and duck, the Canadian bacon, the remaining sausages, and finally, the remaining beans. Carefully pour the garlic-broth mixture over; the liquid should just cover the top layer of beans. Add freshly ground pepper to taste.

7. In a small bowl, toss the bread crumbs and parsley and sprinkle over the cassoulet.

8. Bake for 20 minutes. Push the crumbs into the cassoulet with the back of a spoon and return it to the oven. Bake for 40 more minutes, until the crumbs are crisp and brown and the cassoulet is bubbling. Serve at once.

*Cal. **495** Carb. **50g** Protein **36g** Chol. **74mg** Fat **18g/32%***

Vegetable Cassoulet

SERVES 8

1 cup dried white, great Northern, or cannellini beans, soaked overnight

1 celery stalk, 6 inches long

6 carrots, cut into 2-inch pieces

2 sprigs fresh thyme

4 sprigs fresh sage

2 sprigs fresh rosemary

1 teaspoon fennel seeds

1 bay leaf

5 whole cloves

6 black peppercorns

1 teaspoon olive oil

8 garlic cloves, finely minced

2 cups chopped red onion

1 fennel bulb, coarsely chopped, fronds reserved and minced

4 cups white or wild mushrooms, cleaned and stemmed

1 medium eggplant, cut into 3/4-inch cubes

6 tomatoes, coarsely chopped

1 teaspoon chopped fresh thyme

2 tablespoons chopped fresh sage

2 tablespoons chopped fresh rosemary

3 tablespoons tomato paste

1 cup white wine

1/2 cup red lentils

1/2 cup chopped fresh Italian parsley

1 cup Parmesan shards

1 cup bread crumbs

1. Drain the beans and place them in a large saucepan with 3 cups of water. Add the celery, one carrot, and the thyme, sage, and rosemary sprigs, the fennel seeds, bay leaf, cloves, and peppercorns. Place over high heat, bring to a boil, cover, and boil for 10 minutes. Reduce the heat and simmer for 50 minutes, or until the beans are tender.

2. Remove the vegetables and spices and discard. Drain the beans, reserving the cooking liquid. Pour the liquid back into the pot and reduce it to 1½ cups. Set the reduced liquid aside.

3. Preheat the oven to 375°. Lightly spray or wipe a 9 x 13 x 2-inch casserole with vegetable oil.

4. In a large skillet, heat the oil and sauté the garlic, onion, and fennel until lightly browned, about 10 minutes. Add the mushrooms, eggplant, tomatoes, herbs, tomato paste, and wine, and sauté for 8 minutes, until most of the liquid has evaporated. Add the lentils and the reserved stock and simmer for 15 minutes.

5. Transfer this mixture to the casserole, add the reserved beans, and mix well. Add ¼ cup fennel fronds and the parsley. Sprinkle with the Parmesan and bread crumbs, and bake for 30 to 40 minutes, until golden brown. Serve immediately.

*Cal. **339** Carb. **51g** Protein **19g** Chol. **10mg** Fat **6g/16%***

Bistro Salmon on a Lentil Bed

High heat and quick cooking seal in the flavor. And if you cook the salmon on one side only, its own oil is enough to baste it.

SERVES 8

*1 salmon fillet (2 pounds), boned but
    not skinned*
2 large garlic cloves, chopped
1 to 1½ teaspoons dried thyme
Salt and freshly ground pepper
1 tablespoon olive oil
1 lemon, cut into wedges
1 recipe Bed of Green Lentils (page 229)

1. Preheat the oven to 500°. Place a heavy metal ovenproof steak platter in the oven while it is heating.

2. Rinse the salmon and pat it dry. Place the salmon, skin side down, on a large plate; rub the surface with the garlic. Season the salmon heavily with thyme, salt, and freshly ground pepper to taste; set aside at room temperature for 20 minutes.

3. Carefully pour the oil into the hot platter or a large cast-iron skillet. Quickly transfer the salmon fillet to the platter, skin side down. Roast the fish for 7 minutes. Remove the platter from the oven and cut into serving pieces, leaving the skin behind. Garnish with wedges of lemon and serve at once on a Bed of Green Lentils.

*Cal. **441** Carb. **47g** Protein **46g** Chol. **44mg** Fat **8g/17%***

LENTILS

Lentils are really legumes or seeds, which means that they are very high in protein and energy. They are also an excellent source of cellulose fiber, carbohydrates, pectins, and gums. The gums and pectins can help lower blood cholesterol. Lentils are a good source of B vitamins (including niacin and folacin), and deliver calcium, phosphorus, potassium, zinc, magnesium, and iron, too.

Alsatian Guinea Hen

The classic smoky bacon, heaps of steaming moist cabbage, and the zip of caraway.

SERVES 4

1 guinea hen or free-range chicken (3½ pounds)
Salt and freshly ground pepper
2 cups chicken broth
  (see Basics)
2 ounces Canadian bacon, trimmed of
  fat and finely minced
½ cup white wine
1 head Savoy cabbage
  (about 2¼ pounds), shredded
2 carrots, peeled and diced
4 garlic cloves, minced
1 onion, diced
2 sprigs fresh thyme
4 bay leaves
¼ cup apple cider vinegar
1 tablespoon caraway seeds
1 cup finely chopped fresh Italian parsley

1. Preheat the oven to 400°.
2. Rub the guinea hen inside and out with salt and pepper. Place the hen in a roasting pan and pour the chicken broth over it. Roast for 40 minutes, basting twice.
3. Meanwhile, sauté the Canadian bacon in a large casserole or Dutch oven over medium heat for 5 minutes, stirring occasionally. Add the white wine and deglaze the casserole, scraping up the brown bits. Add the cabbage, carrot, garlic, onion, thyme, and bay leaves. Cover and cook over medium-low heat for 30 minutes, stirring occasionally.
4. Remove the hen from the oven. Quarter the hen and add it to the casserole. Collect any juices remaining in the roasting pan, defat them, and add them to the casserole. Add the vinegar and caraway seeds; cover and cook 30 minutes more.
5. Remove the hen to a platter and add the parsley to the cabbage. Season the cabbage with salt and pepper to taste. To serve, make a bed of cabbage on each plate and set one piece of hen atop each bed.

*Cal. **353** Carb. **29g** Protein **41g** Chol. **102mg** Fat **10g/23%***

Experiment with game to find your taste preferences. Grouse, for instance, is quite rich and somewhat gamy. Woodcock, the only bird with white legs and red breast, is superbly sweet. Farmed guinea hen is like full-flavored chicken.

Guinea Hen with Chestnuts

SERVES 8

1 pound dried prunes, pitted

1/2 cup Armagnac

4 cups dry red wine

1 large onion, coarsely chopped

1/4 cup red wine vinegar

1/4 teaspoon coarsely ground pepper

2 guinea hens (about 3 1/2 pounds each), cut into 8 pieces each

1 teaspoon canola oil

6 garlic cloves, finely minced

3 1/2 cups chicken broth (see Basics)

Bouquet garni *of 2 sprigs parsley, 2 sprigs thyme, and 3 bay leaves*

3/4 pound chestnuts

1. Macerate the prunes in the Armagnac overnight, turning occasionally.

2. Meanwhile, combine the red wine, onion, vinegar, and pepper in a noncorrosive bowl.

3. Add the hens and marinate overnight. Remove the hens from the marinade, strain the marinade, and reserve the marinade and the onions separately. Heat the oil in a large casserole or Dutch oven. Add the hens and brown them on all sides, about 8 minutes; you may have to do this in batches. Set the browned hens aside. Add the garlic and onion to the casserole and sauté for 5 minutes, until the onion is soft. Add the reserved marinade and deglaze the pot for 1 minute, scraping up the brown bits. Add the broth, *bouquet garni*, and hens, and simmer for 1 hour. Add the chestnuts, prunes, and Armagnac, and simmer 1/2 hour more.

4. Remove the *bouquet garni* and discard. Using a slotted spoon, remove the hens, prunes, and chestnuts to a serving platter. Strain the broth and place all but 1/2 cup of the onion and broken chestnuts on the platter with the hens. Return all but 1 cup of broth to the casserole. Reduce the broth to about 3 cups.

5. Place the 1 cup of broth, the remaining 1/2 cup of onion, the broken chestnuts, and about 8 prunes in the blender and purée. Whisk the purée into the broth in the casserole and reduce by one-third, about 20 minutes. Pour the sauce over the hens, chestnuts, and prunes, and serve immediately.

*Cal. **357** Carb. **38g** Protein **32g** Chol. **94mg** Fat **9g/21%***

Beef Daube

SERVES 8

2 teaspoons olive oil

2 pounds beef stew meat, trimmed of all fat and cut into
  2-inch cubes

1 cup minced onion

3 tablespoons minced fresh garlic

12 baby carrots, scraped and cut into 1½-inch pieces (4 cups)

1 medium eggplant, cut into 1-inch cubes (2 cups)

1 sprig fresh rosemary

2 cups beef broth (see Basics)

1 cup apple cider

1 cup red wine

3 whole cloves

1 tablespoon slivered orange zest

2 cups sliced mushrooms

Salt and freshly ground pepper

1 cup finely chopped fresh Italian parsley

1. In a large casserole, heat the oil over medium-high heat.
Brown the beef on all sides, a few pieces at a time; transfer
the browned pieces to a plate and set aside.
2. Add the onion and garlic, and sauté until translucent,
about 5 minutes.
3. Add the carrot, eggplant, rosemary, beef broth, cider, wine,
cloves, and orange zest to the casserole. Return the meat and
any accumulated juices to the casserole. Cover and simmer
for 1½ to 2 hours, until the meat is tender. Skim off any fat as
it rises to the surface.
4. Add the mushrooms and cook for 20 more minutes, uncovered. Season to taste with salt and pepper. Transfer the daube to
a serving dish, garnish with chopped parsley,
and serve at once.

*Cal. **271** Carb. **17g** Protein **27g** Chol. **83mg***

*Fat **11g/36%***

Cold weather makes us want
to get cozy indoors and eat
more robust dishes, like
stews and casseroles. Traditionally, red meat is often
the centerpiece of such
preparations. This is the
time to be conscious of the
amount of protein we want
to eat each day—6 ounces is
all the human body needs.

I generally decrease the
amount of meat in a stew in
proportion to the amount of
vegetables. Doing so doesn't
seem to compromise the
hearty quality of the stew.
And when choosing meats,
look for the new leaner varieties, particularly of beef.

Regardless of grade, the
leanest cuts come from the
parts of the animal that do
the most work: the legs. Leg
meat is generally densely
muscled, with little marbling.

"Loin" meat cuts, which
come from the back of the
animal, are often low in fat as
well. When buying, choose
cuts such as sirloin chops
and the super-lean tenderloin. To select lean meats,
stick with those labeled
"round" or "loin."

Some believe lean cuts lack
flavor, and that they can't be
cooked to tenderness, regardless of time or technique.
Both are misconceptions.

LAMB

Regard tender, delicate-tasting lamb with a bit of caution. Of course it has all of the "complete" protein of other animal meats. But it also has a higher proportion of saturated fatty acids and more cholesterol. A 4-ounce serving has 104 calories, 4 grams of fat, 88 mg. cholesterol, and, like all meats, no fiber or carbohydrates. But lamb is an excellent source of B vitamins and iron.

Ragoût of Lamb, Leeks, and Lentils

A slow-simmered stew cooked until the meat falls apart in tender chunks.

SERVES 8

$2^{1}/_{2}$ pounds lamb shoulder or shank end of leg, trimmed of all
   fat and cut into 2-inch chunks
2 tablespoons all-purpose flour
Salt and freshly ground pepper
2 teaspoons canola oil
1 can (28 ounces) plum tomatoes, drained and quartered,
   juice reserved
2 cups chicken broth (see Basics)
$^{1}/_{2}$ teaspoon dried thyme
1 teaspoon fresh rosemary
8 medium carrots, scraped and halved
24 pearl onions (about 1 inch in diameter), peeled
1 small rutabaga, peeled and cut into 1-inch chunks
4 garlic cloves, chopped
1 tablespoon sugar
1 cup cooked red lentils
1 medium green bell pepper, cut into $^{1}/_{2}$-inch-wide strips (1 cup)
3 leeks, white part only, cut into $^{1}/_{2}$-inch pieces (3 cups)

1. Wipe the meat dry with paper towels. On a plate combine the flour, salt, and pepper. Dredge the meat in the flour and shake off excess.
2. In a large ovenproof casserole, heat 1 teaspoon of the oil over medium-high heat. Brown the lamb on all sides, a few pieces at a time; remove the meat with tongs as it is cooked. Return the browned meat to the casserole. Add the tomatoes, chicken broth, thyme, and rosemary. Cover and simmer over low heat for 45 minutes.
3. Meanwhile, in a large skillet, heat the remaining oil over medium heat; add the carrots, onions, rutabaga, and garlic. Shake the pan to coat the vegetables with oil, then sprinkle with sugar. Cook, turning the vegetables frequently, until glazed and golden, about 10 minutes.
4. Add the vegetables to the lamb. Stir in the cooked lentils. Cover and simmer for 35 minutes.
5. Add the pepper and leek and simmer for 10 minutes longer, or until all the vegetables and the lamb are tender. Serve immediately.

Cal. **421** *Carb.* **42g** *Protein* **37g** *Chol.* **87mg** *Fat* **12g/25%**

Braised Leeks

Those larger-than-life symbols of Wales, gently braised and even more gently glazed.

SERVES 4

1 teaspoon canola oil
4 pounds leeks, trimmed, washed, and quartered lengthwise
1 cup chicken broth (see Basics)
2 tablespoons sugar

1. In a medium skillet with a lid, heat the oil over medium heat. Add the leeks and chicken broth and cover. Braise for 10 to 15 minutes, or until the leeks are tender, stirring occasionally.
2. Remove the lid, keeping the heat at medium-high, and cook for 10 to12 minutes, until the broth has almost evaporated.
3. Increase the heat to high and sprinkle the sugar over the leeks. Cook 10 minutes more, stirring frequently, until the leeks are lightly caramelized. Serve immediately.

*Cal. **100** Carb. **20g** Protein **2g** Chol. **0mg** Fat **1.7g/15%***

Flageolets and Garlic

SERVES 8

1 teapoon olive oil
1 medium onion, chopped
4 large garlic cloves, chopped
2 cups flageolet or giant lima beans, sorted and soaked overnight
1 can (16 ounces) Italian plum tomatoes
1 teaspoon sugar
2 tablespoons tomato paste
¾ cup dry red wine
½ cup chopped fresh Italian parsley

In a Dutch oven with a tight-fitting lid, heat the oil over medium heat. Add the onion and garlic, and sauté until softened. Drain the beans and add them to the onion; stir until evenly coated with oil. Add the tomatoes with their juice, the sugar, tomato paste, and red wine, and bring to a boil. Reduce the heat and simmer, covered, for 1½ hours, until the beans are just tender. If all the liquid has not been absorbed, uncover the pot, and cook for an additional 15 to 20 minutes. Add the parsley and serve immediately.

*Cal. **182** Carb. **35g** Protein **11g** Chol. **0mg** Fat **1g/5%***

Fennel

Fennel bulbs are white and firm, with crisp stalks and feathery, green, anise-flavored fronds. Generally available between October and April, fennel has a crisp texture and a satisfying sweetness not unlike that of celery or certain herbs, yet it is a member of the carrot family.

★ **GOOD FOR YOU** ★

Fennel is very low in calories—about 30 per cup—and rich in protein, vitamin A, calcium, and potassium.

Fennel Purée

SERVES 12

$1^{1}/_{2}$ pounds potatoes (about 4 medium), peeled and quartered
2 fennel bulbs, trimmed and chopped (about 8 cups)
1 cup chicken broth (see Basics)
$^{1}/_{2}$ cup skim milk
2 tablespoons unsalted butter, melted
Salt and freshly ground white pepper

1. Boil the potatoes in water until tender, 30 to 40 minutes. Drain well. Transfer to a large mixing bowl and mash.
2. Meanwhile, in another large saucepan, combine the fennel and chicken broth and cook over medium-high heat until tender, about 20 minutes. Drain. Purée the fennel in a food processor; add to the potatoes.
3. Beat in the milk, butter, and salt and pepper to taste. Serve immediately.

Cal. **75** Carb. **13g** Protein **2g** Chol. **6mg** Fat **2g/26%**

Roasted Fennel and Onions

SERVES 4

3 medium onions, peeled and cut into wedges
2 fennel bulbs, cut into wedges, with fronds reserved
1 tablespoon olive oil
2 tablespoons balsamic vinegar
Freshly ground pepper

1. Preheat the oven to 400°.
2. Quarter the onions. Wash and trim the fennel bulbs and cut them into quarters. Reserve the fronds and chop to make ¼ cup.
3. In an 8-inch square baking dish, place the olive oil, vinegar, onion, and fennel bulbs, and toss well to coat . Season generously with pepper. Bake for 1 hour, uncovered, tossing occasionally, until tender and roasted to a char. Toss with reserved fronds and serve immediately.

Cal. **94** Carb. **15g** Protein **2g** Chol. **0mg** Fat **4g/32%**

Baba au Rhum

SERVES 12

2 tablespoon currants

½ cup plus 1 tablespoon dark rum
   (preferably Mount Gay)

½ cup skim milk

3 tablespoons unsalted butter

1 package dry yeast

2 tablespoons plus 1 cup sugar

2 eggs, at room temperature

½ teaspoon finely grated lemon zest

1⅔ cups sifted all-purpose flour

½ teaspoon salt

4 cups mixed fresh fruit, such as blueberries, raspberries, sliced
   strawberries, or sliced peaches

1. In a small bowl, combine the currants and 1 tablespoon of
the rum. Set aside to macerate for 30 minutes.

2. In a medium saucepan, scald the milk. Remove from the
heat and stir in the butter until melted; cool to 115°.

3. In a large mixing bowl, combine the yeast, 1 tablespoon hot
water, the milk, and 2 tablespoons of sugar. Beat in the eggs
one at a time. Add the lemon zest and macerated currants.
Beat in the flour and salt. The batter should be smooth and
silky; cover with a towel and let rise in a warm place until
doubled in bulk, about 1 hour.

4. Lightly spray or wipe twelve 3½-inch ring molds or one
8½-inch ring mold with vegetable or canola oil.

5. Preheat the oven to 350°.

6. Stir down the dough with a wooden spoon. Divide the
dough evenly among the individual molds or spread it in the
large mold. Cover with a towel and let the dough rise to the
top(s) of the mold(s), about 20 minutes for small molds, 40
minutes for the large mold.

7. Bake small rings for 20 to 30 minutes, large ring for 30 to
45 minutes, until lightly browned.

8. Meanwhile, in a medium saucepan, combine the cup of
sugar and 1 cup of water over medium-high heat, and bring to
a boil. Stir in the remaining ½ cup rum and cool to lukewarm.

9. Remove the cake(s) from the oven and cool in the mold(s)
for 5 minutes. Place a cake rack on a baking sheet. Invert the
cake(s) onto the rack and pour lukewarm syrup over. Spoon
the syrup that drains into the pan over the cake(s) until all is
absorbed.

Ali Baba

Baba au Rhum is attrib-
uted to the greediness of
Poland's King Stanislas
Lesczyinski. During his
exile to Lorraine in the
sixteenth century, he
found the traditional
Kugelhopf too dry and
had it improved by adding
rum. A dedicated reader
of the *Thousand and One
Nights*, this genie king
named the new cake after
his favorite character, Ali
Baba.

   Later, around 1850, the
cake was made in a ring-
shaped mold and named
a "savarin" after Brillat-
Savarin.

Chestnuts

The Chinese, who consume 40% of the world's supply, add chestnuts to porridge, juice them, and make them into honey-coated snacks. The Japanese eat 2 pounds per person per year. Italians use chestnut flour in pasta and sweets. In New York and Paris they've long been sold by vendors on the street, sweet and steaming. But while the French purée them and make candies, we Americans do little more than add a few to our holiday stuffings.

Too bad. Chestnuts are the perfect food, sometimes called "the grain that grows on a tree." Nutty and rich, they're surprisingly low in fat, with a nutritional breakdown close to that of brown rice and potatoes: 40% complex carbohydrate, 40% water, 10% protein, and just 2 to 3% unsaturated fat. And chestnuts have a natural sweetness all their own.

Chestnuts are available year-round and should not be once-a-year treats. Check health-food stores for the Chestnut Hill brand of flash-frozen, organically grown chestnuts from northern Italy. Or call Chestnut Hill Orchards at (800) 745-EASY to order.

10. To serve, turn the babas right side up and spoon fresh fruit into the center of each cake. Serve at room temperature.

*Cal. **201** Carb. **38g** Protein **4g** Chol. **38mg** Fat **4g/18%***

Chocolate-Chestnut Soufflé

SERVES 6

1 cup peeled whole chestnuts
½ cup milk
3 ounces semisweet chocolate, coarsely chopped
2 tablespoons Grand Marnier
1 teaspoon vanilla extract
2 egg yolks, at room temperature
1 teaspoon finely minced orange zest
4 egg whites, at room temperature
Pinch cream of tartar
¼ cup superfine sugar

1. Preheat the oven to 400°.
2. Lightly spray or wipe six 6-ounce soufflé dishes with vegetable oil.
3. Place the chestnuts and ½ cup water in a saucepan and simmer, covered, for 10 minutes. Uncover and add the milk. Simmer, stirring occasionally, for 10 to 12 minutes, or until all the milk is absorbed. Stir in the chocolate until melted; add the Grand Marnier and vanilla. Pour the mixture into a food processor. Add the egg yolks and orange zest. Process for 3 minutes, or until smooth, scraping the sides of the bowl once or twice. The batter will be stiff; transfer it to a mixing bowl.
4. Beat the egg whites and cream of tartar with an electric mixer until soft peaks form. Gradually beat in the superfine sugar, and continue to beat until stiff, shiny peaks form.
5. Gently stir one-third of the egg whites into the chocolate mixture. Once incorporated, gently fold in the remaining whites and continue until well blended.
6. Pour the mixture into the soufflé dishes, and run your thumb around the inside edges to promote even rising. Level the tops. Place the dishes on a sheet pan and place the pan in the center of the oven. Reduce the oven temperature to 375°. Bake for 16 to 17 minutes, until the soufflés are puffed and lightly browned; do not open the oven during the first 15 minutes. Serve immediately.

*Cal. **184** Carb. **26g** Protein **4g** Chol. **63mg** Fat **7g/33%***

Beans and Other Legumes

Basics

Beans and peas are the fresh or dried edible seeds of leguminous plants, a large group of flowering plants that produce double-seamed pods with single rows of seeds. Every culture through the ages has relied on beans for survival. Long called "poor man's meat," beans have been rediscovered with the current interest in healthful eating, freshened with new and exciting flavors, and used in a broad array of dishes. Heirloom beans and new hybrids are also coming back into cultivation and onto the market.

In the Market

Beans are available in four basic categories:

Fresh-shelled beans: Available in season.

Dried beans: Found in supermarkets, specialty stores, and ethnic and natural food shops. Buy from stores with good turnover and avoid beans sold in bulk—they may have been exposed to insects.

Frozen beans: Frozen quickly after harvest, they maintain their flavor and nutrition.

Canned beans: When you're in a hurry, they're better than none. But they lose much of their nutrients in canning and most of their distinguishing taste.

At Home

Freshly shelled beans should be kept (refrigerated in plastic bags) only a few days to remain plump and nutritious.

Dried beans are a pretty addition to your kitchen or pantry, stored in airtight glass containers. Keep in mind that the longer beans are kept, the longer they will need to cook.

In Cooking

Fresh beans should be steamed or cooked in a microwave oven just until they are crunchy tender. Roasted, they become rich and nutty-tasting. All dried beans except lentils and split peas need to be soaked for at least 4 to 6 hours before cooking. Soaking helps to break down the indigestible sugars that cause flatulence. If a bean floats to the surface during soaking, it's old—discard it. If beans are from a fairly recent crop and don't require long soaking, they will absorb only the amount of water they can hold.

★ GOOD FOR YOU ★

Beans are brimming with soluble fiber, which aids in the digestion of fat and protein. The gums and pectins found in dried beans appear to effectively lower cholesterol and blood pressure. Beans are an excellent source of protein and iron, and rich in B vitamins, potassium, magnesium, zinc, and calcium. They are very low in fat and contain no cholesterol. When combined with whole grains or other complex carbohydrates, they make a complete protein.

DRIED BEANS	FLAVOR	DRIED	SOAK	COOK (min)	YIELD (cups)
Adzuki, Azuki Small, oval, russet with thin white lines	Nutty	1 c.	Yes	30–45	3
Appaloosa Large, creamy white with black	Rich, robust	1 c.	Yes	45–50	2¼
Black Turtle Medium, oval, matte, small white lines	Rich, earthy, sweet, mushroomlike	1 c.	Yes	55–60	2¼
Broad or Fava Large, oval, light brown	Nutty, creamy	1 c.	Yes	35–40	2
Boston, Haricot, Navy Small, ¼", plumpish, oval	Mild and creamy	1 c.	Yes	40–45	2
Cannellini Navy/White/Kidney/Haricot, Swedish Brown	Creamy	1 c.	Yes	40–45	2¼
Red or Black Kidney	Robust, full-bodied	1 c.	Yes	45–60	2¼
Great Northern Large, white	Creamy	1 c.	Yes	90–120	2⅔
Flageolet Small to medium; pale green	Nutty and robust	1 c.	Yes	60	2¼
Pinto/Painted Oval buff w/ freckles	Earthy, full-bodied	1 c.	Yes	45–60	2¾
Lima/Christmas Lima Large or small	Starchy, distinctive, like chestnuts	1 c.	Yes	45	2
Jacob's Cattle Kidney-shaped, maroon with creamy white splotches	Robust and earthy	1 c.	Yes	35	2⅔
Black Soybean Small, black or yellow	Rich and robust	1 c.	Yes	25–60	2
Black-Eyed Pea Medium creamy, white ovals with black spots	Vegetablelike	1 c.	Yes	60	2
Chick-Pea Medium to small, plump and hard, buff-colored	Nutty	1 c.	Yes	60	2
Dried Pea Small, greenish-gray yellow, or white	Earthy, sweet	1 c.	Yes	55–60	1½
Lentil Tiny, brown, russet, green, and red	Earthy	1 c.	No	25–30	2¼

T·R·A·T·T·O·R·I·A

Clams Casino

SERVES 12

3 dozen littleneck clams, scrubbed and opened
8 ripe plum tomatoes, minced
3 tablespoons olive oil
Juice of 6 lemons
Zest of 6 lemons, chopped
6 garlic cloves, chopped
6 slices Canadian bacon, trimmed of fat, cut into ¼-inch strips
Freshly ground pepper

1. Preheat the broiler.
2. Loosen each clam from its shell and return to a half-shell. Top each clam with 1 teaspoon tomato, drizzle lightly with oil, and sprinkle with lemon juice and zest; place a few strips of bacon on top.
3. Place the clams on a baking sheet and place the sheet under the broiler, about 4 inches from the heat. Broil for 4 to 6 minutes, or until the bacon is crisp. Serve immediately.

*Cal. **99** Carb. **5g** Protein **9g** Chol. **23mg** Fat **5g/44%***

Rosemary and Olive Focaccia

SERVES 12

1 recipe Plain Focaccia dough (see Basics)
2 tablespoons olive oil

TRATTORIA

The Italian love of food is highly contagious. From them, we've learned passion, spontaneity, genuine respect for fine, fresh ingredients and natural flavors, and a healthy culinary tradition. At the same time, the Italians taught us that food should always be associated with warmth and hospitality, focused on friends and family.

The spirit of Italian home cooking is best exemplified in the trattoria, where an Italian finds his home-away-from-home. A trattoria is often a small, homey restaurant run by the family that owns it, though there are quite elegant and sophisticated versions as well. Often, the menu is limited, but it may change daily and is not always written down. Simple tables are

334

usually covered with plain white cloths, though the red-and-white-checked ones may occasionally show up. The china is heavy and white, and a single glass is used for water and wine. Sometimes the tables are crowded together, but the level of conversation—and laughter—is always high.

Contorni

Salads and vegetables are listed separately from the rest of the menu at most trattorias. Known as *contorni*, they are usually ordered to be shared at the table. Generally, these are home-style dishes, simple, straightforward, well seasoned, and generously portioned.

The following are dishes in this book that will make a good *contorni* at your table, particularly with the simply prepared entrées typical of trattorias.

Braised Leeks • Limas with Prosciutto • Tuscan Beans • Roasted Onions and Raisins • Garlic Cabbage • Bed of Green Lentils • Flageolets with Garlic • Roasted Fennel with Onions • Roasted Ginger Squash • Honey-Glazed Root Vegetables • Sherry Broccoli • Fennel and Leek Gratin • Lentils and Leeks • Ginger Cabbage • Potatoes and Chanterelles

1 cup imported black olives
1 tablespoon fresh rosemary
1 teaspoon coarse sea salt or kosher salt

1. Prepare the Plain Focaccia recipe according to the directions through step 5.
2. Lightly spray or wipe a 14-inch round deep-dish pizza pan or a 15½ x 10½-inch baking pan with cooking oil.
3. Punch the dough down and turn it into the pan. Press the dough evenly into the pan and let it rise, loosely covered, in a warm place for 45 minutes.
4. Preheat the oven to 400°.
5. Brush the dough with olive oil. Scatter the olives and rosemary over the dough and press them in slightly. Sprinkle the surface with salt.
6. Bake the focaccia for 40 to 50 minutes, or until it is golden and sounds hollow when lifted and tapped on the bottom. Let it cool on a rack and serve it warm or at room temperature.

*Cal. **219** Carb. **38g** Protein **5g** Chol. **0mg** Fat **5g/21%***

Tuscan Beans

SERVES 6
1 pound dried Jacob's Cattle or cannellini beans, rinsed, sorted, and soaked overnight
3½ to 4 cups chicken broth (see Basics)
1 tablespoon olive oil
1 dried red chili, crumbled, or ¾ teaspoon crushed red pepper flakes
2 tablespoons slivered garlic
¼ cup packed fresh sage leaves
Salt and freshly ground pepper

1. Drain and rinse the beans.
2. Place the beans in a large Dutch oven; add 3½ cups broth and bring to a boil. Simmer, partially covered, for 1 hour, or until the beans are tender, adding additional broth if necessary. Drain the beans well.
3. In a large heavy skillet, heat the oil over medium heat. Add the chili, garlic, and sage. Cook, stirring, just until the garlic begins to brown; do not let it burn.
4. Add the beans to the oil; stir to coat and heat through. Season with salt and a generous grinding of pepper.

*Cal. **248** Carb. **40g** Protein **16g** Chol. **0mg** Fat **3g/10%***

Minestrone & Wheat Berries

SERVES 8

1 teaspoon olive oil
3 cups chopped onion
2 tablespoons minced garlic
2 cups chopped carrot
1 cup chopped celery
8 cups chopped cabbage
4 cups chopped spinach
1 teaspoon dried thyme
5 bay leaves
½ teaspoon cayenne
1 cup chopped fresh Italian parsley
Freshly ground pepper
Salt
1 tablespoon minced fresh rosemary
2 tablespoons minced fresh sage
1 can (28 ounces) plum tomatoes, chopped, with juice
1 can (16 ounces) chick-peas, with juice
2 cups wheat berries

1. In a 5-quart soup pot over medium-high heat, add the olive oil and sauté the onion and garlic until tender. Add the carrot and celery and sauté for 3 to 5 minutes. Add the cabbage, spinach, thyme, and bay leaves, and cook for 1 to 2 minutes, stirring constantly.

2. Add 3 quarts of water and the remaining ingredients, and bring to a boil. Lower the heat and simmer, covered, for 50 minutes to 1 hour. Taste and adjust seasonings.

*Cal. **316** Carb. **64g** Protein **12g** Chol. **0mg** Fat **3g/7%***

Herbed Breadsticks (Grissini)

YIELD: 48 BREADSTICKS

1¾ teaspoons active dry yeast
Pinch sugar
4 tablespoons olive or canola oil
4 cups all-purpose flour
1½ teaspoons salt
1 tablespoon skim milk
One of the following: 2 tablespoons fresh rosemary; 2 cups chopped fresh spinach; 2 tablespoons dried oregano;

Minestrone

In Italy, *minestrone* usually means a vegetable soup, though sturdy chicken or meat broths may be the base. Wonderful seasonal ingredients are added to the slow-simmering broth at intervals to allow perfect cooking for each. Vegetables vary from recipe to recipe and region to region. Often pasta, beans, and rice are added as well. As with many soups, reheating only heightens the flavors. Minestrone is sometimes served with pesto stirred in or with Parmesan grated on top.

You can vary your minestrone by including combinations of most vegetables:

peas • spinach • artichokes
lettuces • fresh herbs
pasta • carrots • celery
green beans • potatoes
cabbage • zucchini
tomatoes • white beans
rice • garlic • leeks
pumpkin • fava beans

2 tablespoons minced garlic, or 2 tablespoons fresh dill, grated Parmesan, sesame or poppy seeds

1. In a small bowl, combine the yeast, sugar, and ¼ cup warm water. Set aside for 10 minutes, or until foamy.
2. Combine 1½ cups cold water with the oil.
3. In the mixing bowl of an electric mixer fitted with a dough hook, combine the flour and salt; add the water and oil.
4. Add the yeast mixture and blend until the dough forms a ball around the hook.
5. Turn out onto a lightly floured surface and knead until smooth and elastic.
6. Add one of the herbs and knead to distribute well.
7. Cover and let rise in a warm place until double, about 1 hour.
8. Preheat the oven to 375°. Lightly spray or wipe a baking sheet with vegetable oil.
9. Divide the dough into 48 pieces and roll each into a skinny 16-inch length. Brush with the skim milk and sprinkle with the cheese or seeds.
10. Place the pieces of dough on the sheet, leaving 2 inches between them. Bake for 15 to 20 minutes, or until lightly browned. Serve warm or cool to room temperature.

*Cal. **48** Carb. **8g** Protein **1g** Chol. **0mg** Fat **1g/22%***
(analyzed per breadstick)

Roasted Onions and Raisins

SERVES 4
½ cup golden raisins
2 tablespoons brandy or cognac
4 onions, halved horizontally, unpeeled
1 teaspoon canola oil

1. In a small bowl, combine the raisins and brandy; set aside to macerate for 1 hour or longer.
2. Preheat the oven to 375°.
3. Lightly spray or coat a baking sheet with vegetable or canola oil.
4. Brush the onions with the canola oil; place them, cut side down, on the prepared baking sheet and bake for 20 minutes. Turn the onions over and bake for 10 minutes, or until slightly charred. Spoon the raisins and brandy over the onions and bake for 5 minutes. Serve immediately.

*Cal. **103** Carb. **23g** Protein **2g** Chol. **0mg** Fat **1.4g/10%***

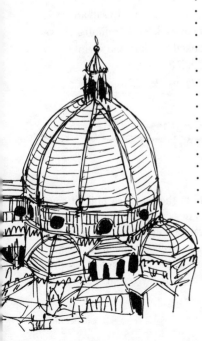

Saucing the pasta

Puttanesca Sauce

This classic spicy sauce is here made with far fewer olives than traditional versions and no additional olive oil. Even I was surprised that simply slow cooking the sauce made the flavors as full as ever.

SERVES 4

1 can (2 ounces) anchovy fillets, undrained
6 garlic cloves, crushed
1 can (35 ounces) plum tomatoes
2 tablespoons sun-dried tomatoes, chopped
1 jar (2½ ounces) capers, drained
½ cup pitted coarsely chopped black olives
½ cup dry red wine
Crushed red pepper flakes
Pinch sugar
Sage
2 tablespoons balsamic vinegar
Freshly ground pepper

1. Place the anchovies and garlic in a heavy medium-size saucepan. Mash thoroughly into a paste.
2. Add the tomatoes, capers, and olives, and stir over medium heat. Reduce the heat to low and add the remaining ingredients; simmer, uncovered, for 1 hour. Taste and adjust the seasonings. Serve over 8 ounces of cooked thin spaghetti.
*Cal. **115** Carb. **16g** Protein **7g** Chol. **12mg** Fat **4g/27%***

Amatriciana Sauce

Every August, the Italian town of Amatrice holds a gala celebration marking the year's harvest. Its principal attraction is this sauce, served with the thick, hollow spaghetti called *bucatini*.

SERVES 4

1 teaspoon olive oil
2 medium-size yellow onions, coarsely chopped
4 ounces pancetta or Canadian bacon, trimmed of fat and cut into ½ x 1-inch strips
4 garlic cloves, chopped
3 cups chopped fresh plum tomatoes
1 ounce capers, drained
Pinch sugar
Pinch crushed red pepper flakes
½ cup dry white wine
Salt and freshly ground pepper

1. In a heavy medium-size saucepan over medium-high heat, heat the olive oil. Add the onion and sauté for 10 minutes.
2. Stir in the pancetta and garlic and sauté for 5 minutes. Stir in the tomatoes, capers, sugar, pepper flakes, and wine. Season with salt and pepper. Simmer, uncovered, for 30 minutes. Serve with 8 ounces of cooked linguine and sprinkle with Romano cheese, if desired.
*Cal. **112** Carb. **11g** Protein **9g** Chol. **16mg** Fat **4g/26%***

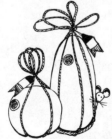

Parmigiano-Reggiano

The name can only be borne by cheese made from the skimmed milk of cows raised in a territory of the provinces of Parma and Reggio Emilia. This completely natural process has remained unchanged for seven centuries and includes eighteen months of aging. The result is a rich, round-flavored cheese that melts readily.

Ask for Parmigiano-Reggiano cut from the wheel at the time you buy it—pre-cut pieces may have begun to dry out. And *never* buy already-grated cheese.

Eggplant-Tomato Sauce

The eggplant melts into this vegetable-filled tomato sauce that's great on ziti or pappardelle.

SERVES 8

1 eggplant (2$^{1}/_4$ to 2$^{1}/_2$ pounds)
Salt and freshly ground pepper
2 pounds fresh ripe tomatoes, cored and
  coarsely chopped
2$^{1}/_2$ cups coarsely diced zucchini
6 sprigs fresh oregano
4 sprigs fresh thyme
2 bay leaves
2 garlic cloves, minced
$^{1}/_4$ teaspoon salt
$^{1}/_4$ teaspoon freshly ground pepper
Pinch cayenne

1. Preheat the oven to 500°. Lightly spray or wipe a baking sheet with vegetable oil.
2. Cut the eggplant in half lengthwise. Make two long lengthwise slits in each half, cutting to but not through the skin. Generously season the cut sides with salt and pepper. Place the eggplant, cut sides down, on the pan and bake for 20 minutes, or until the skin has shriveled and the flesh is very tender.
3. When cool enough to handle, scrape the flesh into a saucepan Add the tomatoes, zucchini, oregano, thyme, bay leaves, garlic, salt, pepper, and cayenne. Bring to a slow boil over medium heat. Reduce partially, cover, and simmer for 20 to 30 minutes. Taste and adjust the seasonings.

Cal. 66 Carb. 15g
Protein .3g Chol. 0mg
Fat .8g/9%

My Favorite Carbonara

The story goes that this sauce was created in the last days of World War II. American soldiers brought bacon and eggs to Italian cooks, requesting that they be made into pasta sauce. It's one of my favorites.

SERVES 6

$^{1}/_4$ pound pancetta,
  diced
$^{3}/_4$ cup coarsely chopped
  onion
2 cups dry white wine
1 pound linguine, cooked
1 egg, lightly beaten
1 cup finely grated
  imported Parmesan
$^{1}/_2$ cup finely chopped
  fresh Italian parsley
Salt and freshly ground
  pepper

1. In a large skillet over low heat, cook the pancetta slowly until it begins to crisp, 8 to 10 minutes. Drain off the fat, add the onion, increase the heat to medium, and cook until the onion is translucent, about 5 minutes.
2. Add the wine to the skillet, increase the heat to medium-high, and reduce to 1$^{1}/_2$ cups, about 5 minutes; keep warm.
3. Quickly pour the hot bacon-wine mixture over the pasta; add the egg and toss to combine thoroughly. Add $^{3}/_4$ cup of the Parmesan and toss; season with salt and pepper to taste.
4. To serve, divide the pasta among four heated plates. Sprinkle with the remaining cheese and garnish with the parsley. Serve immediately.

Cal. 391 Carb. 60g Protein 18g Chol. 45mg
Fat 8g/17%

Linguine with Braised Garlic

One-hundred-year-old vinegar makes the difference.

SERVES 6

1 teaspoon olive oil
¼ cup slivered garlic
1 pound fresh or imported dry linguine
3 tablespoons chicken broth (see Basics)
1 cup freshly grated imported Parmesan
A few drops 100-year-old balsamic vinegar, or 2 tablespoons 25-
  year-old balsamic vinegar mixed with 1 teaspoon brown sugar
Salt and freshly ground pepper
1 cup finely minced fresh Italian parsley

1. In a medium skillet, heat the oil over medium heat. Add the garlic and lower the heat to a simmer. Cook the garlic, covered, for 5 minutes. Remove the cover and continue to cook the garlic just until it begins to brown lightly, 6 to 8 minutes. Do not let the garlic become too dark or burn.
2. Meanwhile, cook the pasta according to directions. Drain and place in a large heated serving bowl. Add the chicken broth, braised garlic, and Parmesan, and toss. Add the vinegar and salt and pepper to taste. Sprinkle with minced parsley and serve immediately.

*Cal. **320** Carb. **46g** Protein **16g** Chol. **55mg** Fat **8g/21%***

Garlic & Swiss Chard Fettuccine

SERVES 4

1 teaspoon extra-virgin olive oil
4 garlic cloves, slivered
¾ cup chicken broth (see Basics)
8 ounces fettuccine (plain, spinach, carrot, tomato,
  or a combination)
1 pound Swiss chard, rinsed, patted dry, stemmed, and shredded
1 tablespoon minced lemon zest
3 tablespoons fresh lemon juice
Salt and freshly ground pepper
½ cup freshly grated imported Parmesan
½ cup chopped fresh Italian parsley

1. In a stockpot or a deep skillet, heat the oil over medium heat. Add the garlic and sauté until golden brown; do not

Balsamic Vinegar

The sweet and tart vinegar of Italy's Trebbiano grape is aged in Modena in a series of wooden casks for at least six years. But *balsamico* can be—and often is—aged for much longer. Needless to say it grows quite expensive with time—very old balsamic, say fifty years or more, can cost upwards of $100 for a 250-milliliter bottle. Someday, when you're feeling flush, try Antica Acetaia dei Carandini; it's so thick and sweet, just a tiny drop creates a memory.

burn. Add the chicken broth and reduce the heat to a simmer.

2. Meanwhile, bring a large pot of salted water to a boil. Add the pasta and cook until al dente, according to package directions.

3. When the pasta is added to the water, bring the chicken broth back to a boil. Add the chard, cover, and lower the heat slightly. Cook for 2 to 3 minutes, stirring once or twice.

4. Drain the pasta and place it in a heated bowl. Add the lemon zest and lemon juice, and toss gently. Pour the chicken-broth mixture over the pasta and toss again.

5. Season with salt and pepper to taste. Add the Parmesan and parsley and divide among four heated plates.

*Cal. **262** Carb. **38g** Protein **13g** Chol. **50mg** Fat **6g/21%***

Pasta with Black Olives

SERVES 6

1 teaspoon canola oil
4 garlic cloves, peeled and crushed
2 pounds fresh button mushrooms,
  cleaned and sliced
¾ cup imported niçoise olives in brine,
  pitted and chopped
¼ cup brine from olives
12 ounces penne
⅛ teaspoon freshly ground pepper
⅔ cup minced fresh Italian parsley

1. In a large skillet, heat the oil over medium heat. Add the garlic and sauté for 2 minutes. Add the mushrooms and cook for 2 to 3 minutes, stirring frequently. Reduce the heat to low, cover, and cook for 7 to 10 minutes, or until the mushrooms are cooked and have released their liquids. Stir in the olives and olive brine, and cook for 3 minutes. Cover and keep warm over very low heat.

2. Meanwhile, bring a large pot of water to a boil. Stir in the pasta and cook until tender but still firm. Drain immediately.

3. Stir the cooked pasta into the mushroom-and-olive sauce, add the parsley, and heat through. Grind plenty of black pepper over the pasta and serve immediately.

*Cal. **329** Carb. **48g** Protein **9g** Chol. **0mg** Fat **12g/32%***

Wild Mushroom & Mint Risotto

SERVES 8

1 ounce dried porcini or morel mushrooms
1 teaspoon olive oil
4 shallots or scallions, finely minced
6 garlic cloves, finely minced
1 pound porcini, portobello, or
    chanterelle mushrooms, stems
    removed and large ones quartered
2 tablespoons finely chopped fresh rosemary
2 cups Arborio rice
1/4 cup red wine
5 cups beef broth (see Basics)
1/2 cup finely minced fresh Italian parsley
1/2 cup chopped fresh mint
Freshly ground pepper

1. In a small bowl, place 1 cup of boiling water and the dried mushrooms, and soak for 20 minutes. Remove the mushrooms with a slotted spoon and coarsely chop them. Strain the liquid through cheesecloth or a coffee filter and reserve.
2. In a large stockpot over medium-high heat, heat the oil. Add the shallot, garlic, porcini, and rosemary. Sauté for 5 minutes, or until the garlic is slightly softened, stirring constantly. Add the rice and reduce the heat to medium; stir until the rice is coated with oil and slightly translucent, about 3 minutes. Add the wine and scrape up the browned bits from the bottom of the pan; simmer until the liquid is absorbed. Add the reserved mushroom liquid and 1/2 cup of the beef broth, stirring constantly until the broth is absorbed. Continue adding broth, 1/2 cup at a time; the rice should be cooked but firm to the bite, and the mixture creamy.
3. Remove from the heat, stir in the parsley, and mint, and season generously with pepper. Pass grated Parmesan at the table, if desired.

Cal. **218** *Carb.* **47g** *Protein* **6g** *Chol.* **0mg** *Fat* **2g/8%**

"The trouble with eating Italian food is that five or six days later you're hungry again."

George Miller

Risotto

The secret: First blanch the outer shell of the rice so that the grains will swell as broth is added. Blanching is accomplished during the important first step, sautéing the Arborio rice—traditional for making this classic dish. Broth quantities in most recipes approximate what is needed to achieve the desired results—a creamy, tender, but not mushy, texture. Add only a little stock or broth at a time. Stir, then wait for the liquid to be absorbed before you add more. Risotto making takes time and care but is highly satisfying. At the end of the process, the grains should be tender but firm to the tooth (al dente). Risotto can accommodate almost any flavor you desire, but some choices are truly superb: seafood, truffles, asparagus, wild mushrooms, chicken, or just first-class Parmigiano-Reggiano, the underpinning of the best-known version, risotto Milanese, which often accompanies osso buco.

Serve risotto in a shallow bowl and eat from the outer edge inwards to keep it hot until you enjoy every bit.

Everyday Red-Wine Risotto

SERVES 8

1 teaspoon olive oil
1 cup finely minced onion
2 tablespoons finely minced garlic
3 fresh rosemary sprigs
1 bay leaf
4 cups beef broth (additional as needed; see Basics)
2 cups Arborio rice
2 cups dry red wine
1 cup freshly grated imported Parmesan
Salt and freshly ground pepper
1/2 cup chopped Italian parsley

1. In a large Dutch oven over medium heat, combine the oil, onion, garlic, rosemary, and bay leaf. Turn the heat to low, cover, and simmer until the onion is soft and translucent, about 15 minutes; do not brown. Stir occasionally.

2. In a medium saucepan, heat the beef broth.

3. Uncover the onion and increase the heat to medium. Add the rice and stir to coat. Sauté, stirring with a wooden spoon, for 2 to 3 minutes, or until the rice begins to turn golden.

4. Stir in 1 cup of the red wine; continue to stir until the wine is absorbed. Add the remaining wine and stir until absorbed.

5. Stir in the broth, 1 cup at a time, until absorbed. The rice should be creamy but still a little crunchy. Add additional broth 1/4 cup at a time, to reach the desired consistency.

6. Remove the bay leaf and rosemary. Stir in the cheese and parsley; season with salt and pepper to taste.

*Cal. **239** Carb. **38g** Protein **10g***
*Chol. **15mg** Fat **5g/19%***

MUSHROOM M A G I C

Basics

Morels, chanterelles, porcini, shiitakes, cèpes, Trompettes des morts. In spring and fall, they pop up overnight under damp leaves near oak and fruit trees.

Mushrooms are an ancient food, long shrouded in myth and folklore. It wasn't until well into the eighteenth century that "fairy rings" in the woods were no longer regarded as evil omens but were linked to the magic of mushrooms. Throughout the nineteenth century they were a food of the rich—the only food that noblemen prepared themselves. Today, wild mushrooms are still a specialty food. But no longer is it necessary to forage for them, for many varieties are available in the markets. Some are really wild; some, wild varieties that are cultivated. Each type has its distinctive taste.

Remember that many mushrooms are toxic and some are deadly, so, when foraging, don't take chances if you have any doubt regarding a variety.

At Home

Wild and cultivated mushrooms should be refrigerated as soon as you're home, in a paper bag or covered loosely with a damp paper towel.

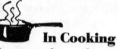

In Cooking

Never wash mushrooms. They're like sponges, absorbing water almost immediately, losing flavor and becoming soggy in the process. Instead, wipe mushrooms with damp paper towels if cleaning is needed at all. Wild mushrooms may be sandy and require brushing. Trim the stems and cut the caps according to your recipe.

For a quick sauté, instead of butter, use a small amount of olive oil and chicken broth, cook over high heat, and toss quickly. This keeps them firm.

In The Market

Wild mushrooms are more intensely flavored than tame types, but price is not necessarily your best guide. Know what you want and, if necessary, ask your greengrocer for advice. Be sure that you're getting what you want. Look for firm, tight mushrooms that are dry, not the least bit slimy. They're very perishable, so use them within two days.

Concentrated Flavor

One of the best ways to intensify the deep, woodsy flavor of wild mushrooms is to combine reconstituted dried mushrooms with fresh. Soak dried cèpes, shiitakes, morels, or chanterelles in warmed red or white wine, beef or chicken broth, or a fortified wine—Madeira, Marsala, or port—for one to two hours. Drain, squeeze out excess moisture, and mince finely; it's the flavor, not texture, that you want. Add the soaking liquid to your dish, watching for sand that may have accumulated.

    Dried mushrooms are pricey, but a few go a long way.

★ GOOD FOR YOU ★

A cup of mushrooms has only 20 calories. Folklore is filled with tales of their mysterious healing powers. Today, we know that they're high in protein, carbohydrates, and fiber, and a good source of riboflavin, vitamin D, and potassium.

    In recent studies, shiitakes were found to be effective in lowering blood pressure and cholesterol; black cloud-ear mushrooms in thinning blood; and enoki in boosting the immune system. Enoki and oyster mushrooms were found to be anticarcinogenic.

Angel Trumpet
White to almost transparent.
Delicate flavor. Tame.

Chanterelle
(Girolle)
Trumpet-shaped.
Mild-flavored. Very delicate; should be prepared
shortly after picking. Peppery when raw;
tastes like apricots. Wild/tame.

Cremini
(Roman)
Cocoa-colored.
More intense flavor than
button mushrooms. Tame.

Champignon de Paris
(button)
White or cream-colored.
Very mild flavor.
A trusty all-purpose mushroom. Tame.

Enoki
(Enokidake or Christmas)
Tiny white caps w/long stems.
Fruity, with a fresh tang.
Wild is prettier, slightly meatier.

Fairy Ring
Taupe w/little brown rings on stems.
Delicate garlic flavor (and smell). Wild.

Hen-of-the-Woods
Smoky gray to gray/brown.
Spoon-shaped fluffy clusters w/feathery edges.
Grows at base of trees. Rich flavor. Tame.

Matsutake
Grown wrapped in a veil.
Spicy, earthy flavor.
Grow on pine logs. Meaty texture. Wild/tame.

Straw
Taupe parasol cap; white stem.
Mild flavor.
Good for stir-frying. Wild.

Puff Ball
Faint flavor, very adaptable.
They have been known to grow as large as
16 feet and weigh 20 pounds. Wild.

Morel
Beige to dark brown.
Meaty texture with an earthy, nutlike taste.
Can be very sandy. Grows in Michigan, Massachusetts, and Connecticut, near aspens and
abandoned orchards. Wild/tame.

Shiitake
Large brownish-black.
Parasol-shaped cap;
creamy-colored inside.
Grows on oak logs. Rich, smoky flavor.
Most intensely flavored
mushroom available. Wild/tame.

Oyster
(Pleurotte)
Light gray, beige, or white w/bluish tinge.
Fan-shaped.
Soft taste of shellfish. Mild, with a silky texture.
Should not be washed. Wild/tame.

Trompettes des morts
(Horns of Plenty)
Black, trumpet-shaped.
Nutty flavor. Wild/tame.

Pom Pom
(Forest, Coral, Lobster)
Cauliflowerlike leaves.
Taste reminiscent of seafood. Tame.

Wood Ear
(Cloud Ear, Tree Ear)
Black or brown, nearly transparent;
ear-shaped.
Crunchy; mild, nutty flavor. Tame.

Porcini
(Cèpe, King Bolete, Boletus)
Taupe to brown.
Parasol-shaped caps.
Earthy, pale, pungent, silken flesh,
smoky, robust.
Large caps can measure up to 6 inches. Wild.

Truffles
Italian White, French Black.
The flavor of the woods at its most intense.
Only use fresh. Wild.

Portobello
Taupe to brown.
Saucer-shaped cap.
Woodsy and pungent taste reminiscent of filet
mignon, meaty. Wild/tame.

Tuscan Pork Loin with Sage

SERVES 4

1 pound pork loin, trimmed of all fat, sliced into 8 slices
8 large sage leaves
2 paper-thin slices imported prosciutto
1 teaspoon olive oil
1 tablespoon unsalted butter
1½ cups Marsala or white wine
Salt and freshly ground pepper
2 tablespoons minced fresh Italian parsley

1. Flatten each slice of pork between two pieces of waxed paper by pressing with the heel of your hand.
2. Lay one sage leaf in the middle of each slice of pork. Cut the slices of prosciutto into quarters. Lay one piece over each slice of pork. Hold the prosciutto, sage, and pork together with a toothpick.
3. In a large heavy skillet, heat the olive oil and butter over medium heat. Add the slices, pork sides down, without letting them touch, and cook until lightly browned, about 4 minutes. Turn and cook 2 more minutes, or until the prosciutto is crisp. Remove to a serving platter and keep warm.
4. Drain any fat from the pan. Add the Marsala and cook over high heat, scraping up all the bits from the skillet, until the sauce is reduced to ½ cup, 4 to 5 minutes. Season with salt and pepper to taste. Pour the sauce over the pork and garnish with parsley.

*Cal. **265** Carb. **11g** Protein **29g** Chol. **102mg** Fat **11g/29%***

Veal Chop Balsamico

SERVES 4

2 teaspoons olive oil
4 veal chops (6 ounces each, ¾ inch thick)
Salt and freshly ground pepper
¼ cup white wine
¼ cup balsamic vinegar
Salsa Puttanesca (at right)

1. Heat the oil in a large skillet until very hot. Add the veal chops and sear them well on both sides. Season to taste with salt and pepper; add the wine.

Leaning Toward Pork

Avoiding pork as a fatty relic of feasts past? Surprise! Today's pork has been bred to have 30% less fat than it did thirty years ago and rivals even chicken in leanness. In fact, the tenderloin of a well-trimmed pork loin is leaner than chicken, with only 79 mg. cholesterol and 59 mg. sodium, which strikes it off the high-cholesterol hit list.

Salsa Puttanesca

SERVES 4

1 tablespoon olive or canola oil
2 tablespoons finely minced garlic
2 cups diced Roma (plum) tomatoes
4 tablespoons capers
¼ cup niçoise olives
Salt and freshly ground pepper

1. Heat the oil and garlic in a heavy medium-size saucepan.
2. Add the tomatoes, capers, and olives. Stir and heat just to simmering over medium heat. Season with salt and pepper to taste.

*Cal. **78** Carb. **5g** Protein **1g** Chol. **0mg** Fat **6g/68%***

2. Reduce the heat and cook the chops until they are slightly underdone and still juicy, about 6 minutes. Remove the chops from the skillet, cover, and keep warm.

3. Add the vinegar to the oil and juices remaining in the skillet. Stir the liquid, scraping any browned bits from the pan, until it is reduced to a glaze. Pour 1 tablespoon over each veal chop, and garnish with Salsa Puttanesca.

*Cal. **138** Carb. **1g** Protein **17g** Chol. **64mg** Fat **7g/46%***

Rabbit

Firmer, leaner, and whiter than chicken and as tasty as veal. Given our fondness for "Bugs," "Peter," and "Brer," chances are that the rabbit you buy will be from Australia or Canada and will be frozen. There are some very good commercial rabbit raisers in this country, however, and you can expect more as this healthful and palate-pleasing meat catches on. Fresh is best, of course. But rabbit is firmer and freezes better than chicken. The delicate flavor is best in small rabbits—a gamy taste can be apparent in the large wild rabbits called hares.

The flavors to pair with rabbit include fennel, juniper, sage, rosemary, lemon, red and white wines, Marsala, pine nuts, raisins, and prosciutto. Think of rabbit as a tastier chicken. You can't go wrong.

Rabbit with Fresh Apricots

SERVES 6

1 rabbit (3 pounds), dressed and cut into serving pieces
1 teaspoon olive oil
3 cups halved and thinly sliced onion
1 cup carrots in 2-inch chunks
2 teaspoons honey
1 cup coarsely chopped celery
  stalks and some of the leaves
1 teaspoon fresh thyme
1 bay leaf
1 teaspoon ground coriander
Salt and freshly ground pepper
1 tablespoon ouzo or Pernod
1 pound fresh apricots, pitted and
  quartered
½ cup chicken broth (see Basics)
1 tablespoon red wine vinegar
2 cups cracked wheat, cooked according to package directions

1. Preheat the broiler.

2. Rub the rabbit pieces with a little of the oil (about ½ teaspoon). Arrange the pieces on a broiler rack and broil until lightly browned on both sides, 10 to 12 minutes. Remove and set aside.

3. In a large heavy skillet over medium heat, add the remaining oil, onion, and carrot. Sauté gently until the onion softens and becomes transparent. Stir in the honey, celery, thyme, bay leaf, coriander, and salt and pepper to taste; add the ouzo. Simmer for 2 to 3 minutes. Add the apricots, chicken broth, and vinegar, and stir gently. Add the rabbit pieces along with any accumulated juices, cover, and simmer gently until the meat is tender, about 45 minutes. Serve with cracked wheat.

*Cal. **439** Carb. **55g** Protein **35g** Chol. **28mg** Fat **8g/18%***

Pheasant with Wine Grapes

SERVES 8

1 cup raisins
½ cup Armagnac
2 free-range pheasants (2½ pounds each)
Salt and freshly ground pepper
2 garlic cloves, smashed
4 sprigs fresh sage
12 garlic cloves, peeled
2½ cups red wine
2 pounds assorted seedless wine and "champagne"
* grapes on the vine, with leaves if possible*
2 teaspoons honey

1. Macerate the raisins in ⅓ cup of the Armagnac overnight; set the remaining Armagnac aside.
2. Preheat the oven to 325°.
3. Rinse the pheasants and pat them dry, inside and out. Rub inside and out with salt and pepper. Rub the breasts with the smashed garlic cloves, then place them in the cavities. Tuck the sage between the legs and the breast. Arrange the pheasants in a large flameproof roasting pan. Scatter the whole garlic cloves around. Pour 2 cups of the red wine over the pheasants. Add the raisins and Armagnac. Arrange the grapes around the pheasants. Roast for 1½ hours, basting every 15 minutes, until the pheasants are tender.
4. Transfer the pheasants to a serving platter. Arrange the grape clusters around the pheasants. Place the roasting pan on the stove over medium-high heat. Deglaze the pan with the remaining wine and the reserved Armagnac. Crush any loose grapes with the back of the spoon; transfer the contents of the roasting pan to a small saucepan, and reduce for 5 minutes, until thickened. Whisk in the honey, strain the sauce over the pheasants, and garnish with clusters of grapes.
*Cal. **334** Carb. **52g** Protein **27g** Chol. **73mg** Fat **7g/16%***

Venison with Leeks

SERVES 4

1½ pounds loin of venison, trimmed and cut into 1½-inch-
* wide strips*
2 tablespoons minced fresh ginger
1 tablespoon low-sodium soy sauce

Venison in a Jiff

Spray or wipe a skillet with olive oil and 1 tablespoon of melted butter. Sauté a tenderloin of venison or medallions over fairly high heat. Deglaze the pan with balsamic vinegar and a pinch of sugar to smooth the edge, then add cider, cream, beef broth, or skim milk to make a pan sauce. The vinegar gives a rich depth of flavor, the perfect match for venison's robust taste.

350

- ¼ *cup rice wine vinegar*
- ½ *cup dry sherry*
- ½ *tablespoon sesame oil*
- 3 *garlic cloves, minced*
- 4 *large leeks (about 2 pounds), coarsely chopped*
- ¾ *cup chicken broth (see Basics)*
- 1 *tablespoon tomato paste*
- ¼ *cup finely chopped fresh cilantro*

1. Marinate the venison in the ginger, soy sauce, vinegar, sherry, and oil for 1 hour. Drain. Reserve the marinade.
2. In a large nonstick sauté pan, sauté the venison over medium-high heat until lightly browned, about 3 minutes. Do this in batches if necessary in order not to overcrowd the pan. Transfer the meat to a bowl. Add the ginger and leeks to the pan. Sauté, stirring, for 3 minutes, until the leek is softened. Add the reserved marinade, the chicken broth, and the tomato paste. Return the venison to the pan and simmer for 5 to 7 minutes, until the liquid has reduced a bit and thickened. Add the cilantro and serve on a bed of rice.

Cal. **298** *Carb.* **21g** *Protein* **41g** *Chol.* **144mg** *Fat* **6g/17%**

Wines for Game

Barolo

Cabernet Sauvignon

Gamay

Brunello di Montalcino

Merlot

Barbaresco

Pomero

Bordeaux

Burgundy

Pinot Noir

Leg of Young Goat

Delicate young goat is becoming more available—seek it out.

SERVES 4

2 *legs of young goat (1½ pounds each)*
1 *garlic clove, smashed*
1 *garlic clove, slivered*
1 *teaspoon olive oil*
4 *sprigs fresh rosemary*
Salt and freshly ground pepper

1. Preheat the oven to 450°.
2. Wipe the meat dry with paper towels; rub it all over with the smashed clove of garlic. Make small slits here and there with the tip of a sharp knife, and insert the garlic slivers.
3. Rub the legs with olive oil. Place the legs on a rack in a roasting pan with the rosemary sprigs on top. Season with salt and pepper to taste. Place the meat in the oven and immediately turn the heat down to 350°. Roast for 1 hour, or until the internal temperature registers 180°. Let the meat rest for 10 minutes before serving.

Cal. **321** *Carb.* **2g** *Protein* **57g** *Chol.* **156mg** *Fat* **8g/22%**

Pears with Grape Syrup

SERVES 6

6 large Bosc pears (about 3 pounds), halved and cored
Juice of 2 large lemons
Finely minced zest of 1 lemon
1/2 teaspoon ground cinnamon
1 1/2 cups Fresh Grape Syrup (below)

1. Preheat the oven to 375°. Lightly spray or wipe a 2-quart baking dish with vegetable oil.
2. Dip the pear halves in the lemon juice and arrange them in the dish. Sprinkle with the lemon zest and cinnamon. Baste the pears with half the grape syrup. Bake for 1 hour, basting every 20 minutes with the remaining grape syrup. When the pears are easily pierced with a knife, remove them from the oven.
3. Remove the pears to a serving dish with a slotted spoon and set them aside. Pour all of the pear juices into a small saucepan. Reduce the juices over high heat for 3 minutes, or until thickened and syrupy. Pour the juices over the pears. Serve warm or at room temperature.

Cal. 276 Carb. 73g Protein 3g Chol. 0mg Fat 2g/6%

Fresh Grape Syrup

YIELD: 2 1/2 CUPS

4 1/2 pounds red grapes, stemmed
8 whole cloves
1 cup dry red wine

1. In a food processor, chop the grapes very finely. (You will need to do this in batches.) Place the grapes in a non-corrosive bowl, cover, and refrigerate for 48 hours.
2. Strain the grapes, pressing down on the skins with a spoon to extract all the juice; you should have 5 1/2 cups. Discard the pulp.
3. Pour the grape juice into a medium saucepan. Add the cloves, and boil for 30 minutes, until the juice is reduced to 2 to 2 1/2 cups. Skim off any foam as it boils, then strain out the cloves. Add the wine and boil for 5 minutes. Serve at room temperature, or cool and store in the refrigerator.

Cal. 34 Carb. 9g Protein .4g Chol. 0mg Fat .3g/7%
(analyzed per tablespoon)

> ★ **GOOD FOR YOU** ★
> **Pears**
>
> One medium-size pear provides 50 calories, and lots of vitamins A and C, is high in carbohydrates and fiber, and also provides iron and potassium. Eat the skin, too, for most of the vitamin C and fiber. Make a perfectly ripened pear one of your five fruits a day throughout the fall.

Figs in Sauternes

SERVES 4

1½ cups Sauternes
2 tablespoons sugar
1 whole vanilla bean, seeds
   removed and pod reserved
Zest of 1 lemon, finely
   minced
Juice of 1 lemon
1 pound fresh figs
2 tablespoons finely chopped mint

1. In a medium saucepan, combine the Sauternes, sugar, vanilla bean pod and seeds, zest, and juice. Simmer over medium heat for 13 to 15 minutes, until slightly syrupy.
2. Add the figs and simmer for 8 to 10 minutes, until tender. If the syrup becomes too thick, stir in 1 tablespoon of water.
3. Remove the vanilla pod and stir in the mint. Cool the figs in the syrup and serve at room temperature.

Cal. **155** Carb. **40g** Protein **1g** Chol. **0mg** Fat **.4g/1%**

Dark Chocolate Sauce

YIELD: 1 CUP

1 tablespoon unsalted butter
½ cup unsweetened cocoa
¼ cup sugar
1 cup light corn syrup
1 tablespoon low-fat sour
   cream

In a medium-size saucepan, combine all of the ingredients except the sour cream. Heat the mixture, stirring constantly, until the sauce begins to boil. Remove the pan from the heat and stir in the sour cream.

Cal. **88** Carb. **20g**

Protein **.7g** Chol. **2mg**

Fat **1.2g/14%**

(analyzed per tablespoon)

Mascarpone Frozen Yogurt

The tart taste of mascarpone may be complemented by Dark Chocolate Sauce.

SERVES 8

1½ cups Yogurt Cheese (see Basics)
1 cup mascarpone
1 cup sugar
1¼ cups skim milk

1. In a large mixing bowl, whisk all of the ingredients. Chill the mixture for 1 hour.
2. Transfer the mixture to an ice cream machine and freeze according to the manufacturer's directions.

Cal. **213** Carb. **33g** Protein **9g** Chol. **18mg**

Fat **5g/22%**

Biscotti with Nuts

YIELD: 45 COOKIES

2 eggs
2 egg whites
1 teaspoon vanilla extract
1 cup sugar
2 cups all-purpose flour
1 teaspoon baking soda
1/4 teaspoon salt
3/4 cup nuts, such as hazelnuts, almonds,
    pistachios, toasted

1. Preheat the oven to 325°. Lightly spray or wipe a large baking sheet with vegetable oil.
2. In the large bowl of an electric mixer, combine the eggs, egg whites, and vanilla. Mix until well combined. Add the sugar, flour, soda, and salt; beat until a dough forms. Stir in the nuts.
3. Turn the sticky dough onto a lightly floured board. With clean floured hands and with the aid of a spatula or pastry scraper, knead the dough several times. Divide the dough in half.
4. With floured hands, form the dough into two flattish logs, about 15 inches long and 2 inches wide. Place the logs on the baking sheet, 3 inches apart. Bake for 40 minutes. Remove and cool for 10 minutes.
5. Reduce the heat to 275°.
6. On a cutting board, cut the logs diagonally into 3/4-inch-thick slices. Arrange the slices on the baking sheet and bake for 10 to 12 minutes. Turn and bake for another 10 to 12 minutes. Turn the heat off, and leave the biscotti to crisp in the oven for 15 minutes. Remove from oven and cool completely.

*Cal. **58** Carb. **10g** Protein **1g** Chol. **4mg** Fat **1.4g/24%***
(analyzed per cookie)

Variations
Three-Ginger: Eliminate the nuts and add 1½ teaspoons ground ginger, 3 tablespoons minced crystallized ginger, and 1 tablespoon grated fresh ginger.
Pistachio-Orange: Use 2/3 cup pistachio nuts, and add 2 tablespoons orange zest and 2 tablespoons Cointreau.
Anise: Use 2/3 cup whole almonds, 1 tablespoon anise seed, and 2 tablespoons Sambuca.

Biscotti Bravi!

Those addictive Italian cookies meant for after-dinner dipping are just as delicious when munched alone. Though biscotti are dry and low in fat, their delicious flavors can delight at any hour of the day—with morning coffee, as a lunchtime sweet, with midafternoon cappuccino. The word *biscotti* refers to their preparation—they are baked twice. It's also generally conceded that no one can eat just one.

With Biscotti

Vin Santo and grappa, two of Italy's great fortified wines, are a good way to finish off just about any meal.

Vin Santo, or "holy wine," is a rich, sweet, dry wine, made from semi-dried Trebbiano and Malvasia grapes left on the vine long after harvest. The best come from Tuscany: Avignonesi, Isolee e Olena, and Castello di Ama. My favorite way to serve Vin Santo is with biscotti to dip into it and soften the crunch.

Throat-searing grappa is a marvelous *digestif*. Poured into espresso it becomes *caffé corretto* or "corrected coffee." Some grappas that have caught my fancy are Masi, Lungarotti, Ceretto, and Novino.

Chocolate Biscotti

YIELD: 32 COOKIES

2 eggs
2 egg whites
1 teaspoon vanilla extract
$^1/_2$ teaspoon almond extract
1 cup sugar
2 cups all-purpose flour
$^1/_3$ cup unsweetened cocoa, preferably Dutch process
2 tablespoons instant espresso granules
1 teaspoon baking soda
Dash salt
$^1/_2$ cup sliced almonds or hazelnuts
12 ounces best-quality bittersweet chocolate

1. Preheat oven to 325°. Lightly spray or wipe a baking sheet with vegetable oil.
2. In the large bowl of an electric mixer, combine the eggs, egg whites, and extracts. Mix until well combined. Add the sugar, flour, cocoa, espresso, soda, and salt. Beat until a dough forms. Stir in the almonds.
3. Turn the dough onto a lightly floured board. With floured hands and the aid of a spatula or pastry scraper, knead the dough several times. Divide the dough in half.
4. With floured hands, form the dough into two flattish logs, about 15 inches long and 2 inches wide. Place the logs on the baking sheet 3 inches apart. Bake for 40 minutes. Remove and cool for 10 minutes.
5. Reduce the heat to 275°.
6. On a cutting board, cut the logs diagonally into ¾-inch-thick slices. Arrange the slices on the baking sheet and bake for 10 to 12 minutes. Turn and bake another 10 to 12 minutes. Turn the heat off, and crisp in the oven 15 minutes. Remove from the oven and cool completely.
7. In a double boiler or heavy saucepan, melt the chocolate over very low heat. Holding the cookies by one end, dip them halfway into the melted chocolate. Place on waxed paper to cool and dry. Store in an airtight container.

*Cal. **80** Carb. **13g** Protein **1g** Chol. **8mg** Fat **3g/29%** (analyzed per cookie)*

The Earth *laughs* with a Harvest

Roasted Ginger Squash

SERVES 4

1 butternut squash (about 2 pounds)
3 tablespoons frozen orange juice concentrate, defrosted
1½ teaspoons peeled and minced fresh ginger
¼ teaspoon ground ginger

1. Preheat the oven to 350°.
2. Cut the squash in half lengthwise. Scoop out and discard the seeds and place the halves, skin sides up, in a shallow pan. Pour in ¼ inch of water. Bake until tender, 1 to 1¼ hours.
3. Remove the pan from the oven and let the squash cool slightly. Scoop the flesh out of the skin, place it in a serving dish, and mash with the remaining ingredients. You may want to add more juice if it's too thick or too gingery for your palate. Serve immediately or cover and keep warm in a low oven.

Cal. **108** *Carb.* **28** *Protein* **2g** *Chol.* **0mg** *Fat* **.2g/2%**

"Earth is here
so kind, that
just tickle her
with a hoe and
she laughs with
a harvest."

Douglas Jerrold

Acorn Squash and Wild Rice

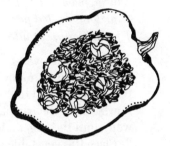
SERVES 4

2 acorn squash (about 1½ pounds each)
½ pound small Brussels sprouts
2 teaspoons canola oil
1 cup diced onion
1 teaspoon fennel seeds
1 teaspoon dried marjoram
¼ cup minced fresh sage
¼ cup fresh orange juice
2 teaspoons fresh lemon juice
⅛ teaspoon freshly ground pepper
2 cups cooked wild rice

1. Preheat the oven to 350°.

2. Cut each squash in half and remove the seeds and pulp. In a large baking dish, place the squash, cut side down, with about 1 inch of water. Bake until tender, about 45 minutes.

3. Pour about 2 inches of water into a large stockpot. Place a collapsible steamer in the pot, cover, and bring to a boil. Place the Brussels sprouts in the steamer, cover, and steam for 5 to 7 minutes, or until tender. Set aside.

4. Meanwhile, in a large skillet, heat the oil over low heat. Add the onion and sauté for 10 minutes, stirring frequently. Stir in the fennel, marjoram, sage, orange juice, lemon juice, and pepper, and simmer for 3 minutes. Stir in the cooked wild rice and the Brussels sprouts and heat through.

5. Spoon the wild rice and Brussels sprout mixture into the squash cavities. Serve immediately.

*Cal. **254** Carb. **55g** Protein **8g** Chol. **0mg***

*Fat **3g/10%***

Honey-Glazed Root Vegetables

SERVES 4

2 tablespoons honey
1 tablespoon fresh lemon juice
1 teaspoon curry powder
1 teaspoon ground cumin
1/2 teaspoon ground coriander
1 teaspoon fennel seeds
1/2 cup fennel fronds, chopped, scraped and trimmed
1 1/2 cups baby carrots
1 large peeled turnip, cut into 1/2-inch chunks (1 cup)
2 medium peeled parsnips, cut into 1/2-inch chunks (1 cup)
1 fennel bulb, cut into 1/2-inch chunks

1. Preheat the oven to 350°.
2. Combine the honey, lemon juice, curry, cumin, coriander, fennel seeds, and half the fennel fronds in a large mixing bowl. Stir in the carrot, turnip, parsnip, and fennel, and toss well, until the vegetables are well coated.
3. Place the vegetable mixture in a shallow baking dish. Place the dish in the oven and bake until golden brown, 45 minutes to 1 hour, tossing occasionally. Remove from the oven and toss with the remaining fennel fronds. Taste and adjust the seasonings—you may want an extra dash of lemon juice.

Cal. **110** *Carb.* **27g** *Protein* **2g** *Chol.* **0mg** *Fat* **.6g/5%**

Oven-Roasted Baby Vegetables

SERVES 6

2 pounds mixed baby vegetables, such as zucchini, yellow
  crookneck squash, or patty pan squash (trimmed), carrots,
  and turnips
2 teaspoons olive oil
Coarse salt
1 tablespoon finely chopped fresh rosemary
1/2 tablespoon balsamic vinegar
1 tablespoon freshly grated Parmesan

1. Preheat the oven to 500°.
2. Lightly spray or wipe a baking sheet with vegetable oil.
3. Choose vegetables roughly the same size or roast in batches on separate baking sheets. Place the vegetables on the baking sheet, brush with the oil, and sprinkle with salt and

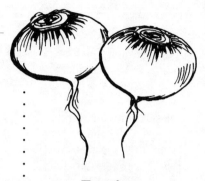

Turnips

Turnips often inspire reflexive nose-crinkling, which is undeserved. They're an excellent addition to casseroles and stews, delicious braised, baked, or mashed.

Buy turnips that are moderately sized, firm, and rather heavy, with only a few leaf scars around the purple crown ends. Avoid them if they are very large, wrinkly, or excessively blemished.

Small turnips are best—about 2 inches across; they appear at farmers' markets and fancy greengrocers from midsummer on.

★ GOOD FOR YOU ★

Both the roots and the greens of turnips are cancer fighters, with high levels of vitamin C, potassium, and calcium. All this, and only 28 calories a cup.

Parsnips

Hardy, humble, and homey, a true fall crop. And surely, one of the most underrated of all root vegetables.

Parsnips are traditionally added to wintry soups and stews. But they also are delicious grated raw into salads and cut into sticks to include with crudités. They can even be cooked, mashed, and added to savory sauces and gravies as a thickening agent. Cook parsnips simply: Sauté them in canola oil or a little butter; finish them off with a little salt and pepper.

Choose medium-size, smooth, firm parsnips. Very large ones probably have flavorless, woody cores, while wilted or flabby parsnips can be fibrous and pithy.

> ★ **GOOD FOR YOU** ★
>
> Parsnips are high in carbohydrates, fiber, and vitamin C and moderately high in calcium, potassium, and protein; ounce for ounce, they're well worth their 102 calories per cup.

rosemary. Place in the oven and roast until tender, 5 to 10 minutes, depending on the size of the vegetables.

4. Place the vegetables on a serving plate and sprinkle with balsamic vinegar and Parmesan.

*Cal. **49** Carb. **7g** Protein **2g** Chol. **1mg** Fat **2g/37%*** %

Parsnips & Marigolds

The marigolds bring fun and color to this dish, but these parsnips are as good without them.

SERVES 4

1½ cups fresh orange juice
1 teaspoon grated orange zest
1 tablespoon dried marigold
*   petals (optional)*
⅛ teaspoon ground cinnamon
1 teaspoon honey
1 pound parsnips, scraped and cut into
*   ⅛-inch slices*
1 tablespoon unsalted butter, at room temperature
1 tablespoon all-purpose flour
Salt and freshly ground pepper
2 tablespoons finely chopped fresh Italian parsley
½ cup halved and thinly sliced fresh orange

1. In a large saucepan, combine the orange juice, zest, marigold petals, cinnamon, and honey. Bring to a boil and add the parsnips. Reduce the heat to medium and simmer until the parsnips are just tender, 20 to 25 minutes. Remove the parsnips with a slotted spoon; place them in a heated serving dish and keep them warm.

2. In a small bowl, beat the butter and flour together with a wooden spoon to make a *beurre manié*.

3. Bring the liquid to a gentle boil. Add the *beurre manié* a little bit at a time, whisking until smooth, until the desired thickness is reached. Cook for 2 to 3 minutes. Season to taste with salt and pepper.

4. Pour the sauce over the parsnips and sprinkle with parsley. Garnish with orange slices. Serve immediately.

*Cal. **166** Carb. **33g** Protein **2g** Chol. **8mg** Fat **4g/19%***

Cheesy Broccoli

SERVES 4

1½ pounds broccoli , washed, and stems trimmed (3 cups)
⅓ cup low-fat ricotta
⅛ cup grated Parmesan
⅛ teaspoon freshly ground pepper
Freshly grated nutmeg

1. Pour about 2 inches of water into a large stockpot. Place a collapsible steamer in the pot, cover, and bring the water to a boil. Place the broccoli in the steamer, cover, and steam for 5 minutes, or until tender-crisp.
2. Meanwhile, in a large saucepan, combine the ricotta, Parmesan, and black pepper, and warm over low heat. Stir in the broccoli and mix well.
3. Transfer to a serving dish and garnish with freshly grated nutmeg. Serve immediately.

Cal. 105 Carb. 6g Protein 9g Chol. 18mg Fat 5g/44%

Curried Broccoli

SERVES 4

1½ pounds broccoli, washed, stems trimmed (3 cups)
1 cup fresh orange juice
3 tablespoons fresh lemon juice
1 teaspoon unsalted butter
1 tablespoon curry powder
Freshly ground pepper

1. Pour about 2 inches of water into a large stockpot. Place a collapsible steamer in the pot, cover, and bring the water to a boil. Place the broccoli florets in the steamer, cover, and steam for 5 minutes, or until tender-crisp.
2. Meanwhile, in a large skillet, bring the orange and lemon juices to a boil over medium-high heat, and reduce to ¼ cup. Reduce the heat to low; stir in the butter and curry powder. Stir in the cooked broccoli florets and heat through.
3. Transfer to a serving dish, and season with pepper to taste. Serve immediately.

Cal. 64 Carb. 12g Protein 3g Chol. 3mg Fat 2g/20%

> ### ★ GOOD FOR YOU ★
>
> Recent medical research shows that eating lots of brassica family plants such as broccoli may actually help prevent cancer. Broccoli offers large doses of vitamin A, more vitamin C than orange juice, vitamins E and K, and potassium. It's one of the top vegetable sources of calcium, an aid in preventing osteoporosis and lowering blood pressure. And it contains virtually no fat, but lots of fiber and protein. A large head of broccoli yields 4 cups, cut up, and only 40 calories per cup.
>
> Lightly steam or blanch fresh broccoli in hot water for the maximum impact of this nutritional powerhouse. It loses a lot of vitamin C if started in cold water. Better yet, eat it raw!

BROCCOLI

Consider it the "good guy" in the vegetable garden, with more nutrition than virtually any other commonly consumed vegetable in the United States. Its often-discarded leaves have even more vitamins A and C and minerals than its power-packed buds.

Broccoli comes in hues of purple, white, chartreuse, or dark green, the latter being the most common in the market. Sprouting broccoli is a pretty, leafy, less-compact variety, with multiple small white or purple florets. Romanesca has a small, compact head that looks like a cauliflower and is made up of tiny spirals that look like conch shells. Broccoli rabe, or rape, actually the flowering shoots of a turnip, has tiny yellow buds and a slightly acrid flavor, and can be cooked like regular broccoli, though it's generally not eaten raw. *Gai long,* or Chinese broccoli, is leafy with white flowers, has a mustardlike flavor, and is excellent raw with dips or in any broccoli recipe. Regardless of type, choose crisp-looking broccoli with good color and nonwoody stems. It's available year-round.

Lemon Broccoli

SERVES 4

1½ *pounds broccoli, washed, stems trimmed (3 cups)*
2 *tablespoons fresh lemon juice*
Zest of 2 lemons
Freshly ground pepper
2 *tablespoons Parmesan shards*

1. Preheat the broiler.
2. Pour about 2 inches of water into a large stockpot. Place a collapsible steamer in the pot, cover, and bring the water to a boil. Place the broccoli in the steamer, cover, and steam for 5 minutes, or until tender-crisp.
3. Transfer the cooked broccoli to a baking tray. Sprinkle with the lemon juice, lemon zest, pepper, and Parmesan shards. Place directly under the broiler; broil until the cheese is melted and slightly charred, about 1 minute.
4. Transfer to a serving dish and serve immediately.

Cal. **54** *Carb.* **5g** *Protein* **5g** *Chol.* **6mg** *Fat* **2g/25%**

Sherry Broccoli

SERVES 4

1½ *pounds fresh broccoli, washed, stems trimmed (3 cups)*
1 *teaspoon salt*
2 *teaspoons slivered garlic*
½ *cup dry sherry*
1 *teaspoon olive oil*
1 *tablespoon fresh lemon juice*
Freshly ground pepper
1 *tablespoon toasted sesame seeds*

1. Peel the broccoli stems and cut them into 3-inch-long pieces; cut the pieces lengthwise. Place the broccoli stems and florets in a large bowl and sprinkle with salt; add water to cover. Set aside for 30 minutes.
2. Preheat the oven to 500°.
3. Drain and rinse the broccoli. Place the broccoli in a shallow baking dish large enough to hold it in one layer. Scatter the garlic over the broccoli. Pour the sherry over the broccoli and drizzle it with olive oil.
4. Roast for 7 to 8 minutes, or until tender-crisp.
5. Season the broccoli with the lemon juice and pepper and garnish with the sesame seeds.

Cal. **67** *Carb.* **10g** *Protein* **4g** *Chol.* **0mg** *Fat* **3g/31%**

Fennel & Leek Gratin

SERVES 8

1 tablespoon olive oil
1 tablespoon slivered garlic
2 cups finely shredded leek
3 fennel bulbs, trimmed and sliced into
    $^{1}/_{2}$-inch juliennes (about 10 cups), fronds
    reserved if available
2 cups canned plum tomatoes, chopped, with
    about $^{1}/_{4}$ cup juice
$^{1}/_{2}$ cup chicken broth (see Basics)
2 tablespoons Pernod or Sambuca
1 cup bread crumbs, preferably made from day-old French bread
$^{3}/_{4}$ cup finely grated imported Parmesan
$^{1}/_{4}$ cup finely minced fresh Italian parsley
Salt and freshly ground pepper

1. Preheat the oven to 350°. In a medium skillet, heat the oil over medium-high heat. Add the garlic and leek and sauté for 3 to 5 minutes, until the leek softens. Remove from the heat and transfer to a large mixing bowl.
2. Add the julienned fennel, tomatoes and juice, broth, and Pernod to the bowl. If you have the fennel frond, mince it—you need about 2 tablespoons—and add it; stir to combine.
3. Lightly spray or wipe a 9 x 13-inch gratin dish with canola or vegetable oil. Add the vegetables, cover tightly with foil, and bake for 30 minutes.
4. Meanwhile, in a medium bowl, combine the bread crumbs, cheese, parsley, and salt and freshly ground pepper to taste.
5. Remove the foil and sprinkle the vegetables with the crumb mixture. Bake for 20 minutes, until the crumbs are nicely browned. Serve immediately.

Cal. 140 Carb. 20g Protein 7g Chol. 8mg Fat 4g/25%

Rosy Garlic-Sautéed Cabbage

SERVES 4

2 teaspoons canola oil
12 garlic cloves, cut in half lengthwise
$^{1}/_{2}$ cup plus 2 tablespoons chicken broth (see Basics)
1 head green cabbage (1 to 1$^{1}/_{2}$ pounds)
$^{1}/_{4}$ teaspoon paprika
Freshly ground pepper

Organic Foods

It's not a fad anymore but a reflection of the growing consumer demand for cleaner foods, grown without the use of artificial fertilizers and pesticides. Happily, availability and quality have been increasing in recent years—naturally grown fruits and vegetables now account for 65% of all organic products sold, while whole foods such as grains, flours, and oils account for another 25%. Meat, dairy products, and juices make up the rest. Still, organic produce accounts for less than 0.2% of the total food market.

   Price is the major obstacle to getting more organic food to more of the public. Many organic products are grown by small farmers entirely by hand; it's a labor-intensive and therefore expensive proposition. Only increased demand can bring costs down and change the equation.

1. In a large skillet, heat the oil over medium heat. Add the garlic and sauté for 3 minutes, stirring constantly. Stir in ½ cup of chicken broth; cover and cook for 15 minutes. Remove the cover and cook until all the liquid has evaporated, stirring constantly as the last few tablespoons of liquid evaporate.

2. Add the cabbage; sprinkle with the remaining chicken broth, paprika, and pepper to taste. Cook for 3 to 5 minutes, or until the cabbage is wilted, stirring constantly. Transfer to a serving bowl and serve immediately.

Cal. 62 Carb. 9g Protein 2g Chol. 0mg Fat 3g/22%

Baby Lima Beans and Garlic

SERVES 6

*1 pound dried baby lima beans, soaked
  overnight and drained*
4 cloves
2 shallots
2 dried jalapeño peppers
1 teaspoon dried thyme
1 head garlic, peeled
1 teaspoon salt
½ teaspoon olive oil
½ teaspoon freshly ground pepper
½ cup finely minced fresh Italian parsley
¼ cup finely minced fresh sage

1. Cover the beans with water by 2 inches in a large stockpot. Stick the cloves into the shallots and add them to the beans. Add the jalapeño pepper and thyme. Bring to a boil, lower the heat, partially cover, and simmer for 30 minutes.

2. Break three cloves of garlic off the head and reserve; tie the rest in a cheesecloth bag and add the bag to the beans. Simmer for 30 minutes. During the last 5 minutes, add the salt.

3. Finely mince the reserved garlic. Heat the olive oil in a small sauté pan and add the garlic. Sauté for 1½ to 2 minutes, until lightly colored.

4. When the beans are tender, remove the garlic bag, shallots, and jalapeño pepper, and discard. Drain and discard all but ½ cup of liquid from the beans. Place the beans and liquid in a serving dish, and add the sautéed garlic, the freshly ground pepper, the parsley, and the sage.

Cal. 287 Carb. 54g Protein 17g Chol. 0mg Fat 2g/5%

Brussels Sprout Leaves

SERVES 4

14 ounces fresh Brussels sprouts
1/2 cup chicken broth (see Basics)
4 sprigs fresh thyme
Freshly ground black pepper

1. Separate the individual Brussels sprout leaves from the cores.
2. In a large skillet, bring the chicken broth, thyme, and pepper to a simmer over low heat. Stir in the Brussels sprout leaves, cover, and simmer for 5 minutes, or until tender.
3. Transfer to a serving dish and serve immediately.

Cal. 47 Carb. 10g Protein 3g Chol. 0mg Fat .6g/9%

Caraway Cabbage

SERVES 4

1/2 cup cider vinegar
3 tablespoons sugar
1 tablespoon caraway seeds
6 cups coarsely chopped cabbage
1 cup julienned cooked beets

In a large sauté pan over medium heat, combine the vinegar, sugar, and caraway seeds. Stir until the sugar has completely dissolved. Add the cabbage and cook, stirring, over medium-high heat for 3 to 5 minutes, or until the cabbage is tender. Stir in the beets and heat through. Serve immediately.

Cal. 83 Carb. 20g Protein 2g Chol. 0mg Fat .4g/4%

Lima Beans with Prosciutto

SERVES 6

1 teaspoon olive oil
2 garlic cloves, finely minced
1 medium onion, finely minced
1/2 cup dry white wine
1/2 pound large plum tomatoes, coarsely
  chopped
1 tablespoon tomato paste
Salt and freshly ground pepper
1 package (10 ounces) frozen baby lima beans, thawed

Brussels Sprouts

Native to Belgium since the thirteenth century. Grown, harvested, and cooked properly, they have excellent flavor. The fresh, firm, tightly packed sprouts are even sweeter and more tender after being nipped by frost or placed in the freezer after harvesting—cold turns the starch into sugar. It also makes them a great source of vitamins A and C during cold-weather months.

Brussels sprouts also contain four substances that help prevent cancer. They are high in protein, carbohydrates, fiber, calcium, potassium, and phosphorus.

Seven to ten minutes should be all the cooking time needed for tender-crisp sprouts.

Ginger Cabbage

SERVES 4

2 tablespoons minced fresh
  ginger
2 medium zucchini, thinly
  sliced
1 green cabbage, shredded
1/4 cup minced fresh cilantro
2 teaspoons sesame oil
2 large garlic cloves, minced
1 tablespoon chicken broth
  (see Basics)
Zest of 2 limes
Juice of 2 limes
2 tablespoons toasted sesame
  seeds

1. Place the ginger, zucchini, cabbage, and cilantro in a large bowl, and toss very well.
2. In a large heavy skillet or a wok, heat the oil over medium-high heat. Add the garlic and sauté for 1 minute. Add the mixed vegetables and stir-fry for 3 to 4 minutes, until the cabbage just begins to wilt. Add the chicken broth as needed.
3. Remove from the heat and return to the bowl. Add the zest and juice, and sesame seeds, and toss well. Serve immediately.

Cal. **150** Carb. **24g**
Protein **7g** Chol. **0mg**
Fat **5g/28%**

1/4 cup prosciutto (about 1 ounce), trimmed and finely minced
1/2 tablespoon finely minced fresh rosemary
1 large zucchini (about 1/4 pound), julienned
1 tablespoon grated Parmesan

In a large nonstick skillet, heat the oil over medium heat. Sauté the garlic and onion for 4 to 5 minutes. Stir in the wine, tomato, tomato paste, and salt and freshly ground pepper to taste. Add the lima beans, prosciutto, and rosemary. Cover and simmer for 5 minutes. Add the zucchini; cover and simmer for 5 minutes. Remove from the heat. Place in a serving dish and sprinkle with the Parmesan. Serve immediately.

Cal. **107** Carb. **17g** Protein **6g** Chol. **5mg** Fat **2g/15%**

Lentils and Leeks

SERVES 8

2 cups dried green or brown lentils, rinsed and drained
1 onion
2 whole cloves
2 bay leaves
1 tablespoon chopped fresh marjoram
Salt
2 teaspoons olive oil
3 pounds leeks (about 6 medium), white parts and about 2
  inches of light green only, quartered lengthwise, washed,
  and finely chopped
3 garlic cloves, finely minced
4 large tomatoes (about 2 pounds), diced
Freshly ground pepper
1/4 cup chopped fresh parsley

1. Bring the lentils and 4 cups of water to a boil. Stick the cloves into the onion and add to the lentils with the bay leaves and marjoram. Cover and simmer for 15 minutes. Add salt to taste. Simmer 10 minutes more.
2. Heat the oil in a large skillet. Add the leek and garlic and sauté over medium heat, stirring, for about 5 minutes, or until the leek is softened. Add the tomatoes and freshly ground pepper. Cover and simmer for 5 minutes.
3. When the lentils are tender, discard the onion and the bay leaves. Drain the lentils and combine with the leeks. Simmer for 2 minutes to heat through. Stir in the parsley.

Cal. **242** Carb. **43g** Protein **16g** Chol. **0mg** Fat **2g/18%**

POTATOES are HOT!

My Favorite Hash Browns

SERVES 8

10 potatoes, unpeeled, cut in half horizontally
2 tablespoons olive oil
2 cups coarsely chopped red onion
12 garlic cloves, finely minced
2 tablespoons unsalted butter
2 tablespoons chopped fresh sage
1 cup chopped fresh Italian parsley
Salt and freshly ground pepper

1. In a large saucepan over medium heat, add the potatoes and cover with water; cook for 20 to 30 minutes, until just tender. Remove from the heat, drain, and cool. Cut the potatoes into ¼-inch-thick rounds, then into quarters.
2. In a large skillet over medium heat, heat 1 tablespoon of oil. Add the onion and garlic, cover, and sweat until translucent.
3. Add 1 tablespoon of butter, let it melt, then add the potatoes. Continue to fry and turn the potatoes as needed to keep them from burning, scraping the crisp bits from the bottom of the skillet. Add additional oil and butter only if absolutely necessary. When the potatoes begin to turn golden brown, stir in the sage and parsley, and season with salt and pepper to taste. Continue to sauté and scrape the potatoes from thee bottom of the pan until they are deep golden brown.

*Cal. **165** Carb. **25g** Protein **3g** Chol. **8mg** Fat **7g/35%***

"My idea of heaven is a great big baked potato and some-one to share it with."

Oprah Winfrey

366

They're the darlings of the culinary world, from the most elegant restaurants in New York and Paris to modest bistros and dinner tables. Potatoes haven't been talked about this much in centuries—except, perhaps, in Ireland.

Potatoes epitomize the rebirth of that cozy culinary style called "home cooking." They're healthful and very low in calories, a feature long obscured by the oil, butter, sour cream, and cheese routinely slathered on them.

Thanks to a broader range of new and old-fashioned varieties, potatoes taste better every year. There seems to be a potato for every purpose: marble-sized new potatoes that take only moments to cook; organically grown russets; buttery-flavored Yukon Golds; Yellow Finns, the European favorite; Irish Cobblers; and Maine's Kennebecs. The most addictive potatoes of all may be Centennial Russets from the San Luis Valley in Colorado. Different varieties have their own starch contents and textures. As they become available, we can learn the distinction between a merely good and a truly great potato, a subtlety that becomes increasingly important as cooking becomes simpler.

Juniper Berry Spuds

SERVES 4

1¼ pounds new potatoes, lightly scrubbed
20 juniper berries
6 cloves garlic, peeled
1 tablespoon extra-virgin olive oil
¼ teaspoon freshly ground sea salt
¼ teaspoon freshly ground pepper
1 tablespoon minced fresh tarragon
2 tablespoons minced fresh Italian parsley

1. Preheat the oven to 350°.
2. Place the potatoes on a baking sheet and bake for 45 minutes to 1 hour.
3. Meanwhile, place the juniper berries in the bowl of a mortar and crush them with a pestle. Add the garlic, one clove at a time, and crush thoroughly. Add the oil, salt, and pepper, and mix well to a paste consistency.
4. Transfer the baked potatoes to a serving bowl and toss with the ground mixture. Add the tarragon and parsley and toss again. Taste and adjust seasonings. Serve immediately or let cool to room temperature.

*Cal. **160** Carb. **29g** Protein **3g** Chol. **0mg** Fat **4g/20%***

Potato Purée with Basil Oil and Chives

SERVES 8

2 pounds Yukon Gold potatoes, peeled and cut into 2-inch chunks
⅔ cup skim milk
½ teaspoon salt
1½ tablespoons Basil Oil (page 289)
¼ cup finely chopped fresh chives
¼ cup chopped fresh basil
Freshly ground pepper

1. Cook the potatoes in a large pot of water until tender, about 20 to 25 minutes. Drain them well and place them in the bowl of an electric mixer.
2. Beat the potatoes slowly until partially mashed. Add the milk and salt and beat until smooth. Slowly drizzle in the basil oil. Add the chives, basil, and pepper to taste. Set aside and keep warm until ready to serve.

*Cal. **98** Carb. **16g** Protein **2g** Chol. **.6mg** Fat **3g/24%***

Sage Potato Salad

SERVES 4

1 pound new potatoes
5 tablespoons sherry vinegar
4 ounces haricots verts (about 1½ cups)
½ cup julienned yellow bell pepper
½ cup thinly sliced red onion
2 tablespoons extra-virgin olive oil
3 tablespoons finely minced fresh sage
1 tablespoon minced fresh Italian parsley
2 teaspoons whole mustard seeds
1 teaspoon Dijon mustard
Freshly ground pepper

1. Place the potatoes in a large stockpot and cover with water. Bring the water to a boil and cook until the potatoes are tender, 15 to 20 minutes. Drain and rinse under cold water. Coarsely chop the potatoes into 1-inch chunks; place in a large bowl and toss with 2 tablespoons of the vinegar.
2. In a saucepan, bring 4 inches of water to a boil. Add the *haricots verts* and blanch until tender-crisp and bright green, about 4 minutes. Drain, rinse under cold water, drain well again, and add to the potatoes.
3. Add the bell pepper and the onion to the potatoes and toss well.
4. In a small jar, place the remaining ingredients, including the remaining 3 tablespoons of vinegar; cover and shake well.
5. Pour the dressing over the vegetables, tossing well, and adjust the seasonings. Cover and refrigerate for at least 1 hour. Serve cold or at room temperature.

Cal. **188** *Carb.* **27g** *Protein* **4g** *Chol.* **0mg** *Fat* **8g/36%**

Warm Potato Salad

SERVES 8

1 pound red onions, thinly sliced
2 pounds new potatoes, quartered
1½ cups red wine vinegar
1 tablespoon olive oil
1 teaspoon Dijon mustard
⅔ cup finely chopped celery
¼ cup finely chopped fresh dill
Freshly ground pepper

Potato Seasonings
Basil
Caraway
Cardamom
Cayenne
Chives
Coriander
Dill
Fennel
Garlic
Lemon juice
Lovage
Marjoram
Mint
Mustard
Nutmeg
Olive oil
Onions
Oregano
Parsley
Pepper
Rosemary
Sage
Tarragon
Thyme

1. Preheat the oven to 500°. Lightly spray or wipe a baking sheet with vegetable oil.
2. Arrange the onion slices on the sheet and roast for 12 minutes; turn and roast for an additional 8 minutes. Coarsely chop the onion.
3. Meanwhile, boil the new potatoes for 15 minutes, or until just tender. Drain and transfer to a mixing bowl.
4. Bring the vinegar to a boil in a small saucepan and cook for 10 minutes, until reduced by half. Pour half the reduced vinegar over the warm potatoes. Return the remaining vinegar to the stove and add the olive oil; return to a boil and whisk in the mustard.
5. Pour the dressing over the potatoes and combine with the onions, celery, and dill. Season to taste with pepper. Serve warm.

*Cal. **135** Carb. **28g** Protein **3g** Chol. **0mg** Fat **2g/13%***

Kay's Lettuce and Potatoes

SERVES 8

3½ to 4 pounds baking potatoes, peeled and chopped
3 tablespoons canola oil
1 cup finely diced Canadian bacon, trimmed of fat
1 cup cider vinegar
½ cup skim milk
2 cups thinly sliced scallion
8 cups arugula, watercress, or romaine lettuce, washed and coarsely chopped
Salt and freshly ground pepper

1. Place the potatoes in a large pot and cover with water. Bring to a boil, then lower the heat to medium-high and cook for 40 to 45 minutes, or until the potatoes can be pierced with a fork.
2. Meanwhile, heat 1 tablespoon of the oil in a medium skillet over medium-high heat; add the bacon and sauté for 4 to 7 minutes. Heat the vinegar and remaining oil in a saucepan over medium heat for 3 minutes.
3. Drain the potatoes and beat with an electric mixer until smooth, slowly adding the milk until there are no lumps. Place the arugula on top of the potatoes but do not stir it in.
4. Working quickly, pour the bacon over the arugula, then the hot vinegar and oil. Slowly stir into the potatoes. Add salt and pepper to taste. Serve immediately.

*Cal. **228** Carb. **34g** Protein **10g** Chol. **10mg** Fat **7g/27%***

Lighter Potatoes

This Miller family favorite is a Dutch classic usually made with one pound of fried bacon and its drippings. We were all surprised at how fresh and terrific this tasted without the lure of crisp bacon.

Potatoes and Chanterelles

SERVES 4

1¼ pounds new potatoes, scrubbed lightly
¼ cup chicken broth (see Basics)
2 garlic cloves, minced
½ pound fresh chanterelles, cleaned
¼ cup minced fresh sage
2 tablespoons minced fresh chives
2 tablespoons minced fresh Italian parsley
1 tablespoon extra-virgin olive oil
¼ teaspoon freshly ground sea salt
¼ teaspoon freshly ground pepper

1. Preheat the oven to 350°. Place the potatoes on a baking sheet, and bake for 45 minutes to 1 hour, until tender.
2. In a small skillet over medium-low heat, warm the chicken broth. Add the garlic and sauté for 1 minute. Add the chanterelles and sauté for 2 minutes, tossing frequently. Add the sage, chives, and parsley; cover and cook for 2 to 3 minutes.
3. Transfer the baked potatoes to a serving bowl and toss with the oil, salt, and pepper. Add the chanterelles and toss again. Taste and adjust seasonings. Serve immediately.

*Cal. **166** Carb. **28g** Protein **5g** Chol. **0mg** Fat **4g/20%***

Scalloped Potatoes

SERVES 8

¾ pound yellow onions, thinly sliced
6 garlic cloves, peeled
1½ cups skim milk
2 pounds boiling potatoes, peeled and thinly sliced
3 tablespoons finely minced fresh sage
Salt and freshly ground pepper
1 tablespoon unsalted butter

1. Preheat the oven to 500°.
2. Lightly spray or wipe a baking sheet with vegetable oil. Arrange the onion slices and garlic cloves on the sheet. Lightly spray or brush the onion slices and garlic with oil. Roast for 12 to 14 minutes, turning once after 8 minutes. Be careful not to burn the garlic—it may cook more quickly than the onion; if it does, remove it. Remove the vegetables and roughly chop the garlic. Lower the oven to 425°.

Eat Your Potatoes

The average American eats 140 potatoes a year, 17 of which are in the form of potato chips. We may be missing the point. A serving of French fries equal in weight to one medium potato contains 480 calories. Boiled, that same potato has only 90. It also has a lot of fiber and more potassium than a banana. With its skin included, it delivers half the recommended daily allowance of vitamin C, the protein of half an egg, and virtually no fat.

★ **GOOD FOR YOU** ★

The fiber in potatoes helps lower cholesterol. Their high level of potassium can reduce blood pressure. Eat the skins—they contain a chemical that helps block early stages of cancer.

Roasted Potatoes

SERVES 6

*2 pounds firm and floury
  baking potatoes, peeled
  and quartered*
2 tablespoons all-purpose flour
¼ teaspoon cayenne
Coarse sea salt
Freshly ground pepper
3 tablespoons olive oil

1. Preheat the oven to 400°.
2. In a medium-size saucepan over medium heat, bring to a boil enough salted water to cover the potatoes. Add the potatoes and cook for 5 minutes, until just slightly tender. Drain and let cool slightly.
3. Place the flour, cayenne, and generous pinches of salt and pepper in a brown paper bag. Shake the potatoes in the mixture, a few at a time, until they are well coated.
4. Place the potatoes in a single layer in a roasting pan. Drizzle with 2 tablespoons oil, and shake the pan to coat evenly. Place the pan on the top rack of the oven and bake for at least 2 hours, or until very crisp, turning occasionally. Add the remaining oil only if necessary. Serve immediately.

*Cal. **159** Carb. **22g** Protein **3g** Chol. **0mg** Fat **7g/38%***

3. Spray or wipe an 8 x 8-inch baking dish with vegetable oil.
4. Gently heat the skim milk in a saucepan; do not boil.
5. Layer the potatoes in the baking dish, alternating with the onion, garlic, sage, and salt and pepper to taste. Pour the milk over the potatoes—it should cover the potatoes to a depth of about three-quarters. Dot the top layer with the butter. Bake for 1 hour to 1 hour 10 minutes, basting twice with the milk that collects around the edges of the dish. The potatoes should achieve a golden top crust. Serve immediately.

*Cal. **116** Carb. **22g** Protein **4g** Chol. **5mg** Fat **2g/13%***

Potatoes Anna

This classic, created in the Second Empire and dedicated to a woman of fashion, is usually loaded with goose fat or butter. We've trimmed the fat down—and they're still tasty.

SERVES 8

2 teaspoons olive oil
2 teaspoons unsalted butter
3 pounds new potatoes, peeled and thinly sliced
½ cup chopped fresh Italian parsley
¼ cup finely minced fresh rosemary
Salt and freshly ground pepper
¾ cup chicken broth

1. Preheat the oven to 425°.
2. Lightly spray or wipe a 10-inch cast-iron skillet with vegetable oil and place it in the oven; heat the skillet for 20 minutes. Carefully remove the skillet and place it on a burner over high heat. If necessary, wipe out any burned oil with a paper towel. Heat the olive oil and butter in the skillet and swirl in the pan to coat it evenly. Overlap the potato slices, beginning in the center of the pan and continuing up the sides. Working quickly, layer in all the potatoes, seasoning with parsley, rosemary, salt, and plenty of freshly ground pepper between the layers. Pour the chicken broth over the potatoes. Lightly spray or wipe the outside and bottom of a 9-inch cake pan with vegetable oil and place it on the potatoes. Weigh the cake pan with pie weights or beans.
3. Return the pan to the oven and bake for 1 hour, or until the potatoes are tender. Run a metal spatula around the edge of the skillet. Invert the potato cake onto a platter, cut it into eight wedges, and serve immediately.

*Cal. **173** Carb. **33g** Protein **4g** Chol. **3mg** Fat **3g/15%***

POTATOES APLENTY

Basics

Given the time and land needed for cultivation, potatoes yield more protein and calories than any other food crop. China grows 19% of the world's supply.

Potatoes can be thin- or thick-skinned, red, pink, white, yellow, pale tan, or dirt-brown in color. They range from as tiny as a pea to as large as a softball. Their textures vary with age and type, and many heirloom varieties are now being planted anew.

Sweet potatoes, not yams, are grown in the United States. There are two varieties: one with buff-colored skin and a dry, yellow interior, the other a red-skinned variety that's orange-fleshed and moist.

In the Market

Look for firm, heavy potatoes with no cuts or soft, watery spots. Avoid potatoes with green skins or sprouting eyes.

New potatoes, available January through September, are young, very small potatoes of any variety, harvested while the leaves of the plant are still green. They have flaky skins and a waxy texture, and keep their shape after boiling.

Main-crop potatoes are larger, mature potatoes with harder, thicker skins. Harvested after the foliage has withered, they're available August through November and "wintered over."

Sweet potatoes have one crop per year—August through October.

At Home

Remove potatoes from plastic or paper bags and store in a cool, dry place—never in the refrigerator or the starch will turn to sugar. The longer a potato is stored, the sweeter—less palatable—it will taste. Don't store with apples or onions or the potatoes will spoil.

In Cooking

Potatoes can be boiled, cooked in a microwave oven, steamed, fried, mashed, scalloped, baked, roasted in coals, or sautéed. They are good at breakfast, lunch, and dinner, or as a snack. They have fascinated home cooks and chefs for years with their versatile, delicate flavor, which provides an ideal palette for endless preparations. Americans love potatoes and consume an average of 140 each per year.

Sweet potatoes become sweeter as they cook. Cook them at 400° for 1¼ to 1½ hours, pricked well all over, and they'll be sweet as can be and won't need much—or any—butter.

★ GOOD FOR YOU ★

Potatoes are low in calories—about 145 per large potato. They're also high in carbohydrates and fiber, which aids in lowering cholesterol. Potato skins contain a chemical—chlorogenic acid—which acts as an anticarcinogen. An average potato contains more than half the recommended daily allowance of vitamin C, loads of potassium (which helps lower blood pressure), thiamine, and niacin.

Sweet potatoes have four times the U.S. recommended daily allowance of vitamin A, one of the leading nutrients in the prevention of cancer. The darker the sweet potato, the more beta-carotene it contains. They also have attention-getting amounts of potassium and calcium, vitamin C, iron, and fiber—the kind that soaks up cholesterol.

POTATO	TYPE	BEST FOR
Round Reds Often called "new"; medium-thick skin	Waxy	Boiling, roasting, mashing
Small Redskins	Low starch, waxy	Steaming, roasting
Russets, Burbank Thick-skinned	High starch, dry, mealy	Boiling, baking, mashing
Round Whites Russet Arcadia, Maine; dirty, dark, thick-skinned	Starchy, with high water content	Steaming, boiling
Idaho Bakers Thick-skinned (graded and sorted according to size)	Floury, fluffier	Baking
White Rose, Reds, Creamers Thin-skinned	Waxy	Boiling, roasting, steaming
Baby Yellow Finns	Medium starch	Steaming, roasting
Large Yellow Finns Yukon Golds Buttery flavor	Waxy	Steaming, roasting
Peruvian Blue	Medium starch	Roasting, mashing
Fingerling, Ruby Crescent	Low starch	Steaming, roasting
Sweet Potato	Floury	Baking, frying, mashing, puréeing

Acorn Squash with Lobster

SERVES 4

4 acorn squash
1 tablespoon unsalted butter
2 tablespoons all-purpose flour
1½ cups clam juice or fish stock
½ cup dry white wine
2 cups thinly sliced mushroom caps
4 sprigs fresh thyme
1 teaspoon minced fresh tarragon
2 tablespoons fresh lime juice
Zest of 1 lime, grated
Freshly ground pepper
2½ cups cooked wild rice
2 lobsters, boiled and cut into ½-inch chunks

1. Preheat the oven to 350°.

2. Cut off 1½ inches from the stem end of each squash, and remove the seeds and a layer of flesh about ¼ inch thick. Wash and dry the squash. Brush the outside of each shell with canola oil and place the shells, cut sides down, in a large baking dish with ½ inch cold water. Bake for 30 to 40 minutes, until cooked but still firm enough to hold their shape.

3. Meanwhile, in a stockpot, melt the butter over low heat and add the flour, whisking until it is blended. Add the clam juice, ½ cup at a time, whisking well to blend after each addition, then add the wine. Add the mushrooms, thyme, tarragon, lime juice, zest, and pepper to taste. Simmer for 15 minutes and taste, adjusting the seasoning if necessary. Stir in the rice and lobster pieces and heat through.

4. Spoon the hot mixture into each acorn squash and serve immediately.

Cal. **362** *Carb.* **75g** *Protein* **13g** *Chol.* **21mg**

Fat **4g/10%**

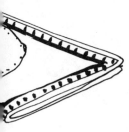
Orange and Leek Pilaf

SERVES 10

1 teaspoon olive oil

3/4 cup washed and shredded leeks

1 cup bulghur

2 cups chicken broth (see Basics)

1 cup finely chopped carrot

1/2 cup finely chopped celery, including some of the leaves

1/2 teaspoon dried marjoram

1 cup trimmed and halved pea pods

1 cup finely chopped scallion, white parts and some of the green

1/2 cup halved, cored, seeded, and finely chopped red bell pepper

1/2 cup halved fresh orange sections

1 cup finely minced fresh Italian parsley

Salt and freshly ground pepper

1 teaspoon finely minced fresh ginger

1/2 cup toasted and chopped pecans

1. In a Dutch oven, heat the oil over medium heat. Add the leek and sauté for 2 to 3 minutes, until softened. Stir in the bulghur thoroughly to coat with oil. While stirring, slowly add the chicken broth. Add the carrot, celery, and marjoram. Cover and simmer for 40 minutes, or until the bulghur is cooked. Remove and fluff with a fork.

2. Fold in the pea pods, scallion, and red pepper. Cover the Dutch oven and let stand to heat through, about 2 minutes.

3. Just before serving, stir in the oranges, parsley, salt and pepper to taste, grated ginger, and toasted pecans. Transfer the pilaf to a heated bowl and serve at once.

*Cal. **120** Carb. **18g** Protein **3g** Chol. **0mg** Fat **5g/33%***

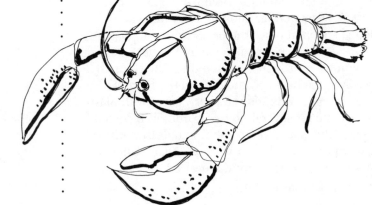

Pears with Poire William

SERVES 6

1 cup sugar
2 tablespoons slivered lemon zest
¼ cup plus 2 tablespoons fresh lemon juice
1 cinnamon stick (3 inches)
1 cup white wine
6 pears, preferably Comice
½ cup Poire William

1. In a saucepan large enough to hold all the pears, combine the sugar, 3 cups water, lemon zest, ¼ cup lemon juice, the cinnamon stick, and the wine. Bring to a boil, lower the heat slightly, and simmer gently for 5 to 8 minutes, until the sugar has dissolved.

2. Meanwhile, peel the pears with a potato peeler, leaving the stems intact. Work quickly and place each pear in a bowl of water with the remaining lemon juice.

3. Place the pears in the poaching liquid and increase the heat so that the pears boil gently. Turn the pears with a wooden spoon and poach for 4 minutes. Remove the pan from the heat and cool the pears in their liquid for 15 minutes.

4. With a slotted spoon, remove the pears from the poaching liquid and set aside. Return the saucepan to the heat and boil for 15 to 20 minutes over high heat to reduce the syrup to 2 cups. Remove from the heat and cool. Stir in the Poire William and transfer to a large bowl. Add the pears, cover with plastic wrap, and refrigerate for several hours, or until well cooled.

5. To serve, place the pears, stem sides up, in dessert dishes with the syrup. Sprinkle each pear with chocolate, Chocolate Leaves (opposite), or a sprig of mint, if desired.

*Cal. **235** Carb. **60g** Protein **.8g** Chol. **0mg** Fat **.7g/2%***

Party Pace

Every party has a beginning, a middle, and an end. The best are carefully orchestrated to build to a climax, not just wind down. To enhance the ebb and flow of an event:

• Serve each course in a different room.

• Have a timetable in your mind, a sense of how and when you want to proceed, but be the only one to know you're keeping the pace.

• Set cocktails for one hour only, then begin dinner promptly.

• When you can, begin indoors and serve dessert outdoors—or vice versa.

• Serve miniature desserts, finger food that allows guests to listen to entertainment or circulate once again.

• Invite guests to explore the grounds or the house at their leisure. Lead them or give them some guideposts.

"The Leaves of Life keep falling one by one."

Edward FitzGerald

Chocolate Leaves

YIELD: 12 LEAVES
8 ounces semisweet chocolate
12 fresh nontoxic leaves,
* such as ivy, herb rose, or*
* scented geranium, washed*
* and dried*

1. Melt the chocolate in a small bowl in a microwave oven set at high for 1 minute, stirring twice.
2. With a bread knife, spread the chocolate ¼ inch thick on the leaves.
3. Place the leaves, chocolate sides up, on a plate and refrigerate for 2 to 3 hours.
4. Carefully peel the leaves from the chocolate and discard them.

*Cal. **95** Carb. **11g** Protein **1g**
Chol. **0mg** Fat **7g/57%**
(analyzed per leaf)*

Pear Frozen Yogurt

SERVES 6
1 tablespoon fresh lemon juice
½ cup sugar
1¾ pounds ripe pears
1 cup Yogurt Cheese (see Basics)
⅓ cup plus 1 tablespoon skim milk
¼ cup Poire William or other pear brandy

1. In a large saucepan, combine the lemon juice, 1½ tablespoons water, and ¼ cup of sugar; keep warm over low heat. Peel, core, and coarsely chop the pears and add them to the saucepan. Bring to a boil, cover, and simmer for 15 minutes, or until the pears are very soft. Transfer the mixture to a blender or food processor and purée for 1 minute. Transfer the mixture to a mixing bowl and refrigerate until well chilled.
2. Add the yogurt cheese, milk, pear brandy, and the remaining sugar to the chilled purée. Whisk until thoroughly combined.
3. Transfer the mixture to an ice cream maker and freeze according to the manufacturer's instructions.

*Cal. **185** Carb. **37g** Protein **5g** Chol. **1mg** Fat **.4g/2%***

Pear Sorbet

SERVES 6
*4 cups fresh pears, preferably Comice, peeled, cored, and cut
  into chunks*
½ cup fresh lemon juice
½ cup sugar
3 tablespoons Poire William or other pear brandy

1. In a food processor, combine the pears, lemon juice, and sugar; process until smooth. Add the Poire William and refrigerate until very cold.
2. Pour the mixture into an ice cream maker and freeze according to the manufacturer's directions. Serve at once.

*Cal. **169** Carb. **39g** Protein **1g** Chol. **0mg** Fat **.5g/2%***

White Lightning Chili

SERVES 8

1 pound dried great Northern beans, soaked
  overnight in cold water and drained
1 teaspoon canola oil
1½ cups chopped onion
3 garlic cloves, minced
1 tablespoon minced jalapeño pepper
2 teaspoons dried oregano
Pinch cayenne
2 teaspoons ground cumin
Pinch ground cloves
Juice of 2 limes
8 cups chicken broth (see Basics)
½ cup chopped fresh cilantro
⅓ cup grated Parmesan

1. Heat the oil in a large soup pot over medium-high heat.
Add the onion and sauté until translucent. Stir in the garlic,
jalapeño pepper, oregano, cayenne, cumin, and cloves.
Sauté, stirring, for 3 minutes.
2. Add the beans, lime juice, broth, and cilantro, and bring
to a boil. Reduce the heat and simmer, covered, for 1½ to 2
hours, until the beans are tender. Adjust the seasoning.
3. Ladle into individual soup bowls and garnish with the cheese.

Cal. **256** *Carb.* **41g** *Protein* **16g** *Chol.* **3mg** *Fat* **3g/10%**

Pinto Bean Chili

SERVES 12

1 teaspoon canola oil
2 cups diced onion
6 garlic cloves, minced

Menu

Root Chips

White Lightning Chili

Pinto Bean Chili

Pennsylvania Dutch Slaw

*Mixed Greens with Sweet-
and-Sour Splash*

Party Pumpkin

Vanilla Frozen Yogurt

2 pounds lean boneless chuck, cut into ½-inch cubes
2 teaspoons paprika
2 teaspoons ground cumin
2 tablespoons minced fresh oregano
2 tablespoons chili powder
2 cans (28 ounces each) plum tomatoes, coarsely chopped, with their juice
1 cup coarsely chopped red bell pepper
1 cup coarsely chopped yellow bell pepper
1 cup coarsely chopped orange bell pepper
3 cups beef broth (see Basics)
3 cups pinto beans, soaked overnight and drained
½ cup minced fresh basil
½ cup minced fresh cilantro

1. In a large stockpot, heat the oil over low heat. Add the onion and garlic and sauté for 5 minutes. Add the meat and cook over medium heat, stirring constantly, until browned. Sprinkle with the paprika, cumin, oregano, and chili powder, and cook for 5 minutes, stirring frequently. Stir in the tomatoes, peppers, broth, and beans. Bring to a boil, partially cover, and simmer for 2½ hours, or until the beans are tender. **2.** Taste and adjust the seasoning; stir in the basil and cilantro.

Cal. 351 Carb. 42g Protein 29g Chol. 55mg Fat 8g/20%

Pennsylvania Dutch Slaw

SERVES 4

½ head green cabbage, thinly sliced
1 egg
3 tablespoons sugar
4 tablespoons cider vinegar
3 slices crisp bacon, cooked until crisp and crumbled, 2 tablespoons drippings reserved
Salt and freshly ground pepper

Crisp the cabbage in ice water for 1 hour. Drain thoroughly and place in a large bowl. In a small bowl, whisk the egg, sugar, and vinegar. Place the reserved drippings in a small saucepan and add the egg mixture to the pan. Place the pan over low heat, and stir constantly until thickened. While hot, pour over the cabbage, add the bacon, and toss well. Season to taste.

Cal. 160 Carb. 14g Protein 4g Chol. 54mg Fat 4g/48%

Ratatouille Meat Loaf

A meat loaf wrapped in a robe of eggplant slices. You'll be surprised how rich yet light this layered masterpiece tastes. This has become the favorite meat loaf at my house. The recipe may look forbidding, but it isn't really difficult.

SERVES 8

2 medium eggplants
1 tablespoon olive oil
Salt and freshly ground pepper
20 ounces fresh spinach
1 medium onion, chopped
2 garlic cloves, minced
12 ounces fresh mushrooms, minced
3/4 cup chicken broth (see Basics)
2 teaspoons ground cumin
1/2 cup minced fresh Italian parsley
1/2 cup minced fresh basil
1/4 cup minced fresh oregano
3/4 pound lean ground beef (sirloin or round)
3/4 pound lean ground turkey (99% fat free)
1 egg white
1/2 cup dry bread crumbs
2 tablespoons baking soda
2 tablespoons tomato paste
1 tablespoon balsamic vinegar
6 ripe Roma (plum) tomatoes, cut in wedges

1. Preheat the oven to 400°.
2. Trim the tops of the eggplants and cut the eggplants into

Menu

Spinach-Dill Dip with Pumpernickel

Arugula and Balsamic Vinaigrette

Ratatouille Meat Loaf

Potatoes Anna

Mascarpone Frozen Yogurt with Dark Chocolate Sauce

Roasted Garlic Pesto

YIELD: ⅔ CUP

2 tablespoons brandy
¼ cup currants
Cloves from 8 heads of garlic,
*   peeled*
¾ cup chicken broth
4 teaspoons extra-virgin
*   olive oil*

1. Preheat the oven to 400°.
2. In a small bowl, combine the brandy and currants and set aside.
3. Place the garlic cloves on a baking sheet with the chicken broth. Place the sheet on the top rack of the oven and roast for 30 minutes, or until tender and golden, stirring occasionally.
4. In a blender or food processor, combine the roasted garlic and remaining liquid, currants, and oil. Purée. Scrape into a covered container and refrigerate until needed.

Cal. 19 Carb. 2g

Protein .5g Chol. 0mg

Fat .6g/29%

(analyzed per teaspoon)

¼-inch lengthwise slices. Lightly brush each side with ½ teaspoon of the olive oil. Season with salt and pepper to taste. Place the seasoned slices on a baking sheet. Bake for 5 to 7 minutes, until tender and lightly brown. Remove from the oven and set aside to cool. Meanwhile, rinse the spinach leaves well and place them, with just the water clinging to the leaves, in a large saucepan. Cook over medium-low heat, covered, until just wilted, about 4 minutes. Rinse under cold water, drain thoroughly, and squeeze gently to remove as much moisture as possible. Set aside.

3. Heat the remaining oil in a heavy skillet over medium-high heat. Add the onion and sauté for 10 minutes. Add the garlic, mushrooms, and ¼ cup of the chicken broth, and continue to sauté until all the moisture has evaporated, about 10 to 15 minutes. Stir in the cumin, parsley, basil, and oregano. Remove from the heat and set aside.

4. In a large mixing bowl, thoroughly combine the ground beef and turkey, egg white, and bread crumbs. Stir in the onion mixture. Mix the remaining ½ cup chicken broth and baking soda together. Add to the meat-loaf mixture and combine thoroughly.

5. Combine the tomato paste and balsamic vinegar in a small bowl and set aside.

6. Assemble the meat loaf. Line the bottom and long sides of a 9 x 5 x 3-inch loaf pan with overlapping eggplant slices. Layer the remaining ingredients in the following order: one-third of the meat mixture, one-half of the spinach, one-third of the meat, one-half of the spinach, one-third of the meat. Brush the final layer with the tomato-paste mixture. Top with the tomatoes in two lengthwise rows.

7. Place the assembled meat loaf in oven. Reduce the heat to 350° and bake for 1½ hours, until crusty and brown on top. Remove from the oven and let rest for 10 minutes or more. Carefully invert onto a serving platter. This may be served hot or at room temperature.

Cal. 312 Carb. 33g Protein 28g Chol. 50mg Fat 10g/27%

Allspice

Dried spice berries, slightly larger than peppercorns. Taste of cinnamon, cloves, and nutmeg; hence, the name.

Available

Dried whole berries, ground, oil
Grind in pepper mill.

Origin

West Indies, Jamaica

Best Use

Excellent in cakes, cookies, pies, breads, steamed puddings, barbecue sauce, catsup, pickles, sausages, pâtés, corned beef, soups, meats, vegetables. Good whole for pickling and marinating and in stews, casseroles, sausages, curries.

Cardamom

Fragrant cinnamonlike seed; white, pale green to black. Lemony flavor, mellow aroma, a little bitter, but warming and agreeable. Seeds—not pods—hold the flavor. Green seeds are best; the paler the husk, the older the seed (younger is better).

Very expensive; a member of the ginger family.

Available

Dried whole seeds, ground

Origin

India; popular in Scandinavia

Best Use

Use in spice cakes and cookies, apple and pumpkin pies, sweet dishes like ice cream, curries; with winter squash, sweet potatoes, vegetables, pilafs.

Cayenne

Pungent, zestful spice made from a blend of small ripe chilies; the heat is from cayenne chile, a red pepper of the capsicum family, most often used dried.

Available

Dried whole pods, but more usually ground (sometimes labeled "ground red pepper")

Origin

East Indies, Africa

Best Use

Use for a little heat in any dish, especially with eggs and cheese.
Add by the pinch.

Chili Powder

Pungent commercial mix of darker dried ground chilies and cumin, oregano, and other herbs and spices.

Available

Whole, flaked, ground

Origin

Originally from Mexico, now grown far and wide

Best Use

Used in bean and meat stews and soups, with eggs and cheese.

Cinnamon

Sweet and woody spice bark of the cassia tree; sweet-hot flavor. Tender bark is peeled and draped in the sun. Fragrance comes from the oil of cinnamon.

Available

Dried whole sticks, ground, or powdered

Origin

Tropical regions

Best Use

Use in spice cakes, cookies, fruit and squash pies, custards, puddings, baked goods, chocolate; with fruit for sauce and conserves; with lamb, tagines, sausages, salads.

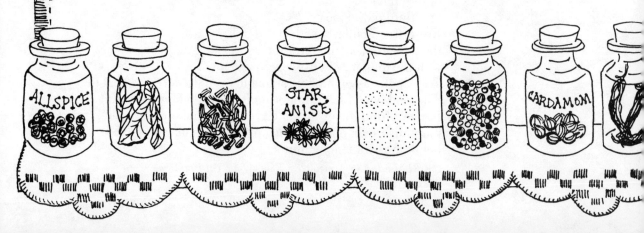

Cloves

Spice of winter holidays, pungent and sweet; dark, warm, rich flavor. Part of the myrtle family; buds are picked just before opening and dried in the sun.

Available
Dried whole, ground
Origin
Spice Islands, Moluccas, Zanzibar, West Indies
Best Use
Goes with sweet-savory foods, mulled wines, soups, meat dishes, apples, ham, mincemeat, baked onion, sweet potatoes, winter squash, carrots, pâtés. Ground added to spice cakes, cookies, quick breads, fruit pies, sauces.

Coriander

Small, slightly oval, nutty-tasting seeds are called coriander and come from the cilantro plant. Agreeably soapy, slightly burnt orange flavor.

Available
Dried whole and ground
Origin
China, Middle East, Egypt

Best Use
Use whole seeds for pickles and ground with rice, dried beans, fish, shellfish, poultry, vegetables, salsas, salads, curry, stuffing, sausage, roast pork, lamb, sweet dishes and cakes.

Cumin

Small, hot bitter seed; strong, heavy taste; sharp, warm, and pungent.

Available
Dried whole seeds and ground
Origin
Casmir, Pakistan, Iran (grows in hot climates)
Best Use
Used in Indian, African, Middle Eastern, and Mexican dishes; essential spice for curry and chili powder mixtures. Good with curried vegetables, beans, fish, lamb, and poultry, pickles, as well as with stews, cheese, sausages, chutney, and yogurt dip.

Filé Powder

Herb ground from dried sassafras leaves, tasting like sassafras or root beer.

Available
Dried ground
Origin
Native to North America
Best Use
Essential for gumbo; added after the dish is removed from the heat but still hot, a thickening agent.

Juniper

Fruit of a small evergreen shrub; strong spice berries the size of small blueberries. Purple when fresh, dark brown when dried. Crush to release flavor—a spicy overtone of pine. Tastes like gin—most are used to make it.

Available
Dried whole berries
Origin
Southern Europe
Best Use
Use in marinades for fish, game, poultry, pork, and beef; in sauerkraut and choucroute; with apple, jelly, roasts, sausages, cabbages, elk, garlic, rosemary, Beca, brandy

Mace

Lacy outer covering of nutmeg, seed of a tropical evergreen tree. Gentle flavor is similar, but slightly milder than nutmeg.

Available

Dried blades and ground coarsely or fine

Origin

Spice Islands
Orange-red: Indonesia
Orange-yellow: Grenada

Best Use

Good in spice cakes and cookies, custards, soufflés, fruit desserts—especially plums, peaches, and apples. Also with carrots, broccoli, brussels sprouts, chutney, fish, and potatoes

Nutmeg

Sweet, nutty spice seed of the nutmeg tree—the size of an olive. Crisp, dry quality; used in rich foods.

Available

Whole seeds and ground. Ground quickly loses its flavor; buy whole and grate as needed with a nutmeg grinder.

Origin

Philippines, Moluccas, West Indies

Best Use

Best in cream sauces and soups, with vegetables (especially dark green), beans, broccoli, carrots, cauliflower, spinach, Brussels sprouts, onions; with cheeses, oysters, soups; but especially for cakes, cookies, pies (pumpkin), pastries, custard, and of course, eggnog.

Paprika

Ground spice of dried red sweet capsicum peppers. Rich, bright red and lightly pungent, with a warm, sweet aroma. Loses its flavor quickly, becoming brown and stale.

Available

Dried ground. Hungarian paprika is most flavorful, available sweet or hot.

Origin

Hungary, Mexico, Spain, Morocco

Best Use

Good in cooked salads—especially potato and egg; salad dressings, dips; with fish, shellfish, poultry; in rices and casseroles. Essential in goulash and paprikash, Hungarian foods.

Saffron

Fragrant spice made from the dried stigmas of crocus. The world's most expensive spice because it is hand-picked and 250,000 are needed to yield one pound. A little saffron goes a long way, while too much lends an unpleasant medicinal flavor. Threads are a deep, rich red, the deeper the color the better.

Available

Dried whole stigmas and ground. Threads ground in a mortar or dried whole threads are of better quality.

Origin

Morocco is the main producer; also Turkey and Spain (La Mancha)

Best Use

Use in paella, bouillabaisse, risotto, tomato and cream soups, sauces, couscous; with seafood; in Swedish cakes and breads; with fish, poultry, beef; in liquor.

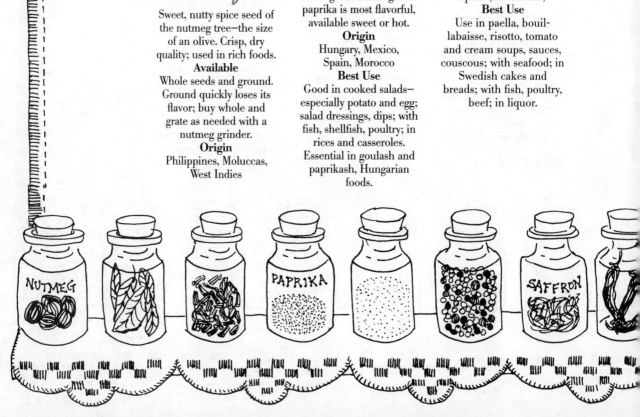

NUTMEG · PAPRIKA · SAFFRON

Star Anise

Eight-pointed stars from a tree of the magnolia family; licorice-flavored and slightly sweet.
Available
Whole, ground
Origin
China, Vietnam
Best Use
Use in cookies, breads, cakes, syrups, jams, soup, stir-frys, stew, Chinese five-spice powder (pagra, cassia, cinnamon, cloves, fennel seeds), with poultry, pork, fish, scallops, leeks, pumpkin; the flavoring for pastis and anisette.

Turmeric

Brilliant yellow spice with warm, mild aroma, fresh taste. A member of the ginger family.
Available
Dried ground
Origin
India is the main producer; also southern Asia
Best Use
Essential to mustard, curry powder, pickles, and relishes; used in chutneys, bean and lentil dishes; with poultry, fish, shellfish, potatoes; also used in moderation in rice dishes for its yellow color.

SPICE TIP

Juniper berries, cloves, nutmeg, and other spices lose some of their pungency after a long time in the package.

To revive them, roast whole in a preheated 350° oven for a few minutes. When their aromas become noticeable, remove them from the oven and use according to your recipe.

You can also dry-sauté them in a skillet to release their flavor or grind them and then moisten them with beef or chicken broth or wine, making a paste. Whenever possible, buy whole spices and grind them yourself. The flavors will be much more rewarding.

TURMERIC

Cajun Meat Loaf & Cool Tomato Salsa

The warm, deep flavors of this meat loaf, with its Cajun
spices, are balanced by Cool Tomato Salsa.

SERVES 8

1 tablespoon canola oil
2 medium yellow onions, chopped
4 garlic cloves, minced
3 tablespoons minced jalapeño pepper
2 tablespoons minced sun-dried tomatoes
1/4 cup drained capers
1/3 cup tomato paste
3 teaspoons chili powder
1 teaspoon ground cumin
1/2 teaspoon cayenne
1/2 pound lean ground beef
1 1/2 pounds lean ground turkey (99% fat free)
1/2 cup bread crumbs
1/2 cup skim milk
Cool Tomato Salsa (page 238)

1. Preheat the oven to 350°.
2. Heat the oil in a skillet over medium-low heat. Add the
onion and garlic and sauté until soft, about 10 minutes.
Transfer to a large mixing bowl.
3. Add the jalapeño pepper, tomatoes, capers, tomato paste,
chili powder, cumin, and cayenne to the onion mixture, and
mix thoroughly. Add the ground beef and turkey, bread
crumbs, and skim milk, and combine thoroughly.
4. Place the meat loaf in a 9 x 4½ x 2½-inch bread pan.
Place in the oven and bake for 1½ hours, until crusty-brown
on top. Remove from the oven and allow to rest for 10 minutes. Serve with salsa.

*Cal. **246** Carb. **12g** Protein **32g** Chol. **83mg** Fat **8g/28%***

Menu

Herbed Potato Skins

*Cajun Meat Loaf and
Cool Tomato Salsa*

Flageolets with Garlic

Pear Compote

Herbed Potato Skins

SERVES 4

6 large baking potatoes
½ cup finely minced herbs, such as chives, rosemary, oregano,
*   savory, alone or in combination*
Ground sea salt and freshly ground pepper
Malt vinegar
Lemon wedges

1. Preheat the oven to 425°.
2. Remove the skins from the potatoes in large strips with a sharp knife or a vegetable peeler, including some potato with each sliced skin.
3. Soak the skins in ice water for 15 minutes. Remove and pat very dry.
4. Spread the pieces of skin out on a large baking sheet. Spray them with a fine mist of olive oil, toss, and spray again. Bake the skins for 10 minutes, and lightly spray both sides again. Bake for another 5 minutes, then sprinkle with the herbs. Return the skins to the oven and bake for 5 minutes longer. The skins are done when lightly browned and crisp. Salt and pepper and serve immediately with malt vinegar or lemon wedges on the side.

*Cal. **170** Carb. **38g** Protein **4g** Chol. **0mg** Fat **1g/5%***

Pear Compote

Fresh pears, with the get-up-and-go of ginger.

YIELD: 4 CUPS

4 cups fresh pears, peeled, cored, and cut into large chunks
¼ cup sugar
1 tablespoon fresh lemon juice
2 tablespoons minced lemon zest
½ teaspoon finely grated fresh ginger

In a large heavy saucepan, combine the pears, sugar, lemon juice, and lemon zest over medium heat. Cook, stirring constantly, for 2 minutes. Simmer gently for 8 more minutes, stirring occasionally, until the fruit begins to soften. Stir in the ginger and cook a moment longer. Serve immediately or store, covered with plastic wrap, in the refrigerator.

*Cal. **37** Carb. **10g** Protein **.2g** Chol. **0mg** Fat **.2g/4%***
(analyzed per ¼ cup)

Perfectly Moist Wild Goose

SERVES 6

1 wild goose (about 3½ pounds)
6 sprigs fresh sage
12 juniper berries
2 oranges, quartered
Freshly ground pepper
10 garlic cloves, peeled
¼ cup red wine

1. Preheat the oven to 375°.
2. Wash the goose well and pat dry. Place four sprigs of sage, the juniper berries, and the oranges in the cavity. Grind the fresh pepper over the goose breast and lay the remaining two sprigs of sage on it, along with the garlic cloves.
3. Place the goose in a large plastic self-basting cooking bag, add the red wine, tie tightly, and place on a baking sheet. Bake for 1¾ hours, until the goose is tender. Carve and serve immediately.

Cal. **268** *Carb.* **10g** *Protein* **29g** *Chol.* **92mg** *Fat* **12g/42%**

Apple and Hazelnut Wild Rice

SERVES 6

1 cup wild rice, rinsed and drained
¼ cup coarsely chopped hazelnuts
1 teaspoon canola oil
2 scallions, finely sliced
1 rib celery, finely sliced
½ medium green bell pepper, seeded and finely diced
½ cup coarsely chopped mushrooms
1 Jonathan apple, cored and diced
¼ cup finely minced sage
2 tablespoons chopped fresh thyme
Salt and pepper
½ cup chicken broth (see Basics)

1. Preheat the oven to 325°.
2. In a medium-size saucepan, place the wild rice and 3 cups of water and bring to a boil. Reduce the heat and simmer for

The Canada Goose

The honking comes first, almost every day from early September through October. Looking up into the sky, we spot hundreds of black-headed Canadian geese flying in V formation. Many are on the long migratory route south, while others are merely making the daily flight from nighttime retreat to daytime feeding ground.

Menu

Perfectly Moist Wild Goose

*Apple and
Hazelnut Wild Rice*

Broccoli-Spinach Purée

Leek and Potato Purée

Parsnip and Apple Purée

*Watercress with
Sliced Mixed Apples
and Apple Spray*

Mom's Apple Crisp

40 minutes, or until the rice is tender but has not burst.

3. Toast the hazelnuts in the oven for about 8 minutes, until lightly golden. Set aside

4. In a large sauté pan, heat the oil over medium heat. Add the scallion, celery, green pepper, mushrooms, apple, sage, thyme, and salt and pepper to taste. Sauté for 6 to 8 minutes, or until tender. Add the cooked wild rice and chicken broth, and heat through, 2 to 3 minutes, or until the chicken broth is absorbed. Remove from the heat and garnish with the chopped hazelnuts. Serve immediately.

*Cal. **170** Carb. **27g** Protein **5g** Chol. **0mg** Fat **5g/27%***

Broccoli-Spinach Purée

SERVES 6

1 teaspoon olive oil

2 ribs celery, diced

1 onion, diced

1 medium baking potato (about $^1\!/_2$ pound), peeled and diced

1$^1\!/_2$ cups chicken broth (see Basics)

*1 bunch broccoli (about 1$^1\!/_4$ pounds), florets cut off, stem
    peeled and chopped*

3 cups fresh spinach leaves, trimmed and washed

$^1\!/_4$ teaspoon ground coriander

Salt and freshly ground pepper

1 tablespoon finely grated lemon zest

1. In a large saucepan, heat the olive oil over low heat. Add the celery and onion and sauté for 3 to 5 minutes, until softened.

2. Add the potato and chicken broth and bring to a boil. Add the broccoli, reserving 1 cup of florets. Reduce the heat, cover, and simmer for 30 minutes.

3. Meanwhile, bring a small saucepan of water to a boil, and add the reserved florets. Simmer for 2 minutes; drain, rinse under cold water, and set aside.

4. Add the spinach to the cooking broccoli and cook for 1 minute; drain the vegetables, reserving the liquid.

5. Transfer the mixture to a food processor and purée. Add enough reserved liquid to achieve a saucelike consistency. Season with the coriander, salt, and pepper. Transfer to an ovenproof dish and fold in the lemon zest; garnish with the reserved broccoli florets.

*Cal. **67** Carb. **12g** Protein **4g** Chol. **2mg** Fat **1g/16%***

*"The goose
and the gander
begin to meander,
The matter is
plain — they are
dancing for
rain."*

Anon.

Crab on a Red Sea

SERVES 4

4 lasagna noodles, uncooked
2 cups cooked fresh crabmeat, picked
  over
2 teaspoons fresh lemon juice
¼ cup minced fresh basil
¼ cup minced fresh dill
½ cup minced fresh Italian parsley
Freshly ground sea salt
Freshly ground pepper
2 cups Red Pepper Aïoli (page 218)

1. Bring a large pot of water to a boil. Add the noodles
and cook until tender but still firm. Drain and set aside.
2. In a medium-size mixing bowl, combine the crabmeat,
lemon juice, basil, dill, parsley, and salt and pepper to
taste. Mix well.
3. Lay the noodles out on a flat surface and cover each with
½ cup of the crab filling. Roll up the noodles to form fairly
tight rolls. Set on a platter, seam sides down; cover and
refrigerate for 15 to 30 minutes, not longer, to firm the rolls.
4. Remove the rolls from the refrigerator, and with a sharp
knife, cut each in half. Spread ¼ cup of the Roasted Red Pepper Aïoli in the center of each of four dinner plates in a circle
5 to 6 inches in diameter. Place one crab roll, ruffled side up,
in the center of each plate. Place a second roll directly atop
the first. Serve immediately with extra aïoli on the side.

Cal. **328** *Carb.* **33g** *Protein* **19g** *Chol.* **68mg** *Fat* **12g/35%** 🔘

Braised Lamb Shanks with Garlic

SERVES 4

4 lamb shanks (about ¾ pound each)
4 garlic cloves, slivered
Freshly ground pepper
24 garlic cloves, peeled
4 tablespoons coarsely chopped fresh rosemary
3½ cups beef broth (see Basics)
1 tablespoon potato starch

Menu

Crab on a Red Sea

Braised Lamb Shanks
with Garlic

Garlic Potatoes

Rum-Plum
Frozen Yogurt

Rum-Plum Frozen Yogurt

SERVES 4

6 fresh red plums, pitted,
* skinned, and coarsely*
* chopped (1 cup)*
½ cup sugar
1¾ cups nonfat plain yogurt
1½ teaspoons dark rum

1. Place the plums in a food processor, and purée for 1 minute. Add the sugar and purée for 30 seconds more.
2. Place the plum mixture in a medium-size mixing bowl. Fold in the yogurt and rum and mix well. Chill for 1 hour.
3. Transfer the mixture to an ice cream maker and freeze according to the manufacturer's directions.

Cal. **176** *Carb.* **37g**
Protein **4g** *Chol.* **0mg**
Fat **.8g/4%**

1. Preheat the oven to 450°.
2. Make slits in the lamb shanks and place the slivered garlic in them. Sprinkle the shanks generously with ground pepper and rosemary. Place the shanks in a shallow roasting pan. Add the whole garlic cloves and roast, uncovered, for 20 minutes, or until the shanks are beginning to brown. Add 1¾ cups broth to the roasting pan, cover, and bake for 1 hour, basting at least twice.
3. Add the remaining broth. Baste and cook for ½ hour, covered. Remove the cover and cook for another ½ hour, basting every 10 minutes. Remove from the oven.
4. Place the shanks on a platter, cover, and place in the turned-off oven to keep warm. Scrape the collected juices into a shallow saucepan and place over medium heat. Reduce the juices by half; sprinkle in the potato starch, whisking constantly—do not allow the mixture to boil. Pass the sauce at the table.

Cal. **267** *Carb.* **13g** *Protein* **33g** *Chol.* **105mg** *Fat* **9g/31%**

Chunky Potato, Carrot, & Garlic Purée

SERVES 4

2 large potatoes, peeled and cut into chunks
4 medium carrots, peeled and sliced
6 garlic cloves, peeled and chopped
1 tablespoon unsalted butter
Salt and freshly ground pepper
½ cup finely minced fresh chives

1. In a large saucepan, combine the potatoes, carrots, and garlic. Cover with water, bring to a boil, and boil until the potatoes and carrots are tender but still firm. Drain well.
2. Place in a food processor and purée, leaving some visible chunks of carrots. Return the purée to the saucepan to keep warm. Add the butter and salt and pepper to taste. Serve immediately, garnished with the chives.
NOTE: The vegetables can also be mashed in a large bowl if desired.

Cal. **247** *Carb.* **50g** *Protein* **6g** *Chol.* **8mg** *Fat* **4g/12%**

Herbed Eggplant Slices

SERVES 4

1 clove garlic, minced
1 tablespoon fresh minced oregano
¼ cup fresh basil leaves
½ cup fresh minced Italian parsley
1 eggplant (1½ pounds)
Salt and freshly ground pepper

1. Preheat the oven to 400°. Lightly spray or wipe a baking sheet with vegetable oil. Set aside.
2. In a small bowl, combine the garlic, oregano, basil leaves, and parsley. Mix well. Set aside.
3. Slice the eggplant into twelve ¼-inch rounds. Generously season each side with salt and pepper. Place on the prepared baking sheet and set on the top rack in the oven.
4. Bake each side until tender and lightly browned, about 5 to 7 minutes per side. Brush each eggplant slice with the herbs and place under the broiler 30 seconds. Transfer to a serving plate and serve immediately.

*Cal. **51** Carb. **10g** Protein **2g** Chol. **0mg** Fat **1g/21%***

Leek and Potato Purée

SERVES 6

1½ pounds baking potatoes (about 3), peeled and cut into eighths
½ cup low-fat buttermilk
½ teaspoon baking soda
4 garlic cloves, minced
2 teaspoons olive oil
3 pounds leeks (about 6 medium), quartered lengthwise, washed, and chopped
Salt and white pepper

1. In a medium saucepan, cover the potatoes with cold water. Bring to a boil and cook for 30 to 40 minutes, or until tender. Drain and pass through a food mill fitted with a medium screen, or mash by hand, or with an electric beater. Add the buttermilk and baking soda and stir to combine.
2. In a large saucepan, heat the oil. Add the garlic and leeks, cover, and sweat for 10 to 12 minutes, until the leeks are softened; stir occasionally.
3. Place the leeks in a food processor. Add ½ cup of the

Paula Red
Bright red with yellow; mildly tart and sweet.

Wealthy
Large, red and yellow; sweet; crisp and juicy.

Winesap
Small, deep red; spicy, sweet-tart; crisp and very juicy.

Wolf River
Red with yellow blush; sweet and crisp.

York Imperial
Deep red striped with green; tart honey flavor.

puréed potatoes. Purée. Fold the leeks into the remaining potatoes. Season with salt and white pepper to taste.

*Cal. **153** Carb. **31g** Protein **4g** Chol. **1mg** Fat **2g/12%***

Mom's Apple Crisp

SERVES 9

7 Granny Smith apples, peeled, cored, and quartered
6 ounces frozen apple juice concentrate, defrosted
¼ cup light brown sugar
1 teaspoon ground cinnamon
1½ cups Vanilla Granola (page 14)
1 tablespoon unsalted butter

1. Spray or wipe a saucepan lightly with vegetable oil. Add the apples, apple juice, sugar, and cinnamon. Cook over high heat until the apples are tender and the juice is reduced and caramelized, about 15 minutes.
2. Lightly spray or wipe a 6 x 8-inch baking dish with vegetable oil. Place the apples in the bottom of the dish. Reserve the juice.
3. Preheat the oven to 350°.
4. Cover the apples with granola, pour over the reserved juice, and dot with butter. Bake for 20 to 30 minutes, or until golden.
5. Serve warm; top each serving with ¼ cup of Vanilla Frozen Yogurt (page 275), if desired.

*Cal. **269** Carb. **51g** Protein **5g** Chol. **14mg** Fat **6g/19%***

Pheasant with Cèpes and Chestnuts

SERVES 6

3/4 cup Armagnac
1 cup dried tart cherries
1 teaspoon canola oil
3 pheasants (2 1/4 pounds each), rinsed and patted dry
3 onions, finely chopped
1/4 cup finely diced Canadian bacon, trimmed of fat
3 cups chicken broth (see Basics)
3 cups dry white wine
Bouquet garni: 2 bay leaves, 2 parsley sprigs, and 2 thyme
  sprigs, tied together
Salt and freshly ground pepper
1/2 pound chestnuts, peeled
2 pounds cèpes or shiitake mushrooms, wiped clean and sliced

1. Place 1/2 cup of the Armagnac in a small bowl. Add the dried cherries and macerate overnight.

2. Heat the oil in a large stockpot with a lid. Add the pheasants and brown on all sides for about 7 minutes. Remove the birds and add the onion and Canadian bacon. Sauté for 5 minutes until the onion is softened. Return the pheasants to the pot. Strain the Armagnac from the cherries into the pot and add the chicken broth, white wine, *bouquet garni*, and salt and pepper to taste. Bring to a boil, then reduce the heat; cover and simmer for 45 minutes. Skim off any fat from the surface of the liquid while the pheasants are cooking. Remove the pheasants and purée the liquid in a blender. You should have about 3 1/2 cups of liquid.

3. Return the pheasants and the liquid to the stockpot. Add the cherries, the remaining 1/4 cup Armagnac, the chestnuts, and the cèpes to the stockpot. Simmer for 15 minutes more. Carve the pheasants and divide the sauce among the plates, or serve it in a bowl on the side.

*Cal. **532** Carb. **66g** Protein **43g** Chol. **113mg** Fat **12g/16%***

Mustard-Dill Carrots

SERVES 4

1 1/4 pounds carrots, peeled
  and cut into 2-inch pieces
1 cup fresh orange juice
3 teaspoons dried mustard
1/2 teaspoon mustard seeds
1 tablespoon dry vermouth
1 tablespoon minced fresh
  dill

1. Place the carrots in a pot with water to cover, and bring to a boil. Cover and gently boil for 7 to 10 minutes, or until the carrots are tender. Drain.

2. Meanwhile, in a wide sauté pan, bring the orange juice, mustard, and mustard seeds to a boil and reduce to 1/4 cup. Reduce the heat to low and stir in the vermouth and dill; stir well to blend. Add the cooked carrots and toss to coat evenly. Serve immediately.

*Cal. **102** Carb. **22g***
*Protein **3g** Chol. **0mg***
*Fat **1g/10%***

IT'S ALL IN THE GAME

Looking for leaner protein? Find a great local source for game.

Farm-raised game is naturally lean and tender, high in protein, iron, and vitamin B$_{12}$, and low in the bad stuff—calories, fat, cholesterol, and sodium. The flavor is delicate and mellow, not gamy—just exactly right.

Be sure you know the pedigree of the game you're buying. A coop-raised pheasant, for example, is tender, but may also be flavorless and fatty from its lazy ways. "Walking around" pheasants raised under nets and fed a diet of nuts and berries will be tender, tasty, and lean. (Their wild brethren are a bit leaner, with a slightly wild flavor and almost no fat.).

Cooking Game

• Gamy flavor results in part from the aging process. Know your source and let your taste preferences be known.
• Lean meats don't freeze well, so try to use game while it's fresh.
• Marinades can tone down gamy flavors and tenderize flesh.
• Robust herbs and spices— rosemary, sage, thyme, winter savory, and garlic—complement game best.
• Game is low in fat—5 to 7% compared to 30 to 45% for beef. Baste with stock, fruit juices, wine, or spirits, and barding to add moisture will not be necessary.

Poultry w/skin	Calories*	Fat g.*	Cholesterol mg.*	Protein g.*
Chicken	230	17.9	83	18.2
Quail	168	6.8	56	25.0
Pheasant	151	5.2	49	24.3
Guinea Hen	156	6.4	53	23.1
Meat				
Beef *bottom round*	214	9.76	92	31.0
Beef *ground*	265	18.4	85	24.0
Pork *shoulder*	219	10.6	101	29.0
Rabbit	143	8.2	69	17.6
Venison	159	3.3	66	25.0

Game Nutritional Analysis from U.S. Department of Agriculture and ESHA research.　　*3.6-ounce serving*

Chicken with Figs

SERVES 4

One chicken (3½ pounds), cut into serving-size pieces
¾ teaspoon toasted cumin seeds
1¼ teaspoons coriander seeds
¾ teaspoons black peppercorns
½ teaspoon salt
1 cup halved and thinly sliced onion
20 whole garlic cloves, peeled
1 bay leaf
18 fresh Black Mission figs
1 cup ruby port
Zest of 1 lemon
½ cup coarsely chopped fresh Italian parsley

1. Preheat the oven to 350°. Place the chicken pieces in a 9 x 13-inch glass or enamel baking dish.
2. In a spice grinder, place the cumin, coriander, and peppercorns, and grind until pulverized; transfer to a small bowl and add the salt. Sprinkle the spice mixture over the chicken, and rub it into the flesh.
3. Scatter the onion, garlic, bay leaf, and figs among the chicken pieces. Pour the port over the chicken and distribute the zest evenly on the top. Cover the dish tightly with foil and bake for 50 minutes. Uncover and continue baking until the chicken is very tender, 15 to 20 minutes more. Sprinkle with the parsley and serve immediately.

*Cal. **529** Carb. **64g** Protein **45g** Chol. **127mg** Fat **12g/17%***

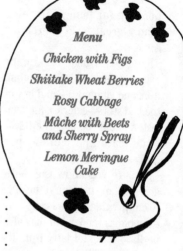

Menu

Chicken with Figs

Shiitake Wheat Berries

Rosy Cabbage

Mâche with Beets and Sherry Spray

Lemon Meringue Cake

Shiitake Wheat Berries

SERVES 4

1 cup winter wheat berries, soaked overnight, rinsed, and drained
¾ ounce dried porcini mushrooms
¼ cup sliced almonds
2 teaspoons olive oil
6 garlic cloves, minced
4 shallots, minced
½ pound shiitake mushrooms, trimmed and sliced

2 tablespoons finely chopped fresh thyme
Salt and freshly ground pepper
1/2 cup beef broth (see Basics)
1/4 cup Marsala
2 tablespoons finely chopped fresh chives

1. Place the wheat berries and 3½ cups cold water in a medium saucepan. Bring to a boil, cover, and simmer for 50 minutes, or until tender. Drain.

2. Bring ½ cup of water to a boil. Pour over the porcini and set aside for 20 minutes. Strain the liquid through a coffee filter. Drain and reserve the liquid. Coarsely chop the mushrooms.

3. Preheat the oven to 350°. Toast the almonds for 5 minutes, or until lightly golden; set them aside.

4. Heat 1 teaspoon of the oil in a large sauté pan. Add the garlic and shallot and sauté for 4 to 5 minutes, or until softened. Add the remaining teaspoon of oil and the shiitakes, and sauté for 4 minutes. Add the thyme, salt and pepper to taste, and the chopped porcini, and sauté for 4 minutes. Add the reserved mushroom liquid, broth, and Marsala, and bring to a boil. Add the wheat berries. Cover, reduce the heat, and simmer for 8 to 10 minutes, or until the liquid is absorbed. Remove from the heat, transfer to a bowl, and sprinkle with the toasted almonds and chives.

*Cal. **290** Carb. **54g** Protein **10g** Chol. **0mg** Fat **7g/18%***

Lemon Meringue Cake

SERVES 16
½ recipe White Wine Cake (page 455)
1 recipe Lemon Curd (page 285)
5 egg whites
½ teaspoon vanilla extract
1 tablespoon sugar

1. Preheat the oven to 450°.

2. Place the cake layer on a cookie sheet. Spread the lemon curd over the cake, leaving a 1-inch edge.

3. In a mixing bowl, beat the egg whites until foamy. Add the vanilla and beat until soft peaks form; add the sugar and beat until stiff glossy peaks form. Spread the meringue over the entire cake, evenly. Place in the oven and bake for 5 to 10 minutes, until golden brown. Cool before serving.

*Cal. **191** Carb. **28g** Protein **3g** Chol. **48mg** Fat **8g/33%***

Chicken Stroganoff

SERVES 4

4 cups chicken broth
¼ cup dried porcini, shiitake, or cèpes
2 whole chicken breasts, split in half, with skin and bone
Freshly ground pepper
1 pound whole fresh porcini, shiitake, or cèpes
½ cup Low-Fat Blend (see Basics)
½ cup chopped fresh chives

1. Preheat the oven to 350°.
2. Heat 1 cup of the chicken broth and pour over the dried mushrooms in a small bowl. Set aside for 2 hours. Drain and reserve the liquid. Finely mince the mushrooms.
3. Meanwhile, arrange the chicken breasts in a shallow baking pan. Pour in just enough chicken broth to cover the bottom of the baking pan—about 1 cup. Cover the pan with aluminum foil and bake until cooked through, about 40 minutes. Cool the chicken in the liquid, then discard the skin, bone, and liquid. Shred the chicken into bite-size pieces.
4. In a large saucepan, combine the remaining broth, minced mushrooms and reserved liquid, and pepper to taste. Simmer gently for 20 minutes, or until the liquid is reduced by half.
5. Add the fresh mushrooms and simmer for 5 minutes. Gently stir in the Low-Fat Blend and chives. Add the chicken and simmer for 3 to 5 minutes. Adjust the seasoning and serve immediately. Serve over egg noodles or rice if desired.

Cal. **224** *Carb.* **4g** *Protein* **38g** *Chol.* **92mg** *Fat* **5g/22%**

Rye Berries with Dried Cherries

SERVES 6

1½ cups rye berries, soaked for 2 hours, rinsed, and drained
4½ cups chicken broth (see Basics)
1 cup dried tart cherries
½ cup coarsely chopped walnuts
1 teaspoon canola oil

Fresh and Dried Mushrooms

When wild mushrooms appear in the markets and magically in the woods, I often deepen the full impact of their flavor by combining them with dried mushrooms. I then build a cozy dinner around them.

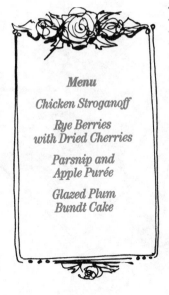

Menu

Chicken Stroganoff

*Rye Berries
with Dried Cherries*

*Parsnip and
Apple Purée*

*Glazed Plum
Bundt Cake*

1 large onion, finely chopped

4 ribs celery, finely chopped

2 tablespoons finely minced fresh sage

2 tablespoons minced fresh thyme

¼ teaspoon freshly ground pepper

Salt

Zest of one lemon, finely minced

½ cup finely chopped fresh Italian parsley

½ cup finely chopped fresh mint

1. Preheat the oven to 375°.

2. Place the rye berries and chicken broth in a medium saucepan, and bring to a boil. Cover, and reduce to a simmer. Simmer for 1 hour, or until tender. Drain, if necessary. During the last 5 minutes, add the cherries.

3. Toast the walnuts in the oven for 6 to 8 minutes, or until lightly golden.

4. Heat the oil in a large skillet and sauté the onion and celery, stirring occasionally, until softened, about 8 minutes. Add the sage, thyme, pepper, and salt to taste. Sauté for 2 minutes. Stir in the lemon zest. Add the rye berries and cherries, and heat through.

5. Remove from the heat and stir in the walnuts, parsley, and mint. Serve immediately.

*Cal. **270** Carb. **43g** Protein **9g** Chol. **6mg** Fat **9g/27%***

Michigan's Cherries

Michigan is the cherry capital of the world, a region where pin, black, and chokecherries thrived long before the first cherry orchards took root. Michigan's cherries are protected from damaging winds by the massive sand dunes along the eastern shores of Lake Michigan, whose warming influence extends the growing season well into the fall and prevents premature spring blossoming with its cold, icy presence.

I love the tart, red Montmorency cherries that are dried in northern Michigan and are sometimes slightly sugared, sometimes not.

To maximize the flavor of dried cherries, macerate them for 30 minutes or so in warmed liquid—apple, cherry, or cran-raspberry juice will do.

Cherry Flavor

chutneys • preserves • oatmeal cookies • stuffing • fruit cakes • cherry pies • cobblers • wild rice • chocolate cakes • fruit salads bread pudding • soups • chicken or duck salad • muffins • gorp • quinoa • pan sauces •

Pork Tenderloin with Chanterelles

SERVES 4

2 teaspoons sugar
1½ teaspoons coarsely ground pepper
1 teaspoon coarsely ground sea salt
½ teaspoon ground coriander
½ teaspoon ground cumin
1 pound pork tenderloin, trimmed of fat and silver skin
1 tablespoon peanut oil
1 tablespoon balsamic vinegar
4 shallots, finely chopped
2 pounds chanterelles, trimmed and quartered
6 fresh sage leaves, snipped, or ½ teaspoon crumbled dried
  sage leaves
1 cup dry white wine
Freshly ground pepper

1. In a small bowl, combine the sugar, pepper, salt, coriander, and cumin. Rub the pork with the spices on all sides and wrap in plastic wrap. Refrigerate for 4 hours or overnight.
2. Preheat the oven to 350°.
3. Lightly spray or wipe a baking dish with vegetable oil. Remove the pork from the plastic and tie it every 2 inches with butcher string, tucking the tail under for uniform thickness. Place the pork in the baking dish, rub with half of the peanut oil, place in the oven, and roast for 15 minutes. Baste the roast with the vinegar, and roast for 30 minutes, basting two or three times with the pan juices. Cook the pork until it reaches an internal temperature of 155°, or just until it is barely pink at the center; do not overcook. Remove the roast from the oven, baste, and let stand for 10 minutes before slicing.
4. While the pork is resting, in a large sauté pan, heat the remaining oil over high heat. Add the shallot, chanterelles, and sage, and sauté for 3 to 4 minutes, or until the mushrooms are tender. Add the wine to deglaze the pan, scraping up any brown bits. Sauté for 5 minutes, or until the liquid is reduced by half. Taste the sauce and adjust the seasonings and pepper.
5. Cut the pork into ¼-inch slices, place on a platter, and spoon the chanterelles and sauce around. Serve immediately.

*Cal. **259** Carb. **11g** Protein **29g** Chol. **83mg** Fat **12g/35%***

Menu

Pork Tenderloin
with Chanterelles

Everyday Herb Rice

Carrot Purée

Watercress with
Sweet-and-Sour
Splash

Baked Pears
with Marsala

A Pig Went to Market

Past and present, pork is the most widely eaten meat in the world, though recent food fashion has led some to believe that it is neither lean enough nor chic. But as home cooking revives, roast loin of pork is regaining popularity.

Home cooks tell me their roasts aren't as moist and juicy as they used to be, which isn't surprising, considering that pork is 30% less fatty than it was thirty years ago. New techniques of breeding and feeding have altered the animal.

The tenderloin of a well-trimmed pork loin is leaner than even chicken (a 3-ounce serving of roasted lean pork contains 79 mg. cholesterol). Cook this new pork by the old methods, and it'll be dried-out, indeed. The trick to that old-fashioned falling-apart pork roast is to slow cook it (at 300°) in a covered pan with 2 cups of apple juice, basting every 30 to 40 minutes, for about 4 hours. Don't dry it out by cooking it beyond an internal temperature of 170°—the point at which pork is safe to eat.

Everyday Herb Rice

SERVES 4

1 tablespoon dried onion flakes
½ tablespoon dried celery flakes
2 tablespoons dried parsley
½ teaspoon dried garlic flakes
1 tablespoon dried green pepper flakes
½ teaspoon ground turmeric
1 tablespoon chicken-flavored granules or bouillon
1 teaspoon sugar
¼ teaspoon salt
Pinch ground cloves
½ cup wild rice or brown rice
1 cup chopped scallion, green parts with some white

1. In a small bowl, combine the first 10 ingredients.
2. In a medium saucepan, combine the rice, 2½ cups water, and the herb mixture. Bring to a boil, partially cover, lower the heat, and simmer for 45 minutes, or until the rice is cooked. Fluff with a fork.
3. Fold in the scallions and serve at once.

*Cal. **174** Carb. **37g** Protein **7g** Chol. **0mg** Fat **.6g/3%***

Baked Pears and Marsala

SERVES 6

6 large firm pears, such as Red Bartlett or Anjou
1 cup dry Marsala
1 cup sugar
1 stick cinnamon

1. Preheat the oven to 325°.
2. Arrange the pears in a large baking dish. Pour the Marsala over the pears and sprinkle with half the sugar. Pour ⅔ cup water into the dish and put in the cinnamon stick. Bake for ½ hour, then turn the pears over. Sprinkle with the rest of the sugar and bake for an additional 1½ to 2 hours. Baste and turn every 20 to 30 minutes.
3. Serve warm or cool, with the syrup from the dish poured over.

*Cal. **274** Carb. **70g** Protein **1g** Chol. **0mg** Fat **.9g/2%***

Shredded Brisket

SERVES 12

1 teaspoon canola oil
1 brisket of beef (about 4 pounds), trimmed of fat
3 cups red wine
2 cups beef broth (see Basics)
1 cup fresh parsley sprigs
1 onion, quartered
12 garlic cloves, crushed
12 whole cloves
10 peppercorns
8 allspice berries
1 cinnamon stick

1. In a large Dutch oven, heat the oil over medium-high heat. Add the brisket and brown well on both sides.
2. Lower the heat to medium. Add the remaining ingredients; bring to a very slow boil. Reduce the heat to low, cover partially, and simmer until the beef is tender, 3 to 3½ hours.
3. Remove the meat from the pan. Use two forks to pull the meat apart, shredding it coarsely. Arrange the meat on a serving platter.
4. Strain the cooking juices through a fine mesh sieve, and skim off any fat. Spoon some of the juices over the meat and pass the rest at the table. Serve immediately on noodles or toasted English muffins.

*Cal. **219** Carb. **6g** Protein **27g** Chol. **98mg** Fat **10g/40%***

Five-Grain Pilaf

SERVES 12

1 cup currants
¼ cup fresh orange juice
1 teaspoon olive oil
1 teaspoon minced garlic
½ cup finely chopped onion
2 cups sliced mushrooms
1 cup barley
½ cup soft winter wheat berries
¼ cup millet

Menu

Bacon and Leek Quiche

Shredded Brisket

Brussel Sprout Leaves

Five-Grain Pilaf

Purple Plums in Port

Designer Beef

A product of pampered herds that graze on lush, green grass and are fed a diet of vegetables, garlic, and beer. They are raised without hormones or antibiotics. A pound of this superior beef sells for upward of thirty dollars.

We did a taste test. The expensive, lean designer beef didn't have any, its thick, rosy appearance and tenderness notwithstanding. Add flavor by marinating? Ridiculous!

Our suggestion: Eat small portions of beef (4 to 6 ounces) less frequently and stick to the kind you like. And talk to your local butcher or breeder. You might find, as we did, that he's experimenting with breeding leaner beef right in your own backyard.

Take heart; as with many new things, in time lean beef should be tastier and cheaper. Markets do respond to demand, don't they?

¼ cup wild rice
¼ cup brown rice
3 cups chicken broth (see Basics)
1 cup chopped scallion
1 cup slivered toasted almonds
1 cup minced fresh Italian parsley
Salt and freshly ground pepper

1. Preheat the oven to 350°. Plump the currants in the orange juice for 20 minutes.

2. In a large ovenproof Dutch oven with a tight-fitting lid, heat the olive oil over medium heat. Add the garlic and onion and sauté for 5 minutes. Add the mushrooms and sauté for 3 to 5 minutes, until softened.

4. Add the barley, wheat berries, millet, wild rice, and brown rice. Stir to coat with the oil, and cook, stirring, for 10 to 15 minutes. The grains should be tender to the tooth.

5. Stir in the chicken broth and bring to a boil. Cover and place in the oven; bake for 30 minutes.

6. Remove the pilaf from the oven; stir in the scallion, currants and soaking liquid, toasted almonds, and parsley. Season with salt and pepper to taste. Serve immediately.

Cal. **205** *Carb.* **30g** *Protein* **7g** *Chol.* **0mg** *Fat* **7g/30%**

Purple Plums in Port

SERVES 12
4 cups port wine
1 cup sugar
2 vanilla beans
8 whole cloves
¼ teaspoon five-spice powder
3 pounds dark purple plums, halved and pitted
Zest and juice of 2 limes

1. In a medium-size saucepan, bring the port, sugar, vanilla beans, cloves, and five-spice powder to a boil, and cook until reduced by half, 15 to 18 minutes.

2. Add the plums, cut sides down, and reduce the heat to a simmer. Cook until tender, about 35 to 40 minutes. Transfer the plums to a serving dish with a slotted spoon. Discard the vanilla beans and cloves and add the lime zest and juice. Pour the sauce over the plums and serve.

Cal. **183** *Carb.* **45g** *Protein* **1g** *Chol.* **0mg** *Fat* **1g/4%**

Baked Tuna Loin & a Green Bouquet

SERVES 4

5 pounds loin of tuna, in one piece (about 3 x 10 inches)
Juice of 4 lemons
Juice of 4 limes
Juice of 2 oranges
3 cups trimmed arugula
2 cups sorrel leaves
1 cup fresh dill
2 cups fresh Italian parsley
1 cup fresh chives
1 cup fresh cilantro leaves
1 cup fresh thyme leaves
2 tablespoons olive oil
Freshly ground pepper

1. Place the tuna in a shallow glass dish, and marinate in the lemon, lime, and orange juice for 1 hour in the refrigerator. Turn the fish every 15 minutes.
2. Preheat the oven to 400°.
3. Drain and reserve the juices from the tuna. Place the tuna in the oven and bake for 30 to 40 minutes, basting frequently with the marinating juices.
4. Meanwhile, wash the greens and herbs and pat them dry. Coarsely chop them and place them in a microwavable bowl. Let stand at room temperature for no more than 1 hour; if longer, refrigerate.
5. Just before removing the tuna from the oven, lightly toss the greens and herbs. Coat your hands with olive oil and toss again to coat the greens and herbs.
6. Cook the greens and herbs for 2 minutes in a microwave oven set on high, just to heat through.
7. Carve the tuna into ¾-inch slices. Serve with the greens and herbs alongside or beneath the slices.

*Cal. **250** Carb. **7g** Protein **43g** Chol. **89mg** Fat **5g/18%***

L'Inspiration

We first tasted this treasure as part of a *dégustation* menu at l'Arpege on rue de Varenne in Paris. At first we thought chef Alain Passard was intriguing us with a roast loin of pork, but in fact he was foxing us with a roasted loin of tuna to be sliced at the table. Our waiter then ground on generous amounts of fresh black pepper and sea salt. This is a great way to serve fish to guests and know it will be done perfectly—and a forkful of the tuna with the satiny greens is sublime. I like to serve ratatouille or puttanesca sauce on the side.

Whitefish with Chanterelles

SERVES 4

4 tablespoons minced fresh
  chives
4 tablespoons minced fresh
  chervil
2 teaspoons fresh lemon juice
2 fresh whitefish fillets (about
  2 pounds)
Freshly ground pepper
4 ounces halved fresh
  chanterelles

1. Preheat the oven to 375°.
2. In a small bowl, combine the chives, chervil, and lemon juice. Set aside.
3. Lightly spray or wipe two pieces of aluminum foil, each large enough to enclose a fillet, with vegetable oil. Place a fillet on each piece of foil, and season with pepper to taste. Sprinkle each fillet with half the herb mixture. Arrange the chanterelles on top of the fillets, sprinkle with the remaining herbs, and season lightly with pepper.
4. Close the packages by folding the foil over the fillets and tightly sealing the ends. Set the packages on a baking sheet and bake for 25 to 35 minutes. Open the packets to see that the fish is opaque and flakes when pierced with a fork. If so, remove from the oven and cut each fillet in half. Serve immediately.

*Cal. **306** Carb. **16g***
*Protein **51g** Chol. **83mg***
*Fat **4g/11%***

Mussel Stew

SERVES 4

1 teaspoon olive oil
4 garlic cloves, minced
5 whole jalapeño peppers, seeded and minced
1 red bell pepper, cored, seeded, and chopped
3 cups thinly sliced onion
1 cup dry white wine
2 cans (28 ounces each) whole tomatoes,
  quartered lengthwise, and their juice
1/4 teaspoon freshly grated nutmeg
1/2 teaspoon ground cloves
1/2 teaspoon or more crushed red pepper flakes
Freshly ground pepper
4 tablespoons chopped fresh tarragon, basil, thyme, or oregano
2 cups chopped fresh Italian parsley
2 pounds fresh mussels, carefully scrubbed and debearded

1. In a wide, deep skillet over medium heat, heat the oil. Add the garlic, pepper, and onion, and cook, stirring occasionally, until the vegetables are tender, about 10 minutes. Stir in the wine, tomatoes, nutmeg, and cloves. Add the peppers to taste. Bring to a boil, reduce the heat to low, add the tarragon and 1 cup of the parsley, and simmer, uncovered, for 20 minutes.
2. Stir in the mussels, cover, and cook until the mussels open, about 5 minutes. Discard any unopened mussels. Stir in the remaining parsley. Taste the liquid and adjust the seasonings before serving.

*Cal. **246** Carb. **39g** Protein **17g** Chol. **25mg** Fat **5g/14%***

S w e e t   D r e a m s

Apple Tart Tatin

SERVES 6

3 Granny Smith or other tart apples, peeled, cored, and quartered
¼ cup light brown sugar
3 tablespoons Calvados
2 tablespoons honey
1 sheet frozen puff pastry (8 x 8 inches), defrosted

1. Preheat the oven to 350°.
2. In an 8-inch cast-iron or other ovenproof skillet, place all the ingredients except the pastry. Stir over low heat until the liquid turns syrupy and deep amber; do not burn. Set aside.
3. On a lightly floured surface, roll out the pastry ⅛ inch thick.
4. Cut out a 9-inch circle of pastry. Place the pastry over the apples and tuck in the edges.
5. Place in the oven and bake for 30 to 35 minutes, or until the pastry is puffed and golden brown. Preheat the broiler.
6. Immediately invert the tart onto a cookie sheet and place it under the broiler for 3 to 5 minutes, watching constantly, until the apples bubble and brown. Serve warm from the oven, with a dollop of Vanilla Cream (page 100) or Vanilla Frozen Yogurt (page 275) if desired.

*Cal. **166** Carb. **28g** Protein **1g** Chol. **17mg** Fat **6g/30%***

Apple Time

Crisp leaves. Cozy flannel shirts. The smell of cinnamon. The warm fragrance of a hot apple pie. It's apple season.

You can buy apples year-round, of course. But once picked, they continue to ripen even when refrigerated. Eventually, they become mealy and dry. So use them now, at their autumn best, to eat out of hand or put into applesauce, pies, cider, and strudels.

Susie's Baked Apples

My sister-in-law's fail-safe, quick-as-a-wink baked apples.

SERVES 8

½ cup brown sugar
1 teaspoon ground cinnamon
1 teaspoon freshly grated nutmeg
1 teaspoon ground cloves
1 cup raisins or currants
8 large Granny Smith apples, cored
¾ cup frozen orange juice concentrate, defrosted
Vanilla Custard Sauce (page 97)

1. In a medium mixing bowl, combine the sugar, cinnamon, nutmeg, and cloves, and mix until well combined. Fold in the raisins. Spoon as much of the mixture as possible into the cores of the apples. Drizzle 1½ tablespoons of orange juice concentrate into each apple.
2. Place four of the apples on a microwavable plate and place in a microwave oven set on high for 8 minutes. Remove the apples and cover them with foil to keep warm. Repeat with the remaining apples and serve at once with the sauce.

Cal. **202** Carb. **51g**
Protein **2g** Chol. **0mg**
Fat **1g/4%**

My Mom's Apple Pie

SERVES 8

2½ pounds Granny Smith apples
Juice of 1 lemon
¾ packed cup light brown sugar
3 tablespoons all-purpose flour
½ teaspoon ground cinnamon
½ teaspoon grated lemon zest
3 tablespoons Calvados
1 recipe Flaky Pie Crust (see Basics)
1 teaspoon skim milk
1 teaspoon granulated sugar

1. Preheat the oven to 400°.
2. Peel, core, and thinly slice the apples; place the slices in a large mixing bowl and sprinkle with the lemon juice.
3. In a small bowl, combine the brown sugar, flour, cinnamon, and lemon zest. Stir in the Calvados. Pour the mixture over the apples and toss well to coat.
4. Roll out half the dough to fit a 9-inch pie plate; line the plate. Spoon the apples, along with the accumulated juices, into the pastry. Roll out the remaining dough and cover the pie; crimp the edges together and slash the top in a few places to allow steam to escape while baking. Brush the top crust with the skim milk and sprinkle with the sugar.
5. Place the pie in the oven and bake for 10 minutes. Reduce the heat to 350° and bake for 40 minutes, or until the crust is golden. Let the pie cool slightly before serving. Serve with a small wedge of cheddar cheese or Vanilla Frozen Yogurt (page 275).

Cal. **449** Carb. **75g** Protein **5g** Chol. **0mg** Fat **15g/29%**

Pear Pudding

SERVES 10

One 10 x 5-inch pound cake
1½ pounds firm pears, such as Bosc, peeled if desired
1½ cups low-fat cottage cheese
1¼ cups low-fat buttermilk
⅓ cup nonfat plain yogurt
⅓ cup superfine sugar
1 vanilla bean, split and seeds removed
½ teaspoon vanilla extract
½ teaspoon almond extract
2 tablespoons brown sugar
Freshly grated nutmeg

1. Preheat the oven to 325°.
2. Remove the seeds and stems from the pears and coarsely chop them.
3. In a blender, blend the cottage cheese, buttermilk, yogurt, sugar, the seeds from the vanilla bean, and the extracts, until smooth.
4. Slice the pound cake into ¼-inch thick-slices and lay them out on a baking sheet with sides. Pour 1 cup of the sauce evenly over the pound cake; the sauce should soak into the cake.
5. Using about two-thirds of the pound cake, line the prepared 2-quart baking dish; spread the pears over the pound cake. Pour ¾ cup of the remaining sauce over the pears.
6. Cut the remaining pound cake into ½-inch strips and scatter over the pears; pour on ¼ cup of the remaining sauce. Refrigerate the unused sauce until serving time; you should have about 1 cup left. Sprinkle the brown sugar and grated nutmeg over the pudding.
7. Bake the pudding in a large dish, filled with water to within 1 inch of the top of the pudding dish, for 50 minutes, or until set. Spoon the warm pudding into serving dishes and top each with 1½ tablespoons of the reserved chilled sauce.

*Cal. **243** Carb. **42g** Protein **9g** Chol. **21mg** Fat **4g/16%***

"The pear is the grandfather of the apple,... a fallen aristocrat..."

François Pierre de la Varenne

Pear and Ginger Sorbet

SERVES 6

6 to 8 ripe Comice pears, peeled, seeded, and cut into chunks (4 cups)
½ cup fresh lime juice
½ cup sugar
½ teaspoon finely grated fresh ginger

1. In a food processor, combine the pears, lime juice, and sugar. Purée the mixture. Add the ginger and process a few seconds longer. Transfer the mixture to a medium bowl, cover with plastic wrap, and refrigerate until very cold.
2. Transfer the mixture to an ice cream maker and freeze according to the manufacturer's directions.
NOTE: Bosc or Bartlett pears may be substituted for Comice.

*Cal. **135** Carb. **35g***
*Protein **1g** Chol. **0mg***
*Fat **.5g/3%***

Pears Perfect

A fine, ripe pear is purely ambrosial, with a scent perfumers label "ethereal" and flesh that's buttery and melting. A pear can be the perfect complement to a good, robust cheese; try one with Stilton or Pecorino. The right wine for this treat is ruby port or Barolo.

Pears have been cultivated for thirty-five to forty centuries; they probably originated in western Asia and around the Caspian Sea. In the court of Louis XIV in seventeenth-century France, they reigned supreme.

Women may cringe at the description "pear-shaped," but in fact, pears can also be round, ovoid, squat as quinces, long-necked as gourds, or clubby and knobbed.

There are some 5,000 varieties, many of which grow all over the world, some only in small locales. Most American pears grow in the region from California through Oregon and into Washington.

"Winter" pears are the common, commercially grown varieties harvested in September, put into cold storage, and marketed from winter through early summer.

Anjou, or D'Anjou

Green and egg-shaped, with tender skin and mild, spicy flavor. For eating and cooking, October through June.

Bartlett

Harvested in mid-August, gone by November. Golden-green, with russet spots and marbling, or rosy and red-skinned. Their flavor is musky. This is a great eating pear that holds its classic bell shape when cooked. Red Bartletts' skin turns crimson when ripe. Bartletts account for a quarter of American pear production.

Bosc

Good eating, with flesh as rich as cream, graceful Modigliani necks and long, curving stems. Boscs have tough, sandy-textured skin with a russet hue. They hold their shape when boiled, baked, or poached.

Comice

Thick-skinned, squat, and green, with flesh that's sweet, juicy, and buttery all at once. This is the crème de la crème of pears, according to the French.

Forelle

Looks like a little Bartlett, though smaller. The Forelle is golden with a crimson blush, and sprouts freckles when ripe. This is the perfect Christmas pear, with or without the partridge.

Nelis

Small-to-medium-sized; shaped like Comice with green and brown russet skin and sweet, creamy flesh.

Seckel/Sugar Pear

Bite-sized and blushing, they range from tiny to small, with reddish-green skin. When good, Seckels are intoxicatingly sweet. Unfortunately, sometimes the ones on the market are like stones. A gentle squeeze should tell.

Ripening Pears

Nature aside, pears need a human touch to achieve perfection. Pick them while they are still green and hard. But take note: If picked *too* soon, they will wilt and shrivel. If, on the other hand, they are picked too late, they'll be bitter and gritty.

Pears ripen inside out, so it's hard to judge. My suggestion: Put them in a bowl of bananas or in a paper bag with holes in a dark or shady spot. Watch carefully—when the stem end gives a little, they're ripe. If you aren't using them immediately, store them in the refrigerator to slow their ripening, but eat them at room temperature to enjoy the full bouquet.

For cooking, use slightly underripe pears. Sprinkle pears with lemon or lime juice—lime is less tart—to prevent browning once they're peeled.

★ GOOD FOR YOU ★

One medium-sized pear provides 50 calories, lots of vitamins A and C, 4.8 grams of fiber, and iodine and potassium. Make a perfectly ripened pear one of your five fruits a day all fall.

Glazed Plum Bundt Cake

SERVES 24

2 cups sugar

1 cup canola oil

4 tablespoons (½ stick) unsalted butter, softened

3 cups all-purpose flour

2 teaspoons ground cinnamon

1 teaspoon baking soda

1 teaspoon salt

1 egg

4 egg whites

1 tablespoon vanilla extract

¼ cup low-fat buttermilk

3 cups pitted and chopped plums

1 cup coarsely chopped walnuts

½ cup light brown sugar

2 tablespoons skim milk

1. Preheat the oven to 350°. Spray or wipe a 12-cup Bundt pan with vegetable oil. Lightly dust the pan with flour.
2. In a large mixing bowl, cream the sugar, ½ cup oil, and butter until fluffy. Add the dry ingredients and mix until blended.
3. Add the egg, egg whites, vanilla, and buttermilk, and blend well.
4. Stir in the plums and walnuts; pour the batter in the pan and bake for 50 minutes, or until a cake tester or toothpick comes out clean.
5. While the cake is baking, in a saucepan heat the remaining ½ cup canola oil and brown sugar until hot. Add the skim milk, stir, and set aside.
6. Cool the cake in the pan, then invert it onto a plate, and spoon the glaze over the top.

Cal. **266** Carb. **36g**

Protein **3g** Chol. **13mg**

Fat **12g/41%**

Heartwarming After-Dinner Drinks

- White Russians made with Vanilla Frozen Yogurt.
- Chartreuse perked up with champagne—elegant, green, and fizzy.
- Cognac, Armagnac, or the wonderful Marc de Bourgogne.
- Aged port.
- Calvados.
- Grappa.
- Framboise.
- Eaux de Vie.
- Amaretto, Grand Marnier, or Frangelico.

Individual Plum Tarts

SERVES 8

$^{1}/_{2}$ *recipe Flaky Pie Crust (see Basics)*
$^{3}/_{4}$ *pounds plums, pitted and coarsely chopped*
$^{1}/_{3}$ *cup frozen cran-raspberry juice concentrate, thawed*
$^{1}/_{2}$ *tablespoon honey*
$^{1}/_{2}$ *vanilla bean*
Generous pinch ground cloves
1 sprig fresh mint
3 tablespoons chopped
  crystallized ginger
8 small plums (about 2 ounces each), halved and pitted
1 tablespoon sugar
Pinch ground cinnamon

1. Preheat the oven to 425°.
2. Lightly spray or wipe a baking sheet with vegetable oil. Roll out the pastry into eight 4-inch rounds, about $^{1}/_{4}$ inch thick. Place the rounds on the baking sheet. Prick the rounds with a fork and crimp the edges in an irregular way to form shallow sides in a rustic manner; refrigerate.
3. Place the chopped plums, cran-raspberry concentrate, honey, vanilla bean, and ground cloves in a medium-size pan. Bring to a boil and continue boiling until thickened, about 20 minutes, stirring frequently to prevent sticking. Once the plums are tender, strain the excess liquid off and discard; there should be no more than about $^{1}/_{4}$ cup in the pan at this point. Remove the vanilla bean. Add the leaves from the sprig of mint and purée in a blender or food processor; you will have about $^{3}/_{4}$ cup purée. Cool the purée to room temperature.
4. Divide the purée among the tarts—about $1^{1}/_{2}$ tablespoons each—and spread almost to the edges.
5. Sprinkle the crystallized ginger evenly over the purée.
6. Bake the tarts for 12 minutes, or until the crust edges are lightly golden. Set aside to cool.
7. Meanwhile, place the plum halves, cut sides up, in a small roasting pan and bake for 8 minutes in the same oven. Remove and slice each half into three wedges.
8. Arrange the plum wedges in a star pattern—points out—in the center of each tart. Sprinkle with the sugar and ground cinnamon. Broil for $1^{1}/_{2}$ to 2 minutes, or until bubbly and golden. Serve immediately.

Cal. **231** *Carb.* **39g** *Protein* **3g** *Chol.* **0mg** *Fat* **8g/28%**

Plums

Santa Rosa, Black Amber, Laroda, El Dorado, Scarlet Heart, Nubiona, Black Beauty... even their names seem to take us on a journey to mysterious places. Their season is short, so enjoy them when you can.

★ GOOD FOR YOU ★

Figure 30 to 60 calories per plum, depending on size. They're high in carbohydrates, and a great source of vitamins A and C, as well as potassium. And they're naturally sweet.

Rice Pudding

SERVES 8

2 cinnamon sticks (each 2 inches long)
2 pieces fresh lime zest (about ½ inch x 4 inches)
1 cup converted rice
4 cups skim milk
½ cup sugar
Salt
1 egg
2 egg yolks
1 teaspoon vanilla extract (preferably Mexican)
½ cup raisins
1 tablespoon chilled unsalted butter
1 tablespoon sliced almonds

1. In a heavy medium-size saucepan, bring 2 cups of water, the cinnamon sticks, and the lime zest to a boil over high heat. Lower the heat slightly and simmer for 5 minutes.
2. Add the rice and bring the water back to a boil. Cover, lower the heat to a simmer, and cook until the liquid is absorbed, about 20 minutes. Stir in the milk, sugar, and salt. Increase the heat to medium and cook until the rice begins to thicken, about 20 minutes, stirring occasionally. Remove from the heat and discard the cinnamon sticks and lime zest.
3. In a small bowl, whisk the egg, egg yolks, and vanilla. Beat about ¼ cup of the hot rice mixture, a tablespoon at a time, into the eggs. Whisk the egg mixture into the remaining hot rice. Stir in the raisins.
4. Preheat the broiler.
5. Spoon the pudding into a shallow 2-quart baking dish. Dot the surface with bits of cold butter, and broil until the top begins to brown, 2 to 3 minutes; do not let the pudding burn. Sprinkle the top with almonds and broil 1 more minute, until the almonds just begin to brown. Serve warm or at room temperature.

*Cal. **185** Carb. **34g** Protein **6g** Chol. **56mg** Fat **3g/15%***

Port

Once considered the province of cigar-wielding gentlemen in private English clubs, Port is still a great after-dinner pleasure. Stilton, walnuts, and chocolate are compatible with port.

Today, Portugal's ports are widely enjoyed. Among the popular types are:
• White ports, produced from white grapes, aged in wooden casks, and blended for a sweet, dry flavor.
• Tawny ports, which are aged longer and have a smoother taste.
• Ruby ports—young, red, and robust.
• Vintage ports, which contain the fruit of a single harvest of outstanding quality.

Cooking with port creates rich sauces for poultry and meats. Reduced and laced with chocolate, a minor flavor miracle occurs—it makes chocolate taste more chocolaty.

Bourbon Nuts

YIELD: 1 CUP

1 cup finely chopped walnuts
2 tablespoons bourbon
2 tablespoons sugar
1/4 teaspoon ground cinnamon
1/4 teaspoon ground cloves
1/4 teaspoon ground nutmeg

1. Position the rack in the center of the oven and preheat the oven to 300°.
2. Combine all the ingredients in a small bowl and toss until the nuts are evenly coated.
3. Transfer the nuts to a baking sheet and spread in a single layer. Bake for 10 to 15 minutes, stirring occasionally, until the nuts are crisp and golden. Transfer the nuts immediately to a plate or bowl to stop the baking process.
4. Store in an airtight container, for up to 2 weeks.

*Cal. **43** Carb. **2g***
*Protein **1g** Chol. **0mg***
*Fat **4g/67%***

Party Pumpkin

SERVES 8

1 small pumpkin (about 3¹/₂ pounds; 8 or 9 inches in diameter)
1 cup chopped Granny Smith apples
1 cup fresh cranberries
1 cup raisins
³/₄ cup toasted and coarsely chopped walnuts
¹/₃ cup sugar
¹/₂ teaspoon ground cinnamon
¹/₄ teaspoon freshly grated nutmeg
1 teaspoon lemon juice
1 cup nonfat plain yogurt

1. Preheat the oven to 350°.
2. Cut off the top of the pumpkin and reserve; scrape the seeds out of the bottom.
3. In a large bowl, combine the remaining ingredients, except the yogurt. Stuff the pumpkin with the mixture and replace the lid. Place the pumpkin in a roasting pan and add 1 to 2 inches of hot water to the pan. Bake the pumpkin for 45 minutes to 1 hour. Remove the lid and set aside; bake the pumpkin for 30 minutes. Replace the lid and bake for 20 minutes. Add more water to the roasting pan if necessary.
4. To serve, scoop out some filling and some cooked pumpkin flesh onto individual plates; add a dollop of yogurt.

*Cal. **223** Carb. **40g** Protein **5g***
*Chol. **223mg** Fat **7g/27%***

Home for the Holidays

CHRISTMAS GREENS

SAUGATUCK VILLAGE HALL

"He that is of a merry heart hath a continual feast."

Proverbs 15:15

Holiday Journal

November

25 Everyone coming for
      Thanksgiving weekend

27 Be good to my "Secret Santa"
28 Christmas shopping weekend

29 Bring paperwhites into the sun

30 Bake and freeze gingerbread

Presents to make
ornaments
cookies
candles
fruitcakes
wreaths

December

1 Find skis, skates, and toboggan
3 Tree-cutting party — meet
                  in the woods

5 Stack logs to get us through the holidays

7 Gather pinecones and cut greens for decorating

8 Address Christmas cards — packages
10 Gingerbread house party   out by today!
11 Finish making ornaments for exchange

ROB

15 String popcorn and cranberries for the tree

16 Find ornaments and check the strings of lights

17 Sleigh ride and caroling — find sheet music

19 WATER THE CHRISTMAS TREE DAILY

21 Garden club Christmas Party

table favors?

22 Wrap presents

Katie

24 Christmas Eve/
    midnight candlelight service

25 CHRISTMAS MORNING BRUNCH — Open House!

26 Black tie to cleaners

29 Mulch flower beds with
    boughs from Christmas tree

30 Cook for New Year's Eve

A Thanksgiving Feast

Corn Chowder

SERVES 12

6 cups fresh corn kernels (about 12 ears)
1 ounce hickory-smoked slab bacon, finely minced
2 teaspoons vegetable oil
4 cups finely chopped leek (about 6 leeks)
2 cups finely chopped onion
4 teaspoons all-purpose flour
6 cups chicken broth (see Basics)
1 pound new potatoes, cut into ½-inch cubes
2 tablespoons chopped fresh thyme
2 bay leaves
1 cup low-fat buttermilk
Salt and freshly ground pepper
Pinch cayenne

1. In a blender or food processor, purée 4 cups of corn; set aside.

2. In a medium-size stockpot, sauté the bacon over medium heat until all the fat is rendered and the bacon is lightly browned, 2 to 3 minutes.

3. Add the oil, leek, and onion; cover and sweat until softened, about 8 minutes. Stir in the flour and cook an additional 2 minutes, stirring constantly.

The month-long holiday season begins with the most American of holidays. This day centers on family and friends, football games, parades, and the official beginning of the "Holiday Season." As Santa and his reindeer are welcomed, this is the time to experience—if only through the young—a child's sense of wide-eyed wonder and anticipation at this season of plenty.

It's also when the temptations are everywhere—the wondrous smells, the cozy warmth of a house filled with baking, celebrations of all sorts. Now it is up to you to plan your own indulgences—make your own wise choices.

Come New Year's, you may have nothing to resolve.

4. Reduce the heat to low, and add the broth, potatoes, thyme, and bay leaf. Simmer, covered, for 30 minutes. Stir in the corn purée and the remaining kernels, and simmer, uncovered, for 3 minutes.

5. Whisk in the buttermilk and simmer until heated through, but do not boil. Season to taste with the salt, pepper, and cayenne. Remove the bay leaf before serving.

*Cal. **185** Carb. **31g** Protein **6g** Chol. **6mg** Fat **5g/25%***

Burgundian Spice Bread

SERVES 10

1 cup sultanas
½ cup Grand Marnier or orange juice
¾ cup honey
½ cup sugar
1½ teaspoons fennel seeds
2 teaspoons ground ginger
¾ teaspoon ground cinnamon
2 teaspoons finely grated orange zest
¼ teaspoon salt
1½ cups unbleached all-purpose flour
½ cup rye flour
1 tablespoon baking powder

1. In a small bowl, combine the sultanas and Grand Marnier, and macerate for 30 minutes.

2. In a large mixing bowl, combine the honey, sugar, ½ cup warm water, spices, zest, and salt. Stir to combine thoroughly.

3. Combine the flours and baking powder and sift the mixture into the honey mixture. Beat well with a wooden spoon to obtain a thick batter. Fold in the macerated sultanas. Cover the mixing bowl with a tea towel and let the batter rest for 1 hour.

4. Preheat the oven to 300°.

5. Lightly spray or wipe a 9 x 4-inch loaf pan with vegetable oil. Line the bottom of the pan with parchment paper and spray or wipe with oil.

6. Stir the batter gently. It should be thick but should fall from a spoon in a thick, silky ribbon. If it seems too thick, add a little water. Spoon the batter into the pan and bake for 1½ hours, or until a skewer inserted in the middle comes out clean. Cool the bread in the pan for 15 minutes on a rack before turning out, then cool completely.

*Cal. **263** Carb. **65g** Protein **3g** Chol. **0mg** Fat **.4g/1%***

Roast Turkey Marsala

SERVES 12
1 fresh turkey (14 to 16 pounds)
1 tablespoon coarse salt
2 cups seeded, cored, and chunked pears
2 cups seeded, cored, and chunked apples
2 cups peeled and quartered onions
8 sprigs fresh Italian parsley
2 sprigs fresh rosemary
2 sprigs fresh thyme
12 sage leaves
1 tablespoon canola oil
1 cup Marsala or white wine
1 cup chicken broth (see Basics)

1. Preheat the oven to 450°.
2. Remove the giblets from the turkey and reserve for gravy. Wash the turkey inside and out with plenty of cold running water; pat dry with paper towels.
3. Rub the turkey cavities thoroughly with salt.
4. Place the pears, apples, onions, parsley, rosemary, thyme, and sage leaves into the cavities. Truss the bird with metal poultry skewers, fold the wings under, and fasten the legs close to the body by tying the ends of the drumsticks together. Rub the turkey with the oil, and place on a rack in an uncovered roasting pan. Place the turkey in the oven and immediately reduce the heat to 325°. Roast for 15 to 20 minutes per pound. Using a pastry brush, baste the turkey with wine and chicken broth every 20 minutes after the first hour of roasting.
5. Remove the turkey from the oven and let it rest for 20 minutes. Remove and discard the fruit, onions, and herbs.
6. Reserve the drippings for turkey gravy.

*Cal. **468** Carb. **2g** Protein **77g** Chol. **200mg** Fat **14g/27%***

Giblet Gravy

YIELD: 7 CUPS
All reserved drippings from roasted turkey, defatted;
 2 tablespoons fat reserved
4 tablespoons all-purpose flour
6 cups Giblet Purée (at right)
Chicken broth (see Basics) or water as needed

Giblet Purée

YIELD: 6 CUPS
Giblets (not the liver) from a
 14- to 16-pound turkey
2 cups coarsely chopped
 celery stalks and leaves
1 cup coarsely chopped onion
1 cup coarsely chopped carrots
5 sprigs fresh Italian parsley

1. In a large saucepan, combine all the ingredients with water to cover. Cover and simmer for 1½ hours. Cool. Remove the neck meat from the bone and discard. Chop the giblets.
2. In a blender, process the giblets, vegetables, and broth in batches until smooth.

*Cal. **5** Carb. **.4g** Protein **.5g** Chol. **7mg** Fat **.1g/20%** (analyzed per tablespoon)*

"Strange to see how a good dinner and feasting reconciles everybody."

Samuel Pepys

Today, you have a choice: frozen, fresh, free-range, Amish, farm-raised "wild," or really wild.

A turkey tastes like what he's eaten—grass, nuts, berries, or a mystery meal. An Amish bird is one of the sweetest and moistest. Wild turkey tastes like the ones I remember as a child. They are richer-flavored, with a leaner, firmer texture, but not "gamy."

You can purchase wild turkeys from specialty game bird suppliers— fresh during the holiday season, frozen the rest of the year. Try to find Bronze or Merriam brands —they're the tastiest.

Slow-roasting is my preferred method. Basting is absolutely necessary if you don't want to add extra fat by barding.

Don't push the "let it rest until the juices gather" myth too far. Hot turkey is wonderful! Twenty minutes is long enough for a turkey to stand before carving.

Leftover turkey stays very moist if packed for the freezer in large chunks. Wrap it first in plastic wrap and then in foil. Wide, flat packages freeze and thaw the most quickly.

¹/₄ cup or more Marsala
Salt and freshly ground pepper

1. In a large skillet or the turkey roasting pan, heat 2 tablespoons of reserved turkey fat over medium heat. Sprinkle the flour over the hot fat and stir well to combine. Slowly, whisking constantly, add the giblet purée until thickened. Stir in the skimmed turkey juices. If the gravy seems thick, thin it with chicken broth or water to achieve the desired consistency. Bring the gravy to a gentle boil and cook for 5 minutes.
2. Just before serving, stir in the Marsala, salt, and pepper to taste.

Cal. **6** *Carb.* **.6g** *Protein* **.5g** *Chol.* **6mg** *Fat* **.1g/18%**
(analyzed per tablespoon)

Cranberry, Cherry, and Walnut Chutney

SERVES 12
2 cups dried tart cherries
1 cup fresh cranberries
1 cup raisins
1 cup sugar
¹/₂ cup apple cider vinegar
¹/₂ cup finely chopped celery
6 tablespoons apple juice
¹/₂ teaspoon crushed red pepper flakes
1 tablespoon chopped lemon zest
1 cup toasted and coarsely chopped black or English walnuts
    or hazelnuts

1. Combine all of the ingredients in a 2-quart saucepan over medium heat. Cook for 20 minutes, stirring well.
2. Cool the chutney to room temperature; cover tightly and refrigerate. The chutney will thicken as it cools and will keep for up to 2 weeks in the refrigerator.

Cal. **232** *Carb.* **50g** *Protein* **3g** *Chol.* **0mg** *Fat* **4g/13%**

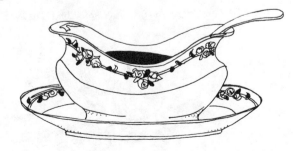

Great Corn Bread Stuffing

My mother-in-law, Kay Miller, taught me to "lift" or lighten stuffing with beaten egg white and baking soda. I like the crunchy crust that develops when you bake the stuffing in a casserole, but of course, you can stuff the bird as well.

SERVES 16

1 pound lean ground turkey (99% fat free)
2 cups coarsely chopped onion
1 teaspoon crushed red pepper flakes
8 cups Crackling Corn Bread (page 178), broken into coarse crumbs
1 cup coarsely chopped pecan halves
1 cup golden raisins
4 medium Granny Smith apples, cored and cut into chunks
2 cups coarsely minced fresh Italian parsley
1/2 cup finely minced fresh sage
3 cups chicken broth (see Basics)
Freshly ground pepper
1 cup bourbon or chicken broth
4 egg whites, at room temperature
1 tablespoon baking soda

1. Preheat the oven to 375°.
2. In a medium sauté pan, place the turkey, onion, and pepper flakes, and brown over medium heat. Drain off the fat.
3. In a very large bowl, combine the turkey mixture, corn bread, pecans, raisins, apples, parsley, and sage, and toss very well. Add the chicken broth and pepper to taste; add the bourbon or more broth.
4. Beat the egg whites until stiff. Gently fold the beaten egg whites and baking soda into the mixture—the mixture will be quite moist. Spoon the stuffing into two 9 x 13 x 2-inch baking dishes and bake for 45 minutes to 1 hour, until golden brown and crisp.

Cal. **350** *Carb.* **39g** *Protein* **15g** *Chol.* **42mg** *Fat 8g/20%*

FLAVORING STUFFING

Corn bread, multigrain bread cubes, wild or brown rice

Dried cherries or cranberries

Turkey sausage, plain or flavored

Fresh sage, rosemary, and Italian parsley

Chestnuts or oysters

Dried prunes, apricots, or figs

Red pearl onions, leeks, or garlic

Pecans, walnuts, or hazelnuts

Fresh apples, pears, or cranberries

Bourbon, Armagnac, Marsala, brandy, or wine

Chilies, cilantro, chorizo, and lime zest

Wild and tame mushrooms, or truffles

Allspice, ginger, or nutmeg

★ Give overnight guests breakfast in bed. Pampering? Sure, but it also keeps them out of the kitchen while you get organized for the big feast.

★ Pace the feast, starting with very light hors d'oeuvres, a first course, entrée, and salad course. You might want to delay dessert until later.

★ Make it special with candlelight, music, flowers, and perhaps a tiny present at each place—maybe a photo taken last Thanksgiving.

★ Encourage everyone to spend the entire afternoon together, rather than disappearing for football or TV, dishes or naps (the tryptophan enzyme in turkey does encourage dozing).

★ During dinner, roast a second turkey so that your guests go home with leftovers.

★ Go for a nice, long walk, all together.

★ Look ahead to the next big day of the season and draw names for Christmas stocking gifts for a Secret Pals grab bag.

Parsnip and Apple Purée

SERVES 6

Juice of 1 lemon
4 large Granny Smith or other tart apples
2 pounds parsnips, peeled and coarsely chopped
¼ cup chicken broth (see Basics)
2 tablespoons light brown sugar
1 teaspoon ground coriander
Dash ground cinnamon
Freshly ground pepper
¾ cup low-fat buttermilk
Fresh mint sprigs

1. Preheat the oven to 375°.
2. Combine the lemon juice and ¼ cup of water in a large bowl.
3. Peel and core the apples, and cut them into eighths, dropping the pieces into the lemon water as you work.
4. Place the parsnips in a shallow baking pan. Drain the apples, reserving the water. Add the apples and ¼ cup of the water to the pan. Add the chicken broth. Sprinkle with the brown sugar, coriander, cinnamon, and pepper. Cover the dish and bake for 1¼ hours, stirring a few times, until the parsnips are tender.
5. Reduce the temperature to 350°. Transfer the parsnips and apples with their cooking juices and the buttermilk to a food processor and purée. Reheat if necessary, in a covered ovenproof dish, for 15 minutes. Garnish with mint.

*Cal. **207** Carb. **48g** Protein **3g** Chol. **1mg** Fat **1g/5%***

Glazed Autumn Medley

SERVES 12

6 large yams
8 carrots, cut into 3-inch pieces
1 cup fresh orange juice
½ cup light brown sugar
1 teaspoon ground cinnamon
2 cups miniature marshmallows
3 mangoes, peeled, pitted, and cut
 into chunks
Juice of 1 lime

1. Preheat the oven to 350°.
2. Place the yams in the oven and bake for 30 minutes. Let them cool, then peel and set aside.
3. Pour 3 cups of water into a medium saucepan. Add the carrots and cook over medium-high heat for 15 minutes, until they are cooked but still crunchy. Drain, cool, and set aside.
4. In a medium-size saucepan, put the orange juice, brown sugar, and cinnamon, and cook over medium heat until well blended. Gradually whisk in the marshmallows, and continue to stir until they are melted and the sauce is smooth.
5. Cut the yams into large chunks. Place them in a 9 x 13 x 2-inch baking dish with the carrots and mangoes. Add the sauce and toss to coat. Bake for 30 to 45 minutes, until the vegetables are tender and golden. Sprinkle with lime juice and serve immediately.

*Cal. **223** Carb. **79g** Protein **4g** Chol. **.2mg** Fat **.6g/2%***

Wild Rice, Black Walnut, and Dried Cherry Stuffing

SERVES 12

8 ounces wild rice
8 ounces brown rice
5 to 6 cups beef broth (see Basics)
½ cup Marsala
1 cup toasted and coarsely chopped black walnuts
1 cup dried sour cherries, plumped in ½ cup Marsala
1 cup finely chopped scallion, white parts and some of the green
1 cup finely chopped fresh Italian parsley
Salt and freshly ground pepper

"The king and high priest of all the festivals was the autumn Thanksgiving. When... the labors of the season were done."

Harriet Beecher Stowe

Thanksgiving Wine

Today, we're inclined to choose American. And though turkey is poultry, it can handle fairly robust wines. Our choices: Zinfandel, Cabernet Sauvignon, Merlot, or a Beaujolais. Prefer white? Try champagne, a Sauvignon Blanc, Chardonnay, or a white Bordeaux.

• Don't use butter or any other fat to baste the turkey. Instead, baste with chicken stock, fruit juices, or fortified wines; the turkey will brown on its own.

• Remove all the fat from the turkey cooking juice before making gravy. Use a fat strainer or let the fat rise to the top in a bowl in the freezer and skim.

• Don't use organ meats in the stuffing. They're full of cholesterol.

• Use apple juice instead of brown sugar and butter when cooking yams.

• Dilute salad dressing with broth or fruit juice and put it in a spray bottle. Mist it on instead of pouring.

• Use nonfat milk in mashed potatoes, and hold the butter.

• Season vegetables with herbs, spices, and lemon or lime juice instead of butter.

• Skip the whipped cream on the pie. If you like, substitute Vanilla Custard Sauce (page 97) or Vanilla Cream (page 100).

1. In a large saucepan or Dutch oven, combine the wild and brown rice, 5 cups beef broth, and the Marsala. Bring to a boil, partially cover, reduce the heat, and cook for 45 to 60 minutes, until the rice is tender; add additional beef broth if needed to prevent the rice from drying out.

2. Stir in the walnuts, the cherries and their soaking liquid, and the scallion. Fold in the parsley and salt and pepper to taste, and heat through. Serve immediately.

*Cal. **268** Carb. **45g** Protein **8g** Chol. **0mg** Fat **8g/22%***

Glazed Pears

SERVES 12

Juice of 2 lemons

16 pears (a mixture of Anjou, green, red, and Bartlett), unpeeled

2 tablespoons unsweetened butter

4 tablespoons brown sugar

1. In a large bowl, combine the lemon juice with several cups of water. Core the pears, slice them lengthwise into wedges, then chop them into bite-size pieces. Place the pears into the lemon water as you work, to prevent them from turning brown.

2. Drain the pears and pat them dry with paper towels. In a large sauté pan, melt the butter. Add the pears and cook over medium heat until the juices are released, about 10 minutes, stirring occasionally. Sprinkle the brown sugar over the pears, and continue to cook until the juices are absorbed and the pears are glazed. Be careful not to burn the pears.

3. Sprinkle with the lemon juice, and cook just a bit longer. Taste and adjust with more lemon, as needed.

*Cal. **162** Carb. **37g** Protein **.9g** Chol. **6mg** Fat **3g/15%***

Homemade Mincemeat Pie

Pie crust is an indulgence anytime. And the dried fruits in mincemeat make it even higher in calories—and truly an indulgence. Here, the saturated fat and cholesterol have been cut out of the crust, along with the suet from traditional mincemeat. A clear sauce replaces the butter-and-egg holiday sauce that was a once-a-year treat in our house.

But Thanksgiving without mincemeat pie at all? I think not. Indulge today, and remember . . . fruit and salad tomorrow.

SERVES 8

4 cups Green Tomato Mincemeat (page 182)
1 recipe Flaky Pie Crust rolled out for a 9-inch pie, according
   to directions (see Basics)
1 tablespoon skim milk
1 teaspoon sugar
⅓ cup apple juice or cider
3 tablespoons blended whiskey

1. Rest a colander over a bowl. Place the mincemeat in the colander and drain for 1½ hours, or until you have ⅓ to ½ cup liquid. Reserve the mincemeat and the liquid.
2. Preheat the oven to 400°.
3. Line a 9-inch pie plate with one of the pie crusts. Pour in the drained mincemeat. Cover with the second crust and crimp the edges. Slash the top with a sharp knife in three or four places. Brush the top with the skim milk and sprinkle with the sugar.
4. Place the pie in the oven and bake for 10 minutes. Reduce the heat to 350° and bake for an additional 25 minutes, until the crust is golden brown.
5. Place the reserved mincemeat juices and the apple juice in a small saucepan. Bring to a boil and reduce to ½ cup. Remove from the heat and stir in the whiskey. Pour into a small pitcher and serve at the table over the pie.

Cal. **509** *Carb.* **88g** *Protein* **6g** *Chol.* **1mg** *Fat* **15g/26%**

*"So once in every
year we throng
Upon a day
apart,
To praise the
Lord with feast
and song
In thankfulness
of heart."*

Arthur Guiterman

For a traditional look: gourds, pumpkins, duck decoys, pears, apples, pine cones, chestnuts, or pomegranate pyramids stacked high. Or use fresh herbs, flowers, or parts of your favorite Americana antique or art collection.

Even if dinner's served early, we still love candlelight, a crackling fire, and soft, classical music drifting through the air. The spirit of this day should be warm, festive, and informal.

Create a party mood with a subdued palette of salmon, peach, and copper. These colors provide a pleasing contrast to the blazing reds and fiery oranges of fall's foliage. Decorate with branches of berries and peach and orange geraniums in terra-cotta pots. Drape your tables with copper gauze, which you can find at a fabric store. Arrange salmon-colored amarylla, champagne roses, and hydrangeas in all their smoky shades. Use peach linen napkins as accent.

Line rows of votive candles along beams, railings, walkways, windows, sideboards, or columns.

Pumpkin Mousse

SERVES 4

¾ *cup pumpkin purée (canned or homemade)*
9 tablespoons nonfat plain yogurt
10 tablespoons low-fat cottage cheese
1 teaspoon unflavored gelatin
2 tablespoons crystallized ginger
⅓ *cup plus 1 tablespoon sugar*
1 egg white, at room temperature
Freshly grated nutmeg

1. Place the pumpkin, yogurt, and cottage cheese in a food processor, and process until just puréed. Set aside.
2. In a small saucepan, soften the gelatin in ¼ cup cold water and let it stand for 1 minute. Dissolve the gelatin over low heat, stirring until completely dissolved. Add the ginger and ⅓ cup sugar and stir until the sugar is completely dissolved. Transfer to a large bowl and whisk until just warm.
3. Slowly whisk the puréed mixture into the gelatin; combine well. Place in the refrigerator for 30 to 40 minutes, until the mixture is quite thick; whisk occasionally to prevent lumps.
4. In another bowl, beat the egg white to soft peaks. Add the remaining sugar and beat until stiff. Gently fold in the egg white and blend well. Transfer to a serving bowl, cover, and refrigerate for 4 hours. Sprinkle with the nutmeg.

Cal. **161** *Carb.* **32g** *Protein* **7g** *Chol.* **4mg** *Fat* **1g/6%**

Leftovers are the **best** part

My Turkey Hash

SERVES 6

1 tablespoon unsalted butter
1 medium potato, scrubbed and cubed
1 green bell pepper, halved, seeded, and cut into 1-inch chunks
2 cups leftover turkey meat, cut into bite-size chunks
½ cup Giblet Gravy (page 420)
2 cups Corn Bread Stuffing (page 422)
¼ cup finely chopped fresh Italian parsley

1. In an 8-inch skillet with 3-inch sides, heat the butter over medium heat. Add, in layers, the potato, pepper, and turkey; dot each layer with gravy. Top with the stuffing.
2. Cover the skillet tightly with foil, reduce the heat, and cook for 35 to 40 minutes, or until the hash is bubbling and the potatoes are cooked through. Serve garnished with the parsley.

*Cal. **216** Carb. **19g** Protein **17g** Chol. **53mg** Fat **8g/32%***

Creamed Turkey Corn Bread

SERVES 4

1 teaspoon olive oil
½ cup finely chopped onion
½ cup diced green bell pepper
2 tablespoons unsalted butter, softened
4 tablespoons all-purpose flour
1 cup chicken broth (see Basics)
1 cup skim milk
¼ teaspoon dried basil
3 cups cooked bite-size turkey meat, preferably white

"No more turkey, but I'd like another helping of that bread he ate."

Anonymous quoted in Joy of Cooking

2 tablespoons Canadian bacon, trimmed, thinly sliced and diced
Salt and freshly ground pepper

1. In a medium skillet, heat the olive oil over medium heat. Add the onion and green pepper and sauté until soft, about 5 minutes; set aside.

2. In a small bowl, beat the butter and flour together with a wooden spoon, to make a *beurre manié*.

3. In a heavy medium-size saucepan, combine the chicken broth and milk over medium-high heat, and bring to a low boil. Bit by bit, whisk in the *beurre manié* and cook, stirring, until it is thick and smooth. Simmer the sauce for 3 to 4 minutes. Stir in the basil, turkey, bacon, and sautéed onion and pepper. Season with salt and pepper to taste. Heat over medium heat for 5 to 7 minutes, or until piping-hot. Serve over a toasted English muffins, toast, or corn bread.

Cal. **322** *Carb.* **12g** *Protein* **36g** *Chol.* **74mg** *Fat* **13g/38%**

Turkey and Wild Rice Salad

SERVES 4
2 tablespoons extra-virgin olive oil
4 tablespoons fresh orange juice
1 tablespoon white wine vinegar
2 tablespoons minced fresh mint
1/4 teaspoon freshly ground pepper
Grated zest of 1 orange
3/4 cup cooked wild rice
3/4 cup cooked brown rice
2 tablespoons finely chopped dried apricots
8 ounces frozen French-style green beans, defrosted
8 ounces turkey breast, cooked and thinly sliced
4 fresh apricots, pitted and cut into thin wedges

1. In a small jar, combine the olive oil, orange juice, vinegar, mint, pepper, and orange zest. Shake well and set aside.

2. In a medium-size bowl, combine the wild and brown rice and dried apricots, and toss well. Pour the dressing over the rice, reserving 1 tablespoon, and toss well.

3. In a small bowl, combine the beans and the remaining tablespoon of the dressing, and toss well to coat evenly.

4. On a large round platter, mound the rice and arrange the beans, sliced turkey, and the sliced apricots around.

Cal. **298** *Carb.* **28g** *Protein* **20g** *Chol.* **42mg** *Fat* **12g/36%**

Apple-Turkey Salad

SERVES 6

1 cup dried cherries
1 tablespoon Sambuca
1 cup Low-Fat Blend (see Basics)
1 tablespoon "light" mayonnaise
1 pound cooked turkey
1 cup cored and diced red apples (skin on)
1 cup cored and diced green apples (skin on)
1/2 cup thinly sliced celery
1/2 cup thinly sliced fennel bulb

1. In a small bowl, combine the cherries and Sambuca; marinate for 30 minutes.
2. Place the Low-Fat Blend and mayonnaise in a blender, and blend until smooth. Set aside.
3. Shred the turkey into bite-size pieces and transfer to a large bowl. Add the apples, celery, fennel, and marinated cherries, and toss well. Add the dressing and toss to coat evenly. Cover and refrigerate for at least 1 hour. Taste and adjust the seasonings before serving.

Cal. **275** Carb. **20g** Protein **35g**

Chol. **83mg** Fat **6g/19%**

Barley

In the race for the newest and best of cholesterol-lowering cures, barley is often overlooked—erroneously. It's loaded with pectin, which is believed to slow the absorption of fats and has an ingredient that blocks the liver's ability to manufacture cholesterol.

Hulled barley has the tough outer hull removed. "Hull-less" is a special softer-hulled hybrid. Pearling abrasively removes the outer husk—as well as most of the fiber and half of the protein, fat, and minerals. Scotch or pot barley has been pearled three times; pearled barley, six times.

Barley's also great for thickening soups, stews, and casseroles.

Turkey-Barley Soup

YIELD: 4 QUARTS

1 meaty turkey carcass, left over from a 14- to 16-pound turkey
4 quarts chicken broth (see Basics) or water
1 tablespoon chopped garlic
3 cups chopped celery
2 cups shredded leek
1 cup chopped onion
2 cups chopped carrot
1½ cups finely chopped fresh Italian parsley
1 rutabaga (1¼ to 1½ pounds), peeled and cut into ¾-inch dice
1 cup barley
Salt and freshly ground pepper

1. In a very large stockpot, combine the carcass, water, garlic, celery, leek, onion, carrot, and 1 cup of the parsley. Bring to a boil, cover, reduce the heat, and simmer gently for 3 hours. Cool.

2. Strain the soup into a large bowl. Discard all skin, bones, and fat. Skim any fat from the broth. Return the broth to the pot.

3. Shred the turkey meat and add it to the broth along with the strained vegetables. Bring the soup to a boil and add the rutabaga and barley. Cover and simmer over low heat until the rutabaga and barley are cooked, about 45 minutes. Season to taste with salt and pepper. Just before serving stir in the remaining parsley.

*Cal. **85** Carb. **18g** Protein **3g** Chol. **3mg***

*Fat **.5g/5%** (analyzed per cup)*

The Christmas Cookie Jar

In this season of plenty, I still want to have my home chockful of goodies for guests to nibble. But when it comes to my favorite baked goods, it's a bit of a trade-off. It's very hard to reduce the fats and still achieve crisp, crunchy cookies. And so I reduce the saturated fats (and therefore the cholesterol) by cooking with canola oil as much as possible, always keeping taste first and foremost. Then I make bite-sized cookies, so guests can make their own smart choices.

Sugar Plums

YIELD: 48 PIECES

4 ounces whole blanched
   almonds
4 ounces walnuts
1 cup cooked millet
Zest of 1 orange, finely minced
4 ounces currants
4 ounces pitted dates
4 ounces golden raisins
4 ounces dried apricots
1/4 cup bourbon
6 ounces coarsely chopped
   walnuts

1. Chop the almonds and walnuts together in a food processor until fine; transfer to a mixing bowl. Combine the chopped nuts with the millet and orange zest.
2. Lightly spray or wipe the food processor blades with vegetable oil. Add the cur-

rants, dates, raisins, and apricots; pulse until finely chopped. Add the bourbon and the nut-and-millet mixture. Process until the mixture comes together in a ball.
3. Shape the mixture into walnut-sized balls. Roll in the coarsely chopped walnuts. Store in an airtight container for 3 days at room temperature to allow the flavors to blend, then store for several months in the refrigerator.
Cal. 82 Carb. 8g Protein 2g Chol. 0mg Fat 5g/51%*

Wood Shavings

YIELD: 30 COOKIES

1 egg
2 egg whites
1/2 cup sugar
1/2 cup plus 2 tablespoons
   all-purpose flour

1. Preheat the oven to 350°. Lightly spray or wipe two baking sheets with vegetable oil.

2. Beat the egg, egg whites, and sugar until thick. Add the flour and continue beating until well blended.

3. Fit a pastry bag with a number-10 pastry tube; spoon the batter into the bag. Press out 6-inch strips 3 inches apart, no more than six strips to a pan. Bake for 3 to 5 minutes, or just until the edges turn brown.

4. Remove from the oven, and while still warm, wrap each strip around a pencil to form a spiral. Remove and continue; the cookies will firm up quickly, so speed is of the essence. Repeat until all the batter is used up.

*Cal. **26** Carb. **5g** Protein **.6g** Chol. **6mg** Fat **.2g/6%*****

Brownie Points

YIELD: 32 MINI-BROWNIES

³/₄ cup all-purpose flour
¹/₄ teaspoon baking soda
¹/₄ teaspoon salt
2 cups semisweet chocolate chips
1 teaspoon vanilla extract
¹/₄ cup canola oil
²/₃ cup sugar
1 egg
1 egg white

1. Preheat the oven to 325°.

2. Lightly spray or wipe a 9-inch square pan with vegetable oil.

3. In a small bowl, combine the flour, baking soda, and salt. Set aside.

4. In a large bowl, combine the chocolate chips and vanilla.

5. In a saucepan, combine the oil, sugar, and 2 tablespoons of water. Bring the mixture just to a boil. Pour the hot mixture over the chips and stir. Add the egg and the egg white, and stir. Stir in the flour mixture. Pour the batter into the pan and spread evenly. Bake for 20 to 25 minutes—don't overcook. These should be slightly underdone for chewy brownies. Cut while still warm into 1-inch squares, and cool before removing them from the pan.

*Cal. **102** Carb. **13g** Protein **1g** Chol. **6mg** Fat **5g/43%*****

*Nutrition information analyzed per piece

Chocolate-Chip Bites

YIELD: 200 COOKIES

$^{1}/_{2}$ cup canola oil

1 cup light brown sugar

$^{3}/_{4}$ cup granulated sugar

1 egg

2 egg whites

$2^{1}/_{2}$ cups all-purpose flour

1 teaspoon baking soda

1 teaspoon salt

$1^{1}/_{2}$ cups semisweet chocolate
chips

1. Preheat the oven to 375°.
Lightly spray or wipe two baking sheets with vegetable oil.
2. In a large mixing bowl,
cream the oil, sugar, egg, and
egg whites until smooth.
3. Add the flour, soda, and
salt, and mix well.
4. Add the chocolate chips
and mix gently.
5. Place the dough, in $^{1}/_{2}$-tea-
spoon mounds, on the sheet.
6. Bake for 7 minutes, or until
brown.

Cal. **22** *Carb.* **3g** *Protein* **.3g**
Chol. **.9mg** *Fat* **.9g/38%***

Chocolate-Pecan Toffee Bars

YIELD: FORTY-EIGHT
1-INCH SQUARES

$^{3}/_{4}$ cup canola oil

1 cup light brown sugar

1 egg yolk

2 cups all-purpose flour

1 teaspoon vanilla extract

1 cup semisweet chocolate
chips

$^{1}/_{2}$ cup coarsely chopped
pecans

1. Preheat the oven to 350°.
2. In a medium-size bowl,
cream the oil and sugar. Add
the egg yolk and beat well.
Stir in the flour and vanilla.
3. Press the dough onto the
sheet. Lightly spray or wipe an
11 x 14-inch baking sheet
with vegetable oil. Bake for 25
minutes, or until golden; cool.
4. Melt the chocolate chips in
a double boiler. Spread the
melted chocolate evenly over
the cooled toffee and sprinkle
with the chopped pecans.

Cal. **88** *Carb.* **9g** *Protein* **.9g**
Chol. **4mg** *Fat* **5g/54%***

Snappy Ginger Cookies

YIELD: 72 COOKIES

1 tightly packed cup dark
brown sugar

$^{2}/_{3}$ cup canola oil

$^{1}/_{4}$ cup molasses

1 egg

$2^{1}/_{4}$ cups all-purpose flour

2 teaspoons ground ginger

2 tablespoons baking soda

$^{1}/_{2}$ teaspoon salt

$1^{1}/_{2}$ tablespoons finely
chopped fresh ginger

$^{1}/_{2}$ cup finely chopped
crystallized ginger

1. In a large mixing bowl, mix
the sugar and oil. Add the molasses and egg and beat well.
2. Stir in the flour, ground
ginger, baking soda, and salt
until well blended. Add the
fresh and crystallized ginger
and mix well.
3. Cover the bowl with plastic
wrap and refrigerate for at
least 2 hours or overnight.
4. Preheat the oven to 300°.
Spray or wipe a baking sheet
with vegetable oil.
5. Shape the dough into $^{1}/_{2}$-
inch balls and place on the
sheet about 2 inches apart.
Bake for 10 minutes or until
crisp; remove from the oven
and cool on a wire rack.

Cal. **47** *Carb.* **7g** *Protein* **.5g**
Chol. **3mg** *Fat* **2g/41%***

Peanut Butter Bites

YIELD: NINETY-SIX 1-INCH
COOKIES

1 cup chunky peanut butter

1 cup sugar

1 egg

1. Preheat the oven to 350°.
Lightly spray or wipe a baking
sheet with vegetable oil.

2. Place all the ingredients in
a medium bowl, and mix until
well blended.

3. Shape the dough into 1-
inch balls and place them on
the cookie sheet.

4. Bake for 7 to 10 minutes,
or until the bottoms are gold-
en brown.

Cal. 25 Carb. 3g Protein .7g

Chol. 2mg Fat 1g/48%*

Oatmeal-Raisin Cookies

My grandmother made
these crisp and crunchy
cookies, and we would eat
mountains of them. Hers
had lots of butter—but this
version still disappears like
crazy at our house.

YIELD: ONE HUNDRED AND
EIGHT 2-INCH COOKIES

1/2 cup golden raisins

3/4 cup fresh orange juice

3/4 cup canola oil

1 cup light brown sugar

1 cup granulated sugar

2 eggs

2 cups all-purpose flour

1/2 teaspoon baking powder

1 teaspoon baking soda

1 teaspoon salt

*1 vanilla bean, split, seeds
    removed*

1 cup quick oats

2 cups corn flakes

*1 cup flaked and
    sweetened coconut*

1. Preheat the oven to 350°.

2. In a saucepan, macerate the
raisins in the orange juice
over low heat for 15 minutes,
or until plumped.

3. In a heavy mixing bowl,
combine the oil, sugars, and
eggs, and mix until smooth.
Add the dry ingredients and
stir until well mixed. Add the
plumped raisins.

4. Lightly spray or wipe a
cookie sheet with vegetable
oil. Drop the dough by tea-
spoonfuls onto the baking
sheet; the cookies will spread
slightly during baking. Bake
for 8 to 10 minutes, or until
the cookies are golden brown;
cool on baking racks.

Cal. 45 Carb. .6g Protein .6g

Chol. 3mg Fat 3g/38%*

**Nutrition information
  analyzed per piece*

Gingerbread House *Party*

Gingerbread

YIELD: THIRTY 4 x 6-INCH COOKIES

1 egg

2 egg whites

³/4 cup light brown sugar

1/4 cup (1/2 stick) unsalted butter, softened

1/4 cup canola oil

1/2 cup molasses

3¹/2 cups all-purpose flour

1/4 teaspoon salt

1 teaspoon baking soda

1 teaspoon ground ginger

2 teaspoons minced crystallized ginger

1 teaspoon ground cinnamon

1/2 teaspoon ground nutmeg

1/4 teaspoon ground cloves

Royal Icing (opposite; optional)

1. In a large mixing bowl, beat the egg and egg whites slightly. Add the sugar, butter, oil, and molasses, and beat until creamy.

2. In a separate bowl, combine the dry ingredients and stir to combine. Slowly add the dry mixture to the wet and beat until well blended.

3. Flatten the dough into a large disc, place on a dinner plate, cover with plastic wrap, and refrigerate overnight.

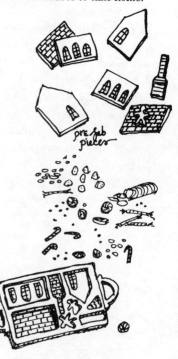

pre-fab pieces

Royal Icing

YIELD: 2 CUPS

3 large egg whites
4 cups confectioners' sugar
2 tablespoons fresh lemon juice

1. In a large mixing bowl, place the egg whites, sugar, and juice. Beat on low speed until blended.
2. Increase the speed to high and beat until stiff glossy peaks form.
3. Color with food coloring or use as is. The icing will keep for up to 3 days when stored in an airtight container in the refrigerator.

Cal. 59 Carb. 15g Protein .3g Chol. 0mg Fat 00g/00% (analyzed per tablespoon)

4. Preheat the oven to 350°. Lightly spray or wipe two cookie sheets with vegetable oil. Lightly flour a flat surface and roll out half the dough ¼ inch thick.
5. Cut out cookies with a cookie cutter. Place the cookies on the sheet and bake for 7 minutes, or until golden brown.
6. Decorate the cookies with Royal Icing, if desired.

Cal. 113 Carb. 18g Protein 2g Chol. 10mg Fat 4g/29%

Lemon Christmas Cookies

YIELD: EIGHTY 2½-INCH COOKIES

4 cups all-purpose flour
1 tablespoon baking powder
½ teaspoon salt
4 eggs
2 cups sugar
Zest of 1 lemon, grated
½ teaspoon mace
Confectioners' sugar

1. Into a large bowl, sift the flour, baking powder, and salt. Set aside.
2. In a large bowl of an electric mixer, at high speed, beat the eggs for 5 minutes, until thick and lemon colored.
3. At medium speed, beat in the sugar, 2 tablespoons at a time, beating well after each addition. Continue to beat the egg mixture for 10 minutes after all the sugar has been added.
4. Remove the bowl from the mixer, and add the flour, lemon zest, and mace, stirring with a wooden spoon until well combined.
5. Divide the mixture into four equal pieces, wrap in plastic, and refrigerate until very cold, at least 3 hours.
6. Preheat the oven to 325°. Line baking sheets with parchment paper. Lightly dust a pastry board and rolling pin with confectioners' sugar. Remove one package of dough from the refrigerator; keep each of the remaining packages chilled until you are ready to work with it. Roll the dough out to about ⅛ inch thick. Cut out the cookies, and with a spatula, place them on the baking sheets. Bake for 12 to 15 minutes, or until just lightly golden. Remove to a wire rack and cool completely.
NOTE: For a shiny cookie, bake for 5 minutes, brush with lightly beaten egg white, and continue baking until done.

Cal. 46 Carb. 10g Protein 1g Chol. 9mg Fat .3g/6% (analyzed per cookie)

Cherry-Walnut Fruitcake

SERVES 24

2 cups dried cherries
2 cups chopped, pitted dates
1 cup cream sherry
¾ cup all-purpose flour
⅓ cup light brown sugar
½ teaspoon baking powder
2 cups chopped walnuts
1 egg
2 egg whites

1. Preheat the oven to 300°. Lightly spray or wipe four 3 x 6 x 2-inch loaf pans with vegetable oil.
2. In a large bowl, combine the cherries, dates, and ½ cup of sherry; set aside for 15 minutes, stirring occasionally.
3. In a separate large bowl, mix the flour, sugar, and baking powder. Add the nuts. Add the egg and egg whites, and mix well. Stir the flour mixture into the fruit mixture. Place 1 cup of batter into each loaf pan.
4. Bake for 1 hour, or until golden brown. Remove from the oven and immediately pour the remaining sherry over the loaves. Keep in a tin, well wrapped with plastic wrap, for up to 2 weeks.

*Cal. **175** Carb. **28g** Protein **4g** Chol. **8mg** Fat **7g/32%***

Deck the Halls, etc.

• Swag columns, window treatments, or walls corner to corner with bolts of wide fabric in intense shades of pink, lavender, green, blue, yellow. Create luminous pools of color with spotlights.
• Have a white Christmas. Use winter white as a theme, varying only shades and textures. Group paper-whites, narcissus, white amaryllis, white poinsettias.
• Make magic everywhere with tiny white Christmas-tree lights; dangle them from the ceiling like stars in the sky, hang them from topiary trees, or nestle them in artificial snow on a tabletop. Let little lights twinkle from beams, railings, banisters, or outside a snowy window.
• Fill the house with greenery. Use pine boughs or boxwood over pictures and mirrors, let it overflow in vases, baskets, and window-boxes, wrap it around pillars, or use it to frame doorways and windows, indoors and out.
• Use tall white candles (18 to 32 inches) in abundance, as a flickering contrast to other lighting.
• Keep a wonderful selection of music playing—Cole Porter, George Gershwin, Irving Berlin, Noël Coward, along with the seasonal classics, the Messiah and oratorios.

438

Pear and Port Fruitcake

SERVES 30

3 large pears, peeled, cored, and
    cut into small chunks
½ cup ruby port
2 tablespoons frozen apple juice
    concentrate, defrosted
2 tablespoons canola oil
2 tablespoons unsalted butter
½ cup light brown sugar
¼ cup molasses
1 egg
4 egg whites
Zest of 1 lemon, finely grated
Zest of 1 orange, finely grated
1½ cups dried cherries
1 cup currants
1½ cups whole-wheat flour
1 cup all-purpose flour
2 teaspoons baking soda
2 teaspoons ground cinnamon
¼ teaspoon salt
1 cup chopped walnuts

1. In a medium saucepan, combine the pears, port, and apple juice concentrate. Bring to a boil and cook for 20 minutes. Drain off ½ cup of the liquid. Mash the pears and remaining liquid together.
2. In a small mixing bowl, place the mashed pears, oil, butter, sugar, molasses, egg, egg whites, and zests. Mix together.
3. Add the cherries and currants to the pear mixture.
4. Preheat the oven to 300°.
5. In a large mixing bowl, combine the flours, baking soda, cinnamon, and salt. Blend in the pear mixture. Fold in the walnuts.
6. Lightly spray or wipe four 3 x 6 x 2-inch mini-loaf pans with vegetable oil. Divide the batter among the pans.
7. Bake for 35 to 40 minutes, or until a toothpick inserted in the center comes out clean.
8. Immediately pour ⅛ cup of the reserved port-and-apple-juice sauce over each loaf; cool the fruitcakes in the pans. Store in a tin for up to 1 week.

*Cal. **142** Carb. **24g** Protein **3g** Chol. **8mg** Fat **5g/28%***

White Christmas Eve

Lobster Bisque

SERVES 8

2 live lobsters (1½ pounds each)
¼ cup Madeira
2 tablespoons unsalted butter
1 cup coarsely chopped onion
1 teaspoon finely chopped garlic
½ cup coarsely chopped celery, including some leaves
½ cup dry white wine
1 cup coarsely chopped fresh tomato
4 whole basil leaves, shredded
½ bay leaf, crumbled
1 cup cubed turnips
2 large carrots, cut into ½-inch cubes (1 cup)
3 tablespoons all-purpose flour
1 cup skim milk
2 teaspoons tomato paste
Salt and freshly ground white pepper

Candlelight Service Supper

Lobster Bisque

Partridges amid Pears

Barolo

Glazed Pearl Onions

Mâche with Champagne Spritz

Cherry-Walnut Fruitcake

"Scented acres of holiday Trees; prickly-leafed holly. Red berries shiny as Chinese bells: black crows swoop upon them screaming. Having stuffed our burlap sacks with enough greenery and crimson to garland a dozen windows, we set about choosing a tree."

Truman Capote
A Christmas Memory

1. In a large heavy skillet with 3-inch sides, bring 6 cups of water to a boil over high heat. Add the live lobsters, cover immediately, lower the heat to medium-high, and steam the lobsters for 10 to 12 minutes. Remove the lobsters from the skillet; reserve the cooking liquid, and set the lobsters aside to cool.

2. When the lobsters are cool enough to handle, crack the shells, remove the meat, and cut it into bite-size pieces. (Discard the stomach, a hard sac near the head.) Reserve all the shells. Place the lobster meat, the coral (roe) if there is any, and the tomalley (the greenish liver) in a bowl; sprinkle with the Madeira and set aside.

3. Pour the cooking water from the skillet into a bowl, and set it aside. In the same large skillet, melt 1 tablespoon of the butter over medium-high heat. Add all the lobster shells and stir to coat with butter. Lower the heat to medium and sauté the shells for 20 to 25 minutes, stirring occasionally. Add the onion, garlic, and celery, and sauté for 10 minutes, stirring. Increase the heat to medium-high and add 4 cups of the reserved lobster cooking liquid, the white wine, chopped tomato, basil, and the bay leaf. Cook, uncovered, until the liquid is reduced by half, about 20 minutes. Strain the mixture through a fine sieve, pressing down hard on the mixture to capture all the juices; you should have 2 cups. Discard the solids and set the reduced liquid aside.

4. Meanwhile, in a separate medium saucepan, combine the remaining 2 cups of lobster cooking liquid with the turnips and carrots. Bring to a boil and cook, covered, for 20 to 30 minutes, or until the vegetables are soft. Purée the vegetables and the cooking liquid in a food processor, and set aside.

5. In a small bowl, combine the remaining butter and the flour, to make a *beurre manié*; set aside.

6. In a large heavy saucepan, bring the 2 cups of reduced cooking liquid to a boil. Whisk in the vegetable purée, the milk, and the tomato paste. Lower the heat and whisk in the *beurre manié* a little at a time. Continue to whisk until the soup is smooth and just thick enough to coat the whisk lightly—you might not need all the *beurre manié*. Bring the bisque to a gentle boil, stir, and cook for 2 minutes.

7. Remove the bisque from the heat and add the lobster meat, tomalley, coral, and Madeira. Season with salt and a dash of pepper, if necessary, to taste. Serve immediately.

Cal. **109** *Carb.* **10g** *Protein* **9g** *Chol.* **33mg** *Fat* **4g/26%**

Partridges amid Pears

SERVES 4

4 partridges (about 1 pound each)
16 Seckel pears
1 cup ruby port
½ cup canned pear juice or nectar
2 tablespoons fresh lemon juice
2 tablespoons unsalted butter
1 tablespoon light brown sugar
1 teaspoon coarsely grated lemon zest
4 thin slices bread, crusts removed

1. Preheat the oven to 350°. Rinse the partridges inside and out and pat dry. Cut four of the pears in half and remove the cores. Stuff each partridge with one halved pear. Truss and place on a rack in a roasting pan.

2. In a small bowl, combine the port and pear juice. Add to the pan and baste. Roast the partridges for 45 minutes, basting them every 8 to 10 minutes.

3. In a medium bowl, combine the lemon juice with 2 cups of water; drop in the remaining pears.

4. In a large skillet, melt the butter over medium heat. Remove the pears from the water and pat dry. Sauté in butter, stirring, until the fruit is fragrant and begins to brown slightly. Sprinkle the pears with the brown sugar and lemon zest, turning them to coat. Remove the birds from the oven. Increase the oven temperature to 500°.

5. Baste the birds with the remaining wine and pear juice, and return them to the oven to brown, about 10 to 12 minutes.

6. To serve, lightly toast the bread on both sides. Place one slice of toast on each of four plates. Place the partridges on the toast and garnish each with three sautéed pears. Serve immediately.

Cal. **388** *Carb.* **50g** *Protein* **22g** *Chol.* **81mg** *Fat* **12g/28%**

Glazed Pearl Onions

SERVES 12

3 pints pearl onions, peeled
$^1/_2$ cup whole garlic cloves, peeled
1 cup chicken broth (see Basics)
1 tablespoon fresh lemon juice
Salt and freshly ground pepper
1 tablespoon unsalted butter
1 tablespoon sugar

1. Preheat the oven to 375°.

2. Place the onions and garlic cloves in a large shallow baking pan; pour the chicken broth over. Add the lemon juice and salt and pepper to taste. Cover the pan tightly with foil and bake for 30 minutes. Remove the foil and bake, uncovered, for 20 to 30 more minutes, until the onions are very tender. Remove from the oven and drain the vegetables.

3. In a very large skillet, heat the butter over medium heat until melted. Add the onions and garlic; sprinkle with the sugar and shake the pan to coat all the onions and garlic. Cook until golden and caramelized, but take care not to burn the vegetables. (This may need to be done in two batches.) Transfer the onions and garlic to a serving dish, sprinkle with lemon zest, if desired, and serve immediately.

NOTE: The cooking broth can be reserved and used for other dishes, such as soups or sauces.

*Cal. **59** Carb. **10g** Protein **2g** Chol. **3mg** Fat **1g/19%***

"So now is come
our joyful'st
feast
Let every man
be jolly
Each room with
ivy leaves is
dressed
And every post
with holly."

George Wither

Christmas Goose with Prunes

SERVES 12

1 package (12 ounces) pitted prunes
1 cup Armagnac
1 goose (12 to 14 pounds), thawed if frozen
Giblet Purée, made with reserved giblets
  (page 420)
1 teaspoon canola oil
2 teaspoons finely minced garlic
2 cups finely chopped celery
1 cup finely chopped onion
8 cups cubed French bread, preferably
  day-old
1 cup finely chopped fresh Italian parsley
¼ cup loosely packed chopped fresh sage
Salt and freshly ground pepper
2 cups dry red wine
8 whole sage leaves
Whole sprigs of sage

1. Soak the prunes in the Armagnac for several hours.

2. Make the Giblet Purée; you should have about 3 cups. Remove every trace of fat from the bird. Rinse the bird and pat it dry inside and out. Rub the cavities of the goose liberally with salt; set aside.

3. In a skillet, heat the oil over medium heat. Add the garlic, celery, and onion, and sauté until softened, 5 to 7 minutes; add the bread and toss well. Add the parsley and chopped sage to the mixture. Drain the prunes and reserve the Armagnac. Chop the prunes coarsely, and add them and the reserved Armagnac to the stuffing. Season with salt and pepper to taste.

4. Preheat the oven to 400°. Loosely stuff the goose with the stuffing and truss it. Place the remaining stuffing in an oven-proof baking dish and add up to 1 cup of the giblet water to moisten. Cover with foil and set aside.

5. Prick the skin of the goose all over with a fork, being careful not to penetrate the flesh. Place the bird on a rack in a roasting pan. Roast for 45 minutes to 1 hour. Spoon the fat from the pan every 30 minutes. Reduce the heat to 325° and roast for 2½ to 2¾ hours more. Bake the stuffing during the last 30 minutes that the goose roasts.

6. Remove the goose from the oven and place on a heated platter; let it rest for 20 minutes.

Christmas Eve Dinner

Crabmeat Soup

Christmas Goose with
Prunes

Apple-Hazelnut Wild Rice

Carrot Purée

Broccoli with Green Sauce

Mesclun with Sherry
Salad Spray

Merry Christmas Trifle

Cognac and Armagnac

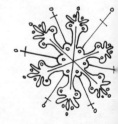

444

7. Meanwhile, drain all the fat from the roasting pan, leaving behind any drippings and browned bits. (A 12½-pound goose will yield about 4½ to 5 cups fat.) Place the roasting pan on the stove over medium-high heat, and add the remaining Giblet Purée and the red wine. Reduce the sauce over high heat until you have 2 cups, about 10 minutes. Season the sauce with salt and freshly ground pepper to taste. Add the sage leaves, and keep the sauce warm until ready to serve.

8. Remove the stuffing from the goose and add it to the baked stuffing. Toss well to combine. Slice the goose and place the pieces on a heated platter. Garnish the platter with sprigs of sage and serve immediately.

*Cal. **485** Carb. **20g** Protein **50g** Chol. **159mg** Fat **17g/33%***

Candied Bourbon Sweets

SERVES 6

4 cups peeled and sliced (¼-inch-thick) sweet potatoes
2 cups fresh orange juice
¼ cup light brown sugar
¼ teaspoon salt
½ cup bourbon, or more to taste
1 vanilla bean, split

1. Preheat the oven to 350°.

2. Lightly spray or wipe an 11 x 7-inch baking dish with canola oil. Place the sweet potatoes in the baking dish in even, overlapping rows.

3. In a medium saucepan, combine the orange juice, sugar, salt, bourbon, and split vanilla bean over medium-high heat. Bring to a boil, stirring, then pour over the potatoes. Bury the vanilla bean under the potatoes. Cover the baking dish tightly with foil.

4. Bake for 30 minutes; uncover and continue to bake, basting frequently, until tender, about 20 more minutes. Serve immediately.

*Cal. **153** Carb. **36g** Protein **2g** Chol. **0mg** Fat .5g/2%*

Snow

We live in the Snow Belt of Michigan. In scientific terms, this is a meterological phenomenon caused by cold air colliding with warmer waters over Lake Michigan. This creates the "lake effect"—snow along the shoreline; a fluffier snow than most, but in greater abundance.

In nonscientific terms, our house is set in a winter wonderland where fluffy snowflakes may drift down every day for weeks.

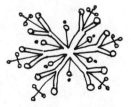

Christmas Capon with Herbs

SERVES 8

1 capon (6 to 7½ pounds)
2 tablespoons minced fresh rosemary
2 teaspoons minced garlic
½ teaspoon coarse salt
1 tablespoon olive oil
Freshly ground pepper
8 sprigs fresh rosemary
1 whole garlic head, outside peel removed, tips trimmed
  with a sharp knife to expose the flesh
3 to 4 tablespoons 25-year-old balsamic vinegar
½ teaspoon light brown sugar

1. Remove the giblets from the capon and reserve for another use. Trim and discard all excess fat from the bird. Rinse the capon and pat it dry.
2. Combine the rosemary, minced garlic, and salt. Rub the capon with the olive oil, then the rosemary-garlic mixture. Season with pepper. Cover loosely with plastic wrap and refrigerate overnight.
3. Preheat the oven to 325°. Place the rosemary sprigs in the cavity along with the head of garlic. Truss the bird and place it on a rack in a roasting pan. Roast the capon 25 minutes per pound, about 2½ to 3 hours, or until it registers 170° on a meat thermometer.
4. Remove the capon from the oven and place it on a heated platter; let it rest for 20 minutes. In a small bowl, combine the vinegar and brown sugar. Drizzle the vinegar mixture over the capon; carve and serve immediately.

Cal. **350** *Carb.* **5g** *Protein* **48g** *Chol.* **145mg** *Fat* **14g/37%**

Christmas Rice

SERVES 8

1 cup white rice
1 cup wild rice
1 teaspoon olive oil
3 tablespoons minced garlic
1 tablespoon minced fresh ginger
1 tablespoon finely chopped and seeded jalapeño pepper
½ cup drained and finely minced sun-dried tomato
1 cup chopped scallion

½ cup finely chopped fresh cilantro
½ cup finely chopped fresh Italian parsley
¼ cup toasted sesame seeds
1 teaspoon sesame oil

1. In a saucepan, bring 2½ cups of water to a boil. Add both rices, lower the heat, and simmer, covered, for 20 minutes, or until the water has evaporated. Set aside.
2. In a large skillet, heat the oil over medium heat. Add the garlic, ginger, and jalapeño pepper. Sauté for 2 minutes, then add the rice. Add the tomato, scallion, cilantro, parsley, and sesame seeds. Add the sesame oil and fry the rice over low heat for 3 minutes. Serve hot.

Cal. **218** *Carb.* **39g** *Protein* **6g** *Chol.* **0mg** *Fat* **4g/18%**

Broccoli with Green Sauce

SERVES 12

8 cups trimmed and chopped broccoli, including peeled stems
1 cup low-fat cottage cheese
4 tablespoons goat cheese
1 tablespoon grated lemon zest
⅛ teaspoon grated fresh nutmeg
Freshly ground pepper
½ cup skim milk
8 cups broccoli florets

1. Bring a pot of water to a boil over high heat. Cook the chopped broccoli until tender, 3 to 4 minutes.
2. Drain the cooked broccoli and put it into a food processor; purée. Set aside.
3. Place the cottage cheese and goat cheese in a processor and blend until smooth. Add the broccoli purée, lemon zest, nutmeg, and pepper to taste, and blend until smooth.
4. Transfer the purée to a saucepan and warm over low heat. Slowly whisk in the milk until thoroughly combined; keep warm over low heat.
5. Prepare the broccoli florets just before serving: Bring 1 inch of water to a boil in a steamer. Place the florets on the steamer rack, cover, and steam until tender yet still crisp and bright green in color, about 3 minutes.
6. Place the florets in a large vegetable dish, ladle the sauce over them, and serve immediately.

Cal. **65** *Carb.* **7g** *Protein* **7g** *Chol.* **4mg** *Fat* **2g/21%**

Chestnut-Potato Purée

SERVES 4

¾ *pound potatoes, peeled and quartered*
1 teaspoon salt
½ *pound chestnuts*
1 cup chicken broth
  (see Basics)
6 tablespoons low-fat buttermilk
¼ *teaspoon baking soda*
½ *teaspoon ground cardamon*
Pinch cayenne

1. Cover the potatoes with cold water in a medium saucepan and bring to a boil. Add ½ teaspoon of salt and boil for 45 minutes, or until tender. Drain and pass through a food mill fitted with a medium screen, or mash by hand or with an electric beater.
2. Place the chestnuts and chicken broth in a small saucepan. Cover and simmer for 30 minutes, or until tender. Transfer the chestnuts with a slotted spoon to a blender or food processor, and process to a purée.
3. Add the buttermilk and baking soda to the potatoes and stir to combine. Fold in the puréed chestnuts.
4. Add the cardamom, remaining salt, and cayenne. Taste and adjust seasonings. Serve immediately.

Cal. **140** *Carb.* **29g** *Protein* **4g** *Chol.* **3mg** *Fat* **1g/8%**

Christmas Day Dinner

Shrimp Sausage

Basil-Cheese Crackers

Christmas Rib Roast

Chestnut-Potato Purée

*Watercress with
Roquefort Salad Spray*

Midnight Torte

Vanilla Chestnut Sauce

Vanilla Frozen Yogurt

Christmas Rib Roast

SERVES 12

*1 standing rib roast (7*½ *to 8*½ *pounds), spinal cord, shoulder
  bone, and chine removed, chine tied back on*
2 tablespoons slivered garlic
*1*½ *tablespoons mixed peppercorns (black, green, pink, and
  white), coarsely ground*
1 tablespoon coarse salt
5 bay leaves
*1 whole garlic head, outside peel removed, tips trimmed with
  a sharp knife to expose the flesh*
4 cups pearl onions
6 large potatoes, peeled
3 cups Madeira

Christmas Crackers

The English have loved to put these colorfully wrapped paper tubes stuffed with toys, poems, confetti, streamers, or marbles on their Christmas tables since Victorian times. Today crackers can also include clever refrigerator magnets, costume jewelry, pens, key rings, and tiny vials of perfume. Tied up with ribbons, crackers also make great place cards.

" not believe in Santa Claus! You might as well not believe in fairies."

Frank Church

2 tablespoons Onion Marmalade (see Basics)
Salt and freshly ground pepper

1. Bring the meat to room temperature before roasting, about 1½ to 2 hours. Pat the roast dry with paper towels.

2. Preheat the oven to 500°. Make small incisions with the tip of a sharp knife all over the roast, except at the meaty eye, and insert all the slivers of garlic. Pack the pepper and salt thickly on the fat on top of the roast. Slip the bay leaves under the butcher strings. Place the roast on a rack in a roasting pan; place the head of garlic under the roast.

3. Place the roast in the oven; reduce the heat to 350°. Roast for 18 to 20 minutes per pound for medium-rare.

4. Meanwhile, prepare the onions and potatoes: Bring a medium pot of water to a boil. Peel the onions and set aside. Peel the potatoes and cut them into pieces about 2 inches long and 1 inch thick. Trim the ends of each piece to give them an oval shape, about 2 to 2½ inches long. Drop the potatoes into the boiling water and parcook them, 10 to 12 minutes. Drain. Thirty minutes before the roast is done, add the onions and potatoes to the roasting pan. Shake the pan slightly to coat the vegetables in the drippings. Baste, and turn the vegetables from time to time until the roast is ready.

5. Remove the roast from the oven and let it stand for 10 to 15 minutes before carving. Keep the vegetables warm until ready to serve. Discard the garlic. Pour off all the drippings from the roasting pan, leaving any brown bits and meat juices, but no fat, in the pan. Place the roasting pan over medium-high heat. Add the Madeira and bring to a boil. Stir up any bits from the bottom of the pan and cook for 10 minutes to reduce the sauce to about 2 cups. Stir in the Onion Marmalade; remove from the heat, and keep the sauce warm.

6. Serve the sliced meat surrounded with onions and potatoes. Add any accumulated juices to the sauce. Pass the sauce at the table.

Cal. **415** *Carb.* **30g** *Protein* **36g** *Chol.* **93mg** *Fat* **17g/37%**

Roasted Harvest Mosaic

SERVES 12

2 Granny Smith apples, cut into chunks
2 cups cubed new potatoes
2 cups trimmed whole Brussels sprouts
6 cups cubed butternut squash
2 tablespoons olive oil
4 tablespoons balsamic vinegar
1/4 cup finely minced fresh thyme
1/4 cup chopped fresh Italian parsley
Salt and freshly ground pepper
1 cup cooked chestnuts

1. Preheat the oven to 375°.
2. Place all of the vegetables, except the chestnuts, in a large mixing bowl and toss with the oil, vinegar, thyme, and parsley to coat well. Divide the vegetables between two 9 x 13 x 2-inch roasting pans.
3. Place the pans in the oven and bake, uncovered, for 50 minutes, tossing with a spoon or spatula every 15 minutes. Add the chestnuts and salt and pepper to taste, and cook for 10 minutes. Transfer the vegetables to a serving bowl and serve immediately.

Cal. 167 Carb. 35g Protein 3g Chol. 0mg Fat 3g/12%

Butternut Squash and Bananas

SERVES 6

1 butternut squash (4 pounds)
Salt
1/2 teaspoon freshly grated nutmeg
3 tablespoons Cointreau or Grand Marnier
1 1/2 teaspoons finely grated orange zest
1 to 2 ripe bananas, mashed (1 cup)
1 tablespoon unsalted butter

1. Preheat the oven to 350°.
2. Lightly spray or wipe a 2-quart baking dish with vegetable or canola oil. Set aside.
3. Cut the squash in half lengthwise. Scoop out the seeds and strings. Place the halves, cut sides down, in another baking dish large enough to accommodate both halves. Add water to reach 1/2 inch up the sides of the squash. Bake for 45 minutes, or until tender.

"...in the depths of winter...we force spring."

Bill Clinton
January 20, 1993

4. Remove the squash from the oven and scoop the flesh into a bowl; use an electric mixer to mash the squash until smooth and fluffy. Add the salt, nutmeg, Cointreau, and zest. Fold the mashed bananas into the squash.

5. Transfer the mixture to the greased baking dish. Dot with bits of the butter and bake until heated through, 20 to 25 minutes. Serve immediately.

Cal. 178 Carb. 41g Protein 3g Chol. 6mg Fat 3g/12%

Ruby Red Sorbet

SERVES 6

1 cup sugar
1 pound cranberries, fresh or frozen, rinsed
1 cup fresh orange juice
1 cup ruby port
1 tablespoon finely minced orange zest

1. In a heavy saucepan over high heat, place 1 cup of water and the sugar, and bring to a rolling boil, stirring occasionally. Boil for 3 minutes, then add the cranberries. Lower the heat to medium and cook for 5 to 8 minutes, until the cranberries soften slightly. Remove the pan from the heat and cool slightly.

2. Transfer the cranberry sauce to a food processor and process until smooth, adding the orange juice and port. Remove from the processor, stir in the zest, and refrigerate until very cold. Freeze the sorbet in an ice cream maker according to the manufacturer's directions.

Cal. 279 Carb. 59g Protein 1g Chol. 0mg Fat .3g/1%

Red and Green Salad

SERVES 4

1 large ripe pomegranate
2 cups loosely packed watercress
6 kiwi, peeled and thinly sliced

1. Cut the pomegranate in half; remove the seeds and juice from the membrane and reserve.

2. Place a bed of watercress on each of four salad plates. Divide the kiwi slices among the plates in a circular pattern. Sprinkle the pomegranate seeds and juice over the kiwi. Serve immediately.

Cal. 111 Carb. 27g Protein 2g Chol. 0mg Fat .7g/5%

Pomegranates

Also known as "Chinese apple," this luscious fruit was brought back by Europeans from the Holy Land. Pomegranates became the basis for a combination as ambrosial today as it was then. Mash the pulp of six pomegranates and place it in a silver bowl. Sprinkle lightly with rose water, lemon juice, and sugar, and serve very cold. This heavenly dessert is loaded with potassium. Pomegranates have some vitamin C, too.

Persimmon Pudding

SERVES 6

2 to 3 ripe persimmons, peeled and puréed to make 1 cup
½ cup skim milk
1 tablespoon unsalted butter, melted
1 egg
¾ cup packed light brown sugar
1 cup all-purpose flour
1 teaspoon baking soda
¼ teaspoon salt
1 teaspoon ground cinnamon
½ teaspoon ground ginger
¼ teaspoon grated nutmeg
Sour Lemon Sauce (below)

1. Preheat the oven to 350°. Lightly spray or wipe a 9-inch pie pan with canola oil.
2. In a small bowl, whisk the persimmon purée, milk, butter, and egg. Set aside.
3. In a large mixing bowl, combine the sugar, flour, soda, salt, and spices. Stir the persimmon mixture into the flour mixture.
4. Pour the mixture into the pie pan. Place the pan in a large shallow pan, and pour boiling water into the larger pan to a depth of ½ inch. Bake for 1 to 1¼ hours, adding water if necessary. The pudding is done when a knife inserted in the center comes out moist but clean.
5. Cool the pudding slightly, cut it into wedges, and serve warm or at room temperature with Sour Lemon Sauce.

Cal. **192** *Carb.* **38g** *Protein 4g Chol.* **36mg** *Fat* **3g/15%**

Sour Lemon Sauce

YIELD: 1 CUP

1 tablespoon cornstarch
¼ cup sugar
1 cup fresh orange juice
1½ tablespoons fresh lemon juice
1 teaspoon finely grated lemon zest
Pinch salt

1. In a heavy saucepan, combine the corn-starch and sugar. Slowly whisk in the orange juice. Cook, stirring, over low heat until the

"Write me down As one who loved poetry, And persimmons."

Shikki

452

mixture is thickened and begins to boil.

2. Stir in the lemon juice, zest, and salt. Remove from the heat. Serve warm or at room temperature.

Cal. 21 Carb. 6g Protein .1g Chol. 0mg Fat .05g/1%
(analyzed per tablespoon)

Merry Christmas Trifle

SERVES 12

1 ripe pomegranate
2 pounds ripe papaya
9 kiwi, peeled and thinly sliced
1 pineapple, cut into ½-inch chunks (2 cups)
1 Sky-High Angel Food Cake, cut into 1-inch cubes (page 98)
2 cups Passionfruit Cream (page 100)

1. Cut the pomegranate in half; remove the seeds and juice and place them in a strainer over a bowl. Set aside.

2. Peel the papayas, remove the seeds, coarsely chop, and place in a blender or food processor. Purée the papaya. Add the pomegranate juice and process for 10 seconds; set aside.

3. To assemble the trifle, place half the cake cubes on the bottom of a 2-quart serving bowl. Spoon half the Passionfruit Cream over the cake cubes. Top with half the papaya purée, and cover with half the kiwi and half the pomegranate seeds. Press down lightly to level the layers. Cover with the remaining cake cubes and press lightly again. Spoon the remaining papaya purée over the cake cubes. Cover with the pineapple. Spoon over the remaining Passionfruit Cream. Top with the remaining kiwi and pomegranate seeds. Cover and refrigerate for at least 4 hours before serving.

Cal. 284 Carb. 64g Protein 9g
Chol .6mg Fat .9g/2%

"Heap on more wood!—the wind is chill;
But let it whistle as it will,
We'll keep our Christmas merry still."

Sir Walter Scott

Noël Cake

SERVES 24

2 layers White Wine Cake (opposite)
1⅔ cups bourbon
2½ cups chopped walnuts
2 cups assorted candied fruits and dried
    cranberries or dried tart cherries
1 cup quartered candied cherries
½ cup light brown sugar
1 cup frozen cran-raspberry juice concentrate,
    defrosted
1 cup halved candied cherries

1. Cut each cake layer horizontally into three layers.
2. Use 1⅓ cups of the bourbon to soak the six layers generously.
3. In a medium saucepan, combine the nuts, fruits, remaining bourbon, sugar, and juice. Stir over medium heat for about 10 minutes, until syrupy and almost caramelized.
4. Using two spatulas, place one cake layer on a serving plate. Divide 1 cup of the fruit mixture over the layer. Repeat with the remaining layers, using the last cup of fruit mixture on top of the cake. Decorate with the halved cherries, placing them around the top rim of the cake.
5. Let sit, covered tightly with plastic wrap, in a cool place for at least 3 to 4 days. Serve in thin slices. This cake will keep for up to 3 weeks.

*Cal. **355** Carb. **51g** Protein **5g** Chol. **8mg** Fat **13g/29%***

Vanilla Chestnut Sauce

SERVES 12

1 pound peeled fresh chestnuts
2 cups sugar
3 whole vanilla beans
¼ cup lemon peel, removed with a vegetable peeler and cut
    into very thin strips
3 tablespoons fresh lemon juice
3 cinnamon sticks (3 inches each)

1. In a large, heavy saucepan, combine all of the ingredients with 2 cups of water. Bring to a boil over medium heat, then reduce the heat and simmer for 40 minutes, or until the

"Exercise is the most awful illusion. The secret is a lot of aspirin and marrons glacés."

Noël Coward

White Wine Cake

A white cake that is light and flavorful without any cholesterol.

YIELD: TWO 9-INCH LAYERS

3 cups dry white wine
1 egg
2 cups sugar
1/2 cup canola oil
2 1/2 cups flour
1/4 teaspoon salt
2 1/2 teaspoons baking powder
1/2 vanilla bean, split, seeds removed
1 tablespoon vanilla
4 egg whites

1. Preheat the oven to 350°. Lightly spray or wipe two 9-inch cake pans with vegetable oil.
2. In a nonreactive saucepan, heat the wine over low heat until the liquid is reduced to one cup; cool.
3. In a large mixing bowl cream the egg, sugar, and oil and beat until smooth. Stir in the wine.
4. Add the flour, salt, baking powder, and vanilla seeds and extract, and mix well until blended.
5. In a separate bowl, whip the egg whites until stiff peaks are formed.
6. Gently fold the whites into the batter. Divide the batter between the pans.
7. Bake for 20 to 25 minutes; or until a toothpick inserted into the center comes out clean.

*Cal. **240** Carb. **41g** Protein **3g** Chol. **11mg** Fat **7g/24%***

chestnuts become somewhat opaque. Cool and store in a covered container in the refrigerator until ready to use.
2. When ready to serve, remove the vanilla bean and lemon peel and discard. Serve the chestnuts warm over ice cream.

*Cal. **182** Carb. **45g** Protein **1g** Chol. **0mg** Fat **.6g/3%***

Chestnut Cheesecake

SERVES 12

1 pound peeled chestnuts
1 cup sugar
1/2 cup cognac
1 vanilla bean, split, seeds removed
1 container (15 ounces) "light" ricotta
8 ounces low-fat cottage cheese
2 eggs, at room temperature
2 egg whites, at room temperature
1 tablespoon vanilla extract
Vanilla Chestnut Sauce (opposite)

1. Preheat the oven to 350°. Lightly spray or wipe a 10 1/2-inch springform pan with vegetable oil.
2. Combine the chestnuts, 1/2 cup of the sugar, the cognac, and the vanilla seeds in a medium saucepan over high heat. Bring to a boil; continue to boil for 5 to 8 minutes, stirring often, until very thick. Cool the mixture and remove the vanilla seeds. Lightly crush the chestnuts.
3. Place the ricotta, the remaining sugar, and the cottage cheese in a blender; process until smooth. Add the eggs, egg whites, and vanilla extract. Pulse just until combined; do not overmix. Transfer the mixture to a mixing bowl.
4. Lace the chestnut pieces through the cheese mixture, creating streaks like a marble cake. Pour the mixture into the springform pan, smoothing the top. Bake for 1 hour; reduce the oven temperature to 325°, and bake for another 15 minutes, or until a knife inserted in the cake 2 inches from the edge comes out clean.
5. Serve at room temperature, or chill until ready to use. Remove from the pan, slice, and serve topped with Vanilla Chestnut Sauce.

*Cal. **226** Carb. **38g** Protein **9g** Chol. **42mg** Fat **4g/17%***

Bûche de Noël

SERVES 12

The cake:

5 egg whites
1/8 teaspoon cream of tartar
1 teaspoon vanilla extract
1/8 teaspoon salt
1/2 cup granulated sugar
1/2 cup all-purpose flour
1/3 cup cocoa
2 tablespoons confectioners' sugar

Mocha filling:

2 cups low-fat ricotta cheese
1/4 cup honey
2 tablespoons Kahlua
1 tablespoon instant coffee
Seeds from 1 vanilla bean

Chocolate meringue:

5 egg whites
1 teaspoon vanilla extract
1/2 cup granulated sugar
1/4 cup cocoa

For the cake:

1. Preheat the oven to 350°.

2. In the bowl of an electric mixer, beat the egg whites until soft peaks form. Add the cream of tartar and vanilla, and beat until the peaks are just stiff.

3. In a small mixing bowl, combine the dry ingredients,

Bûche De Noël

The burning of the yule log has long been a Christmas tradition. Since the 1800s, it has been celebrated at French tables in the form of this chocolate dessert, made with a Genoise sponge cake, spread with buttercream and chocolate to simulate the bark, with almond-paste holly leaves. It's truly a feast for the eyes during the magic of Christmas—and one we wouldn't want to miss!

So I've lightened the chocolate with more egg whites than ever and added no butter. Then I frosted the log with coffee- and honey-flavored ricotta and dotted it with lots of meringue mushrooms. A sight to behold, and a terrific addition to any open-house buffet table.

except the confectioners' sugar. On a slow speed, add the dry mixture to the egg whites.

4. Cover a 12 x 16-inch baking sheet with waxed paper, and very lightly spray or wipe with vegetable oil. Pour the batter onto the sheet.

5. Place the sheet in the oven and bake for 15 minutes; the cake may appear underdone, but do not leave it in the oven.

6. Meanwhile, sprinkle a 12 x 16-inch, or larger, kitchen towel with the confectioners' sugar. Immediately invert the cake onto the towel and peel off the waxed paper. Gently roll the cake, from the long side, into a loose roll. Set aside to cool for 30 minutes.

For the filling:

In a medium mixing bowl, whisk all the filling ingredients until smooth. Unroll the cake and spread the filling evenly over it, leaving 1 inch uncovered on each end. Do not reroll the cake.

For the meringue:

Preheat the oven to 450°. Place the egg whites in the bowl of an electric mixer; beat on high speed until foamy. Add the vanilla and beat on high speed until stiff peaks form. On low, slowly add ¼ cup of sugar and the cocoa until well blended.

To assemble the cake:

1. Roll the cake and filling into a log and place it on the sheet.

2. Cover the log, including the ends, with the chocolate meringue. Sprinkle the top of the log with the remaining sugar and bake for 5 minutes, or just until the meringue begins to brown. Remove the roll from the oven and refrigerate it immediately for at least 2 hours. When ready to serve, cut the roll into 1½-inch slices.

*Cal. **180** Carb. **31g** Protein **8g** Chol. **10mg** Fat **2g/10%***

" I will honor Christmas in my heart, and try to keep it all the year. "

Charles Dickens

The Magical Morn

Baked Pears and Cranberries

SERVES 4

2 pears (preferably Anjou), peeled, halved, and cored
1½ cups fresh orange juice
2 teaspoons unsalted butter
1 vanilla bean, split
1 cup fresh cranberries, rinsed and drained
2 tablespoons sugar
4 cloves
1½ tablespoons grated orange zest
Slices of fresh orange

1. Preheat the oven to 350°.
2. In in a baking dish just large enough to hold them, place the pears, flat sides up, in one layer. Pour ¾ cup orange juice over the pears, and place ½ teaspoon of butter in each cavity. Submerge the vanilla bean in the orange juice. Bake the pears for 20 to 25 minutes, or until tender; do not overcook. Cool slightly.
3. Meanwhile, in a medium saucepan, combine the remaining orange juice, cranberries, sugar, cloves, and orange zest. Bring to a boil, lower the heat slightly, and simmer until the cranberries burst, about 5 minutes. Continue to cook, stirring occasionally, until the liquid reduces and thickens slightly. Cool slightly.
4. To serve, arrange the pears on a dish and spoon the chutney around them; garnish with orange slices.

*Cal. **158** Carb. **34g** Protein **1g** Chol. **6mg** Fat **3g/17%***

Christmas Brunch

*Fresh Orange
and Cranberry Juices*

*Baked Pears and
Cranberries*

Artichokes Benedict

Pecan Strudel

Simple Christmas Brioche

Lemon-Poppy Seed Bread

Walnut-Raisin Loaf

Cappuccino

Artichokes Benedict

SERVES 4

4 large artichokes
Juice of 1 lemon
Zest of 1 lemon
1 bay leaf
12 slices Canadian bacon, trimmed of fat
2 English muffins, split and toasted
Never-Fail Hollandaise Sauce (see Basics)
Paprika
Sprigs of fresh tarragon

1. Trim away the sharp tips of the artichokes, and trim 1½ inches off the tops with a sharp knife. Trim the stem ends. Rub all the trimmed edges with lemon juice, and place the artichokes, stem ends down, in a saucepan large enough to hold them in one layer. Cover the artichokes with water. Add the remaining lemon juice, zest, and bay leaf, and bring to a boil over medium-high heat. Cover, lower the heat, and simmer until the artichokes are tender, about 20 minutes. (If the leaves can be pulled away from the artichokes easily, they are cooked.) Remove the artichokes from the cooking liquid and set them aside to cool. (This can be done ahead.)

2. Pull the leaves off the artichokes; reserve eight and save the rest for another use. Carefully remove the fuzzy chokes from the centers with a spoon. Trim the sides and bottom of each artichoke, leaving four artichoke hearts. Set aside.

3. Heat a medium-size skillet over low heat. Add the sliced bacon and any juices from the package. Heat for several minutes, turning once, until heated through.

4. When ready to serve, place a toasted muffin half on each of four plates. Divide the bacon among the muffins and top them with artichoke hearts and 1 tablespoon hollandaise for each. Garnish with paprika to taste, two artichoke leaves, and a sprig of tarragon. Serve immediately.

*Cal. **205** Carb. **33g** Protein **12g** Chol. **40mg** Fat **5g/20%***

Christmas Day

• Have a leisurely brunch, and then dinner later in the afternoon.

• Go ice skating, sledding, or cross-country skiing.

• Encourage people to stop by during the afternoon.

• Organize a walk or a fortune hunt.

• Have a fire burning all day.

• Let guests bring a dish or help with the meal. Get everybody into the act.

• Stage an after-dinner children's play.

• Sing carols after dinner.

• Sip cordials around the fire. Look at old photographs. Remember.

Pecan Strudel

It wouldn't be Christmas morning without this strudel, which has long been a tradition in our house. It used to take us hours to make—and with more than 2 cups of butter! Now we use frozen sheets of phyllo and butter-flavored vegetable oil, which cuts down the butter a great deal. We still use some of the real thing for flavor, but the calories and fat savings are substantial.

SERVES 28

8 sheets phyllo dough, defrosted
Butter-flavored vegetable oil spray
²⁄₃ cup brown sugar, packed
²⁄₃ cup chopped pecans
1 cup chopped dates
½ teaspoon cinnamon
3 tablespoons unsalted butter, room temperature
1 cup confectioners' sugar
1 tablespoon honey, warmed
Juice of one lemon

1. Spray a 9 x 13-inch jelly roll pan with vegetable spray. Remove one sheet of phyllo from the pile and place it in the center of the pan; spray it lightly with the vegetable oil spray. Place a second sheet on top and spray again. Continue until all the sheets have been used. Preheat the oven to 350°.
2. Spray the center of the phyllo sheets. Sprinkle with half of the brown sugar, pecans, and dates, and ¼ teaspoon cinnamon. Fold one-third of the dough over the center section. Spray, and sprinkle with remaining brown sugar, pecans, and dates, and ¼ teaspoon cinnamon. Fold the final third over the center section and spray the top and sides well. The cake should measure 14 x 16 inches.
3. In a bowl, mix the 3 tablespoons of butter, ⅓ cup confectioners' sugar, and warmed honey. Make three slits in the top of the cake, being careful not to cut through, and spread the honey frosting over the top.
4. Bake for 20 minutes or until golden brown. Remove and cool slightly.
5. In a small bowl, mix ½ cup confectioners' sugar and lemon juice together and drizzle over the warm cake. Cut into 1 x 3-inch strips and serve warm.

Cal. 94 Carb. 17g Protein 1g Chol. 4mg Fat 3g/27%

"First, a gorgeous breakfast: just everything you can imagine—from flapjacks and fried squirrel to hominy grits and honey-in-the-comb... we're so impatient to get at the presents we can't eat a mouthful."

Truman Capote
A Christmas Memory

Candied Citrus Stars

YIELD: 120

*Peel of 3 large grapefruit, or
  8 oranges, quartered*
3 cups plus 1 cup sugar
1/4 cup corn syrup

1. Place 4 cups of water in a large saucepan. Add the peel and bring to a boil; boil for 1 minute. Drain and replace with cold water; bring to a boil for 1 minute. Repeat two more times.

2. In a medium saucepan, heat 3 cups of the sugar, 3/4 cup water, and the corn syrup to a boil. Add the peel, then reduce the heat and simmer for 45 minutes, until the syrup has been absorbed by the peel.

3. Remove the peel with tongs and place on a cake rack to cool until tacky to the touch. Remove to waxed paper and cut with a star-shaped cookie cutter into desired shapes. Place the remaining 1 cup sugar on a plate and roll the peel to cover. Place back on the rack to cool completely. Store in a tin.

*Cal. 30 Carb. 8g
Protein .1g Chol. 0mg
Fat 0g/0%*

Simple Christmas Brioche

SERVES 8

1 cup raisins or candied fruit
2/3 cup brandy or orange juice
3/4 ounces yeast
1/3 cup skim milk
2 1/2 cups all-purpose flour
2 eggs
2 egg whites
6 tablespoons unsalted butter, softened
1 teaspoon salt
1/4 cup sugar

1. Soak the raisins for 1 hour in the brandy, then drain.
2. Preheat the oven to 400°.
3. Pour the yeast into a bowl and whisk in the milk. Fold in 3/4 cup of the flour, then spoon the remaining flour on top. Do not mix in but let sit on top of the mixture until cracks begin to show.
4. Blend in the flour, and add the eggs and the egg whites one at a time and incorporate completely. Mix for 6 to 8 minutes. Gradually mix in the butter. Add the salt and sugar, and completely combine; stir in the raisins.
5. Form the dough into a ball and place it in a bowl. Cover and set to rise in a warm place for 2 to 3 hours.
6. Place on a floured surface and punch down gently, then form into a loaf. Lightly spray or wipe a 10 x 5-inch loaf pan with vegetable oil. Transfer to the pan. Let rise in a warm place for 1 1/2 hours, covered. Bake the loaf for 20 to 25 minutes, until golden.

Cal. 324 Carb. 52g Protein 8g Chol. 70mg Fat 11g/29%

Black-Tie New Year's Eve

Shrimp Sausage

YIELD: THIRTY-TWO 2-INCH-LONG SAUSAGES

1 pound medium shrimp, peeled and deveined
1 pound sea scallops
2 egg yolks
2 cups Low-Fat Blend (see Basics)
1 tablespoon potato starch
1/2 cup chopped fresh dill, chives, or tarragon
Cayenne
1/2 teaspoon paprika
Salt and freshly ground pepper

1. Make sure that all of the ingredients and the bowl are well chilled before starting, and plan on working quickly.
2. Place the shrimp and scallops in a food processor, and purée. Add the egg yolk and pulse until well blended. Transfer to a medium-size mixing bowl and set in a larger bowl of ice.

New Year's Eve

Champagne

Smoked Salmon
with Salmon Mousse

Beluga Caviar

Vanilla Salmon

Tuscan Loin of Veal

Scarlet Plum Salsa

Potato and Rutabaga Purée

Roasted Artichokes

Lucky Red Beans and Rice

Mâche and Maple Salad

Raspberry Soufflé

Venetian Country Cake

Basil-Cheese Crackers

YIELD: 32 CRACKERS

1 cup whole-wheat flour
1 cup white flour
1 tablespoon yellow cornmeal
1 tablespoon dried basil
1/2 teaspoon baking powder
1/4 teaspoon salt
3/4 cup finely grated Romano cheese
1/4 cup canola oil
3/4 cup nonfat plain yogurt

1. In a large bowl, mix the flours, cornmeal, basil, baking powder, salt, and cheese. Add the oil and mix.
2. Add the yogurt and stir until the dough comes together and can be shaped into a mass.
3. Divide the dough in half. Pat each half into a thick disk, flour lightly, wrap in plastic, and refrigerate for 15 minutes.
4. Preheat the oven to 400°. Lightly spray or wipe two baking sheets with vegetable oil.
5. Remove one piece of dough from the refrigerator, unwrap, and place on a lightly floured surface.
6. Roll the dough into a 14-inch round. Cut the round dough into sixteen wedges, and place each on a baking sheet. Prick each wedge with a fork two to three times. Bake for 12 to 14 minutes, or until golden brown. Repeat with the second piece of dough.
7. Store the crackers, tightly sealed, in a plastic bag or a tin.

Cal. **56** Carb. **6g** Protein **2g** Chol. **3mg** Fat **3g/41%**

3. Gently fold in the Low-Fat Blend, potato starch, and dill a little at a time, until blended and smooth. Add the cayenne, paprika, and salt and pepper to taste. Cover, and place in the refrigerator for 15 minutes.
4. When the mixture is well chilled, remove from the refrigerator and place the bowl on a flat work surface. Tear off an 8-inch piece of plastic wrap. Place 2 tablespoons of the mixture in a strip in the center. Fold the plastic wrap over the mixture, roll up to make a 2-inch sausage, and twist the ends. Repeat until all of the mixture is used.
5. Meanwhile, in a large sauté pan fitted with a steamer, bring 1 inch of water to a boil. Keep the sausages chilled until you steam them; you will have to do this this in batches.
6. Place several sausages in the steamer and steam for 7 to 8 minutes, until firm and cooked through. When all the sausages are steamed, remove the plastic and serve warm.

Cal. **37** Carb. **1g** Protein **6g** Chol. **38mg** Fat **.6g/16%**

Crabmeat Soup

SERVES 4

4 cups chicken broth (see Basics)
1/4 cup dry sherry
1/4 cup fresh lime juice
1/4 cup finely minced fresh lemon grass
1 tablespoon minced fresh ginger
1/2 teaspoon curry powder
5 teaspoons potato starch, dissolved in 1 tablespoon water
1 cup cooked lump crabmeat

1. In a stockpot, bring the chicken broth, sherry, lime juice, lemon grass, ginger, and curry paste to a boil.
2. Add the dissolved potato starch and cook, stirring constantly, until the soup thickens. Gently stir in the crabmeat.

Cal. **94** Carb. **10g** Protein **9g** Chol. **34mg** Fat **2g/20%**

Vanilla Salmon

SERVES 4

$\frac{1}{2}$ cup currants

4 tablespoons brandy

1 teaspoon olive oil

2 pounds Spanish onions, peeled and sliced $\frac{1}{4}$ inch thick

$\frac{1}{2}$ teaspoon ground cinnamon

$\frac{1}{2}$ teaspoon freshly grated nutmeg

Salt and freshly ground pepper

1 vanilla bean

4 skinned salmon fillets (about 6 ounces each), rinsed and
  patted dry

$\frac{1}{2}$ cup chicken broth (see Basics)

$\frac{1}{2}$ cup finely minced fresh Italian parsley

1. Soak the currants in the brandy for about 30 minutes.

2. Preheat the oven to 500°.

3. In a large skillet, heat the oil over medium heat. Add the onion and sauté until translucent and soft, 15 to 20 minutes. Sprinkle the onion with the cinnamon, nutmeg, and salt and pepper to taste. Stir in the currants and any remaining brandy. Taste and correct the seasonings.

4. Transfer the onion to a 9 x 13-inch baking dish. Bury the vanilla bean in the onion. Place the fish on the onion, skinned side down. Pour the chicken broth over the fish and bake for 5 to 7 minutes, or until just done; be careful not to overcook.

5. To serve, divide the onion mixture among four heated plates, and top with the salmon fillets. Discard the vanilla bean. Garnish the plates with chopped parsley and serve immediately.

Cal. 365 Carb. 24g Protein 40g Chol. 66mg Fat 12g/27%

Let There Be Light

Illuminate a wonderfully cozy dining scene using firelight and candlelight alone. Use a variety of candle shapes—slender white tapers, fat pillars, rounded balls. Place them on chandeliers, at the table, in sconces, on the mantel, on sideboards.

Tuscan Loin of Veal

For the best flavor, stuff and tie the roast and refrigerate it one day ahead.

SERVES 8

1 boneless butterflied loin of veal (3 to 4 pounds), trimmed of all fat
1 garlic clove, halved
4 ounces finely minced pancetta
2 teaspoons finely minced garlic
¼ cup finely minced fresh Italian parsley
1 teaspoon finely minced lemon zest
Salt and freshly ground pepper
3 sprigs fresh rosemary
1 cup dry white wine
1 cup chicken broth (see Basics)
1 tablespoon lemon juice
1 tablespoon unsalted butter, at room temperature

1. Wipe the meat dry with paper towels and rub all over with the halved garlic. Discard the garlic.

2. In a small bowl, combine the pancetta, minced garlic, parsley, and zest. Spread the stuffing to within 1 inch of the edges of the veal loin. Roll the loin up tightly, and tie at 3-inch intervals with butcher string. Refrigerate overnight, covered with plastic wrap. Return the roast to room temperature before roasting.

3. Preheat the oven to 425°.

4. Place the roast in a shallow roasting pan; season with salt and pepper to taste.

5. Place the roast in the oven and lower the heat to 350°. Roast, uncovered, for 30 minutes, then add the rosemary, wine, and chicken broth. Cover the roast loosely with foil and continue to roast for 1½ hours more, basting occasionally with the pan juices, until the internal temperature reaches 170°. Remove the meat to a heated platter and cover loosely to keep it warm.

6. Skim the fat from the pan juices; remove the rosemary. Set the roasting pan over high heat. Scrape up the bits from the bottom of the pan, and cook for 3 to 4 minutes to reduce slightly. Stir in the lemon juice; taste and correct seasoning. Whisk in the butter just before serving.

7. Slice the meat and serve at once; pass the sauce separately.

Cal. **263** *Carb.* **2g** *Protein* **36g** *Chol.* **141mg** *Fat* **11g/38%**

Mâche and Maple Salad

SERVES 8

3 teaspoons Dijon mustard
1 tablespoon horseradish
3 tablespoons red wine vinegar
2 tablespoons nonfat plain yogurt
1 tablespoon maple syrup
Freshly ground pepper
40 baby beets, washed and trimmed of stems and roots
2 tablespoons canola oil
1/2 cup walnuts, toasted
2 tablespoons finely minced fresh tarragon
1/2 cup finely chopped onion
6 cups mâche leaves

1. Preheat the oven to 350°. In a small bowl, combine the first six ingredients and mix well. Set aside.
2. Place all the beets on a piece of aluminum foil, and brush or spray with the canola oil. Place the beets in the oven and bake for 40 minutes, or until just tender. Remove and cool.
3. Divide the mâche among eight salad plates. Divide the nuts and onion over the mâche and sprinkle with tarragon. Peel the beets and place five beets on each plate. Drizzle lightly with dressing and serve immediately.

Cal. **158** *Carb.* **26g** *Protein* **5g** *Chol.* **.5mg** *Fat* **5g/28%**

Roasted Artichokes

SERVES 4

One package (10 ounces) frozen artichoke hearts, defrosted
20 garlic cloves, peeled
1 small red onion, coarsely chopped
2 tablespoons canola oil
2 sprigs fresh rosemary, coarsely chopped
Juice of one lemon
Freshly ground pepper

1. Preheat the oven to 350°. Combine the artichoke hearts, garlic, onion, oil, rosemary, and half the lemon juice in a shallow roasting pan and mix well. Sprinkle with pepper.
2. Bake for 50 minutes; remove from the oven and sprinkle with the reserved lemon juice. Return to the oven and bake for 10 minutes, or until lightly browned.

Cal. **129** *Carb.* **15g** *Protein* **3g** *Chol.* **8mg** *Fat* **7g/48%**

Scarlet Plum Salsa

YIELD: 1 QUART

1/2 cup frozen cran-raspberry concentrate, thawed
1/8 teaspoon ground cinnamon
4 whole cloves
2 slices fresh ginger, 1/4 inch thick and 1 inch in diameter
Zest of 1 lime
1 sprig fresh mint
Juice of 1 lime
6 scarlet plums, pitted and finely diced
1/4 pound jícama, peeled and finely chopped
1/2 red onion, finely chopped
2 tablespoons fresh cilantro, coarsely chopped
1/2 jalapeño pepper, seeded and minced
2 passionfruits

1. In a small saucepan over low heat, combine the cran-raspberry concentrate, cinnamon, cloves, ginger, lime zest, and mint. Simmer for 8 minutes. Remove from the heat and add the lime juice. Set aside.
2. In a large bowl, combine the plums, jícama, onion, cilantro, and jalapeño pepper, and toss until thoroughly mixed. Strain the juice mixture over the fruit.
3. Scoop out the fruit from the passionfruit; place over the salsa mixture and mix thoroughly. Refrigerate for at least 2 hours before serving.

Cal. **38** *Carb.* **9g** *Protein* **.5g**
Chol. **0mg** *Fat* **.4g/8%**
(analyzed per 1/4 cup)

Potato and Rutabaga Purée

SERVES 8

1 rutabaga (about 1¼ pounds), peeled and roughly diced
2 pounds potatoes, peeled and roughly diced
⅛ teaspoon white pepper
⅛ teaspoon freshly grated nutmeg

1. Place the rutabaga in a medium pot, and cover with cold water. Bring to a boil, reduce the heat, and cook until very tender, 20 to 40 minutes. Drain well.
2. In another pot, place the potatoes and cover with cold water. Bring to a boil, reduce the heat, and cook until very tender, 20 to 40 minutes. Drain well. In a food processor, process the rutabaga until smooth but not finely puréed. Add the potatoes, white pepper, and nutmeg, and process until smooth. If necessary, reheat gently and serve immediately.

*Cal. **89** Carb. **20g** Protein **3g** Chol. **0mg** Fat **.2g/2%***

Lucky Red Beans and Rice

SERVES 12

12 ounces dried red beans, soaked in water to cover overnight
6 cups chicken broth (see Basics)
1 ham bone or ham hock (about 1½ pounds)
2 cups finely chopped onion
2 cups finely chopped celery
1 cup finely chopped green bell pepper
1½ tablespoons finely minced garlic
1 bay leaf
½ teaspoon dried thyme
¼ teaspoon cayenne
½ teaspoon freshly ground white pepper
1 tablespoon finely julienned, well-drained sun-dried tomato
1⅓ cups converted rice
Salt

1. Drain and rinse the beans and place them in a large soup pot with the chicken broth, ham bone, onion, celery, green pepper, garlic, bay leaf, thyme, cayenne, white pepper, and sun-dried tomato. Bring to a boil, cover, lower the heat, and simmer for 1½ to 1¾ hours, until the beans are tender.
2. Add the rice and cook for 25 more minutes. Taste and correct the seasonings. Ladle into bowls and serve immediately.

*Cal. **206** Carb. **40g** Protein **9g** Chol. **0mg** Fat **.6g/3%***

Raspberry Soufflé

SERVES 4

2 cups fresh raspberries
½ banana
2 egg yolks, at room temperature
1 teaspoon vanilla extract
¼ cup superfine sugar
¼ cup low-fat ricotta cheese
3 tablespoons crème de cassis
8 egg whites, at room temperature
Pinch cream of tartar

1. Preheat the oven to 400°.
2. Lightly spray or wipe a 2-quart soufflé dish with vegetable oil.
3. Place the raspberries, banana, egg yolks, vanilla, 1 tablespoon of the superfine sugar, the ricotta, and cassis in a food processor, and purée. Transfer the mixture to a mixing bowl.
4. Beat the egg whites and cream of tartar with an electric mixer until soft peaks form. Gradually beat in the remaining superfine sugar; continue to beat until stiff, shiny peaks form.
5. Stir one-third of the egg whites into the raspberry mixture. Once incorporated, gently fold in the remaining whites, and continue until the two mixtures are well blended.
6. Pour the mixture into the soufflé dish and run your thumb around the inside edge to promote even rising. Level the top. Place the dish on a baking sheet and place the sheet in the center of the oven. Reduce the oven temperature to 375°. Bake for 25 minutes. Serve immediately.

*Cal. **168** Carb. **24g** Protein **10g** Chol. **96mg** Fat **4g/20%***

The Bubbly

Champagne was once reserved for very special occasions and toasts. But in recent years, it has become the preferred wine for many, who like to drink it throughout the evening. To me, the delicate taste of champagne makes it the ideal wine. It seems to go nicely with so many foods—but not all champagnes pair well with all foods:

★ Dry, salty cheeses such as Parmesan or Romano go well with champagne. So do olives, smoked meats, and salted pretzels.

★ Very spicy foods can overpower champagne, so choose carefully.

★ Champagne is best with fish, chicken broth, and bouillons, or consommés or cream- or veloute-based soups such as chowders, purées, bisques.

★ Fish and shellfish, lightly sauced stews, and veal and poultry dishes are great with champagne.

★ The bubbles of champagne tend to lighten fried foods.

★ Champagne is best served with not-too-sweet desserts: fruits, fruit mousses, or tarts, a dark chocolate dessert, nutty desserts, or fairly dry pastries such as Chocolate Biscotti (page 355), Venetian Country Cake (opposite), or pound cake.

★ Stop the flow of alcohol an hour before you expect the party to disband. Leave the mixers out.

★ Have a long dessert-and-coffee period. Make it an event by moving to another room.

★ Have plenty of non-alcoholic alternatives available.

★ Turn up the jazz. ☆Studies show the faster the musical beat, the slower guests sip.

★ Offer a ride home to anyone who would appreciate it.

★ A yawn from the host is a good clue the party's over.

Venetian Country Cake

SERVES 12

2½ cups stale bread crumbs, as fine as possible
¼ cup golden raisins
2 tablespoons dark rum
6 eggs, separated
1 cup sugar
⅓ cup finely chopped candied orange peel
2 tablespoons finely chopped lemon zest
Pinch salt
4 egg whites
1 teaspoon fresh lemon juice
2 tablespoons confectioners' sugar, sifted

To decorate, sprinkle sugar over paper stars, then carefully remove stars to reveal pattern.

1. Preheat the oven to 350°.
2. Sift 2 cups of the bread crumbs onto a piece of waxed paper. Set aside.
3. Lightly spray or wipe a 9½ x 2½-inch springform pan with vegetable or canola oil. Add the remaining bread crumbs, and tip the pan to coat the bottom and sides; discard excess crumbs and set the pan aside.
4. In a small bowl, combine the raisins and rum, and set aside for 15 minutes.
5. In a large bowl, beat the egg yolks and sugar together. Slowly add the sifted bread crumbs, a little at a time. The mixture will become very thick and will barely hold together. Stir in the raisins and rum and the orange peel, lemon zest, and salt.
6. In a large bowl with an electric mixer, beat all 10 egg whites and lemon juice until stiff but not dry.
7. Stir 1 cup of the egg whites into the crumb mixture and combine thoroughly. Fold in the remaining egg whites, a little at a time, mixing carefully but thoroughly after each addition. Pour the batter into the pan and bake for 45 minutes, or until golden. Remove the cake from the oven and cool it on a wire rack for 1 minute. Remove the sides of the springform pan, then the bottom, with the aid of a wide spatula. Allow the cake to cool completely on the rack.
8. Before serving, sprinkle the cake liberally with confectioners' sugar.

Cal. 228 Carb. 43g Protein 6g Chol. 91mg Fat 4g/14%

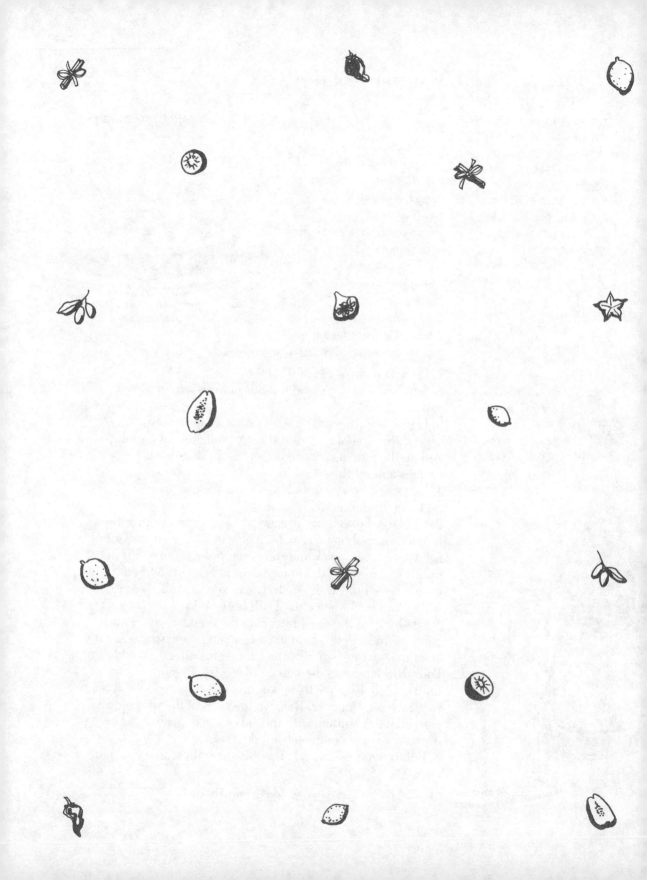

Winter Wonders

"O Winter, king of fire-side enjoyments, home-born happiness..."
William Cowper

Winter Journal

January

1 New Year's Day
Watch fat monitor

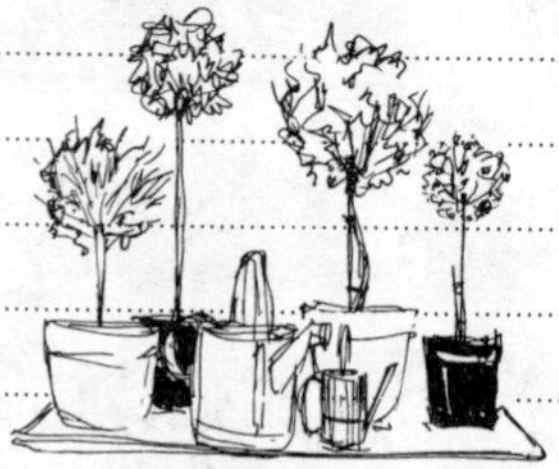

8 Prune and feed
topiaries

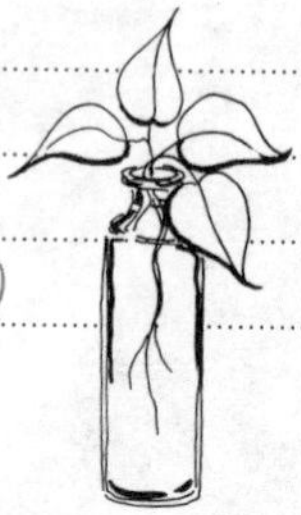

13 Root cuttings
from houseplants

16 Plan spring flower beds

21 Get peat pots and
growing medium

24 Start slow-growing
annuals from seed

31 Snow, snow,
endless snow

February

1 ESCAPE! to St. Barts

8 Home again

10 Prune maples, birches,
and dogwoods before
the sap runs

12 Send VALENTINES

14 *Valentine's Day*

20 *Watch for snowdrop bloom*

27 *Watch for robins*

March

1 *Fertilize shade trees, evergreens, ground covers*

8 *Cut forsythia branches and force bloom*

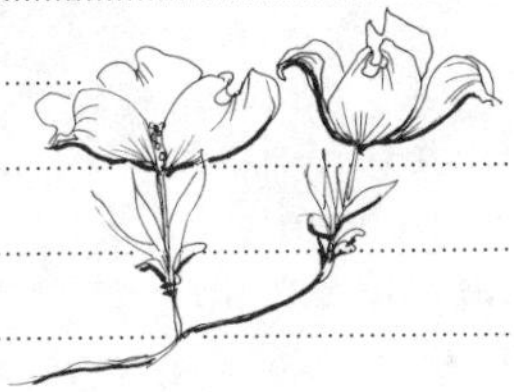

17 *St. Patrick's Day supper*

20 *Feed asparagus*

24 *Cooking workshop in Albuquerque*

29 *Cut back ornamental grasses before new growth*

Warm-Ups!

Rosy Warm Cereal

SERVES 6

1 teaspoon canola oil
1 cup cracked wheat
3½ cups cran-raspberry juice
1 cup dried tart cherries
1½ teaspoons ground cinnamon
¼ teaspoon ground cardamom
⅛ teaspoon ground cloves
2 tablespoons finely minced orange zest
½ cup coarsely chopped pecans

1. In a medium saucepan over medium heat, heat the oil. Add the cracked wheat and toast until golden, 3 to 4 minutes, stirring constantly. Bring the juice to a boil and carefully add it to the wheat—it will splatter. Stir in the cherries, cinnamon, cardamom, and cloves. Lower the heat, cover, and simmer for 15 to 20 minutes, or until the liquid is absorbed. Remove from the heat and let stand, covered, for 5 minutes.
2. Stir in the orange zest and pecans. Serve with skim milk.

*Cal. **204** Carb. **43g** Protein **4g** Chol. **0mg** Fat **2g/9%***

The days are short and cold. The garden draws inward, then lapses into snowy silence. This season's fruits and vegetables are either those already harvested, those flown in from afar, or the few that remain in the dark December ground.

Winter nights are filled with robust flavors: bitter and peppery greens; the licorice taste of fennel; olives; pine nuts; citrus; root vegetables; stick-to-your-ribs beans; one-pot dishes; soups; roasts.

We gravitate to the light and to cozy food that warms body and soul.

Tropical Fruit Salad

SERVES 8

2 cups fresh pineapple chunks
1 ugli fruit, peeled and
    sectioned
2 cups red grapes
2 star fruit (carambola), sliced
2 ripe kiwi, sliced
1 ripe mango, diced
1 ripe papaya, chunked
2 cups frozen orange juice
    concentrate, defrosted
Zest of 1 orange, minced
One 2-inch cinnamon stick
5 whole cloves
1 bay leaf

1. Place all of the fruit in a large bowl and set aside.
2. In a small saucepan over low heat, combine the juice, zest, cinnamon stick, cloves, and bay leaf, and simmer for 20 minutes. Remove from the heat and let cool to room temperature. Remove the cinnamon, cloves, and bay leaf, and discard.
3. Add the juice to the fruit and toss gently. Let marinate for 2 hours, covered, in the refrigerator, tossing occasionally. When ready to serve, allow the fruit to return to room temperature.

*Cal. **226** Carb. **56** Protein **3** Chol. **0** Fat **1g/4%***

Golden Breakfast Couscous

Quick as a wink you can serve warm, light couscous loaded with fruit for breakfast.

SERVES 4

2⅔ cups apple juice
1 cup golden raisins, currants, dried cherries, blueberries,
    cranberries, or apricots
1 cup quick-cooking couscous
1 Granny Smith apple, cored and cut into ½-inch chunks
1 to 2 tablespoons minced crystallized ginger

1. In a small bowl, place 1 cup of the apple juice and the dried fruit. Leave at room temperature overnight.
2. In a medium saucepan, place the remaining juice and bring to a boil. Reduce the heat to medium, add the couscous, and cook for 3 to 5 minutes, until the liquid is absorbed and the couscous is tender. Remove from the heat; add the plump fruit, apples, and ginger. Stir well and serve immediately, drizzled with skim milk if desired.

*Cal. **388** Carb. **91g** Protein **7g** Chol. **0mg** Fat **.7g/2%***

Winter Fruit Salad

SERVES 8

¼ cup fresh lime juice
2 tablespoons honey
3 tablespoons minced fresh
    mint
Zest of 1 lime, grated
1 cup red grapes
1 cup green grapes
8 fresh figs, green or purple
1 honeydew melon, peeled and cut into 24 slices
¼ cup walnuts, toasted and coarsely chopped

honeydew melon
grapes
walnuts
purple figs
with lime, honey, & mint sauce

1. In a large bowl, combine the lime juice, honey, mint, and zest, and mix well. Add the grapes and figs and toss. Allow the fruit to marinate at room temperature for 30 minutes.
2. On a large round platter, arrange the honeydew in a pinwheel pattern. Sprinkle the grapes and figs over and garnish with the walnuts.

*Cal. **213** Carb. **51g** Protein **3g** Chol. **0mg** Fat **3g/11%***

Nonnie's Cinnamon Rolls

These are the kind of soft cinnamon rolls that make you feel pampered and cozy. They're the treat our friend Pam craves on the days she has a soccer match, and her mom, Nonnie, usually fills the bill.

YIELD: 32 ROLLS

1 cup skim milk
¼ cup canola oil
½ cup granulated sugar
¼ teaspoon salt
2 packages active dry yeast
1 egg
2 egg whites
5½ cups white flour
1 cup light brown sugar
2 tablespoons ground cinnamon
½ cup golden raisins
1 cup apple juice frozen concentrate, defrosted
¼ cup chopped walnuts

1. In a saucepan, scald the milk. Add the oil, sugar, and salt, and stir until dissolved. Cool to lukewarm.
2. In a small bowl, combine the yeast and ¼ cup warm water, and set aside until dissolved, about 5 minutes.
3. In a large mixing bowl, beat the egg and egg whites well. Add the flour and the yeast and milk mixtures, and beat until a soft dough forms.
4. Turn the dough onto a lightly floured board and knead until smooth and elastic, about 5 minutes. Cover with plastic wrap and let rise until double in bulk, about 1½ hours.
5. Divide the dough in half and form into two balls. Cover with plastic and set aside to rest for 10 minutes. Lightly spray or wipe an 11 x 14-inch baking sheet with canola or vegetable oil.
6. In a small bowl, combine the brown sugar, cinnamon, and raisins. Set aside.
7. Roll each ball of dough into a 16 x 8-inch rectangle. Spray or wipe the dough with canola or vegetable oil. Cover each rectangle with half of the cinnamon mixture. Roll the dough tightly, starting at the long end. Slice each roll into sixteen 2-inch pieces. Tuck the ends of each roll under and place on the pan. Cover and let rise until doubled in bulk, about 1½ hours.
8. Preheat the oven to 350°.
9. In a saucepan, reduce the apple juice concentrate until it

Winter Fruit Bowl

SERVES 12

2 cups green grapes
1 cup red grapes
1 fresh pineapple, peeled, cored, and cut into bite-size pieces
1 medium-size cantaloupe, cut into bite-size pieces
1 quart blueberries, fresh or frozen, washed
1 tablespoon ground cinnamon
¾ cup frozen orange juice concentrate, defrosted
Sugar or honey

1. In a large bowl, combine the fruit and toss gently.
2. In a small bowl, place the cinnamon. Add the juice, slowly at first, to make a paste, then slowly stir in the rest. Add sugar or honey to taste.
3. Pour the dressing over the fruit and toss well. Place in the refrigerator to chill for 2 to 3 hours. Remove and set aside at room temperature for at least 30 minutes; the fruit should not be ice cold.

*Cal. **93** Carb. **23g***
*Protein **1g** Chol. **0mg***
*Fat **.7g/6%***

is syrupy. Brush each roll with the juice and sprinkle with chopped walnuts. Bake for 15 minutes, until golden brown. Serve warm.

*Cal. **158** Carb. **30g** Protein **3g** Chol. **6mg** Fat **3g/15%***
(analyzed per roll)

Breakfast Focaccia

SERVES 12

1 recipe Sweet Focaccia (see Basics)
1¼ cups assorted dried fruits, such as apples, pears, cherries, cranberries, figs, prunes, and apricots
1 vanilla bean, split
1 egg white
1 tablespoon raw sugar

1. Prepare the Sweet Focaccia dough through step 5.
2. Lightly spray or wipe a 14-inch round deep-dish pizza pan or a 15½ x 10½-inch baking pan with cooking oil.
3. Punch down the risen dough and turn it into the prepared pan; press evenly into the pan and let rise, loosely covered, in a warm place for 45 minutes.
3. Preheat the oven to 400°.
4. Meanwhile, in a large saucepan, combine the dried fruits, vanilla bean, and 4 cups of water. Bring to a boil, reduce the heat, and simmer for 20 minutes, or until the fruit is softened. Drain and reserve the vanilla bean. Pat the fruit dry with paper towels.
5. In a small bowl, whisk the egg white until foaming. Brush the surface of the dough with the egg white. Scatter the poached fruits on the surface, pressing each piece in slightly. Arrange the vanilla bean decoratively in the middle. Sprinkle the surface with the raw sugar and bake immediately for 40 to 50 minutes, or until the crust is golden and sounds hollow when tapped on the bottom. Cool on a rack and serve warm or at room temperature.

*Cal. **271** Carb. **56g** Protein **6g** Chol. **3mg***
*Fat **3g/10%***

Breakfast Focaccia

Focaccia is the original hearth bread from Liguria, on the Italian Riviera. It generally starts out with an olive-oil-enriched dough, the taste and consistency of which we've tried to achieve by using waxy potatoes and just a little fat. It can be fashioned into many styles—sweetened for breakfast, sprinkled with onions and garlic, prosciutto, rosemary, sage, salt or black olives, and even wine grapes.

Whole-Wheat Sourdough Bread

Eddie Parach, our local baker, has saved my soul in Saugatuck with his terrific hearty breads. He's a pro, but he's adapted his bread recipe so that it's just as easy for home baking.

YIELD: 2 LOAVES (12 SLICES EACH)

1 cup Sourdough Starter (see Basics)
1½ teaspoons salt
1 teaspoon active dry yeast
2½ cups bread flour
2½ cups whole-wheat flour

1. In the bowl of an electric mixer fitted with a dough hook, place all of the ingredients plus 1½ cups of water, and mix for 8 minutes. Shape the dough into a ball and place it in a lightly oiled bowl. Cover with plastic wrap or a damp towel, and place it in a warm place to rise until doubled in size, about 2 hours. Place on an oiled baking sheet and shape into two large round loaves; let rise again until doubled in bulk, about 1 hour.
2. Preheat the oven to 400°. Brush the loaves lightly with water and bake for 35 to 40 minutes, until golden brown.

*Cal. **107** Carb. **23g** Protein **4g** Chol. **0mg** Fat **.4g/3%***

The Edgecombs' Rye Bread

Our friend Jean developed this robust bread; it's a real winner.

YIELDS: 4 LOAVES (48 SLICES)

½ teaspoon sugar
3 packages active dry yeast
½ cup molasses
½ cup light brown sugar
2 tablespoons salt
4 tablespoons plus ½ teaspoon vegetable shortening
5 cups rye flour, sifted
6 tablespoons caraway seeds
5 to 7 cups white flour, sifted
1 tablespoon unsalted butter, softened

1. In nonreactive mixing bowl, dissolve the sugar in ½ cup warm water; add the yeast.
2. In another mixing bowl, combine the molasses, brown sugar, salt, shortening, and 3 cups of hot water. Stir until the sugar dissolves. Cool to lukewarm. Stir in the rye flour and

Power Breakfasts

Around the world, breakfast offers great variety. In Egypt, the morning staple is *mudammas* (beans). Latin Americans favor rice, beans, and tortillas, the Japanese, rice and miso soup. Israelis enjoy huge buffets. In Scandinavia, lavish smorgasbords of meats, cheeses, breads, and even vegetables are set out each morning. Perhaps for you, breakfast is a new regime. But with time, it will become a habit you'll look forward to.

beat well. Add the yeast mixture, caraway seeds, and up to 4 cups of white flour. Cover and set aside for 10 minutes.

3. Knead the dough on a well-floured board, adding 2 to 3 cups of white flour with mixture. Place the dough in the bowl, cover, and let rise in a warm place until doubled in size. Punch down and divide into four loaves. Place the loaves on a baking pan and slash them diagonally with a sharp knife or razor blade. Cover and let rise until doubled. The loaves will join together as they bake and rise.

4. Preheat the oven to 375°. Bake the loaves for 25 minutes; turn the oven off and leave the bread in for 5 more minutes. Remove the bread from the oven, brush with the butter, and wait 5 to 10 minutes before separating the loaves.

Cal. 114 Carb. 22g Protein 3g Cholesterol 8mg Fat 2g/14%

Walnut-Raisin Loaf

One slice of this bread loaded with walnuts and raisins, a glass of fresh orange juice, and you're ready for anything.

YIELD: 2 LOAVES (32 SLICES)

1 recipe Basic Bread (see Basics) through step 4
3 cups raisins
3 cups walnuts
1 tablespoon cornmeal
1 egg
½ teaspoon granulated sugar
2 tablespoons raw sugar

1. Spray or wipe a baking sheet with vegetable or canola oil.

2. Punch the dough down and knead in the raisins and walnuts, a little at a time. The dough will be very heavy, and it will seem that all the raisins and walnuts cannot be incorporated; be patient. Divide the dough in half.

3. Shape each loaf to resemble a small football. Sprinkle with the cornmeal and place on the baking sheet. Cover with plastic wrap and let rise until doubled in size, about 1½ hours.

4. Preheat the oven to 425°. In a small bowl, whisk the egg and granulated sugar. Brush each loaf with the mixture and sprinkle with the raw sugar.

5. Bake the bread for 30 to 40 minutes, until it is very brown and sounds hollow when tapped on the bottom. Cool on a wire rack.

Cal. 164 Carb. 23g Protein 4g Chol. 11mg Fat 7g/38%

> "Bread deals with living things, with giving life, with growth, with the seed, the grain that nurtures. It is not coincidence that we say bread is the staff of life."
>
> Lionel Poilane

A Pretzel Party

Warm, soft pretzels, especially really big ones, are a delight to children of every age. I like them best sprinkled with cinnamon and sugar, or frosted as a breakfast treat. But make them any size you like and sprinkle them with kosher salt, fresh dill, chives, sage, rosemary, garlic, or toasted seeds. They may seem like a project—but once you've made them and seen the smiles they bring, you'll realize they're easy and well worth it.

YIELD: TWELVE 12-INCH PRETZELS

2¼ ounces active dry yeast (1¼ packages)
5½ cups sifted all-purpose flour
¼ cup canola oil
2 tablespoons sugar
1 teaspoon salt
¼ cup baking soda
Kosher salt

1. Preheat the oven to 475°. In the large bowl of an electric mixer, pour 1 cup of warm water (115°). Add the yeast and set aside until the mixture is foaming, about 5 minutes. Add 1½ cups flour and the oil, sugar, and salt to the yeast mixture. Beat at medium speed for 3 to 5 minutes. Stir in the remaining flour.
2. Remove the dough to a lightly floured board and knead until the dough loses its stickiness, about 5 minutes.
3. Lightly wipe or spray a large mixing bowl with canola oil. Turn the dough into the bowl and coat it all over with oil. Cover with a damp towel and let rise in a warm place until doubled in size.
4. Lightly spray or wipe a large baking sheet with vegetable oil. Punch the dough down and divide it into 12 pieces. Roll each piece into an 18-inch length about the thickness of a pencil. Follow the illustrations below to shape into pretzels, and place on the baking sheet. Lightly spray with oil; let rise in a warm place until doubled in size, about 20 minutes.
5. Meanwhile, in a large nonreactive pan, bring 2 quarts of water to a boil. Add the baking soda. With a slotted spoon or spatula, carefully lower the pretzels, a few at a time, into the

spin

roll out a strip of dough

pick it up by the ends and

plop down this end first

480

boiling water. Boil for about a minute, or until the pretzels float to the top. Carefully lift the pretzels out of the water and return them to the baking sheet; sprinkle with salt.

6. Bake until crispy and brown, about 12 minutes. Serve at once. Store in an airtight container.

*Cal. **137** Carb. **24g** Protein **4g** Chol. **0mg** Fat **3g/17%**
(analyzed per pretzel)*

Variations:
Caraway-Rye—Substitute 1 cup of rye flour for the all-purpose flour and use caraway seeds in place of salt.
Parsley-Garlic—Remove the pretzels after baking for 9 minutes and brush with skim milk; sprinkle with garlic powder or granules and dried parsley. Return to the oven for 3 minutes.

Glazed Raisin Pretzels

YIELD: 16 GIANT PRETZELS
1 recipe soft pretzels (see above)
6 tablespoons raisins
2 tablespoons skim milk
¾ cup confectioners' sugar
1 teaspoon chopped lemon zest

1. Prepare the dough through step 1.
2. As you knead the dough, incorporate the raisins and continue through step 6.
3. While the pretzels are baking, mix together the remaining ingredients to make the glaze. As the pretzels come from the oven, drizzle with the glaze.

*Cal. **169** Carb. **32g** Protein **5g** Chol. **0mg** Fat **3.3g/19%**
(analyzed per pretzel)*

lay knot over and attach ends

One-Pot Meals

Oxtail Stew

SERVES 8

3 pounds oxtails, cut into 2-inch pieces
2 tablespoons all-purpose flour
Salt and freshly ground pepper
1 teaspoon olive oil
2 cups coarsely chopped onion
¼ cup minced Canadian bacon, trimmed of fat
1 cup coarsely chopped carrot
1 cup coarsely chopped celery
2 tablespoons minced garlic
2 tablespoons tomato paste
2½ cups red wine
2 cups beef broth (see Basics)
2 sprigs fresh thyme
1 piece orange zest (3 x 1 inch)
6 medium turnips, peeled and quartered
16 small pearl onions, peeled
¼ cup finely minced fresh Italian parsley

1. Wipe the oxtails dry with paper towels. Dredge with flour, salt, and freshly ground pepper to taste.
2. In a large ovenproof skillet, heat the oil over medium heat. Brown the oxtails on all sides, about 12 to 15 minutes. Remove the oxtails from the skillet and set them aside.
3. Preheat the oven to 325°.
4. In the oil remaining in the skillet, sauté the onion, bacon, carrot, celery, and garlic until the vegetables are soft, about 5 minutes. Stir in the tomato paste, 2 cups of red wine, and 1½ cups of beef broth. Return the oxtails to the casserole and add the thyme and orange zest. Bring to a boil, cover, and transfer to the oven. Bake for 2 hours.
5. Add the turnips, onions, and remaining wine and broth. Stir to combine, cover, and bake for 45 minutes to 1 hour, or until the turnips are tender. Stir in the parsley, and serve immediately over rice.

*Cal. **512** Carb. **20g** Protein **32g** Chol. **181mg** Fat **39g/67%***

Beef Brisket with Port

SERVES 8

1 beef brisket (3½ to 4 pounds),
  trimmed of as much fat
  as possible
1 teaspoon olive oil
1 cup shredded leek
1 tablespoon minced garlic
1 cup finely chopped carrot
1 cup finely chopped onion
1¼ cups finely chopped celery
4 cups beef broth (see Basics)
1 cup ruby port
Bouquet garni: 1 sprig thyme, 1 bay leaf, 4
  sprigs parsley, tied together
1 cup dried apricots
1 cup dried prunes
1 cup dried pears
1 cup dried Black Mission figs
½ cup minced fresh Italian parsley
Salt and freshly ground pepper

1. Preheat the oven to 325°. Place the brisket in a large
roasting pan.
2. In a large heavy skillet, heat the olive oil over medium-
high heat. Add the leek, garlic, carrot, onion, and celery, and
sauté, stirring, for 4 to 5 minutes, until golden.
3. Transfer the vegetables to the roasting pan with the
brisket. Add 3 cups of beef broth, ½ cup of water, the port,
and the *bouquet garni.* Bring the liquid to a boil, cover tightly
with foil, and transfer to the oven. Cook for 1½ hours.
4. Remove the brisket from the roasting pan and slice it
across the grain. Return the meat to the roasting pan and
add the dried fruits. Cover tightly with foil and bake for 1½
hours, or until the meat is tender. Add the remaining cup of
broth or water if necessary to keep the sauce from drying up;
the meat and fruit should remain moist.
5. To serve, arrange the meat on a platter and, using a slotted
spoon, arrange the fruit around; garnish with the parsley.
Remove any fat from the pan juices, season to taste with salt
and pepper, and pass the sauce at the table.

Cal. **485** *Carb.* **55g** *Protein* **38g** *Chol.* **107mg** *Fat* **13g/22%**

Red Cabbage Stuffed with Lamb

SERVES 8

12 large red cabbage leaves (carefully removed from
a large head of cabbage)
½ pound ground lamb
1 pound lean ground turkey (99% fat free)
2 cups cooked white or brown rice
½ cup currants
1 cup finely chopped scallion, white
part, with some green
½ cup coarsely chopped fresh
Italian parsley
½ teaspoon finely grated nutmeg
1 tablespoon ground cinnamon
1 tablespoon finely minced garlic
2 tablespoons finely minced fresh mint
Salt and freshly ground pepper
4 cups chicken broth (see Basics)
2 teaspoons olive oil
½ cup chopped fresh dill
Never-Fail Hollandaise Sauce (see Basics)

1. Place the cabbage leaves in a deep bowl. Cover them with
boiling water and let stand for 5 minutes.
2. Meanwhile, in a large bowl, combine the lamb, turkey,
rice, currants, scallion, parsley, nutmeg, cinnamon, garlic, mint,
and salt and pepper to taste. Mix together well with a fork or
your hands.
3. Line a 2-quart bowl with a double layer of the leaves,
allowing them to extend somewhat over the edge of the bowl;
you should have a few leaves left. Spoon half the meat mixture into the center of the leaves and pack it down gently.
Place a layer of leaves over the mixture, and spoon the
remaining mixture on top. Fold the extended leaves over the
top; cover the mixture with the remaining leaves.
4. Place the bowl on a rack in a large stockpot. Pour ¼ cup of
broth over the cabbage and drizzle with the oil. Sprinkle the
dill around the edge, and weight the top of the cabbage with
a plate that fits inside the bowl. Pour the remaining broth
into the pot to reach halfway up the sides of the bowl; add
water if the broth is not enough. Cover the pot tightly and
bring to a simmer; steam 1 to 1½ hours, until tender.
5. Carefully remove the bowl from the pot and remove the
plate. Invert the bowl onto a serving platter and carefully lift

it off the cabbage. Cut the cabbage into eight wedges and serve it with Never-Fail Hollandaise Sauce.

*Cal. **263** Carb. **21g** Protein **25g** Chol. **89mg** Fat **9g/29%***

Cabbage Rolls & Tomato Sauce

SERVES 6

12 large cabbage leaves
¾ pound lean ground beef
¾ pound lean ground
   turkey (99% fat free)
¼ cup finely chopped
   onion
1 cup cooked white
   or brown rice
1 egg
½ teaspoon freshly
   ground pepper
Salt
½ teaspoon poultry seasoning or dried thyme
1 tablespoon canola oil
1 tablespoon light brown sugar
1 tablespoon vinegar or lemon juice
1 can (16 ounces) tomato sauce

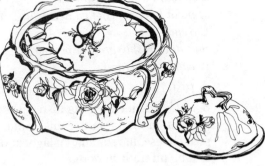

1. Place the leaves in a large bowl. Cover with boiling water and set aside for 5 minutes. Remove the leaves, pat dry, and set aside.
2. In a large bowl, combine the beef, turkey, onion, rice, egg, pepper and salt to taste, and poultry seasoning. Stir thoroughly.
3. Place equal portions of the meat mixture in the center of each leaf. Fold the sides of each leaf over the meat and roll up, starting from the wide end. Place the rolls, seam sides down, on a work surface.
4. In a large skillet, heat the oil over medium heat. Brown the cabbage rolls on all sides, about 8 minutes.
5. In a small bowl, whisk the brown sugar, vinegar, tomato sauce, and water. Pour the mixture over the cabbage rolls and simmer, covered, for 1 hour, basting and turning occasionally. Serve two cabbage rolls, topped with about 3 tablespoons of the sauce, per person.

*Cal. **271** Carb. **18g** Protein **28g** Chol. **106mg** Fat **9g/31%***

"Needles on the pine trees turning to the west means snow."

Anon.

Macaroni & Cheese

SERVES 6

¾ cup low-fat buttermilk
2 cups low-fat cottage cheese
4 ounces "light" cream cheese, at room temperature
2 ounces soft goat cheese, at room temperature
2 ounces skim-milk mozzarella cheese, grated
2 ounces Asiago cheese, grated
2 ounces Parmesan, grated
¾ pound penne, cooked according to package directions
Cayenne
Salt and freshly ground pepper
½ cup bread crumbs

1. Preheat the oven to 350°. Lightly spray or wipe an 8 x 11½ x 2-inch baking dish with vegetable oil. In the blender, place the buttermilk, cottage cheese, cream cheese, goat cheese, mozzarella, Asiago, and half the Parmesan, and blend until smooth.
2. Place the pasta in a large bowl, add the cheese mixture, and toss until well coated. Season with cayenne and salt and pepper to taste. Place the pasta in the baking dish; top with the bread crumbs and remaining Parmesan. Place in the oven and bake until bubbly, 20 to 25 minutes. Place under the broiler for 3 to 4 minutes, until the top is golden brown.

Cal. 460 Carb. 51g Protein 31g Chol. 40mg Fat 15g/29%

Chicken with Artichokes and Garlic

SERVES 4

2 chicken breasts split in half, with skin and bone
1 head garlic, peeled
One box (9 ounces) frozen artichoke hearts, defrosted
1 medium onion, coarsely chopped
½ cup coarsely chopped fresh Italian parsley
2 whole sprigs fresh rosemary
1 teaspoon cracked black pepper
1 cup chicken broth (see Basics)

1. Preheat the oven to 350°. Rinse the breasts and pat dry; arrange them in a baking dish and surround them with all the remaining ingredients except the broth. Pour in the broth and cover with foil.

Artichokes

The artichoke is yet another Italian specialty to be merged into French gastronomy by Catherine de Medici, who brought the edible thistle to the court of Henry II.

In America, virtually all the crop is grown in Castroville, California, the "Artichoke Capital of the World."

My artichoke of choice is the old reliable globe, with its thorns and dullish-green leaves. There are those who seek out frost-damaged artichokes that have rusty or bronze-tinged leaves, in the belief that they have better flavor.

The globe is the commonest type available, and frozen artichokes can be quite satisfactory, depending on the dish they're in.

Artichokes are available year-round, with the peak season falling between March and May. Choose tight, compact heads. Small ones—about 1½ inches in diameter—are almost entirely edible. Plan on one large or four small artichokes per serving. Keep artichokes refrigerated in a plastic bag for up to 1 week.

> ★ GOOD FOR YOU ★
>
> A medium artichoke has only 35 calories and is a good source of potassium and vitamins A and C.

2. Place in the oven and bake, covered, for 30 minutes. Remove the foil and bake for another 30 to 40 minutes, until the liquid has evaporated, basting every 10 to 15 minutes.

*Cal. **240** Carb. **12g** Protein **37g** Chol. **92mg** Fat **5g/18%***

Beef Stew with Eggplant

SERVES 8

2 pounds cubed eggplant,
   with the skin
Salt and freshly ground pepper
2 tablespoons canola oil
2 cups chopped onion
2 pounds cube steak, cut into 2-inch cubes
2 teaspoons ground coriander
1 teaspoon paprika
½ teaspoon ground cinnamon
½ teaspoon ground allspice
½ teaspoon cayenne
6 garlic cloves, finely minced
2 bay leaves
2 pounds fresh ripe tomatoes, cut into chunks, or 2 cans
   (1 pound each) plum tomatoes, drained
2 cups red wine
Zest of 2 lemons
Juice of 2 lemons
1 cup coarsely chopped fresh Italian parsley
¼ cup finely minced fresh mint leaves

1. Place the eggplant in a large bowl, and cover with heavily salted water for 30 minutes. Drain, rinse, and pat dry.
2. In a large pot, heat the oil over medium heat. Add the eggplant and sauté, stirring, until brown on all sides; remove and set aside. Add the onion to the pot and sauté until translucent.
3. Add the meat to the pot, sprinkle with the spices, add the bay leaves, and sauté. Season with salt and pepper to taste.
4. Add the tomatoes and eggplant and simmer for 15 minutes; add the wine, reduce the heat, and simmer, uncovered, until the meat is tender, about 2 hours. Add additional wine or water if necessary. When the meat is tender, add the lemon zest and juice, parsley, and mint, and simmer for 10 to 12 minutes. Serve immediately over rice or noodles.

*Cal. **231** Carb. **18g** Protein **18g** Chol. **51mg** Fat **11g/41%***

Vegetable Lasagne
with Wild Mushroom Sauce

Moist and loaded with vegetables, this recipe looks like it will take hours, but the preparation time should actually be only about half an hour. Best of all, it's so flavorful, no one will ever miss the meat.

SERVES 8

Mushroom Sauce:

1 ounce dried wild mushrooms

1 tablespoon extra-virgin olive oil

1 cup freshly chopped onion

1/2 cup chopped fresh Italian parsley

2 teaspoons finely chopped fresh rosemary

1 can (28 ounces) Italian plum tomatoes with basil

Salt and freshly ground pepper

Cheese Filling:

1 container (15 ounces) nonfat ricotta cheese

1 package (10 ounces) chopped spinach, cooked, drained, and squeezed dry

1/2 cup low-fat buttermilk

1 cup shredded Parmesan

Freshly ground salt and pepper

Vegetables:

1 red bell pepper, roasted, peeled, seeded, and julienned

1 green bell pepper, roasted, peeled, seeded, and julienned

1 yellow squash, thinly sliced and steamed (about 3/4 cup)

1 zucchini, thinly sliced and steamed (about 3/4 cup)

1 pound eggplant, thinly sliced, sprayed or wiped with canola oil, and broiled until lightly browned

2 artichokes, outer leaves and fuzzy cores removed, hearts halved and thinly sliced

Fresh lemon juice

1/2 cup chicken broth (see Basics)

1/2 cup halved and thinly sliced onion

10 lasagne noodles, cooked and drained according to package directions

8 ounces shredded nonfat mozzarella

1/4 cup shredded Parmesan

1. In a small bowl, combine the mushrooms and 1 cup boiling water; set aside for 30 minutes. Remove the mushrooms, and reserve the water. Trim the stems from the mushrooms

Lasagne

Wonderful, delicate, almost weightless layers of pasta are classically lifted by a butter-rich Béchamel sauce and a beefy Bolognese. We've obviously moistened and lightened them in a lower-fat way.

If you can find a source for fresh lasagne dough or can make your own, this is the time to steer away from dried for the best results possible.

and slice the caps.

2. In a large skillet, heat the oil over medium heat. Add the onion and sauté until transparent, about 5 minutes. Stir in the parsley, rosemary, and tomatoes; crush the tomatoes with the back of a fork. Add the sliced mushrooms and reserved soaking liquid. Season to taste with salt and pepper. Simmer the sauce for 20 minutes, uncovered. Set aside.

3. In a medium bowl, combine the ricotta cheese, spinach, buttermilk, 1 cup Parmesan, and salt and pepper to taste. Set aside.

4. In a large bowl, combine the prepared peppers, squash, and eggplant.

5. Squeeze drops of lemon over the artichoke slices to keep them from discoloring. In a medium skillet over medium-high heat, combine the chicken broth and artichokes. Cook until tender-crisp, about 4 minutes. Remove the artichokes with a spotted spoon and add them to the other vegetables. Steam the onion in the remaining chicken broth and add to the vegetables.

6. Preheat the oven to 350°. Lightly spray or wipe a 9 x 13-inch baking dish with canola oil.

7. Spread a few tablespoons of the sauce on the bottom of the dish. Cover with a layer of noodles, half the cheese filling, half the mozzarella cheese, and half the vegetable mixture. Spoon 1 cup of mushroom sauce over the vegetables. Repeat. Add a final layer of noodles and top with the remaining sauce. Sprinkle with ¼ cup Parmesan and bake, covered, for 30 minutes. Remove the cover and bake for 15 minutes longer. Let the lasagne stand for 10 minutes before cutting to serve.

Cal. **280** *Carb.* **34g**

Protein **23g** *Chol.* **12mg**

Fat **7g/23%**

"The flowers of late winter and early spring occupy places in our hearts well out of proportion to their size."

Gertrude Wister

All-Green Vegetable Lasagne

SERVES 8

$^1/_2$ *cup packed fresh Italian parsley, rinsed and dried*
$^1/_2$ *cup packed fresh basil leaves, rinsed and dried*
$^1/_2$ *cup packed fresh spinach leaves, rinsed and dried*
2 cups drained low-fat cottage cheese
$^1/_2$ *cup nonfat yogurt*
$1^1/_2$ *cups freshly grated Parmesan*
Freshly ground nutmeg
Salt and freshly ground pepper
6 cups lightly steamed and thoroughly drained fresh green vegetables, such as chopped broccoli, thinly sliced artichoke hearts, thinly sliced zucchini, chopped green beans, asparagus (thinly sliced if thick), thinly sliced scallions, roasted julienned green pepper
$^1/_2$ *cup chopped fresh Italian parsley*
10 lasagne noodles (about $^1/_2$ pound), cooked and drained according to package directions

1. In a food processor, combine the parsley, basil, and spinach leaves. Process until finely minced. Add the cottage cheese, yogurt, and $1^1/_3$ cups Parmesan. Process until smooth. Season with nutmeg, and salt and pepper to taste. Set this sauce aside.

2. Drain the prepared vegetables thoroughly and combine them in a large bowl. Add the chopped parsley, stir, and set aside.

3. Pat the lasagne noodles dry and preheat the oven to 350°. Lightly spray or wipe a 9 x 13-inch baking dish with canola oil. Coat the dish with a thin layer of sauce (about $^1/_2$ cup). Place a layer of noodles on the sauce. Evenly distribute half of the vegetables over the noodles. Repeat, layering with noodles, sauce, and the remaining vegetables. Put a few drops of sauce on the vegetables. Place a final layer of noodles over the vegetables and cover with the remaining sauce. Sprinkle with the remaining Parmesan.

4. Cover the dish with foil and bake for 30 minutes. Remove the foil and bake 5 more minutes, or until the lasagne is heated through and the sauce is starting to bubble. Do not overcook. Remove the lasagne from the oven and let it stand for 5 minutes before serving.

Cal. **274** *Carb.* **31g** *Protein* **22g** *Chol.* **17mg** *Fat* **7/23%**

Quinoa

This power-perfect grain comes from the Andes. A single cup has as much calcium as a quart of milk and more protein than any other grain—a nearly complete protein, too. In fact, ounce for ounce, quinoa has as much protein as meat, which is almost unknown among grains. In addition, this "super grain" is exceptionally high in lysine, an amino acid, as well as calcium and iron. The Incas called quinoa the "mother grain."

Quinoa is light and nutty, and has just enough of its own taste to serve as a supporting player for other flavors. Serve like rice, or use as a base for salads. Quinoa cooks in just minutes, and as it does, a charming halo develops around each grain.

Pistachio-Mint Quinoa Salad

SERVES 12

2 cups quinoa
4 cups chicken broth
  (see Basics)
Zest of 4 limes
1 cup frozen lime juice
  concentrate, defrosted
1 cup golden raisins
2 jalapeño peppers, split,
  seeded, and minced
1 cup chopped pistachio nuts
32 scallions, white parts only,
  chopped
1 cup chopped fresh mint
1 cup chopped fresh cilantro
Salt and freshly ground pepper

1. In a medium-size saucepan, over medium-heat, place the quinoa and broth. Cook, uncovered, for 12 to 15 minutes, stirring occasionally, until the quinoa is tender and the broth has been absorbed.
2. Meanwhile, in a small saucepan, heat the lime zest and juice until warm. Add the raisins and set aside for 30 minutes.
3. When the quinoa is cooked, transfer to a large mixing bowl and cool to room temperature. When cooled, add the remaining ingredients, including the raisin mixture. Allow the flavors to blend for several hours at room temperature before serving.

Cal. 275 Carb. 48g

Protein 7g

Chol. 0mg Fat 8g/24%

Spicy Turkey Lasagne

SERVES 6

¾ pound Italian turkey sausage, casing removed
½ cup finely chopped onion
1 teaspoon finely minced garlic
½ pound mushrooms, thinly sliced
2 cups chopped canned Italian tomatoes
3 ounces tomato paste
1 teaspoon dried oregano
1 teaspoon dried basil
2 tablespoons finely chopped fresh Italian parsley
¼ teaspoon fennel seeds
Crushed red pepper flakes
Salt
Freshly ground pepper
9 lasagne noodles, cooked according to package directions,
  drained
½ pound part-skim mozzarella cheese, thinly sliced
½ pound low-fat cottage cheese, drained
1 cup Parmesan shards, grated large

1. In a large pot over medium heat, brown the sausage until it is no longer pink, breaking the pieces with the back of a fork. Add the onion, garlic, and mushrooms, and sauté, stirring, for about 5 minutes.
2. Add the tomatoes, the tomato paste, ¼ cup water, and all the seasonings. Reduce the heat to a simmer, cover, and cook for 1 to 1½ hours, stirring occasionally. (The sauce can be made ahead and refrigerated or frozen.)
3. Preheat the oven to 350°. Lightly spray or wipe a 7 x 11-inch baking dish with oil.
4. Coat the baking dish with a little of the sauce. Cover with three lasagne noodles and cover the noodles with half the mozzarella, then half the cottage cheese; sprinkle with a third of the Parmesan. Spoon on just enough sauce to cover. Repeat with noodles, cheeses, and sauce. End with a third layer of noodles, sauce, and the remaining Parmesan. Bake, covered, for 30 minutes. Uncover and bake for 15 minutes longer. Let the lasagne stand for 10 minutes before serving.

Cal. 367 Carb. 22g Protein 41g Chol. 80mg Fat 13g/31%

Beef Tagine with Prunes

SERVES 8

16 ounces pitted prunes

1 teaspoon olive oil

2 pounds lean beef stew meat, trimmed of all fat and cut into 2-inch cubes

4 cups sliced onion

2 teaspoons ground coriander

1½ teaspoons ground cinnamon

1 teaspoon ground ginger

1 can beef broth (10½ ounces), plus enough water to equal 1½ cups

1 preserved lemon (opposite), quartered, pulp discarded

Salt and freshly ground pepper

1. Soak the prunes in warm water to cover. Set aside.

2. In a large heavy casserole, heat the oil over medium-high heat. Brown the meat a few pieces at a time on all sides. Remove the browned pieces to a plate.

The mystique of Morocco is centuries old. Narrow alleys winding between high pink walls create mazes that suddenly open onto bustling bazaars of silk, spice, ivory, silver, ebony, and gem merchants, all bargaining at top voice. Tall palms, pointed cypresses, orchards of oranges and lemons, and acres of silver olive trees provide shade and shadows. Everywhere, tantalizing aromas mix—meats grilling with cumin and cayenne, couscous with saffron and hot peppers, ginger with goat, mint and orange, and very black coffee and hot cinnamon.

3. Add the onion to the casserole and cook until translucent, 5 to 7 minutes. Add the spices and cook for 3 minutes.
4. Return the meat to the casserole. Add the beef broth. Bring to a boil, reduce the heat, and simmer, covered, for about 45 minutes.
5. Drain the prunes and add to the stew. Cook for 20 minutes longer, or until the meat is tender. Add the preserved lemon and cook 5 minutes longer. Season to taste with salt and pepper.
6. Transfer the stew to a warm serving dish, and serve at once.

Cal. 280 Carb. 22g Protein 27g Chol. 83mg Fat 10g/31%

Preserved Lemons

YIELD: 24 SLICES

4 medium lemons
2 cups salt, or more,
*   to cover lemons*

1. Wash and dry the lemons.
2. With the tip of a sharp knife, poke holes all around the middle of the lemons. Place the lemons in a 1-quart mason jar and add salt to cover. Seal the jar.
3. Let the jar stand at room temperature for 2 weeks, turning it upside down occasionally. Refrigerate for up to 6 months.
4. Use the lemons as a garnish for traditional Moroccan dishes or as a seasoning for soups and stews. Rinse the lemons before adding them to dishes.

Cal. 22 Carb. 12g
Protein 1g Chol. 0mg
Fat .3g/5%
(analyzed per slice)

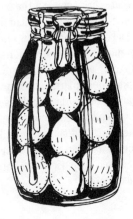

Spicy Lentil Tagine

SERVES 6

1½ cups dry lentils, rinsed and sorted
4 cups chicken broth (see Basics)
1½ teaspoons slivered garlic
1 cup finely chopped onion
1 cup 2-inch carrot pieces
1 cup julienned green bell pepper
2 cups peeled, seeded, and chopped tomato
1 medium sweet potato (about ¾ pound), peeled and cut
*   into chunks*
¼ teaspoon ground ginger
½ teaspoon cayenne
½ teaspoon toasted and ground cumin seeds
½ cup finely chopped fresh cilantro

1. In a Dutch oven, combine the lentils, chicken broth, and garlic. Bring to a boil, lower the heat, cover, and simmer for 20 minutes. Turn the heat off and let the lentils sit for 1 hour.
2. Turn the heat back to medium. Add all the remaining ingredients, except the cilantro. Cook, covered, until the carrot and sweet potato are tender, about 30 minutes.
3. Transfer the lentils and vegetables to a heated serving platter. Garnish with chopped cilantro and serve immediately.

Cal. 259 Carb. 47g Protein 16g Chol. 0mg Fat 1g/3%

Chicken and Olive Tagine

SERVES 8

*2 chickens (3½ pounds each), rinsed
    and quartered*
2 tablespoons coarsely chopped garlic
*½ cup coarsely chopped fresh
    Italian parsley*
½ cup coarsely chopped fresh cilantro
*1 teaspoon lightly toasted and ground
    cumin seeds*
1 teaspoon olive oil
5 tablespoons fresh lemon juice
1 tablespoon freshly ground pepper
1¼ cups grated onion
2 cups chicken broth (see Basics)
*1 preserved lemon (page 493), pulp
    discarded if desired, cut into eighths*
1 cup Kalamata olives
Salt and freshly ground pepper

1. Remove the skin from the chicken and pat dry.
2. In a food processor, combine the garlic, parsley, cilantro, cumin, olive oil, 1 tablespoon of lemon juice, and pepper. Pulse or turn on and off for 15 seconds. Scrape the sides of the bowl and process 5 more seconds. Rub the resulting paste on all sides of the chicken. Place in a large glass bowl, add any remaining paste, cover with plastic wrap, and refrigerate for at least 4 hours, and preferably overnight.
3. In a large stockpot, place all the chicken and the paste. Add ¾ cup of the grated onion and the chicken broth. Cover and simmer for 30 minutes. Add the remaining onion and simmer for 20 more minutes.
4. Add the preserved lemon and the olives, and simmer for 20 minutes, or until the meat is very tender. Remove the chicken, lemon, and olives, and keep warm.
5. Reduce the sauce over medium-high heat to 1½ cups, about 5 minutes. Add the remaining lemon juice and salt and pepper to taste. Pour the sauce over the chicken and serve immediately.

*Cal. **364** Carb. **8g** Protein **43g** Chol. **127mg** Fat **17g/43%***

Typical Tagine

The great specialty of Marrakesh is a *tangia* or *tagine*, a wonderfully aromatic meat or poultry stew named after the pot in which it is cooked—a round dish with a pointed, conical lid made of brown-glazed earthenware.

Any home cook can turn out a dish redolent of the flavors typical of a tagine. What is critical is not the pot but the ingredients—lamb, chicken, saffron, honey, cinnamon, preserved lemons, dates, almonds, ginger, tomatoes, prunes, olives, garlic, and coriander. These tasty components must simmer long and slowly so that the flavors can meld together into a deep, rich, sumptuous stew.

Oasis Olives

YIELD: 3 CUPS

2 tablespoons olive oil
2 teaspoons fennel seeds
2 teaspoons cumin seeds
2 teaspoons coriander seeds
1/4 teaspoon ground cardamom
1/4 teaspoon ground cinnamon
1/4 teaspoon crushed red
  pepper flakes
1/4 teaspoon ground nutmeg
1/4 teaspoon ground cloves
1 vanilla bean, split, seeds
  removed
1/4 cup fresh orange juice
2 tablespoons fresh lime juice
Zest of 1 orange, chopped
Zest of 1 lime, chopped
8 garlic cloves, chopped
3 cups cured olives

1. In a large skillet over medium heat, warm the oil, fennel, cumin and coriander seeds, cardamon, cinnamon, pepper flakes, nutmeg, and cloves. Cook for 2 to 3 minutes to release the aromas.
2. Add the vanilla seeds, the juices, the zest, and the garlic to the spices, and mix well.
3. In a medium bowl, place the olives and the spiced juice mixture, and toss well. Refrigerate for 1 week. Bring the olives to room temperature.

Cal. 37 Carb. 1g

Protein .3g Chol. 0mg

Fat 4g/83%

(analyzed per tablespoon)

Lamb and Quince Tagine

SERVES 8

2 pounds lamb shoulder, trimmed of all fat and cut into
  1 1/2-inch cubes
Salt and freshly ground pepper
1 teaspoon olive oil
1 teaspoon ground ginger
1/4 teaspoon cayenne
1/4 cup grated onion
1/4 cup minced fresh Italian parsley
1/4 cup minced fresh cilantro
2 cups chicken broth (see Basics)
1 1/2 cups pearl onions
1 pound quince, quartered and cored
1 pound Granny Smith apples, quartered and cored
1 teaspoon sugar
1/2 teaspoon ground cinnamon

1. Season the meat with salt and pepper. Set aside.
2. In a large, flat, ovenproof casserole, heat the oil over medium heat. Add the meat. Sprinkle the meat with ginger, cayenne, grated onion, parsley, and cilantro. Cook, stirring, for 5 minutes.
3. Add the chicken broth and bring to a boil. Cover, lower the heat, and cook for 1 1/2 hours, stirring occasionally.
4. Add the pearl onions and cook for 1 hour longer.
5. Meanwhile, poach the fruit in simmering water to cover for 10 to 15 minutes, or until just tender; drain.
6. Preheat the oven to 375°.
7. Arrange the fruit, cut sides down, on top of the meat.
8. In a small dish, combine the sugar and cinnamon. Sprinkle the fruit lightly with the cinnamon-sugar. Bake for 15 minutes, or until the fruit is lightly glazed. Serve immediately over rice.

Cal. 217 Carb. 21g Protein 15g Chol. 51mg Fat 8g/34%

Moroccan Vegetable Soup

SERVES 12

$^1/_2$ cup dried chick-peas, soaked overnight
2 tablespoons olive oil
$^1/_2$ pound lamb shoulder, trimmed of all fat, cut into $^1/_2$-inch
    pieces
1 cup chopped onion
$1^1/_2$ pounds tomatoes, peeled, seeded, and chopped
1 cup diced celery
3 cups chicken broth (see Basics)
$^1/_2$ teaspoon freshly ground pepper
$^1/_4$ teaspoon ground cinnamon
$^1/_4$ teaspoon cayenne
$1^1/_2$ pounds potatoes, peeled and diced
$^3/_4$ pound carrots, scraped and thinly sliced
$^3/_4$ pound zucchini, trimmed and thinly sliced
$^1/_2$ cup finely minced fresh parsley
$^1/_2$ cup finely minced fresh cilantro
1 tablespoon fresh lemon juice

1. Drain and rinse the chick-peas and set them aside.
2. In a large Dutch oven, heat the oil over medium-high heat. Add the lamb, onion, tomato, and celery, and sauté for 8 minutes, stirring. Add the chicken broth and 3 cups of water and bring to a boil. Skim any scum that comes to the surface. Add the chick-peas, pepper, cinnamon, and cayenne. Cover, lower the heat, and simmer gently for 1 hour.
3. Add the potato, carrot, zucchini, half the parsley, and half the cilantro. Cover and simmer for 30 to 45 minutes, or until all the vegetables are tender.
4. Combine the remaining parsley and cilantro.
5. When ready to serve, season the soup with salt and lemon juice to taste. Serve in heated bowls; garnish with the remaining parsley and cilantro.

Cal. **122** *Carb.* **18g** *Protein* **6g** *Chol.* **7mg** *Fat* **4g/27%**

"Manage with bread and butter until God sends the honey."

Moroccan proverb

Moroccan Bread

YIELD: 3 LOAVES (10 SLICES PER LOAF)

1 cup Sourdough Starter (see Basics)
$1^1/_2$ cups whole-wheat flour
$1^1/_2$ cups white flour

Eggplant with Harissa

SERVES 4

2 small eggplants (about
    1¼ pounds each)
Freshly ground sea salt
Freshly ground pepper
1 teaspoon olive oil
½ cup tomato paste
2 teaspoons Harissa
    (page 501)
4 tablespoons freshly minced
    fresh Italian parsley

1. Preheat the oven to 500°.
2. Trim the top of each eggplant and slice in half lengthwise. Cut two deep slits in each eggplant, lengthwise, being careful not to cut through the skin. Season each half with salt and pepper to taste. Place the eggplant halves, flesh sides down, on the prepared baking sheet, and lightly brush the skins with oil if desired. Bake for 15 to 20 minutes, or until the eggplants are tender and the skin is shriveled.
3. Meanwhile, in a small bowl, combine the tomato paste, harissa, and parsley. Mix well.
4. Remove the eggplant from the oven; flip the halves over. Spread each half with the tomato-paste mixture. Place under the broiler for 1 minute. Serve immediately.

Cal. 108 Carb. 23g
Protein 4g Chol. 0mg
Fat 2g/13%

4 tablespoons yellow cornmeal
1 teaspoon salt

1. Lightly spray or wipe two baking sheets with vegetable oil.
2. In a large bowl, combine the starter, flours, cornmeal, salt, and 1½ cups warm water. Beat until the dough is smooth and elastic; add small amounts of additional water as needed.
3. Turn the dough out onto a lightly floured surface and knead for 10 minutes, or until the dough is smooth and elastic.
4. Divide the dough into three equal pieces. Shape them into balls and then into 5-inch-diameter flat rounds.
5. Place the rounds on the baking sheets. Cover with a clean cloth and let rise until doubled in bulk, about 1 hour.
6. Preheat the oven to 400°. Bake the breads for 50 minutes, or until crisp and golden; remove from the sheets and cool on baking racks. Serve with honey for dipping.

Cal. 58 Carb. 12g Protein 2g Chol. 0mg Fat .2g/3%
(analyzed per slice)

Spicy Tomato and Pepper Salad

SERVES 8

4 cups peeled, seeded, and cubed (1-inch) tomato
2½ cups roasted, peeled, and julienned green bell pepper
3 cups halved and sliced hothouse cucumbers
2 tablespoons seeded, deveined, and finely minced fresh red
    chili or jalapeño pepper
1 tablespoon fresh lemon juice
2 tablespoons olive oil
½ teaspoon roasted and finely ground cumin seeds
1 tablespoon finely minced garlic
2 tablespoons coarsely chopped fresh Italian parsley
2 tablespoons coarsely chopped fresh cilantro
Salt and freshly ground pepper

1. In a large bowl, combine the tomato, pepper, cucumber, and chili pepper.
2. In a small bowl, whisk the lemon juice, oil, ground cumin, and garlic. Pour the dressing over the vegetables and toss gently.
3. Fold in the parsley, cilantro, and salt and pepper to taste. Chill until ready to serve.

Cal. 56 Carb. 7g Protein 1g Chol. 0mg Fat 3g/46%

Mandarin Orange and Arugula Salad

SERVES 8

2 teaspoons Dijon mustard
5 tablespoons mandarin orange juice
2 tablespoons sherry vinegar
1 tablespoon olive oil
1 tablespoon minced orange zest
1 teaspoon sugar
1 teaspoon poppy seeds
6 cups arugula, washed and patted dry
¼ cup niçoise olives
¼ cup toasted hazelnuts
1 tablespoon Parmesan shards

1. In a large bowl, blend the first seven ingredients and set aside.
2. Divide the arugula among eight salad plates. Top the arugula with the olives and nuts. Drizzle the dressing over, then place the cheese on the salads. Serve immediately.

*Cal. **69** Carb. **4g** Protein **2g** Cholesterol .**5mg** Fat **6g/70%***

Chicken Kebabs on a Bed of Rice

SERVES 4

1 pound chicken breast, skinned, boned, and cut into
    2-inch cubes
2 tablespoons olive oil
4 tablespoons fresh lime juice
4 garlic cloves, minced
¼ teaspoon cayenne
1 tablespoon minced fresh ginger
½ teaspoon Garam Masala (opposite)
2 cups brown rice
2 green bell peppers, stemmed, seeded, and cut into
    1-inch chunks
2 cups cubed fresh pineapple
8 bamboo skewers, soaked in water for 30 minutes
1 teaspoon canola oil
1 cup chopped scallion, white and green parts
¼ cup slivered almonds, toasted
½ cup chopped fresh mint
Salt and pepper

Moroccan Cuisine

Moroccan cuisine has been shaped by its history—centuries of invasions by Berbers and nomads—and by its proximity to Spain, the Middle East, and even France. The food has been richly influenced by a broad assortment of available products and includes less grain dishes, dried fruits stewed with meats, nuts, olives, mint, oranges, and lemons. Spices are critical to the cuisine. Cinnamon, ginger, cardamom, aniseed, and saffron may be brilliantly combined with honey, olive oil, or orange-flower water.

This is a food style both hearty and delicate, intense and imaginative, and full of surprises.

498

Garam Masala

YIELD: 9 TABLESPOONS

2 tablespoons coriander seeds
2 tablespoons cardamom seeds
1 cinnamon stick
1 tablespoon black peppercorns
1 tablespoon ground cumin
1 tablespoon whole cloves
1 whole nutmeg

1. In a dry skillet, separately roast all the ingredients except the nutmeg. You will know that the spices are roasted when they give off their aromas. When they do, remove them from the heat. Remove the husk from the cardamom seeds.

2. Place the roasted spices in a spice grinder or coffee grinder and finely grind. Grate the nutmeg over the mixture and store in an air-tight container.

Cal. 7 Carb. 1g

Protein .2g Chol. 0mg

Fat .3g/30%
(analyzed per tablespoon)

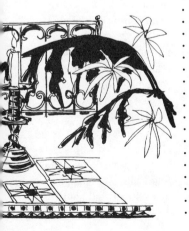

1. In a large bowl, combine the chicken with the olive oil, 3 tablespoons of the lime juice, garlic, cayenne, ginger, and garam marsala. Cover with plastic wrap and marinate in the refrigerator for 2 hours.

2. Cook the brown rice according to the package instructions.

3. Prepare a grill or preheat the broiler.

4. Remove the chicken from the marinade; reserve the marinade. Thread the chicken onto the skewers, alternating with green peppers and pineapple chunks. (Can be made ahead up to this point and refrigerated until ready to cook.)

5. In a large bowl, combine the rice, canola oil, 1 tablespoon lime juice, scallion, almonds, mint, and salt and pepper to taste. Keep warm.

6. Broil the kebabs for 3 to 4 minutes, until the meat is just cooked through, basting occasionally with the marinade.

7. To serve, divide the rice among four plates and top with the chicken kebabs. Serve immediately.

Cal. 394 Carb. 44g Protein 32g Chol. 70mg Fat 10g/23%

Moorish Kebabs

SERVES 8

1 pound pork shoulder, cut into 1/2-inch cubes
1 tablespoon olive oil
1 teaspoon peppercorns
1 teaspoon cumin seeds
1 teaspoon coriander seeds
1 teaspoon cayenne
Freshly ground pepper
8 bamboo skewers soaked in water for 30 minutes
Salt
1 loaf crusty country bread, sliced thickly

1. In a large bowl, place the meat, oil, and spices, and toss to coat. Marinate in the refrigerator overnight.

2. Prepare a grill or broiler for cooking.

3. Thread the meat onto eight skewers, ten to twelve pieces on each. Place the kebabs on the grill over high heat and, turning them frequently, cook until well browned but not dried out.

4. Sprinkle with salt to taste just before removing the kebabs from the heat. Serve the meat on the skewers, with a piece of bread speared on the end of each.

Cal. 323 Carb. 25g Protein 23g Chol. 68mg Fat 14g/39%

Vegetable Couscous

SERVES 12

1 cup dried chick-peas, rinsed, sorted,
   and soaked overnight
1 tablespoon olive oil
2½ cups coarsely chopped onion
4 teaspoons Harissa (opposite)
¼ teaspoon ground allspice
Salt and freshly ground pepper
12 carrots, peeled and cut into
   2-inch pieces
6 cups 2-inch cabbage pieces
3 cups peeled and cubed rutabaga
3 cups quartered plum tomatoes
1½ cups peeled and cut (¾-inch)
   sweet potatoes
1 pound butternut, acorn, or pumpkin squash, peeled and cut
   into 2 x 1-inch pieces
6 medium potatoes, peeled, halved, and quartered lengthwise,
   each piece cut in half (3 cups)
3 cups zucchini pieces (2-inch)
3 cups quick-cooking couscous
Chicken broth (see Basics) or water
1 tablespoon unsalted butter

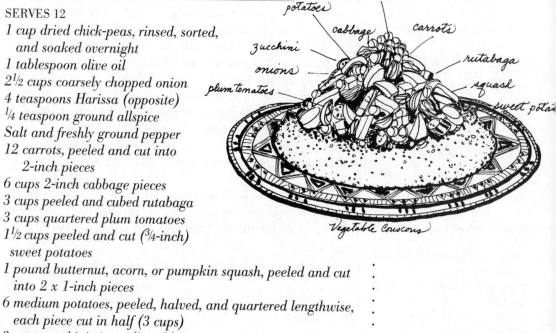

Vegetable Couscous

1. Drain the chick-peas. Place them in a medium saucepan.
Cover with water, bring to a boil, cover, and simmer until just
tender, about 45 minutes.
2. Meanwhile, in a very large Dutch oven, heat 2 tablespoons
of the oil over medium-high heat. Add the onion and sprinkle with harissa, allspice, and salt and pepper to taste. Sauté,
stirring, until the meat has browned, 8 to 10 minutes.
3. Add 3 cups of water, the carrot, cabbage, rutabaga, and
tomato, and bring to a boil. Reduce the heat to low and simmer, partially covered, for 30 to 45 minutes, until the vegetables become tender; transfer them with a slotted spoon to a
large bowl and keep them warm.
4. Add the sweet potato, squash, potato, and zucchini to the
Dutch oven. If necessary, add boiling water to cover the vegetables, and bring back to a boil. Reduce the heat to low, partially cover, and cook for up to 1 hour, or until all the
vegetables are cooked. Transfer the vegetables to the bowl
and keep warm.
5. Cook the instant couscous according to package directions

Couscous

At the end of a Moroccan
feast, traditionally following
an array of tagines, just
when you think you can eat
no more, there arrives a
great mountain of thousands
of tiny pellets of grain on a
huge platter. It's couscous,
the Berber contribution as a
national dish.

Couscous is classically
made of granules of semolina, but it can be made from
other grains as well. Barley,
corn, millet, or wheat can all
become couscous when finely ground and steamed.

Couscous may be served
plain or loaded with vegetables, legumes or sausage.
Sometimes it is spicy, sometimes sweet, but seldom is
there any left over.

Harissa

YIELD: ⅓ CUP

1 cup dried red chili peppers
2 tablespoons coriander seeds
1 tablespoon cumin seeds
2 garlic cloves, peeled
1 tablespoon sea salt
2 tablespoons extra-virgin
  olive oil

1. Remove the stems and seeds from the chili peppers. Place the peppers in a medium bowl and cover with hot water; set aside until very soft.
2. Meanwhile, place the coriander and cumin seeds in a mortar and pound with a pestle until powdered. Add the garlic and salt and pound until smooth.
3. Drain the red peppers; add them to the mortar and pound to a smooth paste. Slowly add the oil until the sauce is smooth and well blended.
4. Transfer to a container, cover, and refrigerate until needed.

Cal. 118 Carb. 13g

Protein 3g Chol. 0mg

Fat 7g/51%

*(analyzed
per tablespoon)*

for six servings, substituting chicken broth for the water and adding 1 tablespoon of olive oil.

6. While the couscous is cooking, return the cooked vegetables to the Dutch oven and bring to a simmer; simmer for 2 to 3 minutes. Stir the butter and salt to taste into the couscous, and put it on a large heated serving platter. Moisten the couscous with about 1 cup of the sauce, then arrange the vegetables on top. Pour the remaining sauce into a heated bowl to pass at the table.

Cal. 246 Carb. 52g Protein 11g Chol. 3mg Fat 5g/12%

Tomatoes with Couscous

SERVES 6

6 medium tomatoes
⅓ cup thinly sliced scallion
1 tablespoon unsalted butter
½ teaspoon ground cumin
¼ teaspoon ground cinnamon
¼ cup currants
¾ cup quick-cooking couscous
¼ cup minced fresh parsley
Parsley leaves

1. Preheat the oven to 350°.
2. Cut the tops off the tomatoes. Carefully scoop out the flesh, taking care not to tear the shells; leave about ¼ inch of the inner walls in place. Reserve the pulp. Lightly salt the cavities and turn the tomatoes upside down on paper towels to drain.
3. Coarsely chop the tomato pulp and set aside. In a skillet, sauté the scallion in the butter for 1 minute. Stir in the cumin, cinnamon, tomato pulp, currants, and 1 cup plus 2 tablespoons water. Bring to a boil and stir in the couscous. Cover, turn off the heat, and let stand for 5 minutes. Stir in the minced parsley. Fill the tomato shells with couscous. Bake for 12 to 15 minutes. Garnish with parsley and serve.

NOTE: Canned plum tomatoes can be substituted. Use a 14-ounce can; drain the tomatoes, chop, and drain again.

Cal. 144 Carb. 26g Protein 5g Chol. 0mg Fat 3g/17%

Bisteeya

One of the truly great dishes of Morocco, *bisteeya* has a complex and unclear origin. Its paper-thin *warkha* pastry could almost be Austrian strudel, Chinese *shao mai*, or Greek phyllo, and its filling of poultry, almonds, and cinnamon could be from Andalusia or Persia. Whatever its provenance, this is a unique and delicious dish. And while it may seem a labor of love, it's most worthwhile—worthy, in fact, of a celebration.

SERVES 12

1 chicken (4 pounds)
1½ tablespoons finely chopped garlic
2 tablespoons coarse salt, or more to taste
1 large Spanish onion, grated (1 cup)
½ teaspoon ground turmeric
1 teaspoon freshly ground pepper
1 tablespoon minced fresh ginger
One 9-inch cinnamon stick, broken into 3-inch pieces
3 cups chicken broth (see Basics)
1 cup slivered almonds, toasted in a 350° oven for 10 minutes,
*   or until light brown*
1 tablespoon confectioners' sugar
4 teaspoons ground cinnamon
½ cup fresh lemon juice
6 eggs
½ cup finely minced fresh Italian parsley
½ cup finely minced fresh cilantro
¾ pound phyllo, thawed according to package directions
1½ preserved lemons (page 493), pulp discarded,
*   cut into eighths*
Butter-flavored vegetable oil spray

1. Cut the chicken into eight pieces. Trim all fat; wash well and pat dry.

2. With a mortar and pestle pound the garlic and salt together to make a paste. Rub the chicken pieces with the paste and let them sit for 30 minutes. Rinse, drain, and place the pieces in a large casserole. Add the onion, turmeric, pepper, ginger, cinnamon sticks, chicken broth, and salt to taste, and bring to a boil. Reduce the heat to low, cover, and simmer for 1 hour.

3. Meanwhile, combine the confectioners' sugar and cinna-

A Moroccan Feast

Mâche,
Mandarin Oranges,
Walnuts, and Citrus Spray

Bisteeya

Spicy Tomato and
Pepper Salad

Honeydew Sorbet

mon in a small bowl, than add to the nuts. Set aside.

4. When the chicken is cooked, remove the pieces, any bones, and the cinnamon sticks from the casserole. Reduce the sauce over high heat to 1¾ cups, about 10 minutes. Stir in the lemon juice and reduce the heat to a simmer.

5. Beat the eggs in a medium bowl until combined. Pour the eggs into the simmering sauce and stir continuously, until the eggs cook and curdle and are stiff-dry.

6. Shred the meat and discard the skin and bones; set aside.

7. Stir the parsley and cilantro into the egg mixture. Adjust seasoning. Cool the mixture completely. The dish can be made ahead up to this point and refrigerated for 1 day.

8. Unroll the phyllo leaves and keep them under a slightly damp towel to prevent them from drying out.

9. Lightly spray the bottom and sides of a 14-inch cake pan or deep-dish pizza pan with vegetable oil.

10. Working quickly, arrange six phyllo leaves so that half of each covers the bottom and half extends over the sides of the pan. Spray the leaves very lightly with vegetable oil so they don't dry out. The pan should be completely covered with phyllo. Fold the additional four leaves in half and let them air dry.

11. Place all of the shredded chicken in one layer on the bottom of the pan, on top of the phyllo; layer the preserved lemon over the chicken. Cover with the egg mixture and then the four dry pastry leaves. Sprinkle the almond-and-sugar mixture over the pastry. Cover with all but two of the remaining pastry leaves, brushing each lightly with oil.

12. Preheat the oven to 425°.

13. Fold the overlapping leaves in over the top to cover the pie. Spray with oil.

14. Bake for 20 minutes, or until the phyllo is golden. Shake the pan to loosen the pie, then remove with a wide spatula to a heated serving dish. Dust the top with a little cinnamon just before serving.

*Cal. **301** Carb. **25g** Protein **24g** Chol. **139mg** Fat **13g/37%***

Casablanca Mint Sorbet

A mint julep for after a Moroccan feast.

SERVES 6

¾ cup sugar
2 packed cups coarsely chopped fresh mint
¼ cup fresh lemon or lime juice
1½ tablespoons finely minced lemon or lime zest

1. Combine 1 quart of water and the sugar in a saucepan and bring to a boil. Add the mint, reduce the heat, and simmer for 5 minutes. Remove from the heat and set aside to steep for 1 hour.
2. Strain the syrup into a bowl. Add the juice and zest; refrigerate until very cold.
3. Freeze in an ice cream maker according to the manufacturer's directions.

Cal. 104 Carb. 27g Protein .4g Chol. 0mg Fat .1g/1%

Honeydew Sorbet

SERVES 6

4 cups ripe honeydew chunks
1 cup fresh lime juice
¾ cup sugar
1 tablespoon finely chopped crystallized ginger

1. Place the honeydew, lime juice, and sugar in a food processor and process until smooth. Stir in the ginger and refrigerate until very cold.
2. Freeze the mixture in an ice cream maker according to the manufacturer's directions. This is best if served immediately or on the day it is made.

Cal. 152 Carb. 40g Protein .7g Chol. 0mg Fat .2g/1%

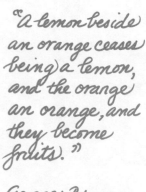

"A lemon beside an orange ceases being a lemon, and the orange an orange, and they become fruits."

Georges Braque

Sugar-Preserved Lemons

Use these sweet and tart lemons as a flavoring for desserts, fruits, or yogurt, or in a cooling lemonade.

YIELD: 24 SLICES

4 medium lemons, washed and dried
2 cups sugar

1. Slice the lemons as thinly as possible. In a 1-quart mason jar, layer the slices alternately with the sugar, filling the jar. Seal the jar.
2. Let the jar stand overnight. The next morning, turn the jar over. By the third day there should be enough liquid in the jar to cover the lemons; if not, add more sugar—do not add water. Let the lemons sit in a cool place for 2 weeks, then refrigerate for up to to 6 months.

*Cal. **68** Carb. **19g***
*Protein **.2g** Chol. **0mg***
*Fat **.1g/1%***

(analyzed per slice)

Lemon Soufflé Pudding

SERVES 6

2 cups skim milk
2 eggs, separated
4 tablespoons all-purpose flour
¾ cup sugar
¼ teaspoon baking powder
Pinch salt
2 tablespoons grated lemon zest
⅓ cup fresh lemon juice

1. Preheat the oven to 350°.
2. In a medium-size bowl, combine the milk and egg yolks. Gradually beat in the dry ingredients. Stir in the zest and the juice.
3. Beat the egg whites until stiff and fold them into the milk mixture. Pour into a 1½-quart baking dish. Set the baking dish inside a larger baking pan and add hot water halfway up the sides of the dish. Bake for 35 to 40 minutes, until the top is slightly puffed and golden brown. Serve immediately.

*Cal. **170** Carb. **35g** Protein **5g** Chol. **62mg** Fat **2g/9%***

Tropical Gratin

SERVES 6

1 ripe mango, peeled, cored, and cut into ¾-inch cubes
1 ripe papaya, peeled, seeded, and cut into ¾-inch cubes
3 oranges, peeled, cut into ¼-inch slices and seeds removed
1 cup sugar
2 tablespoons minced crystallized ginger
1 fresh pineapple trimmed, peeled, cored, and cut into ¼-inch rings

1. Preheat the broiler.
2. In a medium-size bowl, toss the mango, papaya, orange, ½ cup of the sugar, and the ginger, and mix well. Transfer the fruit to a 10 x 8-inch baking dish.
3. Place the pineapple on top of the other fruit and sprinkle with the remaining sugar.
4. Place the casserole under the broiler, about 4 inches from the heat, for approximately 10 minutes, until the crust caramelizes. Serve immediately.

*Cal. **348** Carb. **89g** Protein **2g** Chol. **0mg** Fat **1.4g/3%***

EAST OF THE SUN COOKING

Star-Gazing Soup

A most flavorful clear broth, shimmering with "stars."

SERVES 4

5 cups chicken broth (see Basics)
½ cup fresh orange juice
Zest of 1 orange
3 tablespoons finely slivered fresh ginger
½ cup thinly sliced scallion, white parts only
1 cup stars cut from carrots with a tiny cookie cutter
1 cup stars cut from jícama with a tiny cookie cutter
6 ounces fresh snow peas
Freshly ground pepper

In a soup pot, bring the chicken broth, juice, orange, ginger, and scallion to a boil. Reduce the heat, add the carrot stars, and simmer for 5 minutes. Stir in the jícama stars and snow peas, and simmer for 5 minutes or longer or, until all of the vegetables are tender but still crisp. Add the freshly ground pepper; adjust seasoning. Serve immediately.

Cal. 90 Carb. 15g Protein 4g Chol. 0mg Fat 2g/16%

Many-Moon Soup

SERVES 4

4 cups chicken broth (see Basics)
2 tablespoons dry sherry
¼ cup fresh lemon juice
1 teaspoon sesame oil

Yin and Yang

Chinese cuisine is one of the world's oldest, and surely one of the three or four greatest. Chinese cooking is distinguished by fragrance, texture, color, flavor, and an exquisite sense of balance. Sweet complements sour, crunchy offsets soft, the dull colors of meat are brightened by the bright colors of vegetables.

By A.D. 100, the Chinese had developed and mastered such cooking methods as steaming, grilling, deep-frying, and roasting, and were using garlic, ginger, and scallions as primary seasonings.

During the Hon Dynasty the five essential flavors were first identified and combined: bitter, sour, sweet, salty, and hot. These are the elements common to Chinese cuisines to this day.

Nevertheless, vast and complicated cooking distinctions exist among China's regions. In the north, Beijing was home to emperors and aristocrats for centuries. There, an eclectic style of cooking evolved. The great chefs who cooked for the privileged developed the Mongolian hot pot method for preparing lamb and beef; they learned to barbecue meats and chicken and to salt fish. The noodle and the spring roll are from Beijing. Perhaps the city's most famous dish is the fabulous, ceremonial, and quite complicated Peking duck.

The south's Canton cuisine is the most familiar to the rest of the world. Canton cuisine was exported with those who emigrated to build America's railroads and eventually settled the big cities. Mild but varied, the Cantonese menu includes dim sum, lo mein, lemon squab, and dozens of stir-fried dishes.

To the east is the culinary hub of Shanghai. Its cuisine is mild and delicate. Soy sauce replaces vinegar, and there is a prevalence of sweet-and-sour dishes. Seafood abounds, and many foods are wrapped in lotus leaves for steaming or roasting.

Chinese cooking picks up heat in the western provinces of Szechuan and Hunan, where hot spices, peppers, and oil distinguish a lively, pungent cuisine. Sesame seeds, chili paste, and garlic add depth, while cilantro and other cooling herbs provide the always-present balance.

1 cup thinly shredded boneless, skinless chicken breast
½ cup thinly sliced fresh lemon grass
½ cup sliced scallion
1 cup thinly sliced mushrooms
2 tablespoons minced fresh cilantro
1 tablespoon honey
1 tablespoon potato starch, dissolved in 1 tablespoon water

In a soup pot, bring the broth, sherry, lemon juice, and sesame oil to a boil. Add the chicken, lemon grass, scallion, and mushrooms. Bring to a boil; reduce the heat and simmer for 3 minutes. Add the cilantro and honey and simmer 10 minutes longer. Taste and adjust the seasoning by adding additional sherry, lemon grass, or cilantro as desired. Add the dissolved potato starch and simmer, stirring constantly, until the soup is slightly thickened. Serve immediately.

*Cal. **141** Carb. **16g** Protein **13g** Chol. **27mg** Fat **4g/21%***

Hot-and-Sour Soup

A very light soup that packs a wallop of taste.

SERVES 4

4 cups chicken broth (see Basics)
4 tablespoons distilled white vinegar
2 tablespoons soy sauce
1 teaspoon sesame oil
1 tablespoon Szechuan peppercorns, slightly crushed
½ teaspoon freshly ground pepper
Dash Tabasco
1½ cups enoki mushrooms
1 cup packed fresh spinach, washed and chiffonaded
1 tablespoon potato starch, dissolved in 1 tablespoon water

In a soup pot, bring the broth, vinegar, soy sauce, sesame oil, peppercorns, pepper, and Tabasco to a boil. Reduce the heat and simmer for 10 minutes. Stir in the mushrooms and spinach and simmer for 3 minutes longer. Add the dissolved potato starch, stirring constantly, and cook until the soup is slightly thickened. Taste and adjust the seasoning. Serve immediately.

*Cal. **70** Carb. **9g** Protein **4g** Chol. **0mg** Fat **3g/30%***

WOK AROUND THE CLOCK

Chinese cooking has centuries-old traditions and classic dishes that often require hours of preparation and long lists of special ingredients, some of them hard to find at the supermarket.

A solution for me is what I call my Chinese menu cooking. It allows me to enjoy Asian flavors in a snap with ingredients that are easy to find.

A few tablespoons of one of the sauces on the following pages can be paired with a variety of meats, seafood, fresh vegetables, or other ingredients to create a wonderful meal in moments. Remember to use these sparingly. You want to bring flavor but not overwhelm or add too much fat as you stir-fry your dish.

Chinese Menu Stir-Fry

★
Mung bean shoots
★
Broccoli
★
Celery
★
Chicken breast
★
Sirloin tips
★
Tuna
★
Pork strips
★
Carrots
★
Scallions
★
Lemon grass
★
Chives
★
Sugar snap peas
★
Green beans
★
Cranberry beans
★
Fava beans
★
Lobster
★
Shrimp
★
Zucchini
★
Eggplant
★
Crab
★
Red onions

★
Radishes
★
Orange zest
★
Lemon zest
★
Lime zest
★
Peanuts
★
Almonds
★
Cashews
★
Walnuts
★
Garlic
★
Spinach
★
Watercress
★
Arugula
★
Cabbage
★
Lettuces
★
Bok choy
★
Rutabaga
★
Leeks
★
Artichoke hearts
★
Baby vegetables
★
Celeriac
★
Spaghetti squash
★
Baby artichokes

Pang-Pang Sauce

YIELD: 2 CUPS

1 tablespoon sesame oil

1 tablespoon minced garlic

1 tablespoon minced fresh
   ginger

1 1/2 cups chicken broth
   (see Basics)

1/4 cup chunky peanut butter

3 tablespoons hoisin sauce

2 tablespoons honey

2 tablespoons soy sauce

2 tablespoons thinly and
   diagonally sliced scallion,
   green parts only

1 tablespoon rice vinegar

1/2 teaspoon Chinese chili
   paste

1 teaspoon potato starch, dissolved in 1 tablespoon water

1. In a large skillet, heat the
oil over medium-high heat.
Add the garlic and ginger, and
sauté for 1 minute. Stir in the
chicken broth, peanut butter,
hoisin sauce, honey, soy
sauce, scallion, vinegar, and
chili paste.

2. Bring the sauce to a boil;
reduce the heat and simmer
for 10 minutes. Whisk in the
dissolved potato starch, stirring constantly, until the sauce
thickens slightly. Can be made
ahead and kept refrigerated
for up to 1 week.

*Cal. **37** Carb. **3g** Protein **1g**
Chol. **0mg** Fat **2g/56%***

Black Bean Sauce

YIELD: 1 CUP

1 tablespoon dry sherry

1 tablespoon red wine vinegar

2 tablespoons fresh lime juice

1 tablespoon minced garlic

2 tablespoons minced fresh
   ginger

1 teaspoon oyster sauce

2 teaspoons sugar

1/4 teaspoon chili sauce

1 tablespoon salted black
   beans (whole)

1 tablespoon salted black
   beans (minced)

1 cup chicken broth
   (see Basics)

2 teaspoons potato starch, dissolved in 1 tablespoon water

1. In a large skillet, heat the
sherry, vinegar, and lime juice.
Add the garlic and ginger, and
cook over medium-high heat
for 1 minute. Stir in the oyster
sauce, sugar, chili sauce, black
beans, and chicken broth.

2. Bring the sauce to a boil;
reduce the heat and simmer
for 5 minutes. Whisk in the
dissolved potato starch, stirring constantly, until the sauce
thickens slightly. Can be made
ahead and refrigerated for up
to 1 week.

*Cal. **12** Carb. **2g** Protein **.4g**
Chol. **0mg** Fat **.2g/13%***

**Nutrition information
analyzed per tablespoon*

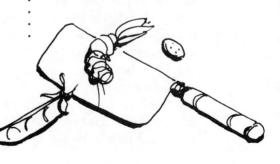

WOK ON THE WILD SIDE

Spicy Peanut Sauce

YIELD: 2 CUPS

2 tablespoons sesame oil
1½ tablespoons minced fresh
  ginger
1½ tablespoons minced garlic
¼ cup minced scallion, white
  parts only
1½ cups chicken broth
  (see Basics)
⅓ cup chunky peanut butter
1 teaspoon Chinese chili paste
2 teaspoons hoisin sauce
2 teaspoons red wine vinegar
2 tablespoons soy sauce
2 tablespoons dry sherry
1 teaspoon potato starch,
  dissolved in 1 tablespoon
  water

1. In a large skillet, heat the
oil. Add the ginger, garlic, and
scallion, and sauté over medium-high heat for 2 minutes.
Whisk in the chicken broth,
peanut butter, chili paste,
hoisin sauce, vinegar, soy
sauce, and sherry.
2. Bring the sauce to a boil;
lower the heat and simmer for
10 minutes. Whisk in the dissolved potato starch, stirring

constantly, until the sauce
thickens slightly. Can be made
ahead and refrigerated for up
to 1 week.

Cal. **28** *Carb.* **1g** *Protein* **1g**
Chol. **0mg** *Fat* **2g/68%***

Orange-Sesame Sauce

YIELD: 2 CUPS

2 tablespoons sesame oil
1 tablespoon minced garlic
3 tablespoons minced fresh
  ginger
½ cup fresh orange juice
1½ cups chicken broth
  (see Basics)
2 tablespoons soy sauce
1 tablespoon minced orange
  zest
3 tablespoons dry sherry
1 tablespoon toasted tahini
2 tablespoons minced fresh
  cilantro

Dash Tabasco
2 tablespoons toasted sesame
  seeds
1 tablespoon potato starch,
  dissolved in 1 tablespoon
  water

1. In a large skillet, heat the
oil over medium-high heat.
Add the garlic and ginger, and
sauté for 1 minute. Stir in the
orange juice, chicken broth,
soy sauce, orange zest, sherry,
tahini, cilantro, Tabasco, and
sesame seeds.
2. Bring the sauce to a boil;
reduce the heat and simmer
for 10 minutes. Whisk in the
dissolved potato starch, stirring constantly, until the sauce
thickens slightly. Can be made
ahead and refrigerated for up
to 1 week.

Cal. **19** *Carb.* **1g** *Protein* **.4g**
Chol. **0mg** *Fat* **2/63%***

510

Lemon-Grass Sauce

YIELD: 1¼ CUPS

1 tablespoon sesame oil
2 tablespoons minced fresh
*   ginger*
½ cup minced fresh lemon grass
½ cup fresh lemon juice
1½ cups chicken broth
*   (see Basics)*
2 tablespoons minced fresh
*   cilantro*
2 tablespoons honey
2 tablespoons potato starch, dis-
*   solved in 1 tablespoon water*

1. In a large skillet, heat the oil
over medium-high heat. Add
the ginger and sauté for 1
minute. Stir in the lemon grass
and lemon juice and simmer for
3 minutes. Add the chicken
broth, cilantro, and honey.
2. Bring the sauce to a boil;
reduce the heat and simmer for
10 minutes. Whisk in the dissolved potato starch, stirring
constantly, until the sauce
thickens slightly. Can be made
ahead and refrigerated for up
to 1 week.

*Cal. **25** Carb. **5g** Protein **.2g**
Chol. **0mg** Fat **1g/32%*** %

Chinese Five Spices

YIELD: 9 TABLESPOONS
2 tablespoons peppercorns
2 tablespoons star anise
Two 10-inch cinnamon sticks
2 tablespoons whole cloves
2 tablespoons fennel seeds

Place the spices in a spice or
coffee grinder. Mix well and
store in a small jar or pot.

*Cal. **26** Carb. **5g** Protein **1g**
Chol. **0mg** Fat **1g/24%***

The Wok

In the Chinese kitchen, the wok
is an essential piece of cooking
equipment. Measuring 14 inches
across the top, this large metal
pan has sloped sides and a small
cooking surface. The design
evolved for its efficiency—the
wok transfers heat quickly and
conserves fuel. It also requires
very little fat for cooking. Stir-
frying, deep-frying, and steaming can all be accomplished in a
wok. Season your wok with oil.
Wipe it immediately after each
use, while it still is hot. Never
use soap or an abrasive.

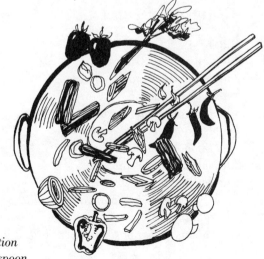

**Nutrition information
analyzed per tablespoon*

Stir-Fried Eggplant

SERVES 6

1 tablespoon finely minced fresh ginger
4 garlic cloves, finely minced
8 scallions, thinly sliced, white and
    green parts
1 dried red chili, seeded and finely
    minced, or ½ teaspoon chili oil
3 tablespoons soy sauce
2 tablespoons light brown sugar
2 tablespoons balsamic vinegar
3 tablespoons chicken broth (see Basics)
1 teaspoon canola or peanut oil
2 eggplants (2 pounds total), cut into 1-inch cubes

1. In a medium-size bowl, combine the ginger, garlic, ¼ cup scallion, chili, soy sauce, sugar, vinegar, and chicken broth. Mix well.

2. In a wok or a large heavy skillet, heat the oil over high heat until hot. Add the sauce and cook until heated through, about 1 minute, stirring constantly. Add the eggplant, stir, then cover and cook for about 5 to 6 minutes. Uncover and continue to cook until most of the liquid is absorbed by the eggplant. Add the remaining scallion and serve immediately.

*Cal. **71** Carb. **14g** Protein **3g** Chol. **0mg** Fat **1g/12%***

Mongolian Beef Stir-Fry

SERVES 4

4 tablespoons soy sauce
2 tablespoons balsamic vinegar
½ teaspoon chili oil
3 tablespoons minced garlic
1 tablespoon chopped fresh ginger
4 tablespoons red wine vinegar
2 teaspoons hoisin sauce
1 teaspoon canola oil
1 pound tenderloin, trimmed of fat and sliced paper-thin
    by a butcher
24 scallions, green parts only, cut into 3-inch pieces

Rice Power

Rice is the staff of life throughout Asia. In China, the greeting "Have you eaten rice yet?" is extended to great leaders and humble peasants alike. The word for rice is the same as the word for food, and a person who has not eaten rice is not considered to have truly eaten. Tradition has it that a full belly indicates that one is well and prosperous. In Tokyo, when our Silver Palate stores opened, each menu contained rice, in a blending of Western and Asian eating traditions. To deny those who enjoy their rice with every meal would have been far too radical.

512

Chinese Caviar

One of the best eggplant caviars ever for spreading on a cracker at cocktail time.

YIELD: 2 CUPS

2 eggplants (1½ pounds each)
2 tablespoons minced garlic
1 tablespoon finely minced
  fresh ginger
¼ cup thinly sliced scallion
½ teaspoon cayenne
1 tablespoon hoisin sauce
3 tablespoons soy sauce
2 teaspoons light brown sugar
2 tablespoons rice vinegar

1. Preheat the oven to 500°.
2. Pierce the eggplants in several places with a fork and place on a baking sheet; bake for 1 hour, turning once, until tender. Remove the eggplants from the oven, slit lengthwise, and set aside to cool.
3. When just warm to the touch, scrape the eggplant pulp into a bowl, using a spoon. Add the remaining ingredients and mix together very well with a fork, until everything is completely incorporated. Serve on crackers or pita bread.

Cal. 13 Carb. 3g Protein .6g
Chol. 0mg Fat .1g/3%
(analyzed per tablespoon)

"*East of the Sun and West of the Moon*"

East of the Sun — Saugatuck)

1. In a small bowl, mix the first seven ingredients together thoroughly.
2. In a large skillet or wok, heat the canola oil over medium-high heat. Add the beef one or two slices at a time, and cook to sear, until just browned. Add the soy-sauce mixture, ¼ cup at a time; at first, the liquid will be absorbed and will evaporate, but then will start to create a sauce.
3. When the meat is browned and all the sauce ingredients have been added, add the scallion. Cover for several minutes, just long enough for the scallion to soften, stirring several times. Work quickly—the total cooking time should be about 5 minutes. Serve the beef and sauce over white or brown rice.

Cal. 229 Carb. 12g Protein 24g
Chol. 60mg Fat 9g/36%

Stir-Fried Crunchy Chicken

SERVES 4

1 cup white wine vinegar
½ cup honey
¼ cup soy sauce
2 garlic cloves, minced
2 teaspoons minced fresh ginger
½ teaspoon crushed dried red chili pepper
1 pound chicken breast, boned, skinned, and cut into strips
2 cups 2-inch asparagus pieces
1 cup thickly sliced mushrooms
1 cup chicken broth (see Basics)
8 scallions, green parts only, quartered lengthwise

1. In a large skillet over medium-high heat, combine the vinegar, honey, soy sauce, garlic, ginger, and chili pepper. Bring to a boil and cook, stirring occasionally, until reduced by about half. Taste and adjust the seasonings.
2. Stir in the chicken, asparagus, and mushrooms, and cook over high heat for 2 minutes. Slowly add the chicken broth, and cook for 2 to 4 minutes. Remove from the heat and stir in the scallion. Taste and adjust the seasonings. Serve immediately.

Cal. 321 Carb. 45g Protein 31g Chol. 70mg Fat 3g/9%

Walnut Chicken Stir-Fry

This is reminiscent of a typical Cantonese chicken dish. The flavorful sauce is made from ingredients you probably have in your cupboard.

SERVES 6

1 cup walnut halves
3 tablespoons soy sauce
3 tablespoons cornstarch
½ teaspoon salt
1 teaspoon sugar
1½ pounds chicken breast, bone and skin removed,
    cut into strips
2 tablespoons peanut oil
3 small heads Chinese cabbage, washed,
    patted dry, and cut crosswise into
    ⅛-inch-thick slices
6 stalks celery, cut into 2-inch pieces, then julienned
2 large onions, cut in half, then sliced thin
1 pound snow peas or sugar snaps, trimmed
1 can (8 ounces) sliced water chestnuts, drained
½ cup chicken broth (see Basics)
2 tablespoons chopped fresh tarragon

1. In a small saucepan, boil the walnuts in water to cover for 3 minutes; rinse in cold water and drain. Set aside.
2. In a small bowl, combine the soy sauce, cornstarch, salt, and sugar, and stir well. Add the chicken strips and toss to coat. Set aside.
3. Heat a large wok or skillet over medium-high heat; add 1 tablespoon of oil and all the vegetables. Stir-fry until tender-crisp, about 3 minutes. Remove the vegetables and set aside. Add the walnuts to the wok and sauté until lightly browned. Add a bit more oil if necessary. Add the water chestnuts and sauté for 1 to 2 minutes longer. Add the walnuts and water chestnuts to the vegetables.
4. Heat the remaining oil until very hot. Remove the chicken from the marinade, and allow the excess to drip off; reserve the marinade. Stir-fry the chicken until cooked through, 3 to 4 minutes. Add the chicken broth and marinade. Cook until bubbling, return the vegetables to the wok, toss, and heat through. Stir in the tarragon and serve immediately over steamed rice or crisp noodles.

*Cal. **455** Carb. **31g** Protein **38g** Chol. **70mg** Fat **21g/40%***

Water Chestnuts

An edible bulb the Chinese call *ma ti* or "horse hoof," in reference to its shape, it is actually the crunchy, slightly sweet fruit of the water plant *trapa*. Water chestnuts are grown in clumps, much like peanuts, harvested by hand at six months old, then hand peeled. They are a favorite crunchy addition to stir-fries, stuffings, and poultry dishes.

Roasted Chicken with Lemon Grass

Every bite of this chicken has the gentle mist of lemon grass.

SERVES 6

1 roasting chicken (about 4 pounds)
10 lemon grass stalks, outer stalks removed and thinly sliced
1 small whole lemon, rind pierced with a fork
1½ cups fresh cilantro sprigs
½ cup finely minced fresh cilantro
2 tablespoons minced lemon zest
Freshly ground pepper
2 cups chicken broth (see Basics)
14 garlic cloves, peeled

1. Preheat the oven to 350°.
2. Rinse the chicken well inside and out and pat dry. Sprinkle the cavity with 1 thinly sliced lemon grass stalk. Place the whole lemon in the cavity. Arrange the cilantro sprigs around the lemon and tie the chicken's legs together.
3. In a small bowl, mix the remaining sliced lemon grass, ¼ cup minced cilantro, and lemon zest. Gently lift the skin (being careful not to break it) from the neck end of the chicken and spread the lemon-grass mixture over the flesh.
4. Place the chicken in a roasting pan and season with the ground pepper. Pour in the chicken broth and scatter the garlic and the remaining minced cilantro in the roasting pan.
5. Place the chicken in the oven. Roast for 2 to 2½ hours, basting every 15 minutes. Remove the chicken from the oven and let it rest for 10 minutes before serving.

Cal. **237** *Carb.* **6g** *Protein* **33g** *Chol.* **97mg** *Fat* **8g/32%**

Lemon Grass

A pot of lemon grass grows in every Thai house. This plant also imparts a subtle, lemony flavor to the dishes of Vietnam, Laos, Cambodia, and Malaysia. It can now be found in Asian markets and gardens across the U.S.

Use lemon grass to accent everything from hot-and-sour soups to chicken and curries. Lemon grass has a "sour power" roughly equivalent to an equal amount of minced lemon peel. To use, remove the few outer layers from the lower part and sauté the chopped inner fiber.

Fresh is best. Dried is just okay. Use powdered lemon grass as a last resort. To start your own pot, stand a stalk in water. Once it is rooted, plant the lemon grass in a pot and set it in a sunny spot—it grows like a weed.

Mongolian Hot Pot

SERVES 4

1 pound beef, lamb, pork tenderloin, boned and skinned
  chicken breast, or medium-size shrimp, peeled and
  deveined
2 quarts beef broth (see Basics)
3 thin slices fresh ginger
1 head green cabbage, quartered, or 4 baby bok choy
4 medium leeks, washed, white parts cut into
  1/2-inch rounds
16 fresh white mushrooms
4 carrots, cut into 1/2-inch pieces
2 turnips, cut into 1/2-inch pieces
1 pound spinach, washed, patted dry, and slivered

1. Cut the meat into paper-thin slices or have the butcher do
it. If you do it yourself, freeze the meat first and use a very
sharp knife. Cut the chicken breast into strips and the
shrimp in half down the middle.
2. Place 4 ounces of meat, in a single layer, on each plate and
chill.
3. Place the broth in a saucepan. Add the ginger and bring to
a boil. Transfer to an earthenware or cast-iron pot and place
over a heat source on the table.
4. Arrange the vegetables, except the spinach, and the sauce
in bowls, and arrange the bowls around the pot. Have your
guests use chopsticks to cook their own meat and vegetables
in the broth. After the meat and vegetables are finished, add
the spinach to the broth, cover for 2 minutes, then ladle the
soup into bowls.

*Cal. **328** Carb. **38g** Protein **27g** Chol. **53mg** Fat **8g/22%***

Mongolian Hot Pot

This communal dish was
first introduced to China in
the thirteenth century, after
the invasion of Mongolian
nomads. Eventually, a version called shabu-shabu
became a Japanese classic.

Guests at a round table
are served an assortment of
uncooked meats, shrimp or
other seafood, and vegetables. The ingredients are
very thinly sliced. At the
center of the table, over a
flame, stands a huge pot of
steaming broth. Each guest
uses chopsticks to dip the
morsels into the hot broth,
where it cooks quickly, and
then into a sauce to enjoy
immediately. The broth,
which becomes increasingly
tasty throughout the pro-
cess, is ladled into small
bowls and drunk at the end
of the meal.

Mongolian Hot Pot Sauces

These sauces are served with Mongolian Hot Pot. For the first three, whisk the ingredients together. Serve the sauces in individual dishes.

Sesame Sauce

1 tablespoon chopped garlic
4 tablespoons tahini or peanut butter
1/2 cup chicken broth (see Basics)
2 tablespoons mirin or sweet sherry
2 teaspoons sugar
2 tablespoons saki
1/2 teaspoon chili oil

Daikon Sauce

4 scallions, finely chopped
1 small daikon, peeled and grated
4 lemon wedges
1 cup soy sauce
1 tablespoon hoisin sauce
1/4 cup chopped cilantro

Hot Tomato Sauce

4 scallions, coarsely chopped
3 tablespoons soy sauce
2 tablespoons tomato paste
4 tablespoons beef broth (see Basics)
2 tablespoons hot bean paste or 1/2 teaspoon chili oil
1 tablespoon sesame oil

Chinese Mustard

For fullest flavor, make this about 1 hour—but not much more—in advance. Place the mustard in a bowl and slowly whisk in the liquid.

4 tablespoons Coleman's dry mustard
6 tablespoons vodka, gin, white wine, or water

Three-Glass Chicken

When Wills and I are in New York, we never miss a chance to track down the ultimate version of Three-Glass Chicken, a traditional dish made with three liquids—soy sauce, rice wine, and water. When they're in season, I make this with wild spring onions that grow in the orchard behind our cottage; other times, scallions are fine.

SERVES 4

1 ounce dried Chinese black or shiitake mushrooms
2 cups chicken broth (see Basics)
1 tablespoon canola oil
1 chicken (3 pounds), cut into small (1- to 3-inch) pieces
2 bunches scallions, white and green parts, cut into 2-inch pieces
2 bunches watercress, stems removed, washed and coarsely chopped
Two 2-inch pieces fresh ginger, peeled and sliced lengthwise
20 whole cloves garlic, peeled
1 pound fresh cultivated mushrooms
1 cup soy sauce
1 cup rice wine, white wine, vodka, or water
2 tablespoons hoisin sauce
Coarsely ground pepper
1 cup minced fresh cilantro leaves

1. Marinate the mushrooms in the chicken broth for at least 1 hour in a warm place.
2. Preheat the oven to 350°.
3. In a large skillet, heat the oil and lightly brown the chicken pieces.
4. Place the chicken, scallion, watercress, ginger, garlic, and fresh mushrooms in a roasting pan. Drain the marinating mushrooms, reserving the broth except that at the very bottom, where it might have collected sand. Coarsely chop the marinated mushrooms and add to the roasting pan.
5. Add the broth, soy sauce, white wine, and hoisin sauce to the pan. Roast, covered, for 45 minutes and uncovered for an additional 45 minutes. Add the cilantro 10 minutes before removing from the oven. Serve over rice or with new potatoes.

Cal. **415** Carb. **24g** Protein **49g** Chol. **109mg**
Fat **15g/28%**

Red-Hot Mexico!

Spicy Bean Dip

YIELD: 4 CUPS

2 cups dry pinto beans
2 tablespoon ground cumin
10 garlic cloves
2 tablespoons minced jalapeño pepper
4 tablespoons cider vinegar
2 tablespoons paprika
2 tablespoons chili powder
Tabasco, to taste
1 cup chopped fresh cilantro

1. Bring about 6 cups of water to a boil. Add the beans and boil until tender, about 2 hours.
2. Drain the beans and place them into a food processor. Add the remaining ingredients and process until smooth. Refrigerate until ready to serve.

*Cal. **24** Carb. **4g** Protein **1g** Chol. **0mg** Fat **.2g/7%**
(analyzed per tablespoon)*

Mexican Cooking

The food of Mexico is rooted in the drama of its history, with geography proving an inescapable influence. The sun over Mexico can be harsh and unforgiving, and much of the land is historically barren.

Nevertheless, an agrarian culture evolved that flourished for more than six and a half million years. This was one of the most important horticultural systems in the history of mankind.

Corn was at the heart of the system, as it has been at the center of all American civilization. Around it developed an ancient culture of trading, growing, roasting, grinding, and cooking. Other early discoveries included beans, chilies, and squash.

By the 1500s, when the Spaniards made their conquering march into the flourishing center of Aztec culture, there were orchards of avocados, coconut, papayas, pineapples, and prickly pears. The first red tomato, a little green husked "tomato," the tomatillo, chilies, manioc, sweet potatoes, four kinds of squash, and at least five major strains of beans were being cultivated. The basis of Mexican cooking had firmly been established.

With the conquering Cortés came cattle, pigs, olives, wheat, and rice.

Although the Aztecs had hunted, mostly for birds, they had not raised animals for the table or for travel and working the land. In what was thereafter known as New Spain, changes and additions occured that would result in the incredibly varied modern Mexican cuisine.

Lime Tortilla Soup

A classic of the Yucatán, where a small, very tart lime grows. But the more common darker Peruvian variety available in most markets will make an equally great soup.

SERVES 8

1¾ pounds chicken pieces
4 cups chicken broth (see Basics)
1 onion, quartered
2 bay leaves
¾ teaspoon cumin seeds
2 teaspoons dried oregano
10 peppercorns
½ teaspoon freshly ground sea salt
1 poblano pepper, roasted
1 to 2 chopped jalapeño peppers
1 teaspoon olive oil
½ cup thinly sliced onion
2 medium tomatoes, diced
Juice of 1 lime
2 corn tortillas, cut into strips
  ¼-inch wide by 3 inches long and toasted

1. Rinse the chicken well and trim off all excess fat. Place the chicken in a large soup pot. Add the broth, 4 cups of water, onion, bay leaves, cumin seeds, oregano, peppercorns, and salt. Bring to a boil. Cover partially, reduce the heat, and simmer for 1 hour.
2. Remove the chicken from the pot. Discard the skin; remove the meat from the bones and shred it into bite-size pieces. Set aside. Strain the stock through a fine-mesh sieve into a bowl, reserving 7 cups. Skim off any fat.
3. In a blender, combine the poblano and jalapeño peppers, remaining cumin seeds, remaining oregano, and ½ cup chicken stock from the soup; save the rest for another purpose. Blend until the peppers are puréed. Set aside.
4. Heat the oil in a large soup pot. Add the sliced onion and sauté over medium heat for 5 minutes. Stir in the tomato and sauté for 5 minutes. Add the remaining chicken stock, the chicken meat, and the pepper mixture, and simmer for 15 minutes. Stir in the lime juice, adjust the seasonings, and serve immediately, garnished with the tortilla strips.

*Cal. **94** Carb. **7g** Protein **11g** Chol. **29mg** Fat **3g/26%***

Pepper Quesadillas

SERVES 8

2/3 cup low-fat goat cheese
4 tablespoons Broccoli Pesto (page 48)
2 jalapeño peppers, minced
Freshly ground pepper
1 teaspoon crushed red pepper flakes
2 large flour tortillas
4 scallions, minced
1 cup minced red onion
1/2 cup roasted, peeled, and diced red bell pepper
1/2 cup roasted, peeled, and diced yellow bell pepper
1/2 cup shredded Monterey Jack cheese
1/2 cup shredded white cheddar cheese

1. Preheat the oven to 450°.
2. In a small mixing bowl, combine the goat cheese, pesto, jalapeño pepper, ground pepper, and red pepper flakes. Place the tortillas on a cookie sheet. Place half the cheese mixture on each tortilla, and spread to 1/4 inch of the edges.
3. Sprinkle each tortilla with scallion, onion, and pepper, and top with the cheeses. Place one tortilla on top of the other and bake until the cheese melts, 8 to 12 minutes.
4. Slice into wedges and serve warm.

*Cal. **157** Carb. **12g** Protein **8g** Chol. **19mg** Fat **9g/50%***

Avocadoes

Cultivated by the Aztecs, the avocado is probably America's oldest tree crop—and an important commercial one, especially just before Superbowl Sunday, when the avocado has its biggest sales days. By the time the game ends, about 6,000 tons of guacamole are consumed in America. Is the avocado the national fruit?

Basil Quesadillas

SERVES 8

1/4 cup low-fat goat cheese
2/3 cup low-fat cottage cheese
1 cup shredded mozzarella cheese
3 large flour tortillas
1 cup white wine
1/2 cup sun-dried tomatoes packed in oil
4 garlic cloves, minced
1/2 cup chopped fresh basil
1 cup chopped Canadian bacon, trimmed of fat
1 cup chopped scallion, green parts only
1 teaspoon minced jalapeño pepper, seeded, membranes removed

1. Preheat the oven to 425°.
2. In a blender, purée the goat cheese, cottage cheese,

and ½ cup of the mozzarella. In a small bowl, place the wine and the tomatoes, and marinate until soft.

3. Spread half the cheese mixture on two of the tortillas to within ½ inch of the edges.

4. Drain and chop the sun-dried tomatoes. Place one tortilla on a cookie sheet. Sprinkle half the tomatoes, garlic, basil, bacon, scallion, and jalapeño pepper over it. Place the second tortilla on top of the first. Sprinkle the remaining tomatoes, garlic, bacon, scallion, and jalapeño pepper over it.

5. Place the third tortilla on top and sprinkle the rest of the mozzarella on top of it. Bake for 8 to 10 minutes, or until the cheese begins to brown. Slice into wedges and serve warm.

Cal. 186 Carb. 18g Protein 14g Chol. 27mg Fat 7g/30%

Spinach Quesadillas

spinach · cheeses · tomato · onion
garlic · jalapeños · parsley and chives

SERVES 8

¼ cup low-fat goat cheese
⅔ cup low-fat cottage cheese
1 cup shredded mozzarella
Freshly ground pepper
2 large flour tortillas
1½ cups chopped onion
½ cup chopped tomato
¾ cup chopped fresh spinach
2 tablespoons chopped fresh cilantro
2 tablespoons chopped fresh chives
2 tablespoons minced, seeded jalapeño pepper, membranes removed
4 garlic cloves, minced
2 tablespoons chopped fresh parsley

1. Preheat the oven to 425°.

2. In a blender, purée the goat cheese, cottage cheese, half the mozzarella, and pepper to taste.

3. Spread half the cheese mixture on each tortilla to within ½ inch of the edges.

4. Sprinkle half of each remaining ingredient over each tortilla.

5. Place one tortilla on a cookie sheet; place the other on top of it. Sprinkle the top with the remaining mozzarella.

6. Bake for 8 to 10 minutes, or until the cheese begins to brown. Slice into four wedges and serve warm.

Cal. 119 Carb. 10g Protein 8g Chol. 17mg Fat 5.5g/40%

Quesadillas

Those wonderful flour tortillas are layered with scrumptious good things and then made with as little cheese as possible to still create an oozing, luscious consistency. They're baked, not fried, but still should be an infrequent indulgence. Cut into pie-shaped wedges, quesadillas are a terrific appetizer or light lunch when accompanied by a green salad.

Drunken Beans

SERVES 8

4 cups pinto beans
1 tablespoon canola oil
3 garlic cloves, minced
1 cup diced onion
2 jalapeño peppers, seeded and sliced thin
2 teaspoons minced fresh oregano
2 teaspoons ground cumin
1/2 teaspoon ground cloves
1/8 teaspoon salt
Freshly ground pepper
1 1/2 cups beer
2 tablespoons dark brown sugar
1 cup finely grated aged Monterey Jack cheese
2 cups Pico de Gallo (at right)

1. In a large bowl, cover the beans with water and soak them overnight. Drain the beans, sort out stones, and set aside.
2. In a large skillet, heat the oil over medium heat. Add the garlic and onion, and sauté for 3 minutes. Reduce the heat to low; add the jalapeño, oregano, cumin, cloves, and salt and pepper to taste. Sauté for 10 minutes, stirring frequently. Add the drained beans, beer, and sugar. Bring to a boil, cover, lower the heat, and simmer for 1 1/2 hours. Preheat the oven to 300°.
3. Transfer the bean mixture to a large casserole dish. Stir in the cheese, cover, place in the oven, and bake for 1 hour. Place the beans in a shallow serving bowl and top with the salsa.

*Cal. **438** Carb. **71g** Protein **25g** Chol. **13mg** Fat **8g/15%***

Pico de Gallo

Embraced throughout Mexico for its pure tastes of tomato, avocado, and chili, pico de gallo is often the salsa of choice. It can perk up tortilla chips, grilled fish or poultry, or drunken beans.

YIELD: 4 CUPS

3 cups chopped tomato
1/2 cup chopped onion
1/2 teaspoon sugar
2 jalapeño peppers, seeded and finely chopped
3 tablespoons fresh lime juice
1 cup loosely packed chopped fresh cilantro

In a large mixing bowl, combine all of the ingredients.

*Cal. **3** Carb. **.7g** Protein **.1g***
*Chol. **0mg** Fat **0g/0%***
(analyzed per tablespoon)

Tequila Scallops

SERVES 4

1/2 cup fresh lime juice
2 tablespoons tequila
4 tablespoons finely minced fresh mint
2 tablespoons minced crystallized ginger
Grated zest of 2 limes
1 1/2 pounds sea scallops

1. In a shallow glass dish, combine the lime juice, tequila, mint, ginger, and lime zest. Add the scallops and toss gently to coat. Marinate at room temperature for 10 minutes.

Tacos

Sometimes, when a corn or flour tortilla is stuffed and then baked or fried, it becomes a taco. Tacos can be soft or hard, rolled or baked to take on the shape of a cup. They have become popular from coast to coast in the United States. My Spicy Chicken is seasoned with spices and then can be layered with shredded lettuce, diced tomatoes, red onions, cheese, minced olives, chopped cilantro, minced jalapeños, garlic, avocado, radishes, or lime zest.

Spicy Chicken

SERVES 4

2 whole chicken breasts
3 cups chicken broth
¼ teaspoon Tabasco sauce
½ teaspoon chili powder
1 tablespoon crushed red
    pepper flakes
1 teaspoon paprika
1 tablespoon seeded and
    minced jalapeño pepper

1. In a large stockpot, combine all of the ingredients and bring to a boil for 5 minutes. Reduce the heat to low, cover, and simmer for 40 minutes. Uncover and simmer for 20 minutes.
2. Remove the pot from the heat and set aside for 1 hour. Remove the chicken and shred.

Cal. 180 Carb. .1g
Protein 34g Chol. 0mg
Fat 4g/19%

2. Preheat the broiler.
3. Divide the scallops among twelve skewers; reserve the marinade. Place the skewers on a pan directly under the broiler. Broil for 2½ minutes, turn, and broil for 1½ minutes, brushing once or twice with the marinade.

Cal. 177 Carb. 12g Protein 29g Chol. 56mg Fat 1.4g/7%

New Spanish Rice

SERVES 6

1 tablespoon olive oil
½ cup seeded and diced Anaheim pepper
1 cup coarsely chopped onion
1 tablespoon finely chopped garlic
1 cup converted white rice
1 cup Herbed Vegetable broth (see Basics)
1½ cups chicken broth (see Basics)
1 cup peeled, seeded, and diced tomato
1½ cups fresh or thawed frozen corn kernels
½ cup frozen petite peas, thawed
½ teaspoon salt
Freshly ground pepper
1 cup finely chopped fresh cilantro

1. In a large saucepan or Dutch oven, heat the oil over medium heat. Add the pepper, onion, and garlic, and sauté for 2 minutes. Add the rice and sauté until the rice begins to brown, 6 to 8 minutes, stirring constantly.
2. Add the vegetable and chicken broths. Cover, reduce the heat, and simmer for 15 minutes.
3. Stir in the tomato, corn, peas, and salt and pepper to taste. Cook for 5 minutes.
4. Just before serving, stir in the cilantro. Serve immediately.

Cal. 230 Carb. 45g Protein 6g Chol. 5mg Fat 4g/15%

Veracruz Snapper

SERVES 4

3 pounds red snapper, cleaned

Marinade:

1/4 cup extra-virgin olive oil

3 tablespoons fresh lime juice

2 garlic cloves, minced

1 teaspoon dried oregano

1 bay leaf, crushed

1/8 teaspoon sea salt

Sauce:

1 tablespoon olive oil

5 garlic cloves, minced

2 1/2 cups finely chopped white onion

2 1/2 pounds finely chopped tomato

1/3 cup finely chopped pimiento-
stuffed green olives

1/4 cup capers, drained

1 to 2 jalapeño peppers, seeded
and thinly sliced

2 teaspoons dried oregano

1 sprig fresh thyme

1 sprig fresh marjoram

2 bay leaves

1. Place the fish in a large baking dish. In a small bowl, combine all the marinade ingredients and mix well. Pour the marinade over the fish and turn to coat. Place the dish in the refrigerator for 1 hour.

2. In a large skillet, heat the tablespoon of oil over medium heat. Add the garlic and onion and cook for 10 minutes, or until the onion is soft. Add all of the remaining sauce ingredients. Simmer for 1 hour, uncovered, or until the sauce is well seasoned and thick, stirring occasionally. Keep warm.

3. Preheat the oven to 375°.

4. Remove the fish from the dish, drain, and brush off any excess marinade. Place the fish on a piece of aluminum foil large enough to enclose it. Fold the foil over and seal the edges tightly. Place the package on a baking sheet and bake for 25 to 35 minutes.

5. Divide the fish among four dinner plates and top each with a generous serving of the sauce. Serve immediately.

*Cal. **394** Carb. **24g** Protein **51g** Chol. **83mg** Fat **11g/24%***

Regional Cooking

In central Mexico, one finds the duality of *lo mexicano*: the Spaniard and the Aztec, the modern and the primitive. *Mole poblano*, made the same way for centuries, is the culinary centerpiece.

In southern Mexico, Oaxaca particularly, a vital Indian heritage mixes a remarkable variety of dried peppers into Mexico's most varied sauces and stews.

West-central Mexico is thoroughly mestizo: the essence of native flowers scattered on crisp-fried pork *carnitas* or sprinkled in a bowl of *posole*. The home of mariachis and tequila, fried tacos and red-chili enchiladas, the region represents what may be Mexico's most prominent profile.

In the warm, tropical Gulf states, known for growing coffee, one finds simple, well-seasoned cooking, with a European and Caribbean character to the spicing and garnishing: fish with tomatoes, herbs, and olives; spicy crab soup; turnovers.

The Yucatán is Mayan, with regional specialties among Mexico's most unusual, from pork in banana leaves to wild turkey with *masa*-thickened white sauce to chicken with vinegar and spices.

In Mexico's north, flour tortillas prevail; in the south, those of corn. For beans— the staff of life of Mexico— there are no boundaries.

Mixed-Spice Paste

YIELD: 3 TABLESPOONS

1 whole head garlic
½ cup chicken broth
  (see Basics)
¼ teaspoon cumin seeds,
  pan-toasted until fragrant
6 whole cloves
1 teaspoon black peppercorns
¼ teaspoon coriander seeds
2 teaspoons dried oregano
¼ teaspoon ground allspice
Salt
1 quarter-sized piece of flour
  tortilla, torn into pieces
1 tablespoon cider vinegar

1. Peel away the excess papery skin on the garlic, leaving the head intact. Slice off the tips with a sharp knife, exposing the flesh. In a small heavy pan, combine the garlic and chicken broth over medium heat. Cover and simmer for about 20 minutes, turning occasionally, until the flesh is soft when pierced with the tip of a knife.
2. In a spice grinder, combine the cumin seeds, cloves, peppercorns and coriander seeds. Pulverize the seeds, then add the oregano, allspice, and salt, and process for a few seconds. Transfer the spices to a mortar.
3. Combine the tortilla and vinegar and soak for 5 minutes.
4. Meanwhile, slip the garlic cloves out of their skins. Pound the cloves into the spices, making a smooth paste. Pound the soaked tortilla and vinegar into the mixture. Transfer to a small dish, cover tightly with plastic wrap and set aside for several hours. Refrigerate unused portion.

*Cal. **26** Carb. **5g** Protein **.9g**
Chol. **0mg** Fat **.6g/17%**
(analyzed per teaspoon)*

Trout in Corn Husks

SERVES 4

1 package corn husks
4 freshly dressed whole trout (about 8 ounces each)
4 Anaheim peppers, stemmed, halved, and seeded
1½ tablespoons Mixed-Spice Paste (at left)

1. Prepare the corn husks in advance: Bring a large pot of water to a full boil. Remove from the heat and add the husks, keeping them submerged with a weight (such as a smaller pot lid). Let stand for about 2 hours to soften; they are ready when they are pliable.
2. Rinse the fish inside and out and pat dry. Fill the cavity of each fish with one whole pepper.
3. Rub the surface of the fish with a thin layer of seasoning paste. Set aside to marinate for at least 1 hour.
4. Separate the largest, longest, and most pliable husks. You will need to overlap some of the husks to get enough length and width for each package. Pat the husks dry with paper towels.
5. Place a trout in the center of each husk. Fold the sides of the husks over the fish to enclose it. Fold the ends over the middle. Tear off long thin pieces from the extra husks, and use them to tie the packages.
6. Set a collapsible vegetable steamer into a large deep skillet. Add about 1 inch of water to the skillet, making sure it does not reach the steamer. Line the steamer with additional corn husks and bring the water to a boil. Lay the trout packages in one layer on the steamer. Cover, reduce the heat to medium, and steam the fish for 15 minutes, or until it flakes easily. Serve immediately.

*Cal. **130** Carb. **8g** Protein **18g** Chol. **45mg** Fat **3g/23%***

Chicken Thighs & Roasted Peppers

SERVES 4

8 chicken thighs (about 3 pounds), boned and skinned,
   bones reserved
1 whole head garlic
1 bay leaf
1/2 teaspoon cumin seeds, lightly toasted
Generous grinding fresh pepper
1 teaspoon salt
1 1/2 tablespoons Mixed-Spice Paste (page 525)
1 teaspoon olive oil
2 cups halved and thinly sliced onion
8 fresh Anaheim chilies, roasted, peeled, seeded,
   and cut into long strips about 1/2 inch wide
2 tablespoons cider vinegar
4 tablespoons coarsely chopped fresh cilantro

1. Fold the edges of each thigh together and secure with toothpicks to form neat packages. Trim the excess papery outside peel from the garlic, leaving the head intact; cut to expose the tops of the cloves.

2. In a large heavy saucepan, combine the thighs, bones, garlic, and 6 cups of water. Bring to a boil and skim off any scum that rises to the surface. Add the bay leaf, cumin seeds, and pepper and salt to taste. Cover, reduce the heat, and simmer gently for 20 minutes, until the meat is tender. Cool the chicken in the broth. Remove the chicken, pat it dry, and set it aside. Bring the broth back to a boil over medium-high heat and reduce it to 3 cups, about 20 minutes. Strain the broth, discarding the bones and spices, and skim off any fat; set aside.

3. Make sure the thighs are dry. Rub 1 tablespoon of the spice paste into the thighs; reserve the remaining 1/2 tablespoon. Set the thighs aside for 1 hour.

4. Meanwhile, in a large heavy skillet over medium-high heat, combine the oil and onion. Sauté for 4 to 5 minutes, until the onion softens, then add the chilies. Stir in the remaining 1/2 tablespoon spice paste and the vinegar. Remove from the heat and set aside.

5. To serve, place two thighs on each serving plate and top with a little sauce. Garnish with the cilantro.

Cal. **345** *Carb.* **25g** *Protein* **40g** *Chol.* **110mg** *Fat* **11g/26%**

Hot Tomato Salsa

This salsa is delicious with either of these chicken dishes.

SERVES 4

4 small anchovy fillets,
   mashed
2 shallots, finely minced
4 garlic cloves, finely minced
4 scallions, finely minced
3 tablespoons minced
   jalapeño pepper
1 1/2 pounds very ripe tomtoes
   (about 3), diced,
   juices retained
1/4 cup coarsely chopped fresh
   basil
1/4 cup coarsely chopped fresh
   cilantro or 2 teaspoons
   dried cilantro
1/4 cup coarsely chopped fresh
   Italian parsley
1/4 cup balsamic vinegar
2 teaspoons olive oil
Freshly ground pepper

In a large mixing bowl, combine the anchovies, shallot, garlic, scallion, and jalapeño pepper. Stir in the tomato and juice, basil, cilantro, parsley, vinegar, and oil. Season to taste with the pepper. Refrigerate for 4 hours, or overnight. Adjust seasoning again and serve well chilled.

Cal. **76g** *Carb.* **12g**
Protein **3g** *Chol.* **1mg**
Fat **3g/31%**

Chicken & Peppers

SERVES 4

2 chicken breasts, split in half, with bone and skin
12 plum tomatoes, coarsely chopped
1 yellow bell pepper, thinly sliced lengthwise
1 red bell pepper, thinly sliced lengthwise
2 tablespoons minced sun-dried tomatoes
1 tablespoon capers
2 garlic cloves, finely minced
¼ teaspoon crushed red pepper flakes
¼ cup minced fresh Italian parsley
½ cup chopped fresh basil
¼ cup Parmesan shards

1. Preheat the oven to 350°. Rinse the chicken breasts and pat dry. Arrange them in a shallow baking dish and surround with the plum tomatoes, yellow and red peppers, sun-dried tomatoes, and capers. In a bowl, combine the garlic, red pepper flakes, parsley, and ¼ cup basil. Pour the liquid into the baking dish; cover with aluminum foil.
2. Bake the chicken, covered, for 30 minutes. Remove the cover and bake for another 40 minutes, basting every 10 to 15 minutes.
3. Remove the chicken from the oven, sprinkle with the remaining basil, and baste well with the liquid. Using the baster, remove any remaining liquid. Sprinkle with the Parmesan and bake for an additional 10 to 15 minutes. Serve immediately.

Cal. **270** *Carb.* **15g** *Protein* **39g** *Chol.* **96mg** *Fat* **6g/21%**

Mole Rojo

YIELD: 2½ CUPS

1 pound Roma (plum) tomatoes
½ pound tomatillos
1 corn tortilla
½ cup coarsely chopped onion
2 to 3 canned chipotle chilies in adobo sauce, seeded
½ teaspoon salt
½ teaspoon ground cinnamon
½ teaspoon ground allspice

1. Preheat the broiler. Place the tomatoes on a baking sheet and roast on the upper rack, turning, until they are charred on all sides. Preheat the oven to 500°.
2. Husk the tomatillos and rinse well. Place them on a baking sheet and roast for 5 minutes, or until slightly softened. Reduce the heat to 300°.
3. Place the tortilla in the oven and bake until crisp, 3 to 4 minutes.
4. Place all of the ingredients in a blender and blend until smooth.
5. Heat a heavy skillet over medium heat. Pour in the sauce and cook for 3 minutes, stirring constantly. Serve the sauce warm.

*Cal. **9** Carb. **2g** Protein **.3g** Chol. **0mg** Fat **.1g/8%***
(analyzed per tablespoon)

Mole Verde

YIELD: 3 CUPS

6 ounces tomatillos
1 corn tortilla
1½ cups chicken broth (see Basics)
6 poblano chilies, roasted, peeled, seeded, and chopped
¼ teaspoon salt
½ teaspoon cumin seeds
1 jalapeño pepper, seeded, membrane removed
¼ cup chopped fresh cilantro
1 cup chopped fresh parsley
1 cup coarsely chopped fresh romaine

1. Preheat the oven to 500°. Husk the tomatillos and rinse well. Place the tomatillos on a baking sheet and bake for 5

Mole

In Mexico, *mole* has been the subject of debate for hundreds of years: Does the term refer to the sauce as we use it today? Or to the finished dish, which is how the Spanish invaders interpreted the Aztec's word for their impressive stews?

In any case, *mole* is made throughout Mexico, with regional versions of many sorts. It is a paste, generally made from ingredients that are pounded together and used to season particular dishes. Sometimes *mole* is green, thickened with tomatillos, green chilies, herbs, nuts, or seeds. Sometimes it is red, hot, and thick from chiles. Some *moles* include unsweetened chocolate, which gives them a dark, rich color and flavor. *Mole* can be used with meat, fowl, fish, or fruit. This ancient category of sauces is sophisticated, complicated, and the first step to dozens of great dishes.

minutes, until slightly softened. Remove the tomatillos from the oven; reduce the heat to 300°. Place the tortilla in the oven and bake until crisp, 3 to 4 minutes.

2. Place the tomatillos and tortilla in a blender, and blend to form a paste. Add all of the remaining ingredients, and blend until smooth.

3. Heat a heavy skillet over medium heat. Pour in the sauce and cook for 3 minutes, stirring constantly; serve the sauce warm.

*Cal. **5** Carb. **1g** Protein **.3g** Chol. **0mg** Fat **0.1g/13%***
(analyzed per tablespoon)

Guajillo Mole

YIELD: 2 CUPS

*3 ounces whole dried guajillo
    chilies*
1 corn tortilla
*1¹/₂ pounds Roma (plum)
    tomatoes, finely chopped*
1 jalapeño pepper
¹/₂ cup chopped fresh cilantro
1 cup chopped fresh Italian parsley

1. Preheat the oven to 250°. Remove the stems from the chilies. Slit them open and remove and discard the seeds. Place on a baking sheet and roast for 5 minutes. Transfer the chilies to a bowl and pour 2 cups of boiling water over them. Let them steep for 5 minutes.

2. Increase the heat to 300°. Place the tortilla in the oven and bake until crisp, 3 to 4 minutes.

3. Preheat the broiler. Place the tomato on the baking sheet and broil on the top rack until charred. Remove and set aside.

4. In a blender or food processor, combine all of the ingredients and purée. Pour the purée into a heavy sauté pan and stir to combine.

5. Place the sauté pan over medium heat and cook for 3 minutes, stirring constantly. Serve the sauce warm.

*Cal. **16** Carb. **3g** Protein **.6g** Chol. **0mg** Fat **.3g/17%***
(analyzed per tablespoon)

Chicken Mole

Truly one of the most festive dishes of Mexico. This is the mole we're most familiar with—it has just a touch of semisweet chocolate.

SERVES 8

1 tablespoon canola oil
6 dried ancho chilies, stemmed, seeded, and deveined
1 dried Anaheim chile, stemmed, seeded, and deveined
1 dried chipotle chile, stemmed, seeded, and deveined
¼ cup husked and coarsely chopped fresh tomatillos
3 tablespoons sesame seeds
5 cups chicken broth (see Basics)
¼ cup finely chopped onion
1 teaspoon finely minced garlic
2 tablespoon raisins
One 6-inch flour tortilla
1 ripe banana, sliced
¾ cup peeled, seeded, and chopped fresh tomato
½ teaspoon dried oregano
¼ teaspoon dried thyme
⅛ teaspoon ground cloves
½ teaspoon ground cinnamon
1 ounce semisweet chocolate, chopped
2 chickens (about 2½ pounds each), quartered, backbones removed
¼ cup coarsely chopped fresh cilantro

1. Preheat the oven to 350°.
2. In a large skillet, heat the oil over medium heat. Sauté all the chilies briefly on both sides until they turn slightly brown; drain thoroughly on paper towels and transfer to a large bowl. Set the skillet aside. Cover the chilies with boiling water and soak for 1 hour; weigh them down with a plate to keep them submerged.
3. Simmer the tomatillos in water to cover until they are tender, about 20 minutes.
4. Toast the sesame seeds in the oven in a small pan or oven-proof skillet for 10 minutes; don't let them burn. Remove from the oven and set aside.

Mexican Fiesta

The vibrant colors of sunny Mexico are vivid orange, green, turquoise, yellow, and purple. Used in bright splashes, they heat up a party room and generate excitement. Use Mexican colors in undercloths for serape-draped table covers, in napkins to set off oversized black plates. And if you are renting, get black chairs. Decorate with huge, bright Mexican paper flowers, piñatas, parrots, cowboy boots, garlands of peppers, and potted cacti.

5. Drain the chilies and cut them into small pieces. In a blender, purée the chilies in two batches, using ½ cup chicken broth each time. Scrape down the sides of the blender a couple of times with a rubber scraper; the purée should be smooth. Set the purée aside.

6. Pour off and reserve all but 1 to 2 teaspoons of oil from the skillet. Sauté the onion and garlic for 6 to 8 minutes, until softened; transfer to a large bowl with a slotted spoon. Sauté the raisins for 1 minute, and add to the onion and garlic. Sauté the tortilla on both sides until lightly brown. Shred the tortilla and add to the above. Add a few drops of the reserved oil if necessary, and sauté the banana until it begins to brown; add it to the onion. Finally, add the tomato, tomatillos, and sesame seeds to the mixture, and stir well to combine.

7. Purée the mixture in a blender in two batches, using ½ cup of chicken broth for each batch. Scrape down the sides of the blender a couple of times with a rubber scraper. Add a little more broth as needed to make a smooth purée. Pass the purée through a mesh strainer, pushing down hard with the back of a wooden spoon. You should have about 2 cups of sauce; set it aside.

8. In a large nonreactive Dutch oven, heat 1 teaspoon of the reserved oil over medium heat. Add the chili purée and stir constantly for 3 minutes, until slightly thickened and darkened. Stir in the other purée, the oregano, thyme, cloves, cinnamon, chocolate, and remaining chicken broth. Simmer gently for 45 minutes; the mixture should reduce slightly, to about 5 cups. Taste the sauce and season to taste with salt and pepper.

9. Preheat the broiler.

10. While the sauce is simmering, place the chicken quarters on a broiler rack and broil on both sides until nicely browned, 15 to 20 minutes.

11. Add the chicken to the sauce. Cover and cook for 25 to 30 minutes, or until the chicken is cooked through. Remove the chicken to a serving platter and serve immediately, garnished with the cilantro. Pass any additional sauce separately at the table.

*Cal. **310** Carb. **15g** Protein **33g** Chol. **91mg** Fat **13g**/38%*

Lamb Shanks with Bean Sauce

SERVES 4

4 lamb shanks, trimmed of fat (about 3½ pounds after trimming)
Salt and freshly ground pepper
½ teaspoon dried oregano
3 tablespoons olive oil
1 cup finely chopped onion
1 cup finely chopped celery
1 cup finely chopped carrot
2 tablespoons plus 1 teaspoon finely chopped garlic
2 cups dry red wine
2 cups beef broth (see Basics)
1 teaspoon drained anchovies, patted dry
2 large bay leaves
3 sprigs fresh thyme
1 can (28 ounces) crushed tomatoes
1 cup Jacob's Cattle beans, rinsed and sorted
2¼ cups chicken broth (see Basics)
¼ teaspoon salt
¼ cup white wine
2 garlic cloves, smashed
4 tablespoons finely chopped fresh Italian parsley

1. Pat the shanks dry with a paper towel. Sprinkle with salt and pepper to taste and the oregano.
2. In a large oven- and heatproof casserole with 3-inch sides, heat 1 tablespoon of oil over medium-high heat. Brown the shanks, two at a time, on all sides, about 5 minutes. Remove the shanks and place them on a platter; set aside.
3. Preheat the oven to 325°.
4. Add the onion, celery, carrot, and 2 tablespoons of chopped garlic to the skillet, and sauté until the vegetables begin to soften and brown slightly, 6 to 8 minutes.
5. Add 1 cup of the red wine, and turn the heat to high. Cook, stirring constantly, for 1 minute, scraping up the brown bits off the bottom. Add the remaining red wine, the beef broth, the anchovies, one bay leaf, one sprig thyme, and the tomatoes. Stir to combine and return the shanks to the pan, turning to coat them in the sauce. Cover the pan tightly and transfer to the oven; bake for 1¾ to 2 hours, or until the meat is tender.
6. Meanwhile, in a large pot, combine the beans, chicken broth, salt, white wine, remaining bay leaf, smashed garlic,

532

Pipián Verde

YIELD: 2½ CUPS

½ pound tomatillos
1 corn tortilla
1 cup raw pumpkin seeds
1½ cups chicken broth
  (see Basics)
2 serrano chilies, seeded
½ teaspoon salt
½ teaspoon freshly ground
  pepper
¼ teaspoon ground cumin
¼ teaspoon ground cinna-
  mon
Pinch cloves
1 cup chopped fresh parsley
1 cup chopped fresh romaine
  lettuce

1. Preheat the oven to 500°.
2. Husk the tomatillos and
rinse them well. Place the
tomatillos on a baking sheet
and bake for 5 minutes, until
slightly softened. Remove
the tomatillos from the oven
and reduce the heat to 300°.
Place the tortilla in the oven
and bake until crisp, 3 to 4
minutes.
3. In a large skillet, dry-roast
the pumpkin seeds over low
heat for 5 to 7 minutes, or
until they finish popping.
4. Place the tomatillos and
pumpkin seeds in a blender,
and blend to a paste. Add all
the remaining ingredients and
blend until smooth.
5. Heat a heavy skillet over
medium heat. Pour in the
sauce and cook for 3 minutes,
stirring constantly. Serve the
sauce warm.

*Cal. **24** Carb. **2g** Protein **1g**
Chol. **0mg** Fat **1.7g/59%***
(analyzed per tablespoon)

and remaining thyme. Bring to a boil, reduce the heat to low,
and cook until the beans are soft, about 1½ hours. Add additional broth if necessary.
7. Remove the pot from the heat; remove the bay leaf and
thyme sprigs and discard. In a food processor, purée the beans.
8. With the machine running, add the remaining chopped
garlic and the remaining olive oil. Return the purée to a
saucepan, season with salt and pepper to taste, and keep
warm until ready to use.
9. Transfer the shanks to a serving platter; cover and keep
warm.
10. Skim the fat from the surface of the sauce. Strain the
sauce through a strainer, pressing down hard on the vegetables to release all the juices; you should have 3 to 3½ cups.
Return the sauce to the skillet, and over medium heat,
reduce it to 2 cups, 20 to 25 minutes. Taste and adjust the
salt and pepper to taste.
11. To serve, place ½ cup of the bean purée on each of four
plates. Top the purée with a lamb shank, and nap with a little
sauce. Garnish with the parsley and serve immediately. Pass
the remaining sauce at the table.

*Cal. **384** Carb. **40g** Protein **35g** Chol. **78mg** Fat **10g/23%***

Mexican Beef Stew

SERVES 6

2 pounds Roma (plum) tomatoes,
    chopped
2 corn tortillas
1 to 2 canned chipotle chilies in
    adobo sauce, seeds removed
1 tablespoon canola oil
1½ pounds stewing beef
¼ teaspoon freshly ground pepper
1½ cups thinly sliced onion
1½ cups beef broth (see Basics)
½ pound fresh tomatillos, husks
    removed, rinsed well, each cut into
    6 wedges
½ cup raisins
1 canela stick or cinnamon stick
4 whole cloves
¼ teaspoon sea salt

1. Preheat the broiler. Place the tomatoes on a baking sheet and set the sheet under the broiler, about 4 inches
from the heat. Broil the tomatoes until charred. If your
broiler is inside your oven, place the tortillas in the oven and
toast until crisp, 3 to 4 minutes.
2. Preheat the oven to 300°. In a blender or food processor,
combine the tomatoes, tortillas, and chilies, and blend until
smooth. Set aside.
3. In a large pot, heat the oil over medium heat. Add the beef
and pepper, and sauté until the meat is browned on all sides.
Add the onion and sauté for 5 minutes. Stir in the tomato
mixture, broth, tomatillos, raisins, canela stick, cloves, and
salt. Bring to a boil, cover partially, reduce the heat, and simmer for 1 hour. Serve over brown rice or noodles.

Cal. **277** *Carb.* **30g** *Protein* **19g**
Chol. **51mg** *Fat* **11g/33%**

534

Saffron Rice

SERVES 6

6 packaged sun-dried tomatoes, cut into small pieces
Pinch saffron
1 cup Arborio rice
4 garlic cloves, finely minced
$\frac{1}{4}$ teaspoon salt
Freshly ground pepper
2 cups chicken broth
(see Basics)
1 cup finely chopped fresh
Italian parsley
$\frac{1}{4}$ cup finely chopped
fresh mint

1. Place the tomato in a small
bowl and add $\frac{1}{2}$ cup of boiling water; set aside for 15
minutes. Remove the tomato
with a slotted spoon and set
aside; reserve the liquid.
2. Place the saffron and $\frac{1}{2}$
cup of boiling water in a bowl,
and steep for 15 minutes;
strain and reserve the liquid.
3. Crush the tomato with a
mortar and pestle. Place the
crushed tomato in a medium
saucepan with the tomato
soaking liquid. Add the rice,
garlic, and salt and pepper to
taste. Simmer for 1 to 2 minutes, until the liquid evaporates. Stir in the chicken
broth, the saffron, and the
saffron soaking liquid. Cover
and simmer for 15 minutes
over medium heat.
4. Remove the rice from the
heat and set it aside, covered,
for 15 minutes more, until
the liquid is absorbed. Stir in
the parsley and mint and
serve immediately.

Cal. **137** Carb. **29g**

Protein **5g** Chol. **2mg**

Fat **1g/6%**

Pepper Sirloin Sauté

SERVES 6

1 teaspoon canola oil
1 tablespoon sliced garlic
1$\frac{1}{2}$ pounds boneless sirloin, cut into $\frac{3}{4}$-inch cubes
2 cups halved and thinly sliced onion
1 can (28 ounces) plum tomatoes, drained, coarsely chopped,
juice reserved
$\frac{1}{2}$ cup beef broth (see Basics)
1 teaspoon dried marjoram
1 bay leaf
3 poblano peppers, roasted, peeled, seeded, and cut into cubes
Salt and freshly ground pepper

1. In a large heavy skillet, heat the oil over medium heat.
Add the garlic and sauté, stirring constantly, until it begins to
brown. Remove with a slotted spoon and set aside. Add the
beef and sauté until it is brown on all sides but still rare.
Remove with a slotted spoon and set aside. Add the onion
and sauté until it begins to soften.
2. Add to the skillet the garlic, the tomato with its juice, beef
broth, marjoram, bay leaf, chili peppers, and salt and pepper
to taste. Lower the heat and simmer for 10 minutes. Remove
the bay leaf.
3. Return the beef, with any accumulated
juices, and heat through. Serve
immediately.

Cal. **197** Carb. **13g** Protein **23g**

Chol. **59mg** Fat **7g/29%**

Mesquite Breast of Turkey

SERVES 10

1 cup fresh lime juice

½ cup tequila

¼ cup chicken broth (see Basics)

6 garlic cloves, smashed

2 teaspoons Tabasco or other pepper sauce

2 teaspoons ground cumin

Freshly ground pepper

1 turkey breast (5 to 6 pounds)

2 to 3 cups mesquite wood chips, soaked in water
according to directions

1. The day before serving, whisk the lime juice, tequila, broth, garlic, Tabasco, cumin, and pepper in a large bowl. Place the breast and the marinade in a self-sealing plastic bag and refrigerate overnight, turning occasionally.
2. When ready to cook, prepare a kettle-type grill for cooking.
3. Remove the turkey from the bag and reserve the marinade. Place a drip pan with 2 cups of water in the center of the coals. Place the breast on a meat rack, skin side up.
4. Just before cooking, sprinkle the wet wood chips evenly over the coals. Replace the grill rack on the grill, and place the turkey on the rack. Place the cover on the grill with the vents open, and roast the breast for 1 hour. At this point, begin to baste the breast with the reserved marinade every 10 minutes until the turkey is done, for a total cooking time of 20 to 25 minutes per pound. Remove the meat from the grill and let it rest for 10 minutes before slicing. Serve warm or cold, with or without Chipotle Sauce (at right).

Cal. 335 Carb. 4g Protein 49g Chol. 124mg Fat 13g/35%

Chorizo

These spicy sausages may be made into links or simply shaped into patties.

SERVES 8

3 dried ancho chilies

3 dried pasilla chilies

½ cup cider vinegar

1 pound pork shoulder, cut into 1-inch cubes

1 pound lean ground turkey (99% fat free)

Chipotle Sauce

YIELD: ABOUT 1¼ CUPS

1 canned chipotle chili,
packed in adobo sauce

1 cup Low-Fat Blend
(see Basics)

½ cup peeled, seeded, and
coarsely chopped fresh
tomato

3 tablespoons finely chopped
fresh cilantro

1 teaspoon or more fresh lime
juice

1. In a food processor, purée the chili, scraping down the sides of the bowl a couple of times. Add the Low-Fat Blend and process until smooth.
2. Transfer the mixture to a bowl. Stir in the tomato, cilantro, and lime juice.

Cal. 8 Carb. 1g Protein 1g

Chol. .3mg Fat .1g/12%
(analyzed per tablespoon)

Chorizo Ways

The spiciness
of chorizo allows a little to go
a long way in:
pasta sauce • rice casseroles •
• taco salads •lasagne •
• baked bean dishes •
breakfast tortillas • pita and
vegetable sandwiches • grain
salads • and tacos

Fresh Chilies
Mild to Hot

Bell Pepper
Hungarian Sweet Chile
Hungarian Cherry Pepper
Pimiento
Anaheim
New Mexico
Chawa
Chilaca
Poblano
Jalapeño
De Agua
Dutch
Güero
Serrano Verde
Fiesta
Huachinango
Fresno
Thai
Tepín
Santa Fe Grande
Korean
Rocotillo
Peruvian
Peter Pepper
Serrano Rojo
Manzana
Tabasco
Ají
Amatista
Brazilian Malagueta
Macho
Jamaican Hot
Scotch Bonnet
Habanero

2 tablespoons finely minced garlic
5 whole cloves
$1/4$ teaspoon coriander seeds
$1/2$ teaspoon dried oregano
$1/2$ teaspoon freshly ground pepper
$1/8$ teaspoon freshly grated nutmeg
$1/2$ teaspoon ground cinnamon
2 tablespoons paprika
$1^{1/2}$ teaspoons salt
About 6 feet pork casings, rinsed if packed in salt

1. Stem and seed the chilies and tear them into pieces. Place in a shallow bowl and cover with the vinegar; soak them for 30 minutes, until softened. Transfer the chilies and vinegar to a food processor and process until quite smooth, scraping down the sides frequently; transfer to a large bowl.
2. In the same bowl of the food processor, coarsely grind the pork in batches; be careful not to overprocess, or the meat will be mushy. Add to the chilies with the turkey and garlic.
3. In a spice grinder, pulverize the cloves and coriander seeds; add to the pork and turkey. Add the oregano, pepper, nutmeg, cinnamon, paprika, and salt. Combine the chilies, meat, and seasonings thoroughly. Cover with plastic wrap and refrigerate overnight.
4. Before beginning to use the casings, check for tears or holes by running water through them. Using the sausage-stuffing attachment on an electric mixer or grinder according to the manufacturer's directions, or a hand-held sausage-stuffing funnel, proceed to stuff the casings in the following manner: Slip the casing over the attachment or funnel, leaving several inches hanging. Feed the sausage through the feeder until the first bit comes through the casing; clamp the casing. As the stuffing accumulates, the casing should stretch to about 1 inch in diameter. When the link is 5 inches long, pull off an additional inch of casing and proceed with another link. Repeat this process with the remaining meat mixture. When finished, tie the links at both ends with pieces of string.
5. Hang the sausage in a cool, dry place for 36 hours to dry. Store in the refrigerator, covered, for up to 1 week.
6. To cook, charcoal-grill or fry in a small amount of olive oil until cooked through, about 15 minutes.

*Cal. **190** Carb. **6g** Protein **28g** Chol. **76mg** Fat **6g/26%***

Walnut Cake

SERVES 8

1¼ cups toasted walnuts
2 tablespoons all-purpose flour
1½ teaspoons ground cinnamon
1 egg, separated
6 tablespoons orange marmalade,
   preferably imported, not too sweet
1 tablespoon orange liqueur
4 egg whites
Orange Yogurt Sauce (recipe follows)

1. Preheat the oven to 400°.
2. Lightly spray or wipe an 8½-inch springform pan with vegetable or canola oil; dust the pan with flour.
3. Grind the nuts in a food processor. Transfer the ground nuts to a medium-size bowl. Add the flour and cinnamon, and toss to combine with a fork.
4. In another bowl, beat the egg yolk with a whisk until light. Stir in the marmalade and orange liqueur. Combine the nut mixture and yolk mixture thoroughly.
5. In a large bowl, with clean beaters, beat the 5 egg whites until stiff but not dry. Stir a little of the whites into the nut mixture, then fold in the remaining whites. Pour the batter into the pan. Bake for 30 to 35 minutes, or until a toothpick inserted in the center comes out clean. Transfer the pan to a wire rack to cool for 5 minutes. Run a knife around the edge and carefully remove the sides. Cool completely. Serve with Orange Yogurt Sauce.

Cal. **187** *Carb.* **17g** *Protein* **5g** *Chol.* **23mg** *Fat* **12g/56%**

Spiced Coffee

In Mexico a slightly sweeter, very aromatic version of coffee is served from morning to late night: To strong coffee, add orange zest and a pinch of ground cloves. Sweeten to taste with dark brown sugar. Add milk, if desired, and stir with a fragrant cinnamon stick.

Orange Yogurt Sauce

YIELD: 1 CUP

8 ounces nonfat plain yogurt
1½ tablespoons honey
1 tablespoon marmalade, preferably imported

In a medium bowl, whisk the ingredients. Refrigerate until ready to serve.

Cal. **17** *Carb.* **4g** *Protein* **.8g** *Chol.* **0mg** *Fat* **.1g/4%**

(analyzed per tablespoon)

Cool Melon Water

SERVES 6

1 ripe seeded cantaloupe
¼ cup superfine sugar
Juice of one lemon

Halve the melon and remove the rind. Cut into
1-inch cubes and place in a blender with ½ cup
cold water, the sugar, and the lemon juice. Stir
well. Transfer to tall ice-filled glasses.

Cal. 52 Carb. 13g Protein 1g Chol. 0mg Fat .2g/4%

Orange Flan

SERVES 8

1 cup sugar
1 cup fresh orange juice
5 eggs, lightly beaten
2 egg yolks, lightly beaten
2 tablespoons evaporated skim milk
1 tablespoon Grand Marnier or other orange liqueur
½ teaspoon vanilla extract

1. Preheat the oven to 350°.
2. Combine the sugar and 3 tablespoons of water in a heavy
saucepan. Cook over medium-high heat until the mixture is
thick, bubbling, and amber-colored. Watch carefully to prevent burning. Wash down any sugar crystals that form on the
sides of the saucepan with a wet pastry brush. Pour into a 5-
cup ring mold and swirl around to coat evenly.
3. Combine the remaining ingredients in a large bowl and
whisk until smooth. Pour the custard into the coated ring
mold. Set the mold in a large baking pan and pour in enough
hot water to reach halfway up the sides of the mold. Bake for
30 minutes, or until the top is firm to the touch.
4. Cool slightly, then refrigerate for 2 hours or
until cold. Unmold onto a serving dish.
Slice and serve.

Cal. 170 Carb. 30g Protein 5g Chol. 159mg

Fat 4g/21%

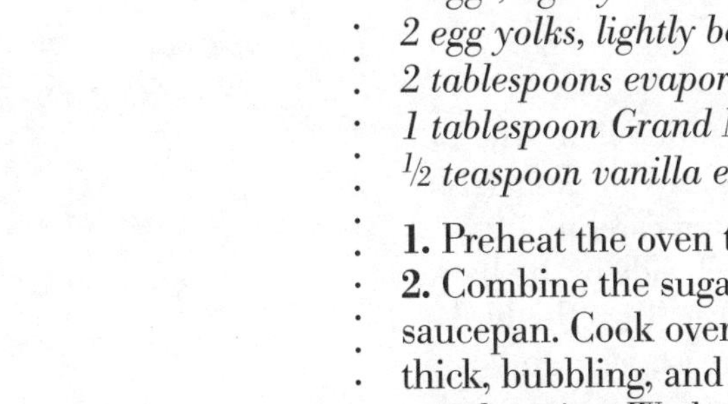

Be My Valentine

A Honey of a Hen

SERVES 4

1 whole chicken (2 to 2½ pounds)
2 lemons, thinly sliced
1 packed cup fresh mint leaves, or four
    4-inch sprigs fresh rosemary
4 tablespoons honey
2 tablespoons fresh lemon juice

1. Preheat the oven to 400°.
2. Rinse the chicken inside and out and pat dry. Place the chicken upside down on a work surface. With your fingers, gently separate the skin from the flesh, being careful not to tear the skin. Insert one lemon slice on each side of the backbone. Truss the opening with a metal skewer. Turn the bird over. Carefully loosen the skin from the breast, legs, and thighs. Insert slices of lemon to cover as much flesh as possible. Place the remaining lemon slices and mint in the cavity, and truss with a metal skewer. Place the chicken on a rack in a foil-lined baking pan.
3. Combine the honey and lemon juice. Place the chicken in the oven. Cook for 1 to 1¼ hours, basting with the honey-lemon mixture every 10 minutes, or until the juice runs clear when the thigh is pierced with a fork. Cut into serving pieces; discard the lemon and mint. Serve immediately.

*Cal. **289** Carb. **12g** Protein **38g** Chol. **109mg** Fat **7g/25%***

Chicken Creole

SERVES 6

1 teaspoon olive oil
2 cups coarsely chopped onion

"Love is a many-splintered thing."

R. Buckminster Fuller

540

1 cup coarsely chopped green bell pepper
1 cup coarsely chopped celery
2 teaspoons minced garlic
1 cup tomato juice
12 ripe plum tomatoes, peeled and coarsely chopped,
  or 4 cups canned tomatoes, drained
2 medium bay leaves
1 tablespoon paprika
$\frac{1}{2}$ teaspoon cayenne
Salt and freshly ground pepper
2 pounds chicken breast, boned, skin removed, and cut into strips

1. In a Dutch oven, heat the oil over medium heat. Add the onion, pepper, celery, and garlic, and sauté for 8 to 10 minutes.
2. Add the remaining ingredients, except the chicken, and simmer for 25 to 30 minutes over low heat.
3. Add the chicken and simmer, stirring occasionally, for 20 to 30 minutes, until the chicken is cooked through. Taste, adjust the seasonings, and serve over rice.

Cal. **242** *Carb.* **12g** *Protein* **36g** *Chol.* **94mg** *Fat* **5g/20%**

Chicken Stew

SERVES 4
2 boneless, skinless chicken breasts
2 garlic cloves, minced
1 cup minced fresh dill
$\frac{1}{4}$ cup minced fresh chives
$\frac{1}{8}$ teaspoon ground nutmeg
$1\frac{1}{2}$ cups peeled baby carrots
$1\frac{1}{2}$ cups coarsely chopped onion
$1\frac{1}{2}$ cups chicken broth (see Basics)
2 cups sugar snap peas
1 cup Low-Fat Blend (see Basics)
Freshly ground pepper

1. In a large stockpot, place the chicken, garlic, ½ cup dill, chives, nutmeg, carrots, onion, and chicken broth. Bring to a boil, reduce the heat, and simmer, covered, for 20 minutes, or until the carrots are tender. Add the sugar snap peas and simmer for 10 minutes, until the sugar snaps are tender.
2. Add the remaining dill, Low-Fat Blend, and pepper to taste. Serve warm.

Cal. **395** *Carb.* **23g** *Protein* **61g** *Chol.* **142mg** *Fat* **7g/15%**

Jambalaya

SERVES 8

1 ounce minced prosciutto or Canadian
   bacon, trimmed of fat
2 cups cubed boiled country ham, trimmed of fat
1 pound spicy smoked turkey sausage
   (99% fat free), cut into ½-inch pieces
1 cup coarsely chopped onion
1 cup cubed green bell pepper
1 tablespoon slivered garlic
3 cups peeled, seeded, and chopped fresh plum tomatoes
1 cup chicken broth (see Basics)
1 cup tomato juice
¾ teaspoon dried thyme
1 bay leaf
½ teaspoon Tabasco, or to taste
½ teaspoon freshly ground pepper
¾ cup white rice
1 pound sea scallops or large bay scallops
1½ pounds shelled and deveined jumbo shrimp
½ cup finely chopped fresh Italian parsley

1. In a very large ovenproof skillet with 3-inch sides, sauté
the prosciutto over medium heat until it just begins to get
crisp around the edges. Add the ham, sausage, onion, green
pepper, and garlic; increase the heat to medium-high and
sauté for 4 to 5 minutes, until the meat begins to brown.
2. Add the tomato, broth, tomato juice, thyme, bay leaf,
Tabasco, and pepper; cover and simmer for 8 minutes.
3. Preheat the oven to 350°.
4. Stir in the rice; cover and simmer for 15 minutes.
5. Add the scallops and shrimp. Cover the skillet and place it
in the oven. Bake for 30 minutes, stirring once or twice.
6. Transfer the jambalaya to a large heated serving platter.
Garnish with chopped parsley and serve immediately.

Cal. **377** *Carb.* **25g** *Protein* **42g** *Chol.* **158mg** *Fat* **12g/28%**

"When one does not love too much — one does not love enough."

Pascal

Fresh Herbs in Winter

Year-round fresh herbs are
still hard to come by. Specialty food stores and supermarkets try to stock them,
but all too often they're
neglected. My solution for
obtaining quantities of the
fresh herbs I like to cook
with (in a tiny town of 1000
people): the local herb lady,
Nancy Baker. A former physi-
cist, she supplies the best
restaurants with herbs from
her greenhouse every week,
and she's willing to make a
stop at our house, too.

With a little investigating
in your own neighborhood,
my guess is you'll find a
"secret source" you can tap.

Goat Cheese and Dill Soufflé

SERVES 4

¼ pound baking potato (about ½ potato), peeled and diced
½ cup chicken broth (see Basics)
¼ cup "light" ricotta
¼ cup low-fat cottage cheese
2 egg yolks, at room temperature
Freshly ground pepper
3 ounces low-fat goat cheese
¼ cup finely chopped fresh dill
5 egg whites, at room temperature
Pinch cream of tartar

1. Preheat the oven to 400°.
2. Lightly spray or wipe four 8-ounce soufflé dishes with vegetable oil. Make a collar out of a strip of foil placed around the inside circumference of each soufflé dish, overextending the rim by 4 to 6 inches, to assist the soufflé in rising.
3. Place the potato and chicken stock in a medium saucepan and simmer, uncovered, for about 15 minutes, until the liquid is absorbed and the potato is tender. Transfer the mixture to a food processor. Add the ricotta, cottage cheese, egg yolks, and pepper to taste; purée. Transfer the mixture to a large mixing bowl and fold in the goat cheese and dill.
4. Beat the egg whites and cream of tartar with an electric mixer until stiff peaks form. Gently stir one-third of the whites into the cheese mixture. Fold in the remaining whites and blend well.
5. Pour the mixture into the soufflé dishes and run your thumb around the inside edges to promote even rising; the batter will be mounded in the center. Place the dishes on a sheet and place the sheet in the center of the oven. Reduce the oven temperature to 375°. Bake for 17 minutes, or until the soufflés are puffed, set, and lightly golden; do not open the oven door during the first 15 minutes of baking. Serve immediately.

Cal. **120** *Carb.* **7g** *Protein* **12g** *Chol.* **102mg** *Fat* **5g/36%**

Variation:
Substitute ½ cup grated Parmesan and 2 tablespoons finely minced fresh basil for the goat cheese and dill; add freshly ground nutmeg to taste. Reserve a bit of the Parmesan to sprinkle on top of the soufflés before they go into the oven.

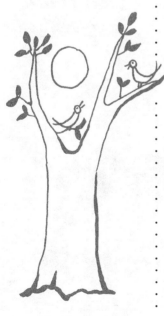

Planning the Garden

• Send for seed catalogues.
• Begin planning spring flower, vegetable, and herb gardens. (Don't forget plans to rotate crops.)
• Repair gardening tools.
• Protect flower beds by covering them with branches from your Christmas tree.
• Watch for early-blooming bulbs, such as snowdrops.
• Prune fruit trees during a mild spell.
• Begin cutting branches of spring-flowering shrubs for forcing.
• Scrub pots and flats needed for starting seeds.

Midnight Torte

Til Midnight, my favorite nearby restaurant, is run by a gentle six-foot-tall woman—Spring TenKley—who never cooked a subtle dish in her life, this dessert included. It is a decadence through and through, perfect for Valentine's Day. When you love chocolate, why not indulge with the real thing?

YIELD: 16 SLICES

1 pound high-quality semi-sweet baking chocolate
1 pound (4 sticks) unsalted butter
6 eggs

1. In the top of a double boiler over medium-high heat, melt the chocolate and butter together. Place the mixture into a medium mixing bowl. Wash the top of the double boiler.
2. In the double boiler over medium-high heat, whisk the eggs until warmed through. Remove the eggs from the heat, and, using an electric mixer set on high, beat for 6 minutes, or until thickened.
3. By hand, fold the thickened eggs into the chocolate, one-quarter at a time, until completely blended.
4. Preheat the oven to 425°.
5. Pour the batter into a 16-inch springform pan. Place the pan in a glass pan, and add enough water to come to 1 inch from the top of the springform pan. Bake for 15 minutes.
6. Remove the torte from the oven and cool for 1 hour at room temperature. Refrigerate 24 hours before slicing with a hot knife. Serve topped with fresh fruit.

*Cal. **371** Carb. **8g** Protein **5g** Chol. **130mg** Fat **40g/87%***
(analyzed per slice)

> "... there are terrible temptations that it requires strength, strength and courage to yield to."
>
> Oscar Wilde
> An Ideal Husband

Key Lime Pie

SERVES 8

1 cup finely crushed graham crackers
³/₄ cup plus 2 tablespoons sugar
3¹/₂ tablespoons canola oil
1 teaspoon unflavored gelatin
¹/₂ cup Key lime juice
Zest of 2 limes, grated
2 cups Low-Fat Blend (see Basics)

Snow Ice Cream

Just pour fruit juice over freshly fallen snow. Orange, cranberry, and pineapple are best. Or heat maple syrup to 260° without stirring and pour over a bowl of clean snow.

1. Preheat the oven to 325°.

2. In a medium-size mixing bowl, combine the crushed graham crackers and the 2 tablespoons of sugar. Mix in the oil until thoroughly moistened. Press the mixture firmly into a 9-inch pie plate. Bake for 6 to 8 minutes. Cool and refrigerate until needed.

3. In a small saucepan, soften the gelatin in ¼ cup water. Place the saucepan over low heat and stir until the gelatin has completely dissolved. Add the lime juice, lime zest, and remaining sugar, stirring until the sugar has completely dissolved and the mixture is slightly thickened. Transfer to a large mixing bowl, and whisk the mixture until it is just warm to the touch. Fold in the Low-Fat Blend and whisk until well mixed.

4. Pour the mixture into the pie shell and refrigerate for at least 4 hours, or until the filling is firm. Serve chilled.

Cal. 219 Carb. 34g Protein 6g Chol. 0mg Fat 7g/30%

Yummy Bread Pudding

SERVES 4

2 cups cubed day-old French bread (about 3 slices)
2 eggs
½ cup sugar
¼ teaspoon salt
1 can evaporated skim milk
½ cup boiling water
1 teaspoon ground cinnamon
1 teaspoon freshly grated nutmeg
½ cup raisins
2 teaspoons vanilla extract

1. Preheat the oven to 350°.

2. Lightly spray or wipe a 1½-quart baking dish with canola or vegetable oil. Place the bread cubes in the dish.

3. In a medium-size bowl, beat the eggs. Add the sugar, salt, and milk. Stir in 2 tablespoons of boiling water, then add the remaining 6 tablespoons water, cinnamon, nutmeg, raisins, and vanilla. Pour the egg mixture over the bread cubes.

4. Bake the pudding until set, about 45 minutes. Serve warm, at room temperature, or cold.

Cal. 192 Carb. 42g Protein .8g Chol. 89mg Fat 3g/13%

Dark, Rich Real Chocolate

Imagine a life without chocolate. Chocolate bewitches. It attracts us like no other food. In fact, it's estimated that the average American consumes 11 pounds of chocolate every year. That's $5 billion spent every year to satisfy our chocolate habit.

Cocoa trees grow only in the hot, rainy climates 20 degrees either side of the equator. Each tree produces 20 to 30 pods a year, and every pod yields 25 to 40 seeds or beans. Four hundred beans are required for 1 pound of chocolate. Cocoa beans are roasted at temperatures from 250 to 350°, 30 minutes to 2 hours. Manufacturers' formulas vary. So does the quality of chocolate.

After roasting, the beans are shelled, leaving behind a "nib" containing 50 to 54% cocoa butter. The nibs are pressed, and the liquified cocoa butter removed, leaving a dark, thick paste called "liquor." Poured into molds and cooled, it becomes unsweetened chocolate. When more cocoa butter is removed, the remainder solidifies and is ground into cocoa powder. Sugar and more cocoa butter are added back to make sweetened chocolate. Dried milk is added for milk chocolate.

At the Market

Read chocolate labels. Know what's in the product you're buying. Quality's defined by the beans and production, not by price. The best beans come from the Caribbean. Good production can take up to three months. Chocolate purchased in the fall is most likely from the new crop. A few months' aging seems to make it better.

Remember: The finished product will only be as good as its ingredients. Buy right and choose according to your own tastes.

Working with Chocolate

For obvious reasons, I always wear brown!

Mold chocolate using shiny, scratch-free surfaces. Chocolate becomes imprinted with the finish upon which it is molded.

Grate sweet and semisweet chocolate over wax paper, holding a large piece of chocolate in paper to keep heat from your hands from melting the chocolate. A Mouli grater is good for

this, since you don't touch the chocolate. When grating in a blender or food processor, first cut into small chunks so that heat from the blades doesn't melt the chocolate. Grate or grind unsweetened chocolate by chopping coarsely with a chef's knife, not in the blender.

Make chocolate leaves. Choose dry, nontoxic leaves (lemon, rose, geranium, plastic). Use semisweet or a mixture of semisweet and milk chocolate. With a narrow knife, cover the back of the leaf ⅛ inch thick with melted chocolate. Allow to cool completely. Peel off the leaf.

Make chocolate curls. With room-temperature chocolate, using a swivel-blade stainless steel vegetable peeler, make curls with long strokes. Let them fall on a sheet of waxed paper. Use the wide side of the chocolate bar for big curls, the narrow side for small curls. Pick up carefully with a spatula when ready to use. If you're not serving immediately, you will want to chill the curls on a sheet of waxed paper.

Tempering chocolate makes it more flexible to work with and keeps it glossy when you want to

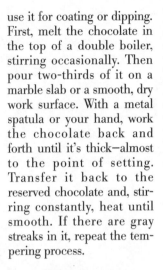

use it for coating or dipping. First, melt the chocolate in the top of a double boiler, stirring occasionally. Then pour two-thirds of it on a marble slab or a smooth, dry work surface. With a metal spatula or your hand, work the chocolate back and forth until it's thick—almost to the point of setting. Transfer it back to the reserved chocolate and, stirring constantly, heat until smooth. If there are gray streaks in it, repeat the tempering process.

Chocolate in the Garden

Lately I've been using the hulls of dry-roasted cocoa beans as a dark rich brown mulch in my garden, making every step outdoors after a summer rain smell like a chocolate cake is baking.

	Cal. (1 oz.)	Prot. (g)	Carb. (g)	Chol. (mg)	Fat/% (g)	Sat. Fat
Cocoa	61	5.4	14	0	3.6/29%	16%
Bittersweet Chocolate	135	2.2	13	0	11/62%	35%
Semisweet Chocolate	135	1.2	18	0	8.4/50%	29%
Dark Chocolate	143	3	8.2	0	15/75%	42%
Milk Chocolate	145	2	17	6.2	8.7/51%	30%

Definitions:

Chocolate liquor: The material obtained from grinding, liquifying, and pan-cooling the edible portion of the roasted cocoa bean.

Cocoa butter: The vegetable fat pressed from the chocolate liquor under pressure. Responsible for chocolate's unique texture. The higher the content, the higher the quality.

Unsweetened chocolate (bitter or baking): Pure chocolate, heated and poured into molds. 53% cocoa butter.

Cocoa powder: What's left when all but 22% of the cocoa butter is removed from chocolate liquor. The resulting cakelike substance is ground and sifted. The Dutch process treats the cocoa with an edible alkali for a less acidic, more easily digested cocoa that's darker and richer-flavored. You must add more leavening (baking powder) when using Dutch cocoa.

Premelted unsweetened baking chocolate: A blend of cocoa and vegetable oil. Use for convenience, not flavor.

Semisweet or bittersweet chocolate (dark chocolate): Chocolate liquor with sweeteners and cocoa butter added. 35% chocolate liquor and 35 to 50% sugar; the remainder is cocoa butter. The varying amounts of sugar provide the subtle difference between semisweet and bittersweet chocolate. Both have flavoring added: either vanillin or pure vanilla. German sweet chocolate is a special blend with sugar and cocoa butter.

Milk chocolate: A smooth eating chocolate made by adding whole milk solids, sugar, additional cocoa butter, and vanilla to chocolate liquor. Must contain 10% chocolate and 55% cocoa butter.

White chocolate: A product containing no chocolate liquor; cannot legally be called chocolate. Contains cocoa butter, sugar, milk solids, flavoring, and occasionally vegetable fat. The best contains all cocoa butter, no vegetable fat.

Imitation chocolate (compound chocolate or confectioners' chocolate): Labeled "chocolate-flavored." All contain natural ingredients, cocoa and vegetable fat other than cocoa butter (usually palm kernel oil, coconut oil, cottonseed oil, or soya oil). Does not have to be tempered. Compound chocolate is used to cut costs in candy bars and cookies.

Commercial coating chocolate or couverture: Can be real or compound chocolate. A higher percentage of cocoa butter gives it a shiny finish and more flexibility, suitable for decorating. Make your own couverture by adding 1½ ounces of cocoa butter to 1 pound of high-quality chocolate.

★ GOOD FOR YOU ★

Like other beans, cocoa beans are a good source of protein, carbohydrates, fiber, B vitamins, phosphorous, iron, and potassium. Cocoa butter, or the fat in cocoa bean has no cholesterol but is second only to coconut oil in its level of saturated fat.

St. Patrick's Day Supper

Corned Beef and Cabbage

Corned beef is brisket pickled in brine. This dish is especially popular as a St. Patrick's Day tradition in America.

SERVES 12

5 pounds corned beef, trimmed of fat
3 bay leaves
1 tablespoon caraway seeds
Freshly ground pepper
12 large onions
12 large carrots, cut into 3-inch pieces
3 large green cabbages, quartered
1 cup chopped fresh Italian parsley
Mustard Sauce or Horseradish Sauce (both opposite)

1. Place the meat in a large stockpot and cover it with water. Bring to a boil and skim the surface. Add the bay leaves, caraway, and pepper. Reduce the heat and simmer, covered, for 1 hour. Add the onions and carrots; cover and cook for 30 minutes. Add the cabbage and cook another 30 minutes.
2. Slice the meat and arrange it on a large platter, surrounded with the vegetables and sprinkled with fresh parsley. Pass the sauce at the table.

*Cal. **535** Carb. **46g** Protein **32g** Chol. **131mg** Fat **27g/44%***

"It's no use boiling your cabbage twice."

Irish proverb

548

Menu

Bourbon Nuts

Corned Beef and Cabbage

Horseradish Sauce

Mustard Sauce

Potatoes in a Bag

Mixed Spring Greens with Sweet-and-Sour Splash

Orange Flan

Tropical Gratin

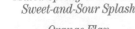

Horseradish Sauce

Use with corned beef, roast beef, or smoked fish, or as a dip.

YIELD: 1 CUP

3 tablespoons finely grated fresh horseradish

1 teaspoon Dijon mustard

1 cup Low-Fat Blend (see Basics)

Combine all of the ingredients and refrigerate until needed.

*Cal. **11** Carb. **1g** Protein **1g** Chol. **.3mg** Fat **.2g/14%***
(analyzed per tablespoon)

Mustard Sauce

Use with fish, New England boiled dinner, or hamburgers.

YIELD: ¾ CUP

6 tablespoons Dijon mustard

¼ cup chopped fresh dill

¼ cup Low-Fat Blend (see Basics)

Combine all of the ingredients and refrigerate until needed.

*Cal. **12** Carb. **.3g** Protein **.4g** Chol. **.1mg** Fat **1g/77%*** %
(analyzed per tablespoon)

Potatoes in a Bag

SERVES 8

36 tiny red or white new potatoes, scrubbed

2 teaspoons olive oil

2 tablespoons chopped fresh Italian parsley

1 tablespoon chopped fresh thyme

1 tablespoon chopped fresh rosemary or sage

Kosher or sea salt

1. Preheat the oven to 350°. In a medium bowl, toss the potatoes with the oil, using your hands to coat the potatoes evenly, then sprinkle them with the herbs.

2. Transfer the potatoes to a sheet of parchment paper or heavy-duty aluminum foil large enough to enclose them. Sprinkle the potatoes with the salt, fold the paper loosely, and seal it by crimping the edges together.

3. Bake for 45 minutes. If you use parchment paper, it is fun to split the packet open at the table. Serve immediately.

*Cal. **165** Carb. **34g** Protein **4g** Chol. **0mg** Fat **1g/8%***
(analyzed per tablespoon)

"Events are
sometimes the
best calendar."

Benjamin
Disraeli

Index